From Words to Numbers

This book illustrates a set of tools – story grammars, relational data models, and network models – that can be profitably used for the collection, organization, and analysis of narrative data in sociohistorical research. A story grammar, or subject-action-object and their modifiers, is the linguistic tool the author uses to structure narrative for the purpose of collecting data on protest events. Relational database models make such complex data collection schemes practically feasible in a computer environment. Finally, network models are a statistical tool best suited to analyze this type of data. Driven by the metaphors of the journal (from . . . to) and the alchemy (words into numbers), the book leads the reader through a number of paths, from substantive to methodological issues, across time and disciplines: sociology, linguistics, literary criticism, history, statistics, computer science, philosophy, cognitive psychology, and political science. The book mitigates its quest for rigor in the social sciences with a subtle irony for that quest.

Roberto Franzosi obtained an Honors BA in Literature at the University of Genoa (Italy) (1975) and a Ph.D. in Sociology at Johns Hopkins University (1981). After spending a year as a postdoctoral Fellow at the University of Michigan, he taught for several years in the Sociology Department at the University of Wisconsin-Madison. Between 1995 and 1999, Franzosi held a lectureship in Sociology at the University of Oxford, with an official fellowship at Trinity College. He took the post of head of the department in Sociology at the University of Reading in 1999. He has served as consulting editor for the *American Journal of Sociology* and is currently a managing editor for the *Journal of Historical Sociology*. The substantive and methodological study of social protest has been at the heart of Franzosi's research agenda with several published articles and the book *The Puzzles of Strikes* (Cambridge University Press, 1995).

Structural Analysis in the Social Sciences 22
Mark Granovetter, editor

The *Structural Analysis in the Social Sciences* series presents approaches that explain social behavior and institutions by reference to *relationships* between such concrete entities as persons and organizations. This contrasts with at least four other popular strategies: (1) reductionist attempts at explanation by focusing on individuals alone; (2) explanations stressing the causal primacy of ideas, values, and cognitions; (3) technological and material determinism; (4) explanations using "variables" as the main analytical concept, as in "structural equation" models, where the structure connects variables rather than actual social entities.

An important example of structural analysis is the "social network" approach. However, the series also features social science theory and research that is not framed explicitly in network terms, but stresses the importance of relationships rather than the atomization of reductionism or the determinism of ideas, technology, or material conditions. Such efforts typically deal with the complex balance between structure and agency, increasingly a key issue in the human sciences. Examples of the structural approach are scattered across many disciplines, and it is the goal of the *Structural Analysis* series to expose this very fruitful style of analysis to a wider public by bringing all the approaches together under a single rubric.

Other books in the series:

Continued on page following the Index

From Words to Numbers

Narrative, Data, and Social Science

ROBERTO FRANZOSI
University of Reading

CAMBRIDGE
UNIVERSITY PRESS

PUBLISHED BY THE PRESS SYNDICATE OF THE UNIVERSITY OF CAMBRIDGE
The Pitt Building, Trumpington Street, Cambridge, United Kingdom

CAMBRIDGE UNIVERSITY PRESS
The Edinburgh Building, Cambridge CB2 2RU, UK
40 West 20th Street, New York, NY 10011-4211, USA
477 Williamstown Road, Port Melbourne, VIC 3207, Australia
Ruiz de Alarcón 13, 28014 Madrid, Spain
Dock House, The Waterfront, Cape Town 8001, South Africa

http://www.cambridge.org

First published 2004

Printed in the United States of America

Typeface Times New Roman 10/12 pt.   *System* WordPerfect   [AU]

A catalog record for this book is available from the British Library.

Library of Congress Cataloging in Publication Data
Franzosi, Roberto.
From words to numbers : narrative, data, and social science / Roberto Franzosi.
    p.   cm. – (Structural analysis in the social sciences)
Includes bibliographical references and index.
ISBN 0-521-81520-7 – ISBN 0-521-54145-X (pb.)
1. Social sciences – Research – Methodology. 2. Content analysis (Communication) 3.
Discourse analysis, Narrative. I. Title. II. Series.
H61.F637   2003
300'.1'41–dc21   2003051548

ISBN 0 521 81520 7 hardback
ISBN 0 521 54145 X paperback

Andreae patri carissimo, in memoriam.
Sit tibi terra levis.

Non chiederci la parola che squadri da ogni lato
l'animo nostro informe, e a lettere di fuoco
lo dichiari e risplenda come un croco
perduto in mezzo a un polveroso prato.

Ah l'uomo che se ne va sicuro,
agli altri ed a se stesso amico,
e l'ombra sua non cura che la canicola
stampa sopra uno scalcinato muro!

Non domandarci la formula che mondi possa aprirti,
sí qualche storta sillaba e secca come un ramo.
Codesto solo oggi possiamo dirti,
ciò che non siamo, ciò che non vogliamo.

Eugenio Montale (from *Ossi di seppia*)

Do not ask us for the word that will square off our shapeless soul from every angle, and proclaim it in characters of fire and shine like a crocus lost in a dusty field. Ah, the man who goes through life with confidence, a friend to others and to himself, unconcerned with his shadow cast by dog days on a flaking wall! Do not ask us for the formula that will open worlds for you, but only some twisted syllables as dry as a branch. Today, we can tell you only this, what we are *not*, what we do *not* want (Montale, 1965).

Contents

List of Tables

List of Figures

Acknowledgments

Long projects inevitably end up with long lists of accumulated debts to people and institutions. This project is no exception. I developed the ideas at the heart of this book at the Center for Research on Social Organizations at the University of Michigan, where I spent the 1981–82 academic year as a postdoctoral Fellow. Charles Tilly, director of CRSO, and Nancy Horn, a graduate student working on Tilly's Great Britain Study, were very generous with their time in clarifying the inner workings of Tilly's approach to coding text for historical research. Charles Tilly's influence on my work did not stop with the year spent at CRSO; neither did it confine itself to methodological issues. What has lived in me through the years is the legacy of Tilly's passion for historical questions that can be addressed through rigorous methods, an unfailing excitement for the new and the innovative.

A grant from Ente Nazionale Idrocarburi (ENI) allowed me to spend a year in Rome after Ann Arbor exploring new ways of collecting text data, taking Tilly's scheme as a point of departure. Gustavo DeSantis played a crucial role in making it happen. Anna Maria Ventrella, director of ISVET, one of ENI's research institutes, gave warm hospitality to my research team, as did all the members of the institute. Annella Centis, one of the team members, stuck with the project till the very end. Her help was invaluable.

In 1986, I started the long and bumpy ride of data collection in Genoa, Italy. If the beginnings were exciting, by the time I finished data collection in 1990, I had run out of steam, amidst financial and operational difficulties. Throughout those years, Giorgio Sola did more than one can reasonably expect of a friend and a colleague. Many students from the University of Genoa worked on the project as coders; they are too numerous for me to thank individually. Alberto Devoto, of the Isitituto Nazionale di Fisica Nucleare of the University of Cagliari, and Corrado Salvo, of the Department of Physics of the University of Genoa, provided the VAX accounts that made possible computer communications between Madison and Genoa. Between 1995 and 1997, Piero Squillante, Mauro Giorgetti, and Daniela Mariani worked on data cleaning and data analysis. I am particularly grateful to Pier Paolo Mudu for his role in data analysis.

Several institutions provided research funds: the Graduate School of the University of Wisconsin, Formez, Confindustria, Intersind, Consiglio Nazionale delle Ricerche (*Progetto strategico "Il conflitto e le relazioni di lavoro nel prossimo decennio"*), and the National Science Foundation (SES-8511632 and SBR 94-11739). The following people played key roles in securing the grants: William Bainbridge, Mario Brutti, Gian Primo Cella, Piero Celli, Innocenzo Cipolletta, Giulio De Caprariis, Benedetto de Cesaris, Enzo Grilli, Charles Manski, Enrico Micheli, Mario Micossi, Filippo Peschiera, Giuseppe Rosa, Carlo Sampietro, and Goffredo Zappa. In am particularly indebted to David Ward at the University of Wisconsin-Madison who gave me the initial funds (and confidence) to embark upon this long journey.

Thomas Mitchell, Shawn Pourchot, and Josè Carlos De Almeida Manganaro proved to be the most competent and most reliable programmers in the development of the data-entry software PC-ACE (Program for Computer-Assisted Coding of Events). Charles Palit and John Nitti at the University of Wisconsin, both involved in different projects based on "words" and on PC technology, provided constant and invaluable technical help and support (and so did my colleague Halliman Winsborough).

In 1986, I submitted my first manuscript on the methodological approach I had developed to *Sociological Methodology*. The comments I received from one of the reviewers indicated that I should fundamentally change my thoughts, away from artificial intelligence and closer to linguistics. Clifford Clogg, editor of the journal, strongly encouraged me to address the reviewer's recommendations ("a foremost linguist in the country," in Clogg's words). Charles Scott at the University of Wisconsin-Madison guided my first steps through an unfamiliar terrain: linguistics. To that anonymous "foremost linguist" goes my deepest gratitude. Perhaps, s/he may never know how deeply her/his review changed the course of my intellectual and professional trajectory. Thanks to you as well, Clifford Clogg. *Tibi quoque sit terra levis*. Peter Marsden, successor to Clifford Clogg at the helm of *Sociological Methodology*, and J. Scott Long, editor of *Sociological Methods and Research*, were just as supportive with further publications on my method.

Several years were still to pass between the time I submitted a collection of published papers to Cambridge University Press (fall 1992) and the time I submitted the completed manuscript for final review (June 2000). Many things came in between – the writing of *The Puzzle of Strikes*, three successive moves of institutions, houses, and even countries, the birth of our daughter, Anna Giulia, in December 1995, and, more to the point, a change in my intellectual trajectory that forced upon me a slow and painful rethinking of my work along interdisciplinary lines.

Many people played key roles in providing guidance and insights in this wild-goose chase across disciplinary boundaries. I list them here in alphabetical order: Ronald Aminzade, Alberto Devoto, James Jaffee, Donald Levine,

Diana Lewis, John Markoff, Larry Scanlon, Biljana Scott, Charles Tilly, Louise Tilly, and Harrison White. Harry Eckstein, Edward McDill, James Rule, Rudy Rummel, and Raymond Tanter were kind enough to illuminate aspects of the history of the process of quantification in which they were involved. But many more than I can list offered occasional references and suggestions. Several research assistants at Oxford helped me with the extensive literature: Michael Elliot, Michelle Jackson, Richard Lim, Shepley Orr, and Daniel Viehoff. Desmond King, Nader Sohrabi, Charles Tilly, and Gavin Williams provided helpful comments on chapters of the manuscript. "Sraffa had the power to force Wittgenstein to revise, not this or that point, but his whole perspective," Ray Monk tells us (1991, p. 260). I had a few Sraffa of my own who, sometimes with off-hand comments, pushed me to explore new directions or substantially revise the manuscript: Richard Gipps, Mark Greengrass (to whom I owe the metaphor of the journey), Daniel Schwartz, Giorgio Sola, and Daniel Spizzo.

At the University of Oxford I found an exciting intellectual atmosphere that will be hard, if not altogether impossible, to replace. Michael Inwood, Desmond King, and Gavin Williams played deeply key roles in my intellectual development during those years. The Department of Applied Social Studies and Social Research provided a comfortable, friendly, and supportive atmosphere for work. At the Taylorian Library and Rhodes Library I spent many days and some wonderful summers research and reading. There, Ms. Elisabeth Tabouis and Mr. Allan Lodge provided unfailing help and always with a smile. At Trinity College, I constantly broke the fundamental rule of convivial life: "Never talk about work." Instead, at the senior common room lunches and dinners I picked everyone's brain at every opportunity; the historians, the philosophers, the mathematicians, the classicists, and even the scientists, all had to put up with my questions. I lived a childish dream that close physical proximity with so many different scholars may somehow transfer their knowledge onto me. Alas, the only knowledge that I did acquire was a humble and unequivocal sense of the limits of my own knowledge. Many of those conversations simply sparked in me a lost gusto for a good story. In many ways, this book is the result of the Trinity Senior Common Room. There, I most acutely experienced the tension of the "two cultures," so deeply ingrained in my own biography. Besides Mike Inwood, I am deeply indebted to several of my Trinity fellows for their constant suggestions: Dinah Birch, Peter Brown, Clive Griffin, Martin Maiden, Jonathan Mallinson, Bede Rundle, and Brian Ward-Perkins.

Needless to say, the final product had little to do with the 1992 book proposal. The beginning of that final product goes back to January 1996 when I started writing in the wee hours of the night, in between nightly feeds of Anna Giulia – a labor of serenity and love – born 21-12 (1995) at 21:12 in Oxford (the magic of numbers!). It continued in earnest till 1999, when I took a job as head of department at the University of Reading. The demands of rebuilding a department fallen under receivership took a heavy personal and professional toll. Lazarsfeld assures us that "educational innovations are, by definition, intellectual as well as administrative tasks" (Lazarsfeld, 1993, p. 269). Then, it was not in vain. For sure, a free hand in setting up new undergraduate and graduate curricula and to hire several new colleagues forced me to bring into sharp focus what I fundamentally believe sociology to be and how to best convey that view to students and colleagues. Nonetheless, the manuscript laid untouched in my laptop for a few more years. I am grateful to Mark Granovetter, editor of the series "Structural Analysis in the Social Sciences," who saw the beginning of my journey, for believing in this travel diary, and to Lewis Bateman, the social science editor at Cambridge University Press, for pushing me to finally let the manuscript go. I am also grateful to Richard Laver for his excellent work with the index, Paul Luna for typesetting advice, and Sophie Doyle for checking and rechecking everything in the final stages of production. The camera-ready copy of the book was printed at the University of Trento where, in the fall of 2003, I resumed data collection on the 1919–22 period, with research grants from the University of Reading and the University of Trento.

This journey from words to numbers has been long and difficult. It has been both personally and professionally taxing, with some painfully humiliating moments. Several friends never gave up on me through it all: Alberto Devoto, Mauro La Noce, Alberto Palloni, Giorgio Sola, Charles Tilly, and Erik Wright. Their friendship and belief in my journey was crucial for me to finally reach a safe harbor. From 1997–1998, I increasingly retreated within myself and within the world of this book. Isolation bought me freedom but delivered grief. The family paid a high price for my enstrangement. My wife, Svetlana Kropp, has been a constant source of both professional and personal support throughout most of these years, and certainly, throughout the hardest ones. She worked as a supervisor on the project in Genoa in 1990. She read more than her share of my work. She helped with data cleaning. She carried out a great deal of the early statistical analyses. She also did what no other had to do: She put up with me through it all. *Mea culpa.*

The following individuals and publishers have kindly given me permission to reprint material from the publications listed below for the poems and epigraphs used in this book:

American Historical Association (American Historical Review), Beacon Press, Cambridge University Press, Columbia University Press, Edinburgh University Press, Free Press, Giulio Einaudi Editore, Robert Fogel, Dori Ghezzi, HarperCollins Publishers, Johns Hopkins University Press, MIT Press, Arnoldo Mondadori Editore, Mouton de Gruyter, Oxford University Press, Palgrave McMillan Publishers, Penguin, The Random House Group (Jonathan Cape; Doubleday & Company; Knopf), Routledge, Charles Tilly, University of California Press, Yale University Press, Kurt H. Wolff.

Barthes, Roland. 1977[1966]. "The Death of the Author." In: pp. 142–8, Roland Barthes, *Image Music Text*. Essays Selected and Translated by Stephen Heath. London: Fontana Press.

Benson, Lee. 1957. "Research Problems in American Political History." In: pp. 113–83, Mirra Komarovsky (ed.), *Common Frontiers of Social Sciences*. Glencoe, IL: Free Press.

Berelson, Bernard. 1952. *Content Analysis in Communication Research*. New York: Free Press.

Berger, John. 1972. *Ways of Seeing: Based on the BBC Television Series with John Berger*. Harmondsworth: Penguin.

Campbell, Norman. 1952. *What is Science?* New York: Dover.

Clark, Kitson G. 1962. *The Making of Victorian England*. London: Methuen.

Columbus, Christopher. 1969. *The Four Voyages of Christopher Columbus*. Edited and translated by J. M. Cohen. Harmondsworth: Penguin.

de Andrè, Fabrizio. 1999. *I testi e gli spartiti di tutte le canzoni*. Milan: Mondadori. (Fabrizio de Andrè and Maurizio Pagani. 1983. *Creuza de mä*. Milan: Ricordi.)

Derrida, Jacques. 1974[1967]. *Of Grammatology*. Baltimore, MD: Johns Hopkins University Press.

Descartes, Renè. 1960. In: *The Rationalists*. Garden City, NY: Doubleday & Company.

Dijk, Teun A. van. 1972. *Some Aspects of Text Grammars: A Study in Theoretical Linguistics and Poetics*. Paris: Mouton.

Dirac, Paul A.M. 1980. "The Excellence of Einstein's Theory of Gravitation." In: pp. 42–6, Maurice Goldsmith, Alan L. Mackay, and James Woudhuysen. *Einstein, the First Hundred Years*. Oxford: Pergamon Press.

Elton, Geoffrey R. 1963. *Reformation Europe 1517–1559*. London: Collins.

——— 1983. "Two Kinds of History." In: pp. 71–121, Robert William Fogel and Geoffrey R. Elton, *Which Road to the Past? Two Views of History*. New Haven, CT: Yale University Press.

Fogel, Robert W. 1975. "The Limits of Quantitative Methods in History." *The American Historical Review*, Vol. 80, No. 2, pp. 329–50.

Frye, Northrop. 1957. *Anatomy of Criticism*. Harmondsworth: Penguin.

Gerth, Hans H. and C. Wright Mills (eds.). 1946. *From Max Weber: Essays in Sociology*. Translated, edited, and with an Introduction by Hans H. Gerth and C. Wright Mills. Oxford: Oxford University Press.

Goethe, Johann Wolfgang. 1987. *Faust*. Part I. Translated with an Introduction by David Luke. Oxford: Oxford University Press.

Jakobson, Roman. 1960. "Closing Statement: Linguistics and Poetics." In: pp. 350–77, Thomas A. Sebeok (ed.), *Style in Language*. Cambridge, MA: The MIT Press.

Kristeva, Julia. 1980. *Desire in Language: A Semiotic Approach to Literature and Art*. New York: Columbia University Press.

Leamer, Edward E. 1983. "Let's Take the Con Out of Econometrics." *American Economic Review*, Vol. 73, No. 1, pp. 31–43.

Le Roy Ladurie, Emmanuel. 1979. *The Territory of the Historian*. Chicago, IL: The University of Chicago Press.

Lévi-Strauss, Claude. 1992[1955]. *Tristes Tropiques*. New York: Penguin Books.

Lieberson, Stanley. 1985. *Making it Count. The Improvement of Social Research and Theory*. Berkeley: University of California Press.

Marcuse, Herbert. 1964. *One-Dimensional Man. Studies in the Ideology of Advanced Industrial Society*. Boston: Beacon Press.

Montale, Eugenio. 1948. *Ossi di seppia*. Milan: Mondadori.

1965. *Selected Poems*. Translated by Glauco Cambon. Edinburgh: Edinburgh University Press.

Pigafetta, Antonio. 1969[1524 ca.]. *Magellan's Voyage. A Narrative Account of the First Circumnavigation*. Translated and edited by R. A. Skelton. New York: Dover.

Richardson, Lewis F. 1960. *Statistics of Deadly Quarrels*. Edited by Quincy Wright and Carl C. Lienau. Chicago, IL: Quadrangle.

Saba, Umberto. 1963. *Antologia del canzoniere*. Turin: Einaudi.

Simmel, Georg. 1950. *The Sociology of Georg Simmel*. Translated, edited, and with an Introduction by Kurt H. Wolff. Glencoe, IL: Free Press.

1955. *Conflict and The Web of Group-Affiliations*. Translated by Kurt H. Wolff and Reinhard Bendix. Foreword by Everett C. Hughes. New York: Free Press.

1959. *Georg Simmel, 1858–1918. A Collection of Essays*. With translations and a bibliography. Edited by Kurt H. Wolff. Columbus: The Ohio State University Press.

1978. *The Philosophy of Money*. Translated by Tom Bottomore and David Frisby. London: Routledge & Kegan Paul.

Stone, Lawrence. 1981. *The Past and the Present*. Boston: Routledge & Kegan Paul.

Tilly, Charles. 1981. *As Sociology Meets History*. New York: Academic Press.

Tolstóy, Leo. 1934. *On Life and Essays on Religion*. Translated with an Introduction by Aylmer Maude. Oxford: Oxford University Press.

Unamuno, Miguel de. 1931. *The Tragic Sense of Life in Men and in Peoples*. Translated by J. E. Crawford Flitch with an Introductory Essay by Salvador de Madariaga. London: Macmillan.

Wilkinson, John. 1981. *Egeria's Travels to the Holy Land*. Revised Edition. Newly translated with Supporting Documents and Notes by John Wilkinson. Jerusalem: Ariel Publishing House.

Zeller, Richard and Edward Carmines. 1980. *Measurement in the Social Sciences. The Link Between Theory and Data*. Cambridge: Cambridge University Press.

Before

It might be told that I made the voyage and saw with my eyes the things
hereafter written, and that I might win a famous name with posterity.

Antonio Pigafetta (1969[1524?], p. 37)

For myself, the book is a sort of termination, a last employment of the past
concept-formations. I am now changing sails and seeking an untrod land. To
be sure, the voyage will probably find its end *before* [reaching] the coast. At
least, what happens to so many of my colleagues shall not happen to me: To
settle down comfortably in the ship itself so that eventually they think that the
ship itself is the new land.

Georg Simmel (1959[1912], pp. 241–2)

The Ant and the Cicada

One day the ant said to the cicada, 'I am tired of this life of mine. I run
around all day; always working hard, never a moment of rest. I look at
you and you really seem to enjoy life, singing away to your heart's
content, day after day. Could I do that?' 'Sure,' was the cicada's
prompt reply. 'Why don't you just become a cicada?' Some time later,
the ant and the cicada met again. 'Fancy seeing you,' said the ant. 'I
have tried very hard to follow your advice and turn into a cicada, but
I have had no luck. Just how would I do that?' 'Well,' replied the
cicada. 'That's for you to find out. I just gave you the general idea.
You will have to work out the details for yourself.'[1]

The general idea at the core of the research project behind this book – that of
story grammars – came to me in a flash one night in 1985. Within two days I had

fully developed the grammar that I subsequently used in my data collection projects. But the design of the computer program that would allow me to practically implement the grammar, the involvement in the collection of a large body of historical data, the refinement of the technique and a clear understanding of its limitations and power, the development of the tools of data analysis, and the pursuit of the epistemological implications of the new technique, were a different story. Working out the details took years of hard work, across several disciplines and subdisciplines – from sociology to linguistics, literary criticism, history, cognitive psychology, philosophy, computer science, and statistics. The quest is still ongoing and far from finished.

Surely, having the good sense to recognize the "doability" of a problem should be part of a scientist's intuition. Perhaps, I failed. Durkheim warned us a long time ago that there are problems that sociology can successfully tackle and problems that it cannot realistically approach with a glimmer of hope of providing a solution "in the foreseeable future." Although those problems may become doable at one time or another, "that time ... is so distant that it is not worth it to tackle those problems" (Durkheim, 1898, pp. v, vi). Wittgenstein, in his lapidary style, thus prefaced his *Tractatus Logico-Philosophicus*: "What we cannot talk about we must pass over in silence" (Wittgenstein, 1961, p. 3).[2]

Only one problem. Whether a problem is "doable" or "undoable" we may only find out at the end of a long struggle. In a letter to Professor Black dated October 24, 1796, James Watt, the inventor of the steam engine, wrote:

> I did not invent this method piece meal but all at once in a few hours in 1765 I believe. The first step was the idea from the elastic nature of steam of condensing in a separate vessel, 2d the getting out the water by a long pipe and the air by a pump, 3d that the pump would extract the water also 4th that grease might be used in place of water to keep the piston tight, 5th that steam might be employed to press upon the piston in place of air 6 to keep the cylinder warm. The next day I set about it.[3]

And the next day, and the next day, and the next day ... Watt's biographer, Samuel Smiles (1865, p. 130) tells us: "[T]hough the invention was complete in Watt's mind [in 1765], it took him many long and laborious years to work out the details of the engine." Even those "few hours in 1765" must be read in context. "There is no question here of any precocious or sudden inspiration," warns French historian Paul Mantoux (1983, p. 319). Watt was well familiar with "fire engines." He had started steam experiments in 1761 (or 1762) and had thoroughly studied Newcomen's engine a couple of years later (Mantoux, 1983, pp. 319–20). My own "night of 1985" had been preceded by years of work spent searching for alternative ways of studying historical processes. The story of those years sheds light on the concerns that have motivated this project.

"It Takes Two to Tango": In Search of the Actor

In the early 1980s, by the end of my dissertation work – an econometric analysis of official strike statistics in the Italian postwar period – I had come to a depressing conclusion. Quantitative strike research had produced an abundant literature in its one hundred or so years of history (Franzosi, 1989a). But that literature was remarkably repetitive and uninspiring (Merton's pathology of science number two, in Diesing's rendering: "Repeated publication of trivial work and academic recognition for sheer quantity of publication"; Diesing, 1991, p. 156). For decades, it had focused narrowly on the statistical relationship between the number of strikes and one measure or another of economic activity – price index, unemployment rate, import figures, production figures, and the like. Occasionally, there would be forays into studying other measures of strike activity (for example, number of workers involved in strikes). But pinning down statistically the determinants of the temporal ups and downs of these other strike indicators proved to be less tractable. As a consequence, that task was seldom embarked upon. Scores of scholars continued to pour their energies into producing countless studies on the empirical relationship between the number of strikes and economic activity – incidentally, this is how scientists proceed: They focus on relationships they can positively support, even to the point of boredom, and ignore what proves to be recalcitrant to their efforts.

The general lack of innovation was not the only problem with the quantitative strike literature. More damagingly, that literature simply missed the point. The exclusive emphasis on what workers do – strike – and at a very aggregate level at that, ignored a basic fact: Strikes represent only one aspect of the broader relationship between workers and employers in a legal/political framework set and guaranteed by the state. To understand what workers do, we must understand what employers and the state do. In other words, "if it takes two to tango, it takes at least two to fight" (Franzosi, 1995, p. 16). Strikes are a multiple-actor, multiple-action phenomenon. Alas, official strike statistics – originally collected to monitor the "moods" of the laboring classes to the benefit of worried elites – do not allow us to say anything about any of that. But, what if you do want to say something about that? What are the empirical prescriptions of that view of history? Which kind of research design? Which kind of data, of method?

Michael Shalev once put it to me very cogently in the course of a conversation we had in Washington, D.C., at the Fourth International Conference of Europeanists in October 1983:

> Roberto – he more or less said – your econometric and spectral analyses of Italian strike data have squeezed official strike statistics for their last drop. Perhaps, it's time to move on. You see, if you have a lemon, you can squeeze it by hand to get some juice out of it. If you

squeeze it with a juicer you get more juice. If you put the lemon in a centrifuge you'll get all the juice in the lemon. But if you need more juice, you'd better get yourself a grapefruit.

The Lemon and the Grapefruit

My work as a "science grocer" had already started during the academic year 1981–82 at the Center for Research on Social Organization (CRSO) at the University of Michigan. At CRSO, Charles Tilly, William Gamson, Jeffery Paige, and their graduate students raised the level of dignity of newspapers as sources of sociohistorical data. Indeed, the "thick" descriptions of newspaper articles on social conflict (strikes, demonstrations, riots, and so on) seemed to provide the key to my search for the actor.

The technique traditionally used in the social sciences to extract a set of characteristics from a text is known as *content analysis*. In content analysis each characteristic of a text of interest to an investigator is formalized as a "coding category" – the set of all coding categories known as "coding scheme." The scheme is then systematically applied to a text to extract uniform and standardized information: If a text contains information on any of the coding categories of the coding scheme, the relevant coding category is "ticked off" (a process known as "coding" in content analysis and carried out by a "coder"). Content analysis then turns words into numbers by counting each tick for each category to obtain basic frequency distributions of the occurrence of certain types of information in the texts. Thus, a coding scheme works like a survey questionnaire administered to a sample of texts rather than to a sample of human respondents. Coder and interviewer play similar roles. In neither case are these figures simple transcribing devices. But in content analysis, the coder plays a greater role in the production of "data" through the interpretation of texts.

Upon my return to Rome, I put into practice the idea of using content analysis on newspaper data for a project on industrial conflict in postwar Italy (1945–80). Nothing substantive came out of that work, only a methodological innovation: A paper-based coding scheme that pushed one step further toward a more fully relational design the scheme adopted by Tilly in his project on popular protest in Great Britain.[4] A year later, at the University of Wisconsin-Madison, I used that scheme as the springboard for the development of a more general computer-assisted and linguistics-based approach to the collection of narrative data.[5] By 1986, at the dawn of the PC era, I had succeeded in developing a first version of a computer-assisted, fully relational coding scheme. With that tool – not to mention several research grants and teams of coders – between 1986 and 1990 in Genoa, Italy, I collected newspaper data on Italian social conflict for the years 1919–22 (over 15,000 articles coded from *Il Lavoro*) and 1986–87 (almost 14,000 articles coded from *L'Unità*).

The approach to text coding that I took differed from traditional content analysis not simply because it was based on direct computer data entry (hardly a claim to innovation given that computers were not around in the 1940s and 1950s when content analysis was first developed). The real difference was my grounding of the coding scheme to underlying structural, linguistic properties of a text, rather than to an investigator's theoretical framework. What I eventually adopted is known as a "semantic grammar" or "text grammar" (as opposed to a "syntax grammar") or "story grammar" (because it works particularly well – if not "only" well – when applied to stories or narrative texts). Basically, a story grammar is nothing but the simple linguistic structure subject-action-object or actor-action-actor with their respective modifiers (for example, number of actors involved, type of actor, time and space of action, reason, outcome).

A story grammar was the ideal tool for my "search for the actor," given the grammar's focus on actors, their actions, and their attributes. And during data analysis (carried out at the University of Oxford between 1996 and 1999) the grammar had more surprises in store for me. The relational properties of the grammar allowed me to use powerful new tools of analysis that promised to get sociology closer to history in its concern with social actors: network models.

Over a twenty-year period (and through many of Watt's sleepless nights), I had succeeded in getting myself a grapefruit, a magic grapefruit that would turn words into numbers and deliver the actor and more.

Of Journeys and Alchemies

From words *to* numbers. This is a journey – the book, a fair account of what I saw during this twenty-year voyage from words to numbers across continents and countries and several academic disciplines – a journey often exhausting, occasionally humiliating, but always exhilarating.

The metaphor of the journey runs through the book providing the imageries that hold the plot together. There is a rich literary tradition built around this metaphor: Life as a journey, as embraced by Christian eschatology; death as a journey, as held by the many ancient cultures that buried the dead with a boat and enough food to undertake the last journey to the other world. You even find that imagery in the unlikely world of science (as in a scientist's journey *to* a discovery). In Claude Lévi-Strauss's *Tristes Tropiques*, the physical journey (to the Brazilian Amazon), the personal, and the scientific journeys fuse together in one of the most beautiful social science books of the twentieth century.

I set off on this journey in search of the actor and to find an answer to a simple substantive sociological question: If "it takes two to tango," how can I document the role of the social actors involved in conflict situations? From sociology, I was forced to march across the territory of linguistics, computer science, and statistics in order to get to the numbers. Occasionally, I would make rapid incursions into the fields of cognitive psychology, literary criticism, political science, anthropology, and philosophy. And the territory of the historian – to insist on Le Roy Ladurie's image (1979b) – provides the very background of the journey. And this is not only because in the book I entertain a constant dialogue with history, but because I look at the many problems we encounter in this journey through the lenses of time: How other travelers, close and distant, saw those same problems and the solutions they adopted is a fundamental part of the way I write my travel book.

I entertained a constant dialogue with the close and distant travelers I met along the road. My *per agere* – the pilgrimage, the voyage – an academic *per agere*, a traversing of fields, and a *per agere* across time. After all, Descartes (1960, p. 42), who spent a great deal of his life traveling, tells us that "to hold converse with those of other ages and to travel are almost the same thing." I took to heart Giordano Bruno's reproach that I am an "ass," that I am modern out of ignorance of the past. I traced the development of arguments in time, I chased after long-dead authors and precursors in this archeology of knowledge. As French historian Lucien Febvre (1932, p. 9) put it:

> We have lingered, and not without reason, over these distant precursors. There is nothing more essential in the study of any scientific question than to consider the manner in which the first investigators stated the terms of the problem before them, and seldom do we fail to find therein the deep-seated reason for many delays and difficulties.

True. I read countless medieval accounts of *peregrinationes maiores*, fifteenth- and sixteenth-century voyages of discovery, medieval alchemic tracts, and Renaissance treatises on the art of memory. But the past catapulted me into the future. Myself a late twentieth-century reader of Egeria and Saewulf, of Albertus Magnus and Columbus, in writing this book I increasingly started taking the point of view of a reader in the year 2520. Why should you, 2520 reader, be interested in my writing? What's in it for you?

It is the potential for innovation that attracted me to the metaphor of the journey. After all, metaphors are figures of speech that, by definition, link different worlds together (as in "Nancy is a gem," or "time is money"). "*The essence of metaphor is understanding and experiencing one kind of thing in terms of another.*"[6] "The metaphor doubles or multiplies an idea," wrote Giacomo Leopardi,[7] one of the great poets of the early nineteenth century; "it represents more than one idea at the same time." By multiplying images, metaphors provide opportunities for imaginative creativity. For Leopardi, metaphors are a true sign of a poet's "inventive and creative faculty."[8] Lakoff and Johnson (1980, p. 193) go one step further:

> metaphor ... unites reason and imagination. Reason, at the very least, involves categorization, entailment, and inference. Imagination ...

involves seeing one kind of thing in terms of another kind of thing. ...
Metaphor is thus *imaginative rationality*.

And that "imaginative rationality" should be all the more imaginative for the
metaphor of the journey. Even by itself, the concept of the journey conjures up
complex imageries.

A journey occurs simultaneously in space, in time and in the social
hierarchy. Each impression can be defined only by being jointly related
to these three axes, and since space is itself three-dimensional, five
axes are necessary if we are to have an adequate representation of any
journey. (Lévi-Strauss, 1992, p. 85)

But what did the "imaginative rationality" of the metaphor of the journey help
me to see that I could perhaps not have seen without it? Basically, the metaphor
exposed me to different types of journeys – religious, military, scientific, and
journeys of geographic exploration – and to the accounts left behind by these
different travelers. There is a "fundamental link," writes Tucker (1996, p. 29),
"between the phenomenon or the idea of travel and the process of reading or
writing." The metaphor highlighted different ways of seeing among these
different travelers. But it also brought out fundamentally similar linguistic
mechanisms across very different types of travel diaries, in particular, the
systematic emphasis on certain aspects of the journey and the silence on others.
The accounts of the early explorers and conquistadores of the new world tell us
very little of the brutality with which they treated local populations in the name
of God and of the kings. They tell us very little about the encounters between
local women and the European newcomers. But they do tell us a great deal about
the riches to expect from further geographical explorations and expeditions. If
they could only have more money, more ships, more men ... (does this remind
anyone of the modern scientific research proposal?) (Ife, 1992, p. 18). Similarly,
early Christian pilgrims to the Holy Land only had eyes and ears for what is
Christian. They tell us nothing of the dangerous mixture of sacred and profane
that such long journeys entail (particularly on ships; particularly for women), of
the liminal and liminoid aspects of these experiences.[9] Surprisingly, they are
even silent about their emotional experience. The autobiographic and personal
element is almost entirely absent in the genre, particularly in the earlier period
(Richard, 1981, p. 21). These same mechanisms of silence and emphasis are at
work in the media production of news, of those accounts that serve as the basis
(as data sources) for the many studies that go "from words to numbers" in the
social movement literature. Even our scientific texts – those accounts of our own
journeys – present that same odd mixture of silence and emphasis.

While the metaphor of the journey allowed me to see new things, the metaphor
also gave me a powerful tool to recount what I saw in new ways – the metaphor
as both "ways of seeing" and "ways of telling." The metaphor offered the
illusion of artistic creativity: Of enlivening an otherwise dry methodological

text, of drawing parallels and connecting distant worlds, of forging new things (beautiful things) on top of and above the scientific creativity expressed in the sociological imagination, in the development of new tools for answering historical and sociological questions (from words to numbers). The metaphor promised to annul the difference between art and science not only in terms of their common creative spirit – "the motivations, desires, rhythms, and itches which lie behind creativeness in any realm" – but also in terms of the very mode of expressing in writing the scientific products of the sociological imagination. I pursued that promise, treading the common terrain (of aesthetics and problems of knowledge) between artistic and scientific inquiry (Nisbet, 1976, pp. 4, 10).

ALCHIMISTA MEDIEVALIS. *From* words *to* numbers. A journey, you say. But it seems to me more like an alchemy, an alchemic transformation of words *into* numbers.

AUTHOR. Why would I need yet another metaphor for the book, yet another way of reading the text? Don't I have enough as is?

ALCHIMISTA MEDIEVALIS. A book is not interesting unless it is complex. One of your contemporaries, certain Pierre Boulez, wrote:

> A work of which you can discover all its paths once and for all in one go is a flat work, lacking in mystery. The mystery of a work consists, rightly, in this polysemy of levels of reading. Be it a book, a painting or a piece of music.[10]

AUTHOR. This is a scientific text, not a work of art! And even for a work of art, neither Hegel nor Croce (1923) were too fond of allegory and hermeneutic readings, which they regarded as a killer of artistic inspiration.

ALCHIMISTA MEDIEVALIS. Suit yourself. But I don't believe either Croce or Hegel are remembered for their poetry. They have the one-sided view of art as creative illumination, typical of those who are not artists themselves. In any case alchemy would allow you to understand some of your own social science twentieth-century work as alchemy. You do have much to learn from us!

"The Law of Genre"[11]

Genres have their laws – and laws are always constraining.[12] Thus, the content of medieval pilgrims' travel books quickly became ritualized. Was the display of Christian pity that we find in these diaries part of the genre? Was the silence on the nonreligious aspects of one's journey – those aspects you find in Chaucer's *Canterbury Tales* – also part of the genre? What was real and what was fictional in these narratives? With different pilgrims often copying full handedly from other pilgrims' diaries, the line between these two worlds often blurred, a characteristic that was true even for the diaries of the early Renaissance transoceanic explorers.

Scientific texts are particularly subservient to the "law of genre." Having rejected a view of social science as art in our quest for scientific status, we have worked hard at suppressing the stylistic freedom that comes with a view of social science as art.[13] The cost of nonconformity to the "canons" are high. No one knew this better than Georg Simmel (1858–1918), who got his first permanent academic appointment at the age of fifty six in the peripheral University of Strasbourg. Even the warmest of Simmel's supporters were dismayed by his "personal ... disorganized, even irritating" writing style (Wolff, 1950, p. xix). With no explanatory footnotes or endnotes, no references to any of his contemporaries' or predecessors' work, Simmel "speaks for himself, along with the immortal dead" (Levine, 1971, p. x). He broke the norm of academic specialization, publishing widely across a range of topics in literature, art, philosophy, psychology, and sociology. He broke the norm of academic jargon, largely addressing his work to a nonacademic audience, and increasingly so in his life (Coser, 1965, pp. 34–6).

In an attempt to unravel the riddle of Simmel's work and life Wolff asked: "Is there a relation between a man's biography and his work?" (Wolff, 1950, p. xvii). Coser provided a brilliant sociological answer to that question. Relying on Merton's work on science and on Merton's concept of *role set* – "the differing expectations as to the behavior of a person occupying a particular status" (Coser, 1965, p. 32) – Coser teased out the close connection between the personal and the professional in Simmel's life. "Simmel's very quest for originality stemmed in part from his self-image as a scholar. ... Simmel conformed to the goals of the academy, but he rejected the norms governing the ways and means for their attainment" (Coser, 1965, p. 37). Not surprisingly, Simmel increasingly put his energies where he found rewards. With a continued low status in the German academy in the face of a growing international reputation as a scholar and of a vast following as a histrionic and brilliant lecturer, Simmel increasingly wrote in the same style in which he lectured, addressing in print that same public that faithfully followed his lectures in the Berlin classrooms.

But if the relationship between life and work may be an appropriate subject of social scientific investigation – particularly when this involves the lives of others and when we can bring to bear sociological concepts to the interpretation – the investigation of the relationship between *our* personal and professional lives is out of the question. Science demanded (and obtained) the head of the personal. And in the name of science, the personal has been publicly and repeatedly executed. No differently from the Bordeaux Pilgrim, who traveled to the Holy Land in 333 A.D. and who left behind the first extant account of a pilgrim's journey, we have no eyes or ears for the personal. Few voices have risen to its defense. Among them, C. Wright Mills was a passionate advocate of a social science based on "the interplay of man and society, of biography and history, of self and world."[14] A few years later, Peter Berger revisited the connection between biography, sociology, and history. "Sociological consciousness ... is

... a live option for the individual seeking to order the events of his own life in some meaningful fashion" (Berger, 1963, p. 68). In a perhaps overly optimistic view of the "debunking and relativizing" power of sociology, for Berger, sociological consciousness provides the individual with the insight that every world view is "*socially grounded*," that "every *weltanschauung* is a conspiracy" perpetrated by those "who construct a social situation in which the particular world view is taken for granted" and the basic assumptions are shared unconsciously (Berger, 1963, p. 78). Understanding one's biography as a continuous process of reinvention of the self in light of forever changing social relations, of selection of personal events to fit the current construction of the self, is equivalent to the historian's constant selection and reselection of past events in light of the present's point of view (Berger, 1963, pp. 68–80). Coming from a different discipline, Claude Lévi-Strauss (1992, pp. 58–9) had put it in remarkably similar words: "Anthropology affords me intellectual satisfaction: As a form of history, linking up at opposite ends with world history and my own history, it thus reveals the rationale common to both. ... It allows me to reconcile my character with my life."

C. Wright Mills made the following recommendation to the young scholar: To read widely here and there, to take good notes, to keep open files on many simultaneously ongoing projects, and, more to the point, to "not split their work from their lives" (Mills, 1959, pp. 195–9). In Mills's view (1959, pp. 5, 6, 13), the "sociological imagination" is the key instrument that

> enables its possessor to understand the larger historical scene in terms of its meaning for the inner life ... to grasp history and biography and the relations between the two within society. That is its task and its promise. ... our most needed quality of mind.

Not a popular view of social science, Mills painfully acknowledged. "Of late the conception of social science I hold," he wrote, "has not been ascendant" (Mills, 1959, p. 20). Rather, ascendant is a view of social science that takes a detached view of the scientific process, "value-free social science." The personal, the biographical has no place in science. Durkheim (1938, pp. 32, 34) had no doubts on the issue:

> Our political and scientific beliefs and our moral standards carry with them an emotional tone that is not characteristic of our attitude toward physical objects; consequently, this emotional character infects our manner of conceiving and explaining them. ... Sentiment is a subject for scientific study, not the criterion of scientific truth.

And yet, for all our concerted efforts to keep the personal out of our texts, to situate ourselves *outside* the text can we *really* escape the personal? Can we *really* step outside the play, as in Brecht's theatrical innovation? Do not our texts often emplot our deeply personal world views in unconscious ways – a metahistory in the writing of history, a metascience in the writing of science:

Michelet the romantic, Marx the tragic, Burckhardt the ironic (White, 1973, 1987)? Even Max Weber, with his life-long inability "of directly revealing himself" and his single-minded pursuit of objectivity as a scholar, ends up revealing something of himself in that very quest for objectivity. "What was most personal to him is accessible and at the same time hidden by the objectification of his work" (Gerth and Mills, 1946b, p. 27). And *he* himself wrote: "[T]he 'personal' element of a scientific work is what is really valuable in it, and that personality must be expressed in every work if its existence is to be justified" (Weber, 1949, p. 82).

"Methodological Pestilence"

For all his obsession with objectivity and rigor, one thing is certain: Max Weber was not very fond of methodological pursuits, in his view, a "methodological pestilence."[15] "The type of social science in which we are interested is an empirical science of concrete reality," not methodological or epistemological reflections (Weber, 1949, p. 72). For Weber,

> Sciences are founded and their methods are progressively developed only when substantive problems are discovered and solved. Purely epistemological or methodological reflections have never yet made a decisive contribution to this project. (Cited in Oakes, 1977, p. 14)

Weber was airing in this passage an idea that Hegel had already put forward a century before. Hegel saw art in his age in a state of terminal decline. "The beautiful days of Greek art," he wrote in his *Introductory Lectures on Aesthetics* (1993, pp. 12–3), "and the golden time of the later middle ages are gone by. ... Art is ... a thing of the past." The multiplication of work of literary and art criticism was for the master a clear sign of the decline. Art and critical reflection upon art do not go well together and Hegel saw his age as an age of criticism and rationality (Inwood, 1993, pp. ix–xi). "Our present ... is not favorable to art. ... the *science* of art is a much more pressing need in our day" (Hegel, 1993, p. 13). George Bernard Shaw (1959, p. 217) was to give this concept its familiar popular culture epitaph: "He who can, does. He who cannot, teaches." To which, Lazarsfeld added (1993, p. 257): "And those who have nothing to teach, become methodologists." You will find plenty of those in sociology, indeed, "the science with more methods and fewer results," in Poincaré's judgment, where "every new doctoral thesis proposes a new method" (1997, p. 13).

Yet, in complex projects, of whatever nature, the very complexity of the tasks, the very length of the "sequence of purposes," induces an "expedient attitude" of concentrating "one's energies on that stage of the sequence of purposes that should be realized next," and that is often purely technical, as Simmel explains.[16] The next stage in the sequence, only a means to the next purpose, tends to become the final purpose itself, the means tends to become the end. But this focused attention on intermediate ends, on the means, brings with it the danger that the means displace the ends. We lose sight of the final purpose, we get lost in the early stages of the teleological sequence of purposes. Such danger is increasing in modern societies. "A larger proportion of civilized man remains forever enslaved, in every sense of the word, in the interest in *technics*. The conditions on which the realization of the ultimate object depends claim their attention, and they concentrate their strength on them, so that real purposes completely disappears from consciousness. Indeed, they are often denied." Sociologists' increasing interest in methodology, perhaps this very journey from words to numbers, is indeed a case in point.

And yet, what are our choices? For Simmel, the concentration on the inter-mediate purposes/means that the attainment of great purposes requires "is of immensurable value to mankind." Wouldn't, otherwise, the sheer magnitude of large projects cripple us, "if we had to be constantly aware of the whole sequence of means for the ultimate purpose while working on each subordinate means." Wouldn't we lose "the strength ... [or] the interest for the immediate task, if we ... realized the logical insignificance of the means in relation to the ultimate ends?" Nobel Prize winner James Watson could not agree more with that. In his upbeat account of the discovery of the double helix he wrote:

> In England, if not everywhere, most botanists and zoologists were a muddled lot. Not even the possession of University Chairs gave many the assurance to do clean science; some actually wasted their efforts on useless polemics about the origin of life or how we know that a scientific fact is really correct. (Watson, 1969, p. 53)

Worrisome words for me, as I now hold a University Chair in England (thank God, not in botany or zoology!). More to the point, worrisome words, in light of my own involvement in the philosophy of science in a methodological text ... C. Wright Mills dedicated a scathing chapter ("Abstracted Empiricism") of his *The Sociological Imagination* to a critique of this "methodological pestilence." He wrote: "As a matter of practice, abstracted empiricists often seem more concerned with the philosophy of science than with social study itself. What they have done, in brief, is to embrace one philosophy of science which they now suppose to be The Scientific Method" (Mills, 1959, p. 57).

Hopefully, the fundamental concern for deeply substantive problems that has motivated my methodological quest can rescue this work from Weber, Poincaré, Mills, and Watson's scorn. After all, Galileo's discovery of solar sunspots, of the four satellites of Jupiter, and of the craters and valleys on the moon – which showed that the moon was not a sphere and not the perfect heavenly body held by Aristotelian cosmology, another blow to the medieval world of authority – was the result of Galileo's involvement in technique: in June or July 1609 he constructed his first three-powered spyglass, he presented an eight-powered version to the Venetian Senate in August, and used a twenty-powered instrument to explore the skies in October or November 1609.

If politics is too important for us to leave it in the hands of politicians, perhaps methodology is also too important for us to leave it in the hands of methodologists. Theoretical and methodological concerns inextricably intertwine in substantively driven research. For one thing, "at any given time knowledge depends on the particular state of methods in use; future knowledge will depend on the development of today's methods" (Cicourel, 1964, p. 7). As Comte put it: "In every science, conceptions which relate to method are inseparable from those which relate to the doctrine under consideration" (1896, vol. 2, p. 210). Certainly in my own research journey, if substantive concerns led me deep into the world of methodology, in its turn, what I found there led me back into the world of substance and theory. Remember: Nothing could be said about what employers do or what the state does on the basis of official strike statistics. The analyses of Chapters 2 and 3 in Part I paint a much richer historical picture than available official strike statistics could ever hope for. More broadly, the kind of epistemological reflection that I undertake in this book would have been unthinkable without my close involvement with the methodological and theoretical aspects of my research agenda.

In any case, regardless of the substantive and theoretical concerns that push us into methodological work, measurement itself, consciously or unconsciously, presupposes some theory about what is measured. What is measured, counted, classified, or analyzed presupposes a certain view of the social world, a certain understanding of social facts, and the construction of objects of scientific inquiry. In Cicourel's words (1964, p. 29): "Every methodological decision presupposes some theoretical equivalent even though our present state of knowledge may not be adequate for determining precisely what the correspondence is." And some would even argue that our theories may be nothing but "necessary consequences of our modes of measurement" – the link between theory and measurement being reduced to an identity.[17]

There is another sense in which methodological work spills over into further theoretical work: What is methodology for some is theoretical work for others. Thus, it was mostly linguists who carried out the theoretical work behind story grammars, the methodological tool I used to structure narrative text. But when we step into the linguists' world with the spirit of settlers rather than that of academic raiders, we are sure to find there a bountiful cornucopia of concepts and tools that could prove very useful to the social scientist settler. Thus, linguists push us into a much more nuanced interpretation of texts and their meanings. They cast long shadows of doubts where people used to handling numbers only see certainties. They push us to consider texts – all texts, alas, even scientific texts (even numbers!) – as cultural artefacts produced under certain conditions, for certain purposes, according to certain rules, and for certain audiences – the product of a period, reflecting specific social arrangements. From there, the stride is short toward a view of our (scientific) work as rhetoric, or, worse yet, as ideology (that is, as cultural artefacts that, regardless of intentions, substantive issues, theoretical frameworks, and methodological approaches, operate to support existing social relations of power). Linguistics would uncover the implicit narratives hidden behind the facade of statistical models ("from numbers to words"). Linguistics would unveil the language conventions that help to underpin our views of an "objective" science (for example, through the use of active rather than passive, metonymic rather than metaphorical constructs).

Yet, in stepping into unfamiliar disciplines, I am also well aware of another intellectual risk: Of embarking upon a journey that will take me across a number of disciplines. George Lundberg's warning of "the incredible absurdities of which even brilliant scientists are capable when they venture into other fields than their own specialty" is as good a currency today as at the time of the 1929 crash when Lundberg wrote it (Lundberg, 1929, p. 393). With no claims on my part of brilliance or science, what will save me from Lundberg's scorn? Yet, for as frightening as I found the idea of blabbering absurdities, I found the alternative even more frightening, of perhaps blabbering trivialities by treading closely to disciplinary paths. "Transgression of disciplinary boundaries," stated Bourdieu, "is a prerequisite for scientific advance."[18]

An Antiquarian in a Modern World

I have worked on this book with the spirit of an aesthetic antiquarian.[19] From the antiquarian I borrowed a passion for the old and the forgotten and the pleasure of bringing it back to life. It is that passion that imparts the book with an old-fashioned ring: the division in parts, the prologues, the epilogues, the epigraphs, the Latin titles, the symmetric structure, the looking back to by-gone worlds. Psychologist Michael Billig put it best when he wrote:

> Psychologists are supposed to be modern. Take a look at any professional journal which reports the latest pieces of research, and you will see how up-to-the-moment most psychologists are. Each article will refer to a clutch of other articles, published not more than five years ago, mostly in the same journal, and some, tantalizingly, just about to be published. Perhaps, some older articles will creep into this showroom of intellectual modernity, often under the guise of being 'classics' or 'pathfinding researches.' It would not be good form to write an article in the 1980s which was filled with references to work done in the 1970s and 1960s. As for the 1950s, that would be stretching matters too far. (Billig, 1987, p. 1)

Lévi-Strauss (1992, p. 103) similarly wrote:

> Our students wanted to know everything but, whatever the field of interest, only the most recent theory seemed to them to be worthy of

being memorized. They were indifferent to all the intellectual feats of the past, which in any case they only knew of by hearsay since they did not read the original works, and were always ready to enthuse over new dishes. But in their case fashion is a more appropriate metaphor than cooking: Ideas and theories had no intrinsic interest for them; they were merely instruments of prestige and the important thing was to be the first to know about them.

I share Lévi-Strauss's and Billig's ambivalence toward the tantalizingly modern. I share Billig's "pathological" obsession of haphazardly reading "passages from old and not-so-old books," of collecting notes and quotations from different ages, of gathering material with "the enthusiasm of the amateur" to illustrate my points. "The antiquarian psychologist will seek out older psychologies, leaving the modern colleague to track down the latest references" (Billig, 1987, p. 2).

I only wish I had Billig's confidence to just pursue the old and ignore the new. Yet, I would find many on my side. Niebuhr wrote:

> Neither in my earlier studies nor during the course of my lectures did I use the most recent works on Roman history. Thus I was not tempted to engage in controversies which would have been inappropriate to this work and which in any case are of little benefit to science; they should be replaced by as complete an analysis as possible.[20]

Hobbes was more dismissive: "If I had read [these research papers] as much as other men," he wrote, "I should have known as little."[21] Descartes (1960, p. 60) tells us: "I was nevertheless prosecuting my design, and making greater progress in the knowledge of truth, than I might, perhaps, have made had I been engaged in the perusal of books merely." And to a young admirer, bewildered by the scarcity of books in Simmel's private library, Simmel confessed: "I don't read any more!"[22]

As for myself, I read the old and the new, including the tantalizingly new, the unpublished papers delivered at conferences, as suggested by well-meaning colleagues and not-so-well-meaning anonymous reviewers. Like the best of antiquarians, I got involved in a great deal of detective work in trying to track down the origin and development of debates to establish the thin trickle of ideas across time and space. Who first used the term "content analysis"? Where do numbers come from? Where did Ted Robert Gurr or Charles Tilly get their design of complex coding schemes for collective action research? What is the origin of the motto of the State of Maryland *fatti maschi, parole femmine* (something like "masculine deeds, feminine words")? I cannot honestly say that reading on the effects of light and sitting posture on human errors kept me up at night with excitement; yet, I pursued that literature with the same intensity that I devoted to the artificial art of memory or number magic. But little by little, what were haphazard questions at first almost became a method of inquiry. I systematically crucified colleagues in other disciplines with such questions: "Have you ever heard of the problem of ...?" "How do you see the issue of ...?" "Do you have any suggestions for some readings?"

Take the daunting problem of classifying human actions into a manageable set of categories from the thousands of language verbs that express those actions. I looked, first, at the literature on collective action – the closest to my immediate concerns. Finding no acceptable solution there, I turned to game theory, network, and power models. Dismayed not only by the diversity of solutions on offer but by their ad hoc nature, I moved to the philosophical and linguistic tradition of verb classification. Finally, intrigued by the issue of classification, I started asking questions not clearly or closely related to my specific problem: Is there a general problem of classification and categorization? Where did Darwin get his idea of classifying the natural world? Did his classification scheme lead him to the discovery of evolution? Will children confronted with the task of sorting objects in separate bins similarly distribute their objects? And bringing it all back to base, what does this tell us about the task at hand of classifying human actions as expressed in language verbs?

So, what answers did I find to all these questions? Where did this work lead? Wittgenstein, in the preface to his *Tractatus Logico-Philosophicus*, wrote:

> The book deals with the problems of philosophy ... the *truth* of the thoughts that are here communicated seems to me unassailable and definitive. I therefore believe myself to have found, on all essential points, the final solution of the problems. (Wittgenstein, 1961, pp. 3–4; emphasis in the original)

That confidence was not to be long lasting. A slow, critical rethinking of his positions ultimately led him to fundamentally reject the claims of the *Tractatus*. Never again in his life did Wittgenstein find himself in the enviable position of when he wrote the preface.

"All I knowe: And more (I know) then yet in any other," wrote John Florio (1598) in "The Epistle Dedicatorie" of his English-Italian Dictionary, *A Worlde of Wordes*. I could say the same (without the "yet in any other"). Despite such effort, I have never come even close to having solved the fundamental problems of content analysis, in spite of the modesty of that claim. After twenty years of work – that long I have spent on this journey of going from words to numbers – a rigorous and formal solution to "the fundamental problems of content analysis" still eludes me. Although a grammar provides a more rigorous classification scheme for text information than traditional content analysis schemes, the tool works well for narrative texts *only*. Text coding within the categories of a story grammar is probably a more natural process than coding within the abstract categories of traditional content analysis. Even so, the process of going from text to coding categories – be these the categories of a story grammar or of a traditional content analysis scheme – is as shrouded in mystery as ever. The coder's mind is still a "black box."

No doubt, from time to time, I have had my moments of enthusiastic euphoria *a la* Wittgenstein: In 1985, when I first formalized a story grammar approach to content analysis; in 1990, when I reexpressed a story grammar into a set theoretical notation, the same mathematical principles laying behind both models of data collection and of data organization and retrieval that I had adopted (story grammars and relational database systems); in 1997, when I pushed the mathematical link between words and numbers one step further, with set theory underlying the statistical models of data analysis as well (network models).

Novel Penelope – *mutatis mutandis* – I spent ten years patiently twisting the mathematical thin thread that links words to numbers. The linguistic tool that I adopt to structure narrative – story grammars – can be reexpressed in set theoretical notation; that same notation provides the mathematical underpinnings of the relational database management systems (RDBMS) that make a grammar practically feasible in a computer environment; the statistical models that are most compatible with the kind of relational structure of story grammars and relational database management systems – network models – are also based on set theory. What I have to offer, then, is a thin thread from words to numbers and a handful of clear solutions to the many problems encountered along the way. For the rest, I tried to narrow down and circumscribe the range of acceptable solutions, to show the relative value of some solutions in light of a long historical tradition, and, last but not least, to clearly highlight the points of weakness (rather than sweep them under the rug).

Captain James Cook, on his return from his second voyage of discovery to the South Pacific (1772–75), wrote on March 22, 1775, from Table Bay Cape of Good Hope a letter to the Admiralty Secretary that concluded (Cook, 1961, Vol. II, p. 693):

> If I have failed in discovering a Continent it is because it does not exist in a Navigable Sea and not for want of looking after ... Whoever has resolution and perseverance to find one beyond where I have been, I shall not envy him the honour of the discovery ...

Far from me the idea that I failed to find a solution to the many problems I unsuccessfully tackled "because it [a solution] does not exist." I did not discover it, not "for want of looking after." I just failed to find it. A solution is out there *somewhere*. No doubt, someone with a better mind than mine eventually will. One thing I did learn from this intellectual meandering of mine: That where a discipline runs into a dead end, another will open a highway, and that the new comes out of the old in often unpredictable and even paradoxical ways. Out of a centuries-old tradition in the artificial art of memory, with its Renaissance epigones in the occult arts, came Leibniz's work on infinitesimal calculus.[23] In Newton, the modern scientist lived side by side with the medieval alchemist. And Columbus's strictly medieval world-vision ushered in a new Renaissance world. When linguists abandoned the semantic field of text grammars as unfruitful, cognitive psychologists picked up the ball and kept it rolling. In the process, they lost much of the complexities and subtleties that linguists had brought to the topic, but added novelties of their own (namely the role of story grammars in cognition: from narrative competence in children, to the role of macrostructures in text understanding). And when computer scientists found themselves in need of a simple model for computer understanding of natural languages, they turned to the simple structure of story grammars (for example, Schank and Riesbeck, 1981). Again, they picked and chose from the linguists' and psychologists' tool bags. And while they have not fulfilled their early promises of an artificial intelligence solution to automated text processing, their goal is getting closer. And when they will get there – all too soon, I am afraid – the methodology of content analysis, even in its linguistic variant described in this book, will be a thing of the past, indeed, an antiquarian's curiosity.

Breaking the Law

"Genres are not to be mixed," cries out Derrida, "I will not mix genres. I repeat: Genres are not to be mixed. I will not mix them" (Derrida, 1992, p. 223). Yet, even Derrida (1992, p. 230) acknowledges that "Every text *participates* in one or several genres, there is no genreless text, there is always a genre and genres, yet such participation never amounts to belonging." The metaphor of the journey, with its multiple axes and complex imageries, offered a tantalizingly appealing way to mix genres, to push boundaries (*limen*), weaving into the text different threads of meaning – a discourse on science, on beauty, on content analysis, on scientific innovation, on theory. Narrative is the binding glue of this text. "Story" grammars, one of the tools we use in getting numbers out of words, heighten our consciousness of stories and narrative; and so does the basic metaphor of the book: the journey, with its close association with narrative. "The repetition of stories throughout the book, this insistence on a narrative scheme ultimately gives the reader an interpretative structure. ... [L]eitmotifs and repetitions bind the text together, linking beginning, middle and end."[24]

The postmodern vogue has made us all familiar with the idea of texts containing "layers of meaning." We have rediscovered the polysemic nature of texts, with writers and readers, authors and audiences locked into an implicit contract, where the division of labor is clear: The ones encode, the others decode. I say "rediscover" because, in fact, medieval culture had taken polysemy very seriously, turning it into a complex art.[25] And even more complex was the occult art of magic that flourished well into the Renaissance. Indeed, nothing, in the medieval eyes was as simple as it looked, as simple as it read. We will get a few glimpses in this book of those old games with words.

You, the reader, may not like this. You may, understandably so, reject this pact that subordinates your role to finding out what I, the author, have managed to cram into the text. If this text is all about me, the author, why should you get involved? Why should you want to play? I would not be surprised if you rather wished the death of the author.[26] And, naturally, this is my turn to rebel. After all, I have worked hard to embed these "layers of meaning." I have worked hard at playing a number of leitmotifs, of building the pillars over which the many bridges span that link the text. I have worked hard at exploring the infinite possibilities of our journey. Of Simmel's lectures, a student later recalled: "Just about the time when ... one felt he had reached a conclusion, he had a way of raising his right arm and, with three fingers of his hand, turning the imaginary object so as to exhibit still another facet."[27] Throughout the book I will keep raising my arm. I will keep turning my imaginary objects.

Journeys; "magic caskets full of dreamlike promises" (Lévi-Strauss, 1992, p. 37). Journeys; with their points of departure and arrival. From words *to* numbers. Are numbers our teleological destination? Indeed, in this journey, I do eventually lead the reader to numbers. Yet, it may not be through a straight "royal road" (Sorokin, 1956, p. 315), but, rather, through the tortuous path of many blind alleys and narrow dirt lanes – at times opening up the way as we journey along – with occasional stretches of broad, open highways. But, remember, "it behoves a man who wants to see wonders sometimes to go out of his way" (Mandeville, 1983, p. 113). Worse yet, when we eventually get there, the pilgrims' ecstasy and joy of finally being *there*, of having attained a life-long dream, of being one with God, is not for us. This journey ends on an ironic note. Having set out on this journey in search of the actor, when the actor we do find, we come to realize that we can only understand actors through their actions. But the meaning of action is largely beyond the reach of the tools developed for capturing the actor – story grammars. T. S. Eliot writes in *The Dry Salvages,* one of the *Four Quartets:* "We had the experience but missed the meaning." We are on the road again. If "irony ... is the product of the union of an artistic sense of life with the scientific spirit," in Schlegel's words, then, perhaps, it is only fitting that a book that tries so hard to break the boundaries between art and science (to trespass the *limen*) should end that way.[28] Or, perhaps, its ironic ending betrays the book's fundamental humanistic stance. As Peter Berger put it in his *Invitation to Sociology. A Humanistic Perspective:* "[T]he mere presence in an intellectual discipline of ironical scepticism concerning its own undertakings is a mark of its humanistic character."[29]

So, in the end, we may get nowhere in this journey of ours; although this black-and-white masculine language of hate *or* love, success *or* failure, victory *or* defeat precludes the possibility of infinite compromises, of *still* getting somewhere. Like the Celtic monks of the early centuries of the Christian era aimlessly traveling across Europe, as we travel from words to numbers, the journey may even be more telling than where we get. At least for now, the numbers may have to settle for a partial victory over words (or defeat, depending on whose side you are on). There may be some consolation in that. In Nietzsche's (1954, p. 160) words: "You may have only enemies whom you can hate, not enemies you despise. You must be proud of your enemy: Then the success of your enemy are your successes too." *Chapeau bas* to the words!

Chapeau bas to the words, for sure. Yet, again, you may not like this. You may find such an anticlimactic ending not to your taste. As C. Wright Mills wrote:[30]

> Certain types of critics judge work in social science according to whether or not its conclusions are gloomy or sunshiny, negative or constructive. These sunshine moralists want a lyric upsurge, at least at the end: They are made happy by a sturdy little mood of earnest optimism, out of which we step forward fresh and shining.

In your eyes, I may have *broken the law* (of genres). I may not have kept the author's promise (almost a guarantee) of delivering *something* at the end, according to the law of genres. I provide no closure to the quest. Yet, as Simmel put it in his *Soziologie*: "The individual can attain closure here only in the subjective sense that *he communicates everything that he has been able to see.*"[31] And that I have faithfully (even painstakingly) done. But, if this is not enough, I propose a compromise that, hopefully, you will find acceptable. "This book consists of many books," wrote Julio Cortázar in the "Author's Note" to his *Rayuela* (Cortázar, 1967). And he then proceeded to offer his readers at least two options on how to choose the book they want to read. I should do the same, for "the sunshine moralists": Stop reading at Part I, where I recount all the marvelous things we have seen in this journey. Alternatively, consider this as an episode in an ongoing saga, like the serial publication of many of Hugo's or Zola's novels, where the end of a story is the prelude to a new story, the end a new beginning. "The end is nothing but the beginning," one reads in the *Turba Philosophorum*, an anonymous alchemic tract of Arabic origin falsely attributed to Arisleus, "death is the cause of life and the beginning of the end."[32] In T. S. Eliot's beautiful verses of *Little Gidding, Four Quartets*:

> What we call the beginning is often the end / And to make an end is to make a beginning, / The end is where we start from. / ... / We shall not cease from exploration / And the end of all our exploring / Will be to arrive where we started / And know the place for the first time.

Then, the lack of closure will be nothing more than a rhetorical device to entice you to journey together in the future. This I am willing to promise to you; this pact with the reader I am willing to sign; this law of genre I am willing to obey: That "business as usual" should never be "ritualism as usual."[33]

Of Prefaces and Introductions: Guidebook for the Journey

The philosopher Georg Hegel was not fond of prefaces or introductions – and perhaps that is why he faithfully wrote prefaces to his books ... to deny their function. The inherent contradiction of the genre did not escape the great master: Its *raison d'etre* in a knowledge before knowledge, in a writing *before* writing, but which, of necessity, must be written *after* what follows, in order to be able to summarize it.[34] In the preface to his *Phenomenology of Spirit*, he explained:

> In the preface of a book it is customary to explain the author's aim, the reasons why he wrote the book, and what he takes to be its relationship to other treatments, earlier or contemporary, of the same subject. In the case of a philosophical work, however, such an explanation seems not only superfluous but, owing to the nature of the subject matter, altogether improper and unsuited to the end in view.

That may well be for philosophy. "Philosophical truth," Hegel continued, "cannot be presented in this manner" in a preface. Gerard Genette, in a seminal study on paratexts,[35] highlights that fundamental function of prefaces to "inform the reader about the origin of the work, the circumstances in which it was written, the stages of its creation" (Genette, 1997, p. 210). This is exactly what I have done in the first sections of this Preface/Before. But prefaces or introductions may also perform other functions. To the preface, ancient rhetoric assigned the risky and difficult task of catching the reader's interest, "*to get the book read*"[36] – risky, because an author is investing years of work in a handful of pages – in light of this, short prefaces, or no prefaces, may be the best strategy, as recommended by Quevedo "God spare thee, reader, long prefaces";[37] difficult, because, in a preface, an author has to tread the fine line between exalting one's contribution without appearing too arrogant. In the old days, the typical approach was: Exalt the topic and excuse one's inadequacy; *amplificatio* and *excusatio propter infirmitatem*. Genette (1997, p. 200) credits Rousseau with having taken the first bold step into the modern world of advertising when he wrote: "I am undertaking a work which has no example, and whose execution will have no imitator." And yet, this is no match to Giordano Bruno's dedication of his *De umbris idearum* (The shadows of Ideas) to Henry III, king of France:

> Who would ignore, most holy majesty, that to the greats are due precious gifts, to the majors more precious gifts, and to the maximums, the most precious of gifts? For this reason no one will be surprised if this work (*which must be counted among the most important for the nobility of the subject dealt with, the originality of the findings upon which it rests, and the depth of reasoning through which it is communicated*) is dedicated to you. ... (Bruno, 1997[1582], p. 39; emphasis added)

Bernal Díaz, a soldier who accompanied Cortés in the expedition that led to the conquest of Mexico, takes a different approach. He introduces himself to the reader of his *Historia verdadera de la conquista de la Nueva España* as a simple man (*idiota sin letras*), as "an old man, over eighty-four years of age ... [who has] lost both sight and hearing" and who has "gained no wealth to leave to ... [his] children and descendants." He undertakes the writing of his "true story ... a most remarkable one" "as an honest eyewitness, without twisting the facts in any way," contrary to Francisco Lopez de Gomara and Bartolomé de Las Casas who never give the truth "neither in the beginning, nor in the middle, nor the end" (Díaz, 1963, p. 14). From the start, Díaz sets up his narrative strategy to win the reader's sympathy to his side of the story.[38]

Certainly, one of the main purposes of prefaces is that of providing a synopsis of the arguments of the book, a summary of what is to come. This often takes the form of a chapter by chapter, if not section by section, explanation of the table of contents. Again, Hegel was critical of such introductory summaries: "For the subject matter is not exhausted by any aim, but only by the way in which things are worked out in detail; nor is the result the actual whole, but only the result together with its becoming." In this book, perhaps more so than in most social science books, the "becoming" is as important as the point of arrival, the details as telling as the "actual whole." It was Guy de Maupassant (1938, p. 334) who wrote that "an artist's originality is signaled first and foremost by small things rather than the big ones." And Ruskin echoed: "Greatness can only be rightly estimated when minuteness is justly reverenced. Greatness is the aggregation of minuteness."[39] Yet, summaries are helpful in providing a snapshot of the journey ahead, of what to expect. So, let me give you one, trusting that you will read beyond, to get the small things – the becoming and the details.

Part I takes the reader through the demanding *tour de force* of going from words to numbers. In Chapter 1, I show that a theoretical tool developed at the crossroad between linguistics and cognitive psychology, called "story grammar," has properties that make it a far more attractive "coding scheme" than traditional content analysis schemes for the collection of narrative data in sociohistorical research. Chapter 2 relies on computer science to offer practical solutions to the problem of storing and retrieving the huge mass of information that "story grammars" potentially deliver. In Chapter 3, it is statistics that shows us ways of analyzing narrative data (network models, in particular).

The illustrative examples of text coding based on a story grammar should give the reader enough tokens of the power of the tool. But the real touchstone of that power ultimately depends upon a positive answer to the question: Does the technique work with "real" data, rather than toy examples? "After all," as Descartes (1960, p. 40) writes, "it is possible I may be mistaken; and it is but a little copper and glass, perhaps, that I took for gold and diamonds." In Chapters 2 and 3, I put the technique to the test of "real" data, as collected from some 15,000 newspaper articles taken from the Italian newspaper *Il Lavoro*. The data capture all instances of social conflict in Italy during the 1919–22 period, a period that "may well have produced the highest level of involvement in collective violence ... in Italy's modern history" (Tilly et al., 1975, p. 126). The first two years (1919–20, the *Red Years*) witnessed the highest burst of working-class mobilization to that date (and, in any case, surpassed only by the 1969 "Hot Autumn"). The *Black Years* of 1921–1922 saw a rapid increase in fascist violence until October 1922 when Mussolini's "march on Rome" precipitated the collapse of the liberal state and the beginning of twenty years of dictatorship.

Throughout Chapters 2 and 3, history looms in the background. Yet, as a historian, you may be disappointed not to find here any serious engagement with the historians' views of this period. To avoid disappointment, I have to add another clause to my pact with the reader. *Do not expect a book on the origins of Italian fascism.* This is a book on ways of going from words to numbers, of using qualitative data for quantitative purposes. The 1919–22 period only provides the illustrative data on how this alchemy works. It is only the first step in "a sequence of purposes." You will have to wait for that book on fascism (but I promise, it will come).[40]

The analyses of Chapters 2 and 3 – however illustrative, however provisional – leave no doubt about the power of the technique of going "from words to numbers." The richness of the information made available by the combination of newspaper narratives and computer-assisted story grammars, the organizational structure of the data in relational form, and the application of such tools of analysis as network models bring out stark patterns in the historical evidence. In Lundberg's (1929, p. 390) vocabulary of science: "[T]he final test of the validity of any method must lie in its results. Whatever technique achieves the result sought is *ipso facto* a valid technique." And the technique delivered exactly what it had been designed to deliver. Certainly, traditional available data would not have provided the same richness of empirical evidence. Official strike statistics – with their high level of temporal and sectoral aggregation, their exclusive focus on what workers do, and on only one of their actions at that (strike) – would not have allowed me to say anything about state and employers' actions, or the array of actions workers engage in. In the world of official strike statistics, workers' actions occur in a vacuum of social relations. And certainly, traditional approaches to content analyses would not have allowed the kind of fine-grained analyses performed here. They would have not allowed me to query the database in search of an answer to a very basic question: Who did what, where, when and why? Perhaps, it was gold and diamonds after all.

Having completed the task of getting numbers out of words, Part II takes a different turn. It asks the disquieting questions: What's in the numbers? Why should we have turned words into numbers in the first place? What is the social context of such project? What world view does it imply, what interests does it hide? The approach to those questions starts in the epilogue to Part I, where I undertake an excursus into the texts left behind by medieval pilgrims in their journeys of penance and by renaissance explorers in their journeys of discovery. The analysis of these travel accounts reveals that two fundamental mechanisms are behind the production of these texts: ways of seeing and silence and emphasis. The question is: Could the same mechanisms operate in the production of other text genres?

Chapter 4 looks at the types of error we can incur in the process of measurement: reliability and validity. Reliability – more specifically intercoder reliability as it is known in the field of content analysis – measures repeatability: The results obtained by one coder can be repeated by other coders using the same techniques on the same material with the same set of rules.[41] Content analysis canons maintain that coders should achieve that result solely on the basis of a clearly written set of coding instructions. Linguistics and philosophy of language debunk that myth. The first thing we learn from these disciplines is that meaning is in context. In the process of text understanding we unconsciously rely on such wealth of background knowledge (context) that no handbook of coding instructions could ever come close to mimicking. "One cannot lay down a set of handy instructions," Cicourel argued (1964, p. 19). "One cannot write a handbook ..." Validity addresses a different question: Do the data that I collected from newspapers on the 1919–22 period reflect a newspaper reality or a historical reality? "We do not measure protest per se," Rucht and Neidhardt (1999, p. 77) acknowledge, "but protest covered in the media." I show that, no doubt, newspaper information on protest event is "biased" and that bias is the result of ways of seeing and silence and emphasis rather than outright "lies."

The analyses of Chapter 5 reveal that those same mechanisms – ways of seeing and silence and emphasis – are at work in the production of (social) scientific texts. The traditional emphasis of textbooks of content analysis on issues of reliability, sampling, measurement, efficiency and the neglect of far more fundamental (but unresolved) issues of meaning, interpretation, and role of the reader highlight a general mechanism in the historical development of the social sciences: Emphasis on what we know and silence on what we do not know. Silence and emphasis, backgrounding and foregrounding; the same mechanisms seem to be at work in the production of *all* texts, texts that are the product of specific discursive communities that share similar assumptions and beliefs about the world ("ways of seeing"). The linguistic analyses of Chapter 5 highlight the overall effect of those devices, the subtle manipulation of meaning through syntax (for example, passive or active sentences), vocabulary (for example, terrorists or freedom fighters/martyrs), "master tropes" (in particular, metonymic versus metaphorical discourse), and sentence sequence. It is those linguistic practices that characterize the ideological aspects of text. The production of text is inseparable from the production of ideology, of *"meaning in the service of power."*[42] "All knowledge produced in the human and social sciences lends itself to use by a given ideology" (White, 1987, p. 81).

The critical analyses of Chapters 4 and 5 seem to call into question the entire scientific apparatus that I had so painfully constructed in Part I. Claude Lévi-Strauss, in one of the many beautiful passages of his *Tristes Tropiques*, wrote:

> We were approaching Le Pot-au-Noir (the Doldrums), which was greatly feared by the old navigators. The winds peculiar to both hemispheres stop on either side of this area, and the sails would hang for weeks on end without a single breath of wind to stir them into life. The air is so still that one might think oneself in some confined space instead of out on the open sea; dark clouds, with no breeze to disturb

their balance, are affected only by gravity, and slowly disintegrate as they drift down toward the sea. (Lévi-Strauss, 1992, p. 73)

Have I reached Doldrums of my own? A standstill between the buoyant optimism of Part I, in my single-minded forced march toward the numbers, and the disappointment of what I actually find when I get there? Can I find my way back to my lost scientific course?

It is in Chapter 6 that I finally lead the reader out of the Doldrums, and "steer[ing] north to find the strong westerlies,"[43] I reestablish some of the shaken confidence in our scientific procedures and methods. There, I take a bird's-eye view of those methods and procedures. Coming to the end of our journey, I try to grasp its broader meaning, to understand its full implications, to bring it all together. And the implications of using a story grammar to structure narrative as a way of going from words to numbers are far broader than implied by our ability to run a regression equation. With data as sets of chrono-logically (indeed, temporally *and* logically) ordered "semantic triplets" new epistemological representations of social reality become available: Actors instead of variables, diachronic time instead of synchronic time, events and event narratives instead of structures, narrative causality, as the position of a specific action in a sequence of actions, instead of statistical causality, as crudely interpreted as a set of independent variables "causing" a dependent variable within multivariate statistical models. (One *caveat*. In going from words to numbers are we also going from thin explanations to "thick descriptions," the very richness of the data luring investigators into a purely descriptive approach?) More to the point, several disciplines seem to come together at this unlikely juncture in assigning a privileged position to action over actors, verb over noun: linguistics, sociology, and history. In the end, the methodological tools developed along the way open up a theoretical world; they push us into a view of sociology as "social relations." I bring to life a theoretical vision that flourished in the first few decades of the twentieth century, waxed and waned thereafter, only to gain prominence in recent years with a "manifesto" of its own (Emirbayer, 1997): from Weber and Simmel to Vierkandt, von Wiese, Park, Ross, and Burgess, in the 1920s and 1930s, and later yet to Parsons and Coleman. Their views of the social world and sociology provide the theoretical underpinnings of our methodological work. They open up "unbelievably" immense vistas. I feel close to Egeria, this fourth-century nun who came to the Holy Land "right from the other end of the earth."[44] After climbing the Sinai, the Mount of God, a mountain so high "almost too much for us to climb," she annotated in her travel book: "From there we were able to see Egypt and Palestine, the Red Sea and the Parthenian Sea ... as well as the vast lands of the Saracens – all unbelievably far below us" (Wilkinson, 1981a, pp. 94–5).

At the end of our journey, I consider our problem of measurement – that of measuring the role of social actors in sociohistorical research – in light of other attempts at measuring ... within the metaphor of the journey: The measurement problems posed by longitude and the steam engine. For all the criticisms and *caveats* raised in Part II about our journey from words to numbers, one thing is clear: Like other fields of human endeavor, our ability to measure social phenomena has steadily increased. As for the bookend – "And after"– I really should not give it away ...

Prefaces as occasions to tell the origin of a book; prefaces as sales pitch for what's to come; prefaces as opportunities to introduce authors in the most favorable light; prefaces as summaries of arguments. With all that entrusted to the preface, it is not surprising that Schlegel, in one of his 1797 fragments of the *Lyceum*, wrote: "A good preface is, at the same time, the square root and the square of the book," both synopsis and expansion of the ideas contained in the book.[45] And there is even more to a preface. Because prefaces not only attempt to ensure that a text is read, but *"that the text is read properly."*[46] "The preface provides direction for using the book," wrote Novalis (cited in Genette, 1997, p. 209). A preface gives an authorial privileged stamp on ways of reading. If so, what would my stamp be? Which way would *I* want *you* to read this text? As a methodological text? A substantive text? An epistemological text? As a miscellaneous collection of fragments of stories? As a desperate attempt to escape the dryness of technique, the caducity of science by turning to literature and art? Or, perhaps, even as a personal, deeply personal account of a science pilgrim? After all, "any book with a readable title-page is, to some extent, autobiographical."[47] And that may be true to an even greater extent for a book dealing with narrative. After all, narrative is nothing but "recapitulation of past experience," "the temporal character of human experience" (Labov, 1972, p. 359; Ricoeur, 1984, p. 52). In the end, you will choose, perhaps even in ways that I have not foreseen. After all, these are times of active audiences,[48] of omnipotent readers, and dead authors. But whichever way you choose to read this work, please do not take the one option I have not offered: Of putting the book down, reading no further. *"Ricorditi di me che son la Pia."* With these words – remember me, who am the Pia – Pia de Tolomei beseeched Dante not to forget her (Dante, *Purgatory*, Canto V, line 133).

Ricorditi di me. I will only live through you.

Part I

From Words to Numbers: A Journey

Thou hast ordered all things by measure and number and weight.

Bible (Wisdom, 11, 21)

Many issues that turn crucially on quantitative dimensions are disguised by words; they are not apparent because they are put forward in words instead of in numbers or equations. ... Equations have always been a part of historical literature. Prior to the appearance of quantitative historians, however, these equations were implicit, covert, and subliminal. The contribution of historical quantifiers is that they have made implicit mathematics explicit. ... The prohibition of explicit equations will not eliminate mathematics from historiography. It will merely impede the effort to determine whether the implicit equations embedded in important arguments are true or false, whether these equations are adequate depictions of the reality with which historians are concerned.

Robert Fogel (1975, pp. 330–41)

Do not guess, try to count, and if you cannot count, admit that you are guessing.

G. Kitson Clark (1962, p. 14)

Prologue

Of science Hobbes (1985, Part I, chap 5, 7, p. 115; emphasis in the original) wrote in *Leviathan*:

By this it appears that Reason is not a Sense, and Memory, born with us; nor gotten by Experience onely; as Prudence is; but attayned by Industry; first in apt imposing of Names; and secondly by getting a good and orderly Method in proceeding from the Elements, which are

Names, to Assertions made by Connexion of one of them to another; and so to Syllogismes, which are the Connexions of one Assertion to another, till we come to a knowledge of all the Consequences of names appertaining to the subject in hand; and that is it, men call SCIENCE.

This 1651 recipe of science is remarkably modern. In Part I of this book, I develop a way of going from words to numbers based on precisely such an Industry: An orderly Method of finding Names (called "coding categories" in the vocabulary of content analysis) and imposing Connexions among them (or "relations"). By systematically studying these Connexions (through "network models") "we come" if not "to a knowledge of all the Consequences of names" at least " to a knowledge of all the" Causes and, in particular, of the matrix of social relations involved in the period 1919–22.

The same mathematical thread – set theory – runs thorough these Names, Connexions, and Causes if not Consequences. A story grammar easily converts into a set theoretical framework. That should be hardly surprising. The linguists Chierchia and McConnell-Ginet (1990, p. 1) wrote that, in Chomsky's view, "theoretical linguistics is a branch of (applied) mathematics and in this respect like contemporary theoretical physics and chemistry." But those same set theoretical properties also underlie complex data organizational models found in computer science for the storage of text data collected via a story grammar (relational database management systems, RDBMS). Finally, set theory provides the mathematical underpinning of network models, the models best suited to analyze this kind of relational data. Thus, the same mathematical framework – set theory – lies behind story grammars, relational computer data models, and network analysis, the three tools that I adopt for the collection, organization, and analysis of text data. A thin thread runs from words to numbers. Aaron Cicourel (1964, p. 25) had said as much, in one of the most thought-provoking books on methods, when he wrote: "Current measurement systems have their foundations in formal logic, set theory, and derivations therefrom."

Let's follow Hobbes in this pursuit that "men call SCIENCE."

1

"In the Beginning Was the Word"[1]

MEPHISTOPHELES. ... hold fast to words! They'll guide / You on the road to certainty, / And Wisdom's gates will open wide. / STUDENT. But words must have some sense, it seems to me. / MEPHISTOPHELES. Yes, yes, but don't be bothered / overmuch by that. / It's just when sense is missing that a word comes pat / And serves one's purpose most conveniently. / Words make for splendid disputations / And noble systematizations; / Words are matters of faith; as you'll have heard, / One can take no jot nor tittle from a word!

Johann Wolfgang Goethe (*Faust*, 1987, 1990–2000)

Content analysis is a research technique for the objective, systematic, and quantitative description of the manifest content of communication.

Bernard Berelson (1952, p. 18)

Poetics ... provides theoretical understanding of one important type of text [literary text]. ... Poetics might even provide the models for the study of other types of texts such as propaganda, the language of politics and advertising, psychiatric reports, and so on, which are now mainly studied in the theoretically rather poorly developed interdisciplinary content analysis.

Teun A. van Dijk (1972, p. 183)

"In the Beginning Was the Word"

Consider the following narratives of events that took place in Avranches, France, in 1639, in St. Louis, USA, in 1917, again in Paris, France, in 1789, and in Northenden in Cheshire, England, in 1790.[2]

La Besnadière Poupinel, *lieutenant particulier* of the Présidial at Coutances, came to Avranches on Saturday, July 16, 1639, for the purpose to carry out a commission for the Parliament of Rouen which related to justice and had nothing to do with fiscal matters. ... The men chosen to check on visitors, the priest Bastard and a certain Bonniel, went to inspect his room at the hostelry and saw "on the table the *arrêt* which he had come to execute ..." Without even reading these papers and without trying to understand them, they sent warning to the sieur de Ponthébert, a small squire who was a great talker, and a certain Champmartin, and spread the story that a commission had been issued for suppressing the salt pans of Avranches. This happened on a market day. People hastened to warn "the peasants working on table salt," the salt makers on the sand below Avranches. An hour and a half later, four hundred people, mostly salt makers and wood porters, were kicking and punching Poupinel and beating him with sticks and stones. The wretched man, his flesh in shreds, died about half past twelve noon. The spinning women put out his eyes with their spindles.

A large group of whites marched through the streets shouting that colored people should leave East St. Louis immediately and permanently; ... By the early afternoon, when several Negroes were beaten and lay bloodied in the street, mob leaders calmly shot and killed them. ... Near Main and Broadway, white prostitutes grabbed ... fleeing Negro women ... A few yards away two or three Negro men held their hands high in a gesture of surrender, but were clubbed with gun butts. When they fell, young girls got blood on their stockings while kicking the victims, and the sight amused the rioters. ... Shacks at Main Street and Brady Avenue, Third and Brady, and Third and Railroad Avenue were surrounded and set afire. ... Fires destroyed over two hundred houses ... By midnight the South End was bright with flames which could be seen miles away ... With the flames illuminating the night sky, hundreds of tired, terrified refugees were brought by military escort to the City Hall auditorium. Some suffered from burns or beatings; many were separated from their families. The moaning and wailing of these people 'raised a Bedlam that at times drowned out the bark of pistols and the crackling of fires.' The lights suddenly went out in the building and 'the negroes screamed in terror, believing this was a new plan to murder them wholesale. In a moment, the lights returned; there had been a slight accident to the electrical machinery.'

On the morning of 5 October the revolt started simultaneously in the central markets and the Faubourg Saint-Antoine; in both cases women were the leading spirits; ... women of every social class ... both fishwives and stall-holders of the markets, working women of the *faubourg*, smartly dressed *bourgeoises*, and '*des femmes à chapeau.*' In the markets, according to a Châtelet witness, the movement was started by a small girl, who set out from the District of Saint-Eustache beating a drum and declaiming against the scarcity of bread; this drew together a large crowd of women, whose numbers rapidly increased. ... Meanwhile, in the Faubourg Sainte-Antoine, women compelled the bellringer of the Sainte-Marguerite church to ring the tocsin and call the citizens to arms; ... From these beginnings the women now converged on the Hôtel de Ville. ... groups of women [were] stopping strangers in the streets and compelling them to go with them to the Town Hall, '*où l'on devait aller pour se fait donner du pain.*' The guards were disarmed and their arms were handed to men who followed behind the women and urged them on. ... [A] cashier in the Hôtel de Ville, described how, about half past nine, large numbers of women, with men amongst them, rushed up the stairs and broke into all the offices of the building. ... Having sounded the tocsin from the steeple, the demonstrators retired to the Place de Grève outside at about 11 o' clock.

In about 1790 Alice Evans the wife of a weaver, and a powerful athletic woman 'chastised her own lord and master for some act of intemperance and neglect of work' – 'This conduct (of hers) the neighboring lords of creation were determined to punish, fearing their own spouses might assume the same authority. They therefore mounted one of their body, dressed in female apparel, on the back of an old donkey, the man holding a spinning wheel on his lap, and his back toward the donkey's head. Two men led the animal through the neighborhood, followed by scores of boys and idle men, tinkling kettles and frying pans, roaring with cows' horns, and making a most hideous hullabaloo, stopping every now and then while the exhibitioner on the donkey made the following proclamation:
Ran a dan, ran a dan, ran a dan,
Mrs Alice Evans has beat her good man;
It was neither with sword, spear, pistol, or knife
But with a pair of tongs she vowed to take his life ...'

It is narrative documents of this kind that historians have long since used and produced in the study of protest events. But social scientists (and of late, an increasing number of historians) have approached those same events with a different spirit. By and large, they have tended to work on event counts rather than on narratives of individual events, with the help of an impressive array of statistical techniques.

Words and numbers. Social scientists, dug into opposing trenches like so many World War One soldiers, have fought bitterly over issues of methodological approach in social research. It is quite ironic that these two worlds should have grown so far apart in light of what Leonard Bosman writes in *The Meaning and Philosophy of Numbers* (1932, p. xiii):

What then is a number? Skeat states that the Indo-Germanic root of the word is *nem*. This is similar to the Sanskrit *nam* or *nama,* the origin of the word *name*. To name a thing is to individualize it or distinguish it (N) from the mass (M), and it is difficult to understand the difference between name and number, since the roots are practically the same.[3]

Even closer the etymological roots of the words "count" (numbers) and "recount," as in narrate or tell a story (words).[4] The word "recount" was imported into English from the French *reconter* in the fifteenth century. In French, the verb *reconter*, a close proxy of *conter*,[5] had been adopted in the twelfth century from the Latin *computare* (meaning reckon and calculate). And *computare* has its root in *putare*, which simply means, to think. Thus, words and numbers, telling and measuring, counting and recounting, were once simply intellectual activities, involving thinking, or, more appropriately, enumerating or going through a sequential list.

The "two cultures" were once unified![6] Is there a way to recover their original unity? Is there a road (or can we trace one) that will wind through those worlds, back and forth, out of one and into the other? Is there any merit in searching for or tracing that road? "Let the masters of Alchemy know," said Aristotle (384–322 B.C.), "that the species of things cannot be changed" (cited in Albertus Magnus, 1958, p. 9). If so, is this a project doomed to failure? After all, an early pioneer, Pitirim Sorokin, wrote (1937, p. 268; see also, pp. 282, 399):

> The main *methodological* difficulty ... is the impossibility of making a 'perfect translation' into purely quantitative language of any phenomenon that is *qualitative-quantitative*. Most sociocultural phenomena, including the phenomena of war and revolutions, are of this nature.

All Sorokin got out of the thousands of historians' pages on wars that he consulted were simple counts of wars, their duration, size of armies, number of casualties, and "no other aspect of the war phenomena" (Sorokin, 1937, p. 282).

Content Analysis: "Objective, Systematic, and Quantitative"

Consider the following definitions.[7]

> Content analysis is the statistical semantics of political discourse.

> Content analysis provides a precise means of describing the contents of any sort of communication – newspapers, radio programs, films, everyday conversations, verbalized free associations, and so on.

> A distinguishing characteristic of content analysis, as contrasted with other techniques of describing communications, is its quantitative

aspect. Content analysis aims at a classification of content in more precise, numerical terms than is provided by impressionistic 'more or less' judgements of 'either-or.'

Content analysis is a research technique for the objective, systematic, and quantitative description of the manifest content of communication.

We propose to use the terms 'content analysis' and 'coding' interchangeably, to refer to the objective, systematic, and quantitative description of any symbolic behavior.

Content analysis is any research technique for making inferences by systematically and objectively identifying specified characteristics within text.

Content analysis is a research technique for making replicable and valid inferences from data to their context.

Do not these definitions contain the magic words – research technique, statistics, inference, quantitative, systematic, objective, communication, text – that promise a solution to our problem of going from words to numbers? No doubt, of all the roads before us, this is the one we should travel first.

Who coined the label "content analysis" is unclear. According to Kaplan (1943), the term originated within the research group directed by Lasswell, the *Experimental Division for the Study of War Time Communications.*[8] Indeed, the first printed use of the label is found in titles of documents that the Experimental Division put out between 1941 and 1945.

It was Lasswell who first used the label in the title of one of the Experimental Division's early documents.[9] In that same year, 1941, Douglas Waples, another professor at the University of Chicago, and a graduate student, Bernard Berelson, had an unpublished monograph with "content analysis" in the title (Waples and Berelson, 1941). Yet, Laswell himself, in the early stages of development of the technique, was also using other labels: "[S]ymbol analysis," "content of mass communication," "content of the press," "coding editorial content."[10] A year later, in 1942, we have Nathan Leites and Ithiel de Sola Pool's and Janis and Fadner's documents in the Experimental Division for the Study of War Time Communications. In 1943, we find the label "content analysis" in the first journal articles.[11] Finally, with the publication of the collective results of the Experimental Division's work in 1949[12] and of the first methodological monograph on the technique (Berelson, 1952), the label is there to stay.[13]

If the 1940s bring us a new label, there is much déjà vu in the technique itself. A trickle of scholars in political science, journalism, and sociology had shown an interest in newspaper content since the late 1800s. In 1924, at the second "national conference on the science of politics," American political scientists argued that:

Table 1.1. *Rough Number of Published Studies Based on Content Analysis (Five-year Intervals, 1921–1950)*

1921–25	1926–30	1931–35	1936–40	1941–45	1946–50
10	15	25	40	60	130

Source: Berelson (1952, p. 22)

It might be possible to study the effects of different sorts of newspaper publicity upon elections. The election results might be studied in relation to such factors as amount of newspaper space for and against, number of papers for and against, as well as their circulation, amount of logical and emotional writing, and other factors. (*The American Political Science Review*, 1925, p. 17)

In the 1930s, the growing number of totalitarian regimes (communist, fascist, nazi), and their militaristic and belligerent stance, brought out a wealth of studies on propaganda.[14] Those studies multiplied during World War Two under the sponsorship of different projects.[15]

In the field of journalism and mass communication – particularly at the School of Journalism of Columbia University – scholars had shown an early interest in the systematic study of American newspapers.[16] They were concerned with the effects on news content of the increasing concentration of newspapers into fewer corporate hands and of the growing weight of advertising.

Sociologists had no particular questions of their own, but they did start looking at newspapers early on, producing some of the best monographs of the time, and bringing to the field a concern with measurement and method that was generally lacking (for example, Willey, 1926).

Thus, coming from different directions and traveling on different roads, content analysis slowly came of age (see Table 1.1). In this journey, Lasswell and his associates did more than just coin a new label. They took a methodology that had produced research that is remarkable for its lack of rigor and tried hard to define, measure, and quantify (Krippendorf, 1980, p. 16). When compared to earlier work, their work has the very modern ring of a social *science* that, in its attempt to become *science*, is increasingly concerned with methodological issues.

The great majority of studies in the prewar literature had approached the study of newspaper content by classifying information into a set of news categories and then providing extensive quotes for each category. Exemplar of this approach is the massive, two-volume study of public opinion in England (on the Eastern Question of 1876 in particular) by Thompson (1886). "We have no precise numerical test of the volume necessary to constitute an opinion public," writes Thompson (1886, p. 36), "nor need we look for numerical accuracy on such a point." Instead, Thompson accumulates his evidence in the form of a large number of quotes from various sources on such issues as "antiTurkish" or "antiwar" sentiments, and so on.

Early studies of newspaper content measured everything in terms of inches of space dedicated to a set of issues. And issues in that set were rarely defined.[17] Willey took an important "step in the development of a quantitative methodology," (1926, p. vii) – dedicating two chapters or thirty pages of a small book to issues of measurement, definitions, and classification. And yet, this coding scheme design simply builds upon previous and largely similar designs. More to the point, Willey's design does not move beyond the ad hoc approach of his predecessors.

> The following method was used in devising such a classification system. For two weeks every item of reading matter in the *New York Sun* was read and 'the what' established. ...[18] 'The whats' so found were recorded, and subsequently regrouped under more inclusive headings. In this manner ... [forty nine] subheadings, or categories, were found ... then arranged under ... [ten] major headings. (Willey, 1926, pp. 35–7)

No doubt, the first road we traveled has born fruit. Along the way, we have encountered an array of concepts and techniques, developed by several different traditions, that merged into the royal road of content analysis. That royal road does lead us "from words to numbers." But other roads were parting from approximately the same point where I took the royal road. Along one of these roads we find scholars also looking at newspapers, also interested in getting numbers out of words. These scholars were certainly familiar with the techniques of content analysis. Yet, they rarely referred to their pursuits in those terms. Some even coined (less successfully) their own labels (for example, "polimetrics," Gurr, 1972). Follow me along this road and see where it takes us.

From Event Counts to Event Characteristics

Upon his death in 1953, Dr. Lewis F. Richardson left behind an unpublished manuscript titled *Statistics of Deadly Quarrels*.[19] The title is somewhat misleading. The book does contain a compilation of all violent events throughout the world between 1820 and 1949. But the book also contains a great deal more.

A member of the Society of Friends, Richardson became obsessed with the quantitative study of war after serving in World War One in the Friends' Ambulance Unit. True to the Quaker spirit, Richardson's motivation was to understand wars to avoid them. A mathematical physicist by training, he went on to obtain a degree in psychology in 1929, and continued to gather data on wars while working at the Meteorological Office (1919–20), while heading the physics department at Westminster Training College (1920–29), and being the principal of Paisley Technical College and School of Art (1929–40). He retired early at the age of forty nine to dedicate his full energies to research on wars. To the book *Statistics of Deadly Quarrels* Richardson brought the rigor and weight of his mathematical training. The mathematical and statistical treatment of the data is extensive – Moreno would have loved the matrix representation of the relationships between quarreling parties (see Moreno, 1951, 1953). Indeed, it would be decades before that representation would become standard in the literature on conflict events. To the book, Richardson also brought the breaking of conventions and rules of academic style that comes from being an outsider to the profession. Ironic about the enterprise of quantifying, Richardson intersperses his tables, figures, and formulae with dialogues between "author" and "critic," "mentor," "chorus of enemies of Britain," and so on (for example, pp. 1–2, 174–5, 243–5). The book is a wonderful postmodernist text *ante-litteram* ... without the gibberish. Yet, it is also an old-fashioned book, perhaps the last in a long tradition dedicated to the simple counting of events.

Gaston Bodart (1916) had opened that tradition providing measures of duration, size of armies, and number of casualties for each war in which Austria-Hungary and France had been involved between the early seventeenth century[20] and 1913.[21] Compared to Bodart's simple treatment, Sorokin's (1937) work stands out as the work of a giant. His attempt at measuring violent events (wars and revolutions) in various European nations since 600 B.C. in terms of duration, size of armies, and number of casualties is part of a much bolder project aimed at measuring a variety of sociocultural phenomena.[22] The result is a massive four-volume treatment, *Social and Cultural Dynamics.*[23] Quincey Wright's *A Study of War* (1942) closes the trickle of quantitative studies on wars before Richardson. Like Sorokin, Wright is concerned with the timing of violent events, assembled hierarchically into battles, campaigns, and wars, and with their magnitude – duration, scale, intensity.

Wars, however, do not just bring about devastation as captured by Bodart, Sorokin, Wright, and Richardson's figures. With wars comes state making.[24] With wars comes technological innovation. The pace of that innovation soars under the pressure of war. Sorokin noted (1928, p. 339):

> The unusual stimulation of the inventive power of a nation for the sake of military victory has often facilitated the invention of a new method or the improvement of the old methods of wealth production. In this way it has indirectly contributed something toward economic progress and has, sometimes, at least partly compensated for its economic damages.

More generally, "by its strong stimulation, excitement, and extraordinary conditions, the war situation has been responsible for the enlargement of human knowledge" (Sorokin, 1928, p. 351). The more devastating the war, the more incentive belligerent parties have to find innovative technical solutions to tame the enemy. In that respect, World War Two, with its devastation on an unprecedented scale, provided the greatest of incentives. If the analysis of war propaganda spurred social scientists to new developments in content analysis (Krippendorf, 1980, p. 16), cracking enemy coded messages hastened the development of computers.[25] And computers greatly increased scholars' ability to measure social phenomena. Ted Robert Gurr (1974, pp. 250-1) posed the question in the right terms:

> The essential research question is whether it is more appropriate to measure the *properties* of conflict such as its duration, intensity, scale, and impact, either in single events or at the national level; or to concentrate on the *incidence* of conflict, that is, on the number of distinguishable events which occur.

The question for Gurr was mostly rhetorical. In his mind, the answer was quite clear: Researchers "repeatedly and mistakenly ... treat counts of conflict events as though they were conflict properties" (Gurr, 1974, p. 251). That question, unfortunately, was a luxury that Bodart, Sorokin, Wright, or even Richardson could not afford asking. The technology was simply not there to handle the kind of data that a focus on event properties would yield. No computers, no quantitative study of conflict events based on event properties.

Harry Eckstein, directly and indirectly, was one of the key figures in taking the next step toward measuring event properties. In the late 1950s, Eckstein was a professor of Political Science and Fellow at the Center of International Studies at Princeton University. From *The New York Times Index* he had collected data on twelve different measures (kinds) of domestic conflict for 113 countries for the years 1946–59.[26] Eckstein's measures were: internal warfare, turmoil, rioting, large-scale terrorism, small-scale terrorism, mutinies, coups, plots, administrative actions, quasi-private violence, total number of unequivocal acts of violence (UE), and total number of unequivocal plus equivocal acts of violence (UE+E).[27] Compared to Sorokin or Richardson's, Eckstein's work provides a broader scope of actions: We go from a concern with single macroevents of earlier studies – namely war, revolutions, or deadly quarrels – to a wider range of forms of conflict. Projects carried out under the sponsorship of private foundations and the National Science Foundation (in particular, the Dimensionality of Nations Project carried out at Northwestern University) were similarly focusing on a variety of both domestic and international forms of conflict.[28] Once again, war – the Cold War, this time – was providing the impetus behind these efforts.[29]

In 1961, Eckstein obtained a three-year grant from the Carnegie Endowment for Peace. Eckstein solicited doctoral and postdoctoral research applications from both Gurr and Tilly. They both arrived to the Center of International Studies in the fall of 1962 and stayed for the length of the academic year. As a graduate student in the Department of Government and International Relations at New York University, Gurr had been working on a dissertation titled *The*

Genesis of Violence: A Multivariate Theory of Civil Strife. Charles Tilly was an assistant professor in sociology at the University of Delaware. He had just completed his dissertation at Harvard on the counterrevolutionary activities of the Vendée region from 1793 to 1800 (Tilly, 1964). Both were interested in issues of conflict. Both had reasons to want to escape their institutions, given an opportunity. Harry Eckstein offered them both that opportunity.

Eckstein (1964) eventually published an edited volume titled *Internal War: Problems and Approaches* that summarized the collective experience of the activities of the Center. Gurr turned his dissertation work into the success story of *Why Men Rebel* (1970) and Tilly followed suit with success stories of his own on the basis of the work started at the Center (*Strikes in France, 1830–1968*, with Edward Shorter, 1974; *The Contentious French*, 1986).

While at the Center, both Gurr and Tilly developed yet more complex schemes of data collection of events. Following Eckstein, their schemes included measures of the forms of events. But Gurr and Tilly also recorded the sequences of actions, the relationship of events to other events, the organizations and actors involved and their goals.[30]

With the seminal work of Eckstein, Gurr, and Tilly at the Center of International Studies at Princeton, we enter a new era in the study of conflict events. The coding schemes developed at the Center, give or take a few coding categories, remarkably survived virtually unchanged for several decades. They provided a blueprint for scores of studies of collective action.[31] And yet, some scholars started experimenting with the design of more complex coding schemes, in particular, schemes that would keep track of the relationships between coding categories for a given event.

Markoff, Shapiro, and Weitman took an early step in that direction.[32] Their task was to code the information contained in the *cahiers de doléances,* a set of documents produced in 1789 at the eve of the French Revolution. The *cahiers* provide a rich list of grievances (*doléances*) by some 40,000 corporate and territorial entities of the old regime. The coding scheme that Markoff, Shapiro, and Weitman developed to quantify all that information is made up of four main categories: Institution, Action, Conventional Remarks, and Free Remarks. The "Institution" field provides the means to code the identity of the actors involved in the demands. In the "Action" field, coders can store information on any action undertaken by the actors. For both fields of Institution and Action a set of nonbinding symbolic precoded items (1,000 for Institutions and 50 for Actions) are available to coders. Conventional remarks are used to link the categories Institution/Action and Free Remarks; relationships between sentences, such as "if," "provided that," and "if not," would be coded in this relational category. Given a complex sentence, characterized by the presence of subordinate clauses, the information provided in the main clause would be coded in a structured way in the categories Institution and Action. The subordinate clause would be freely coded in the Free Remarks category and the type of relationship between main and subordinate clause would be coded under Conventional Remarks.

Tilly himself continued to push for the development of more complex coding schemes that would yield "richer, more flexible records than ever before" (Tilly, 1981, p. 76). In 1975, Tilly started working on a project of data collection on "collective gatherings" in England. The coding scheme that he devised for that project is based on an elementary relational framework, with a set of actors (formations) and actions (action phase) connected via identifying numbers (Tilly, 1978, pp. 287–306; 1995a). Actors and actions are recorded in terms of the very words used by the source documents.

In 1982, when I started working on a project on industrial conflict in postwar Italy, I borrowed from Tilly the idea of using a relational scheme. What I eventually came up with was a code book divided into several sections: scene, workers, unions, employers, state, and other actors (Franzosi and Centis, 1988). The scene allowed coding of spatial and temporal information;[33] each of the other sections contained a list of actors, actions, and main objects. Connections between scenes, subjects, actions, and their modifiers were externally made by the coder: Each scene was assigned a progressive identification number; this number would then be written next to the appropriate actor, action, and object in the appropriate section of the code book. The scheme also provided some capacity to relate sets of subject/action/object, particularly in hypothetical clauses (for example, "workers will strike *if* employer fires two workers").[34]

This road, as well, seems to have much to offer, with the added advantage of dealing with the familiar substantive problems that had originally spurred me on my methodological quest: the study of conflict events. Traveling along this road, as we have done, shows that, little by little, the coding of event narratives slowly increased in complexity. At first, throughout the interwar years, from Sorokin to Richardson, scholars focused their attention on a single macroaction – wars – and tabulated their number, duration, and intensity. Eckstein widened that concern to a number of macroactions, from warfare, to turmoil, rioting, terrorism, and so on. To this set of actions, Gurr and Tilly added actors and organizations. Finally, Markoff, Shapiro, and Weitman, and Tilly, in his later work, formally related actors to their actions. They also started collecting a number of microactions (for example, leaflet, speak, open fire) within larger macroactions or events (for example, strike). Little by little, on each event, we came to know much more than the handful of counts we had found at the beginning of the road. In this, technology probably had a greater effect in spurring scholarly imagination to new heights than the stimuli that come from our own theoretical or methodological traditions.

But other scholars had been looking at narrative (not necessarily the same types of narrative of conflict events, but narrative nonetheless). They were not interested in getting numbers out of those narratives. But about those narratives they knew more than either content analysts or event analysts had ever come close to (or, probably, ever cared for). Yet, with hindsight, that road should have been traveled first. But the signpost for that road was written in a language I could not understand. And from the first steps I had taken along that road, I knew it would be a hard road to travel; and where it would lead I wasn't sure.

Turning to Linguistics for Help

In the winter of 1955, the Committee on Linguistics and Psychology of the Social Science Research Council called a work conference on content analysis. It took place at the University of Illinois in Monticello. Participants included members of the committee, researchers engaged in content analysis, and invited guests. The conference was called to "bring together" "contiguous approaches" between linguists and practitioners of content analysis:

> the psychologist, the propaganda analyst, the critic. ... [S]ince they are working on verbal texts, it is also clear that what the linguist discovers about the formal properties of the code must in some ways be relevant to what they are doing. (de Sola Pool, 1959, pp. 1, 5)

The conference proceedings were eventually published in 1959 as *Trends in Content Analysis* (de Sola Pool, 1959). In a section of his summary chapter titled "Linguistics and content analysis," de Sola Pool (1959, p. 224) wrote:

> On the face of it, the relation of linguistics to content analysis should be a close one, but historically it has not been. Both linguists and content analysts analyze texts and are concerned with language patterns, but ... differences in their approaches have kept them apart.

That plea for linguistics was later repeated by Hays (1969, pp. 66–7):

> The method of assigning properties to words and counting appearances of properties is insufficient ... The action program I am calling for is a difficult one ... It calls for contributions from linguists ... Linguistic theory has advanced a long way in ten years, and is now flourishing; content analysis based on theory already published could be exciting, but the work of the next few years is likely to improve our theory ...

Writing in 1975, Markoff, Shapiro, and Weitman (1975, p. 8) lamented:

> the linkages between content analysis and linguistics have generally been tenuous. Whatever else it is, content analysis is clearly a particular kind of study of language. We find it disturbing that the extensive methodological literature on content analysis has only recently made its first serious contacts with the discipline of linguistics, which has made such impressive advances in recent decades.

Still in 1989, Roberts remarked: "Social scientists' writings on content analysis either mention linguistics only in passing or ignore it altogether."[35]

While pleas to bring linguistics to the aid of content analysis methodologies multiplied, practical solutions and cross-fertilizations remained remarkably lacking. The Monticello conference, no doubt, had the great merit of calling attention to neglected issues of meaning. Among the participants, George (1959) drew a clear distinction between quantitative and qualitative content analysis. Osgood (1959) similarly clearly highlighted the limits of an approach to content analysis based on manifest versus latent meanings. Yet, of the seven chapters of *Trends in Content Analysis,* only one deals explicitly with linguistics (Saporta and Sebeok, 1959). And even those authors have no practical solutions to offer, only more caveats against some gross claims of quantitative content analysis (for example, word frequency versus contingency analysis, or words in context), a call to pay closer attention to issues of meaning and semantics. I wonder what linguists working in the field of semantics would have to say about de Sola Pool's (1959, p. 5) statement:

> The linguist starts out in most cases excluding problems of meaning from his ken. It is clear that he thereby leaves another area for exploration, that which *is* specifically concerned with the meanings communicated by texts.

The title of Roberts's paper (1989) "Other Than Counting Words: A Linguistic Approach to Content Analysis," seems to finally hold the solution to the plea, but, the paper delivers less than it promises. Linguistics, there, is really nowhere to be seen.

Syntax Grammar

There is some truth to de Sola Pool's claim that "the linguist starts out in most cases excluding problems of meaning from his ken." Noam Chomsky had claimed as much in his *Syntactic Structures* (1957), a work that was to revolutionize the field of linguistics.

For Chomsky, a relatively large number of words (lexical elements) is structured into a handful of prototypical phrases (phrasal categories), such as NP (noun phrase), AP (adjective phrase), VP (verb phrase), AP (adverb phrase), and so on (Radford, 1981, p. 53). A set of syntactic sentence-formation rules, called grammar, specifies how sentences are generated out of these basic building blocks. A grammar, in other words, specifies precisely what combinations of the basic elements of a language (morphemes and lexemes) are permissible or well formed. The grammar is said to generate all and only the sentences of the language (Lyons, 1970, p. 24). Thus, the following set of rules "generates" the (S)entence "this boy will speak very slowly to that girl," in terms of a set of Noun Phrases (NP), auxiliaries (AUX), Verb Phrases (VP), Determiners (DET), Nouns (N), Adverbial Phrases (ADVP), Adverbs (ADV), Prepositions (P), and Preposition Phrases (PP).

(1)	S	$\rightarrow$ NP AUX VP
(2)	NP	$\rightarrow$ DET N
(3)	VP	$\rightarrow$ V ADVP PP
(4)	ADVP	$\rightarrow$ DEG ADV
(5)	PP	$\rightarrow$ P NP
(6)	DET	$\rightarrow$ {this, ..., that}
(7)	N	$\rightarrow$ {boy, girl, ...}
(8)	AUX	$\rightarrow$ {will, ...}
(9)	V	$\rightarrow$ {speak, ...}
(10)	DEG	$\rightarrow$ {very, ...}
(11)	ADV	$\rightarrow$ {slowly, ...}
(12)	P	$\rightarrow$ {to, ...}

The rules (also called productions or rewrite rules) state that an initial symbol (S) is rewritten (the symbol $\rightarrow$ must be read as "is rewritten") as the string of symbols NP AUX VP. The latter are nonterminal symbols, also called syntactic categories or variables; they provide the most general structures of a language. Through the successive applications of productions, general categories can be broken up into simpler and simpler units until they cannot be broken any further. Each of these resulting units will constitute a new nonterminal symbol, unless it cannot be further decomposed; in this case it will be referred to as a terminal symbol of the language. The set of terminal symbols of a grammar constitutes the lexicon of a language. Notationally, nonterminal symbols are capitalized, while terminal symbols are in lower case. Rewrite rules specify the relations between strings of terminal and nonterminal symbols allowed in the language. This system of rules constitutes a phrase-structure grammar.[36] Transformational rules can also be applied (see Lyons, 1970, p. 121 ff.). Given a basic structure (such as NP VP), a set of transformational rules can map this elementary sentence structure into more complex structures. Thus, the active sentence "John ate the apple" is generated by the set of generative rules outlined above but it is transformed in its passive form "the apple was eaten by John" through a series of transformational rules. The two sentences are said to have the same deep structure and different surface structures (that is, syntactical categories). In Chierchia and McConnell-Ginet's (1990, p. 1) words:

> a grammar of a language can be viewed as a set of abstract devices, rule systems, and principles that serve to characterize formally various properties of the well-formed sentences of that language ...

A sentence grammar would seem to be exactly what we need: A glorified coding scheme, where there is a place for every word (lexical element) of a text but in a handful of categories, only. The grammar simplified the complexity of stories, reducing them to a handful of categories. As Eco put it, it is not that "there are more things in a text than are dreamt of in our text theories. But [that] there are fewer ... " (Eco, 1979, p. 38). Why not use such a refined and detailed scheme to collect verbal information? Simply because there are several problems in using a sentence grammar as a structured basis for data collection for sociohistorical research. To illustrate these problems, let's take the sentence "Workers have handed out leaflets to passersby." This sentence (S) would be decoded by a sentence grammar as workers (N) have (AUX) handed (V) out (PRT, particle) leaflets (N) to (P) passersby (N). It is certainly of no interest from the substantive point of view of a study of collective events that the lexemes "out" and "to" are coded respectively as particle (PRT) and preposition (P) or that "have" is coded as an auxiliary (AUX). On the other hand, lexical elements such as "workers," "leaflets," and "passersby" are bunched together under the same label (N) despite their differences, again, from the substantive viewpoint of collective action research. Thus, paradoxically, if we were to use a sentence grammar to collect textual data, we would collect both too much information and not enough. Sentence grammars have yet another problem: They take the sentence as their basic unit of analysis. Suppose that the sentence next to the one just coded reads "The workers were young and skilled." This sentence provides two basic pieces of substantive information: young and skilled. Other information provided by the new sentence (such as "workers") has already been given by the previous sentence; we are simply not interested in the lexemes "the," "were," and "and." There is no need to code a whole new sentence for two relevant pieces of information that modify the main actor of the previous sentence. Coding sentences seriatim, one sentence at a time, may be quite useless and very time consuming.

Thus, if our interest lies with event characteristics, particularly what kinds of actions certain actors perform, what we need is a technique that would allow us to extract functional categories (that is, properties of events) from a text as a whole (for example, a newspaper article, a police report, and so on, or even a series of articles or reports on an event), rather than syntactic categories from each individual sentence in the text. We want to be able to read text selectively, picking up only certain thematic units and/or certain semantic structures, leaving the rest behind. Thus, in the two sentences above, we are interested in the fact that an actor (workers), with certain characteristics (male, skilled), performs a function (hand out leaflet) toward an object (passersby). The tense information contained in the auxiliary can be used to infer the time of the function (past).

Semantic Text Grammar

Approximately ten years after the publication of Chomsky's *Syntactic Structure*, a second revolution was stirring the field of linguistics; only, this time it was in semantics (Dascal and Margalit, 1974). The new debate centered on the issue: text grammars versus sentence grammars. In van Dijk's words (1972, p. 1):

> many relevant and systematic phenomena of natural language are properties of 'discourse' [text], and these properties cannot be

adequately described in the existing types of grammar. ... Such a grammar, accounting for the formal structure of texts, will be called TEXT GRAMMAR, abbreviated as T-grammar. The existing types of structural and generative-transformational grammars are, at least in practice, limited to the formal enumeration and structural description of the sentences of a language and therefore will be called SENTENCE GRAMMARS or S-grammars. (Emphasis in the original)

A text, in other words, is not just a sequence of unrelated sentences, however syntactically well formed (Kintsch and van Dijk, 1978, p. 365). A text is a unitary whole, with sentences organized around a dominant theme or topic within this unit. If a text is a whole, then, perhaps it too, like the sentence, has a basic structure. Semantic Text Grammars have been used to analyze this structure, just like Sentence Grammars have been used to analyze the structure of sentences.[37] Van Dijk has argued that there are two basic levels of semantic structure in a text – microstructures and macrostructures.

Microstructures and macrostructures organize successive sentences of a text into a hierarchical sequence of propositions through the application of three basic rules of macrostructure formation (macrorules):

1. deletion – propositions that are not central to the local and global comprehension of a text are deleted;
2. generalization – each sequence of propositions in the text can be generalized into a higher level macrostructural proposition;
3. construction – each sequence of propositions denoting some facts can be substituted by a proposition denoting a more comprehensive fact, of which the facts narrated in the lower-level propositions are part (for example, the actions "cheer," "leaflet," and "picket," part of the macroaction "strike").[38]

Macrorules are repeatedly applied, first, on the surface propositions directly making up the text, then, on the macropropositions generated through the generalization/construction operation of the first pass, then on macropropositions resulting from the generalization/construction operation of the second pass, and so on until at the end one is left with only one macroproposition – basically, a summary title for a whole text.[39]

At an intermediate level between such top-level, superordinate, macrostructure as a title, and the microstructures, which are closely linked to the sequence of sentences in the text, one finds a set of macrostructures that provide the "schema" or "global schematic form" of a discourse. A schema does not directly organize the sequence of propositions of a discourse, but its macrostructures; it is not given by specific actor/action sequences, but by sequences of macro-propositions derived from them. "A schema or superstructure is a functional organization of the macrostructure of a discourse" (van Dijk, 1983, p. 36). Different schemata, among other things, characterize different discourse genres (van Dijk, 1983, p. 24). Thus, for instance, the schema of a research report is made up of the following macrostructural functional categories: introduction, statement of the problem and literature review, data and methodology, empirical results, discussion, and conclusions. News articles, as well, have been shown to be characterized by fairly fixed, deep macrostructures (van Dijk, 1983, 1985). It is in the genre of narrative, though, that functional categories have been most widely studied. As early as 1928, Propp (1968[1928]) provided one of the first functional models of textual macrostructures (van Dijk, 1972, p. 136). In Propp's schema, thirty-one functions, corresponding to the actions that the hero of the story performs, provide the deep, underlying structure of Russian folktales. These thirty-one functions were subsequently reduced by Greimas (1966; 1971) to five basic semantic macrostructures: 1) disruption of a state of equilibrium; 2) arrival and mission of the hero; 3) trial of the hero; 4) task accomplished by the hero; 5) return to the original state of equilibrium. Colby, in his study of Eskimo folktales, focuses on three main classes of narrative actions: "motivation," "engagement," and "resolution," each, in their turn, comprised of several, lower-level elements (called "eidons"), similar to Propp's functions.[40,41]

The problem with Propp's or Greimas's schemata, is that both reduce "narrative structure to functions denoting ONLY one macro-semantic category of the macro-proposition: ACTIONS" (van Dijk, 1972, p. 287; emphasis in the original). The arguments of the basic narrative function, such as subject or object, are not analyzed, presumably because the hero is the main protagonist of folktales. If we want to generalize the macrostructures to contexts where more than one actor plays a role, we need to introduce the different actants (subjects and objects) and their actions (van Dijk, 1972, p. 287). Furthermore, we need to show how deep structures (schemata) are related to higher-level structures.

Perhaps not unsurprisingly, Dascal and Margalit concluded their survey of the field with the following statement: "Far from being the beginning of a promising 'revolution' in the field of linguistics, the T-grammar research program looks, so far, more like a doomed 'coup d'état'" (1974, p. 213). But while the study of T-grammars never really took off in the field of linguistics,[42] it thrived in psychology throughout the 1970s and early 1980s with a flurry of titles.[43]

Psychologists' Story Grammars

In 1975, David E. Rumelhart, a young professor at the University of California-San Diego with a degree in mathematical psychology from Stanford, made a bold entrance into the field of study of stories with a paper unpretentiously titled "Notes on a Schema for Stories." The paper opened simply: "Just as sentences can be said to have an internal structure, so too can stories be said to have an internal structure."[44] And that structure, according to Rumelhart, can be captured by a simple "story grammar," that is, "a set of syntactical rules which generate the constituent structure of stories and a corresponding set of semantic

interpretation rules which determine the semantic representation of the story."
Less than twenty rules can generate any simple story, starting from

Rule 1: Story   →   Setting + Episode ...
Rule 3: Episode →   Event + Reaction
Rule 4: Event   →   {Episode | Change-of-state | Action | Event + Event} ...

The "setting" is "a statement of the time and place of a story as well as an
introduction to its main characters. ... Episodes are special kinds of events
which involve the reactions of animate (or anthropomorphized) objects to events
in the world." In the last paragraph of his paper, Rumelhart acknowledges the
work of linguists: "[T]he approach developed here is, to some degree, designed
to be a systematization of Propp's (1968) analysis of Russian folktales. ... [This]
work should be compared to that of Colby (1973) on Eskimo folktales." Other
than these fleeting remarks, Rumelhart makes no attempt to link his work to the
body of work done by linguists on stories and story grammars. As such, the
paper does not move beyond what linguists already knew; in fact, Rumelhart
ignores developments which could have been beneficial to his understanding of
stories.[45] Yet, Rumelhart's paper has considerable appeal. It is brief and clearly
written, condensing into a handful of pages Propp's cumbersome work. It has a
simple, rigorous formalism. Best of all, it brings to the field of psychology a
novel tool (novel for psychologists, that is) – story grammar. Rumelhart's
"notes" – "obviously only a tentative beginning of a theory of the structure and
summarization of stories," in his own summary (1975, p. 234) – are about to
become very influential in psychology and cognitive science.

Jean Mandler, a colleague of Rumelhart in psychology at San Diego, was
among the first to pick up the ball and run with it.[46] Her fields of interest are
memory and cognition. She approaches the study of story grammars for what
they have to offer as simple templates for text understanding and recall. In her
first published paper on story grammars,[47] Mandler acknowledges "David
Rumelhart['s] ... many helpful suggestions"; she acknowledges that her
"analyses are based on Rumelhart's (1975) characterization of story structure."
But she also acknowledges that her "attempts to apply his [Rumelhart's]
analyses to new stories frequently failed. ... [Rumelhart's story grammar]
depended on a set of dual structures ... syntactic ... [and] semantic ... which are
unwieldy to work with and frequently redundant." As a result, Mandler proposes
a more elaborate type of story grammar.[48] "A story grammar," in her definition,
"is a rule system which specifies canonical sequences of units occurring in
stories and the conditions under which they can be changed, deleted, or moved"
(Mandler, 1982, p. 307). Her main interest, in other words, is on narrative
sequences and on the rules of their behavior. There is not much new here. What
is new, however, in Mandler's and other psychologists' work on story grammars,
is their experimental work on the validity of a story grammar approach to
cognition.[49] Their research clearly shows that people use something like a story
grammar when interpreting and recalling stories and that breakdown in

comprehension occurs for stories not "confirming to an ideal schema … [not] matching a canonical structure."[50]

A Story Grammar for Sociohistorical Research

Whether carried out by linguists or psychologists, most of the research work on stories focused on macrostructures, narrative units, and their sequences. The basic unit of analysis was an elementary, minimal sentence, such as we find in Mandler and Johnson – "the people came down to the water," "they began to fight," "many were killed" (Mandler and Johnson, 1977, p. 136) – or in Prince – "the Wolf pulled the bolt," "he threw himself on the good woman," "he devoured her in no time" (Prince, 1973, pp. 92–3). There was no interest in breaking down further this basic unit. Mandler and Goodman (1982, p. 509) acknowledge that the rewrite rules of story grammars operate on several clauses and sentences at a time; "The rewrite rules are thus closer in conception to the macrostructure of a story, not the microstructure." Furthermore, the link between surface structures (that is, how the text actually reads) and deep macrostructures was never clearly specified. Back in 1977, in their seminal paper on story grammars, Mandler and Johnson wrote (1977, p. 148): "Before the grammar can make even modest claims to adequacy, it must be expanded to include more precise transformational rules governing the relationships between the surface and underlying structures." But that research program was never carried out, either by Mandler herself (still writing about story grammars in 1987) or others. Yet, if we are to use story grammars for sociohistorical research, we do need to solve these problems, since, there, knowledge of the actors ("the people," "the Wolf," "the good woman") and their actions ("came," "fight," "kill") is crucial.

It is these unresolved issues that Labov tackled in his work on vernacular narratives of New York Harlem blacks. Not only did Lavob find a structure in these narratives very similar to that of Greimas;[51] he also showed that this deep semantic structure can be mapped into surface structures, namely through adverbial elements (for time and space), a subject-noun phrase, and a verb phrase (see Labov, 1972, p. 375 ff.). Narrative, in other words, is shown by Labov to have a simple surface structure patterned after the canonical subject-action-object structure with some modifiers. Todorov found that same structure in Boccaccio's *Decameron*. Todorov first reduces the story to its paraphrase; and, from the paraphrased sentence, he then extracts three basic symbols: proper name, adjective, and verb. In Todorov's words:[52]

> A narrative grammar is made up of three primary categories that are: the proper name, the adjective, and the verb. … Syntactically, the proper name corresponds to the agent. But the agent can be either subject or object. … The appearance of an object depends upon the transitive or intransitive character of the verb.

Van Dijk (1972, p. 145) proposes the following formal representation[53] of a text grammar at the microstructural level:

(i) T $\rightarrow$ $Pred_2\ (Arg)^2$

(ii) $Pred_2$ $\rightarrow$ $g(-,-)$

(iii) $(Arg)^2$ $\rightarrow$ (x, y)

where T, the initial symbol of the grammar and the equivalent of S in a syntax grammar, is basically the text, $Pred$ is the predicates (verb), and Arg is the arguments (namely, subjects and objects, x and y), and $\rightarrow$ is a rewrite rule.[54]

Following Labov, van Dijk, and Todorov, we can develop a story grammar (or text grammar, or semantic grammar) for use in sociohistorical research, in particular, a grammar that would allow us to structure narratives of social conflict, protest, and violence. The grammar that I propose is centered around the basic S-A-O structure, subject-action-object (or "semantic triplet") and their respective modifiers. Both the object and the S-A-O modifiers are enclosed in square brackets because their presence is optional.[55] The expression "three terrorists kidnaped the president of the Employers' Association" has a subject – three terrorists – an action – kidnaped – and an object – president of Employers' Association; the expression "workers strike" has no object.

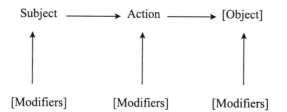

This simple, horizontal, relational structure can be aggregated, vertically, into a set of hierarchical structures, such as events and disputes.

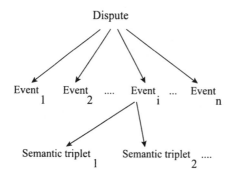

Using a set of rewrite rules,[56] we can build a story grammar for the collection of event data for sociohistorical research.

<dispute>   → {<event>}
<event>   → {<semantic triplet>}
<semantic triplet> → {<subject>} {<action>} [{<object>}]][57, 58]

These few lines show that the initial symbol <dispute> can be rewritten (→) as a set of one or more (as indicated by the curly brackets) <events>, and the <event> can be rewritten as one or more <semantic triplets>, that is, the set of subject, action, and object.[59] Subjects, actions, and objects can be rewritten further in order to capture substantively relevant attributes of actors and actions. One would like to know whether a subject is an institution, an individual, or a set of individuals. In the latter case, one would like to know the number of individuals involved; the name, profession, rank, marital status, age of an individual; the demographic characteristics (young, old, male, female, black, white), and the organizational affiliation of individuals and groups. Organizations operate in different societal spheres (religious, political, social, economic); economic organizations operate in different sectors (chemicals, textiles, banking, and so on), at different levels of aggregation (for example, shop, plant, firm, and so on). Using the rewrite rules and the familiar symbols, we can translate the foregoing discussion into the following formalized structure:

<subject>   → <actor> [{<actor modifier>}]
<actor>   → <individual> | <set of individuals>|
          <institution>
<individual>   → <improper name> [<proper name>]
<improper name> → (mayor | president | ...)
<proper name>   → (Agnelli | Giolitti | Mussolini | ...)
<set of individuals> → [{<number>}] (workers | shop stewards | ...)
<number>   → <quantitative expression>
<actor modifiers> → [{<type>}] [{<organization>}] ...
<type>   → (male | young | black | skilled | ...)
<institution>   → <organization>

The rewrite rules for <quantitative expression>[60] allow us to code both definite ("three," "five") and indefinite ("some," "hundreds") quantitative expressions, uncertainty ("approximately"), and single values or a range of values ("from three to five"). Furthermore, the rules explicitly identify the combinations that are allowed under the grammar ("several 200," "from 100 to hundreds" are not allowed). Similarly, the rewrite rules for <organization> allow us to code a variety of information about an organization. Consider the sentence:

One hundred workers according to plant management – two hundred according to union officials – struck today at the painting shop of the

Turin Mirafiori auto plant where the FIAT firm employs several thousand workers.

This brief account provides, among other things, four levels of aggregation for the organization involved: shop, plant, firm, economic sector. Furthermore, for each level, several other items of information are given: for all four levels, the proper name of the unit (Mirafiori or FIAT) or the improper name (painting, auto); for the plant level, the number of workers employed (several thousand) and the geographical location of the unit (Turin). All this information can be easily coded with a story grammar.

As for an action, there are several items of information of interest. First, an action occurs in time and space, the fundamental categories of narrative. There is no story without time. Narrative time has three aspects: order, duration, and frequency, each dealing with three different sets of questions: When? For how long? And how often?[61, 62] In comparison, the narrative category of space occupies a less central role in narrative analysis.[63] An action also has a reason and an outcome. For example, an action such as "strike" could occur over "contract renewal" and result in"ten percent wage increase" or "one extra paid vacation day." That same strike action can be of several different types: "general," "wildcat," "sit-in," or "to rule." The action may be based on different instruments. Thus, the police might attack a crowd using "batons," "tear gas," and so on. A crowd, in turn, might use "rocks," "sticks," or "molotov bombs." Finally, there may be a need to relate actions to objects through the case in order to eliminate semantic ambiguity. There is no ambiguity in understanding the semantic triplet <subject> trade unions <action> organize strike <object> workers (<organization> Ford) even if the specification of the case is missing (trade unions organize a strike *for* Ford workers); but the triplet <subject> workers (<organization> Pirelli) <action> collect signatures <object> workers (<organization> Breda) is semantically ambiguous as it is unclear whether signatures are collected on behalf of, or among Breda workers. Explicit links (<case>) can thus be specified to connect actions to objects (for example, "for," "from," and "to"). In conclusion, the nonterminal symbol <action> may be rewritten as follows:

<action>	→	<action phrase> [<negation>][<modality>] [<tense>] [{<action modifier>}]
<action phrase>	→	(strike | demonstrate | hand out leaflets | ...)
<negation>	→	(not)
<modality>	→	(can | could | may | might | will | would | shall | should | must | ought)
<tense>	→	(past | present | future)
<action modifiers>	→	[{<time>}] [{<space>}] [{<case>}] ...

For <time> the grammar allows a coder to specify whether it is a date and/or a time of day; whether it is expressed in definite or indefinite form; it also allows sorting action and events in partial time ordering.[64] The apparent variety of temporal expressions is reduced by the grammar to a few fixed forms. The grammar, indeed, allows great flexibility in coding temporal forms, while at the same time providing a tight framework where any temporal expression can be placed in a unique way.

For <space>, the grammar allows a coder to specify whether the geographical location of an action is a territorial extension or a precise locality – a city. A territory can either be properly named – Austria, Illinois, Piedmont – or have an improper name, such as "state," "county," "region," "department," "province," or "commune" that are legally defined administrative units and whose specific names vary from country to country. For instance, the territory of the United States is divided into states, counties, cities, and townships; the territory of Italy is divided into regions, provinces, and communes; the territory of France is divided into departments and communes. A city has neighborhoods, streets, and squares. Space can be static (in, at) or dynamic (from, to).

Finally, the grammar rewrites the <object> as either an actor (that is, a human agent), an inanimate noun (for example, factory, road, and so on), or even another triplet. This way expressions such as "workers occupy the factory," "protesters set fire to cars," and so on, can easily be coded in the grammar.

<object>   →   <actor> | <inanimate object> | <semantic triplet>
<inanimate object>   →   (factory | road | car | ...)

There are obvious similarities between sentence and text grammars (notably, in their formal representations through rewrite rules, terminal and non-terminal symbols). But, while a sentence grammar would specify a story in terms of syntactic categories, a story grammar specifies the same story in terms of functionally relevant, semantic categories, avoiding the unnecessary level of detail of sentence grammars (unnecessary, for our purpose). As categories are functionally defined (that is, defined in terms of the function that they perform either in the text or in the context of a researcher's substantive problem), one can preserve as much as needed of the lower-level structure of sentence grammars. And while some of these functions are invariant with respect to the type of narrative analyzed (for example, <time> and <space>), others may be specific to specific types of narrative. For example, you will find such modifiers as <trade union> in a narrative of strikes; but it is unlikely that, in these narratives, you will find references to personal physical attributes, such as the color of hair, eyes, and so on, much more typical of folktales. In a story grammar, one can specify any number of modifiers without altering its basic structure. The modifiers presented here are, thus, to be taken only as examples of how the grammar works. Researcher will tailor the grammar to their specific needs.

Examples of Coding

Consider the story of Poupinel's ill-fated death as told by Mousnier at the opening of this chapter. In chronological order, the information could be coded as follows.

<semantic triplet 1> <subject> Parliament (<space> Rouen) <action> dispatches (<time> prior to time of semantic triplet 2 <space> to Avranches <reason> commission of justice (*arrêt*)) <object> La Besnadière Poupinel (<role> *lieutenant particulier* <organization> Présidial <space> Coutances)

<semantic triplet 2> <subject> La Besnadière Poupinel <action> comes (<time> Saturday, July 16, 1639 <space> to Avranches <reason> to carry out a commission)

<semantic triplet 3> <subject> Bastard (<occupation> priest) & <subject> Bonniel <action> inspect room (<space> at the hostelry <case> of) <object> La Besnadière Poupinel

<semantic triplet 4> <subject> Bastard & <subject> Bonniel <action> see <object> *arrêt* papers (<space> on the table)

<semantic triplet 5> <subject> Bastard & <subject> Bonniel <action> read (<negation> not) <object> *arrêt* papers ·

<semantic triplet 6> <subject> Bastard & <subject> Bonniel <action> sent warning <object> sieur de Ponthébert (<occupation> small squire <comment> a great talker) & <object> Champmartin

<semantic triplet 7> <subject> Bastard & <subject> Bonniel <action> spread the story (<time> a market day)

<semantic triplet 8> <triplet relation> that <subject> ? <action> issues commission & <action> suppresses <object> salt pans (<space> Avranches)

<semantic triplet 9> <subject> people <action> hasten to warn <object> peasants (<organization> working on table salt> <space> Avranches)

<semantic triplet 10> <subject> people (<number> four hundred <occupation> salt makers & <occupation> wood porters) <action> kick & <action> punch & <action> beat (<time> an hour and a half later <instrument> sticks & <instrument> stones) <object> Poupinel

<semantic triplet 11> <subject> Poupinel (<comment> wretched man; his flesh in shreds) <action> die (<time> half past twelve noon)

<semantic triplet 12> <subject> women (<occupation> spinners) <action> put out eyes (<instrument> spindles)

Or consider the similar ill-fated death of the negroes of East St. Louis in 1929 brought to light by Rudwick.

<semantic triplet 1> <subject> group (<number> large <race> white) <action> march (<time> unknown <space> through the streets) & <action> shout (<tense> past)

<semantic triplet 2> (<triplet relation> that) <subject> people (<race> colored) <action> leave (<modality> should <space> East St. Louis <time> immediately <duration> permanently)

<semantic triplet 3> <subject> ? <action> beat <object> Negroes (<number> several)

<semantic triplet 4> <subject> Negroes (<number> several <type> bloodied) <action> lay (<space> in the streets)

<semantic triplet 5> <subject> mob leaders <action> shoot & <action> kill (<type> calmly <time> by the early afternoon) <object> triplet number 4

<semantic triplet 6> <subject> prostitutes (<race> white) <action> grab (<space> near Main and Broadway) <object> women (<race> Negro <type> fleeing)

<semantic triplet 7> <subject> men (<race> Negro <number> two or three) <action> hold hands high (<tense> past) & <action> surrender (<tense> past) <space> a few yards away)

<semantic triplet 8> <subject> ? <action> club (<instrument> gun butts) <object> subject of semantic triplet 7

<semantic triplet 9> <subject> girls (<type> young) <action> kick <object> victims (<comment> got blood on their stockings)

<semantic triplet 10> <subject> rioters <action> are amused (<reason> semantic triplet 9)

<semantic triplet 11> <subject> ? <action> set afire <object> shacks (<space> at Main Street & <space> Brady Avenue & <space> Third & <space> Brady & <space> Railroad Avenue)

<semantic triplet 12> <subject> fire <action> destroys <object> houses (<number> over two hundred) (<comment> by midnight the South End was bright with flames which could be seen miles away)

<semantic triplet 13> <subject> military escort <action> bring (<space> to the City Hall auditorium) <object> refugees (<number> hundreds <type> tired & <type> terrified & <type> injured)

<semantic triplet 14> <subject> refugees <action> moan & <action> wail (<type> loudly)

<semantic triplet 15> <subject> lights <action> go out (<type> suddenly <space> in the building <reason> slight accident to the electrical machinery)

<semantic triplet 16> <subject> negroes <action> scream (<type> in terror <reason> fear of being murdered wholesale)

<semantic triplet 17> <subject> lights <action> return (<time> in a moment)

These examples[65] of coding on the basis of a story grammar show that coded output preserves much of the flavor of a natural-language narrative, with output organized in chrono-logical order (temporal *and* logical), in storylike structures. Coded output also preserves most of the original information. As James Watt wrote about his steam engine: "You need not fash yourself anymore about that, man; I have now made an engine that should not waste a particle of steam."[66]

Running into Problems with Story Grammars

The examples of coding provided in the previous section seem to confirm the power of a story-grammar approach to text coding. Yet, that power may be overstated. Consider a paragraph that follows Mousnier's narrative of the events in Avranches in 1639 that opened this chapter.

> The rebel area had a granite soil, impermeable and poor. Its landscape was already that of the Bocage: small fields enclosed by dykes, that is, banks planted with trees and hedges; deeply embanked rivers; rounded ridges; deep and winding roads; country where one could not see far ahead and where it was difficult to get about. The crops were poor ... Wheat had to bought in Brittany. Pastures and grasslands were rare and there was extensive heathland. *Without the fine table salt and the fishing, this district could not survive. The peasants' holdings, which were too small and too much broken up, were always on the brink of ruin. ... As the good Président Bigot de Monville wrote, they [the peasants] were 'capable of undertaking any action, owing to their extreme wretchedness, which caused them to fear nothing worse than what they were already enduring' and which made them highly susceptible to any agitation.* (Mousnier, 1970, p. 101; emphasis added)

Where are the actors in this excerpt? Where are the actions? The sentences merely provide descriptions – which work themselves into an explanation in the last few sentences.

And some sentences provide neither description nor action, but interpretation and analysis. Consider E. P. Thompson's narrative of Alice Evans's *charivari* (or rough music) in 1790 (another narrative that we encountered at the beginning of this chapter). After taking the reader through the events, E. P. Thompson writes:

> The forms are dramatic: They are a kind of "street theatre." As such, they are immediately adapted to the function of publicising scandal. Moreover, the dramatic forms are usually processional. Perhaps, one should say, indeed, that they are antiprocessional, in the sense that horsemen, drummers, banners, lantern-carriers, effigies in carts, and so on, mock, in a kind of conscious antiphony, the ceremonial of the processionals of state, of law, of civic ceremonial, of the guild and of the church. (Thompson, 1991, p. 478)

Consider the following text, taken from Georges Lefebvre's *The Coming of the French Revolution* (1947), a masterpiece of twentieth-century historiography.

> It was on Sunday morning, July 12, that Paris heard of the dismissal of Necker. The day was fair, and a crowd assembled at the Palais-Royal in the afternoon. Amazement and consternation soon turned into

indignation and fury. Orators gathered audiences ... Camille Desmoulins ... at about half past three raised the call to arms, brandishing a pistol. Soon demonstrators swarmed in the streets. ... A unit of cavalry now intervened. (Lefebvre, 1947, p. 110)

How can we code some of the sentences of this excerpt within the categories of the grammar? Where are the human agents in: "It was on Sunday morning," or "the day was fair," and "amazement and consternation soon turned into indignation and fury?" These sentences provide description rather than action. And many sentences in Lefebvre's book are devoid of both description and action. They contain interpretation and analysis only. Consider this:

> There is no foundation to the charge often made against the National Assembly, that it incited people to believe in an unlimited and arbitrary liberty and to demand a perfect equality. From Article IV it follows expressly that liberty is limited by law, and the first article stipulates that men are equal *in rights*, an equality carefully defined in other articles as an equality before the law. Nor would we be rash to suppose that the Assembly, in deciding not to mention 'general felicity' as the purpose of political association, wished to prevent the transformation of juridical or civil equality into social equality, and to forestall those who might appeal to equality in demanding improvement of the lot of the poor. Even these precautions were not generally considered sufficient. Some deputies, notably churchmen such as Grégoire, suggested that the Declaration of Rights be supplemented with a Declaration of Duties ...

Neither descriptive nor analytical discourse easily fit into the categories of a grammar. Should we skip coding this type of sentences? If we are interested in *who did what, where, when, and why* perhaps there is little harm in doing so – but, then, we would not understand Mousnier's passage based on an explanation constructed on purely descriptive sentences ... Clearly, an understanding of the power and limitations of story grammars for the collection of text data requires a deeper understanding of narrative. What exactly is narrative and narrative discourse?

Narrative Discourse

"Narrative," for Labov, is "one method of recapitulating past experience by matching a verbal sequence of clauses to the sequence of events which (it is inferred) actually occurred."[67] That definition has survived, more or less intact, through the years and through a number of hands that have pulled and pushed it from different angles. We find it in Rimmon-Kenan: "[N]arrative fiction ... [is] a *succession of events*"; in Cohan and Shires: "The distinguishing feature of narrative is its linear organization of events"; and in Toolan: "A minimalist definition of narrative might be: A perceived sequence of non-randomly connected events."[68]

It is not surprising that all these definitions are in basic agreement. After all, they have common roots in the work of the Russian formalists of the beginning of the twentieth century, Propp and Tomashevski in particular. It is the Russian formalists who introduced the distinction between story versus plot in narrative (*fabula* versus *sjužet*). Building upon Aristotle's idea of plot-structure – *mythos*, in the master's own words: "[B]y this term 'plot-structure' I mean the organisation of the events"[69] – Tomashevski (1965, p. 67) wrote: "Plot is distinct from story. Both include the same events, but in the plot the events *are arranged* and connected according to the orderly sequence in which they were presented in the work. [Continued in a note; the story is] "the action itself, … [the plot] how the reader learns of the action." A *story*, in other words, refers to a skeletal description of the fundamental events in their natural logical and chronological order (perhaps, with an equally skeletal listing of the roles of the characters in the story) (Bal, 1977, p. 4; Toolan, 1988, p. 9).

The French structuralists adopted the basic distinction *fabula* versus *sjužet*, coined their own terms for the dichotomy, *histoire* versus *discours*,[70] story versus discourse, and further subdivided the plot/discourse level into *text* (or, more generally, discourse) and narrating or *narration*.[71] In the words of French linguist Gérard Genette (1980, pp. 25–6), there are at least three different meanings to the word "narrative."[72]

> A first meaning … has *narrative* refer to the narrative statement, the oral or written discourse that undertakes to tell of an event or a series of events [plot/text/discourse or *narrative* proper for Genette] … A second meaning … has *narrative* refer to the succession of events, real or fictitious [story/*histoire*] … A third meaning … has *narrative* refer once more to an event: Not, however, the event that is recounted, but the event that consists of someone recounting something: The act of narrating taken in itself. [narrating/*narration*]

It is the story – the chronological succession of events – that provides the basic building blocks of narrative. Without story there is no narrative. "The presence or absence of a story is what distinguishes narrative from nonnarrative texts" (Rimmon-Kenan, 1983, p. 15). "A story," wrote Tomashevski (1965, p. 70), "may be thought of as a journey from one situation to another."

A story, in other words, implies a change in situations as expressed by the unfolding of a specific sequence of events. The chronological sequence is a crucial ingredient of any definition of story. Tomashevski, Labov, Prince, Bal, Todorov, Rimmon-Kenan, Cohan and Shires all drum that same point.[73] Not every sequence of any two temporally ordered events can constitute a story (Rimmon-Kenan, 1983, p. 19). Two sentences such as "Joan took her plane at 5 P.M." and "Peter drove to the airport at 8 P.M." would constitute a story only if later sentences established a logical connection between those two sentences, such as "They had both been looking forward to spending the weekend together." The temporal ordering of events in a story is a necessary but not sufficient condition for the emergence of a story. The events in the sequence must be bound together by some principles of logical coherence.[74] At the level of plot the events of a story can form complex sequences by combining events in a variety of ways through enchainment, embedding, and joining.[75] Finally, the events in the story must disrupt an initial state of equilibrium setting in motion an inversion of situation, a change of fortunes: from good to bad, from bad to good.[76]

"The inversion of an event is one of the essential features of a story," sums up Prince (1973, p. 28) – the other essential feature being the temporal ordering of events in a story.[77] In classical Aristotelian poetics, the turn of fortunes – a *reversal* – is the key characteristic of comedy and tragedy. "Reversal," wrote Aristotle, "is a complete swing in the direction of the action" (Halliwell, 1987, p. 42). While comedy marks an improvement of a situation, tragedy marks a worsening, the "transformation to prosperity or affliction."[78] Reversals can occur repeatedly in a story along the sequence: initial state → disruption → new state → disruption → new state → … → final state (equilibrium). Each new state is both a point of arrival and a point of departure, sort of a temporary equilibrium between the "before and after," the past and the future. In Todorov's (1990, p. 30) words: "[T]he elements [of a story] are related [not] only by *succession*; … they are also related by *transformation*. Here finally we have the two principles of narratives."

In a sequence, not all events are as equally consequential for change of a situation. For Tomashevski (1965[1925], p. 70) "Motifs [basically, actions and events] which change the situation are *dynamic motifs*; those which do not are *static*." This distinction between those actions and events that fundamentally alter a narrative situation and the ones that do not is quite recurrent in the field. Roland Barthes (1977[1966], pp. 93–4), for instance, distinguishes between *cardinal functions* (or *nuclei*) and *catalysers*. Catalysers "merely fill in the narrative space," while cardinal functions alter current state of affairs, either by bringing them to a new equilibrium or by disrupting an existing equilibrium. "Catalysers are only consecutive [that is, chronologically ordered] units, cardinal functions are both consecutive and consequential" (Barthes, 1977[1966], p. 94). Chatman (1978, pp. 32, 53–6) adopted Barthes's basic distinction but in a different language: kernel and satellite events (Rimmon-Kenan, 1983, p. 16, also talks about kernel and satellite events). "Kernels cannot be deleted," writes Chatman (1978, p. 53), "without destroying the narrative logic." Kernels open up narrative choices.[79]

Dynamic motifs, cardinal functions, or kernel events have corresponding linguistic markers. For Labov (1972, pp. 360–1) "a *minimal narrative* … [is] a sequence of two clauses which are *temporally ordered*. … The skeleton of a narrative … consists of a series of temporally ordered clauses" (called *narrative clauses*). Time, in narrative, has a dual function; according to Rimmon-Kenan, it "is constitutive both of the means of representation (language) and of the object represented (the incidents of the story). ... [I]t can be defined as the relations of chronology between story and text" (Rimmon-Kenan, 1983, p. 44). In any story, the sequence of clauses can coincide with the sequence of the narrated events. Story and plot coincide, with minimum plot development. That is rather typical of simple stories. The plot is the realm where the narrative abilities of different authors can make something out of the basic raw material of a story (a sequence of events).

While there may be no narrative without narrative clauses, not all clauses found in narrative are *narrative clauses*.[80] Consider Labov's (1972, p. 361) example:

> a   I know a boy named Harry.
> b   Another boy threw a bottle at him right in the head
> c   and he got seven stitches.

In this narrative passage, only clauses *b* and *c* are *narrative clauses*. Clause *a* is not. It is a *free clause*, in Labov's terminology; a clause that has no temporal dimension attached to it; a clause, therefore, that can be moved freely up and down in the text without altering its meaning. Not so with *narrative clauses*. A rearrangement of narrative clauses typically results in a change in meaning ("I punched this boy/and he punched me" versus "This boy punched me/and I punched him."[81]

In general, a narrative text will comprise a mixture of both narrative and nonnarrative clauses. Stories (or narrative discourse) are a particular kind of action discourse, that is, "discourse which is interpreted as a sequence of actions and their properties" (van Dijk, 1980, p. 13). Not each sentence in an action discourse must necessarily be about action, but most of them are.

Historians have long recognized that, in historical writing, narrative and nonnarrative elements (descriptive and analytical, the latter in particular) mix together.[82] No doubt, the narration of actions and events has dominated historical writing, at the expense of both description and analysis. But in the twentieth century, analytical prose has become increasingly dominant. Lawrence Stone argues that the "new history"

> organizes its material in a new way; books are written in an analytical, not a narrative, arrangement, and it is no coincidence that almost all of what are regarded as the outstanding historical works of the last quarter century have been analytical rather than narrative. Second, it asks new questions; why did things happen the way they did and what were the consequences, rather than the old questions of what and how. It is to solve these new questions that the historian is obliged to adopt an analytical organization of his material. (Stone, 1987, p. 21)

In analytical writing, the forces that operate in history become impersonal. They lose the faces of Poupinel, the spinning women of Avranches, of Alice Evans. They become structural, or natural.

"Non-story elements may be found in a narrative text just as story elements may be found in a nonnarrative text. A novel may well include the description of a cathedral, and the description of a cathedral, say in a guidebook, may include the story of its construction" (Rimmon-Kenan, 1983, p. 15). In particular, descriptive and expository propositions typically enter into a minimal narrative.[83] Narrative texts are those where "the distinctive traits of the narrative genre ... are quantitatively predominant" (Bal, 1977, p. 13).[84] There is never either a pure narrative or nonnarrative text. "Description alone is not enough to constitute a narrative; narrative for its part does not exclude description."[85]

"In modern theories of literature," states Bal (1977, p. 89), "description occupies a marginal role. The structural analysis of narrative relegates it to a secondary function: It is subordinate to the narration of action. It can occupy the *catalyser* function but never that of *nucleus.*" "Description [is] a narrative luxury ... with an essential ornamental function" (Bal, 1977, pp. 89–90). Typically, the narrative characteristics of a story are linguistically marked by the use of finite (rather than nonfinite) verbs (for example, walks or walked, rather than to walk). In Toolan's (1988, pp. 34–5) words: "The finite verb ... is the unmarked, preferred and unexceptional vehicle for expression of plot events." Narratives are further grammatically characterized by the use of dynamic verbs that depict events and active processes, rather than stative verbs that describe state of affairs or descriptions (Toolan, 1988, pp. 34, 266). In the most explicit attempt at linking narrative macrostructures to grammatical features, particularly of verbs or "processes," Chatman writes: "[Narrative] statements are of two kinds – *process* and *stasis* – according to whether someone did something or something happened; or whether something simply existed in the story. Process statements are in the mode of DO or HAPPEN ... Stasis statements are in the mode of IS."[86]

What Have We Gained?

What have we gained by approaching text via story grammars? The language of gains and losses, of advantages and disadvantages is always a language of comparisons. Gains (or losses), with respect to what? With respect to content analysis as a social science technique for turning quality into quantity? To the text itself and the way we understand it directly through reading? To other linguistic tools, such as syntax grammars? To scripts and schemata, in computer understanding of natural languages? One The account of gains and losses partly depends upon where we look. And, for now, let's look inside the social science's camp and compare story grammars to the coding schemes of content analysis.

1. *Content analysis*. The design of coding categories closely follows the substantive and theoretical interests of the investigator. The demands that a protest group puts forward could be classified as ideal, material, particularistic, or universalistic. The actions could be proactive or reactive; violent or nonviolent.

   Story grammar. The coding categories of the grammar are functional, linguistic-based categories. They reflect properties of the text itself, rather than the researchers' theoretical interests.

2. *Content analysis*. Coding categories are abstract, general, and highly aggregated. The microactions that make up macroactions are typically disregarded (for example, "cheer," "shout," "hand-out leaflets," "collect solidarity funds," "picket" for the macroaction "strike"). As a result, macroactions lose in specificity and richness of detail. Similarly, events lasting over long periods of time (days, weeks, or months) or spreading across a large territory, lose their temporal and spatial depth. Although the total duration of an event may be recorded (and generally is), specific sequences of microactions within events are lost.

   Story grammar. Through a set of rewrite rules, the grammar generates an event (or collective campaign) in terms of nonterminal and terminal symbols. Terminal symbols are given by the very words and expressions found in the text. The action modifier <demand> would not be coded as "material," "ideal," "universalistic," or "particularistic," but as "ten percent wage increase," "ten-hour day," "dissolution of Parliament."

3. *Content analysis*. Since coding categories and their level of aggregation directly reflect the theoretical concerns of the researcher who first designed them, "a researcher interested in a different theoretical use of the text will almost certainly find the categories inappropriate" (Markoff, Shapiro, and Weitman, 1975, p. 41). That would even be true of the original researcher wishing "to pose new questions to the source material" after the completion of data collection (Markoff, Shapiro, and Weitman, 1975, p. 41). In both cases, new coding is necessary. As Stone (1987, p. 37) remarked:

   > [Given] these highly costly and labour-intensive quantitative studies ... If any variable is missed in setting up the code book – for example, the social distribution of literacy as evidenced by signatures in the 1427 Florentine *catasto* – it is too late to go back and do it again once the omission is discovered.

   Story grammar. In a grammar-based coding scheme all relevant factual information can be coded, with a high degree of disaggregation in ways that closely resemble the original narrative. As a result, the data collected using a story grammar are more nearly hypothesis free than traditional ones. That should allow a number of secondary data analyses, independently of the particular theoretical concerns that guided the original design of the coding scheme. The wealth of available information should also allow rich and fine grained analyses, the empirical testing of hitherto untested and untestable propositions.

4. *Content analysis.* Coders play a major role in trying to fit concrete text into a set of highly abstract categories. However much researchers may try to reduce the coder's discretion through written coding rules, abstract coding categories invariably result in the contamination of the measurement (see Krippendorf, 1980, p. 84). Coders play "surrogate scientist" (Markoff et al., 1975, p. 37; Shapiro and Markoff, 1998, p. 64).

   Story grammar. By keeping closer to the source material, coders do not have to make a theoretical judgment as to whether a demand of "ten percent wage increase" is universalistic or particularistic. This decision would be made at a later stage, by researchers themselves. "The coder," as Markoff, Shapiro and Weitman write (1975, p. 41), "transcribes a set of symbols which are intended to be as close as possible to the level of concreteness in the original document ... The coder translates; the scientist analyzes."

5. *Content analysis.* Links and connections between categories are not usually specified (nor easily specifiable).[87] If two people are injured in a clash between demonstrators and the police, and the injuries are due to police charges, it is not possible to link the actors "police" and "demonstrators" via the action "baton charge."

   Story grammar. In a grammar, the connections between coding categories are explicitly specified by the grammar itself, with subjects linked to actions, actions to objects, and subjects, actions, and objects linked to their modifiers.

6. *Content analysis.* Coded output will bear little or no relationship to the original text input. The original words are lost. And so are the connections between words.

   Story grammar. Coding text in terms of terminal symbols (that is, the very lexicon found in the text) within explicitly linked linguistic categories gives coded output the flavor of a natural-language narrative. Coded output is organized in chronologically order sentencelike structures.[88] Little original information is lost in the process of coding.

2

Ars Memoriae

Danger arises from problems of scale. A peculiar combination of circumstances came together in the 1960s which made it possible for the first time to assemble and manipulate enormous quantities of data[:] ... the advent of the computer ... and a cornucopia of research funds suddenly made available for hiring large teams of helots to work on vast collective projects. The result was the emergence of the huge quantitative research project.

Lawrence Stone (1981, pp. 36, 38, 39)

These symbols are then arranged as follows. The first thought is placed, as it were, in the forecourt; the second, let us say, in the living-room; the remainder are placed in due order all around the *impluvium* and entrusted not merely to bedrooms and parlours, but even to the care of statues and the like. This done, as soon as the memory of the facts requires to be revived, all these places are visited in turn and the various deposits are demanded from their custodians, as the sight of each recalls the respective details ... We require, therefore, places, real or imaginary, and images or symbols ...

Quintilian (1922, 21, p. 223)

The Artificial Art of Memory: The Old and the New

The Introduction to the 1744 edition of Giambattista Vico's *Principj di Scienza Nuova* was titled: *Idea dell'opera. Spiegazione della dipintura proposta al frontespizio che serve per l'introduzione dell'opera*.[1] The Introduction is a long explanation of a frontispiece painting that, in Vico's words, "should help the reader to get an idea of the work before actually reading it and to commit to memory more easily ... after having read it" (Vico, 1959, p. 239). Vico was not the first philosopher to introduce his work by means of a painting.[2] Bacon's 1620 edition of the *Novum Organum* was prefaced by a painting. And so was

Hobbes's 1651 edition of *Leviathan* with its dramatic painting of the state/monster (Hobbes, 1985, p. 71). In fact, Bacon, Hobbes, and Vico were following a time-honored tradition known as the "artificial art of memory" that stretched at least as far back as the Greeks.

The purpose of this practical "art" was to increase one's memory by linking concepts to symbols, notably places. That art would certainly come handy if we are to analyze within the categories of a story grammar more than just a handful of sentences. Quintilian has left us one of the early accounts on how the art worked.[3]

> It is an assistance to the memory if localities are sharply impressed upon the mind ... For when we return to a place after considerable absence, we not merely recognize the place itself, but remember things that we did there, and recall the persons whom we met and even the unuttered thoughts which passed through our minds ... (Quintilian, 18, 1922, p. 221)

On the basis of that principle, Quintilian recommended linking one's thoughts and ideas to various objects carefully arranged in a house, room after room, for later collection, in the same order, when needed (Quintilian, 1922, 21, p. 223). By Vico's time, Quintilian's practical advice to orators had developed into a complicated "art" through the Middle Ages and the Renaissance, in fact, into an occult art closely linked to magic and to the cabalist tradition.[4] Raymond Lull was an early medieval champion of that tradition with his work on the combinatorial wheels (Yates, 1992, pp. 175–96). In this new approach, Cicero's and Quintilian's practical art is slowly turned into an occult art that found later Renaissance champions in Giulio Camillo and Giordano Bruno (Yates, 1992, p. 155). Of the classical art, Giulio Camillo retained a commitment to images and memory places. But Camillo put those images to a different use. He made his goal clear when he wrote (1554, p. 63):

> The ancient orators, wanting to place day by day the parts of their speeches they had to make, they assigned them to fleeting places, as fleeting those speeches were; but because we want to commit for eternity the eternal essence of all things ... we must assign them to eternal places.

And in search of those eternal places, Camillo turned to the cabalist tradition,[5] to the seven pillars of wisdom, the seven days of creation, the seven planets, the seven sephirot, the seven angels. "This seven is a perfect number," Camillo writes (1554, p. 62), "because it contains one and the other sexes, because it is made up of the odd and the even ..."

Regarded as "the divine Camillo" in his own time, and for at least another century,[6] this man spent his life in the pursuit of a project: Write the ultimate book on memory and build the perfect memory theater. The great book he never wrote (Merton's pathology of science number four, in Diesing's rendering:

"Withdrawal into fantasies of future glory when one's masterpiece is finally published and acclaimed" Diesing, 1991, p. 156). His collected works – letters, rhymes, and miscellaneous essays – amount to a three-by-five inch, tiny little book published in Venice in 1554. Among the essays, *L'idea del theatro* (Camillo, 1554, pp. 59–146) can hardly be considered a definitive statement on the art of memory.[7] Neither did Camillo ever complete his work on the theater. This "very wonderful theater, fame of which has spread throughout Italy," in the prefatory words of Lodovico Dolce,[8] was not supposed to be just a textbook project for Camillo, but a physical construction, a real theater. Few of his contemporaries actually saw it. The king of France, Francis I, was among the privileged and must have been sufficiently impressed to advance Camillo 500 ducats to continue his work. A certain Viglius Zuichemus also saw a miniature wooden model of the theater in Venice and left us a description in a letter to Erasmus of 1532. According to Zuichemus, the model theater was big enough for two adults to stand up in the middle and look around its seven grades, full of images and drawers containing "masses of papers" reporting speeches based on Cicero's work and relating to the figures (Yates, 1992, p. 148). It is "a work of wonderful skill," Zuichemus informs Erasmus, "into which whoever is admitted as spectator will be able to discourse on any subject no less fluently than Cicero" (cited in Yates, 1992, p. 135). Camillo's theater represents a vision of the world – hence the contemporaries' label of *theatrum mundi*, theater of the world.[9]

With Camillo's, Cicero's, and Quintilian's old "practical" art of memory to commit speeches to memory had come to an end. A new art was now being sought and practiced, an art that promised not only storage and retrieval of hard-won knowledge, but the very creation of new knowledge, in fact, of *true* knowledge. Giulio Camillo made that clear when he wrote in his *L'idea del Theatro*:

> This high and incomparable placing serves not only the purpose of storing things, words, and arts which we confide to it, so that we may find them at once whenever we need them, but also gives us true wisdom from whose founts we come to the knowledge of things from their causes rather than from their effects. (Camillo, 1554, p. 11; see also Yates, 1992, p. 147)

Giordano Bruno reiterated that same point in his approach to the art of memory: "This art," Bruno wrote in *De umbris idearum* (1997, p. 55), "is not only useful for the acquisition of simple memory techniques, but for opening new ways and leading to the discovery of many new faculties." If the *memory theater* is Camillo's tool of "true wisdom," Raymond Lull's *combinatorial wheels* are Bruno's tool for "the discovery of many new faculties."

The wheels, as Bruno represented them in *De umbris idearum* (1997, pp. 154–87, in particular), consist of concentric rings in a circle, each ring subdivided into thirty slices containing one of thirty alphabetic letters (the twenty-three letters of the Italian alphabet, A–Z, plus the four Greek letters Ψ,

Φ, ω, θ and the three Hebrew letters ע, צ, ש). Each letter on a wheel has a specific mnemonic and iconographic image attached to it (for example, Licaon attached to the letter *A* on the outer wheel). A set of such concentric wheels can be used to represent different things. The outermost wheel represents the "agents." The immediately adjacent wheel represents the "actions." The third wheel represents the "instrument" (or *insignia*). These three wheels provide the basic structure, but more wheels can be added to represent "assisting elements," "conditions," and more (Bruno, 1997, p. 174).

Each wheel can be kept fixed, each letter and image under another to convey a fixed meaning (for example, *AA,* agent and action, "Licaon in a banquet"; Bruno, 1997, pp. 159–61; *AAA,* agent, action, and instrument, "Licaon in a banquet with a chain"; Bruno, 1997, pp. 162–3). But by appropriately sliding one wheel inside another, a large number of *combinations* can be produced with any agent being able to perform any action with the help of any instrument (Bruno, 1997, pp. 165–7, 172). Bruno was proud of his discovery. "How magnificent this discovery is," he would write, "you will be able to understand better through practice and through the application to other cases" (Bruno, 1997, p. 171).

But the proponents of another Renaissance art, of another method (the "scientific method") were far less enthusiastic. They saw the art of memory as a tool to acquire knowledge without effort, a shortcut to knowledge. Neither Bacon nor Descartes had anything good to say about Lull's or Camillo's approach to the art of memory – an art, however, in which they were both well versed. Descartes, in his *A Discourse on Method,* wrote of "the art of Lully, in speaking without judgment of things of which we are ignorant" (Descartes, 1960, p. 50). Bacon similarly scornfully wrote of this "method, which is not a lawful method, but a method of imposture; which is to deliver knowledges in such a manner, as men may speedily come to make a show of learning who have it not" (cited in Yates, 1992, p. 361). And yet, magic and science combined in Bacon himself.[10] Leibniz was well versed in the Lullian art of memory.[11] It is out of Raymond Lull's work on the use of symbols, and not just places, to denote concepts, out of Lull's complex scheme where symbols could be combined in an infinite number of ways by turning them around on wheels – albeit, not just to recall knowledge but to produce new knowledge – that later came Leibniz's work on infinitesimal calculus, one of the pillars of modern mathematics.[12]

As for Quintilian's *practical* art of memory, the appearance of the printed book made the connection between knowledge and memory far less imperative. The figure of the medieval scholar who journeyed from library to library committing manuscripts to memory became a thing of the past – the metaphor of knowledge as a journey had a metonymic value after all … And, of course, the advent of the computer has dealt the final blow to the art. No need to clutter one's brain with information readily available at one's fingertips. Yet, the computer era has brought out a new art of memory, a new art of assigning knowledge to memory, only, this time, it is computer memory. And in curious ways, with the past recaptured to new ends, such operating systems as Microsoft Windows rely heavily on "icons" and "shortcuts," language itself being reminiscent of practices of old. Indeed, what makes story grammars of practical use as data-collection schemes is the fact that they can be implemented in a computer environment. With pencil and paper the use of such complex coding schemes as story grammars is out of the question. Let us take a closer look at this new art of (computer) memory.

Database Design for a Story Grammar

On August 31, 1920, one reads in *Il Lavoro*, a socialist newspaper published in Genoa, Italy:

> The struggle of metallurgical workers
> The lockout of a Milanese firm provokes factory occupation
>   Milan, August 30, evening
> Following yesterday's incidents, the Romeo Company announced a lockout. Naturally, the metallurgical workers of other plants in the area did not accept this decision passively and the leaders of the labor movement immediately decided, in protest, that all workers should occupy their factories. The order was issued and immediately executed. In all the Milanese plants involved in the metallurgic workers dispute, the workers did not leave their factories, and ... they are still in there, without doing any work. At first, all technical personnel, the factory managers, and some of the owners were kept inside the plant by the workers. In the evening, however, almost all of them were freed. In the evening, in many plants, workers' families brought in dinner. All in all, no serious incidents have occurred ... (*Il Lavoro,* August 31, 1920, p. 2, c. 3)

That day, August 31, and that factory, the Romeo Factory in Milan, mark the beginning of the factory occupation movement, the most salient event in a two-year period of turmoil known in Italian history as the *Biennio rosso*, the Red Years (1919–20). Within a day or two, at the beginning of September, most metallurgic factories throughout the country came under workers' control. Starting September 3, article titles of *Il Lavoro* on the factory occupation ran the width of the page, a palpable sense of a social revolution in the air. But the factory occupation ended in failure a month after it had started, opening the doors to a reactionary period of widespread fascist violence (the *Biennio nero*, the Black Years of 1921–22).

Several articles from *Il Lavoro* address the Romeo factory labor dispute; several hundred the factory occupation movement, and over 15,000 the Red Years and the Black Years, between 1919 and 1922. Now, suppose that you wanted to "memorize" all the information contained in these articles. Perhaps, not even Pico della Mirandola, a Renaissance champion of Quintilian's art famed for his prodigious memory, could have mastered that feat. In any case, the memory of that art of memory has now faded (although you do still find it in remarkably unchanged form in books of advice on how to build up your memory). A computer database is what we really need. After all, C. J. Date, one of the engineers who contributed to the development of the field, tells us that a database is "nothing more than a system whose overall purpose is to record and maintain information," "a computer-based recordkeeping system."[13]

All databases share some basic concepts, such as "entities," "entity sets," "domains," and "relationships." An "entity is a thing that is distinguishable; that is we can tell one thing from another."[14] In our grammar, such words as "strike," "lockout," or "demonstrate" are entities, since a "competent reader of the language" can tell them apart from actors or time. Groups of similar entities form entity sets. Entities can have characteristics called "attributes." Thus, all actions and actors form an action set and an actor set; all actor and action modifiers (for example, <number of actors>, <time>, <space>) are attributes.

Typically, in a database, each entity set is stored in a separate file (for example, one file for such entity sets as events, triplets, actors, actions, time, space, and other modifiers or attributes).[15] The question is: If information is stored in separate files, how do we link information across files? Without these links there would be no way to know which actors perform which actions, or where and when each action occurs. The links, in database jargon, are known as relationships – different types of relationships yielding different types of data models: network, hierarchical, and relational.[16] These different data models have different properties, and different advantages and disadvantages. Until the late 1970s, commercial database systems were almost exclusively based on the network or hierarchical model (Ullman, 1980, p. 100). But relational databases systems (RDBMS) were becoming increasingly popular.[17] The ready availability of relational database software for PC platforms (for example, Access, Oracle, FoxPro) have now made RDBMS the dominant type of data model.[18]

Table 2.1 provides a relational database representation for the handful of categories of a story grammar required to store the information of the article on the Romeo Factory lockout.[19] The subject_table, action_table, and object_table all have six attributes: the current table, dispute, event, triplet, and subject/action/object identifiers, and the subject/action/object name. The number_table has seven attributes: the identifiers for current table, dispute, event, triplet, upper table and upper-table entity, and the number itself.[20] In this example, the hierarchical levels of the grammar (dispute, event, and triplet) have been linearized, that is, they have been rendered in terms of a unique identifier (_id) that is repeated in all tables.[21] In addition, the tables also share other common attributes (for example, the table_id and the upper_table_id between the subject_table, action_table, object_table, and number_table).

Table 2.1. *A Relational Database Representation of a Story Grammar*

Subject_table

table_id	dispute_id	event_id	triplet_id	subject_id	subject_name
1	1	2	1	1	firm
1	1	2	2	2	workers
1	1	2	3	3	leaders
1	1	2	4	4	workers
1	1	2	5	5	workers
1	1	2	6	6	workers
1	1	2	7	7	workers
1	1	2	8	8	families

Action_table

table_id	dispute_id	event_id	triplet_id	action_id	action_name
2	1	2	1	1	announce lockout
2	1	2	2	2	do not accept decision
2	1	2	3	3	decide factory occupation
2	1	2	4	4	do not leave plant
2	1	2	5	5	do not work
2	1	2	6	6	keep inside the factory
2	1	2	7	7	free

Object_table

table_id	dispute_id	event_id	triplet_id	object_id	object_name
3	1	2	6	1	technical personnel
3	1	2	6	2	managers
3	1	2	6	3	owners
3	1	2	7	4	technical personnel
3	1	2	7	5	managers
3	1	2	7	6	owners
3	1	2	8	7	workers

Number_table

current table_id	dispute_id	event_id	triplet_id	upper table_id	upper tuple_id	number_value
4	1	2	4	1	4	all factories
4	1	2	6	3	1	all
4	1	2	6	3	3	some
4	1	2	7	3	4	almost all
4	1	2	7	3	5	almost all
4	1	2	7	3	6	almost all

Links between entities stored in different tables can be made through these overlapping attributes. Thus, for instance, the same triplet_id in the subject, action, and object tables tell us that the corresponding actor_name(s) and action_name(s) go together as part of the same sentence (for example, the triplet_id = 6 in the subject_table corresponds to the actor_name "workers," to the action_name "keep inside the factory" as action in the action_table, and to the object_name technical personnel, managers, owners in the object_table, which corresponds to the properly formed English sentence "workers keep technical personnel, managers, and owners inside the factory").[22]

Computer-Assisted Content Analysis

The period between 1760 and 1830 – the boundary dates set by historian T. S. Ashton for the Industrial Revolution – was a remarkable period in English history. The number of patents registered through the period gives a tangible indicator of the "great transformation": Less than twelve up to 1760, thirty six in 1769, 64 in 1783, 85 in 1792; the pace hastened to 107 patents ten years later in 1802, 180 in 1824, and 250 in 1825. Behind those numbers, there are a handful of well-known (and lesser known) inventors: John Kay (flying shuttle in 1733), James Hargreaves (spinning jenny in 1764–7), Richard Arkwright, the "inventor"[23] of the water frame in 1768, James Watt (steam engine patented in 1769), Samuel Crompton (mule in 1789), Edmund Cartwright (power loom in the 1780s).[24]

Two centuries later, give or take a year or two, history repeats itself. The development of microcomputers (the "PC") would draw a similar pattern of harsh-paced innovation: From a handful of megahertz in speed and megabytes of hard disk drive to the current 3,000 megabytes and hard drives now measured in gigabytes. Software innovation followed suit (but sometimes set the pace, in the typical see-saw pattern of challenge and response highlighted by Landes, 1969): from CPM, to DOS and Windows operating systems. The number of software applications in support of a variety of different problems skyrocketed, with an ever-increasing number on offer. Such is the case for computer software for the analysis of qualitative data.[25] Names such as NUD*IST have become as familiar as SPSS. This new generation of software promises not just solutions to methodological problems of data analysis but "powerful processes of … theorizing." Tantalizingly close seem to be the days when the computer can offer solutions to fundamental problems of a discipline (linking methods and theory) and not just to egoistic worries of individual academics (McCloskey's PUBPER, the "publish or perish" computer program, 1985, p. 167). Long live the computer, reader of the year 2520!

With a computer on every social scientist's desk, each one of us has become an inventor of sorts, developing specialized software for specialized problems. Indeed, most of these new software applications are home-baked products, arising out of specific research needs and commercialized out of someone's backroom. The entrepreneurial route for academics is not without dangers. Samuel Crompton, the inventor of the mule in 1789, went bankrupt trying to exploit his invention commercially, and, embroiled in legal suits over patent infringement, died indebted and poor in 1827 (Mantoux, 1983, pp. 234–8).

It is to the category of home-baked products that belongs the software I developed between 1985 and 1995 to carry out a content analysis of protest event narratives on the basis of a story grammar: PC-ACE, Program for Computer-Assisted Coding of Events. And it is of Edmund Cartwright I was thinking, to keep at bay the lure of riches through the sales of the software. So, I will give you "the general idea" of the software for free, but keep in the drawer my old-fashioned PC-ACE written in an already defunct language (Turbo Pascal) – life is short in the fast lane. My recommendation to you is to build your application of a story grammar on a PC database engine such as Access, Paradox, or FoxPro. These programs will do a lot of the ground work for you. You can get a basic story grammar up and running in a short time. But beware! Even slight increments in performance – which you are bound to want after you get going – will require a great deal of programming (and you may end up displacing means for ends, engulfed in "mind-absorbing," "soul-entrapping" "technical problem-solving"; Bailyn, 1982, p. 6). *Experientia docet!*

Basic Features of the Software

What will you need to do? Simple: Just follow the grammar. And the first item in the grammar is the article key. You need to record the information that uniquely identifies each qualifying article (or any document for that matter)[26]: the newspaper name, date, page number (and page title, if given), column number, and position of the article in the column.[27] Current database software relies on "forms" for data entry, where each required item of information has a data-entry field. Within each field, the software should allow you to enter default values wherever possible to increase efficiency and to enter information either verbatim or by choosing it from a dictionary of precoded items.[28] It should also allow you to perform all standard operations of adding, deleting, and editing fields (including cutting and pasting information). The software should make all necessary data reliability checks (for example, December 33, 1920 for the newspaper date is not a valid date and the software should automatically flag it as an error).[29]

The next step is to record the name of the dispute(s) the article deals with. Is this a new dispute or an ongoing dispute? You will need to have a list of all coded disputes, each identified by name and perhaps by the date of the first article that provided information on the dispute. If the article key just coded is that of the first article of a new dispute, you will need to open a new dispute and assign it a name (for example, Romeo Factory lockout). The names given to disputes play an important role in coding. They supply a brief mnemonic description of what the story is all about. Such a description will help you to identify a coded story. It serves the same purpose as a title.[30] The dispute provides the overall organizing principle for the incoming articles. Its title constitutes a superordinate proposition that facilitates the process of understanding and organizing the material.[31] The more meaningful the description, the easier it will be for you (or other users) to determine the content of a dispute without having to read it. While the software should allow you to supply your own dispute names, the software could promote greater uniformity in dispute names by requiring you to supply information on specific aspects of a dispute (for example, location, actor, macroevent, demands/reasons) and then automatically compose a title by collating this information.

You have identified the relevant articles. You have collated them in appropriate aggregates (for example, disputes, events). The software will have kept a running count of the cross-references between articles and disputes, displaying the number of disputes for each article and the number of articles for each dispute. Next, you need to code the information contained in each article, assigning it to a set of coding categories, or, in the notation of a text grammar, to actors, actions, and the characteristics of actors and actions (semantic triplet).[32, 33] How should these coding tasks be organized? The structure of the grammar around the basic canonical form of the language noun phrase/verb phrase – subject, action, object, and their modifiers – suggests that a computer implementation of the grammar should organize coding along the familiar and natural lines of sentence formation: First, the subjects and respective modifiers, then, the actions with their modifiers, and, finally, the objects and object modifiers, along the natural lines of the linguistic structure of simple narrative discourse. This presumes that the information in an article is presented sequentially and in the same order expected by the grammar – which, of course, is doubtful. The software should rather allow you to enter information in whichever way you want and, then, check for the well formedness of each semantic triplet. To the very minimum the software should ensure that both subject and action are present in a completed triplet. But data reliability can be further improved by establishing automatic "selection restrictions" between two or more syntactically linked lexical items (Bierwisch, 1970, p. 171). Thus, the two triplets "<subject> employer <action> strike," and "<subject> employer <action> lay off," should be flagged as errors by the software since employers do not strike and the <action> "lay off" requires an <object>. The grammar also calls for the classification of actors and actions. The software should automatically classify all unambiguous cases (for example, "kill" is undoubtedly an action of violence), but ask for your input in all ambiguous ones.

Finally, actor and action modifiers need to be coded. Some of these have a simple structure (for example, <type of action>); but others have complex rewrite rules (for example, <organization>, <space>, <time>). Regardless of complexity and no differently from the data-entry forms for the article key or the dispute name, data entry for modifiers will require the design of specific forms.

Some Lessons From Cognitive Psychology

Confronted with a coding task, you first coded the article keys of all qualifying articles. Then, you collated those articles into disputes, coding a handful of information for each dispute that gave you a mnemonic title for the dispute. Finally, you coded in detail, within the categories of the grammar, the information contained in each article for each dispute. Only one problem: You had to read each article at least three times. Wouldn't it make more sense in a computer environment to perform all three coding steps at once when first reading a qualifying article? After all, previously coded information is at your fingertips.

Indeed, it would make sense. You could start recording information as you read it, article after article, dispute after dispute, actor after actor, action after action. Yet, as you jump around from article to article, from dispute to dispute, it will not be long before your brain starts experiencing an information overload, with the consequence that either your coded output is not very reliable or that coding takes you much longer than expected (or, worse yet, both). Experimental work by cognitive psychologists on text understanding and recall, much of it based on the use of story grammars, has amply confirmed that people will take more time and make more errors when reading, comprehending, and recalling stories where important elements of a story grammar are missing or scrambled (particularly with elements taken from other stories), independently of story length.[34]

Perhaps a better alternative to a one-pass coding is a two-pass or even a multiple-pass coding. In the first pass, you record the information required to locate each relevant article (the article key) and you assemble articles in disputes, providing a general title for each dispute and cross-referencing each article to the appropriate dispute. In the second pass, you code each dispute separately, dealing only with the articles pertaining to one dispute. In two-pass coding you focus on one story at a time, from beginning to end without time lapses or interference from other intervening stories. This uninterrupted focus greatly reduces the risk of duplicating events, facilitates reliable chronological ordering of information, and helps to detect inconsistencies in the information found in different documents on the same event.

One-pass coding may appear intuitively appealing and efficient, particularly in a computer environment. Yet, two-pass coding is much more reliable. And despite the two passes, it may even be cheaper: Total coding time of multiple-article disputes is likely to decrease, since the coding time required by the first pass is more than offset by savings in coding time during the second pass.[35] The data-entry software should allow you to choose between alternative approaches to the coding task (namely, one-pass and a variety of multiple-pass approaches). Furthermore, if the articles to be coded are selected on the basis of a sample of disputes, rather than all disputes, the software should automatically implement the sampling framework.

Reliability versus Efficiency

Newspapers typically report one story/event/dispute per article. But reporting of several different and unrelated stories/events under the same article headline is not infrequent. In my 1920 data, over 98% of the articles dealt with only one story/dispute. The corresponding figure for my 1972 data is 78%. In absolute figures, only 75 articles covered more than one dispute in 1920, compared to, 1865 such articles in 1972. These differences in reporting practices can greatly affect data collection costs. Depending upon the organization of the coding task, multiple-dispute articles may result in higher coding time (and therefore costs) than single-dispute articles. Although two-pass coding of multiple-article disputes is more reliable than one-pass coding, it is very inefficient if you have multiple-dispute articles. In these cases, you have to return to the same article as many times as the number of disputes, n, in the article. This would involve n repetitions of some tasks (certainly reading the article, but also returning to a given article in a stack of papers, microfilm reader, or computer file).[36]

The higher the average number of disputes reported in a single article (and of multiple-dispute articles), the higher the cost paid for the increased reliability of multiple-pass coding. In one-pass coding, you never have to return on the same article. All the information in an article is coded as soon as a qualifying article is found, regardless of the number and type of disputes reported in it. Thus, two-pass coding increases data reliability in the presence of multiple-article disputes, but decreases efficiency in the presence of multiple-dispute articles. The software of data entry should allow you to select the most appropriate approach for coding each individual dispute.[37]

On Sampling: More on Reliability versus Efficiency

In one of the earliest studies aimed at assessing the impact of sampling on the results obtained through content analysis, Mintz (1949, p. 127) wrote:

> If the material ... investigated involves a large number of items, ... [content analysis] takes much time and labor. This suggests sampling of the material as a labor-saving device; instead of classifying and counting all available items, one may consider using only a part of the material, thus saving much effort.

Mintz's recommended strategy was to draw "nonconsecutive-day samples."[38] That early recipe for "saving much effort" by sampling newspaper issues has been followed faithfully by the practitioners of the art of content analysis. Kriesi and his associates relied on Monday issues of newspapers in their study of Swiss protest events (Kriesi et al., 1981). And so did Rucht and Neidhardt in their studies of German protest events (1999, p. 80) and Koopmans in his cross-national work (1995b; 1999, p. 102).[39]

This sampling strategy, unfortunately, runs into a fundamental problem in historical research. The question is: If sampling increases task efficiency what does it do to data reliability? Contrary to mass media investigators, historical researchers are interested in the characteristics of the events reported, rather than in the characteristics of newspaper reporting of events. They are interested in the signified, rather than the signifier. They use newspapers as mirrors of reality. These goals conflict with standard sampling procedures.

Sampling presupposes a known population from which a sample is drawn. When we sample newspaper issues by date, we use the total number of newspaper issues as our population; then, we adopt a systematic sampling rule of drawing a sample from this population (for example, every other issue). In so doing, we sample indirectly a set of events from the population of events reported by the newspaper in all its issues. The sample of events includes all the events reported in the newspaper issues sampled. This sample of events, however, is not random. It has not been drawn from a population of events with known characteristics and according to known sampling rules. Rather, it is the by-product of a sampling strategy based on newspaper issues, rather than event characteristics. The consequence of such a sampling strategy is that the sample of events available for analysis is biased. And this is in addition to the bias introduced by the nonrandom nature of the sample of events selected by the newspaper (Weede, 1973).

Furthermore, events are strategically linked in chains (my disputes or van Dijk's episodes). The event sequence, rather than the single event, constitutes a higher-level unit of aggregation of information (for example, a labor dispute, rather than a single work stoppage or a whole war, rather than a single combat operation). Collecting data from a sample of articles drawn on the basis of newspaper properties, rather than event properties, is likely to provide incomplete accounts of events or to alter the mix of events within higher-level units of data aggregation.[40]

These problems suggest a sampling strategy where researchers sample the disputes to be coded from all the disputes reported by a newspaper, regardless of issue, rather than the newspaper issue. Which brings us back to a two-pass approach to coding: First, you assemble into disputes all the qualifying articles from all the issues, and, second, you code only a sample drawn from this population of disputes (perhaps stratifying the sample by the importance of the dispute, as measured by the number of articles in the dispute).[41] Thus, two-pass coding increases not only data reliability, but provides a known population of disputes from which to draw a sample with desired characteristics.[42]

And More Lessons from Linguistics: Text Schemata

It is not just narrative discourse that is characterized by a deep structural schema. According to van Dijk,[43] newspaper articles have a similar fixed, deep schema

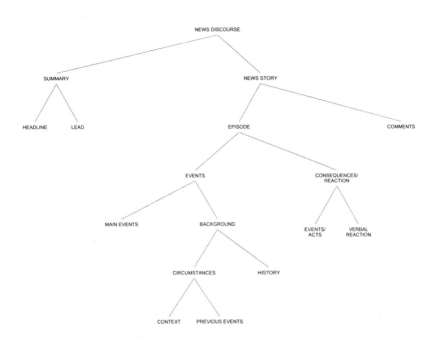

Figure 2.1. *Van Dijk's Schema of News Discourse*

of organization of the information (Figure 2.6). The schema provides a convenient catalogue for different types of news information. By clearly highlighting the news categories where either a language of evaluation or narrative "facticity"[44] is likely to prevail, the schema helps to map the relationship between a story grammar and news reports. It will also help to gauge the expected performance of the grammar as an instrument of measurement, in relation to different types of news information.

Consider the *episode*. The episode comprises the facts that make up the story, often with references to antecedent and consequent events, and verbal reactions, but where the *main event* is the *raison d'etre* of the article. The grammar is particularly well-suited for coding the information contained in the more factual categories of *main event, previous events,* and the *events/acts* of *consequences/ reactions*. In these categories of the schema we are likely to find the basic elements of a story grammar: Actors doing some actions (or saying something) for or against some other actors.[45]

The grammar will be less helpful in coding *comments*. The lexicon and syntax of these categories of discourse are likely to be abstract, more complex than the simple S-A-O structure of the grammar (van Dijk, 1985). Constraining this type of surface representation into the deep structure of the grammar may be an impossible task. The same may be true for *verbal reactions,* except for the most trivial cases (such expressions as "reject accusations," "blame," and "are satisfied with the outcome" do find a place in the grammar).

The schema helps to highlight where you can expect troubles, where you are more likely to experience difficulties, where coding errors are more likely to occur. As cognitive psychologists Mandler and Johnson (1977, p. 134) have argued: "Distortions in recall [and understanding of a story] will occur at points where ambiguity or violation of an ideal structure occurs in the surface structure." In other words, we can expect a greater likelihood of coding errors and/or intercoder differences (leading to lower reliability), the further the distance between the structure of a story grammar and the surface structure of the story being coded (as in the comments and verbal reactions).

But van Dijk's schema also helps to identify when you can expect to find repeated information both within and across articles. Certainly the category *summary* will contain information provided in greater detail in the body of the article. The category *previous events* is likely to report information already provided in previous articles. The *events/acts* of consequences and reactions may be further expanded in future articles.[46] What should you do when documents provide information on previous events? Very likely, that information will have already been reported in previous articles. And those articles – if they fall within the temporal range of the project – will have already been coded. Should you code repeated information again or should you disregard it? If the purpose of data collection is not newspaper reporting practices but the reconstruction of an historical event, duplicate coding would be not only unnecessary but inappropriate. It would lead to the duplication of "real" events.[47] Similarly, information contained in the *summary* and *background* categories can be skipped, provided the information had already been coded from a previous article and did not add any new information.[48] Cutting out repetitious information could lead to great savings in coding time. The lower the amount of new information reported, the more time will be saved.[49, 50]

Data Verification

You have now coded all your information. No doubt, a well-designed data-entry software based on any commercially available relational database management system (RDBMS) would have alerted you on line to any error you may have inadvertently committed.[51] Yet, errors may have still slipped through.[52] And if they have, you (or an independent verifier) want to catch them. The property of a linguistic approach to content analysis of preserving in coded output the structural properties of narrative can be of great help in detecting and eliminating error.[53] Like the original input narrative text, coded output must be semantically coherent. It must make sense to any "competent user of the language." There are two basic levels of coherence, linguists tell us: local and global.[54]

When each sentence in a text is meaningfully well formed and sequential sentences are meaningfully related – in our case, the well formedness of the basic linguistic construct on which the grammar is based (subject, action, object, and their respective modifiers) – the text has local coherence. When each sentence or sequence of sentences is meaningfully related to one or more dominant themes or topics appearing in the text as a whole, the text has global coherence. A "competent" reader should recognize as errors intrasentence violations of "selection restrictions" (for example, "workers lay off employer"). Intersentence well formedness in natural languages can be deduced through explicit surface relations and constraints, such as pronominalization (for example, "I would like to buy a PC. *It* is not too expensive for me.") and the use of intersentence conjunctions and adverbs (for example, "I would like to buy a PC. *However*, I do not have the money.") (see van Dijk, 1972, p. 124).[55] In coding, the data-entry software should have an implicit "and" as the default relation between triplets with the option of specifying a different relation (for example, "so that," "because").

Perhaps the most critical aspect of intersentence coherence is tense continuity and the temporal sequence of clauses – in our case, the temporal ordering of semantic triplets. As Labov and Waletzsky (1967) have argued, in simple narrative, units of linguistic expression are connected to one another principally through a relation of temporal order; in fact, they define "a minimal narrative" as "a sequence of two clauses which are temporally ordered."[56] A story is coherent if the chrono-logical sequence of sentences or macropropositions squares with the reader's understanding of the order of real-life activities. Thus, the software should allow time ordering (and reordering) of triplets. It should also allow reaggregation of information without having to do any recoding of material previously coded.[57] After all, in narrative, the boundaries of macro-actions – where one episode ends and another one begins – are often blurred.[58]

Given the relationship between semantic coherence and output readability, the software should provide a range of alternative printing formats of the coded information: printing each item of coded information with all the coding labels (using the article on the Romeo Factory lockout):

<dispute 1> metalworkers *<event 1>* incidents *<time>* yesterday *<event 2>* lockout *<semantic triplet 1>* *<subject>* firm (*<name>* Romeo) *<action>* announces lockout *<event 3>* factory occupation (*<comment>* no serious incidents have occurred) *<semantic triplet 2>* *<subject>* workers (*<organization>* all other plants (*<space>* in the area)) *<action>* do not accept decision *<semantic triplet 3>* *<subject>* labor leaders *<action>* decide factory occupation (*<time>* immediately *<reason>* protest) *<semantic triplet 4>* *<subject>* workers (*<economic sector>* metalworking; *<number>* all factories *<space>* Milanese) *<action>* do not leave plant …

with all the information in basic narrative format but without the annoying labels firm (Romeo) announces lockout; workers (all other plants, in the area) do not accept decision; labor leaders decide factory occupation (immediately, protest); workers (metalworking, all factories, Milan) do not leave plant ...

or even without the modifiers for quick access to the basic skeleton triplet structure of subject, action and object.[59]

firm announces lockout
workers do not accept decision
labor leaders decide factory occupation
workers do not leave plant

Different types of display allow coders to check for different types of breakdown in coherence. Printing output with the appropriate coding labels would enable a reader to catch text coded under the wrong category (for example, "pro-availability of abortion" wrongly coded under the label <instrument> rather than <demand>).[60] But a quick glance to the coded output without labels and perhaps without modifiers would allow a reader to gauge intrasentence and intersentence coherence (in particular, the chrono-logical ordering of actions and events).

The coder's continuing involvement in understanding the data and in producing a coherent output should greatly reduce the incidence of error. To the extent that output maintains much of the linguistic structure and lexicon of text input, linguistic rules of both intra- and intersentence well formedness can be used to check coded output and to achieve higher levels of data reliability. Such powerful validation tools of text grammars should offset the greater likelihood of error that comes with working with a more complex coding scheme.[61]

Verification for semantic coherence, no doubt, provides a powerful tool for checking the accuracy of coded information either directly by the coder or, at a later stage, by an independent verifier. Yet, it only guarantees general readability and acceptability of output; it does not guarantee correspondence between input (source) and output (code). Output can make perfect sense, but ... be the product of a coder's imagination. A second type of output verification is then required: a direct comparison of the coded output to the original source material (input versus output verification).[62] Verification can check for both document omission and accuracy of information entered.[63, 64, 65, 66]

When the original input material is not readily accessible in the computer, input versus output verification is time consuming and expensive and you may want to adopt Acceptance Sampling schemes.[67] Acceptance Sampling provides quality control through the inspection of only a sample of output production units. If the inspected output does not meet some predetermined standards (that is, too many errors are found in the sample or the types of error are too severe), then the entire lot should be inspected and all errors rectified. Acceptance Sampling cannot guarantee an "error free" product, but it can guarantee, at a relatively low cost, that errors will be kept within predetermined limits of tolerance (technically defined as the Average Outgoing Quality Limit; see Naus,

1975, p. 102).[68] Again, the data-entry software should perform the tasks involved in drawing the sample. It should allow verifiers to select the population to sample (for example, a single coding session, a week's worth of coding), the unit to be sampled for inspection (for example, a collective campaign, an event, an article, a single coding category), and the percentage of units to be sampled. The software should then randomly draw the sample of units to be verified and keep track of the status of each sampling unit (for example, sampled, unverified, verified with no errors found, verified with errors found).

Navigating a Relational Database

In reducing to six Propp's thirty-one original functions of Russian folktales, French linguist Greimas (1966, pp. 192–203) grouped together, under the label "trial of the hero," many of the functions centered on the hero's actions. You may start feeling that keeping up with this book is such a trial. If so, there is good news from Propp. Because, in the end, after much traveling along perilous roads in far away lands on the other side of the earth, and much fighting dragons and villains, the hero always emerges victorious, the reward no less than a bride and a kingdom (function XXXI, "the hero is married and ascends the throne," Propp, 1968, p. 63). But, as for ourselves, I am in no position to promise you brides and kingdoms, and, in any case, we are not at function XXXI, yet. Even with all the information a) efficiently organized in a relational format and b) entered in a computer via a data-entry software that closely reflects the linguistic underpinnings of the grammar in its design, we need to take one more step. We need to access all that information, somehow.

Most database systems have their own way of searching and retrieving data, which makes switching systems a costly experience. Computer scientists, however, have also produced a standard query language, SQL (Structured Query Language).[69] SQL is particularly simple, a handful of general commands allowing users to "query" a database, that is, to search and retrieve information. In particular, the commands *select* and *from* form the basic query engine.[70] The *select* statement tells the RDBMS which columns to retrieve; the *from* statement tells the RDBMS the name of the table where the column is to be found. The syntax of the two commands is:

select column name(s)
from table name

Thus, the query:

select subject_name
from subject_table

when applied to the simple database of the Romeo lockout would yield a list of all the eight subject names available in the table of subjects: firm, workers, leaders, workers, workers, workers, workers, families. To eliminate duplicate entries in a table, we could qualify a query with the *distinct* statement. The query:

> *select distinct* subject_name
> *from* subject_table

results in the following list of the four unique subjects involved in the Romeo lockout: firm, workers, leaders, families.

Names can also be sorted (in ascending or descending order) or grouped in specific ways. More generally, queries can be qualified, that is, subjected to search conditions, via the *where* statement. The query:

> *select* object_name
> *from* object_table
> *where* triplet_id = 6

yields a list of names for the objects of triplet 6: technical personnel, managers, owners.

The *count* function within a select clause is particularly useful for our purposes, as it provides a tally of the number of occurrences of elements in a given column. The query:

> *select* object_name = "owners"
> number = *count* (*distinct* triplet_id)
> *from* object_table

gives the total number of distinct triplets in which the word "owners" appears as objects; the result of the query is stored in a column labeled "number" (in this case, number = 2). Needless to say, we could compute the frequency distribution of certain entities within each of the aggregation levels specified by the grammar: semantic triplet, event, dispute. The query:

> *select* object_name = "owners"
> number = *count* (*distinct* dispute_id)
> *from* object_table

would compute the same frequency distribution of the previous query for the object "owner," but with reference to disputes, rather than triplets, yielding the result: number = 1.

Single table operations are certainly useful. But the power of SQL stems from its ability to operate on several tables at a time. With information stored in separate tables it is imperative that SQL should link information across tables. For instance, the subject_table stores information on subjects, the action_table on actions, and the object_table on objects. To reconstruct the basic skeleton framework of the newspaper narrative of the Romeo lockout, we would need to

Table 2.2. *The Skeleton Triplets of the Romeo Factory Lockout Article in Relational Format*

Triplet_id	Subject_name	Action_name	Object_name
1	Firm	Announce lockout	
2	Workers	Do not accept decision	
3	Leaders	Decide factory occupation	
4	Workers	Do not leave plant	
5	Workers	Do not work	
6	Workers	Keep inside the factory	Technical personnel
6	Workers	Keep inside the factory	Managers
6	Workers	Keep inside the factory	Owners
7	Workers	Free	Technical personnel
7	Workers	Free	Managers
7	Workers	Free	Owners
8	Families	Bring dinner	Workers

join the three tables. On the basis of the common field, triplet_id, the following query would yield the list of Table 2.2 of the skeleton triplets (without their modifiers) contained in the newspaper article in proper chronological sequence:

select s.triplet_id, s.subject_name, a.action_name, o.object_name
from subject_table s, action_table a, object_table o
where s.triplet_id = a.triplet_id *and* a.triplet_id = o.triplet_id
group by triplet_id

Via similar queries operating on all the tables of the database we could easily reconstruct the entire story given in the article.

Toy Examples and "Real" Data: The Test of Large Data Sets

"*Parturient montes, nascetur ridiculus mus*" [the mountains will be in labor, a ridiculus mouse will be born], wrote Horace in his *Ars Poetica*. Could that be the case of story grammars, of all the linguistic paraphernalia of rewrite rules, all the mathematical much-ado-about-nothing of set theory and cardinal numbers ("all to tell me in the end that to get numbers out of words … you count them!"), all that computer jargon of pointers and relations? A case of "large-scale bureaucratic research into small-scale problems," in C. Wright Mills's words?[71] There is only one way to find out: Apply a grammar to a real problem, coding a large volume of text, and analyzing the data. The results will tell which kind of animal was born out of that labor. After all, in Le Roy Ladurie's words: "The computer … [will only tell us] what everyone knew in the first place … What matters is not so much the machine as the questions one asks it."[72]

From the "Red Years" to the "Black Years" (Italy, 1919–1922)

The questions I ask focus on a turbulent period of Italian history, right after World War One, known as the *Biennio rosso* (the Red Years) of 1919–20 and the *Biennio nero* (the Black Years) of 1921–22. The Romeo Factory lockout played a key role in the unfolding of events, in sparking the factory occupation movement, "the watershed between the revolutionary and reactionary phases of the postwar crisis" (Lyttleton, 1973, p. 36). Of those years, Charles, Louise, and Richard Tilly (1975, p. 126) wrote: "Those three years [1919, 1920, and 1921] may well have produced the highest level of involvement in collective violence of any trio in Italy's modern history." Indeed, when viewed in historical perspective, the unique character of those years becomes immediately apparent (see the plot of the yearly number of strikers in Figure 2.2). In the years 1919 and 1920, the number of strikers soared to unprecedented levels (to over four times the highest prewar levels). Figure 2.3 zooms in on the 1919–22 years. The monthly figures give the tempo of mobilization, with peaks centered around May–July 1919 and January–June 1920. Then, in the fall of 1920 the pace of mobilization of the Italian working class slowed down, with one last flurry of protest in June 1922. What has intrigued generations of historians and social scientists alike about those years is the sudden turn from mobilization to countermobilization, from the revolutionary situation of the Red Years to the fascist takeover of power in October 1922. How did that happen? How could that have happened? Who was involved? What were their actions? What was at stake?

We will search in vain for answers to those questions using official strike statistics as evidence. The plots of Figure 2.2 and Figure 2.3 go as far as those statistics can take us. To go further in sociohistorical research, we have to abandon counts and rely on such "thick descriptions" as police reports, newspaper articles, or witness accounts. And that is precisely what I did. With the help of computerized story grammar (PC-ACE, Program for Computer-Assisted Coding of Events) and "a large team of helots" – in Lawrence Stone's biting words – I coded over 15,000 of those narratives taking them from the socialist daily *Il Lavoro*. The figures of Table 2.3 give a rough idea of the scale of the project – over 15,000 newspaper articles in input, more than 3,000 disputes and 16,000 semantic triplets in output.

Simple Counts Tell Complex Stories

What do those data reveal? Let us start by querying the database for the actors involved as "subjects" using the following SQL query:

select subject_name, frequency = *count (distinct* dispute_id)
from subject_table

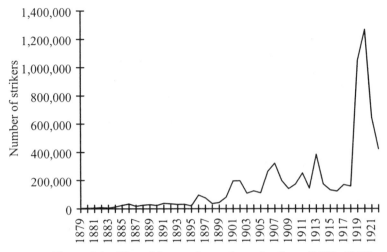

Figure 2.2. *Plot of the yearly number of strikers (1879–1922)*

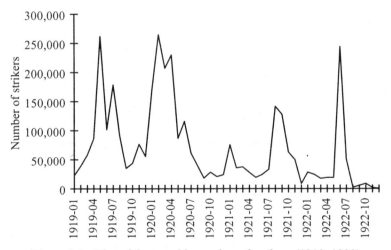

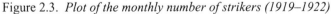

Figure 2.3. *Plot of the monthly number of strikers (1919–1922)*

For the year 1919, the query yields the frequency distribution (by dispute) of Table 2.4. In the four-year period over two thousand of those actors occur with a frequency lower than three.[73] We need to aggregate, accounting for synonyms and equivalent actors. Table 2.5 shows the results of aggregation. The results leave no doubt about the shift away from working-class actors in the early years

Table 2.3. *Frequency Distribution of Articles, Disputes, and Triplets in the 1919–1922 Database*

	1919	1920	1921	1922	Total
Number of articles	4,213	4,329	3,715	2,889	15,146
Number of disputes	597	622	1,132	926	3,277
Number of triplets	5511	5078	2961	3195	16745

Table 2.4. *Frequency Distribution of Actors (Subjects and Objects) in 1919 (Number of Disputes)*

Actor name	#	Actor name	#	Actor name	#
Workers	231	Firm	30	City Hall	15
Trade unions	200	Employer	29	Police	14
Bargaining parties	83	Mayor	28	Workers	14
White-collar workers	76	Association	27	Prefecture	13
Counterparty	65	Committee	25	MP (*Parlamentare*)	12
Commission	63	Blue-collar workers	24	Sailors	12
Government	62	Railway workers	24	Teachers	12
Unknown actor	62	Commune	22	...	
Management	57	Prime Minister	19	People	2
Strikers	51	*Carabinieri* (police)	19	MP (*Onorevole*)	2
Union representative	47	Employers	18	...	
Prefect	41	Administration	18	Boys	1
Secretary	40	Minister	16	Proletarians	1
Representative	39	Authority	16	Father	1
Citizens	31	Collective employers	15	Tailors	1

Table 2.5. *Frequency Distribution of Most Common Actors (Number of Disputes)*

Types of actors	1919	1920	1921	1922
Trade unions	215	175	160	176
Employers	133	155	97	239
Workers	337	440	385	92
Government	71	56	42	70
Parliament	26	59	92	66
Ministries	78	65	57	40
Prefect	47	50	27	32
Police	32	108	106	74
Political activists	12	126	652	759

(the Red Years 1919–20; for example, trade unions, workers) toward employers, particularly in 1922. Remarkable, also, is the soaring presence of political activists during the Black Years. The government is notably absent during the crucial years of 1920–21, during the factory occupation movement, and the aftermath, during the first wave of backlash from the right. That, indeed, had been Prime Minister Giolitti's strategy against the Left and the Right, a strategy that turned out to be politically very costly to both Giolitti and the country.

This simple frequency distribution of actors thus seems to highlight the process of mobilization from below during the Red Years and countermobilization process from above during the Black Years and to underscore a shift in class power from the Left to the Right during the same period.

The query:

select action_name, frequency = *count* (*distinct* dispute_id)
from action_table

provides a frequency distribution of available actions in 1919 (over 3,000 of which with frequency less than three) (see Table 2.6). Properly aggregated, those actions yield the counts of Table 2.7. The counts support the story of Table 2.5: A widespread mobilization in the early years where claim making, collective actions, and labor contracts prevail, followed by a sharp decline in working-class activism and a surge in political activism and violence during the Black Years.

Again, the frequency distributions of demands of Table 2.8 confirm the view of a working class on the offensive during the first two years against both the state and employers (for example, 307 disputes with economic demands in 1919 versus 80 of them in 1922, but also demands of improved working conditions, trade union rights, contract renewals). The number of disputes characterized by offensive demands sharply dropped in 1921 and 1922 while defensive disputes (for example, against layoffs) increased. The number of defensive disputes against political violence increased but not nearly in proportion to the increase in the frequency of violent actors and actions. The Italian working class seems to have even lost its ability to protest defensively by 1922.

For all the clarity of the message of Table 2.5, Table 2.7, and Table 2.8, the high level of aggregation of the data does not do justice to the mobilization process that characterized the 1919–20 Red Years. A more fine-grained look at the information available in the database would reveal that mobilization took on many forms and involved a variety of social actors during those years: From women to students, from war veterans to the unemployed, from agricultural laborers to industrial workers – all took to the streets in a crescendo of demands. Italy was on the brink of revolution (Lyttleton, 1977, p. 63). The cause for such widespread mobilization generally stemmed from the problems related to war demobilization and conversion of war production. *Caroviveri* (inflation) and unemployment figure high among the "economic" demands of Table 2.8. As such, Italy was no different from what was going on in a number of other countries across Europe in those years (Maier, 1975).

Table 2.6.   *Frequency Distribution of Actions in 1919 (Number of Disputes)*

Action name	#	Action name	#	Action name	#
Protest	195	Call for public meeting	33	...	
Hold assembly	191	Threaten to strike	32	Assault	6
Make claims	164	Refuse to deal	30	Appeal	6
Strike	138	Threat	29	Intervene	6
Announce assembly	105	Sign contract	22	Send letters	6
Hold meeting	95	Announce intervention	22	...	
Call off strike	66	Layoff	21	Receive	5
Plead intervention	66	Agitate	21	Approve proposal	5
Reach agreement	61	Vote	20	...	
Meet with speech	61	Break agreement	20	Take part in meeting	4
Continue strike	55	Explain situation	20	...	
Hold meeting	54	Approve	20	Accept deal	1
Accept demands	54	Criticize	19	Accept contract	1
Express solidarity	35	...		Despair	1
Declare a strike	34	Accept requests	18	...	

Table 2.7.   *Frequency Distribution of Most Common Actions (Number of Disputes)*

Types of actions	1919	1920	1921	1922
Claim making	196	91	37	4
Collective actions	335	328	228	249
Meetings	236	221	186	131
Labor contracts	142	111	99	35
Verbal critiques and accusations	21	29	121	22
Violence	47	168	550	525

Table 2.8.   *Frequency Distribution of Most Common Demands (Number of Disputes)*

Types of demands	1919	1920	1921	1922
Economic	307	239	165	80
Quick settlement of a dispute	118	60	51	60
Employers' unwillingness to bargain	115	96	28	35
Working conditions	177	71	79	35
Trade union rights	112	43	23	47
Contract renewal	99	29	40	31
Political demands against the state	64	26	51	31
Against layoffs	32	50	43	90
Against violence	15	33	45	43

Knowing the most typical actors, actions, and demands is certainly an improvement over the rough counts of the numbers of strikes, strikers, and hours lost of official strike statistics.[74] Of even greater interest would be to find out who did what and why. What specific actions did some of the actors in Table 2.5 perform? What did workers or employers do? Who were the political activists? Was the increase in the frequency of those activists related to the increase in violence? To answer those questions, let us query the database, one more time:

select a.action_name, frequency = *count* (*distinct* a.dispute_id)
from subject_table s, action_table a
where s.triplet_id = a.triplet_id *and* s.subject_name = "workers"

The query would provide a frequency distribution of the actions performed by workers – actions that, when properly aggregated, give the figures of Table 2.9. Those figures confirm not only the wide repertoire of actions workers engage in, but also the rapid mobilization and demobilization processes that characterized the 1919–20 and 1921–22 years. Large-scale mobilization in the form of general and national strikes made up many of the collective actions of the early years (91 in 1919, down to 23, 20, and 21 in 1922). Labor mobilization peaked in 1920. In the countryside, episodes of land occupations, particularly of uncultivated land in the south, became more and more common during the spring. In September 1920, industrial metal workers occupied their factories (Spriano, 1964, pp. 179–90). The brief newspaper article on the Romeo lockout at the opening of this chapter announced the beginning of that vast mobilization. The occupation involved practically all of Italy, from such large factories as Romeo, Fiat, or Ansaldo to the small semiartisanal workshops more typical of the Italian productive structure, from the big cities to the small towns, from the north to the south.

The "great fear" that traveled the country during that month of September 1920, followed by a socialist electoral victory in November, set off a countermobilization process that eventually ended with Mussolini's march on Rome on October 28, 1922, and twenty years of fascist dictatorship. Indeed, the first fascist "hit squads" and "black shirts"[75] started operating in the fall of 1920, right after the factory occupation and the November administrative elections.[76]

The data of Table 2.10 show that the majority of political activists encountered in Table 2.5 were Fascists. The query:

select a.action_name, frequency = *count* (*distinct* a.dispute_id)
from subject_table s, action_table a
where s.triplet_id = a.triplet_id *and* s.subject_name = "Fascists"

would allow us to find out whether the simultaneous rise in the frequency of both political activists and violence is due to the Fascists' actions. The aggregated results reported in Table 2.11 leave no doubt about that: The rise of fascism went hand-in-hand with the rise of violence. Indeed, violence was the hallmark of the early fascist movement. According to Snowden (1986, pp.

Table 2.9. *Frequency Distribution of the Most Common Actions Performed by Workers (Number of Disputes)*

Types of actions	1919	1920	1921	1922
Meetings	101	109	68	57
Make claims	83	37	7	0
Protest	81	78	50	40
Rally	4	11	5	2
Public speech	39	42	25	15
Strike	78	160	60	11
Occupation	2	28	1	0
Solidarity	11	19	12	7

Table 2.10. *Frequency Distribution of the Actor "Fascists" (Number of Disputes)*

Type of actor	1919	1920	1921	1922
Fascists	1	38	524	564

Table 2.11. *Frequency Distribution of the Actions Performed by Fascists (Number of Disputes)*

Types of actions	1919	1920	1921	1922
Clash	0	27	228	164
Wound	0	3	46	87
Kill	0	1	41	35
Assault	0	2	48	133
Destroy	0	0	35	29
Set on fire	0	0	27	11
Occupy	0	0	3	47

186–7), Apulian fascism was quite distinctive in relying entirely on physical force.

Distinctive, perhaps, but by no means unique. In Tuscany, "hit squads" carried out both punitive expeditions and "extortion, protection rackets, and sheer plunder."[77] In the provinces of Ferrara and Bologna violence played a central role in smashing socialist strongholds.[78] By the 1921 elections, many local prefects informed Prime Minister Giolitti that they could not guarantee order (Maier, 1975, p. 315). What the prefects were not saying is that much fascist violence occurred with police compliance if not outright collusion.[79]

Table 2.12. *Frequency Distribution of the Actors with Whom Fascists "Clash" (Number of Disputes)*

Types of actors	1919	1920	1921	1922
Police	0	2	13	1
Republicans	0	0	0	9
Popolari	0	0	7	9
Socialists	0	20	35	23
Communists	0	2	145	72
Workers	0	0	21	16
Strikers	0	1	0	4
Peasants	0	2	1	3

But, to probe further into the database, with whom did the Fascists clash?[80] The data in Table 2.12 provide an answer to that question: The Fascists clashed most frequently with the Communists, the Socialists, and the militants of the Partito Repubblicano and Partito Popolare. Their enemies were anywhere from the center of the political spectrum to the extreme left. Occasionally workers, peasants, and strikers were the target of fascist violence. Interestingly enough, it appears from the data that in 1922 the police let the Fascists run their show undisturbed, occasionally joining in with them.[81] And what did the forty-seven occupations of 1922 shown in Table 2.11 involve? Land, as for the peasants in 1919? Factories, as for the workers in 1920? A query on another object of fascist violent actions ("occupy") would show that contrary to the peasants' and workers' actions in 1919 and 1920, the Fascists did not occupy land or factories. They mostly occupied buildings (for example, trade union and socialist party locals, city halls) and, occasionally, entire towns and cities with large-scale military-style operations.[82]

Stitching the Thread

There is a concept in mathematics that allows us to understand such collections as we have found in the grammar (for example, <action>: Announce lockout, decide factory occupation, ...): the *set*.[83] Indeed, a set is nothing but a collection of objects of whichever kind – cars in a parking lot, children in a school, oranges in a fruit bin, or words. Thus, in the newspaper article on the Romeo lockout, the <subjects> {firm, leaders, workers, ...} constitute a set; and so do the <actions> {announce lockout, decide factory occupation, do not leave plant, do not work, keep inside the factory, free, bring dinner}. The entire grammar can be expressed conveniently in set theoretical notation, with a set R of actoRs (subjects or objects), a set N for actioNs, a set M for Modifiers, and so on. In a notation called the *set-builder form* of a set, the set of <subjects> S can be expressed as S = {s | s is subject} which reads "S is the set of subjects s such that (the symbol | reads "such that") s is a subject." The notations s ∈ S and s ∉ S read respectively "s belongs to S" and "s does not belong to S." Thus, the element "workers" belongs to the set of <subjects> but the element "police" does not.

In set theory we also find tools – "Cartesian product," "sentence," and "relation" – that allow us to express the links between the categories of a grammar in a tight mathematical formulation. The *product set* or *Cartesian product* of any two sets A and B consists of all ordered pairs (a,b) where a ∈ A and b ∈ B. It is denoted by A x B (reads "A cross B"). Using the set-builder notation, this is A x B = {(a,b) | a ∈ A, b ∈ B}. Thus, if S is the set of subjects S = {firm, leaders, workers, ...} and A is the set of actions A = {announce lockout, decide factory occupation, ...}, the Cartesian product of S and A consists of all ordered pairs (firm, announce lockout), (firm, decide factory occupation), ... (workers, announce lockout) ... More generally, the Cartesian product of n sets S_1, S_2, ..., S_n is denoted by S_1 x S_2 x S_3 x ... x S_n and consists of all n-tuples (s_1, s_2, s_3, ..., s_n) where $s_1 \in S_1$, $s_2 \in S_2$, ..., $s_n \in S_n$. Thus, a semantic triplet is a Cartesian product S x A x O, where the set O would contain a null element to account for triplets with no object (for example, "workers strike," as opposed to "employer fires workers").

Only a subset of the 2-tuples or 3-tuples that result from the Cartesian product S x A x O will be semantically well formed. Thus, the 2-tuples (firm, decide factory occupation) or (workers, announce lockout) do not make sense in light of capitalist social relations of productions – firms lockout and workers occupy factories, but not viceversa. The concepts of *sentence* and *relation* restrict the combinations that result from joining sets to semantically acceptable n-tuples. A *propositional function* or *sentence*, P(a,b), has the property that P(a,b) is either true or false for any ordered pair (a,b) ∈ A x B. The *relation* R = (A,B,P(a,b)) is the Cartesian product of sets A and B subject to the constraint of the sentence P(a,b). If R = (A,B,P(a,b)) is a relation, the solution set R* of the relation R consists of the elements (a,b) in the Cartesian product A x B for which P(a,b) is true. Notationally, R* = {(a,b) | a ∈ A, b ∈ B, P(a,b) is true}. Thus, the set of semantic triplets of the grammar is the subset of acceptable 3-tuples obtained from the Cartesian product of the sets of subjects, actions, and objects S x A x O, that is, T = {S ∪ A ∪ O | (s,a,o) ∉ C, s ∈ S, a ∈ A, o ∈ O} where ∪ is the set symbol for a *union* or sum of sets (in this case, of the sets S, A, and O) and C is the set of "selection restrictions," that is, the set of invalid 3-tuples.

Both linguistic and mathematical representations of a story grammar underscore the fact that 1) a text is made up of similar items of information that can be conveniently filed together – spatial information within the category (or set) <space>; temporal information within the category/set <time>; and so on – and 2) the information filed in one category/set may be linked with information filed in another category/set. The grammar, indeed, is nothing but a powerful filing system. And that is no silly matter. A generation of Taylorites and "scientific managers" in the early twentieth century made their fortune simply by rationalizing office work, inventing "virtually every piece of office equipment we are familiar with today ... [including] equipment used in filing, such as file cabinets, loose-leaf binders, rolodexes, and card indices."[84]

Further Advantages of Story Grammars

The pace of our journey from words to numbers seems to have picked up in this chapter: from linguistics to set theory, data models, query languages, Italian history, and the art of memory. Let me retrace our steps to catch our breath and get our bearings.

We set forth on this journey because the poverty of information contained in event counts (more specifically, official strike statistics) ultimately cripples our understanding of historical processes. Historical agents are typically nowhere to be seen in the world of event counts. A view of history as agency (who did what) requires us to move away from counts and toward the "thick descriptions" typically found in such documents as police dispatches and newspaper articles. But it is one thing to deal with a handful of documents (as many historians do), and another to construct as complete an enumeration as possible of events and their characteristics (a sociologist's obsession). The latter research strategy may involve thousands of documents; a feat that only a quantitative approach to those texts may accomplish.

Indeed, quantification partly results from the amount of material available. Toynbee (1946, pp. 45–6) provides the following explanation for the old Aristotelian distinction in the techniques of history, science, and fiction:

> [T]he techniques of history, science and fiction ... differ from each other in their suitability for dealing with 'data' of different quantities. The ascertainment and record of particular facts is all that is possible in a field of study where the data happen to be few. The elucidation and formulation of laws is both possible and necessary where the data are too numerous to tabulate but not too numerous to survey. ... [F]iction is the only technique that can be employed or is worth employing where the data are innumerable. ... *The techniques differ in their utility for handling different quantities of data.* (Emphasis added)

No doubt, ethnographers who have had to sift through pages of field notes, reading and rereading them, highlighting themes and picking quotes, will appreciate the appearance on the market of computer programs that make it easier to handle large bodies of text.[85] Consider the alternative: Confine all that evidence to memory with the risk of distorting it (Ayedelotte, 1969, pp. 4–5). And that risk remains even if you practice Quintilian's long lost art of memory!

The linguistics and computer-assisted approach to content analysis described here is another step in the direction of quantification of large bodies of data. In

Chapter 1, we saw how "story grammars" present several advantages over traditional content analysis. And to that list, we must now add several other advantages.

1. Set theory provides a powerful mathematical notation (namely, Cartesian product, sentence, relation) for expressing the complex set of relations between the building blocks of a grammar.

2. Set theory serves as the mathematical foundation of relational database management systems (RDBMS). RDBMS provide powerful models of computer data organization and storage. It is precisely because a grammar of data collection can be implemented in a computer environment through relational database technology that content analysis based on such complex coding schemes as story grammars becomes practically feasible.

3. In set theory we find the tool that allows us to go "from words to numbers": the cardinal number.

4. Set theory is not a fancy cover for very mundane practices (namely, counting words). Because set theory is behind the coding schemes used to collect text data (text grammar), and behind the models used to organize them (relational structures) and analyze them (cardinal number), set theory provides a single unifying thread and a general framework for the various phases of a linguistic approach to content analysis. It is precisely because we can rewrite a grammar in set theoretical and relational terms, that we can use such mundane tools as relational DBMSs to collect, organize, and query even complex text data, making a linguistic approach to content analysis well within the reach of any PC user. It does seem that, no differently from Propp's hero, we did acquire a "magical element" with set theory! (Function number XIV, Propp, 1968, p. 43).

5. A computer-based story grammar is not just a toy that works well on a handful of contrived examples. It works well even when applied to the collection of large bodies of data, such as the 15,000 newspaper articles of my 1919–22 project.

6. Within the realm of numbers, we find a host of statistical tools for the quantitative analysis of large bodies of data. We will need to explore those.

Scientists' Bitter Fate

Microfilm readers, DOS operating systems, coders, SQL. This vocabulary has an old-fashioned ring to it. If the technology it describes is not obsolete yet, it soon will be, all too soon. Artificial intelligence (AI), no doubt, will live up to its promise of finding a solution to computer understanding of natural languages. Then, this chapter, this entire book, in fact, will be a thing of the past. For all I know, in fact, you, reader of the year 2520, may be just such an AI machine. Perhaps a machine that is not just a tool of scientific research – reading texts, this text (!), so that through you a *human* scientist can draw inferences from the text – but a machine reading this text for your own pleasure. You have a personal interest in this archeology of knowledge, in these times before your times when words were still words and numbers were numbers, before people like me started subverting "the order of things," tinkering with such sacred things as the words.

Yet, whoever you are, dear reader, don't take the transiency of this work as a negative sign. Merton wouldn't. If anything, transiency is the very hallmark of science (Merton, 1968, pp. 27–30). And so it was for Weber. In his "Science as a Vocation" Weber wrote (in Gerth and Mills, 1946a, p. 138):

> In science, each of us knows that what he has accomplished will be antiquated in ten, twenty, fifty years. That is the fate to which science is subjected. ... Every scientific 'fulfilment' raises new 'questions'; it *asks* to be 'surpassed' and outdated. Whoever wishes to serve science has to resign himself to this fact. Scientific work certainly can last as 'gratifications' because of their artistic quality, or they may remain important as a means of training. Yet they will be surpassed scientifically – let that be repeated – for it is our common fate and, more, our common goal. We cannot work without hoping that others will advance further than we have.

"Science is a cemetery of dead ideas," Unamuno wrote, "even though life may issue from them. Worms also feed upon corpses."[86] In science, we must resign ourselves to early death. "Science," wrote physicist Max Planck (1936, p. 77), "does not mean an idle resting upon a body of certain knowledge, it means unresting endeavor and continually progressing development." And that means early death for the scientist, *qua* scientist. Most scientists will accept this bitter fate. It is part of the ethos of science, Merton tells us. So, I should be happy if my name and my work will elapse into oblivion, engulfed in the stream of scientific innovation, an inch ahead of my precursors, miles behind my successors. Or should I? Does not this go against the lessons of the world's most powerful myths, from Gilgamesh to Icarus? Isn't Diotima's speech on love and beauty, as reported by Socrates in Plato's *Symposium,*[87] a celebration of immortality? "Why procreation?" asks Diotima. "Because procreation is as close as a mortal can get to being immortal and undying." "It's a divine business; it is immortality in a mortal creature, this matter of pregnancy and birth." Beauty and immortality go hand in hand because "the object of love ... is birth and procreation in a beautiful medium." We do all we can "to achieve immortality and live for ever." And the easiest thing "for ordinary men" to do is biological reproduction, physical pregnancy. By reproducing in their children ordinary men achieve a form of immortality. But there is another way, a nobler way, where human beings seek immortality through mental pregnancy. If physical pregnancy produces children that are the result of love in a beautiful medium, that is, love with a beautiful woman, mental pregnancy, too, produces "offsprings [that] are particularly attractive and are closer to immortality than ordinary children." It is these children who earn immortality to their fathers, not the human children. "We'd all prefer to have children of this sort." The search for immortality "is what motivates people to do anything, and that the better they are, the more this is their motivation. The point is, they're in love with immortality."

At the beginning of the twentieth century, Unamuno championed that theme in his *The Tragic Sense of Life*. "The longing not to die, the hunger for personal immortality" are, for Unamuno, the very essence of that tragic sense. That is "the affective basis of all knowledge and the personal inward starting-point of all human philosophy." Everything starts from there, from that "yearning for immortality" – be that even "a shadow of immortality." Nearly a biological, built-in drive, as Darwin would have it, a "Struggle for Existence ... [manifesting itself in the] success in leaving progeny" (Darwin, 1996, p. 53). Unamuno continues: "[U]nderlying the enquiry into the 'why,' the cause, there is simply the search for the 'wherefore,' the end" – our end. Passion – "a tremendous passion" – drives man to avoid oblivion. "For the sake of a name man is ready to sacrifice not only life but happiness – life as a matter of course." As Pascal had put it: "The sweetness of fame is so great that whatever we pin it to, we love, even death" (Pascal, III, 71, 1995, p. 16). We contend a place in the small and crowded hall of fame with both the dead and the living in "this violent struggle for the perpetuation of our name."[88]

But if man is involved in this eternal struggle against death, in this struggle for immortality, how can scientists, how do scientists accept their bitter fate of early death? If the nemesis of scientific work is obsolescence and early death, how can we survive? Weber gives us a hint of a possible strategy when he alludes in the passage quoted previously to the "artistic quality" of scientific work. "What kind of temporality belongs to aesthetic being?" asks Gadamer (1997, p. 121). "Timelessness" is his answer. The works of art, not the works of science, have universal validity, *for all times*. Beauty is the way to immortality for Socrates. "The gods smile on a person who bears and nurtures true goodness ... it is he who has the potential for immortality" (Plato, *Symposium,* 212a, 1994). And the way to goodness is through beauty.

> The proper way to go about or to be guided through the ways of love is to start with beautiful things in this world and always make the beauty I've been talking about the reason for your ascent. You should use the things of this world as rungs in a ladder. You start by loving one attractive body and step up to two; from there you move on to physical beauty in general, from there to the beauty of people's activities, from there to the beauty of intellectual endeavours, and from there you ascend to that final intellectual endeavour, which is no more and no less than the study of *that* beauty, so that finally you recognize true beauty. (Plato, *Symposium,* 211c, 1963; for a similar ascent see *Republic,* 511b–c, 1994)

Centuries later historian Jakob Burckhardt, in his essay on "The Great Men of History," would still assign the highest echelons to philosophers, artists, and poets. To philosophers is given truth; "to poets and artists ... is given beauty."[89] Yet, having given priority to philosophers over poets and artists, contrary to Plato's and Bentham's better judgment, Burckhardt goes on to cite a passage from Schiller's letter to Goethe: "One thing is certain, that the poet is the only true *man*, and the best of philosophers is a mere caricature in comparison with him" (Burckhardt, 1979, p. 279; emphasis in the original).

> [The poets] alone can interpret and give *imperishable form to the mystery of beauty*. Everything that passes by us in life, so swift, rare, and unequal, is here gathered together in a world of poems, in pictures and great picture cycles, in color, stone, and sound, to form a second, *sublimer world on earth*. Indeed, in architecture and music *we can only experience beauty through art*; without art we should not know that it exists. (Burckhardt, 1979, p. 280; emphasis added)

Indeed, beauty became Burckhardt's obsession, his scholarly work increasingly "motivated by his thirst for beauty" (Dietze, 1979, p. 12). After publishing *The Civilization of the Renaissance in Italy* (1860) and *The History of the Renaissance* (1867) both concerned with the arts and understanding the Renaissance culture that had produced such great works of art, being only fifty, and being himself no artist capable of producing such beauty, "for the rest of his life, Burckhardt never published a line" (Dietze, 1979, p. 12). Burckhardt's engagement with art and beauty, the pinnacle of creativity and originality in Burckhardt's mind, led him to a "passive deviant response" to the pressures of originality: *Retreatism*, in Merton's words, that is, the abandoning of one's own goal of scientific production (Merton, 1973, pp. 317–20; see also Diesing's discussion, 1991, p. 156).

Beauty, then, can be dangerous. A brush with beauty can lose for ever those who, like Burckhardt, are not artists or poets, the only creators of beauty. Even more dangerous is to attempt to achieve long-lasting immortality in science by turning science into art, by imparting universal value to scientific work by creating beauty. Not even English school children remember Erasmus Darwin, the grandfather of the more famous Charles Darwin, for his poetry where he molded his scientific work on plants into verses.[90]

So, escaping scientific death through art will not do for the scientist. A more promising route of escape is priority; getting there first, perhaps linking one's name to a discovery – often quite literally, as in eponymy: the Copernican system, Planck's constant, Keynesian economics, Halley's comet (Merton, 1973, pp. 298–302). Geographic explorers' claim to fame rested in a ritual that established priorities. "Cortés took possession of that land for the King, performing the act ... in this way: He drew his sword, and, as a sign of possession, made three cuts in a large silk-cotton tree ..."[91] Priorities are no less important for us, academic voyagers. Charles Darwin, having just finished a first sketch of his theory on the origin of species wrote to his wife in 1844:

> [M]y theory ... will be a considerable step in science. I therefore write this in case of my sudden death, as my most solemn and last request, which I am sure you will consider the same as legally entered in my will, that you will devote £400 to its publication.[92]

"The history of science is punctuated by disputes ... over priority of discovery."[93] Indeed, priority, for a scientist, is the most coveted of all prizes, as Merton's work on science shows. The best known scientists got embroiled in these "sordid," "tedious," "harsh, and ugly" disputes, from Galileo to Newton and Cavendish. "Science," Merton argues, "with its ... emphasis on originality ... makes recognition of priority uppermost," quite independently of scientists' personality traits (egomaniac or egotistic). Homages, rewards, and prizes play as much a role in the scientist's world as in Cortés's or Magellan's. And a book, a book on a library shelf, is still for many of us the most coveted prize. Temple Grandin, an autistic scientist, frankly confessed to Oliver Sacks who had come to interview her:

> I have read that *libraries are where immortality lies* I don't want my thoughts to die with me. ... I want to have done something. ... I'm not interested in power, or piles of money. I want to leave something behind. I want to make a positive contribution – know that my life has meaning. *Right now, I'm talking about things at the very core of my existence.* (Sacks, 1995, p. 282; emphasis added)

Not power. Not money. Nothing less than immortality. "Eternity, Eternity! – that is the supreme desire!" similarly confesses Unamuno. "I do not want to die – no. ... I want to live for ever and ever and ever. I want this 'I' to live – this poor 'I' that I am ... the problem of the duration of my soul ... tortures me."[94] He adds confidently: "The man of letters who shall tell you that he despises fame is a lying rascal."[95]

3

"Everything Is Number"

This is the common fault of history books. Out of such vague data only the crude preliminaries of science can be made. So let us now leave narrative history and go on to quantitative history.

> Lewis F. Richardson (1960, p. xvi)

Scientific historians ... have found evidence and means for a meaningful study of a good many questions ... However, the very nature of their methods compels them to eliminate large areas of enquiry from their agenda ...

> Geoffrey R. Elton (1983, p. 80)

One can, in principle, master all things by calculation.

> Max Weber (in Gerth and Mills, 1946a, p. 139)

This tendency [to dissolve quality into quantity] may never absolutely attain its goals by mortal means.

> Georg Simmel (1978, p. 278)

A theory with the beauty and elegance of Einstein's theory *has* to be substantially correct.

> Paul A. M. Dirac (1980, pp. 43–4)

"Friends of Friends": Grammars and Network Models

It did not happen very often. But it did happen. And when it happened, no doubt, it would enrage the members of the Inquisition tribunals – men all too accustomed to having their way; men of such "stiff-necked arrogance which could prevent even a group of three from functioning as a unit" (Monter, 1990,

p. 58). Here and there, in the surviving records of the Inquisition trials, we find references to names against whom even the all too powerful tribunal would be impotent. In the language of the Inquisition, the "untouchables" had "honorable relatives" (Monter, 1990, p. 89). In Dutch anthropologist Jeremy Boissevain's (1974) language, they were "friends of friends."

Is it, indeed, the characteristics of the social relations in which individuals find themselves, rather than the characteristics of institutions and individuals, that crucially shape social outcomes? Boissevain certainly seems to think so. He writes (1974, p. 64):

> Behaviour cannot be explained solely in terms of norms and values: There are other forces at work besides normative constraints which must be taken into account. It was suggested that these 'other forces' lie in the area of interpersonal relations, which can be approached by viewing most interactions as transactions. In order to gain greater insight into the way in which interpersonal relations are structured, they may be viewed as a network. This makes it possible to measure systematically the diverse ways persons are linked to others and the reciprocal influence of interaction and network structure on each other.

And so it was, as Monter tells us, that "conversos" (Jews who had converted to Christianity, forcefully or otherwise) would be systematically tried and convicted by Inquisition tribunals everywhere in the Spanish kingdom. In Seville, however, they were relatively freer. What was different about Seville? The Inquisition tribunals were the same; same procedural rules; same institution, with personnel often rotating among different tribunals to ensure uniformity in trial procedures. And Jews were Jews, with the Inquisition having been set up as "an antijewish institution ... except for a central window where, during a century, it turned its attention on the Old Christians."[1] And yet, Sevillian Jews had been assimilated into the elite power structure of the city through marriages and economic alliances. They were "well networked."[2]

Cosimo de' Medici carefully and patiently constructed a similar network of marital, economic, political, and personal ties among Florentine families in the first quarter of the fifteenth century. It is that network of alliances that ultimately explains the ascendance to power of the Medici family (Padgett and Ansell, 1993). But why should we be surprised? Another Florentine, Niccolò Machiavelli, who was to run into troubles with Cosimo's heirs a century later, so advised a "prince" on his way to power:

> The nobles ought to be looked at mainly in two ways: That is to say, they either shape their course in such a way as binds them entirely to your fortune, or they do not. Those who so bind themselves, and are not rapacious, ought to be honoured and loved; those who do not bind themselves may be dealt with in two ways; they may fail to do this through pusillanimity and a natural want of courage, in which case you

ought to make use of them, especially of those who are of good counsel; and thus, whilst in prosperity you honour yourself, in adversity you have not to fear them. But when for their own ambitious ends they shun binding themselves, it is a token that they are giving more thought to themselves than to you, and a prince ought to guard against such, and to fear them as if they were open enemies, because in adversity they always help to ruin him. (Machiavelli, 1958, p. 53)

If networks of social relations are so important for understanding social behavior and social outcomes, could we put the framework of our story grammar – with actors related to other actors via a set of actions – to good use possibly to extract networks of social relations from our data?[3] As a way to approach an answer to this question, let us go back to the article that appeared on August 31, 1920, in *Il Lavoro*, reporting on the Romeo Factory lockout and the workers' reaction with the occupation of the factory. I opened Chapter 2 with that article. The factory occupation movement of September 1920 opened with that event. Let us go back to Table 2.2. with its lists of the skeleton triplets of that newspaper article (SAO without modifiers). These triplets constitute a set of size twelve.

More generally, we can think of the skeleton semantic triplets of any story or collection of stories as a set T of size T ($T = t_1, t_2, t_3, ..., t_T$).[4] T will be made up of a set of subjects S of size S (with $S = s_1, s_2, s_3, ..., s_S$), a set of actions A of size A (with $A = a_1, a_2, a_3, ..., a_A$), and a set of objects O of size O (with $O = o_1, o_2, o_3, ..., o_O$). While the set of subjects S is made up exclusively of social actors (by the rules of the story grammar), the set of objects O contains both social actors and inanimate objects (for example, <subject> Fascists <action> blow up <object> *building*). From the set of objects O we can select a subset O_I that includes only those objects that are social actors; then, if we join the set S of subjects and the subset O_I of objects, we obtain the set of distinct social actors N of size N (with $N = n_1, n_2, n_3, ..., n_N$). In our case, N has size seven and would contain the following elements: firm, workers, leaders, families, technical personnel, managers, owners. Similarly, eight distinct actions appear in the Romeo Factory lockout article: announce lockout, do not accept decision, decide factory occupation, do not leave plant, do not work, keep inside the factory, free, bring dinner. The set of actions A is thus of size eight. The size of A can be reduced by properly aggregating individual actions into broader spheres of action. Three basic spheres of action make up the Romeo Factory lockout story: *conflict* (announce lockout, decide factory occupation, do not leave plant, do not work, keep inside the factory), *rejection* (do not accept decision), and *facilitation*, that is, actions that benefit other actors (free, bring dinner).

In the SAO representation, the action (or the aggregated sphere of action) operates as a relation between actors – a relation which is both dichotomous and directional: Any member n_i of the set of actors N, where $n_i \in N$, either relates to another member n_j or does not; furthermore, whether an actor occupies the role of subject or object makes a difference (consider the triplets: "Technicians were sequestered by workers" versus "Workers were sequestered by technicians"). Not all social actors present in the database will relate to all other actors. If a tie is present between n_i and n_j, then we say that the ordered pair $<n_i, n_j>$ belongs to a special collection of pairs $\mathcal{L}$. $\mathcal{L}$, in other words, represents the set of triplets that contain a non-null (human) object. In our example, this would exclude the triplets "firm announce lockout," "workers do not accept decision," or "leaders decide factory occupation," "workers do not leave plant," "workers do not work"). If an ordered pair $<n_i, n_j>$ is in $\mathcal{L}$, then the first actor in the pair relates to the second on the relation under consideration; we can write $n_i \rightarrow n_j$.[5] Each relation has a corresponding set of arcs, $\mathcal{L}_r$, containing $\mathcal{L}_r$ ordered pairs of actors as elements (the subscript r ranges from 1 to R, the total number of aggregated relations). In our case, R has a value of two, since the triplet involving the sphere of action of rejection has no object, and therefore is excluded.

The two sets $\mathcal{L}_1$ and $\mathcal{L}_2$ of all ordered pairs of actors and their relations on the two spheres of action of conflict and facilitation provide the basic information on the networks of social interactions found in the article from *Il Lavoro* on the Romeo Factory lockout. But the longer the list of ordered pairs and the more difficult it would be to grasp the patterns of interactions. A graphic representation of the information in the sets $\mathcal{L}_1, \mathcal{L}_2, \ldots \mathcal{L}_s$ would provide a better alternative. The elements of the ordered pairs of relating actors can be represented graphically by drawing a line from the first actor in the element to the second. In this representation, each actor is also known as *node*, and each directed line is known as *arc*. A given set of actors and their corresponding arcs are called *directed graph* and can be visually represented as a diagram where nodes are points in a two-dimensional space and arcs are directed arrows between points.[6] Figure 3.1 reports the graphs of the relations of conflict and facilitation of the article from *Il Lavoro*.

The graphs provide a clear picture of the social relations depicted in *Il Lavoro*'s article. Yet, does one really need to enroll the help of linguistics, set theory, and network analysis to get that picture? No doubt, an old-fashioned but much simpler reading of the articles would do. But would that still do with hundreds or thousands of articles?

Mobilization and Countermobilization Processes (1919–1922): Shifting Networks of Interaction

The simple and exploratory analyses of the 1919–22 data presented in Chapter 2 have a great deal to say about the social relations of those years, as we saw in the last chapter. Yet, network models may allow us to exploit more fully the relational characteristics of those data and to trace more systematically the interactions among social actors.[7]

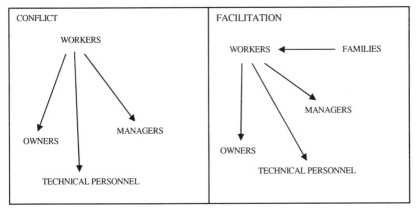

Figure 3.1. *Network Graphs for the Relations of Conflict and Facilitation for the Romeo Factory Lockout Article from* Il Lavoro

Let me start with the social relations involved in the sphere of action of *communication* (Figure 3.2). The graphs give a dramatic picture of the increasing isolation of the working class, at the center of a complex network of interactions with the government and employers in 1919, but disconnected from public discourse by 1921 and 1922 (thicker lines imply at least twice the number of actions measured by standard lines; curved lines have no particular meaning, other than clarity of presentation).[8] The network graphs for *request* (Figure 3.3) similarly highlight the dwindling capacity of the working class to make claims on employers and the state. We go from the rich networks of 1919 and 1920, with unions and workers making a barrage of claims, to the empty picture of 1921 where no actors reach the minimum 5% threshold necessary to be graphed. Surprisingly, the graph of 1922 seems to point to a renewed capacity of the Italian working class to advance demands. What the picture does not show, however, is that, first, the sheer number of actions of request plummeted to a fourth of what they had been, and that, second, the nature of the demands changed from "offensive" to "defensive," from demands mostly centered in the market to demands centered in the political arena, where workers and the unions plead political actors to intervene in their behalf.

That same story is told by the graphs centered around the sphere of action of *conflict* (Figure 3.4), with a great deal of conflict in the economic arena during 1919 and 1920, and with the emergence of a distinct political arena of conflict during the Black Years (Fascists versus Socialists and, especially, unions). In fact, the total amount of political conflict born out by the network graphs is grossly underestimated because many actions of conflict are classified under *violence*. Again, the revival of conflict in the economic arena hides the basic fact that the nature of conflict shifts from offensive to defensive in the four-year period. Furthermore, while in the early years the total number of actions of

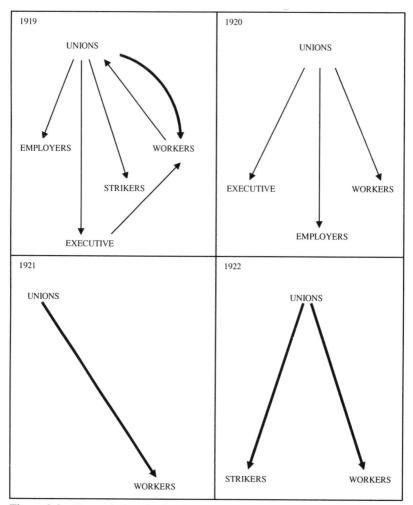

Figure 3.2. *Network Graphs for the Sphere of Action of Communication*

conflict that workers carry out against employers is roughly equal to that of employers against workers (as represented by the double-pointed arrow between employers and workers in the network graphs for 1919 and 1920), in 1921 the employers are on the offensive (as represented by the thicker line going from employers to workers).

The graphs for *violence* (Figure 3.5) clearly bring home the point that things changed drastically from 1919–20 to 1921–22. The graphs for 1919, 1920, and 1921 all show a "star" shape, with one actor at the center of the network of interactions, a hub for relations where actors have no links to one another, except with the star. But, while in 1919 the police (and the army) occupy the center of the star, in later years the "Fascists" take that position. The graph also brings

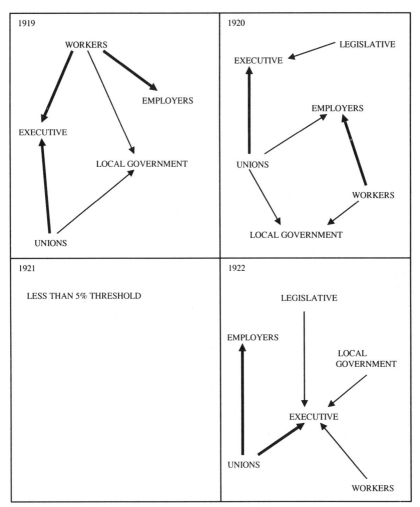

Figure 3.3. *Network Graphs for the Sphere of Action of Request*

home another point: That most violence is actually performed by the police and the army, as a number of studies on protest movements and collective action have underscored (for example, Tilly, 1983, 1985, 1995b). The graph for 1919 highlights an important actor – shopkeepers (and, more generally, the petty bourgeoisie) – the target of people's and workers' violence, particularly during the intense period of mobilization for the *caroviveri* (inflation). Perhaps not surprisingly, the petty bourgeoisie would later embrace fascism wholeheartedly![9]

The double arrow between Communists and Fascists in the network graph for 1922 indicates that the Communists were not mere recipients of fascist violence. They acted as agents in many violent actions against the Fascists. That finding is not surprising. The Communist Party was born out of the controversy between

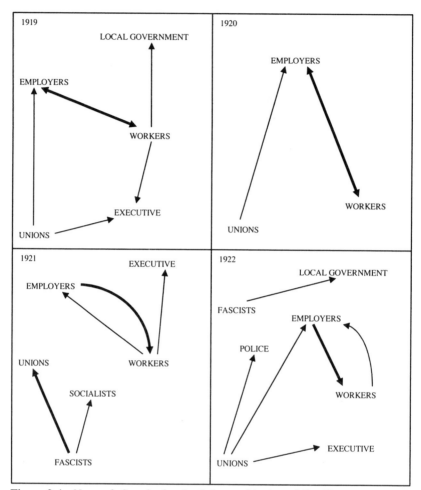

Figure 3.4. *Network Graphs for the Sphere of Action of Conflict*

the reformist and the revolutionary wing of the Socialist Party after the failure of the factory occupation movement. From the beginning, the Communists took the Fascists head on, responding to violence with violence, forming such organizations as the *arditi del popolo* to contrast on the terrain of violence the Fascists' *arditi d'Italia* (Del Carria, 1975, pp. 225–8).

The historical evidence on the reliance of the early fascist movement on physical violence is overwhelming. In Tuscany, in Apulia, in Emilia Romagna, in Veneto, in Lombardy, wherever agricultural workers had successfully organized themselves against landlords, the reaction was brutal.[10] In those areas where proletarian organizations were socialist, the targets of fascist violence were Socialists; where the organizations were catholic, the targets were Catholics.[11] As De Felice (1995a, p. 17) writes: "In 1921, despite its activism,

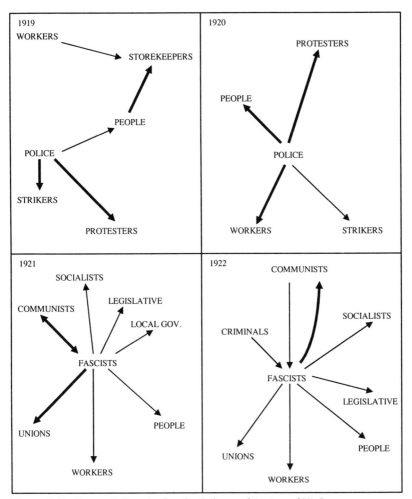

Figure 3.5. *Network Graphs for the Sphere of Action of Violence*

despite its systematic violence, the agrarian fascism did not have a political program. It was reaction, pure reaction only; a local and provincial reaction without perspectives."

Typically, local landlords relied on outside Fascists from nearby cities to carry out punitive expeditions in the countryside.[12] The first expeditions involved just a handful of thugs. During the parliamentary interrogations over fascist violence in December 1920, socialist MP Matteotti, later slain by the Fascists, described one such typical expedition with these words (in Novacco, 1967, p. 167):

> In Pincara, a small country village, a truck pulls up at midnight in front of the *ufficio di collocamento*,[13] a miserable barrack, a tiny room. There is no one inside, but to be sure the Fascists shoot a submachine-gun

volley, the signs of which are still visible on the wall. There is no one; so, out with the gasoline and they burn everything. Then, still after midnight, they move on to the mayor's house; they do not find him by pure chance. The wife is in the hospital; the daughter, a little girl, says: 'my father is not home.' ... [T]hey move on, in the middle of the country, to the house of the *capo lega*,[14] who is asleep. They surround the house. Two hundred musket and revolver shots mark the walls of the poor house on all sides. The wretched man comes down and defends with his body the entrance to his house; fifty shots riddle the door and the man is shot dead in his own home.

By mid-1921, those small, nighttime excursions into the countryside took on the character of full-scale, military-style operations involving thousands of Fascists and large cities.[15]

Just as the Fascists' tactics changed in the course of the Black Years, so did the targets of their violence. According to Salvemini (1928, p. 110), the nascent fascist movement started out by attacking, first, the *economic* strongholds of the working class, intimidating, beating, and killing trade union leaders and individual workers, attacking and destroying their houses and their organizational headquarters. "What matters to the agricultural landlords is smashing the proletarian economic organizations and organizations of resistance, even more than their political organizations" (Del Carria, 1975, p. 183). Within a few months, sometimes weeks, of systematic violence, village after village, entire provinces and regions would be "purged" (Del Carria, 1975, p. 183). Only then, would the Fascists move on to political leaders and political headquarters.

The network graphs for *control* (Figure 3.6) for 1919, 1920, and 1921 show the typical "star" shape that we have already encountered in the network graphs of violence. The number of actors involved in the network for the year 1920, highlights the effervescent climate of the Red Years, when the Left, participants in collective action, strikers, people, unions, Socialists, and workers, all came under the stick of law enforcement agencies (particularly, the Left, workers, and strikers). The picture changes drastically in 1921, when economic actors (workers, strikers, unions) and other collective actors (participants in collective action and people) retreat from the stage of history to leave it to political actors, political extremists, in particular. By 1922, that picture becomes further polarized, with the forces of order trying to keep both Communists and Fascists at bay. This last finding is somewhat surprising. Surprising, that is, in light of overwhelming evidence that the army, the police, and the *carabinieri* often supplied trucks, arms, and know how to the Fascists for their military-style "punitive expeditions."

Indeed, much fascist violence occurred with police compliance if not outright collusion.[16] Salvemini reports a memorandum of October 20, 1920 from the General Staff that encouraged divisional commanders "to show active favour to the fascist organizations" (Salvemini, 1928, p. 78). Tasca (1995, p. 187) reports

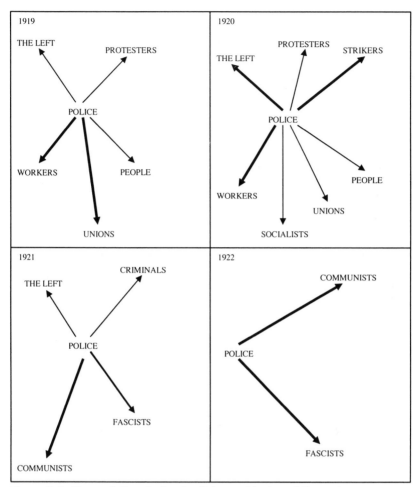

Figure 3.6. *Network Graphs for the Sphere of Action of Control*

the content of a late 1920 memorandum by Minister of Justice Fera that "invites [the magistracy] to stall the dossiers against Fascists' criminal acts." Truckloads of *carabinieri* driving into towns behind the Fascists were reported (Salvatorelli and Mira, 1964, p. 179). Courts began to treat as "extortions" the boycotts and fines set by the workers' leagues against employers and strike breakers (Cardoza, 1982, p. 356). Not surprisingly, the only network graph for 1922 among actions of facilitation (that is, actions that benefit other actors) is that between the judiciary and the Fascists (Figure 3.7). The networks for actions of facilitation in 1919 and 1920 also confirm the enviable position of workers during the Red Years, a position that suddenly came to an end in 1921.[17]

And, yet, for all its stark clarity, this evidence is likely to catch only the tip of the iceberg of the collusion between the Fascists and the police and military

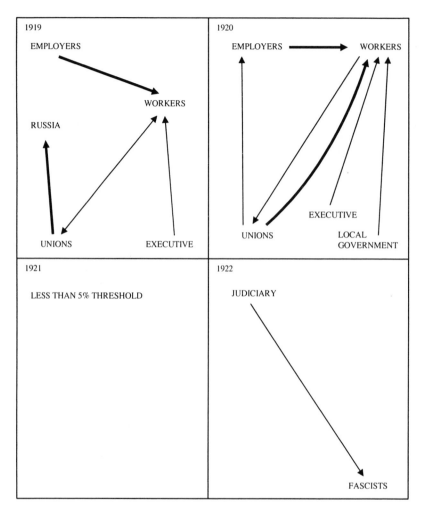

Figure 3.7. *Network Graphs for the Sphere of Action of Facilitation*

authorities. In a book section titled "The Secret of the Fascist Victory," Salvemini (1928, p. 76) points to the role of the police and the military in making the victory possible. The title of another section of Salvemini's book is even more explicit: "The Military Conspiracy" (Salvemini, 1928, p. 107). De Felice (1995a, p. 32) correctly states:

> It is not hazardous to conclude that the cases of open collusion between the army and the Fascists must have been much more numerous than political authorities were ever able to document. One must wonder whether the military commands and, especially, the propaganda, security, secret services, etc. were really as innocent as they claimed.

After all, "the seizure of power by 'force' in a modern state," writes Lyttleton (1973, p. 86), "is never possible, except when the army or police carries out the coup, unless the will to resist of the Government forces has been undermined." For Maier (1975, p. 321), the Ministry of the Interior could have mustered the forces to beat the Fascists, but both the police and the army were sympathetic to the patriotic, militaristic, patriarchal, "law and order" cultural ideology of fascism. In spite of Prime Minister Giolitti's efforts to instruct local authorities to react swiftly against fascism, those instructions fell mostly on deaf ears.[18]

No doubt, the police and the army had their reasons for behaving that way. The antiwar and antipatriotic socialist propaganda had deeply offended the patriotic spirit of army officers and veterans (Chabod, 1961, pp. 38–9). "The militaries look upon the fascist movement with sympathy because of its patriotic spirit," wrote Police Inspector and Vice-Prefect Ricci (cited in Fabbro, 1974, p. 56). The police had been the frequent target of socialist demonstrators (Maier, 1975, pp. 177, 317; Snowden, 1989, p. 195). As a result, the police viewed "the Fascists as an ally in defeating subversive elements who had been the negation of the patriotic idea, who until a few months ago, covered the police force with insults … violence, and even atrocities."[19]

I could continue with this exercise, faithfully describing the network graphs for each sphere of action, each new graph adding more or less detail to, shedding a dimmer or brighter light on basically the same picture of a drastic change in the number and type of actors involved and in the forms of their interactions from the "red" to the "black" years. We can safely leave those analyses without fear of compromising the picture.

"Everything Is Number"

Pythagoras and his followers would have loved that. That a story grammar could be reexpressed as a mathematical problem; that in the mathematician's tool bag we would find the tools to get numbers out of words; that those same mathematical tools would lie at the foundation of computer data models; and that this complex apparatus, drawn from various disciplines and held together by mathematics, could be harnessed to gain a better understanding of the origins of Italian fascism. To the Pythagoreans, "everything is number." Behind the complexity of the universe, they saw a simple key holding it all together: numbers as the *clavis universalis*. "When God called the world into existence, He worked as a mathematician," declared Pythagoras. "Numbers contain the secrets of things" (cited in Bosman, 1932, p. 89). Plato embraced that world vision. For Plato, God had framed the world on numerical principles, its very soul wrought out of a mathematical musical scale.[20]

For the Pythagoreans, different numbers have different magical properties (Bell, 1946, pp. 153–75). The numbers in the "tetrad" (1, 2, 3, 4) and in the "decad" (1, 2, 3, 4, 5, 6, 7, 8, 9, 10) are of particular significance. The numbers in the tetrad not only make up all the other numbers of the decad by addition and multiplication (5=2+3; 6=1+2+3 or 2x3; 7=3+4; 8=2x4; 9=3x3; 10=1+2+3+4). They also establish the relationship between space and numbers (1 being the point, 2 the line, 3 the plane, and 4 the tetrahedron and the pyramid, the simplest of solids). That way, space too is a number. Odd and even numbers form pairs of opposites in the Universe – odd numbers being male numbers, with active, creative characteristics; even numbers being female, passive, and receptive. The Pythagoreans sought to establish the mystical properties of each number.

Number one, unity; number two, opposition, duality (from the Sanskrit *dvi*, divide); three, the result of the unity of one and two (thesis, antithesis, synthesis). Four, as the number of elements that make up all material things: fire, earth, water, and air. Six, the "perfect number."[21] Seven, as the number of planets, seven days of the week, seven notes of the scale, and seven colors of the rainbow. In Plato's account of creation the world was generated from the number seven. "From such constituents, to the number of four [water, air, fire, and earth], was the body of the world formed" (Plato, *Timaeus*, 32 b–c, 1963). And that world was God himself, the number one and the sphere in geometry, with "a soul in its center" made up of three parts – Same, Other, and Being. The number seven as the sum of the tetrad and trinity, 4+3=7. The number seven occurs frequently even in the Bible. Joshua brought down the walls of Jericho using the power of that number. Following the Lord's suggestion, he marched his army around the city walls for seven days, accompanied by seven priests carrying seven trumpets. On the seventh day they marched around the city seven times. Then the priests "blew the trumpets, and when the army heard the trumpet sound, they raised a great shout, and down fell the walls" (Joshua, 6, 20). Twelve as in the twelve signs of the Zodiac, the twelve "moods" of the year, the twelve nerves of the human brain.

There is plenty of mystery in these numbers to keep generations of numerologists busy for centuries to come. Indeed, "millions of man-hours and thousands of lives went into this interminable task" of searching for the inner meaning of things through numbers (Bell, 1946, p. 192). Numerologists tried to convert everything into numbers. And the one thing that was easy to convert into numbers were ... words.

Indeed, there was a long tradition of going from words to numbers in antiquity. And for good reason. The ancient world lacked specific symbols for numbers (such as 1, 2, 3, ...). To express numbers, they relied on the position of the letters of the alphabet (A=1, B=2, C=3, ...). On the basis of that simple correspondence between numbers and letters, the ancient Hebrews developed a system of reducing words to their number values by adding the individual number value of each letter in a word (an intellectual activity known as gematria, a part of the Cabala). Through the conversion of words into numbers, cabalists and numerologists sought to discover deeper meanings in the sacred scriptures. They would reduce words to their number value; they would translate these numbers back into different words of similar value, in the attempt to reveal new and occult meanings in the original words; they would compare words via their number values, and regarded words with the same numerical value as deeply connected (Bosman, 1932, p. xvii). St. Augustine himself – a firm believer that God had "ordered all things in number and measure and weight" – performed an exhaustive numerological analysis of the Bible (Bell, 1946, p. 288).

During the Middle Ages and the Renaissance, different methods of conversions were used as European cabalists adapted their alphabets to the Hebrew alphabet. Cagliostro, who kept sixteenth-century Europe under the spell of his histrionic personality, used the following method:[22]

1	2	3	4	5	6	7	8
A	B	C	D	E	U	O	F
I	K	G	M	H	V	Z	P
Q	R	L	T	N	W		
J		S			X		
Y							

With Cagliostro, and many more like him throughout the Middle Ages and the Renaissance, Pythagoras's numerology turned into pure magic, if not a game, the original pursuit of both scientific and mystical/magical aspects of mathematics severed and lost. Giulio Camillo, the "divine Camillo" we met at the beginning of last chapter, played one such learned game in a letter he wrote from France in 1535 to a certain Lucretia, to whom he professes eternal love (*ardentissime fiamme mie*, "my burning flames," *unico sostegno della mente mia*, "sole support of my mind"; Camillo, 1554, p. 344). He tells her how philosophers working in the tradition of the "wonderful ... ancient Hebrew theology"[23] took the first words of the Bible "In the beginning," and constructed a number of new sentences, each with new deep and occult meaning, simply by changing the order of the letters. "This is not a human thing," he reassures his loved one, "it is divine" (Camillo, 1554, p. 344). "Proceeding the same way, I can form several sentences starting from your name LUCRETIA" with the following result: "[T]he dear light, creates, rare, certain, helps, cures, dark, net, art, irate she tears us apart" (Camillo, 1554, p. 343). As she, no doubt, recognizes these qualities about herself, she "will know to be true what I say." As for Camillo, he can only hope never to experience the "irate she tears us apart" (Camillo, 1554, pp. 343).

Whatever Cagliostro or Camillo are remembered for, if they are remembered at all, it is certainly not for their contributions to mathematics and science. But Pythagoras himself, despite the esoteric aspects of his work and life, was one of the greatest scientists to ever live. He may have also been one of the luckiest. He chose the one problem where the relationship between nature and numbers is just below the surface: acoustics (Bell, 1946, pp. 106–8).[24] Had he chosen to seek mathematical solutions to other natural phenomena (for example, the electric spark from rubbed amber which had fascinated his teacher Thales) "he might be seeking yet" (Bell, 1946, p. 106). The mathematical underpinnings of electricity were discovered only in the twentieth century. "But in acoustics the search was short" (Bell, 1946, p. 107). Not only was it short; it also involved the simplest of numbers – 1, 2, 3, 4 – and of ratios – 1/2, 2/3, 3/4 – which may explain why the tetrad played such a key role in Pythagoras's numerology. Emboldened by this finding, Pythagoras came to believe that "everything is number."

Perhaps, I was just as lucky in picking a problem that afforded a solution, and a mathematical solution at that – a property that is just as desirable in modern academia as in Pythagoras's academia. Perhaps, in embarking upon the journey from words to numbers, I had the good intuition to take the right road – just imagine, I could have chosen the time-honored road of numerology. Lucky or clever? What do my numerological numbers say?[25]

R	O	B	E	R	T	O		F	R	A	N	Z	O	S	I			
2	7	2	5	2	4	7		8	2	1	5	7	7	3	1	=	63; (6+3) = 9

My number name is 9, which, in the chart of the Renaissance cabalist Cornelius Agrippa, stands for great achievement, inspiration, spirituality. Neither lucky nor clever, then; a disappointing answer from numerology. But, each one of us carries two other significant numbers that can be obtained by adding vowels and consonants separately – the vowel number referring to the hidden self in numerology and the consonants to the outer self. For my name, the vowel total OEO AOI is 7+5+7+1+7+1=28; (2+8)=10; (1+0)=1 which stands for purpose, action, ambition, aggression, leadership. The consonant total gives: RBRT FRNZS or 2+2+2+4+8+2+5+7+3=35; (3+5)=8 which stands for material success and worldly involvement. Again, successful, but neither lucky nor clever. Successful?! Close to the age of fifty and still with no permanent academic position? Another disappointing answer from numerology. Perhaps, I was clever after all … to stay away from numerology as a way to go from words to numbers. Or was I?

Renaissance cabalist John Reuchlin ingeniously managed to link the two most powerful words of the cabalist tradition, the 72-letter word Shemhamforash and the four-letter Tetragrammaton,[26] by means of gematria:

Y	=	10
YH	=	15 (10+5)
YHV	=	21 (10+5+6)
YHVH	=	26 (10+5+6+5)
	=	72

Reuchlin must have been as awestruck by this finding as I was when I first saw the statistical results out of the data I had collected on the basis of a computer-based story grammar – the two of us pursuing the relationship between words and numbers our different ways, but probably with the same obstinacy and determination.[27] Will someone still remember my name five-hundred years from now? No doubt, Reuchlin took the right road.

Of Thin Threads and Other Threads

In 1962, the National Science Foundation awarded Harold Guetzkow at Northwestern University a research grant for the study of conflict behavior. It was the beginning of a long-running project, known as the Dimensionality of Nations, that involved several principal investigators (Rummel, 1963, pp. 1, 4; Rummel, 1966, p. 65; Tanter, 1966, p. 41).[28] Rummel (1963, p. 4) writes: "One of the primary aims of the National Science Foundation's Dimensionality of Nations Project ... is to do ... a replication of Cattell's work."

Why Cattell? There are two reasons for Rummel to want to replicate Cattell's work, both having to do with our views of science. First, replication is the very hallmark of science. In his *The Scientific Study of Human Society*, Franklin Giddings (1924, p. 58), an American sociology pioneer, wrote:

> The final verification of an alleged fact (its conclusive establishment as a fact) is attained only through much repeating of observations and measurements. ... Physicists and chemists, astronomers and geologists, biologists and physiologists, are tirelessly repeating their observations and their measurements of presumptive fact. Social psychologists and sociologists must get this habit.

Second, Cattell uses a cutting-edge statistical technique – factor analysis – that was then making its way from psychology into political science and sociology. The association of social scientific work with quantification and statistics was well under way. Cattell himself had published in 1952 a timely book on factor analysis that was to become extremely popular. By that time, Cattell had been using factor analysis for some years, applying to conflict behavior between nations the "new method ... which has already proved so valuable in dissecting out the functional unities of the individual personality" (Cattell, 1949, p. 443). Cattell had high hopes for the new method, because "attempts to formulate laws are hindered by the lack of precise methods of measurement in the description of groups and group behavior" (Cattell, 1950, p. 215). Rummel shared that enthusiasm (but so must have the National Science Foundation and the Department of Defense) when he wrote that factor analysis is a "method ... of great potential value" in the study of conflict events, a method

> ideally suited to determining the nature of interrelationships between a large number of variables. Applied to a collection of variables, factor analysis delineates those which cluster together – which covary more with each other than they do with any of the other variables ...[29]

Table 3.1. *Factor Analysis of Eighteen Types of Collective Actions in the*
1919–1922 Database

Factor	Eigenvalue	% of variance	Cumulative %
1	14.82	82.4	82.4
2	1.90	10.6	93

The Dimensionality of Nations Project took its name from the fact that factor analysis isolates major clusters of variation – dimensions – among a set of variables (in Rummel's case, types of conflict actions). Three separate dimensions of conflict underline Rummel's nine measures of domestic conflict and thirteen measures of foreign conflict.[30] For domestic conflict, the three dimensions are: turmoil (a disorganized, spontaneous conflict behavior), revolutionary (overt and organized conflict behavior), and subversive (covert and illegal conflict behavior) (Rummel, 1963, pp. 11–13). Tanter (1966), in a reanalysis of Rummel's data, found a dual dimension of internal conflict behavior: A dimension of organized and largely legal actions, and a dimension "associated with organized conflict behavior of a highly violent nature" (Tanter, 1966, p. 49).

Would factor analysis highlight similar underlying dimensions in my Italian data? To answer that question, let me extract from the database a set of eighteen types of collective actions: assembly, bargaining meeting, break in, demonstration 1, demonstration 2, intervention, lockout, meeting, occupation, plant closing, protest, public meeting with speech making, rally, reunion, strike, turmoil, violence against people, and violence against things.[31] Table 3. 1 and Table 3.2 report the results. Perhaps not surprisingly, a very similar pattern to that of Rummel and Tanter emerges.

Factor values greater than .5 indicate that the variable belongs to the factor. Thus, the first factor is made up of the following actions: demonstration 1, demonstration 2, intervention, lockout, meeting, bargaining meeting, occupation, plant closing, protest, rally with speech making, rally, reunion, strike, agitation, assembly. The second factor groups together three types of action: break in, violence against people, violence against things. One thing is clear: Factor analysis breaks up the variance space into two basic components, one made up of a broad class of peaceful protest actions, and the other comprising violent actions. *Exactly* like Rummel had found.

No doubt, factor analysis is ideally suited "to make sense out of the innumerable and ever-shifting constellations of variables with which the student of cross-national behavior is confronted":[32] Thirteen measures of domestic conflict for 113 countries for Eckstein's data; twenty-two measures of foreign and domestic conflict behavior for seventy-seven nations for Rummel's data.[33]

Yet, all to find what? That conflict can be organized or disorganized, planned or spontaneous, and violent or nonviolent? Meager results, perhaps; where,

Table 3.2. *Factor Analysis of Eighteen Types of Collective Actions in the*
1919–1922 Database (Rotated Factor Matrix)

	Factor 1	Factor 2
Meeting	0.94092	0.16412
Intervention	0.94223	0.18256
Break in	0.08723	0.83665
Demonstration 2	0.93793	0.31186
Occupation	0.8062	0.47885
Protest	0.96334	0.17521
Reunion	0.97068	0.21727
Strike	0.94889	0.28881
Lockout	0.91806	0.29984
Agitation	0.97522	0.19387
Bargaining meeting	0.9482	0.18331
Violence against people	0.47801	0.8519
Violence against things	0.16873	0.94438
Assembly	0.95716	0.16486
Plant closing	0.94351	0.23743
Rally with speech making	0.96538	0.2089
Rally	0.84809	0.3887
Demonstration 1	0.8868	0.39654

often, the statistical findings deliver less than the underlying elegant mathematics (see Rummel, 1965). Not surprisingly, critics have lashed out at quantitative approaches in the social sciences and history. In an article titled "Roots of a Scientific Paradigm," historian Carlo Ginzburg (1979, p. 276) pessimistically concluded:

> The quantitative and anti-anthropocentric approach of the sciences of nature from Galileo on has placed human sciences in an unpleasant dilemma; they must either adopt a weak scientific standard so as to be able to attain significant results, or adopt a strong scientific standard to attain results of no great importance.

But, in the late 1950s, the mood was positive; the buzz words were about to become familiar: "systematic," "scientific," "data," and "methods" (Rummel, 1963, p. 1); the only way was forward. Indeed, by the late 1960s, social scientists were slowly moving to new tools of analysis: the regression model. The new tool was even more "ideally suited" to meet the social scientist's needs. After all, it appeared to speak the language of causality, where a set of "independent" variables, X_1, X_2, ..., X_k "cause" a change in a "dependent" variable Y. Let us try the power of that magic tool.

The regression model that I propose to estimate – and I could have chosen dozens of others – is one that relates fascist violence to the "red menace." The question that such a model addresses is the following: Does the level of fascist violence in 1921 in a province[34] depend upon 1) the extent of social conflict from below in that province during the Red Years and 2) the percentage of communes in the province that obtained a socialist majority during the administrative elections of November 1920? In other words, the model is:

$$Y_i = \beta_0 + \beta_1 X_{1i} + \beta_2 X_{2i} + \epsilon_i \qquad\qquad 3.1$$

where:

the subscript i indexes the set of provinces upon which the regression is run ($0 \leq i \leq 57$);

Y_i refers to the number of fascist violent actions in province i in 1921;

X_{1i} refers to the number of conflict events on the Left in province i during the Red Years of 1919–20;

X_{2i} refers to percentage of communes in province i that obtained a socialist majority during the administrative elections of November 1920;

and where the expected signs of the parameters are: $\beta_1 \geq 0$ and $\beta_2 \geq 0$. β_0 is a constant measuring the intercept. If the "red menace" hypothesis were correct, we should expect a violent fascist reaction in those provinces were the middle and/or upper classes may have felt threatened by the level of working-class mobilization in their provinces.

Table 3.3 reports the results of the least-squares estimate of Equation 3.1. The coefficients of both independent variables have the expected sign and are highly significant. Unfortunately, the values of leverage, Cook's D Statistics, and Mahalanobis distance all single out the observation for Genoa as a highly influential observation (with values ten times as high or higher than the next most influential observation). Given the potentially distorting effect of influential observations on parameter estimates, Model 2 reports the estimates of Equation 3.1, with the addition of a dummy variable for Genoa (on outliers and influence, see Belsley et al., 1980; Franzosi, 1994b). The results show that the coefficient of the dummy variable for Genoa is, indeed, the most highly significant among the set of independent variables. Nonetheless, the coefficients of both variables of Equation 3.1 remain significant and with the expected sign. The adjusted R-squared increases from .554 to .686. The values of leverage, Cook's D Statistics, and Mahalanobis distance for the new model estimate now point to Milan as a potentially troublesome data point (a problem known as "masking"; see Atkinson, 1988). Model 3 of Table 3.3 reports the estimates of Equation 3.1 with the addition of a second dummy variable for Milan. Model 4 includes a dummy variable for Rome, "unmasked" by the estimates of Model 3 (after which, no more significant influential observations are brought out). Again, the estimates confirm the significance of the dummy variables; but the data values of Genoa, Milan, and Rome do not seem to affect the signs and significance of the substantive coefficients (percent of communes with a socialist majority in the 1920 administrative elections and number of working-class actions of conflict and violence during 1919 and 1920). The regression results

Table 3.3. *Least-squares Estimates of a Regression Model of Fascist
Violence*

	Model 1	Model 2	Model 3	Model 4
Constant	2.835*	1.750**	.970	1.171
	(1.447)	(1.034)	(1.036)	(1.070)
% Socialist communes	.125*	9.893E-02*	.105*	.106*
in 1920 elections	(.033)	(.024)	(.023)	(.023)
Number of working-class	7.176E-01*	.304*	.395*	.358*
actions of conflict and	(.010)	(.045)	(.057)	(.074)
violence (1919–20)				
Dummy variable (Genoa)		-150.811	-208.471*	-185.041*
		(28.836)	(35.999)	(46.642)
Dummy variable (Milan)			-16.155*	-13.313**
			(6.501)	(7.441)
Dummy variable (Rome)				5.036
				(6.341)
R-squared	0.573	0.702	0.734	0.737
Adjusted R-squared	0.554	0.686	0.714	0.711

Note: Standard error in parentheses. **Significant at the .05 level; *significant at the .01 level. Dependent variable: Number of violent actions committed by the Fascists in 1921.

thus seem to confirm an interpretation of fascist violence as a response to a threat from below.

Given, the highly aggregated nature of the data, I am reluctant to dwell upon the substantive interpretation of the results. The point is: It is possible to perform quantitative analyses on data that are fundamentally qualitative in nature, in other words, *it is possible to go from words to numbers*. And ever more tools are becoming available to work on the numbers. Some of these tools are especially well suited to deal with the kind of numbers produced by a quantitative, story grammar approach to narrative, in particular the detailed information on time and space. Thus, knowledge of the timing and duration of each microaction and macroaction lends itself to the application of event history analysis (for an application, see Myers, 1997). The chronological ordering of those actions – their temporal and logical sequence – would allow investigators to apply sequence analysis to these data (for an example, see Abbott, 1983; Abbott and Barman, 1997).[35] The work by Bearman and Stovel (2000) on autobiographical accounts of becoming a Nazi uses a novel representation of narrative sequences as networks to shed light on the process of identity formation. Finally, detailed information on the geographic location of actions and events would allow us to apply geographic information systems to draw the map of conflict. After all, a question of old found in the literature on the rise of Italian fascism and revisited by Brustein (1991) on the pages of the *American Sociological Review* hinges on knowledge of the spatial distribution of conflict: Was Italian fascism a reaction to socialism, a reaction to the "red menace"? If so, wouldn't we expect a close geographic overlap between working-class actions in 1919–20 and employers' or landlords' reactions in 1921–22 (particularly, at the beginning of countermobilization in the fall of 1920)? And diffusion models would allow us to critically link information on both time and space of events (for an application, see Hedström, 1994; Oliver and Myers, 2003). Andrew Charlesworth (1979), in a seminal paper in historical geography, showed how the Swing rebellion of 1830 in England moved south, day after day, along the main routes of communication of the time, in particular, the River Thames. How did the factory occupation movement spread from its beginning in the Romeo Factory in Milan? Crucially, we need to link together time, space, and network information (Oliver and Myers, 2003). It is unfortunate that, by and large, in the growing literature on protest events little use has been made of the temporal and spatial information that researchers will have spared no effort to collect in the greatest detail. As Tarrow has put it: "The fetish of [wasted] thoroughness" runs deep in the social sciences (1989, p. 363).

And Yet, What Do We Know?

Was Horace's little mouse born out of this methodological tour de force? Did I apply Ginzburg's strong scientific standard to attain results of no great importance? I am tempted to answer "no" to those questions – but I should remind the reader of an old Italian saying: "Never ask the wine seller if his wine is good." Both the simple counts of Chapter 2 and the network models of this chapter have told us a great deal about what was happening during the 1919–22 period in Italy. They have disclosed patterns in the unfolding of historical events. They have highlighted networks of social relations. Much more analysis of these hard-won data will be necessary, but the beginnings are encouraging. Ultimately, it is substantive results of this kind – "the questions one asks" – that make social scientists' involvement in methodological pursuits worthwhile. Of course, we can ask questions until we are blue in the face. Perhaps, what matters even more is answers. In the words of another historian, Elton (1967, p. 33): "Too often vast engines are assembled, and blows of enormous weight are struck, only to produce an answer which is either obvious, well known, or manifestly unhelpful." Indeed, was it all worth it? Has anything new come out of the analyses of the 1919–22 data (15,000 newspaper articles coded, tens of helots at work!)? Anything we did not already know?

   Yet, what we know is not easy to pin down. As usual in the social sciences, there is no dearth of knowledge. There are at least two ways in which we can approach the study of the 1919–22 period. On the one hand, we can look at fascism as one of the forms of the modern state. Some of the big names in the social sciences, from Barrington Moore to Lipset, figure prominently in this tradition. On the other hand, we can approach the Red Years and the Black Years as instances of mobilization and countermobilization processes within the social movement literature. More big names, from Tilly to Tarrow, figure in this tradition. The trouble is, there is no agreement among the big names in either tradition as to what constitutes an explanation of fascism or mobilization. As a result, we have a host of theories in search of confirmation.

Take the social science theories of fascism. De Felice dedicated an entire volume to the discussion of those theories and interpretations (plural!).[36] One interpretation that has enjoyed considerable popularity is that of fascism as reaction to socialism. The Communist International gave the first version of that interpretation in its Third Congress in 1921: Fascism is the expression of the monopoly phase of capitalism, of the growing difficulties of the industrial bourgeoisie in maintaining its position in the class struggle against the proletariat, and of its need to resort to political authoritarianism (De Felice, 1995b, pp. 51–66).

The Third Communist International points its accusatory finger toward the industrial bourgeoisie; but others have blamed the petty bourgeoisie for the outcome. For Salvatorelli (cited in De Felice, 1995b, p. 186):

> Fascism represents the 'class struggle' of the petty bourgeoisie, wedged between capital and proletariat ... Fascism has a single reality; but because it stands in opposition to two antagonistic – albeit complementary – social forces at the same time, it will take on different characteristics depending upon whether one considers its anticapitalist or its antiproletariat stance.

Seymour Martin Lipset echoed that view, decades later, when he wrote: "Fascism is basically a middle-class movement representing a protest against both capitalism *and* socialism, big business *and* big unions" (Lipset, 1981, p. 131; emphasis in the original).

Poulantzas (1970) similarly stressed the role of the petty bourgeoisie in bringing about a fascist solution. But the petty bourgeoisie did not act alone. Fascism was the result of the alliance between that class and big capital. Various other social groups were also involved (landlords, peasantry, and so on) but they only played a secondary historical role (Poulantzas, 1970, pp. 85–8, 237–46).[37] What held together this unholy alliance between petty bourgeoisie and industrial bourgeoisie was a common ideology of nationalism and anticommunism.

Poulantzas's work on fascism focuses on class alliances. There is a long tradition on the Left for that kind of analysis, starting with Marx's own work, *The Eighteenth Brumaire of Louis Bonaparte or The Class Struggles in France (1848–50)*. Outside that tradition, it was Barrington Moore (1966) who squarely put the role of class alliances on the agenda of historical sociology in his *Social Origins of Dictatorship and Democracy*. For Barrington Moore right-wing authoritarianism in general, and fascism more specifically, is one of three paths to the modern world, bourgeois democracy and communism being the other two (Moore, 1966, p. 414). Fascism is the political regime that results from the alliance of the landed upper class, the state, and the industrial bourgeoisie (Moore, 1966, p. 436).[38] What drove semidemocratic prefascist states to fascism was their failure to cope with the socioeconomic problems of the day and their reluctance or inability to bring about fundamental structural changes (Moore, 1966, p. 438). For Moore, fascism is inconceivable without democracy; fascism is "an attempt to make reaction popular and plebeian" (Moore, 1966, p. 447).[39]

If theories of fascism look at the behavior of social actors for explanations, theories of mobilization tend to focus on macrolevel characteristics: The resources available to mobilizing groups (resource-mobilization theories), the opportunities for mobilization offered by the political system (political opportunity structure theories), or the ideological frameworks adopted by mobilizing groups (frame alignment theories, Snow et al., 1986).

Briefly, according to resource mobilization theories, all forms of protest require resources, whether material (money, guns, manpower, and so on), organizational (structures for effective mobilization, skilled organizers), or ideological (symbolism, access to media). For Piven and Cloward, lack of resources is the main reason why poor people's movements fail (Piven and Cloward, 1977, pp. 1–37). Mobilization – the process by which movements secure control over those resources (Tilly, 1978, p. 7) – consists of three essential elements: 1) increasing collective claims on the resources of members by eliminating competing claims on those resources; 2) accumulating new resources; 3) building organizational structures that can act effectively and can respond quickly to new developments (Tilly, 1978, pp. 71–3).

Action, particularly successful action, may well be impossible without access to resources, as resource mobilization teaches us. But groups do not act simply because they have resources. Resource mobilization theory deals with the capacity to act, but not the immediate incentive or opportunity to do so. Political opportunity structure comprises those features of the political environment which encourage or discourage groups from acting (Tarrow, 1994, p. 18).[40] It is these features that are largely responsible for the timing of collective action: When costs are low and probability of success high due to fluctuations in these factors, action is more likely to be undertaken (McAdam, 1996, p. 29).[41]

Yet, changes in political structures, no matter how momentous, are opportunities only when they are defined as such by groups sufficiently organized to act. Frame alignment theories examine the processes of formation of grievances and of maturation of the belief that mobilization is the most effective way to address those grievances (Snow et al., 1986). "The social arrangements that are ordinarily perceived as just and immutable must come to seem both unjust and mutable" (Piven and Cloward, 1977, p. 12). It is not the presence of grievances, but their interpretation that matters. Movement must inscribe their grievances in overall ideological and cultural frames (Zald, 1996, pp. 266–7).[42]

So, in the end, what do we know? What we know depends a great deal upon where you look and whom you listen to. Which class and which type of class alliance was responsible for twenty years of fascist dictatorship in Italy? Different theories have different culprits in mind. To summarize:

Moore – Fascism is the result of a class alliance between the landed elite, the industrial bourgeoisie, and the state.

Poulantzas – Fascism is the result of a class alliance between the industrial bourgeoisie and the petty bourgeoisie.

Salvatorelli, Lipset – Fascism is the political outcome of the reaction to socialism by the petty bourgeoisie.

Lenin, Third Communist International – Fascism is the political outcome of the reaction to socialism by the industrial bourgeoisie.

So, "what do we know?" I ask. "What can we actually claim to know about key subjects …?" asks James Rule at the beginning of a wonderful book, *Theories of Civil Violence* (Rule, 1988, p. 5). The answer to that question comes at the end of a tour de force where Rule looks at the theoretical and empirical claims of a wide range of theories of civil violence – precisely the type of theories we are dealing with in our application of a story grammar. And it's not good news. "The case for cumulative progress in theories of civil violence is problematic" (Rule, 1988, p. 310). Fundamentally, social theories come and go on the tide of broader social-political movements. New sociopolitical contexts in society at large bring out new concerns. And with these new concerns come new theoretical *perspectives* (perspective as a point of view, indeed). And the old is typically forgotten after an initial dialogue (or, better, clash of ideas). As Weber put it:

> The history of the social sciences is and remains a continuous process passing from the attempt to order reality analytically through the construction of concepts – the dissolution of the analytical constructs so constructed through the expansion and shift of the scientific horizon – and the reformulation anew of concepts on the foundations thus transformed. (Weber, 1949, p. 105)

In the end, different social theories capture, to a greater or lesser extent, different aspects of reality. They are all true to some extent. They are certainly "true to *someone*'s experience" (Rule, 1988, p. 310; emphasis in the original).

Yet, Rule points to a possible way out of the impasse of social theory. The question is: "Does this account point to evidence not suggested by other accounts; and do actual investigations yield the sort of evidence suggested by this account, rather than those suggested by alternative views?" (Rule, 1988, p. 310). And this is good news for us. After all, the type of data that narrative and story grammars make available squarely address Rule's question. They would lead to a definite solution of the puzzle of Italian fascism. Do not these data provide information on who does what, where, when, and why? Do not network models provide information on the network of social relations in which social actors are embedded? Would not this allow us to find out, once and for all, who allied with whom in bringing out a fascist path to the modern world in Italy? We would be able to tell who was right and who was wrong, Moore or Poulantzas, Lipset or Lenin. In the end, have we not fully lived up to Sorokin's great hopes of forging the science of sociology?

> There is no need to stress the great importance of the factual and 'inductive' studies. To them, primarily, belongs the credit of a real promotion of sociology as a science. They represent the only basis for deciding whether a certain philosophical generalization is valid. Through such studies we are given relatively accurate sociological correlations and causal formulas, and *in such studies mainly lies the hope of a further perfecting of sociology as a science.*[43]

In the Linguists' Tool Bag: Theta Theory

Once again, perhaps not unsurprisingly (remember the story of the wine seller), story grammars emerge as the panacea of social scientific work. Yet, for all their advantages, story grammars do have problems we must face up to. For one thing, the construct subject-action-object mixes syntactic and semantic categories. In accusative languages, grammatical relations are referred to as "subject" and "object." "Subject and Objects are grammatical relations, not [semantic] roles" (Palmer, 1994, pp. 14, 19; see also Chafe, 1970, pp. 95–6). Action is a semantic category – in syntax you find verbs or verb phrases. These are not just linguistic subtleties. They do pose problems in coding passive sentences. Consider the sentence "demonstrators are shot dead by the police." The syntactic subject of the sentence – the demonstrators – is actually the (semantic) object of the police's actions. Active and passive constructs have different ideological import (Trew, 1979a); yet, if the investigator's interest lies with who did what, one can always recover that information by turning passive constructs into active ones.

But if the solution to the problem of coding passive sentences within the SAO structure of the grammar was easy enough, the solution to other problems brought on by the grammar was a different story. In setting up the grammar, I had obviously worked with the implicit assumption that, in narratives of protest events, subjects would be human actors and that, therefore, verbs would be actions. Reasonable assumption. It is one, in fact, that we commonly find even among linguists working on narrative. But when the time came to analyze the newspaper data on the 1919–22 and 1986–87 periods, in the database I discovered hundreds of <subjects> that were not actors, and hundreds of

<actions> that did not sound at all like actions. Such triplets as "Fascists kill socialist mayor" or "police charge protesters," live side by side in the database with "trucks stall" (albeit, trucks full of Fascists), "building blows up," "Government minister is ill" (conveniently), or "wounded victims die." Coders, obviously, had provided their own practical solutions to the limitations of the grammar. But their solutions just postponed the problems. When confronted with the task of classifying the thousands of actions in the database, that varied assortment of verbs/actions turned out to be quite intractable.

The linguistic theory of theta roles (or theta theory or theory of semantic roles) offers a solution to this problem. Theta roles, or thematic roles, or semantic roles[44] "refer to the semantic relations between verbs and their arguments, where arguments are the participants minimally involved in the activity or state expressed by the predicate" (Haegeman, 1991, p. 36).

According to theta theory, verbs in language come with a preconfigured template of information that tells us which *arguments* are associated with the verb. Thus, the verb "to give" has three arguments, as in "John gave Laura a book." The verb "to kill" has two arguments ("The police killed demonstrators.") and "to expire" has one argument ("The license expired."). The template not only contains information about the number of arguments related to the verb, but also about the type of argument, their thematic or semantic roles. In "John gave Laura a book," the verb "to give" assigns the role Agent to the subject argument (John), the role Patient to the Object argument (book), and the role Beneficiary to the dative, or indirect object, argument (Laura) (Haegeman, 1991, pp. 41–2). All main verbs theta-mark their arguments (Haegeman, 1991, p. 41).

Agent, patient, and beneficiary are, no doubt, the three most important roles (Chafe, 1970, pp. 102–4; Palmer, 1994, pp. 6, 8). The *agent* is the instigator of the event. Agents are generally animate beings, although they need not be (for example, "lightning killed the child"). As a result, animacy is often used as a criterion to determine the Agent (Chafe, 1970, pp. 109–12; Palmer, 1994, p. 27). The *patient* undergoes or suffers the action of the agent (again, "police killed demonstrators," where police is the agent and demonstrators the patient; but also "Giulia ripped the book," where the book is the patient).[45] The *beneficiary*[46] refers to entities, typically animate and human,[47] that are indirectly affected by the action of the verb.

But agent, patient, and beneficiary are hardly the only roles.[48] In fact, the "theoretical" number of such roles is probably large, although limited. In practice, a handful of roles – among which agent, patient, and beneficiary occupy a prominent place – would give us a fairly comprehensive list.[49] Consider the sentence "John saw the accident." In which sense is John an agent? – or the accident a patient, for that matter. The roles of *perceiver* and *perceived* may be more appropriate (Palmer, 1994, p. 26).[50] Similarly, the two arguments involved in verbs of emotion (for example, "John liked Mary" and "Municipal councilors feared the Fascists") may be better described semantically as *experiencer* and *experienced*, with the experiencer being normally animate

(Palmer, 1994, p. 27). Other roles, such as *instrumental* and *locative* are most clearly indicated in less familiar languages (Palmer, 1994, p. 10). Our story grammar deals with these roles indirectly as modifiers of the action (<instrument> and <space>).[51]

Working with theta roles, instead of an SAO structure, gets rid of the problem of active versus passive sentences. Active and passive forms change the grammatical roles, but not the semantic roles of a sentence (Palmer, 1994, p. 19). When transforming active sentences into passive, patients are not transformed into agents; they are still patients, although they are now the grammatical subjects (Palmer, 1994, p. 19).[52]

Working with theta roles also provides clues on how to approach the problem of classifying verbs. Halliday (1970; 1994, p. 107), in his approach to the relationship between semantic roles and verbs (or processes in Halliday's language), wrote: "A process consists, in principle, of three components: (i) the process itself; (ii) participants in the process; (iii) circumstances associated with the process [time and space, in particular]." The loose correspondence between semantic roles and verbs allows Halliday to provide a broad classification of verbs.[53]

Of Beauty (and Science)

Everything is numbers. And numbers are beautiful, "the archetype of the beautiful," in the words of the seventeenth-century astronomer-mathematician, Johannes Kepler.[54] Filtered through Plato and Aristotle, Pythagoras's aesthetic beliefs in the power of numbers and of geometric forms and in the celestial "harmony of the spheres" would exert enormous influence for centuries to come.[55] In his *Itinerary of the Mind to God* – a journey of other times – Bonaventure of Bagnoregio would write back in 1259:

> Because all things are beautiful and in some way pleasant, and beauty and pleasure cannot be without proportion; and proportion is first in numbers, it follows that everything is number. (Bonaventure, 1994, p. 114, chap. 2, para. 10)

Tarnas goes as far as claiming that "without the intellectual bias created by a neoplatonically defined aesthetic judgement [that is, the joy of finding pure geometrical forms in nature], the Scientific Revolution might well not have occurred, certainly not in the form it took historically" (Tarnas, 1996, p. 255).

Pythagoras's influence was particularly strong in astronomy where a geocentric view of the universe saw the sun moving in circles around the Earth – circles being the most pure geometrical form. Even the ancient Greeks were aware of discrepancies between observation and theory. In an attempt to reconcile the observed positions of the planets to the aesthetics of perfect circular motion, astronomers started employing an ever-increasing number of mathematical devices: deferents, major and minor epicycles, equants, and eccentrics. When a planet's movement did not appear to move in a perfect circle, another, smaller circle was added, around which the planet hypothetically moved while it continued moving round the larger circle. Further discrepancies were solved by compounding the circles, displacing their centers, positing yet another center from which motion remained uniform (Tarnas, 1996, p. 248).

By Copernicus's time, this cosmographic model had reached enormous complexity, yet still failing to accurately predict the movements of the planets. To simplify matters, Copernicus revived the ancient hypothesis of a heliocentric universe, where planets revolve around the sun. Indeed, this explanation solved many problems. Ptolemy's equants, for one, were no longer needed. But Copernicus continued to uphold the ancient belief in perfect circular motion. He objected to the use of equants "on aesthetic grounds because it violated the rule of uniform circular motion" (Tarnas, 1996, p. 250). In the end, Copernicus's aesthetic beliefs forced him to make continuous adjustments to his simple initial model till it became as complex and inaccurate as that of Ptolemy.

Kepler's work was no less driven by Pythagorean number mysticism. He embraced the heliocentric theory of the universe with the sun at the center and Mercury, Venus, Earth, Mars, Saturn, and Jupiter orbiting around it and separated from one another by an octahedron, an icosohedron, a dodecahedron, a tetrahedron, and a cube. "To Kepler the discovery was fundamental because it showed the mathematical order of the universe" (Debus, 1978, p. 92). Indeed, Kepler's lasting contributions to modern astronomy come from a Pythagorean concern with aesthetic and number mysticism. Later, Kepler used ellipses in place of Copernicus's circles and his own five geometrical solids. His calculations led him to formulate the law that the squares of the lines of revolution of any two planets around the sun are proportional to the cubes of their mean distances from the sun. "A brilliant discovery from our point of view," writes Debus (1978, p. 95). But from Kepler's point of view, this law had a much deeper meaning, as a mathematical expression of the world harmonies. Like Pythagoras, Kepler turned his ear to the skies to hear the voices of the planets. In his *Mysterium Cosmographicum*, Kepler covered the study of the five regular solids and their harmonic ratios, musical harmonies, and their relationship to the universe.

> [But] the eighth book was to be devoted to the four kinds of voice emitted by the planets (contralto, alto, tenor, and bass), and the third law of planetary motion had been made part of a book on the expression of the clefs of the musical scale and the genera of major and minor consonances. (Debus, 1978, p. 95)

The new and the old go hand in hand. Platonic and Neoplatonic revivals during the Renaissance led to the development of geometry and algebra and of a modern mathematical approach to nature *and* to the flourishing of occult investigations of number mysticism of cabalistic and numerological studies

(Debus, 1978, p. 11). But twentieth-century mathematicians and scientists are no less taken by the beauty of numbers and mathematics than Pythagoras himself. "I know numbers are beautiful. If they aren't beautiful, nothing is," claimed Hungarian mathematician Paul Erdős (cited in Hoffman, 1998, p. 44). Richard Borcherds – a Cambridge mathematician winner of a Fields Medal, the mathematics equivalent of the Nobel Prize, for his proof of the "moonshine" conjecture[56] – admits that his work has little practical utility; it is just "a study of beauty – something with a lot of symmetry to it."[57]

Einstein's appreciation for beauty is well known. His first paper on the field equations ends with the words: "Scarcely anyone who fully comprehends this theory can escape from its magic" (cited in Chandrasekhar, 1987, p. 64). Hermann Bondi recalls showing Einstein the mathematical equations of a unified field theory he had worked out. "Oh, how ugly," Einstein's reacted. Bondi continues: "He [Einstein] was quite convinced that beauty was a guiding principle in the search for important results in theoretical physics" (cited in Feuer, 1995, p. 7). "When Einstein was working on building up his theory of gravitation," Physicist Nobel Laureate Paul Dirac remarks, "he was not trying to account for some results of observations. Far from it. His entire procedure was to search for a beautiful theory" (cited in McAllister, 1996, p. 15). And if that was Einstein's goal, he may just have succeeded. Physicist Max Born recalls that Einstein's theory "appealed to me like a great work of art, to be enjoyed and admired from a distance" (cited in Feuer, 1995, p. 8). Even Dirac acknowledges the beauty of Einstein's theory. "One has a great confidence in the theory arising from its great beauty, quite independent of its detailed successes … One has an overpowering belief that its foundation must be correct quite independent of its agreement with observation."[58]

Dirac himself puts aesthetics first as a criterion of theory evaluation. "One should be dominated by considerations of mathematical beauty," he writes, "and not be too much perturbed by discrepancies with observation" (Dirac, 1980, p. 44). "It is more important to have beauty in one's equations than to have them fit experiment" (Dirac, 1963, p. 47). German physicist/mathematician Hermann Weyl who made fundamental contributions to "group theory," would have agreed with Dirac: "My work always tried to unite the true with the beautiful; but when I had to choose one or the other, I usually chose the beautiful" (cited in Chandrasekhar, 1987, p. 52). The beauty of one's equations mirror the mathematical beauty of nature. "It seems to be one of the fundamental features of nature," he concludes, "that fundamental physical laws are described in terms of a mathematical theory of great beauty and power" (cited in Chandrasekhar, 1987, p. 53). Mathematician Jules-Henri Poincaré wrote that, ultimately, it is aesthetic principles that guide scientists not only in the evaluation of scientific work but, unconsciously, in its very production (1997, pp. 47–9; see also Cellucci, 1998, p. 8). Of the various ideas that come to our mind, we pursue the beautiful ones; "the most useful combinations are precisely the most beautiful" (Poincaré, 1997, p. 49).

An appeal to aesthetic criteria is pervasive among scientists even in those disciplines less directly grounded in mathematics.[59] The words "beautiful" and "beauty" appear repeatedly in Darwin's *The Origin of Species*: "[B]eautiful co-adaptations," "beautiful adaptations," "beauty and infinite complexity of the coadaptations between all organic beings," and "beautiful and harmonious diversity of nature."[60] He has numerous passages of truly lyrical tones:

> As buds give rise by growth to fresh buds, and these, if vigorous, branch out and overtop on all sides many a feebler branch, so by generation I believe it has been with the great Tree of Life, which fills with its dead and broken branches the crust of the earth, and covers the surface with its ever branching and *beautiful* ramifications.[61]

And yet, for Darwin, even this beauty is nothing in comparison to the beauty of the one single law that explains all that harmony and diversity, "natural selection ... that gives rise to all the more important modifications of structure, by which the innumerable beings on the face of this earth are enabled to struggle with each other, and the best adapted to survive" (Darwin, 1996, p. 139). We know nothing about the laws of nature. "Our ignorance of the laws of variation is profound." Yet, "the same laws appear to have acted in producing the lesser differences between varieties of the same species" (Darwin, 1996, p. 137). He concludes his enormously influential book with the words:

> There is grandeur in this view of life ... whilst this planet has gone cycling on according to the fixed law of gravity, from so simple a beginning endless forms most *beautiful* and most wonderful have been, and are being, evolved. (Darwin, 1996, p. 396; emphasis added)

One single theory that explains the complexity of the natural world, that brings together the thousand different species on earth. That strikes Darwin as beautiful. Weisskopf, the American twentieth-century physicist, put it this way:[62]

> Most of the scientific insights that are considered beautiful bring together seemingly unconnected phenomena in a surprisingly compact way or express the fundamental features of a large number of natural occurrences with one single system of thought.

In *The Athenaeum* of May, 1919, J. W. N. Sullivan, Beethoven's and Einstein's biographer, wrote:[63]

> The measure of a scientific theory is, in fact, a measure of its aesthetic value, since it is a measure of the extent to which it has introduced harmony with what was before chaos. It is in its aesthetic value that the justification of the scientific theory is to be found, and with it the justification of the scientific method.

James Watson, in his upbeat account of the discovery of DNA similarly reports: "I had just devised a *beautiful* DNA structure."[64] When he reports Rosalind

Franklin's reactions to the DNA structure, Watson writes: "Rosy ... accepted the fact that *the structure was too pretty not to be true*" (Watson, 1969, p. 134; emphasis added). Chemist Nobel Laureate Rick Smally would put his own discovery of buckminsterfullerene or carbon 60 with remarkably similar words. After frantically trying again and again to build a three-dimensional paper model of the molecule, Smally finally taped hexagons to the side of pentagons till he had a stable structure. "That was it. Twelve pentagons and 20 hexagons, and he had the shape of a perfect sphere. *It was so beautiful it had to be true.* This had to be the structure of C60."[65]

> How could they have been so blind? Now it had been pointed out to them, it was all too perfectly obvious. The structure of C60 was not only the most wonderfully symmetrical molecular structure they had ever contemplated, it was also absurdly commonplace. A modern soccer ball ... Heath raced to a sporting goods store in the Village and returned with a real soccer ball, *just so they could admire it.*"

A fellow sociologist, Guillermina Jasso, thus recounts[66] the moment "One afternoon in June of 1976, [when] the justice evaluation function ... jumped out of a regression equation. It was beautiful and full of possibilities. ... [T]he most beautiful thing I had ever seen." She adds, in lyrical tones: "The new justice evaluation function swirled around the room, sparkling and showing the colors of the rainbow, and making a sound like the crystal of a chandelier in the breeze." "Everything changed ... [for me that] day."

Pythagoras, Copernicus, Kepler, Darwin, Einstein, Dirac, Smally, Watson, and Jasso. I am in good company in being captivated by the elegance and beauty of the thin mathematical thread that links words to numbers and by the synthetic power of a handful of network graphs to give such clear and concise snapshot of the complex variety of social relations during the Red Years and the Black Years. For all their diverse equations, consciously or unconsciously, scientists seem to hold one fundamental equation in common:[67]

$$beauty = truth$$

And that equation goes hand in hand with another fundamental equation:

$$beauty = good$$

"Don't you think that anything good is also attractive?" Socrates asks Agathon in Plato's *Symposium*.[68] These equations are deeply ingrained in Western culture.[69] Catholic religious writings have emphatically depicted God and the angels as beautiful, good, and just. The devil, instead, is always ugly.[70] For Dante, the devil has three heads, hairy legs, and looks like a "windmill."[71] Ugly devils are to be found everywhere in medieval art. Sir James Melville, envoy from Mary, Queen of Scots, to Queen Elizabeth describes the event of the witches of North-Berwick calling up the devil and receiving a "sermon" from him:

Now after that the Devil had ended his admonitions, he came down out of the pulpit, and caused all the company come kiss his arse: Which they said was cold like ice; his body hard like iron, as they thought who handled him; his face was terrible; his nose like the beak of an eagle; great burning eyes; his hands and his legs were hoary, with claws upon his hands and feet like the griffin; he spoke with a low voice.[72]

Unlucky to be so ugly, but to have a cold arse as well!

Journeys

Journeys ... magic caskets full of dreamlike promises.

Claude Lévi-Strauss (1992, p. 37)

Umbre de muri, umbre de mainè, dunde ne vegni, duve l'è ch'a nè ...

Fabrizio de Andrè (1999, p. 54)

The further one travels the more one learns.

Christopher Columbus (1969, p. 224)

The way we see things is affected by what we know or what we believe.

John Berger (1972, p. 8)

The scientific abstraction from concreteness, the quantification of qualities which yield exactness as well as universal validity, involve a specific concrete experience of the *Lebenswelt* – a specific mode of 'seeing' the world. And this 'seeing,' in spite of its 'pure,' disinterested character, is seeing within a purposive, practical context.

Herbert Marcuse (1964, p. 164)

"A March it Was"

"A march it was of military speed," wrote Wordsworth of his crossing of the Alps with his "fellow student" Robert Jones – "side by side / Pacing, two brother Pilgrims."[1] A march you may think it was, our going *from* words *to* numbers of the last three chapters, with me incessantly spurring you on – a harsh guide in my single-minded pursuit of the numbers. The linguists' work on narrative, Pythagoras, Quintilian, Camillo and the art of memory, the Spanish Inquisition, the Red Years and the Black Years, and the stories of *The Three Kingdoms* all whizzed by in a flash. On, on we pressed, from content analysis, to linguistics; from linguistics to computer science and statistics.

The proof of the pudding is in the eating; and, perhaps not surprisingly, I have been boasting that my pudding is good, listing advantages after advantages. Yet, I hear some grumbles.

HISTORIAN. Which pudding? Where is the pudding? Show me that your numbers, these hard-won numbers, in the end, add something to our historical knowledge of the rise of fascism. Show me that your numbers prove some scholarly views on the rise of fascism to be mistaken, others partly right or in need of clarification, and still others right on target. That, in my book, is a good pudding! I didn't see any of that.

METHODOLOGIST [in anger]. Who cares about that? What I want to see is more of the technique itself. This is no manual for practitioners of content analysis. What's the use of it? Tell me which content analysis software I should buy!

AUTHOR [*sotto voce*, turning to the audience]. He means: Which buttons I should poke on the computer!

METHODOLOGIST. What has Camillo's life or Pythagoras got do with content analysis? Why waste precious pages on trivia?

HISTORIAN. Indeed! Use those pages to discuss the validity of your data (taken from newspapers!), to present more data analyses, to show me how your results confirm or modify what historians know about the rise of fascism.

METHODOLOGIST. Forget that nonsense about fascism, once and for all. Listen! You have a rigorous and innovative method: linguistics, set theory, network models; state of the art. That's a good pudding. Why spoil it with this postmodern mumbo jumbo about authors and readers? Why do you have to undermine the numbers with all these useless words?

FAUST [arguing with his famulus Wagner]. "Stick to right thinking and sound sense, it tells, / Its own tale, little artifice is needed; / If you have something serious to say, / Drop the pursuit of words! This play / Of dazzling oratory, this paper decoration / You fiddle with and offer to the world ..."[2]

CALVINO. "I'm producing too many stories at once because what I want is for you to feel, around the story, a saturation of other stories. ... You feel a bit cheated, seeing that the stream is dispersed into so many trickles."[3]

AUTHOR. Come now. The lot of you. Your puddings were never in the menu. That's not the deal I struck with you. Do you remember my "pact with the reader?" Perhaps, it was a mistake to give you voice; a book where author and reader do not observe the rule of silence as they journey together from words to numbers. "Side by side ... two brother Pilgrims," you and I never tire of a chattering dialogue. But, alas, it is I who have the last word. Unfair as this is, I get to write the book I want, not you. This journey, having gotten you to the numbers starting from words, this journey is over. That was my pact with you and, unlike you, I am trying my best to keep my end of the bargain.

AUTHOR [muttering to himself]. Yet, are journeys ever *really* over? In what sense was Columbus's first voyage over on Thursday, March 14, 1493, when the Admiral, "at noon, crossed the bar of Saltes and anchored in Palos harbour, from which he had sailed on 3 August of the previous year 1492, seven months and eleven days before" (Columbus, 1969, p. 113). Journeys are transformative, sometimes, of the world around us; most often, of the world inside us. Saul changed his ways and even his name (to Paul) after a journey to Damascus (Acts, 9: 1–9). Perhaps not to the extent of St. Paul, but we are never quite the same after a journey. Journeys never leave us the way they found us. They really are "magic caskets full of dreamlike promises" (Lévi-Strauss, 1992, p. 37). Out of the magic casket of one such long journey, aboard the H. M. S. Beagle, between December 1831 and October 1836, a young naturalist by the name of Charles Darwin would pull his path-breaking theory of evolution (Darwin, 1989; 1996). St. Paul and Darwin, Giordano Bruno, Camillo, Pythagoras, Poupinel, and others, all come out of the magic casket of my own journey from words to numbers. But "dreamlike promises" point to things to come, perhaps to more dreams and more magic to be pulled out of the casket. There must be more to this journey. And indeed, there is!

AUTHOR [turning to the reader]. So, angry reader, forget your anger. Don't use my book to write *your* book. Let yourself slip into *my* book. Let yourself slip into the magic of journeys. In fact, forget Chapters 1, 2, and 3 with their fair account of this armchair journey from words to numbers. Forget the magic casket of story grammars, theta theory, set theory, SQL, network models, linguistics, sociology, theory, and methodology. Forget all that and, together, let's accompany real voyagers on real journeys. Let's go through the pages of the fair accounts left behind by Christian medieval pilgrims in their voyages of penance and by early navigators in their voyages of "discovery."

   Could my journey have anything in common with these journeys, my account anything in common with their accounts? Could we learn anything by looking at other travel accounts? Could the metaphor of the journey teach us anything "sociological"? Let's find out.

CALVINO. "Relax. Concentrate. Dispel every other thought. Let the world around you fade. Best to close the door ... Find the most comfortable position ... Stretch your legs ... Adjust the light so you won't strain your eyes. ... Do you have to pee? All right, you know best."[4]

Pilgrims on the Road

Starting around the fourth century, scores of European pilgrims journeyed to sites of worship.[5] The Holy Land was the Medieval pilgrims' preferred destination.[6] But the Holy Land was very far away, well beyond the means of most ordinary people (Coleman and Elsner, 1995, p. 110). Rome in Italy, Santiago de Compostela in Spain, Canterbury and Walsingham in England, Chartres and St. Martin at Tours in France emerged as the main European pilgrimage sites.[7] By the late Middle Ages most Christian pilgrimage in Europe was local or national, with many shrines of worship closer at hand.[8]

People from all walks of life went on pilgrimage. Saint Francis of Assisi in his *Fioretti* tells us the story of Louis VII, king of France, who paid a visit to Saint Egidio in Perugia under the complete anonymity of a pilgrim's garb and how God revealed to Egidio the true identity of his visitor (Saint Francis, 1957, pp. 91–2). Jerome tells us how his friend Paula, a Roman aristocrat, traveled in poverty to the Holy Land, preferring the sparse hospitality of the Christian monks to the luxury of high-placed family friends (Hunt, 1984, p. 82). The rich, however, often traveled in the relative comfort of their status, as masterly portrayed by Chaucer in his *Canterbury Tales*.[9] Pietro Della Valle, an eccentric and rich Roman nobleman, traveled to the Holy Land and beyond in the early 1600s, with a large company, "nine camels, two good horses and some small donkeys" (Della Valle, 1989, p. 69). "My arrival in Jerusalem," he tells us jokingly (this "will make you laugh"), "had been preceded by some rumour about me ... my arrival with more than a pilgrim's escort and in the manner of someone out of the ordinary ... the common people had taken me for the son of a king ..." (Della Valle, 1989, pp. 69, 71).

The rich could even afford paying someone to go on pilgrimage in their place.[10] A certain Reginald Lombard in 1306 went on pilgrimage to Compostela for Edward I, king of England. King Charles VI of France at the end of the fourteenth century sent a pilgrim to a number of sacred places across France and on to Compostela. An increasing number of wills contained bequests for hirelings to fulfill pilgrimage vows by proxy. Typical is William Newland's, who willed in 1425 that his goods be used to find a man "to go to Rome and to Ierusalem, and to haue their-of for his costes and labour L mare; a-nother for to go fro the Swerd in Fletstrete vn-to Caunterbury, barefot xs.; and a-nother to seynt Iames in Galis" (cited in Davidson and Dunn-Wood, 1993, p. 67).

Over the centuries, pilgrims have left behind a large number of travel diaries. The *Itinerarium Burdigalense*, the Bordeaux Itinerary, is certainly the first extant travel account known to us.[11] We have no name for its author.[12] He is simply known as the Pilgrim of Bordeaux. We do know that he came to the Holy Land starting in Bordeaux, in the *Aequitania* province,[13] in the year of God 333.[14] He left behind a short and terse account of his journey, for the most part no more than a list of staging posts and miles traveled: "City of Maximianopolis (18 miles). City of Jezreel (10 miles) ... City of Scythopolis (12 miles). ... City of Neapolis (15 miles)."[15] Considering that the Pilgrim of Bordeaux traveled by land 1,700 miles each way through the vast expanse of the Roman empire, the "sheer magnitude and extent of such an undertaking" cannot be exaggerated – indeed, a "mammoth effort," as Hunt remarks.[16] And a mammoth effort must have been the journey of another early pilgrim, the nun Egeria who traveled to the Holy Land some fifty years later, between 381 and 384 A.D., from even farther – "right from the other end of the earth," in her own words.[17] Egeria's account offers precious glimpses of a most remarkable woman, when she tells her "loving sisters" at home, with an air of complicity: "You know how inquisitive I am ..."[18] or when she describes her fortuitous encounter with one of her "dearest friends, a holy deaconess called Marthana. I had come to know her in Jerusalem when she was up there on pilgrimage. ... I simply cannot tell you how pleased we were to see each other again." Her desire to see as much as she can transpires through her pages – "the holy men were kind enough to show us everything," she tells us; "the holy men ... took me round all the biblical sites I kept asking to see," despite being "so unimportant a person as me." She is movingly torn between the desire to go home to her "sisters" and to see more.

> It was already three full years since my arrival in Jerusalem, and I had seen all the places which were the object of my pilgrimage, I felt that the time had come to return in God's name to my own country. But God also moved me with a desire to go to Syrian Mesopotamia.

Starting from these early pilgrims' accounts of travel to the Holy Land a literary genre emerged, based on stereotypical codes of writing (and behavior[19]): distances between cities, presence of hospices, hostels and churches, descriptions of worship sites, words in different languages, currencies needed and exchange rates, display of Christian pity, silence on the nonreligious aspects of the journey.[20] The desire to show to the ones who could not travel "the place where the feet of the Lord have stood" or to motivate the undecided to go and "set eyes on the traces of the Nativity, the Cross and the Passion, as though they were newly-made" must be the reason why so many pilgrims left accounts of their journeys.[21] Egeria, in addressing her cloister "loving sisters" back home, makes clear the purpose of her writing: That "*it may help you, loving sisters, the better to picture what happened in these places when you read the holy books of Moses*" (Wilkinson, 1981a, pp. 97–8; emphasis added). Thietmar de Mersebourg similarly wishes to offer his readers, through his account, a glimpse of the pleasure he experienced in visiting the Holy places in 1217.[22]

Authors would abundantly take material from one another – plagiarism must be seen in a context of respect to tradition and authority – some accounts having been produced by authors who never went to the Holy Land.[23] Pilgrims would be familiar with these works, some of which reached immense popularity in the later medieval period.[24] The line between travel account and travel guidebook often blurred. For sure, travel guidebooks were readily available – at the beginning of the thirteenth century, pilgrims could acquire guidebooks to the Holy Land before departure from Venice.[25] The twelfth-century anonymous *The Pilgrim's Guide* to Santiago de Compostela is "one of the classics of the genre."[26] The *Guide*, with its trenchant remarks on people and places, is still a fun read today and not only for the specialist or the religious.

> The Landes of Bordeaux ... is a desolate country, lacking in everything. ... The Gascons are loud-mouthed, talkative, given to

mockery, libidinous, drunken, greedy eaters, clad in rags and poverty-stricken … [In the Basque country] a barbarous tongue is spoken. … [The Navarreses are] a barbarous people … malignant, dark in colour, ugly of face, debauched, perverse …[27]

The guide gives plenty of advice and warns pilgrims against natural and man-made evils: "[T]he rivers between Estella and Longroño … are … poisonous"; the boatmen of the two rivers near the village of Saint-Jean de Sorde delight when their passengers drown because they can "appropriate the possessions of the dead"; "a Navarrese or a Basque will kill a Frenchman for a penny if he can" (Anonymous, 1992, pp. 14, 19, 23–4).

Indeed, danger, for body and soul, is a recurrent theme in the pilgrims' travel literature. And for good reasons, perhaps. According to Davidson and Dunn-Wood (1993, p. 60) the death toll among medieval pilgrims was high (with both weather and people as the enemy). In the twelfth century, one out of ten pilgrims to Compostela died on the way. Alfani reports that tens of pilgrims would die in Rome during jubilee years crumpled and suffocated in the streets and churches by the sheer multitude of people (1750, pp. 14, 30, 60, 63). He tells us that, in 1350, in occasion of the second Roman jubilee year,

> men and women of every state and condition traveled to Rome in incredible and wonderful numbers. … They patiently put up with the discomforts of the body, because it was unbelievably cold, with ice, and snow, and torrential rain; and the roads everywhere broken up and torn … full of people day and night … with not enough hostels and houses to shelter horses and people. But the Germans and the Hungarians, in flocks, and in enormous crowds, huddled together at night to keep warm around big fires. (Alfani, 1750, p. 29)

Nature, no doubt, was not a pilgrims' friend. The Anglo-Saxon Saewulf, who traveled to the Holy Land by sea around 1101–03, left a most vivid description of the perils of sea travel. In the very prologue of his travel book, Saewulf breaks the law of genre by talking about the perils of sea voyage instead of the most typical holy motive of his journey: "[T]he violence of the waves … waves higher than mountains … men and women submerged … pieces of ships strewn all around … terrible noise of the sea … savagery of the wind … bodies cut to pieces floating … more than a thousand men and women died that day. No eye ever saw more misery in one day …"[28] Quite an irony to have a name like Saewulf and be so terrified of the sea! But he was hardly alone. Joinville tells us of "the terror of country folks suffering from sea sickness and the apprehension given by the sight of the depth of the ocean" (cited in Richard, 1981, p. 77). Della Valle may be unique in his witty remarks on sea travel: "[U]s all, even the sailors … vomited in unison, all laughing and making fun of each other" (Della Valle, 1989, p. 4). Yet, not even Della Valle was laughing when aboard the

Venetian galleon *Gran Delfino* that took him to the Holy Land, "there spread ...
a type of infection ... death made sure of its tithes ... before I left the ship I
witnessed the burial of three people" (Della Valle, 1989, p. 3).

But humans were perhaps an even worse enemy. Along the Dalmatian coasts
pirates lurked to make sea travel unsafe, under any weather (Tenenti, 1959,
1961). Saewulf encountered those as well, more than once (Saewulf, in Huygens
and Pryor, 1995, lines 149–56, 565–77, 590). And land travel had its assortments
of brigands, bandits, and highway robbers (Sumption, 1975, pp. 180–3). "Those
who lived on the pilgrimage roads regarded pilgrims as fair game to be
plundered at will" (Sumption, 1975, p. 192). Egeria gives us hints of the dangers
of early travel in the Holy Land: "[W]e dismissed the soldiers who had provided
us with an escort on behalf of the Roman authorities when we went through the
danger areas. We no longer needed military protection ..." (Wilkinson, 1981a,
p. 103). Centuries later, Saewulf reminds his reader that the road from Jaffa to
Jerusalem "was very dangerous, because the Saracens ... were hiding in the
caves ... awake day and night, always keeping a look out for someone to
attack."[29] Thietmar similarly tells us of "caves full of thieves" – *"speluncam
latronum, ubi plures conueniebant latrones"* (in Laurent, 1852, lines X–21–22).
In 1500, for the eighth Roman jubilee, Pope Alexander VI "ordered Governors,
Rectors, and Vicars of the Papal State and the feudal Barons ... to keep the roads
free of assassins" (Alfani, 1750, p. 97).

No less dangerous was travel for the soul than for the body, with the less than
holy crowding the pilgrims' paths. In inns and hostels sleeping arrangements
saw several strangers in the same bed, several beds to a room.[30] After all, beds
were valuable commodities – William Shakespeare willed his second-best bed
to his wife (Loxton, 1978, p. 108). Things were even worse on board of ships
(Hunt, 1984, p. 72). Della Valle's *Gran Delfino* was crowded with

> about five-hundred people, both men and women, including soldiers,
> merchants, and other passengers, among whom there were Catholic
> Christians, heretics of various sects, Greeks, Armenians, Turks,
> Persians, Hebrews, Italians from just about every city, Frenchmen,
> Spaniards, Portuguese, Englishmen, Germans, Flemings ...

"Such mixed company should have been very much to my taste," acknowledges
the young and dazzling Della Valle in search of adventure. And yet, even for
him, "there were just too many of us, and this created all kinds of anxieties and
confusions."[31] No doubt, as Sumption put it (1975, p. 186), a "galley was a scene
of unending chaos."

The Holy places themselves were not so holy, not for everyone anyway.
Burchard of Mount Sion, a Dominican monk of German origin who visited
Palestine in 1280, wrote in his book *Descriptio Terrae Sanctae (A Description
of the Holy Land*, which underwent at least twenty editions): "Whenever
someone was a malefactor such as a murderer, a robber, a thief, or an adulterer,
he used to cross the sea ... Once being here ... they return to their 'vomit,' doing

the worse of the worst" (cited in Coleman and Elsner, 1995, p. 97). In 1217, the German pilgrim Thietmar called Acre, the crusaders' capital, "the city of vice."[32] Not surprisingly, church canons forbade the clergy to enter inns and hostels (Hunt, 1984, p. 70). In letters of advice to professed ascetics, both Gregory of Nyssa and Jerome warned monks and virgins on the hazards of pilgrimages. "How is it possible," lamented Gregory, "to pass impassively through places where passions lurk?" (cited in Hunt, 1984, pp. 70, 91). "Those who go on pilgrimage," Thomas à Kempis put it, "rarely become saints," or, in Erasmus's version of the same tune, "Those who travel widely, rarely become hollowed" (cited in Davidson and Dunn-Wood, 1993, p. 73).

In light of the dangers and of Church's opposition, why would so many be willing to risk going on pilgrimage,[33] although precisely how many, we may never know?[34] No doubt, the first place to look for answers must be the profoundly religious *weltanschauung* of the medieval world. As Jerome put it, in his *epitaphium* for his friend Paula, the main goal of Holy Land pilgrims, surely, must have been:

> To worship at the place where the feet of the Lord have stood is the task of faith, and to have set eyes on the traces of the Nativity, the Cross and the Passion, as though they were newly-made.[35]

Certainly, the material benefits of a pilgrimage were meager. A papal license to Jerusalem (*licentia Romani pontificis*) granted pilgrims:[36] A three-year truce for the security of home and property; assurances against civil and criminal suits during the absence; a grant of stays in suits brought against them for debt; a letter by the Bishop commending them to the hospitality of hostelries and religious houses on the road;[37] access to special facilities for borrowing money. And yet, for as meager as these benefits were, they must have provided enough of an "incentive for the less than spiritually pure to undertake the journey."[38] Already in 396, the Council of Nîmes sought to prevent the abuse of the charity of local churches "on the pretext of pilgrimage" (Hunt, 1984, p. 65).

Religious and material motives notwithstanding, there may well have been other reasons for medieval men and women to venture out into the unknown, leaving everything behind. The quaint sociological traditional society – of Tönnies's *gemeinschaft* and *gesellschaft*, of Simmel's concentric affiliations – may not have seemed so quaint from within, from inside the smallest of the circles; not to all anyway. Pilgrimages, however risky, would have certainly provided for some a welcome break from the overbearing, all-scrutinizing, "panoptical" medieval society (see Foucault, 1979, pp. 195–228). Even war has its morbid appeal, as Ernst Jünger annotates in his diary of World War One: "The war had entered into us like wine. We had set out in a rain of flowers to seek the death of heroes. ... *[A]nything rather than stay at home* ..."[39]

Pilgrimages were one of medieval society's ways of breaking the norms, of passing the limits of the everyday, of seeing new things, of meeting new people, of mixing the sexes, of not shaving, of not bathing,[40] of even walking naked under the pretext of that having been the true way of Jesus.[41] And compared to another way of escaping – joining an army – a pilgrimage was less dangerous.[42]

It is these aspects of the pilgrim's experience that, for Victor and Edith Turner (1978), give pilgrimages a distinctive "liminal" character, where "the social and cultural relations defining a community are temporarily abandoned and individuals are in a social space where very unusual rituals and laws apply." The pilgrimage experience equalizes rich and poor, man and woman, young and old, sick and healthy, all under the same pilgrim costume. It unites people into a *communitas*, however temporary, based on the shared affirmation of their faith.

> Pilgrimage, then, has some of the attributes of liminality in passage rites; release from mundane structure; homogenization of status; simplicity of dress and behaviour; *communitas*; ordeal; reflection on the meaning of basic religious and cultural values; ritualized enactment of correspondences between religious paradigms and shared human experiences; emergence of the integral person from multiple personae ... (Turner and Turner, 1978, p. 34)

And yet, this "melting-pot" power of pilgrimages can only be limited. In fact, for Eade and Sallnow (1991, p. 5), "the maintenance and ... reinforcement of social boundaries and distinctions" may be rather more typical. Pilgrimages are a "realm of competing discourses" (Eade and Sallnow, 1991, p. 5). Pilgrimages mixed the sacred and the profane. The figure of the pilgrim itself masked the holy and the criminal, the religious wanderer and the political exile, the pilgrim of penance and the pilgrim of penalty.[43]

Voyages of Discovery

On October 2, 1492, the Genoese Christopher Columbus "discovered" America.[44] It was not just a lucky event. It had taken nearly two centuries of preparation to get there.[45] That long had passed, almost to the year, since the 1291 ill-fated expedition of two other Genoese, the Vivaldi brothers, Ugolino and Vadino. They had set off from Genoa and had sailed through the pillars of Hercules to go *ad partes Indiae per mare oceanum* never to be heard from again. Their tiny galleys – the *Allegranza* and *Sant'Antonio* – good enough for Mediterranean coastal sailing were no match for the Atlantic. Not that the three caravels of Columbus's first voyage were much bigger: The *Pinta* and *Niña* were about seventy tons each and the *Santa María* was one hundred tons.[46] But the caravel's design – "purely Portuguese in its origin" (Baker, 1937, p. 64) – made it "an ideal ship for [oceanic] exploration" with its combination of safety, speed, size, and maneuverability (Chaunu, 1979, pp. 158, 243–6).

The Portuguese had not only designed the caravel to fit their needs of Atlantic exploration. They had also systematically accumulated a wealth of knowledge on oceanic navigation.[47] As Thomas Stevens, a Jesuit missionary to India, annotated in 1579, "there is not a fowl that appeareth or sign in the air or in the sea that ... [the Portuguese] have not written down" (cited in Landes, 1996, p. 20; also, p. 23). Throughout the fourteenth and fifteenth centuries, little by little, the Portuguese had pushed further and further south along the coast of Africa, until Bartholomeu Dias reached Cape Good Hope (1487–1488). Vasco da Gama's own circumnavigation of Africa toward India, between 1497 and 1499, capitalized on the latest technical equipment and on the accumulated knowledge of prevailing Atlantic currents, winds, and weather.[48]

Columbus was the right man at the right time in the final adventure to the West. "He had assimilated what had been learnt during the long Afro-Portuguese preparation, and applied it all at once to the new demands of sailing east-west" (Chaunu, 1979, p. 159). Columbus himself may have had a different view of Chaunu's use of the expression "all at once." In fact, he would miss no opportunity to tell of the long humiliating years spent waiting at the court of the sovereigns of Spain, "expounding, as well as I could, how great services might in this [voyage to the west] be rendered ..."[49] He opens his letter to the sovereigns, after his third voyage, with that reminder. Everyone "held it [the voyage] to be impossible ... On this matter I spent six or seven years of deep anxiety ... one and all laughed it to scorn ... " And he closes the *lettera rarissima*,[50] after the fourth and last voyage, yet again with that reminder. "I spent seven years at your royal court, where everyone to whom I spoke of this undertaking said that it was ridiculous."

But in spite of everyone's prediction, Columbus succeeded in his voyage and his discovery paved the way to further discoveries and to the colonization of the Americas. The massive work of reconstruction of trade patterns between Seville and the new world performed by French historians Huguette and Pierre Chaunu on the basis of data uncovered at the *Casa de la Contratación* has made one thing clear: From less than a handful of ships a year crossing the Atlantic in the first few years of the sixteenth century the number steadily rose decade after decade throughout the century (Chaunu and Chaunu, 1955).

These sailors crossed the oceans in the name of God and of their sovereigns, in a curious mixture of sacred and profane, of religious and economic motifs. Many, like the earlier Christian pilgrims, left behind journals of their voyages.[51] Columbus annotates in his journal: "I took possession of all these lands in her royal name [Isabel, queen of Spain]" (1969, p. 265). Pigafetta, an Italian nobleman on board Magellan's ship in the first voyage around the world, wrote: "On top of the highest mountain there we [Magellan and his crew] set up a very tall cross, as a sign that the said land belonged to the King of Spain."[52] Magellan also tried "to induce them [local people] to become Christians ... the captain told them how God had made the heaven, the earth, and the sea, and all other things in the world ..." (Pigafetta, 1969, p. 77). Cortés as well "took formal possession of this country in His Majesty's name" (Díaz, 1963, pp. 37, 71, 199).

Religious motifs were dear to the heart of the Portuguese and Spanish Catholic sovereigns – voyages of discoveries of new lands potentially meant more souls to be converted to Catholicism, more souls to be rescued from eternal perdition. Columbus himself was animated by a sort of Franciscan mysticism. Indeed, it was the monks of the Franciscan community La Rábida who, taken by Columbus's messianic vision, had introduced him to the sovereigns of Spain.[53] But economic motifs no doubt played a dominant role. Cortés, in his first encounter with Montezuma, the Aztec king, curiously mixes the sacred and the profane, when he explains to the Aztec ruler the reasons for their journey:[54]

• *The sacred.* "We were Christians and worshiped one God alone, named Jesus Christ ... and what they worshiped as gods were not gods but devils, which were evil things ... Then he carefully expounded the creation of the world, how we were all brothers ... and how such a brother as our great Emperor, grieving for the perdition of so many souls ... had sent us to tell him this, so that they might put a stop to it ... no more human sacrifices ... no more robbery and sodomy ... he begged Montezuma to do as he was asked."
• *The profane.* "Then our Captain informed them ["Indians"] through our interpreters that we came from a distant country, and were vassals of a great emperor called Charles who ruled over many great lords and chieftains, and that *they must accept him as their lord*, which would be greatly to their advantage."

What advantages Cortés had in mind for the Indians is not clear. But the advantages to the Spaniards are clear enough. Gold and spices were the goods Mediterranean people were after. Contrary to the northern economies (based on copper or silver coinage) their economies were based on a gold monetary system (Chaunu, 1979, pp. 103–4). "The seizure of gold at its source was an important development in [Portugal's] trade with Africa" (Chaunu, 1979, p. 99).

"Gold is most excellent," Columbus wrote in 1503 in his *lettera rarissima* to the sovereigns of Spain. "Gold constitutes treasure, and anyone who has it can do whatever he wants in the world. With it he can succeed in bringing souls to Paradise" (Columbus, 1969, p. 300). Columbus meant what he wrote, and not just in light of the lucrative Church business of the sale of indulgences which was about to tear the old Europe apart. Toward the end of his life, Columbus increasingly saw himself as the man entrusted by God to help rebuild Jerusalem and Mount Sion "by Christian hands," as written in the *Book of Prophecy.* "Who will offer himself for this task? ... I pledge myself," Columbus concludes (1969, p. 301; see, Thacher, 1904, vol. 3, p. 501). He would urge the fulfilment of this "wild purpose" onto his son Diego and heirs (Thacher, 1904, vol. 3, p. 502). That is why gold was "most excellent," at least for Columbus.

Gold runs through the pages of all the accounts of the new land.[55] Perhaps not surprisingly the native inhabitants of the Americas had their way of quenching the conquistadores' thirst for gold: "The Indians hated the Spaniards for their tyranny and cruelty ... Those whom they took alive, especially the generals ... they would pour [molten] gold into their mouths ... and taunt them for their greed saying: 'Eat, Christian, eat this gold.'"[56] If captains could find sailors and investors for their enterprises, it was only because of the untold profits to be made. Bernal Díaz (1963, p. 27), in his gripping eyewitness account of Cortés's conquest of Mexico, wrote:

> As the report had spread that these lands were very rich, and ... there was gold, those settlers and soldiers in the island who possessed no Indians were eager and greedy to go. So we quickly collected two hundred and forty companions.

The enormous differences between prices of goods at home and in America, India, and China found people willing to risk their lives and their capital in maritime expeditions.[57] As the Dominican priest Bartolomé de Las Casas wrote of the conquistadores in his *Short Account of the Destruction of the Indies* in 1542 (1992, p. 13): "They have set out to line their pockets with gold and to amass private fortunes as quickly as possible so that they can then assume a status quite at odds with that into which they were born."[58] Even Columbus (1969, p. 270) admits that the aim of the settlers of Hispaniola is "to amass all they can and return home speedily," and that they can do so because "gold is being collected so freely that a man may have five marks in four hours."

Profits were high. But so were the risks,[59] and the ones who made it back were lucky. Chaunu (1969, p. 278) estimates "only one chance in two, on average, for each of those who attempt the adventure [the five-year return journey Seville-Manila], of ever coming back to live the rest of his life with his parents." Chaunu and Chaunu (1955, Vol. VI, Tome VI, pp. 857–957) give a long list by year, cause of loss, and other indicators, of ships lost in the Atlantic traffic between Seville and the new world. But too many returned for all to be lucky. "There was method to their madness," writes Landes of these audacious sea voyagers (Landes, 1996, p. 22). In trying to minimize risks, they coasted as much as possible. Tenenti's map of the Venetian vessels that shipwrecked or ran aground between 1592 and 1609 is full of some 300 dots along the Mediterranean coasts; none in the open seas (Tenenti, 1959, pp. 64–5). They also hopped, whenever possible, from island to island.[60] They traveled in convoys.[61] They took local pilots on boards.[62] They stuck to familiar routes.[63]

By luck or design, the discovery of a new world was to change the course of history. The *mare nostrum* lost to the Ocean Sea its privileged geographic and economic position. And in one of those ironies of history, we know that world not by Columbus's name, but by that of one of his contemporaries: the Florentine Amerigo Vespucci. Columbus – who had bargained with the sovereigns of Spain, for himself, his sons, and his successors, the lofty titles of "Admiral of the Ocean Sea," of Don, Governor, Viceroy; who had bargained for a coat of arms with the royal colors; who had bargained for profitable shares of the riches coming to the crown from his discoveries, insisting to have it all in writing[64] – with history, he did not strike nearly as good a bargain. History denied him the eponymic prize for getting there first (Merton, 1973, pp. 298–302). The *Universalis Cosmographia*, the first geographic map with an image of the new world, published by Martin Waldseemüller in 1507, had the name "America" written over the new continent.[65] In 1509, the time of a second edition of his work, Waldseemüller rectified the error and deleted the name America from the map. Alas, too late. The name America was to stick, even against several more attempts to name the new world "Columbia."

Ways of Seeing

"The way we see things is affected by what we know or what we believe," wrote Berger in a fascinating little book titled *Ways of Seeing*. The Pilgrim of Bordeaux has eyes only for what is Christian, for the holy places of the Old and New Testament. "Seeing, maybe, is believing, but believing also ensures that there is plenty to see," Robin Lane Fox wrote (cited in A. Palmer, 1994, p. 45). Outside the holy places nothing seems to interest the Pilgrim of Bordeaux. The only reference he makes outside that world is to the tomb of Hannibal. Of Rome, which he saw on his return journey, he has nothing to say, just another staging post, dutifully annotated, among countless others. Egeria similarly describes in great detail countryside and gardens, but ignores the beauty of Antioch (not "the product of an urban environment"; A. Palmer, 1994, p. 44).

What Columbus saw and how he interpreted what he saw depended upon his fundamentally medieval world view (Quinn, 1976, p. 637). "Every image embodies a way of seeing. ... Yet, although every image embodies a way of seeing, our perception or appreciation of an image depends also upon our own way of seeing" (Berger, 1972, p. 10). Columbus's deeply Christian beliefs and his knowledge of the classical geography and travel literature led him astray on more than one occasion. In a letter dispatched to the sovereigns of Spain during his third voyage (1498–1500), the Admiral gives full credence to the legends of the Earthly Paradise.[66] "Holy Scripture testifies that Our Lord made the Earthly Paradise in which he placed the Tree of Life" (Columbus, 1969, p. 220). In a few spirited pages, Columbus reviews old and new arguments, he summons old and new authorities, he brings to bear all the evidence that he has personally amassed in his three voyages (Columbus, 1969, pp. 217–18):

> I have always read that the world of land and sea is spherical. All authorities and the recorded experiments of Ptolemy and the rest ... have constantly drawn and confirmed this picture, which they held to be true. Now, ... I have found such great irregularities that I have come to the following conclusions concerning the world: That it is not round as they describe it, but the shape of a pear, which is round everywhere except at the stalk, where it juts out a long way; or that it is like a round ball, on part of which is something like a woman's nipple. This point on which the protuberance stands is the highest and nearest to the sky ... the place where all land and islands end.

He is confident that he has reached that point, and that that point is where the Earthly Paradise lies. "I believe that the Earthly Paradise lies here," he assures the Spanish sovereigns.[67]

It is the Admiral's stubborn conviction of having reached the westernmost shores of China (Cathay) during his voyages that may have deprived him of making a most remarkable discovery: That, in fact, he had discovered a new and unknown continent and thousand more miles separated him from China. Having reached Veragua along the coasts of Central America during his fourth and last voyage, he who listened eagerly to every whisper about gold and uselessly followed the leads, remarkably, paid no attention to the Indians' stories about the province of Ciguare

> which ... lies inland nine days' journey westward. They say that there is a vast quantity of gold there ... that Ciguare is surrounded by water, and that ten days' journey away is the river Ganges. These lands seem to lie in the same relation to Veragua as Tortosa to Fuentarabia or Pisa to Venice. (Columbus, 1969, pp. 287–8)

It appears that the Admiral fully understood the geographical implications of these stories ("in the same relation to Veragua as Tortosa to Fuentarabia or Pisa to Venice"), that he may have sensed that a handful of inland miles away lay an even larger ocean than the one he had crossed. Yet, in that same letter to the sovereigns of Spain, he still talks about the River Ganges and Cathay ("I arrived on 13 May at the province of Mago [in Cuba], which borders on Cathay," p. 294, and, again, on p. 298).[68] He died clinging to his beliefs. In his testament, he insisted that he should be remembered as the Admiral of the Indies and that such title should be bestowed upon his descendants.

In comparison to Columbus's fundamentally medieval world view, Vespucci ushers in a *new world*. For one thing, contrary to Columbus, Vespucci clearly makes a claim of having reached a new world. When his work is first published probably in Florence in late 1502 or the beginning of 1503, the book has the title *Mundus novus*, New World. Second, he consciously challenges the firmly-held Aristotelian belief that there could be no life below the Tropic of Capricorn that he has just visited. "My navigation refutes that theory, clearly showing to everyone that it is false and far from any truth," we read in the very first lines of the *Mundus novus* (Vespucci, 1984, p. 89). In the context of the new Florentine Renaissance culture, this is a major blow to the medieval view of authority, of the *ipse dixit*. When in doubt, trust experience, not authority. Twenty years later, on 18 March 1523, Pietro Pomponazzi, philosopher at the University of Bologna, during a lecture on Aristotle, would tell his students of having heard of a navigator who found hundreds of islands below the Tropic of Capricorn "not only inhabitable, but inhabited."[69] So, whom should we believe, the navigator or Aristotle's arguments? "I am of the opinion," Pomponazzi tells his students, "that when experience is in disagreement with arguments, we must stick with experience and let go of arguments." Vespucci did not just discover a new physical world, but, perhaps more importantly, a new ideal world. Columbus's medieval world gives way, here, to Vespucci's Renaissance world. The new world of Bacon and Galileo's *sensate esperienze* (and *matematiche dimostrazioni*) is not too far away (Galileo, 1964, pp. 130, 150, 165).

"It was not the innocent, but the selective eye which first viewed America" (Elliott, 1976, p. 17). That is certainly true for the gold Columbus saw everywhere. Yet, we know, there was no gold to speak of in the lands he had touched – always to be found in vast quantities in the next island, further to the west, a few days' journey to the north ... Because he *wanted* to see gold. He *needed* to see gold. Whatever his personal dreams were, he needed to entice others with some material inducements to make *his* dreams come true. In a letter to the queen and king of Spain, "written aboard the caravel off the Canary Islands, 15 February 1493," Columbus (1969, p. 122; emphasis added) wrote:

> In conclusion, to speak of the results of this very hasty voyage, their Highnesses can see that I will give them as much gold as they require, *if they will render me some very slight assistance*; also I will give them all the spices and cotton they want ... as much aloes as they ask and as many slaves, who will be taken from the idolaters.

He had similarly deceived himself and others at the start of his journey. "The world is small and six parts of it are land, the seventh part being entirely covered by water" (Columbus, 1969, p. 289). With this claim, and a letter from Toscanelli to back it up, Columbus had approached European sovereigns to obtain funding for his voyage of discovery; with this claim he had tried to convince pilots and sailors to join him. Would Columbus have been able to convince anyone to back his dreams, had he known the real distance (12,000 miles to Chipangu, Japan, instead of his estimated 2,760)?[70] More to the point, would he have embarked upon his journey?

Seeing is relational, always relative to one's "position in time and space," to where and when, to the soldier and the priest, the pilgrim of penance and the pilgrim of penalty (Berger, 1972, p. 18). It "comes before words, and can never be quite covered by them ... We only see what we look at. To look is an act of choice. ...We never look at just one thing; we are always looking at the relation between things and ourselves" (Berger, 1972, pp. 8, 9). Indeed, Columbus's description of both places and people are always *comparative*: To Castile, Andalusia, and Spain; things are always "different from ours."[71] Bartolomé de Las Casas, in his summary of Columbus's log-book of the first voyage, annotated: "SUNDAY, 28 October [1492]. ... The Admiral says he had never seen a more beautiful country. ... He says that this island is the most beautiful that eyes have ever seen" (Columbus, 1969, pp. 75–6). Hernando Colón, Columbus's son, who accompanied the father in his fourth voyage, similarly wrote (Columbus, 1969, p. 83): "This country, Most Serene Highness, is so enchantingly beautiful that it surpasses all others in charm and beauty as much as the light of day surpasses night."

The first images of the new world dispatched by both Columbus and Vespucci build upon, and reaffirm, a long tradition of the marvelous, well established in European popular culture by the first medieval land travelers to the far east, from the merchant Marco Polo to the Franciscan friars Odoric of Pordenone, William of Rubruquis, and John de Piano Carpini. In particular, Marco Polo's account of his travels to the far east, first known by its French title *Livre de merveilles du monde*, had fueled the popular imagination across Europe. Already, at the beginning of the fourteenth century, the book had reached immense popularity in several different languages. And no less popular had been another travel account, real or fictional as it may be, that began to circulate in Europe after 1356, *The Travels of Sir John Mandeville.*[72] The word "marvel" is used by Mandeville throughout his book to convey the idea of something extraordinary.[73] Columbus, after describing the natural beauty of the places he encountered in his first voyage, concludes: "All this is marvellous."[74] "I have not found the human monsters which many people expected," Columbus informs his readers. Even so, he has found plenty of wonders: People who "go naked ... men and women alike"; people with "no religion ... firmly convinced that I have come from the sky ... "; "people ... born with tails" and "people who ... eat human flesh" (Mandeville had talked about cannibals as well; 1983, p. 174). He has also found "Women [who] do not follow feminine occupations but use cane bows and arrows."

The use of such categories as the "wonderful," the "marvelous," and the "fabulous," the mixing of fact and fiction, of the old and the new, are found in the very early documents concerning the new world.[75] In the first extant letter with news of the discovery, that of the Italian Hanibal Januarius to his brother, an ambassador from the Duke of Ferrara to the Court at Milan, we read: "In the month of August last ... one named Collomba ... in thirty-four days ... came to a *great* isle ... where men are born with tails" (in Thacher, 1903, vol. 2, pp. 8–9; emphasis added). The learned Peter Martyr, later to become one of the main historians of *la conquista*, in May 1493 wrote a letter to Count Borromeus with a handful of lines on the news: "[A] certain Christopher Columbus, a Ligurian, ... penetrated to that province which was believed to be *fabulous*" (in Thacher, 1903, vol. 1, p. 54; emphasis added). By September, Peter Martyr had become quite aware of the importance of the news, as we read in another letter to Count Tendilla and the Archbishop of Granada: "Attention, you two most wise and venerable men, and hear of a new discovery. You remember Columbus, the Ligurian, who persisted ... that one could pass over by way of the Western Antipodes to a new hemisphere of the globe ... He is returned safe and declares to have found *wonderful* things."[76]

Yet, it would be Amerigo Vespucci's writings, not Columbus's, that were widely circulated throughout Europe in the early 1500s, deeply shaping people's perceptions of the new world (Quinn, 1976, p. 647). In the first letter sent to Lorenzo de' Medici on 28 July 1500, Vespucci writes of being so overwhelmed by the beauty of the new lands that "we thought we were in the Earthly

Paradise."[77] In the *Mundus novus* he similarly acknowledges: "If there is such thing as an Earthly Paradise, for sure, it must not be far from here." Just like in Mandeville, the word "marvelous" is recurrent in Vespucci's writing. Vespucci's very narrative is full of wonder. In the first encounter between the Europeans and the native Americans, "we saw a grand multitude of people on the beach who stared at us as a thing of wonder." Like Mandeville and Columbus, Vespucci met people who eat human flesh and who spend their time fighting with their neighbors so as to secure their food supply. He met people who go around completely naked, men and women alike, and people "so tall, that each of them was taller, kneeling down, than myself standing."

In a second letter to Lorenzo de' Medici written in 1502, Vespucci goes into greater details on the habits of the people he met, people he now defines as "rational animals," naked, with no laws or religious beliefs, with no private property, no kings nor lords, living together five or six hundred to a house, only eating human flesh taken from enemy populations, and taking as many women as they want (Vespucci, 1984, pp. 79–80). Like Columbus's letters, Vespucci's private letters to Lorenzo de' Medici were copied and circulated in manuscript form among learned humanists. But it is the publication in printed form of Vespucci's *Mundus novus* (New World) that made the images of the new world truly popular across the whole of Europe. Within a few weeks of its first publication, *Mundus novus* was reprinted in Venice, Paris, Antwerp, Cologne, Nuremberg, Strasbourg, and Rostock. It was soon translated from Latin into Flemish and German. In 1507 the book was published in Italian and reprinted five times in twelve years. In *Mundus novus*,[78] he refers again to the unusual customs of the inhabitants, who go naked, eat human flesh, have no private property, kings, or laws, and no religion, market, money, or marriage. He writes of the incredible lustfulness of the women, who, "to satisfy their dishonest pleasure," give men a herbal potion to drink that will "inflate their members so that it grows enormously"; "and when that is not enough, they use certain poisonous animals to bite the member until it enlarges" – a "habit far from any human living." This dream of women and men, not to mention twenty first-century pharmaceutical companies, does have a side effect: "many of the men lose their testicles and become eunuchs." Most unfortunate. In *Mundus novus*, he writes about these people's "truly epicurean way of life," where "everyone has sex with anyone, regardless of family relationships, the son with the mother, and the brother with the sister; they do so publicly, like brute animals; whenever and wherever they meet they copulate."

These images of the "rational animal" would endure in European popular culture, and vie for attention, with later, very different images of the people of the Americas and their great civilizations (in particular, Aztec, Maya, and Incas). Bernal Díaz (1963, p. 214) gives the following vivid image of the first sight from a distance of the Aztec cities around the capital Mexico:[79]

And when we saw all those cities and villages built in the water, and other great towns on dry land, and that straight and level causeway leading to Mexico we were astounded. These great towns and *cues* [temples] and buildings rising from the water, all made of stone, seemed like an enchanted vision from the tale of Amadis. Indeed, some of our soldiers asked whether it was not all a dream. ... It was all so wonderful that I do not know how to describe this first glimpse of things never heard of, seen or dreamed of before.

The description of the capital city of Mexico, as seen from the top of the tallest *cue* gives us one of Bernal Díaz's (1963, pp. 234–5) most powerful passages:

Then Montezuma took him [Cortés] by the hand, and told him to look at his great city and all the other cities standing in the water, and the many others ... So we stood there looking ... We saw the three causeways that led into Mexico ... We saw the fresh water which came from Chapultepec to supply the city, and the bridges ... a great number of canoes ... *cues* and shrines in these cities that looked like gleaming white towers and castles: a marvelous sight. ... [O]n the causeways were other small towers and shrines built like fortresses. ... Some of our soldiers who had been in many parts of the world, in Constantinople, in Rome, and all over Italy, said that they had never seen a market so well laid out, so large, so orderly, and so full of people.[80]

Silence and Emphasis

"Every description of reality must select from it; by leaving certain elements out it produces not just the 'presences' of what it includes but the absences of what it excludes" (Alexander, 1987, p. 34). In an abundant pilgrimage literature of terse narratives consisting mostly of short descriptions of the Holy places themselves, distances between cities, places of hospitality, currencies needed in each country and exchange rates, basic words in the different languages, dangers to guard against – in other words, of what is of interest to a Christian – references to the nonChristian worlds are rare.[81] We may then be surprised to hear Antonino of Piacenza, who traveled to the Holy Land in the second half of the sixth century, tell his readers that "*the beauty of the women* [in the city of Nazaret] is such that they could not be any more beautiful."[82] Nikulas of Munkathvera, an abbot who traveled from Iceland to Jerusalem around 1154, left us a brief description of his voyage – a description mostly made up of distances in miles and days between cities and of any significant churches, hostels, and hospices present in the various cities in a tradition first set by the Pilgrim of Bordeaux. We may be similarly surprised to read what he has to say about Siena, "a beautiful city, with episcopal see at the Church of Santa Maria; here there are *the most attractive women*" (in Stopani, 1991, p. 69, emphasis added).

For those who traveled to the Holy Land, Muslims' polygamy greatly roused their curiosity.[83] Thietmar spent the night in a hotel where he "saw a Saracen sleep with his seven wives in the same bed. And the women all wore trousers, with vests coming down to their knees ..." and that "the pope [in Damascus] keeps several virgins in his house and bedroom, whom he can take where he wants, when he wants, as many times and ways as he wants" (in Laurent, 1852, lines VII–4–5 and XII–7–8; see also IX–1–3 and IX–22–25). If Muslims titillate the curiosity of the medieval European world, Jews are regarded with suspicion. Mandeville (1983, p. 166) reports that "in time of the Antichrist ... Jews will sally out and do much harm to Christian men. ... [A]ll the Jews in the different parts of the world learn to speak Hebrew," so as to recognize each other "by their speech." They will march together "into Christendom to destroy Christian men." Popular culture views of "the other" have deep roots in history.

In their almost complete indifference to the nonChristian world, medieval Christian pilgrims implicitly tell us something about themselves, about what they regarded as important and worth recording (whether in their eyes or in the eyes of their readers). In Roland Barthes's words (1970, p. 149): "We know that the absence of a sign can be significant too." Oddly enough, it is not just the external world that is not worth recording. Most pilgrims are indifferent to their own inner world, to their emotions. Autobiographic and personal references are almost entirely absent in the genre, particularly in the earlier period.[84] "Finding those touches, those glimpses," Davidson and Dunn-Wood remark (1993, pp. 73), "is often the most rewarding aspect of the day's study." We find one of those glimpses in Jerome's *epitaphium* for his friend Paula. Jerome tells us how Paula was overcome by emotions when she reached the Holy Land.

> She prostrated herself before the Cross ... Entering the Sepulchre of the Resurrection, she kissed the Stone ... with faithful lips she touched the place where the Lord's body had lain ... Jerusalem is witness to the tears she shed and to her moanings: The Lord is her witness, to whom she prayed. (Wilkinson, 1981b, p. 20)

Nearly a thousand years later, Anselme Adorno in his *Itineraire d'Anselme Adorno en Terre Sainte (1470–1471)* wrote how visitors to the Holy Land "no matter how hardened and distant from the faith, would cry and humbly beat their chest in remorse" (cited in Richard, 1984, p. 148). Domenico Laffi wrote:

> On seeing it [the city of St James] we fell to our knees, and in our great joy tears fell from our eyes and we began to sing the *Te Deum*. But ... we found ourselves unable to pronounce the words for the abundance of tears which gushed from our eyes ... (Laffi, 1673, p. 49)

Hardened conquistadores are even more silent about their emotions. The emphasis is on other character traits: endurance, toughness, leadership. "Such are the hardships to be endured when discovering new lands," tells us Bernal Díaz (1963, p. 25), "no one can imagine their severity who has not himself endured them." Pigafetta wrote that Magellan was "so valiant and noble a captain ... more constant in a very high hazard and great affair than ever was any other. He endured hunger better than all the others" (Pigafetta, 1969, pp. 88–9). Pigafetta's description of the last few moments of Magellan's life – surrounded by Indians, with arrows, lances, and javelins being hurled at him from all sides – consigns to history the *portrait of a hero*.[85] Díaz is keen to let his readers know in the "Preliminary Note" to his *The Conquest of New Spain* that, "being no scholar," he decided to write the book "to extol the adventures that befell us, and the heroic deeds we performed during the conquest of New Spain" (Díaz, 1963, p. 203). In this world of supermen, it is astonishing to read of soldiers pissing in their pants for fear before a pitched battle with the Aztecs.[86]

Rather than ruthless adventurers motivated by lust and greed, they paint themselves as *disinterested* leaders deeply *concerned* with the welfare of the local populations. "I allowed nothing to be taken, not even the value of a pin," Columbus tells us. "I did not sail on this voyage [the fourth and last voyage, of 1502–4] to gain honour or wealth" (Columbus, 1969, pp. 71, 304). The syntagms they choose to describe their actions are typically "syntagms of leadership" (Barthes, 1970, p. 149; Loesberg, 1983). In a letter written by Dr. Chapa we find a wide range of those syntagms:[87] "The Admiral sent"; "the Admiral went"; "the Admiral would not allow"; "the Admiral asked"; "the Admiral said"; "the Admiral ordered"; "the Admiral dispatched"; "the Admiral decided." The only time "the Admiral could not decide what to do" is when he is a wise and prudent leader who waits "until the facts were better known" before acting. Hernando Colón gives us the following account of the end of Columbus's second journey:

> all the pilots were still at a loss except the Admiral, who ... gave his reason that they were now near Cape St. Vincent. The pilots laughed, some of them saying that they were in the English Channel and others off the English coast. ... From that day onwards he [Columbus] was held by the seamen to have great and heaven-sent knowledge of the art of navigation. (Columbus, 1969, pp. 198–9)

And yet, we know, the Admiral was often wrong in his rudimentary calculations. We know that he was neither a good administrator nor a good judge of characters. We also know that he was not always so disinterested.

Columbus writes that "Hispaniola was reduced to such peace and obedience that all promised to pay tribute to the Catholic sovereigns every three months."[88] "Should your Highness command it all the inhabitants could be taken away to Castile or held as slaves on the island, for with fifty men we could subjugate them all and *make them do whatever we wish*" (Columbus, 1969, pp. 58–9; emphasis added). The Admiral relates the story of a man on a canoe he met on his first voyage, how he welcomed this man on board, "ordered that he should be given bread and honey and something to drink. ... [C]arry him to Fernandina and restore all his possessions to him *so that he may give a good account of us.* Then when, God willing, your Highness send others here, *we shall be favourably received and the natives may give us all they possess*" (Columbus, 1969, p. 63). Pigafetta annotates that if the local populations "agreed to obey the King of Spain, and recognize the Christian king as their lord, *and give us tribute,* they should all be friends. But *if they acted otherwise they should learn by experience how our lances pierced.*"[89] The Europeans meant what they said. Díaz (1963, p. 338) reports that "to strike fear in the neighbouring towns, Cortés ordered that half the houses in the district should be set on fire."[90]

Such open acknowledgments of brutality, even when related with justification, are rare in the conquistadores' accounts. But the Indians did find a champion of their cause in Bartolomé de Las Casas (1484–1576), a Dominican priest who had followed the conquistadores in their expeditions – only "Columbus and Las Casas belong to America," Símon Bolívar would later assert at the Angostura Congress in 1819 (cited in Hanke, 1959, p. 114). Las Casas wrote copiously till the very end of a long life about the horrors of the conquest. In *A Short Account of the Destruction of the Indies* he tells us how the Spaniards treated native inhabitants "not as brute animals – so much as piles of dung in the middle of the road" (Las Casas, 1992, p. 13).

> They forced their way into native settlements, slaughtering everyone they found there … They hacked them to pieces, slicing open their bellies with their swords … They grabbed suckling infants by the feet and … dashed them headlong against the rocks. … [They tied] native leaders and nobles to a kind of griddle … and then grill[ed] … over a slow fire … [the dying] howled in agony … as they died a lingering death … to stop them making such a racket … [the Spaniards rammed] wooden bungs into their mouths. (Las Casas, 1992, pp. 15–6)

Women were a precious commodity in this world of ruthless men of adventure. Again, Las Casas tells us of "the Europeans taking native women and children both as servants and to satisfy their own base appetites" (Las Casas, 1992, p. 14). He tells us how "the European commanders raped the wife of the paramount chief of the entire island" (Las Casas, 1992, p. 14). Even the typically subdued journals of Columbus's four voyages do tell us that men and, especially women are taken prisoners (for example, Columbus, 1969, pp. 85, 135, 187). In a letter addressed to Juana de la Torre, Columbus (1969, p. 271) acknowledges that, in the year 1500 with the first settlers coming to Hispaniola "the cost of a woman is 100 *castellanos* … The trade is very common and there are now many merchants who go about looking for girls; some of nine or ten are now on sale, but whatever their age they command a good price." Hernando Colón, Columbus's son, tells us of a mutiny to the Admiral where "every Spaniard went out among the Indians robbing and seizing their women wherever he pleased" (Columbus, 1969, p. 187).

But typically, conquistadores saw it (or at least told us) differently. In Hernando Colón's biography of the Admiral we read that "a great number of women came in to take a look at the Spaniards ... These women also kissed the strangers' feet and hands in awe and wonder, as if they were holy objects, and proffered the presents they had brought" (Columbus, 1969, pp. 78–9). Pigafetta wrote: "For a hatchet or for a knife they gave us one or two of their daughters ... not ... their wives for anything at all" (Pigafetta, 1969, p. 44). Similarly, Bernal Díaz (1963, pp. 80, 210) tells us of "gifts ... of twenty women ... eight Indian women." Vespucci, in a 1504 letter to Soderini, writes that, in the marvelous lands he saw, the local people "are ... lustful beyond measure, the women more so than the men; ... of disordered lust. They showed great willingness to copulate with us Christians" (Vespucci, 1984, pp. 134–5).[91] But in case the women would not show "great willingness," here is what was likely to happen to them, as related by Michele de Cuneo, one of Columbus's Italian lieutenants during the second voyage:

> I captured a very beautiful Carib woman ... When I had taken her to my cabin she was naked – as was their custom. I was filled with a desire to take my pleasure with her and attempted to satisfy my desire. She was unwilling, and so treated me with her nails that I wished I had never begun. But – to cut a long story short – I then took a piece of rope and whipped her soundly ... Eventually we came to such terms, I assure you, that you would have thought she had been brought up in a school for whores. (In Columbus, 1969, p. 139)

Saracen or Indian, the "other" rarely has a voice in either pilgrims' or conquistadores' accounts. Díaz is unusual in allowing "the other" to break the silence, to express, however faintly, their point of view, which is often critical of "our" point of view. "They [the Indians] answered that we had hardly entered their country," frankly acknowledges Bernal Díaz, "yet we were already ordering them to forsake their *Teules* [Gods], which they could not do. But as for giving obedience to this King we spoke of, this they would do" (Díaz, 1963, p. 191). In the first encounter between Cortés and Montezuma, after Cortés had explained to Montezuma Christian genesis and cosmology, Montezuma replies:

> these arguments of yours have been familiar to me for some time. I understand what you said to my ambassadors on the sandhills about the three gods and the cross, also what you preached in the various towns through which you passed. We have given you no answer, since *we have worshiped our own gods here from the beginning and know them to be good.* No doubt yours are good also ... (Díaz, 1963, pp. 222–3; emphasis added)

Yet, such seemingly objective representation of historical reality should not be exaggerated. Such realism – *mimesis* – had already shown all its limits in

Tacitus's powerful narrative of the revolt of the Germanic legions after the death of Augustus, as brilliantly argued by Auerbach (1953, pp. 33–40, 46–8, 52–60, 84, 94). In Díaz – or Tacitus, a far better historian – the biases are all too clear.[92] They shine through the actions Díaz imputes to the enemy, through his "characterization" of the enemy, through his moral judgment on their religion and savagery (for example, p. 320 "the others" rape enemies' women; so do the Spaniards, but Díaz doesn't say ...).

Even rarer is the view that the "other" may actually be better than the "self." Captain James Cook annotated the following remark in his diary:

> Men women and children go wholy naked ... and are not ashame'd; they live chiefly on Fish and wild Fowl and such other articles as the land naturly produceth ... These people may truly be said to be in the pure state of Nature, and may appear to some to be the most wretched upon Earth: But in reality *they are far more happier that that [sic] we Europeans* ... (Cook, 1955, Vol. I, p. 508; emphasis added)

But, by Cook's time, nearly three centuries had passed since the first encounters with non-Europeans, three centuries of soul-searching questioning who the "other" was. Even so, the view of the other in relation to the self expressed by a young Charles Darwin, at the end of his five-year voyage around the world on board the H. M. S. Beagle, is rather more typical (Darwin, 1989, p. 376):

> It is impossible not to look forward with high expectation to the future progress of nearly an entire hemisphere. Africa, the Americas, Oceania have all been brought under civilization. These changes have now been effected by the philanthropic spirit of the British nation. ... It is impossible for an Englishman to behold these distant colonies, without a high pride and satisfaction. To hoist the British flag, seems to draw with it as a certain consequence, wealth, prosperity, and civilization.

Even the simplest of historical writing, the chronicle, bears witness to the process of silence and emphasis, to the process of selectivity of "the facts of history." Medieval chroniclers listed events sequentially, year after year, one event per year, one year per line, a blank entry for many years. Furthermore, events varied in duration from "Pippin, mayor of the palace, died" (714 A.D.) to "Theudo drove the Saracens out of Acquitaine" (721 A.D.) (White, 1987, pp. 6–9). Yet, even this seemingly random and bizarre selection of facts ("712 flood everywhere; ... 722 Great crops; ... 725 Saracens came for the first time ..."; White, 1987, p. 7) makes sense in light of the authors' fundamentally religious *weltanschauung* where only the "other world" counts and God's intentions for this world are inscrutable.

It is tempting to think that this selectivity depends upon the infancy of historical writing, that ways of seeing and representing depend upon our level of technical development. Thus, Romanesque paintings were flat and static because Giotto had yet to "invent" the perspective. Gothic cathedrals were tall and slim because Alberti, Brunelleschi, and Michelangelo had yet to figure out how to stick a large cupola on a church. Italian art critic Matteo Marangoni wrote in his *Saper vedere*, an enormously influential book, one, in any case, that deeply influenced me during my high-school years:

> Today, anyone with the bare minimum of education is well aware of the errors of the old art criticism ... Who, for example, would criticize a painter of the *Trecento* for the lack of proportion between figures and things, who will still take this for a mistake and justify it with the ill-famed expression 'infancy of art?' (Marangoni, 1964, p. 18)[93]

The church of St. Apollinare Nuovo in Ravenna best exemplifies Marangoni's views. Inside the church, two different layers of mosaics, one above the other, run all around the walls. The mosaics of one layer have flat, frontal, and schematic representations of human bodies in a sea of gold; the others portray the bodies in full and in various positions set against a naturalistic background. Perhaps no more than fifty years separate the artists who worked on the two layers of mosaics. But those were fifty years full of change, most notably, the transfer of the capital of the Roman Empire to Constantinople. The new masters around town brought with them a new and different vision of the world.[94] And that new vision brought new representations expressed in new techniques.

Our relationship with nature, what we think of plants and flowers, of other animals and human beings, similarly changes with new visions. The English historian Keith Thomas (1984, p. 15) has masterfully shown how, during the centuries following the geographic discoveries, between 1500 and 1800, "New sensibilities arose towards animals, plants and landscape." Our sensibilities toward high and dangerous mountains are certainly among these. In crossing the Alps in 1128, a Canterbury monk wrote: "Pardon me for not writing. I have been up on the St. Bernard pass ... shuddering at the hell of the valleys ... 'Lord,' I said, 'restore me to my brethren, that I may tell them, that they come not into this place of torment.'" In 1432, Bertrandon de la Broquière who traveled from Gand to Jerusalem, wrote: "I came to the foot of the biggest and tallest of all mountains, Moncenisio, a mountain that is very dangerous to pass" (in Stopani, 1991, p. 140). Ruskin confirms the medievals' ambivalent feelings toward mountains "regarded with reverence ... [but] also the subjects of a certain dislike and dread."

> The mountains were thus voiceful with perpetual rebuke, and necessarily contemplated with a kind of pain and fear ... It was only for their punishment, or in their despair, that men consented to tread the crocused slopes of the Chartreuse, or the soft glades and dewy pastures of Vallombrosa.[95]

Wordsworth, in his 1805 edition of his autobiographic poem *The Prelude*, would give us quite a different image of his own crossing of the Alps – the "sublime" about to sweep through the Romantic literature: "My heart leap'd up when first I did look down / On that which was first seen of those deep haunts, / ... That day we first / Beheld the summit of Mont Blanc and griev'd / ..." "Those solitudes sublime," far from inspiring fear in Wordsworth, evoke "dreams and fictions pensively compos'd, / Dejection taken up for pleasure's sake, / And gilded sympathies; ... And sober posies of funeral flowers ... / ... / ... many a meditative hour" (Book VI, Cambridge and the Alps; lines 446–61, 481–87). The ingredients of the romantic vision of the sublime are all present in this handful of lines. With Romanticism many long-forgotten traits of a medieval world badly battered by the Enlightenment are rediscovered and rehabilitated.[96] But the medieval fear of the natural world was not one of them, the most fearful of natural scenes incorporated into the concept of the sublime. We never see the same things with the same eyes.

"Journeys ... Magic Caskets Full of Dreamlike Promises"

Magic. Indeed, much magic we did see in these journeys. Spring waters on Mount Sinai where no woman can wash without becoming pregnant, as the Bordeaux's pilgrim assures us (Wilkinson, 1981a, p. 153, lines 586.1–2). And Antonino of Piacenza tells us of stones that emit sounds when shaken, although made of solid rock, and when touched, will prevent a woman from aborting, or when hugged, will take your "measurements" and diagnose any disease and cure you; he tells us of a beam in Nazareth upon which Jesus sat that can be moved and lifted by Christians, but that Jews cannot nudge.[97] Mandeville's travel book is full of wonders, from "trees that bear wool, like that of sheep," to seas, in the land of Prester John, with no water, and yet plenty of fish ("I, John Mandeville, ate them, and so believe it, for its is true"), and "women, who have precious stones growing in their eyes" (Mandeville, 1983, pp. 167, 169, 175).

Dreams. Of being in other times, in other places, along the *via francigena* on the way to the eternal city or aboard a Portuguese caravel. Dreams of altogether being someone else. Bruno, perhaps? Simmel? Columbus? Even this trick you can pull out of the magic casket of a journey. Remember the tragic story of Martin Guerre to whose trial a young Montaigne participated (Zemon Davis, 1983)? Dreams of riches, of "gorging in gold." "Everyone, young and old alike, who journeys to the New World," Las Casas (1992, p. 130) tells us, "is either openly or in secret a fortune-hunter." Dreams of immortality, be this the pilgrims' "hope of immortality in another world" or the explorers' "hope of living in the memory of future generations." "O Posterity, holy and sacred," emphatically wrote Diderot. "Posterity is for the Philosopher what the other world is for the religious" (cited in Becker, 1932, pp. 130, 150). An early fourteenth-century rhyme goes:[98] "Out to sea, far west of Spain, / Lies a land men call Cockaygne. / No land that under heaven is / For wealth and beauty comes near this." If poetry had tried to give peasants' dreams of old of the *land of Cockaigne* and of the magical kingdom of Prester John a realistic character, reality often had the character of dream in many of the eyewitness accounts of the new world. In his second letter to Lorenzo de' Medici of 1502, Vespucci is so conscious of writing about such "wonderful things of God and of nature" that he adds: "I do not want to write more about this [the beauty of the discovered lands], because I fear no one will believe me" (Vespucci, 1984, pp. 76, 79).

Promises. Magic, for sure; and even dreams. But what about those promises of sociological meaning to be found in those pilgrims' and voyagers' travel accounts, of perhaps casting light on the account of our journey from words to numbers by comparing it to the accounts of these other journeys? We may smile at Columbus who believed to have reached the Earthly Paradise. Will you similarly smile, reader of 2520, at my belief to have reached the numbers? We may smile at Columbus's self-deception that the earth is small and that seas are even smaller. But, was I not just as deluded when I thought I could do twenty projects with the generous funds David Ward had first granted me to embark upon this journey from words to numbers – a journey that most colleagues thought to be impossible? We may smile at Columbus who saw gold everywhere. Yet, will "the professor" not recognize in Columbus's way of seeing, in this deception of self and others, the tell-tale signs of the research proposal? "Grant officer of a funding agency give me the requested research funds and I will give you more numbers, better numbers, bigger numbers."[99] Not surprisingly, neither Columbus nor social scientists talk about problems.[100] That's not what those whom we beg for money want to hear. Is what we find at the end of our science journeys shaped by our reasons for looking? Will I find numbers, if numbers is what I want to find? We found rituals of behavior in journeys.[101] We found stylized and stereotypical ways of writing. Is there ritual in the way we conduct our science? Is there a stylized way of writing social science texts? Do we use syntagms of power in our accounts of armchair academic voyages? Do we cast ourselves in a positive light? Do we carefully choose our words (and numbers ...)? And what are scientists *supposed to* talk about? Will I not tell other travelers of the dangers of my road, of the shortcuts I may have taken? Is my "thin thread" thinner than I have disclosed?

The metaphor of the journey has certainly raised many questions. But will it give us answers? It has showed us the way. But will it get us there? Let's follow Faust to find out. "World of magic, land of dreams! / We have entered you, it seems. / Wisp, lead well and show your paces; / We must get there, we must hurry / In these wild, wide-open places!" (Goethe, 1987, 3,871–5)

Part II

Looking Back: What's in the Numbers?

I betook me again to travelling ... And, during the nine subsequent years, I did nothing but roam from one place to another, desirous of being a spectator rather than an actor in the plays exhibited on the theatre of the world; ... I gradually rooted out from my mind all the errors which had hitherto crept into it. Not that in this I imitated the skeptics who doubt only that they may doubt, and seek nothing beyond uncertainty itself; for, on the contrary, my design was singly to find ground of assurance, and cast aside the loose earth and sand, that I might reach the rock or the clay. In this, as appears to me, I was successful enough ...

René Descartes (1960, p. 59)

There are two things you are better off not watching in the making: sausages and econometric estimates.

Edward E. Leamer (1983, p. 36)

Prologue

"I have disclosed to you the meaning, now I will help you to understand the secrets of this art," wrote Albertus Magnus in his *Libellus de Alchimia* (Albertus Magnus, 1958, p. 58).[1] I have done the opposite. In Part I of this book I disclosed to you the secrets of the art of going from words to numbers. I showed you "how to do it." I illustrated a tool borrowed from linguistics (story grammars) with properties that make it useful in sociohistorical research for collecting data from text sources. By providing the templates to structure the information contained in narrative texts story grammars allow the alchemic transformation of words into numbers. The examples of coding that I provided certainly give more than token evidence of the power of the technique. In any case, particularly in Chapter 3, we saw that the tool is not just an interesting toy with desirable properties, but it actually works when applied to collect large volumes of data. More to the point, the innovative empirical results illustrated in that chapter on the mobilization and countermobilization process of the 1919–22 period in Italy could not have been obtained using either available data (for example, strike statistics) or traditional methods of data collection (for example, ethnography, surveys).

But having disclosed "the secrets of this art," what about its meaning? Strangely enough, it is by reflecting upon that meaning that the *real* secrets of the art turn up. Christian pilgrims could count on powerful symbols to help them reflect upon their journeys. At the Chartres cathedral and at the Basilica of St. Vitale in Ravenna complex labyrinths on the floors reminded pilgrims of the tortuous path of their life on the way to salvation in the next.[2] The entire cultural world of a medieval Christian pilgrim came together in the iconography and narrative of bas-reliefs, statues, paintings, stained-glass windows, tombs, and relics. Renaissance men had ways of their own of bringing together their cultural world. Raymond Lull, Giulio Camillo, and Giordano Bruno laid the ground work of that construction. The iconography of medieval cathedrals would, no doubt, help me in this final reflection upon the meaning of our journey. And Camillo's theater would have altogether saved me the trouble of the quest. But my wares are no medieval cathedral; not even Giulio Camillo's miniature theater (more like Horace's "ridiculous mouse?"). I only have Albertus Magnus's advice to go by: Persevere in the efforts.

In Part II, our journey leads us through more perilous paths. The spell of words I invoked relentlessly throughout Part I "as a voodoo magician might his most cherished hobgoblins" – "rigorous," "formal," "scientific," "power" – seems to lose its power.[3] The bright optimism of Part I gives way to a darker pessimism. Will you not find to your taste the critique to the "scientific" approach to content analysis that I bring out in this second part of the book? Perhaps. But, I count on you being like Calvino's reader of *If on a Winter's Night a Traveler* (1993, pp. 4, 9). You do not "expect anything in particular from this particular book. You're the sort of person who, on principle, no longer expects anything of anything. ... You know that the best you can expect is to avoid the worst." Perhaps, if "you go on" with the reading "you realize that the book is readable nevertheless ... it's the book in itself that arouses your curiosity; in fact, on sober reflection, you prefer it this way, confronting something and not quite knowing yet what it is." So, bear with me.

SUNSHINE MORALISTS. "Bear with me!" You gave us the numbers in Chapter 3. You gave us a rigorous way of linking the words to the numbers. You were very careful in spelling out the limitations of your technique. You chastised the social science alchemists, "the pokers of buttons," the ritualistic investigators, the theoretical cataloguers. OK. But that's enough! You don't have to throw it all away, do you? Can't you make up your mind? Are you for rigorous measurement or fluffy words?

MICHEL FOUCAULT. "'Words and things' is the entirely serious title of a problem; it is the ironic title of a work that modifies its own form, displaces its own data, and reveals, at the end of the day, a quite different task. A task that consists of not – of no longer – treating discourses as groups of signs (signifying elements referring to contents or representations) but as practices that systematically form the objects of which they speak. Of course, discourses are composed of signs; but what they do is more than use these signs to designate things" (Foucault, 1972, p. 49).

AUTHOR. What am I guilty of? Of not having silenced the words that things still speak, of not "having boasted of any system"? Perhaps, in your mind, I am guilty of "having confessed my ignorance with greater freedom than those are accustomed to do who have studied a little, and expounded, perhaps, the reasons that led me to doubt of many of those things that by others are esteemed certain" (Descartes, 1960, p. 61). Even Lundberg, not exactly a postmodernist, in the preface to his *Social Research. A Study in Methods of Data Gathering*, wrote:

> The objectives … of the present book are: 1) To emphasize the importance of accurate and objective observation as the first step of scientific method … 2) To inculcate a healthy skepticism of, and a critical spirit toward, statistical data by acquainting the student with the difficulties, danger, and inaccuracies to which the collection and interpretation of social data are especially subject. 3) To give a general knowledge of the technique of gathering original data. (Lundberg, 1942, pp. vii–viii)

"Healthy skepticism"; "critical spirit." Do you hear that? Whatever happened to those commitments?

GALILEO [to his inquisitors]. "I succeeded in procuring a copy of my book [*Dialogue on the Great World Systems*], and … I applied myself with the utmost diligence to its perusal … And as, owing to my not having seen it for so long, it presented itself to me, as it were, like a new writing and by another author, I freely confess that in several places it seems to me set forth in such a form that a reader ignorant of my real purpose might have had reason to suppose that the arguments brought on the false side, and which it was my intention to confute, were so expressed as to be calculated rather to compel conviction by their cogency than to be easy of solution. … *My error, then, has been – and I confess it – one of vainglorious ambition and of pure ignorance and inadvertence*" (in de Santillana, 1961, pp. 255–6; emphasis added).

It was a simple quest for which I had set out on this long journey from words to numbers: If "it takes two to tango, it takes at least two to fight." One cannot understand the dynamic of strikes – what workers do – without, at the same time, understanding what employers and the state do (at least!). An understanding of the actions of a social actor presupposes an understanding of the social relations in which this actor is involved. Newspaper articles (or police reports, for that matter) on conflict events gave me the kind of "thick descriptions" of the social relations I was looking for. And story grammars gave me the methodological tool to structure those narratives in ways that made possible the quantitative analysis of qualitative information. But the journey in search of the actor has taken us across disciplines and, more to the point, from the substantive world of strike and conflict research, to the methodological and epistemological worlds. In this second part, the search will finally lead us to a rich theoretical view of sociology as the study of social relations. For all the limits of the tools discovered in this journey, there are a handful of *memorabilia* for us to take away as bounty. I do try hard to please the "sunshine moralists," to shed brighter light upon darker paths. In a letter to Max Weber dated March 18, 1908, Georg Simmel rebelled indignantly to the accusations of being a "destructive and negative" character, always and only ready to tear down but not to build:

> In some circles, the opinion prevails that I am only critical, even destructive, and that my lectures do nothing but teach to negate. Perhaps I don't have to tell you that this is a disgusting untruth. My lectures, as well as my entire work for several years now, are only directed towards the positive, the proof of a deeper understanding of the world and the spirit, without any polemics against or critique of differing states and theories. (In Gassen and Landmann, 1958, pp. 127–8)

I will have to subscribe to that. Descartes would have done the same (1960, p. 59). So, on you go, reader, with an open mind to the playful games of the intellect. In a letter to his opponent Noel Bédier, Erasmus complained:

> In my opinion, it is quite unnecessary to act in the Schools as you act when playing cards or dice, where any infringement of the rules spoils the game. In a learned discussion, however, there should be nothing outrageous or risky in putting forward a novel idea.[4]

But, just in case, don't forget Unamuno's warning (1931, p. 131):

> The reader who follows me further is now aware that I am about to carry him into the region of the imagination, of imagination, not destitute of reason, for without reason nothing subsists, but of imagination founded on feeling. And as regards its truth, the real truth, that which is independent of ourselves, beyond the reach of our logic and of our heart – of this truth who knows aught?

Follow me!

4

The Word and the World[1]

The trouble with the Word is that it differs by more than one letter from the world.

Geoffrey R. Elton (1963, p. 87)

The question of relations between the word and the world concerns not only verbal art but actually all kinds of discourse.

Roman Jakobson (1960, p. 351)

Two key terms, reliability and validity, provide the essential language of measurement.

Richard Zeller and Edward Carmines (1980, p. 6)

It cannot be emphasized too often that in *good* ... history, the quality of the work on the sources alone decides the quality and the acceptability of the history written.

Geoffrey R. Elton (1983, p. 106)

Great attention must be given to evaluating the quality of the data – and this does not appear to be developing at present in social research.

Stanley Lieberson (1985, p. 216)

Founding Fathers and Disciplinary Mottos

The "Science of Sociology"

It is perhaps only by accident that the academic discipline that we call *sociology* has come down to us by that name. The man who first coined the label, Auguste Comte, had originally chosen a different one: *social physics*. Only when the Belgian social statistician Adolphe Quetelet adopted that term as his own (for example, in his 1869 *Physique sociale, ou, Essai sur le développement des facultés de l'homme)*, did Comte feel compelled to come up with a new label, the one that was to stick (Hankins, 1939).

"Social physics" would, no doubt, have made more immediately transparent the true nature and goal of the new discipline – Political *Science* was luckier in that respect. For, make no mistake, the new discipline was born as a science. It was born with an explicit mandate to emulate the natural sciences in its quest to explain the social, in its ultimate goal of discovering the basic laws of society.[2] Comte, Spencer, Pareto, Durkheim, sociology's "founding fathers," all shared a firm belief in the scientific nature of the new discipline. Comte's "Law of three stages" revealed his vision of history as dominated by general laws of change, from the theological stage, to the metaphysical and, finally, the positive stage, when the human race would achieve its fullest potential through science.[3] The social sciences have an important role to play at this stage of human development. Comte wrote (1896, vol. 2, p. 240):

> We see what is the function of social science. Without extolling or condemning political facts, science regards them as subjects of observation: It contemplates each phenomenon in its harmony with coexisting phenomena, and in its connection with the foregoing and the following state of human development; It endeavours to discover, from both points of view, the general relations which connect all social phenomena; And each of them is explained, in the scientific sense of the word, when it has been connected with the whole of the existing situation, and the whole of the preceding movement.

Durkheim followed closely on Comte's footsteps. In his preface to *Suicide*, Durkheim writes: "We hope to have demonstrated" that "real *laws* are discoverable" in sociology (1951[1897], p. 37; emphasis added). Similarly, in the 1895 "Author's Preface to the First Edition" of *The Rules of Sociological Method* he wrote (1938, p. xxxix; emphasis added):

> Our principal objective is to extend *scientific rationalism* to human behavior. It can be shown that behavior of the past, when analyzed, can be reduced to relationships of *cause and effect*. These relationships can then be transformed, by an equally logical operation, into rules of action for the future.

From there, beliefs in the social sciences as sciences – with the corollaries of general laws and causal explanations[4] – trickled down to us. Ernst Jünger tells us in his diary of his experience in the trenches of World War One: "Courage runs through the ranks like wine" (Jünger, 1930, p. 27). But so do the words that flow through the academic ranks down from our founding fathers, in a re-enactment of the "myth of origin" in the seemingly unlikely world of science. And the academic "ranks" have learned "to babble the words."[5] A June 7, 1880, resolution by the trustees of Columbia College reads:[6]

> The trustees have recently appointed a special professor of sociology
> ... This newly established chair will provide for a thorough study of
> philosophical or general sociology ... By the term 'general sociology'
> is meant the scientific study of society ...

Two traditions ("philosophical or general sociology") mix here in interesting (and confusing) ways (Bernard, 1929, pp. 13–4).[7] But Franklin Henry Giddings, who first occupied that chair at Columbia, was not at all confused. He had no doubt about the nature of sociology: The word science appears several times in his early text *The Theory of Sociology* (Giddings, 1894). His later (1924) more ambitious work, *The Scientific Study of Human Society*, betrays Giddings's view of sociology as science in the very title. A fellow of the American Statistical Association, Giddings (1924, p. 208) thought "necessary that the scientific student of human society should know the essentials of statistical theory" and proceeds to provide basic definitions of mean, median, mode, standard deviation, and Pearson correlation coefficient. "We need rigorously scientific studies of human society," he insisted (1924, p. 37). Such chapter titles as "Scientific Scrutiny of Societal Facts" and "Classification of Societal Facts" bear witness not only to Giddings's view of sociology as science but his close connection with Comte and Durkheim.

At the turn of the nineteenth century many American sociologists were embracing that view of sociology as science. Albion W. Small,[8] professor at the University of Chicago, founder of the *American Journal of Sociology*, and one of the early presidents of the American Sociological Association, raised the question in his journal: "What is a sociologist?" "A sociologist," his reply was, "is a man who is studying the facts of society *in a certain way*. ... The sociologist tries to look upon life from a point of view which commands all that *science* permits us to know about the total *facts* of human life" (1903, pp. 468, 472; emphasis added). Robert Park, Small's successor at Chicago, left us a coauthored *Introduction to the Science of Sociology* – science, notice – that underwent several editions and that "became the most influential introduction to sociology in the United States in the 1920s and 1930s."[9]

In the next generation of American sociologists George Lundberg was to become a fervent advocate of "the more rigorous application of the method of physical science in sociology" (Lundberg, 1929, p. 401). For Lundberg, the objections raised against "the idea of sociology as a natural science" are simply "based on ... confusion" (Lundberg, 1929, p. 395).[10] Sorokin, in the final sentence of his *Contemporary Sociological Theories* (1928, p. 761; emphasis added), best captures sociology's aspirations to the general and the scientific: "Sociology has been, is, and either will be a *science* of the *general* characteristics of all classes of social phenomena, with the relationships and correlations between them; or there will be no sociology."

And if sociology is a science, it *must* concern itself with method, with the specific rules of how to approach the study of social reality. A reflection upon method and a view of sociology as science go hand in hand. We may regret that such preoccupation with method should become in time a "kind of fetishism" and a "pestilence;"[11] that sociologists may "have become so preoccupied with methodological questions that they have ceased to be interested in society at all;"[12] that method from a "means" to approach the study of society should have become an "end" in itself.[13] But no method, no science.

In his survey of American sociological theory in the early decades of the twentieth century, Bain (1929, p. 106) concludes: "1. Sociology is a natural science. ... 2. Sociology will become increasingly statistical. ... [T]he business of sociologists is to generalize human behavior." And by the 1960s, sociologists' business was booming, sociologists having found a way to combine their aspirations to uniformities and general laws, to causal explanations, and to rigorous statistical testing of hypotheses, in an all-encompassing powerful new tool: the statistical causal model (Blalock, 1971). And by that time, Paul Lazarsfeld, professor of sociology at Columbia University, had firmly established himself as the champion of rigorous empirical social research, had most closely linked his name to "methodology" (Boudon, 1993, p. 12).

"Sociologists study man in society," Lazarsfeld wrote, "methodologists study the sociologist at work. In the world of the natural sciences this is a major activity ..." (Lazarsfeld, 1993, p. 236). Lazarsfeld saw himself as a promoter and contributor of that activity in the social sciences. In his presidential address at the fifty-seventh annual meeting of the American Sociological Association held in Washington, D.C., on September 1, 1962, Lazarsfeld confessed to his audience that "To choose a topic for a presidential address is a rather frightening experience." In the end, what did he choose? "I always felt," he acknowledges, that there is "an unfair misunderstanding of methodology, and tonight's occasion seemed an opportunity for clarification" (Lazarsfeld, 1993, p. 257). No doubt, methodology – which he viewed as "a way of reflecting on research procedures," almost an epistemology of social science, rather than as the involvement in specific techniques – was dear to his heart. "[F]or him, methodology was a discipline in itself" (Boudon, 1993, p. 4). But not only did Lazarsfeld define methodology as a new discipline, "he also brought into existence many of its most effective instruments" (Boudon, 1993, p. 14).

"Wie es Eigentlich Gewesen"

It is one thing for a discipline to have a name like political *science* or even sociology, *socios* and *logos*, the study of society. Meaning is in reference to a constellation of other meanings. What gives meaning to a word is its relation to a set of other words. And those names – political science, sociology – conjure up images of science (social *science*), method, general laws, causality. But, consider this. The name of your discipline is *history* where the same word is used to mean two different things: 1) An account of some human events that happened in the past; 2) a fanciful account that is the fruit of someone's imagination. For as close as the words designating these two different meanings are in English (*history* and *story*) they are different enough perhaps not to attract suspicion. But *storia* and *storia*, *histoire* and *histoire*? How can you tell which are historians' writings? What is the historians' business?

Many historians will acknowledge that, "at bottom," they are storytellers. For Trevelyan, the historian's "first duty … is to tell the story." "The principal craft of the historian [is] the art of narrative." "History is, in its unchangeable essence, 'a tale.'" "The art of history remains always the art of narrative. That is the bed rock."[14] George Clark, a Cambridge historian, similarly argued that "every good historian is something of a story-teller" (Clark, 1944, pp. 20–1). The first two chapters of Renier's *History: Its Purpose and Method* (1950) bear the titles: "The story that must be told" and "Nothing but a story." Yet, historians would reject the view that telling a story is all there is to their work. In Bailyn's words: "No working historian, however philosophically sophisticated, can write a sentence of history without thinking that something in fact happened back there; that there was a real world back then" (Bailyn, 1994, p. 74). Historians operate at two different levels. Sure, they do tell a story, but that story must be true, it must tell a tale of events that really happened in some place, at some time.[15] "When truth is removed from history," Polybius wrote, "the remainder turns out to be a useless tale" (Histories, I. 14; in Grant, 1992, p. 158). Yet, how do historians know they are telling the truth? Because they are using sound and reliable evidence, something storytellers do not have to worry about. Thucydides had made that clear (I, 21–22; in Grant, 1992, p. 67): "I do not think that one will be far wrong in accepting the conclusions I have reached from the evidence which I have put forward. It is better evidence than that of the poets …" And how do historians know their evidence is "better"? Because they subject that evidence to relentless critical examination. Indeed, if truth is the criterion that distinguishes between storytelling and history, issues of validity and critical examination of sources become fundamental to the evaluation of a good history, rather than artistic talent expressed in the writing (White, 1987, p. 27).

It is the seventeenth-century antiquarian historians – the erudites – that played a crucial role in laying the foundations of the critical method in history with their work on textual criticism and the evaluation of nonliterary sources – charters, statutes, inscriptions, coins, monuments, and archeological evidence – and their relationship to literary sources.[16] It is unfortunate that *les érudits* should have come under the axe of Voltaire's relentless, vitriolic attacks. Poor antiquarians, they have hardly recovered from the mighty blows! Back in 1898, rising to their partial defense, French historians Langlois and Seignobos acknowledged that antiquarian work was still associated "with lesser and pedantic minds."

Neither Voltaire nor the other *philosophes* had anything positive to say about the antiquarians' "fondness for classification and for irrelevant detail" (Momigliano, 1969, p. 25). "*Malheur aux détails*," Voltaire had thundered in 1738, "*c'est un vermine qui tue les grands ouvrages*" (damn the details; it's a worm that kills all great work; cited in Momigliano, 1969, p. 43). The philosophic historians of the late-eighteenth century had no patience for the erudites' preference for the writing about the sources of history, rather than the writing of history itself; no patience for the learned and lengthy disquisitions over one detail or another. History was about grand theorizing, not quibbling over facts. It should be concerned with the understanding of the general principles of human progress and the development of civilization (Momigliano, 1969, p. 43). The antiquarians' concern for the past, particularly the distant past, is a waste of time. What counts is the present. It is in the present that we find the highest point of human development, the triumph of reason against the obscurity of the past.

And yet, there is much to be salvaged from the wreck of the antiquarians, as Momigliano (1969, p. 27) acknowledges:

> The antiquary rescued history from the sceptics, even though he did not write it. His preference for the original documents, his ingenuity in discovering forgeries, his skill in collecting and classifying the evidence and, above all, his unbounded love for learning are the antiquary's contributions to the 'ethics' of the historian.

Erudition served them well in this task. "Without erudition there is no history," and, certainly, "no reliable history" would write Langlois and Seignobos (1898, pp. 89, 90). Only erudition, in fact, endows the historian with the formidable amount of knowledge that the critical examination of the sources requires, through the faithful reconstruction of the texts, critique of origins, collection and classification of the documents verified.[17]

When modern "scientific history" was born in German universities across the eighteenth and nineteenth centuries, particularly in Jena and in Berlin at Humboldt, in opposition to a philosophical approach to the study of history,[18] it turned to the work of the erudites. Behind von Ranke there was Niebuhr – von Ranke kept a bust of Niebuhr in his office. But behind Niebuhr there was Wolf and a host of minor German academic figures steeped in a philological tradition of critical scholarship of texts to which the erudites had greatly contributed. "Scientific history" had one goal in mind: To develop the critical method, the tools most appropriate to establish the credibility of sources, the validity of evidence. That all-German academic invention of the research seminar became the training ground for a new generation of historians in the critical habit (Krieger, 1977, p. 2). Generations of historians "learned to babble" von Ranke's words: *Wie es eigentlich gewesen* – tell the story the way it actually happened, a story based on established facts, properly subjected to scientific scrutiny and criticism.[19]

There is no work on historiography over the last two centuries that does not deal at length with issues of evidence and their critical appraisal. Six of the seventeen chapters, or one hundred of the three hundred pages of Langlois and Seignobos's wonderful book, *Introduction aux études historiques*, have the word *critique* in the title. In those chapters, the authors dissect every aspect of the critical appraisal of the sources. In their view, the journey that the historian takes is one "from traces to facts. The document is the point of departure; the past fact is the point of arrival. Between this point of departure and this point of arrival, one needs to traverse a complex series of arguments, enchained one to the other ..."[20] Writing a century later Elton still insisted: "Knowledge of all the sources, and competent criticism of them, these are the basic requirements of a reliable historiography."[21]

That has been the long-lasting legacy of Niebuhr's and von Ranke's "scientific history," where "scientific" referred to the use of critical method and evaluation of the sources in the writing of history, in an effort to separate out the real from the imaginary, *storia* from *storia*.[22]

The Newspaper "Black Box"

In the sociological tradition and in the social sciences more generally, you will be hard pressed to find the equivalent of the historians' concern and cumulated body of work on sources and criticism. As Lieberson (1985, p. 216) has remarked: "Great attention must be given to evaluating the quality of the data – and this does not appear to be developing at present in social research." By and large, social scientists do not share the historians' habit of subjecting their data to "intense criticism." We could certainly use Collingwood's metaphor of putting sources "in the witness-box, and ... cross-questioning" them or Langlois and Seignobos's metaphor of the questionnaire, of posing a battery of questions to sources: What reason does the author of a document have to collect some information? What are his/her interests? Who witnessed the events?[23] All taken by the "noble dream" of theory building social scientists tend to forget to test the ground upon which their grand constructions rest.[24] When we have turned to history, we have treated it as a warehouse of data. Historians certainly accuse us of that. "In the eyes of some social scientists history apparently is now regarded as little more than a useful data source for the pursuit of their own theoretical investigations" (Stone, 1987, p. 31). One of sociology's founding fathers, Emile Durkheim, wrote of the sociologist "intruding as a stranger in the domain of the historian in order to steal, in some way, the facts that interest him" (Durkheim, 1898, p. iii).

Yet, in the case of newspapers as sources of sociohistorical data, a large body of critical evaluation of these sources has slowly emerged (Franzosi, 1987; Olzak, 1989). Unfortunately, one thing is clear: Newspapers are very selective in the information they provide.[25] Media news do not simply reflect a reality that is "out there," but filter it in some [at least partially] predictable ways.[26]

But which ways? This much we know: That different events stand different chances of being reported, that there are both temporal and spatial differences in the probability of reporting, that newspapers differ in their reporting practices, and that newspapers as sources of data do not compare favorably to other sources. Let's review the findings in detail.

• *Differences between events.* Not all events are equally likely to make news. "Size, violence and 'political significance'" make the difference (Snyder and Kelly, 1977, pp. 109–10; Mueller, 1997). Large-scale events are typically newsworthy.[27] But small events go largely unreported. In their study of demonstrations in Washington, D.C., in 1982 and 1991, McCarthy et al. (1996, p. 494) conclude: "The vast majority of demonstrations are ignored [around 90%] ... the very large ones are covered. Demonstration size is, by far, the most important characteristic determining the likelihood of media coverage." Unfortunately, "the largest proportions of demonstrations (60%) fall in the smallest size category" with only 2.9 likelihood of media coverage (McCarthy et al., 1996, p. 487). These same results are true for France (Fillieule, 1999, p. 206) and Germany (Rucht and Neidhardt, 1999, pp. 76–7).

Violent events, particularly when involving death, are generally more likely to make news. Azar (1975, p. 4) showed that *The New York Times* is more likely to cover conflict events rather than cooperative events in international affairs. In the McCarthy et al. comparative study (1996), both *The Washington Post* and *The New York Times* were more likely to cover violent demonstrations than peaceful ones. Oliver and Myers (1999), in one of the few studies of different types of events – protest, sport, entertainment, business, and so on – show that protest events fare comparatively well in media coverage. Among protest events, however, those "linked to ongoing chronic issues in the community or polity" are less likely to be reported than events directly linked to current legislative issues.

According to Snyder and Kelly, civil wars, coups d'etat, and mass arrests are more fully reported than exiles, arrests of a few insignificant persons, and crisis within nongovernmental organizations, or strikes (for which there is "drastic underreporting bias"; Snyder and Kelly, 1977, p. 110). But service-sector strikes directly involving the public, violent strikes, and strikes where unions and workers are divided do make the headlines.[28]

• *Geographic differences.* Events closer to either a media or a news service office (for example, AP, UPI, Reuters) are more likely to be reported (Danzger, 1975; Snyder and Kelly, 1977; Mueller, 1997). "Very few protests occurring in U.S. Western cities," Snyder and Kelly wrote (1977, pp. 119–20), "appeared in *The New York Times.*" *The Washington Post*, printed in Washington, D.C., was twice as likely to cover demonstrations occurring in Washington than *The New York Times* (McCarthy et al., 1996). Proximity matters even within a city. "Events occurring away from the downtown area had much less chance of receiving news coverage," report Oliver and Myers (1999, pp. 76–7). For international news, the geopolitical position of a country and the world interest in its domestic affairs are likely to affect the probability of events occurring in a country to be reported in the international press (Rummel, 1966).[29] This distortion is found in both the elite press and the international wire services. A study of the number of foreign stories reported by *The New York Times* in 1974 found a disproportionate number of reports for Great Britain, West Germany, Japan, France, the Soviet Union, South Africa, Egypt, and Israel (Simmel, 1970). In the same study, level of press attention was positively correlated with a country's economic status, size (land area and population), openness to the international economy, and political ties to the United States.[30] An examination of the coverage provided by the four major wire services (UPI, AP, Reuters, and Agence France-Presse) reports similar regional variation (Fenby, 1986). The probability of coverage of protest events in the international press is negatively correlated to the physical distance between country of event and country of newspaper (Mueller, 1997).

• *Temporal differences*. The amount of attention the media give to various issues fluctuates over time. For one thing, given the space or time limitations of the media, protest events compete with other type of events and issues for media attention. This mix varies over time. Even a large event may not be reported if other issues dominate media attention, leading to temporal "variations [that] substantially misrepresent[ed] the shape of the protest cycle" (Oliver and Maney, 2000, p. 497). Second, protest events gain and lose media attention. This "media issue attention cycle"[31] is characterized by the sudden ascendance of an issue from obscurity to a sustained prominence that dominates the news for a period of time before once again fading into oblivion.[32] This cycle, unfortunately, is typically not synchronous with the unfolding of events. For Snyder and Kelly (1977, pp. 113) there is a long-run inverted-U relationship between frequency of reporting and conflict events. Racial disorders occurring in cities with previous or no previous experiences of racial conflict have different probabilities of being reported.[33] Martindale (1985), in her comparative study of the coverage of black Americans in five newspapers, shows that the occurrence of racial conflict in a city increased the probability of subsequent local media attention to racial issues. Capecchi and Livolsi (1971) and my own comparative work (Franzosi, 1994c, pp. 102–25) show that attention to issues of labor relations by the Italian media increased after the 1969 *autunno caldo* more than proportionately to the actual number of conflict events. McCarthy, McPhail, and Smith (1996, pp. 494, 495) also found a positive relationship between issue-attention cycles and likelihood of media coverage of demonstrations: Even small events become more newsworthy during peaks of media attention cycles but larger events may fail to make it during troughs.

• *Differences between newspapers*. There is typically little overlap in event reporting of different news media (Azar et al., 1972; Azar, 1975, p. 4). On the basis of my comparative analysis of twenty-three Italian newspapers I conclude (Franzosi, 1994c, p. 105): "With the exception of a handful of large disputes

... the degree of dispersion is quite high: Out of a total of 56 disputes reported by all papers in 1962, only 26 are reported by more than one paper (19 out of 62 in 1976)." Capecchi and Livolsi's comparative analysis of international press reaches similar conclusions: "[O]ut of 500 news items, only 30 are comparable, and of these 3 or 4 are in complete disagreement; all other items cannot be compared because they appear in only one paper" (Capecchi and Livolsi, 1971, p. 264).

The main discriminatory lines between newspapers are: local versus national and left-wing versus right-wing newspapers (for working-class protest events).[34] The local papers used in my comparative analysis focus almost exclusively on local news. Snyder and Kelly (1977) found differences between national and local newspapers in their reports of size, violence against property and persons, and number of arrests. Using forty-three local papers in as many U.S. cities, Eisinger registered 120 protest events between May and October 1968 (Eisinger, 1973). However, only twenty two of these events (or 18.3%) were reported in *The New York Times*.[35] Paige found that local papers in Peru, Angola, and Vietnam reported "a considerably greater number of events" than *The New York Times* or *The Times* in London (Paige, 1975, pp. 138, 264, 329). In a study of Israeli protests from 1960 to 1967, Lehman-Wilzig and Ungar (1985) found 228 protest events in the *Jerusalem Post* while the *World Handbook of Political and Social Indicators* (1972), based on *The New York Times*, reported only twenty five.[36] In France, events occurring in Paris are six to eleven times more likely to be reported by *Le Monde* and *Libération*, papers published in Paris, than events occurring in Marseille or Nantes (Fillieule, 1999, p. 205). Rucht and Neidhardt (1999, p. 76) "estimate that probably less than 1% of all locally reported protest events may be found in a national newspaper" in Germany.[37]

In one of the few systematic comparative analyses involving both mainstream and radical papers, Hartmann (1979) showed that the *Morning Star*, the daily newspaper of the British Communist Party, reports a much higher number of items of information on industrial relations than any of the other four mainstream British dailies considered in the study (in fact, almost half the total reported by all four other papers combined). Furthermore, Hartmann showed that the *Star* pays much closer attention to the causes of industrial action rather than its consequences on the economy or on the public. My own comparative analyses of twenty-three Italian newspapers for the 1960–80 period show that *L'Unità*, the Italian Communist Party newspaper, provides from two to ten times the number of articles on industrial conflict compared to three leading elite papers (*Corriere della sera, Messaggero, Stampa*) (Franzosi, 1994c, pp. 102–25). Furthermore, in 1962, reporting of news on strikes was almost the exclusive domain of left-wing newspapers (Franzosi, 1994c, p. 103).

• *Differences between newspapers and other sources.* There are few systematic comparisons of newspaper data with data gathered from other, independent, sources. In an early comparative study between data collected by McClelland mostly from *The New York Times* (WEIS data) and data collected from the U.S. Department of State's operational traffic (FRIP data), Lanphier (1975) found great differences in enumeration of events: In a six-month period for seven countries, the WEIS data contained only twelve events against 1,046 of FRIP. In a major critical review of data sources on protest events, Rucht and Ohlemacher (1992, p. 102) point out that the 1972 edition of the *World Handbook of Political and Social Indicators*,[38] largely based on *The New York Times*, reported only seventeen nonviolent demonstrations in West Germany during 1976–77, whereas the German Ministry of the Interior counted 5,843 for the same period. McCarthy, McPhail and Smith (1996) have compared press and TV coverage of 1982 and 1991 demonstrations in Washington, D.C., against the official permit application records of three different police agencies. Their conclusion is: "[T]he picture of Washington demonstrations portrayed in the mass media differs dramatically from that generated from demonstration permit records" (McCarthy et al., 1996, p. 487). Fillieule's comparison of police and newspaper protest-event data for France reaches substantially similar conclusions: "[N]ewspaper accounts report on a very small number [around 2%] of the protest events documented in police sources" (Fillieule, 1999, p. 205). A similar comparison by Hocke (1999, pp. 150, 159) found that 95.4% of protest events recorded by the police in the German city of Freiburg did not make it into national newspapers (although the local press fared better with 62.3% coverage). The researchers of the Glasgow University Media Group (1976, pp. 167, 180–93) write that "there is no consistent relationship between the [work] stoppages recorded during the first five months of 1975 [by the British Department of Employment] and those reported by Television news."[39]

Why, Then, Newspapers? Social Scientists' Line of Defense

The news, when it comes to newspapers as sources of data, is certainly not good.[40] Which raises the question: In relying on newspapers, are social scientists studying patterns of historical events or patterns of news reporting? After all, as Lieberson and Silverman have remarked, newspapers have a tendency "to make the frequency of rapes or other events into a crime wave when in fact the major variable is the frequency of reporting such events."[41] Why, then, have we increasingly relied on newspapers in sociohistorical research (Franzosi, 1987; Olzak, 1989)? Here are some of the arguments social scientists have lined up in defense of newspapers.

• What if newspapers are the only sources of data? Indeed. What would we know on social movements in recent decades without data collected from newspapers? What would we know about peasants' rebellions? Of these, Paige wrote: "No compilation of events ... is available, so that it was necessary to compute event counts directly from newspaper sources."[42] Exclusion of newspaper data would, no doubt, prevent research in fields where no alternative data are available (McAdam, 1982, p. 236).

- In any case, not all items of information or events are equally likely to be misrepresented in the press. Some news is more likely than others to be affected by editorial policies – *soft* news and *hard* news in Tuchman's terminology (1973, pp. 110–13; see also Danzger, 1975). We know that media information on the number of participants in collective events is likely to verge on the fantastic.[43] Newspapers will also vary in their interpretation of events, as perhaps highlighted in the reporting of the reasons given for people's action, or of the particular responsibilities assigned to certain groups (workers versus police, for example) for certain actions (property damage or violence) (see, for example, McAdam, 1982, p. 237). But, perhaps, newspapers are more likely to agree on the type of action involved (strike, demonstration, sit-in, and so on), its location and date, or the general identity of the participants (workers, students, blacks, police, and so on), of whether people were arrested, injured, or killed.[44] In his comparative analysis of police and newspaper data for France in 1989, Fillieule found no difference in reporting "the date, location, and identification of demonstrators" (Fillieule, 1999, p. 204).

- And don't most studies of media coverage agree that large-scale events hardly go unnoticed in the media? You can always reduce the probability of error by raising the minimum threshold that qualify events for collection – fifty individuals instead of ten, acting collectively (Tilly, 1969, pp. 29–30; Snyder and Kelly, 1977, p. 109). And if definitions of qualifying events are kept sufficiently broad, then separate analyses can be performed at various levels of threshold. The statistical results obtained at higher threshold levels – and consequently at higher levels of validity – can then be used as yardsticks against which the results obtained at lower levels can be compared (Tilly, 1969, p. 30). As Tilly (1969, p. 30) writes:

> Comparisons between newspaper events and other sources discouraged any hope of arriving at the same list of disturbances from these diverse sources, but they did indicate that the newspapers provided the fullest enumeration and that their chief bias was toward the over-reporting of events in big cities.[45]

- Perhaps, all data are biased in some ways. What is important is to know the type and form of bias in order to be able to gage its effect on evidence and conclusions. As Robert Fogel has argued (1983, p. 47):

> It is not always appreciated that even proven defects in a given body of evidence do not necessarily deprive it of usefulness. Defects may invalidate the source on one issue but not on another, for one purpose but not for another. ... Sometimes it is possible to demonstrate that the defects in a given body of data are too small to have a significant effect

on the analytical issues that will be addressed to it. So, before dismissing a large body of evidence it is important to determine the nature of the error that affects it.

Opening the Box: Behind the Surface of Our 1919–1922 Data

I cannot think of a better way to represent the *potential* bias in the information contained in my 1919–22 database than through the figures of Table 4.1. Those figures are remarkably clear. They tell us that a great deal of the events available in the database from *Il Lavoro* occurred in Genoa and Liguria, the northern region whose capital Genoa is. *Il Lavoro* was published in Genoa. They also tell us that the spatial distribution of the available events is not stable over time; it shows clear temporal patterns: It goes from close to 70% in 1919 down to almost 40%; even clearer is the increasing weight of "other regions" over the four-year period: from about 20% in 1919 to 55% in 1922.

Both the spatial and temporal distributions of disputes raise several questions. Could Genoa and Liguria alone account for 70% of disputes in 1919? Does the finding make sense in light of the population size of the city/region relative to that of other Italian cities/regions? Better yet, given that, as we saw in Chapter 2, the majority of disputes in 1919 centered on labor conflicts, does the comparative industrial base of the city/region justify that finding?

These questions suggest a clear validation strategy. On the one hand, we need population and industrial census data by region and, possibly, by city. When we look at the demographic evidence we find that Genoa is the fourth largest Italian city in 1921, after Naples, Milan, and Rome with 541,562 people (Liguria ranks eleventh among the twenty regions, with 1,337,979 people). Population data alone do not seem to justify the findings of Table 4.1. Neither do industrial census data. According to the 1911 industrial census (Ministero di agricoltura, industria e commercio, 1913, p. 241), Genoa ranks third, out of sixty-nine provinces, with respect to the total number of industrial firms (10,152), third in terms of total industrial employment (124,897), and fourth in terms of total horse power consumption (109,730). Similarly, out of sixteen regions, Liguria ranks seventh with respect to the total number of industrial firms (11,459), sixth in terms of total industrial employment (132,674), and fourth in terms of total horse power consumption (124,650) (Ministero di agricoltura, industria e commercio, 1913, p. 247). The foundation of what was to become the "industrial triangle" in the years after World War Two between Turin, Milan, and Genoa is already laid by 1911. Clearly a mighty industrial area but hardly alone. The figures do not seem consistent with the finding that 70% of all disputes would be located in Genoa and Liguria.

Of course, knowledge of the "population at risk" cannot tell us the whole story. Numbers are not enough for mobilization. You need opportunities. You need

Table 4.1. *Distribution of Disputes from* Il Lavoro *by Location of Occurrence*

	1919		1920		1921		1922	
	#	%	#	%	#	%	#	%
Genoa and Liguria	367	68.3	256	46.3	393	42.6	304	41.1
Other regions	108	20.1	223	40.3	507	55	413	55.9
Liguria and other regions	62	11.6	74	13.4	22	2.4	22	3.0
Total	537	100	553	100	922	100	739	100.0

organization. Opportunities (political and economic) may well have been similar if not for the entire country at least for the regions of the industrialized Northwest. But as for organization, it was a different story. We do know that local working-class communities typically have different ideological traditions, different forms, and levels of class organization. Genoa certainly had among the most highly organized workers in Italy, as evinced by both unionization figures and electoral support for the Socialist Party. But, again, they were not alone. Bell, in his study of the rise of fascism in the town of San Giovanni near Milan, a working-class stronghold, tells us that as late as April 1921, the Sesto *fascio* apologized for a Milanese fascist attack (Bell, 1986, p. 162). The first raid against the Socialist Party headquarters did not occur there until September 1922, a month before the "march on Rome." Only on October 31, after the "march on Rome," did Fascists from Sesto, Milan, and the Lomellina occupy the Sesto town hall (Bell, 1986, pp. 177–8).

Alas, I don't seem to be able to find convincing empirical support for the findings of Table 4.1. Perhaps, the implicit model of data generation that I have used is not appropriate. The number of disputes (most of which are industrial) may have nothing to do with the size of the working-class population involved or the capacity of this population to mobilize. We know that working-class mobilization fundamentally depends on the state of the labor market: the higher the rate of unemployment, the lower the workers' propensity to strike. After all, that is the clearest finding of one-hundred years of strike research. Given Liguria's higher propensity toward industrial disputes brought out by Table 4.1, could Liguria have enjoyed much lower rates of unemployment when compared to the other industrialized regions? Again, the answer to that question is no.

If so, there is only one conclusion to be drawn from the numbers of Table 4.1: Those numbers are verisimilar but not quite true. Our data are distorted in their spatial distribution. Which prompts another question: What other kinds of distortions lurk behind our numbers? The distribution of the main aggregated actors found in the database may help us to find an answer to that question: Forty-three percent of all actors are either workers (30%) or unions (13%), with all other actors trailing behind. If the place of publication of *Il Lavoro* is perhaps responsible for its focus on Genoa, its ideological position as a socialist paper may be responsible for its focus on working-class actors.[46] In the end, one thing

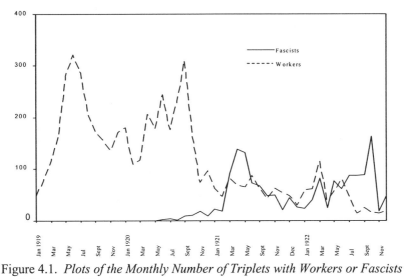

Figure 4.1. *Plots of the Monthly Number of Triplets with Workers or Fascists as Subjects or Objects*

is clear: The data upon which I based the analyses of Chapters 2 and 3 are biased. Yet, despite these empirically-observable biases, the monthly plot of the number of triplets in the 1919–22 database with workers as subjects or objects (Figure 4.1) shows a very close temporal dynamic to that of the number of strikers taken from official strike statistics independently collected by the police (see Figure 2.3 in Chapter 2). Whatever one wants to make of these findings, differences and similarities point to the need of serious validation work.

Silence and Emphasis Revisited

Through the word, then, we construct and know the world. And a strange world that is, turned upside down, deformed like bodies in the mirrors of amusement parks: A world of violent events (peaceful ones go unreported), a world of long and large events (small ones are less newsworthy), a world of class-divisive and disruptive service strikes (all others are ignored). It is a masterful orchestration of silence and emphasis. In 1919, in a letter addressed to von Ficker, a potential publisher of his *Tractatus Logico-Philosophicus*, Wittgenstein explained: "I wanted to write that my work consists of two parts: Of the one which is here, and of everything which I have *not* written. And precisely this second part is the important one" (in Monk, 1991, p. 178). That could not be more true for newspaper information. As Capecchi and Livolsi wrote (1971, p. 264):

> The distortion of news does not operate so much through an obvious alteration of an event (for example: The news 'A loves B' reported by

a right-wing newspaper and that appears as 'A hates B' in a left-wing newspaper), as much as through the downplay or the insistence on some particular features of an event.

Silence and emphasis, light and darkness: Those are the main mechanisms of media bias. The media manipulate information through the use of adjectives, the frequency of certain nouns, the use of synonyms and paraphrases, of comments and editorials, of titles and subtitles, the emphasis on some aspects of an event to the exclusion of others, the break-up of information and its recomposition in such a way as to suggest precise causal relations.[47]

Left-wing, minority political groups (domestic or foreign) do not fare particularly well in the media, since the politics of these groups pose a serious threat to the very socioeconomic foundation of Western societies. Typically, these groups are labeled "terrorists" (rather than "freedom fighters" or "martyrs"), their actions "disruptive" and "violent" (Hartley, 1982, pp. 63–74). The reasons for their existence, the ideas for which they stand are never made clear. There is an overall negative connotation of these groups in the media (Murdock, 1973). But other minority groups do not fare much better. The portrayal of nonwhite minorities as violent, lazy, and drug-using and -peddling is characteristic of the media. The place of women in either the kitchen or the bedroom is pervasive in the media (and not just in advertisement).[48]

Trew (1979a) has convincingly shown how even subtle manipulations of sentence construction can operate profound alterations in meaning. Consider the sentence "Police shot dead Africans." The sentence foregrounds responsibility: Syntactic subject and semantic agent of the sentence coincide (police). In the equivalent passive sentence "Africans were shot dead by the police," agency is backgrounded. And while agency cannot be omitted in active sentences, because the agent is also the subject of the sentence, in passive sentences, it syntactically *can* (for example, "Africans were shot dead"). Trew argues that this and similar linguistic mechanisms of deletions and rewordings contribute to the process of ideological production of news by imparting preferred readings on the same basic material (see also, Kress and Hodge, 1979; van Dijk, 1983).

Extralinguistic mechanisms are also at work. In the organization of news, one finds the same simple dichotomy "good versus evil" and "us versus them" that characterizes entertainment programs.[49] That same dichotomous framework characterizes both the narrative of individual newspaper stories (for example, Russians versus British, Tories versus Labour, Mr. Foot versus Mr. Rodgers within the Labour Party, and so on) and the overall layout of a page (peace, stability, freedom, welfare stories, associated with "us," on one side of a page, and war, violence, racism, poverty, associated with "them," on the opposite side) (Trew, 1979a, 1979b; Hartley and Montgomery, 1985). U.S. television coverage of the 1979–81 Iran hostage crisis shows a similar dichotomous format: Interviews with grieved hostage families became the symbol of the American perspective, while shots of Iranian crowds (both in Iran and inside the United

States) chanting anti-American slogans vividly portrayed the other side (Altheide, 1982, 1985). The oppositional framework of news, regardless of the topic treated, provides a supratextual unity among articles and a master key to the reading of *any* article (Hartley, 1982, p. 116; Trew, 1979a, 1979b).

The combination of linguistic and semiotic processes – the focus on particular aspects of reality (the spotlight mechanism of light and darkness), the hammering repetition of themes, the standardization of formats – virtually ensures that "alternative ... choices are hardly imaginable" (Herman and Chomsky, 1988, p. 2). When "the same underlying premises constantly reappear, they tend to be accepted as natural elements."[50, 51] This way, the bias introduced in the production of news goes well beyond the counts of articles and news items for certain issues, social actors, or actions. Bias is far more pervasive and subtle. It involves the very cognitive processes through which we access social reality, the way the word constructs the world, and the way we know that world through the word.

How to Go about Validating Data:
A Decalogue of Rules

"A term like verification," writes historian Elton (1983, p. 100; see also p. 54), "has virtually no usable meaning in history ... [because] major historical problems do not ever reach final solutions." There is never closure; just different interpretations and approximations. After all, in Burckhardt's view, history is "the record of what one age finds worthy of note in another." And what is worthy depends upon societal shifting value systems. Renzo De Felice dedicated an entire volume to the "interpretations" of fascism. And that book was first published in 1969. De Felice, a professor of history at the University of Rome *La Sapienza*, died in 1997. But were he to publish now his *Le interpretazioni del fascismo*, he would have to dedicate a new chapter to the new studies on the cultural and ideological aspects of fascism (Gentile, 1989; Berezin, 1997).

Yet, even Elton (1983, p. 100) believes that "isolated events – many of the details studied in analyzing the problem – can be settled by a process akin to verification." Dates, or the presence or absence of certain individuals can be verified and validated. After all, that kind of validation is part and parcel of the historian's methodological training. The recipe for data validation is old: Collect information from different sources and compare (for example, Langlois and Seignobos, 1898). As part of the recipe is the caveat: When assembling different sources, make sure that they are, indeed, different sources. All too often, as Danzger (1975, p. 573) observes: "What appear to be numerous sources, is upon closer examination primarily the same source in different guise."

If the recipe for validation is old, the ingredients are simple. Let's look at them in some detail.

- Use the comparative data that you have collected for a "sound" choice of your sources to gauge the extent of bias in your data.
- Make sure that agreement among news from different papers is not due to the fact that the information comes from the same source, such as one of the "big four" press agencies: AP, UPI, Reuters, or Agence-France Press.
- If you are working on current sociohistorical issues, set up independent recording procedures – even if only for a small subset of the territory of interest and for a limited time period. Firms, local trade unions and employers' associations, police departments, or civil rights organizations may be persuaded to collect and provide valuable information "according to standards acceptable to researchers" (Tilly, 1969, p. 31).[52] You can then compare these data with the data reported by newspapers.
- Rely on any other preexisting enumeration of events. Yearbooks, court proceedings, results of investigations of ad hoc parliamentary committees, surveys of specialized data gathering agencies, data found in organization, factory, and police archives[53] can all provide useful information (Tilly, 1969, pp. 23–4, 30). In the case of strikes, government agencies (Ministries of Interiors, Ministries of Labor, or Census Bureaus), have collected data systematically for at least a century. These data are typically highly aggregated and in numeric form. But, for earlier periods, information is often available in narrative form and on each individual event. For the 1919–22 period in Italy the information contained in the *Bollettino del lavoro e della Previdenza sociale* is precisely in that form. If you are studying prison riots, make sure that the Ministries of Interiors or of Corrections, will not have compiled listings of these riots. The same is true for other types of protest events.
- Social scientists, for the most part, do not go to the archives. Von Ranke's sensuous pleasure for "old papers" in which he "steeped" himself, is not for us. "From these flowers – they actually seem very dried up but they have their scent – I draw honey," von Ranke wrote.[54] Yet, if you are studying events distant in time, there may be no better source than the archives. And today's archives are much better organized than in von Ranke's times. You will find that the work of ordering, cataloguing, and sorting the material will have been done for you already. It is unlikely that you will have to write what von Ranke wrote (1981, pp. 68–9):

  > Projects of a systematic collection of its transactions [of the German Diets] have occasionally been entertained, and the work been taken in hand; but all that has hitherto been done has remained in a fragmentary and incomplete state. ... I have long cherished the project of devoting my industry and my powers to this most important work.

- Make use of the historians' own work. Particularly narrativist historians will provide long descriptions of events. Many of the pioneers of the study of wars and deadly quarrels relied predominantly on historians' work to get their counts. Richardson (1960, p. 125) tells us that he derived "most of the information about wars ... from the works of professional historians." And so did Sorokin. And we can get more than simple counts from historians' narratives. Using a story grammar as template, we can extract all the basic material of their stories. Narrative monographs on specific regions can be particularly useful. At least for the Italian case, what you find in regional archives is typically much more detailed than what you find in the central archives. Draw up as complete a list as possible of historians' regional monographs.

• Historians may not only have done the work of going to the regional archives for you.[55] They may have also done the work of collecting systematic lists of events in narrative form. Make sure to check for the existence of this type of work. Chiurco's (1929) five-volume *Storia della rivoluzione fascista* should not be missed by anyone studying the rise of Italian fascism.

• When using historians' work as source of data along with archival material, make sure you are not double counting. Historians will have typically gotten their information from regional or national archives.

• Not just historians but specific organizations may have left behind detailed comparisons of events. The Italian Socialist Party produced such a compilation of violent events perpetrated by the Fascists against the Socialists (*Avanti!*, 1963).

The purpose of collecting "control" data – even if only for a subset of the total sample period, geographical distribution, and types of events of interest – is not to provide either a full-fledged investigation into the nature of newspaper bias or a sample of events as close as possible to the population of events – which by itself may be highly desirable. Rather, it is meant to give us a gauge of the extent of bias for different items of information from different sources, to find out, with some degree of confidence, which information can be trusted and which cannot, the frailty or solidity of the grounds upon which we build our arguments.[56] What we are looking for is simple: a better understanding of the characteristics of events in the newspaper sample. Indeed, the collection of comparative data should be an integral part of the research design of projects involving data collection from newspapers. There are good reasons for doing so. And if social scientists find the historian's obsession with truth alien to them (von Ranke' *wie es eigentlich gewesen* – tell the story the way it actually happened), they should at least appreciate the statistical arguments behind validation: That conflict data are not a random sample and, therefore, standard statistical inference does not hold. Furthermore, as Weede (1973) has argued, conflict data are extremely sensitive to measurement error, especially "few, but large measurement errors." The resulting "asymmetric distributions and outliers" have detrimental effect on statistical estimates. The only solution to these problems is "replication of data-making."[57]

Further Rules: Selecting the Newspaper(s)

It may well be in the nature of academic work. Those who use newspapers to study bias will find it. And they have done so with remarkable consistency, since at least the last century when they first approached the problem. Those who use newspapers as sources of sociohistorical data are more likely to see newspapers as mirrors of reality. Yet, knowing that that is not the case, we need to put more care in the choice of our newspaper sources. Certainly, the research strategy of collecting data from all available newspapers can be prohibitive (Rucht and Ohlemacher, 1992). The only alternative then is: Base your choice on the results of a sound sampling framework. Here is the outline of that strategy.

- Draw your sample from the population of all available newspapers, or, at least, from papers differently located in their ideological and geographical positions.
- Do not just count articles or column inches (as in early studies of newspaper bias). Quality is perhaps even more important than quantity. How "thick" are the descriptions of those news stories? How many different actions and actors are portrayed? How are they portrayed?
- Counting articles is easy. Looking at content implies coding the information provided by each article. And that takes resources. Which means that you can probably count articles for longer time spans and for more newspapers than you can code detailed information on each article. Which also suggests a strategy based on a double-sampling framework. First, you sample a handful of newspapers from a wide population and over a period of a few weeks or months, using article counts as selection criterion. Depending upon the period and the number and sizes of the countries under investigation, you are likely to reduce the sample to a handful of papers. Then, for this small sample, you code detailed information, you compare and, perhaps, you choose further.
- Do not assume that bias is constant over time. We know it is not. Which means that you will have to compare at selected temporal intervals. That is all the more necessary, the longer the time span of your study. But even a study of a short period (my 1919–22 or Tarrow's 1966–73 years) may require repeated sampling. We know that in the case of large mobilization processes (such as, indeed, the 1919–22 or 1966–73 periods in Italy) the temporal dynamics of the movement and of media interest are not synchronous. If you are studying a period of high mobilization – which is very likely if you are studying movements of protest – be ready to sample at repeated intervals.

Barking up the Wrong Tree: Reliability versus Validity

Are the "American Indians"[58] men with rational souls and not lacking in reason or are they demented mistakes of nature, barbarians given to sodomy and cannibalism, no more than beasts (*bestias*), brute animals (*animales brutos*), even worse than asses, dogs, or black dogs (*perro moro*)?[59] The question was debated in a learned dispute held in Valladolid between Bartolomé de Las Casas and Juan Ginés de Sepúlveda, one of Spain's most learned men and a champion of Aristotelian philosophy. For two years, between 1550 and 1551, these two men sparred before a "Council of the Fourteen," summoned by the Emperor Charles V of Spain.

For the Spaniards and Charles V the question was hardly rhetorical – so much so that the emperor had suspended all conquest in the new world, pending the results of the dispute (Hanke, 1959, p. 36). Because if American Indians are inferior beings – "as children are to adults, as women are to men" – then, as Sepúlveda argued, the Aristotelian doctrine of natural slaves could be applied to them. And even less rhetorical was the question for the American Indians themselves. After all, this is what they heard the Spaniards read to them in their first encounter, if they could have only understood their language: "We shall take you and your wives and children, and shall make slaves of them ... and we shall take away your goods, and shall do all the harm and damage that we can, as to vassals that do not obey" (cited in Hanke, 1959, p. 16).

Issues of classification in the social sciences are mercifully less consequential on people's lives (although census categories can be bitterly contested).[60] But they do have consequences on the process of scientific production. Cicourel clearly understood the trick behind numbers, or, if you wish, the key element in the alchemic transformation of words into numbers when he wrote (1964, p. 18): "Our often arbitrary classifications of data become the basis for establishing some form of quantification." In other words, to quantify we classify qualitative data, first, then count the number of occurrences within each class. He also clearly understood that, once in the realm of numbers, a critique of those numbers becomes impossible. Cicourel (1964, p. 18) wrote:

> The validity of our [quantitative] measurement is relative to the arbitrary classification and makes replication and the possibility of rigorously obtained knowledge remote at this time. The most serious problems of measurement, then, arise when we deal with qualitative 'variables.'

A critique of numbers, in other words, must retrace the process of generating those numbers, it must go back to the words. We must go back to Chapter 2 to find out how we classified words; back to the repeated statements "properly aggregated," found there. And to the serious problems of measurement due to classification, we have to add further, and potentially even more serious problems, due to the very process of generating those words. The analyses of this chapter leave little doubt about the general lack of validity of newspaper words (or police or ambassadorial words, for that matter).

Janis (1949, pp. 56–7), one of the "father founders" of the technique of content analysis, put it best when he wrote: "Let us assume that we have tested the reliability of a content-analysis technique ... The question then arises: *What do the content-analysis results describe?*" (emphasis in the original). Indeed, what are we measuring? That question is seldom asked. "Content analysts have been rather casual about validating their results" (Krippendorf, 1980, p. 155).[61] If the silence found in the literature on issues of classification tells us anything, it is that the scholars involved must have either found the issue of classification unproblematic or had no solution to the problems involved. Given the difficulties I personally experienced with classification – a sheer exercise in frustration – I would exclude the former. Which leaves me to think: We have collectively ignored issues of classification, despite their negative effect on validity, because the whole process is based on ad hoc empirical tinkering, the final product one of Leamer's sausages[62] – hardly the view of science we have for ourselves or we want to project to others.

Content analysts are far more likely to ask a different question (one to which they are more likely to have an answer): Are content analysis data reliable? This is the question content analysis methodologists have tackled from the start (for example, Kaplan and Goldsen, 1949; Janis, 1949, p. 56). They have even given it a special name: intercoder reliability. They have proposed various statistical measures to quantify the problem (Krippendorf, 1980, pp. 129–54). No one, in content analysis, could get away with publishing work that did not report the values of the coefficients of intercoder reliability. It would be like publishing regression estimates without reporting the values of the R^2 and t-statistics. But, thank God, those coefficients are always high, safeguarding a basic tenet of science: That results must be reproducible.[63]

Social science researchers have put laudable efforts in attempting to eliminate random errors (reliability) from data collected from newspapers, while generally neglecting nonrandom errors (validity) (again, silence and emphasis). Certainly, most conflict studies go through painstaking efforts to ensure that whatever is reported by newspapers is recorded without error. Is this really worth it? Zeller and Carmines provide a very apt metaphor that may help us to answer that question (1980, pp. 48, 77):

> If a well-anchored rifle is fired but the shots are widely scattered about a target, the rifle is unreliable. But if the shots are closely concentrated around the target, the rifle is considered reliable. ... [I]f the shots ... hit exactly the same location but not the proper target, the targeting of the rifle is consistent (and hence reliable) but it did not hit the location that it was supposed to hit (and hence it is not valid).

What is the point of making sure that a figure of 200,000 for the size of a crowd is properly recorded, when such a figure may actually verge on the fantastic and when, furthermore, there is an equal likelihood of it being overestimated or underestimated?[64] Given that nonrandom error (validity) is much more likely to distort historical data than random error (reliability) and given the disproportionate attention paid to problems of reliability than of validity, I would recommend a shift in focus from problems of reliability to problems of validity. Validation of one's data through alternative and independent measures should be an integral part of any research design involving data collection from newspapers (from any source, in fact). It may well be that we need to rely on imperfect sources for lack of better alternatives, but that does not excuse us from trying to map the exact limits of our data. Only by means of validation studies can we hope to obtain a better understanding of the contours of the population of events of interest and of the mapping rules that link the nonrandom sample of events collected to its population.

In Stone's critical view of the "historical factory": These "vast undertakings" may be impressive as a whole, awesome to contemporaries, as awesome must have been to contemporaries the "satanic mills" at the beginning of the Industrial Revolution. But, to stick to the architectural metaphor, these huge structures will stand only if each constituent part stands, if the pillars and walls on which the structure rests, stand. The tendency is indeed one of standing awestruck before such buildings for the inventive and creative genius of architects without appreciation for the work of structural engineers. To put it with Stone:

> To some extent the conclusions drawn from these highly costly and labour-intensive quantitative studies still depend on the utility and reliability of the variables selected for study by the director before the data collection begins. (Stone, 1987, p. 37)

Data: "Given" or Constructed?

"The critical habit," warned Langlois and Seignobos (1898, p. 49) a century ago, "is not natural; it must be inculcated, and it only becomes ingrained through repeated exercise … and that is often accompanied by real pain." Von Ranke had been among the early proponents of that critical habit. He had pushed for the development of the historical seminar (Krieger, 1977, p. 2). He had insisted that all narrative or literary accounts of events (that is, historians' accounts) must be mistrusted (only second-hand knowledge, in his opinion). All historical knowledge should be based on first-hand, archival information.[65] In Lord Acton's 1886 obituary of von Ranke, von Ranke's achievement lays less in "the display of extraordinary faculties" than in his having "written a larger number of mostly excellent books than any man that ever lived" and in his having "taken pains from the first to explain how the thing is done" (in Krieger, 1977, p. 4). And von Ranke was certainly not a man easily scared by pain. Driven by a Protestant ethic to which he makes repeated references in his writings, he was accustomed to winning the battles of the body. "From time to time," he openly avows to us, "my soul has desired the love of a gentle maiden, [yet] it has never desired a woman, for … I am determined not to pay the least attention to my body in this kind of affair."[66]

Other affairs were stirring von Ranke's passions. "The object of my love is a beautiful Italian, and I hope that together we shall produce a Romano-German prodigy." But that "beautiful Italian," for von Ranke, is a Venetian document, the *relazioni* written from abroad by the *Serenissima*'s ambassadors! A closed archive "is still absolutely a virgin. I long for the moment I shall have access to her and make my declaration of love, whether she is pretty or not."[67]

Driven by this sensuous relationship with the archives and the document, he bought forty-eight *relazioni* on the antiquarian market.[68] These *relazioni* exemplified his "ideal type" document: An eyewitness account presented in terse, lucid, and yet vivid language by great diplomats – after all, the only history that counts for von Ranke is political history – with the added bonus of constituting an almost "continuous narrative" from the 1400s to the 1700s (Benzoni, 1990, pp. 51, 53). In the preface to *The Popes of Rome*, his most popular work, von Ranke writes: "It was from these [*relazioni*] that I derived the idea of a continuous narrative, and the courage to attempt it" (von Ranke, 1981, p. 63; Benzoni, 1990, p. 48).

"The Lunatic, the Lover, and the Poet / Are of imagination all compact," having lost all sense of reality, Theseus tells Hippolyta in *A Midsummer Night's Dream* (Shakespeare, act 5, scene I, lines 7–8). We may have to add "the Historian" to Theseus's list (and "the Social Scientist" and …). Novel Rinaldo,[69] *furioso d'amore* for the Venetian archives and the *relazioni,* von Ranke may have forgone his critical spirit. The *relazioni* are anything but simple, eyewitness accounts, written in the midst of events; rather, "they are highly filtered, deeply pondered texts, and they are not in the least spontaneous" (Benzoni, 1990, p. 53). They are overburdened with stylistic sophistication, with artifice, with strict adherence to a stylistic canon that is immutable over the centuries. Places, events, and protagonists are seen through the eyes of Venice and the Venetian patrician class. The *relazioni* aim to sing the supreme virtues of that class and of the individual writers, both in their political and literary capacities. "There are hundreds of *relazioni* written in different times, by different hands, concerning different countries. And yet, they are all similar to one another and seem to be the work of a single author" (Benzoni, 1990, p. 55).

If there is a sense in which we can talk about the politics of the data, the *relazioni*, von Ranke's favorite source upon which he "staked his scholarly reputation,"[70] illustrate that vividly. The *relazioni* were political documents, written by political figures, about other dominant political figures, and for political purposes. The *relazioni* can hardly be taken as "pure documents serving the interests of pure history" (Benzoni, 1990, p. 55). But if not in the interest of history, in whose interest? Taking the terse ambassadorial reports as "true facts," von Ranke failed to pose to his sources the questionnaire that Langlois and Seignobos suggest (1898, pp. 140–1): What reason does the author of a document have to collect some information? What are its *interests*? Which specific interest does certain information serve? Taking those reports as "eyewitness accounts," von Ranke failed to run the experiment that the great Belgian historian Henri Pirenne used to run with his students (reported in Chabod, 1992, pp. 66–7): He would have a waiter, dressed in flashy clothes, walk through the class. He would then ask the students to write down what they saw. Out of twenty reports, no two would be the same; often, in fact, they would be openly contradictory.

Official acts, according to Langlois and Seignobos, are particularly suspicious. They are even more likely than other documents to have practical reasons – *ragion di stato* – for favoring one or more parties against others (Langlois and Seignobos, 1898, pp. 140–1). Unfortunately, a great deal of the information we use today either as historians or social scientists is "official acts": births, marriages, deaths, tax payments, import, export, unemployment, strikes. Labor statistics are particularly sensitive to the question: in whose interest? Unemployment and strike figures are a good case in point, both subject to government manipulation and changes in definitions. In the 1971 Census for the United Kingdom, 1,365,775 people claimed to be unemployed. The official figure from the relevant week's records from the Department of Employment was half as much at 773,800 people.[71] As for strike statistics, in the nineteenth century, strikes were viewed as crimes under Combination Acts. Their recording was police business; data were kept secret in the hands of Ministries of the Interior (Perrot, 1974). Only after the interpretation of strikes shifted from one of crime to one of "social illness" did strikes become the concern of specialized Labor Ministries in most countries.[72] Despite the shift from "repression" to "cure" the kind of information collected still reflected state concern with rising labor militancy as information was collected on the presence of working class organizations during strikes, on the occurrence of violence and on the outcome of strikes. As Alonso and Starr (1987, p. 3) have made clear, official statistics are not "politicized" "in the sense of being corrupt," but "political judgements are implicit in the choice of what to measure, how to measure it, how often to measure it, and how to present and interpret the results."

If governments were eager to know what workers were up to and to collect data on strikes, they were not nearly as eager to make these data readily available. During the last century in Italy, publication of strike statistics was never timely; often two years or more passed before they were made publicly available. Statistics were published at a highly aggregated level, which made them of little use to working-class organizations.[73] And governments were even less eager to collect information on what employers and the state do. Neither Central Statistical Offices nor Ministries of Labor have ever collected data on state or employers' forms and levels of labor repression or on the timing of employers' introduction of new technologies and new forms of organization of production.[74]

Thus, statistics reflect relations of class and power in the way they are defined, collected, and made available. They provide information in ways that make them more or less useful to different social groups in society. Such skewed knowledge embedded in the very data makes it very difficult to investigate the nature of the social relations among actors. Instead of thinking of the "power of statistics," we should, perhaps, start thinking in terms of "statistics of power" (Franzosi, 1995a, pp. 242–53; see Porter, 1995, pp. 33–7).

One thing is clear: There is nothing *given* in our *data* (data, plural of Latin singular *datum* = given). Language, of course, can be very deceptive. We do, indeed, take our data as given, as granted, as unquestionable facts. As Marcuse put it: "[L]inguistic behavior ... repels recognition of the factors behind the facts, and thus repels recognition of the facts, and of their historical content" (Marcuse, 1964, p. 97). "Facts are what they are as occurrences in this struggle ["this historical struggle of man with nature and with society]. Their factuality is historical ..." (Marcuse, 1964, p. 185). As a result, only historical analysis – Foucault's "archeology of knowledge" – only "the mediation of the past with the present discovers the factors which made the facts, ... it projects the limits and the alternatives" (Marcuse, 1964, p. 100).

"Every researcher grants the status of *data* only to a small fraction of the *given*," Bourdieu says; and that fraction has less to do with the investigators' "problematics" than with "the pedagogical tradition of which they are part" (Bourdieu and Wacquant, 1992, p. 225). Typically, it is specific methodological schools that confer the status of *datum* to specific types of evidence. Data, in other words, are the result of specific types of data collection techniques. And that is true in the social sciences as much as history.[75] In that sense, Collingwood was right on target when he wrote that "when we ask what gives historical thought this datum, the answer is obvious: Historical thought *gives* it to itself, and therefore in relation to historical thought at large it is not a *datum* but a result or achievement" (Collingwood, 1946, p. 244; emphasis added). He would confess:

> Much of what he [the historian] takes for true is not given in this way but constructed by his *a priori* imagination; but I still fancied that this imagination worked inferentially from fixed points given in the same sense. I am now driven to confess that there are for historical thought no fixed points thus *given*: In other words, just as there are properly speaking no authorities, so there are properly speaking no *data*. (Collingwood, 1946, p. 241; emphasis added)

The historians of the *Annales* School (from Labrousse, to Bloch, Febvre, and Braudel), as Ricoeur points out, never doubted that "the facts ... are not given in the documents, rather documents are selected as a function of a certain problem. Documents themselves are not just given" (Ricoeur, 1984, p. 108). And that modern institution that historians have created – the Archive, where historians store and find their documents – "reflect an implicit choice in favor of history conceived of as an anthology of events and as the chronicle of a state" (Ricoeur, 1984, p. 108). Not surprisingly, Bloch remarks that perhaps the best evidence is "evidence of witnesses in spite of themselves," witnesses who never produced their documents with an eye to the Archives.[76]

Content and Form

It was Hegel who popularized in his *Introductory Lectures on Aesthetics* (1993[1835]) an idea of old, that works of art are characterized by two distinct dimensions: content and form. Emphasis on the content of historical narratives had led eighteenth-century erudites and nineteenth-century "scientific historians" to develop the philological and critical tools that would ensure the "truth" of that content. But by the twentieth century, emphasis had shifted to the form of historical narrative, to the purely linguistic features of historians' texts: the type of peculiar sentences used ("narrative sentences"), the balance between story and plot,[77] the reliance on different master tropes, the necessity of story point and coherence. "My method," states Hayden White who championed the approach, "is formalist" to the extent that it "seek[s] to identify the structural components of those [historical] accounts" (White, 1973, pp. 3–4).

"As works of imagination," Collingwood would write, "the historian's work and the novelist's do not differ" (Collingwood, 1946, p. 246). Historical narrative and storytelling differ only in terms of content, rather than form (White, 1987, p. 27). Roland Barthes, in a seminal essay on "The Discourse of History," would ask: "Is there in fact any specific difference between factual and imaginary narrative, any linguistic feature by which we may distinguish historical and fictional discourse?" His answer is "no" (Barthes, 1970, p. 153). Both history and storytelling use similar rhetorical devises and have similar narrative structures. "By its structures alone, without recourse to its content, historical discourse is essentially a product of ideology, or rather of imagination." Not that reference to content would rescue historical writing. "The only feature which distinguishes historical discourse from other kinds," Barthes continues, "is a paradox: The 'fact' can only exist linguistically, as a term in a discourse."[78] "The fictions of factual representation" are deeply ingrained in the historical tradition (White, 1978, p. 121).

Like Barthes, Danto sees no way of distinguishing the two types of sentences, historical and fictional.

> Imagine someone mixing up the history books with the historical novels – or with any kind of novel for that matter – and then asking us to sort them out, by criteria ... internal to the books themselves or the sentences which go to compose them. (Danto, 1985, p. 63)

The only characteristic that distinguishes historical sentences is their truth value, and that truth has nothing to do "with the surface of the sentence ... [but rather] with a relationship between sentences and whatever it is that they are about"

(Danto, 1985, p. 64). There are no intrinsic differences between the novelist's and the historian's sentences, both being "narrative sentences" whose "most general characteristic is that they refer to at least to two time-separated events," one prior, one posterior, one past, one future (Danto, 1985, p. 143). Thus, paradoxically, the writing of history, the writing about the past involves knowledge of the future. "There will always be descriptions of events in 1715 which will depend upon descriptions of events which have not as yet happened."[79] There is never closure in the writing of history. The past is constantly rewritten in light of an ever-changing present. The facts themselves may not change but their interpretation will. "Facts do not speak for themselves, but ... the historian speaks for them" (White, 1978, p. 125). "Historians are the inventors of their documents" (Ricoeur, 1984, p. 110).

To the very least that selectivity involves the constitution of the historians' (or sociologists', for that matter) *object* of inquiry out of their personal *subjective* interests. Max Weber, the sociologist, made that clear.

> The quality of an event as a 'social-economic' event is not something which it possesses 'objectively.' It is rather conditioned by the orientation of our cognitive interest, as it arises from the specific cultural significance which we attribute to the particular event in a given case. (Weber, 1949, p. 64)

Writing nearly a hundred years later, historian E. H. Carr put it in very similar terms:

> The facts of history cannot be purely objective, since they become facts of history only in virtue of the significance attached to them by the historian. Objectivity in history ... cannot be an objectivity of fact, but only of relation, of the relation between fact and interpretation, between past, present, and future. (Carr, 1990, p. 120)

But the process of selection does not stop at the constitution of an object of inquiry – the agrarian sociology of late Roman Antiquity or Soviet history. The sociologist and the historian continue to select further. And selection implies analysis, implies a grand narrative. For Bloch (1953, p. 144) "the historian selects and sorts. In short, he analyzes." And that selection constitutes a theory of history that tells us which actors, which actions, which facts should be included in the narrative. "Narrative history," according to Braudel (1980, p. 11), "consists in an interpretation, an authentic philosophy of history." "The historian is necessarily selective," echoes E. H. Carr.[80] "The belief in a hard core of historical facts existing objectively and independently of the interpretation of the historian is a preposterous fallacy" (Carr, 1990, p. 120).

Again, that process of selection finds its roots in the very linguistic characteristics of historical narratives. For Danto, all stories – true or fictional as that may be – share a fundamental characteristic: They all must have a beginning, a middle, and an end (Danto, 1985, p. 233). It is finding that middle between a beginning and an end that constitutes an explanation.[81] The very word "plot" that we associate to narrative provides the basic organizing principle of the information contained in the narrative, of action in the Aristotelian tradition. The distinction between story and plot, *fabula* and *sjužet*, is a distinction between "what really happened" and "all that he [the reader] ever directly knows" (Brooks, 1984, p. 13). There is no such thing as a purely descriptive narrative. "History is all of a piece. ... there is nothing one might call a pure description in contrast with something else to be called an interpretation."[82] Narrative is a both a form of understanding and explanation.[83] "A narrative describes and explains at once."[84] Although this claim is by no means novel in historiography,[85] Ricoeur, Brooks, Danto, and others give it specific linguistic underpinnings.

As stories, historians' narratives must also posses two essential narrative features: Story point – what's the point of telling the story? – and coherence – the story must make sense. It is history proper that brings "story point" to the fore, in particular, the relationship between historical narrativity and moralizing (White, 1987, pp. 22–5). For Polybius, "serious history is the best education for actual life" (in Grant, 1992, p. 153). "The study of history is the best medicine for a sick mind," wrote Livy. Because in history you will find "fine things to take as models, base things, rotten through and through, to avoid" (in Grant, 1992, p. 296). Bernard Bailyn would put it in remarkably similar words: "Accurate historical knowledge is essential for social sanity" (Bailyn, 1994, p. 12). For Tacitus, "Indeed, it is from such studies – from the experience of others – that most men learn to distinguish right and wrong, advantage and disadvantage" (in Grant, 1992, p. 468). Scores of historians have embraced that classical view of *historia magistra vitae*. History's "only purpose is educative," stated Trevelyan (Trevelyan, 1919, p. 27). It is that view of the pedagogical role of history dating back to the great Greek and Roman masters that led to the idea of a "dignity of history" – that of certain things one should not talk about. What is undignified, of course, depends upon one's point of view, one's position in the social world. For centuries, the dignity of history excluded the lower classes, women, and blacks from serious historical writing.

That process of selectivity imposed by story point is further underscored by another narrative imperative: that of coherence. "The novel and the history must both of them make sense" (Collingwood, 1946, p. 245). "Making his picture a coherent whole" is the most salient resemblance between the historian and the novelist (Collingwood, 1946, p. 245). And to make sense, only what is necessary must be in the story and nothing else, says Collingwood (1946, pp. 245–6).[86] To make sense, in other words, the historian *must* be selective. Danto will put it strikingly similar. Historical narratives, according to Danto, must constitute events into coherent "temporal wholes," with a "narrative unity."[87] For *N* to be a narrative it must possess narrative unity and that implies that "(A) *N* is about the same subject, (B) *N* adequately explains the changes in that subject which is covered by the explanandum, and (C) *N* contains only so much information as required by (B) and no more" (Danto, 1985, p. 251).

Thus, coherence (or narrative unity) implies selection. Historical explanations "represent products of decisions to ignore specific domains in the interest of achieving a purely formal coherence in representation" (White, 1978, p. 57). There is no escape from being selective. We are selective because we could not include either everything that happened in the past or that surrounds us in social reality. In fact, if we did, Danto argues, we would "fail through succeeding" (Danto, 1985, p. 114). We would not produce history, only *temporal structures* with no overall coherence, with no point, and with no story (Danto, 1985, p. 166). Coherence implies tailoring of facts and definite narrative strategies, definite forms of emplotment in the name of constructing *plausible* accounts (White, 1978, pp. 91, 122).

> The events are *made* into a story by the suppression or subordination of certain of them and the highlighting of others, by characterization, motif repetition, variation of tone and point of view, alternative descriptive strategies, and the like – in short, all of the techniques that we would normally expect to find in the emplotment of a novel or play. (White 1978, p. 84)

Gallie endorses that narrativist view of history when he writes: "All history … is basically a narrative of events" (Gallie, 1963, p. 69). "History is a species of the genus story" (Gallie, 1963, p. 66), where a story is nothing but a sequence of actions performed or suffered by certain actors. To understand a story means simply this: The ability to follow that sequence of actions, to find acceptable the unfolding of actions and the conclusions reached. It is our competence to follow stories that enables us to understand history. "Followability" is the key feature of any good story. And to make a story "followable" a historian must subsume individual events into a broader schema, weave them into a narrative. This way, historians, in their stories, select, narrate, and explain at the same time. "Followability" forces the good historians to produce "coherent" texts. And followability and coherence constrain the historian to be selective. And selection implies silence on certain events and emphasis on others. But that selectivity is not so much, or not only, the result of the capricious biases of an historian's values. The writing of history in narrative form imposes its constraints upon historians' narrative through purely linguistic mechanisms.

Language itself imposes further constraints, distorts, and warps the historians' narratives. "The use of language forbids … [the historian] to be neutral," writes E. H. Carr (1990, p. 25). Contrary to the language of natural scientists – often devised with the sole purpose of precision in definitions – historians' language is everyday language imbued with the emotions, passions, and biases of life.[88] "History receives its vocabulary, for the most part, from the very subject-matter of its study," writes Bloch (1953, p. 158). "It accepts it, already worn out and deformed by long usage; frequently, moreover, ambiguous from the very beginning, like any system of expression which has not derived from the rigorously organized efforts of technical experts." "Historians *constitute* their subjects as possible objects of narrative representation by the very language they use to *describe* them" (White 1978, p. 95; emphasis in the original).

By privileging metonymy over metaphor historians have created the illusion of facticity and objectivity (White, 1978, pp. 81–100, 121–34). Through their differential reliance on master tropes (in particular, metaphor, metonymy, synecdoche, and irony) historians fashion very different kinds of stories out of the same basic material (modes of emplotment), they have provided fundamentally different types of historical explanations (modes of explanation), a metahistory of history. To the use of metonymy there corresponds a mode of emplotment characterized by a tragic plot structure and a mode of explanation based on mechanistic causal connections; irony produces satiric plots and pragmatic, contextual explanations; synecdoche tends to generate comic emplotments and organicistic explanations (White, 1978, p. 128; 1973, pp.7–21). These different modes of emplotment and different modes of historical explanation have correspondingly different ideological implications (anarchist, radical, conservative, liberal). "A historiographical style represents a particular combination of modes of emplotment, argument, and ideological implication" (White, 1973, p. 29). Different authors, consciously or unconsciously, produce different historiographical styles based on somewhat standard, although not rigid, combinations of these three different modes of emplotment, argument, and ideological implication.[89]

Bloch's, Barthes's, Ricoeur's, White's, and Danto's emphasis on language and on the configuration of scientific inquiry in the human sciences at the linguistic level casts new light (or ominous shadows) on our journey from words to numbers, on our quest for rigorous and exact measurement that prompted our journey. We have inadvertently stepped out of that comforting technical world of rewrite rules, relational database models, SQL, and networks to confront something new, something perhaps less tangible than Durkheim's social things or von Ranke's historical facts as they really happened. In Cicourel's words:

> The problems of measurement, therefore, can be viewed from the perspective of the sociology of knowledge: The world of observables is not simply 'out there' to be described and measured with the measurement systems of modern science, but the course of historical events and the ideologies of a given era can influence what is 'out there' and how these objects and events are to be perceived, evaluated, described, and measured. (Cicourel, 1964, p. 38)

Our problem of measurement surges here to a different, unexpected plane, takes on new meanings, engages us in a much wider search involving, no less, "the sociology of knowledge," the whole "course of historical events," and "ideologies." A technical tool that we had developed to solve a problem of data collection – story grammar – helps us understand fundamental epistemological problems of how disciplines know what they know. Measurement hardly seems a technical problem any more.

What is *the problem* then? Cicourel is clear on this: "[M]easurement in sociology ... cannot be rigorous without solutions to *the problems* of cultural meanings. [But] understanding *the problem* of meaning requires a theory of both language and culture."[90] Economist Donald McCloskey put it similarly. "Quantification without a rhetoric of the scholarly conversation" does not help us to understand the way we approach the issue (McCloskey, 1985, p. 150). We have stepped here into a new world where language and words, rather than mathematics and numbers seem to take center stage. Two sentences by Durkheim and Barthes best give the sense of the distance that separates these two worlds.[91] For Durkheim: "If there is such a science as sociology, it can only be the study of a world hitherto unknown, different from those explored by the other sciences. *This world is nothing if not a system of realities.*" And for Barthes "*reality is nothing but a meaning.*"

Let's leave behind Durkheim's world and explore Barthes's.

5

"A Worlde of Wordes"[1]

[T]here is nothing outside the text. … [T]here has never been anything but writing.

Jacques Derrida (1974, p. 158)

The text is a tissue of quotations drawn from the innumerable centres of culture.

Roland Barthes (1977b, p. 146)

The only road from grammar to logic … runs through the intermediate territory of rhetoric.

Northrop Frye (1957, p. 331)

Science … can afford no guidance for the life of man.

Leo Tolstóy (1934, p. 229)

Back to the Linguist's World

Is everything really a number, as Pythagoras would have it? Or is it not the case that everything is a word, our world "a worlde of wordes" in John Florio's title of the first English-Italian dictionary (1598)? There are good arguments for this.

• My source material are words: Newspaper and police narratives of protest events.
• The method of data collection – story grammar – reveals in its very name its close association with words.
• The data I extract from my sources via this method are still words – the triplets: "Workers strike"; "Employer fires workers"; "Ministry of labor mediates"; ….

- The thousands of triplets present in the database are crunched in a handful of implicit triplets hidden behind a language of statistics and network graphs (for example, in Figure 3.6, for the year 1920, "the police controls the Left, protesters, strikers, people, unions, Socialists, and workers" or, in Figure 3.7, for 1922, "the judiciary helps the Fascists").
- The way I fashion my story out of this basic building blocks, are yet more words. I tell many stories on my way to the numbers.
- My text is a collage of quotes and citations.

Language, meaning, texts, representations. We have entered a world here where science seems to slip through our fingers, a world where the confident certainties we had built in Part I seem to disappear. We are learning a new vocabulary. Ambiguity, interpretation, selection, rhetoric, rigidity, and data as "socially constructed" are lurking behind the vocabulary of power, rigor, formalism, models, objectivity, and data (as "given"). Just when victory seemed certain for the numbers in this war between words and numbers, the words are mounting a powerful counterattack. The war is far from over. Linguistics that had helped us to pave the way from words to numbers is now turning its back on us.

Stories

An Oxford Story

Writing in the mid-nineteenth century, Mark Pattison, rector at Lincoln College, passionately defended the tutorial system – the one-to-one teaching that has been the hallmark of the University of Oxford for centuries:[2]

> Professorial lectures … are in place at Mechanics Institutes, to convey the elements of knowledge to youthful or ignorant hearers, or in metropolitan lecture halls, to exhibit a superficial view of a serious subject before a fashionable audience. For the … serious student … what is needed is the immediate contact of mind with mind … [3]

Yet, the success of German universities – "where the college and the college tutor were things unheard of"[4] – was there to paint a different picture of professorial lectures. That picture became even clearer during World War One, which exposed the deficiencies of British technology. Critics deplored the tutorial system "regarded as a waste of intellectual resources." Still in the late 1950s, "while for some it [the tutorial system] might be a marriage of true minds, for others it was often an embarrassing and expensive failure."[5]

A contact of mind with mind? Or an embarrassing and expensive failure? The debate continued in the late-twentieth century through several Commissions of Inquiry. For me, the tutorial system, during my years as an Oxford don, allowed me to run daily experiments in the ontology of language (and … science).[6] The moment a student settled into my office, took out the essay, and started reading, I started counting – one, two, three, … – the number of seconds it would take until I heard the sentence, "In this essay it will be shown that …" Few of us are sensitive to such linguistic nuances in grammaticalization. Most of us, in fact, would expect that language. After all, isn't that what we are taught in high school (and British high schools are particularly insistent on the use of passive constructs)? Isn't that what our journals have gotten us used to? Isn't that the very way we write? But, for the sake of scientific experimentation, I often asked the student: "By whom? By whom will it be shown?" To which, a bewildered student typically replied: "Well … by me [you idiot!]." "Then, why didn't you just write: 'In this essay I will show that …?'" "But … but … that's too personal. It's not objective!" There you have it. Your "empirical evidence" on objectivity as the result of a linguistic convention.

A Children's Story

Maddalena and Marianna, my older twin daughters, were probably only two-years old when this event happened long ago in Rome. There had been a small family get together at our house. My mother was there, my sister, her daughter and her husband, my sister in law and her daughter, my mother in law, my wife, and the twins; in all, nine women, young and old, and two men. After lunch, we had decided to all go out for a short walk. My brother-in-law and I were standing in the hall with Maddalena and Marianna, impatiently waiting for everyone else. After a few minutes of waiting, I asked: *"Siamo pronti ad andare, o no?"* (Are we ready to go or not?)

In Italian, as in many other languages, nouns and adjectives are gendered (thus, a mouse is masculine but a chicken is feminine, a tractor masculine but an excavator feminine, and so is a chair, or a cup – go figure that!) Adjectives take the gender of the noun to which they refer. That rule runs into problems when the noun is plural and represents a collection of both feminine and masculine nouns (as in my sentence "are *we* ready to go, or not?" where *we* refers to the eleven people in the house, nine females and two males). Which gender should the adjective take, masculine, feminine, or perhaps neutral? And if masculine or feminine, what should the rule be: Majority wins? Italian, a patriarchal language, solves the problem by conjugating the adjective to the masculine if even only one masculine noun is present. Thus, the grammatical rule of proper sentence formation dictates that in my sentence "Are we ready" the *ready* should be masculine, because the *we* to which *ready* refers includes two males.

The discriminatory nature of that grammatical rule did not escape the two-year-old Marianna, who exclaimed: *"Ma, ma, ma, papà, perchè pronti?"* ("but, but, but, daddy, why ready?") It escaped me, not surprisingly. I did not understand what she was trying to say, until she asked: "But, but, but, aren't we coming?" Now it was clear. Marianna was worried that by using the masculine form of the adjective "ready" (*pronti*, masculine, instead of *pronte*, feminine) I meant to exclude all the women in the house (and most importantly *them*) from going for a walk. It would be years before another thing would become clear to me: The double power of language to include or exclude, and even to deny cognitive access to alternatives. Quite a lesson from a two-year-old!

The Moral of the Stories: "Where Is Anna Giulia?"

In his *Reflections on Language*, Chomsky (1976, p. 4) writes:

> By studying language we may discover abstract principles that govern its structure and use, principles that are universal by biological necessity and not mere historical accident, that derive from mental characteristics of the species.

Notwithstanding the dignity of this goal, I am rather fond of a different goal for the study of language: For what it has to say about our linguistic cognitive processes, about the mechanisms through which reality seems to appear and disappear, like a rabbit out of a conjurer's hat, via the tricks of language.

In a masterful analysis of the functions of language, Jakobson distinguishes among six different functions of language, functions which correspond symmetrically to six different "factors inalienably involved in verbal communication" (Jakobson, 1960, p. 353). Basically, any act of communication involves an "addresser" who sends a "message" to an "addressee," the receiver of the message, on a specific physical medium ("contact" in Jakobson's language) (for example, paper, radio). The "message" includes the set of explicit and implicit meanings verbalized by the addresser in the message ("context" or "referent"). Its intelligibility implies the availability of a common "code" of interpretation between addresser and addressee (Eco, 1979, p. 15). In Jakobson's summary:[7]

CONTEXT

ADDRESSER   MESSAGE   ADDRESSEE
_____

CONTACT
CODE

To this constellation of factors, there corresponds the following constellation of different functions of language:

REFERENTIAL

EMOTIVE   POETIC   CONATIVE
                 PHATIC

METALINGUAL

The "referential," "emotive," and "conative" functions are the most important functions of language.[8] No doubt, the "referential" function, the relationship between message and its implicit and explicit context, is the "leading task of numerous messages ... [with] the accessory participation of the other functions" (Jakobson, 1960, p. 353). The "emotive" (or "expressive") function refers to "the speaker's attitude toward what he is speaking about" (Jakobson, 1960, p. 354), to the addresser's way of seeing, to his inner world. The "conative" function expresses the message's orientation toward the addressee (as expressed particularly in imperative and exhortative forms). The respective emphases of "emotive" and "conative" functions are on author and audience, on writer and reader, on the *I* and the *you*.

Verbal messages are never either purely emotive, or conative, or referential, never one *or* the other. "We could ... hardly find verbal messages that would fulfill only one function," Jakobson tells us (1960, p. 353). "The diversity lies not in a monopoly of some of these several functions but in a different hierarchical order of functions." According to Jakobson, different text genres privilege one or more linguistic functions at the expense of the others. "The particularities of diverse ... genres imply a differently ranked participation of the other verbal functions along with the dominant ... function."[9]

Scientific discourse, as a specific type of text genre, is a good illustration of this "differently ranked participation" of verbal functions to the overall production of the text. Scientific discourse has backgrounded the emotive and conative functions of language and foregrounded the referential function. It has systematically erased any signs of the reader's presence. In Barthes's words:

> It is a remarkable and rather odd fact that literary discourse rarely carries any mark acknowledging the reader's presence; one might even characterize it as (apparently) a discourse without Thou [it] though in fact its whole structure implies a reader as 'subject.' In historical discourse destination signs are normally absent. (Barthes, 1970, p. 148)

Not just the reader, but even the author is denied a presence. The "*I*" of a novel is never the "real" narrator, but an interposed narrator.[10] "I am the man who comes and goes between the bar and the telephone booth. Or, rather: *That man is called "I"* ... I hang up the receiver ... I await the rattling flush ... I push the glass door." Thus, Calvino writes in that masterpiece *If on a Winter's Night a Traveler* – Calvino who had befriended Foucault and Barthes after moving to Paris.[11]

And if silence on the reader's and author's presence is true of "literary discourse," it is even more true of historical and scientific discourse. Historians and scientists have carefully avoided signaling the author's presence, suppressing "all traces of the *I* in their text" (Barthes, 1970, p. 148). In historical writing, by "systematically omitting any direct allusion to the originator of the text ... the history seems to write itself" (Barthes, 1970, p. 148).

> How well I would write if I were not here! If between the white page
> and the writing of words and stories that take shape and disappear
> without anyone's ever writing them there were not interposed that
> uncomfortable partition which is my person! Style, taste, individual
> philosophy, subjectivity, cultural background, real experience,
> psychology, talent, tricks of the trade: All the elements that make what
> I write recognizable as mine seem to me a cage that restricts the
> possibilities. If I were only a hand, a severed hand that grasps a pen
> and writes ... (Calvino, 1993, p. 167)

Fogel and Engerman (1974, p. 3) in their *Time on the Cross* write:

> We have tried to present the findings of the cliometricians on the
> economics of slavery in as dispassionate a manner as possible –
> although we allowed ourselves *some personal latitude in the prologue
> and epilogue*. (Emphasis added)

Indeed, the paratext has become the confine of the personal – in prefaces,
"Narcissism is the law" (Derrida, 1981, p. 45); "the preface ... [is] a monument
to pride," in the words of Charles Nodier.[12] Hegel, typically detached and
impersonal in his style, allows himself the use of the "I" in his prefaces, in a
tradition that dates back to Livy of talking about oneself in the first person *only*
in the preface (Genette, 1997, p. 165). A similarly detached and stern von
Ranke, the "father" of modern history, wrote in his "Introduction" to the *History
of the Reformation in Germany* (1981, p. 70; emphasis added):

> Let no one pity a man who devotes himself to studies apparently so
> dry, and neglects for them the delights of many a joyous day. It is true
> that the companions of his solitary hours are but lifeless paper, but they
> are the remnants of the life of past ages, which gradually assume form
> and substance to the eye occupied in the study of them. *For me (in an
> introduction an author is bound to speak of himself – a subject he
> elsewhere gladly avoids) they had a peculiar interest.*

The overall result of the systematic application of both negative and positive
selections – the adroit elimination of the *I* (author) and the *you* (reader) – is a
strong appearance of impersonal and objective discourse, the discourse of
science. If linguistic change is partly due to changing social relations and
shifting relations of power, the ultimate touchstone of the power of the scientific
community will be a linguistic change where "the objectivity of thought can be
expressed using the verb 'to think' in the impersonal third person: Saying not 'I
think' but 'it thinks' as we say 'it rains'" (Calvino, 1993, p. 171).

For Barthes, historians' reliance on an objectivity carefully constructed at the
language level is nothing but a "referential illusion, where the historian tries to
give the impression that the referent is speaking for himself" (Barthes, 1970,
p. 149). Barthes insists (1970, p. 151):

'Objective' discourse (as in positivistic history) resembles schizo-phrenic discourse; in both cases there is a radical censorship of the utterance, in which negativity cannot be expressed (though it can be felt), and there is a massive reversion of discourse away from any form of sui-reference, or even (in the case of the historian) a reversion towards the level of pure referent – the utterance for which no one is responsible.

It is an interesting language game this game of scientific discourse. I wonder what my three-year-old daughter Anna Giulia would have to say about that. Because she plays a remarkably similar game of her own. She hides her face behind her hands and then asks: "Where is Anna Giulia?" Drawn into this childish game, I start looking around, myself asking: "Where is Anna Giulia? She has disappeared! Oh dear me, I cannot find her any more!" And the game ends in great laughter when Anna Giulia pulls her hands away, opens her eyes, and screams: "Here I am! Here I am!" What would she think of these grown up academics – who rather take themselves very seriously – going around, their faces hidden behind their hands, asking the question: "Where is the author?" "Where is the reader?" but no one's laughing.

"The Body and its Shadow": Play, Aesthetics, and Language Games

And why should they laugh? Children laugh, with an easy laughter. But grown ups have to work hard at it. They had to invent the comic, the humor, the jokes to regain the "lost laughter of childhood," to recapture "the mood of our childhood, when we were ignorant of the comic, when we were incapable of jokes and when we had no need of humour to make us feel happy in our life" (Freud, 1991, pp. 289, 302). Yet, play is a main civilizing factor (Huizinga, 1949, p. 5). "Real civilization cannot exist in the absence of a certain play-element" (Huizinga, 1949, p. 211).

Journeys and play share many characteristics in common. Play presents itself "everywhere as a well-defined quality of action which is different from 'ordinary' life" (Huizinga, 1949, p. 4). Like a journey's liminality, play is "a stepping out of 'real' life into a temporary sphere of activity with a disposition all of its own" (Huizinga, 1949, pp. 8, 9–19). Play "is free, is in fact freedom," freedom "to dare, to take risks, to bear uncertainty, to endure tension – these are the essence of the play spirit" (Huizinga, 1949, pp. 8, 51). Daring journeys and daring plays always raise the question: "[W]ill it come off?" (Huizinga, 1949, p. 47)

We play "for" something, typically for victory (Huizinga, 1949, p. 50). You cannot have a game by yourself, confirms Gadamer. There is always to-and-from movement in play.[13] Yet, play does not necessarily have to result in winners and losers. For Gadamer (1997, p. 106) "the real subject of the game ... is not the player but instead the game itself." In the end, "the players ... no longer exist, only what they are playing" (Gadamer, 1997, p. 112). Play, in fact, is first and foremost "self-presentation ... the player achieving ... his own self-presentation by playing" (Gadamer, 1997, p. 108). This way, play is always intimately connected to the self. Play "is always self-realization, sheer fulfillment, energeia" (Gadamer, 1997, p. 113). In that sense, play is a way to be young, a way of keeping old age and death at bay: If I play, I am alive! Not only alive, but alive at the start of my life, a child again with a whole life in front of me. In Samuel Beckett's *Endgame*, Clov says to Hamm: "Let's stop playing." "Never!" replies Hamm. And after a pause: "Put me in my coffin." To which Clov answers: "There are no more coffins."[14] Play, and its associated laughter, is a temporary path to immortality, another path in man's obstinate refusal of death. For as long as I play I know I am alive: *Rideo ergo sum.* "The Aristotelian *animal ridens* characterizes man as distinct from the animal almost more absolutely than *homo sapiens*" (Huizinga, 1949, p. 6).

We journey and play to run away from death, to step out of ordinary life, to escape routine – "an intermezzo, an interlude." And some are luckier than others. As Einstein put it, in a speech delivered at a celebration of Max Planck's sixtieth birthday: "I believe with Schopenhauer that one of the strongest motives that leads men to art and science is escape from everyday life with its painful crudity and hopeless dreariness, from the fetters of one's own shifting desires" (1973, p. 225). Nisbet would agree: "The unity of science and art exists most luminously in the motivations, desires, rhythms, and itches which lie behind creativeness in any realm" (1976, p. 4). Creativity, then, as the truest expression of freedom – after all, when we proffer the word "Creator" don't we refer to nothing less than God? But Gods, unfortunately, we are not – if anything playthings in the hands of the Gods; so our freedom is only limited freedom.

The play-element, perhaps even more so than the journey, betrays its close connection to beauty and aesthetics. "Many and close are the links that connect play with beauty," wrote Huizinga (1949, p. 4). Right at the beginning of his *Critique of Judgment*, Kant emphasizes "disinterestedness" as one of the essential characteristic of aesthetics, conceived as the judgment of taste: "*The delight which determines the judgment of taste is independent of all interest.*" "*Beauty* is the form of *finality* in an object, so far as perceived in it *apart from the representation of an end.*"[15] It is this same sheer pleasure of contemplation, regardless of any practical utility or application, that Schiller stresses in his writings on aesthetics (of art, one should not be "asking after its purpose"). Schiller insists on the "play impulse" of art, on art as freedom.[16] Since playful activities have these same characteristics of sheer pleasure, playful activities must be included "in the realm of the aesthetic" (Huizinga, 1949, p. 7). "Man with beauty must only play, and he must play only with beauty," Schlegel wrote. "Man plays only insofar as he is a man ... and he is truly man only when he plays."[17]

Behind that playful spirit there is a search for beauty and immortality: Step by step, like "rungs in a ladder," from the beauty of a human body, to physical beauty in general, the beauty of people's activities, the beauty of intellectual endeavors, and *that* beauty, true beauty, as Socrates would have it. "Too late came I to love thee, O thou Beauty," confesses Augustine, "both so ancient and so fresh, yea too late came I to love thee" (Augustine, X, XXVII; 1912, p. 147). The gods will smile on that man. He alone will have the *potential* for immortality. The symmetric organizational structure of this book and its literary character, the reflections upon mathematics, the use of the narrative form, my game with the reader, my play with forms and ideas perhaps betray this concern with beauty and death (or its negation). The very narrative plot of the book, with its beginning, middle, and end, "is the internal logic of the discourse of mortality" (Brooks, 1984, p. 22). The open-ended finale of the book, the lingering with the reader, the reluctance to put the word "end" at the bottom of the last page, is a refusal of that logic, a refusal of death.

But if the place of play is in the realm of the aesthetic, in that realm we find the comic as well. Freud, in his *Jokes and Their Relation to the Unconscious*, agrees with philosopher Kuno Fischer that "a joke is a *playful* judgment"; that

> the aesthetic attitude towards an object is characterized by the condition that we do not ask anything of the object, especially no satisfaction of our serious needs, but content ourselves with the enjoyment of contemplating it. The aesthetic attitude is *playful* in contrast to work. (Cited in Freud, 1991, p. 41; see also pp. 138–9; emphasis in the original)

He agrees with novelist Jean Paul Richter that at the heart of the comic is aesthetic freedom. "Freedom produces jokes and jokes produce freedom." Thus, both the play-element of culture and the comic need freedom. Like metaphor, joking is the creative "ability to find similarity between dissimilar things" (cited in Freud, 1991, p. 41). "Joking is merely playing with ideas" (cited in Freud, 1991, p. 41). Pirandello, writing his essay on *Humor* only three years after Freud's *Jokes*, would agree with Freud that playing with ideas and the comic go together. In fact, he would push that further. Humor is not just playing with ideas. It is playing with ideas in a disruptive and desecrating way, playing with ideas to mock established creed. The comic is fundamentally about transgression. Pirandello writes: "The humorist does not know heroes; or at least lets others represent heroes."[18] "He knows what legends and stories really are and how they are fashioned ... their pretense of reality" and he enjoys exposing them. It is a sentiment of the contrary that characterizes the humorist. He is drawn to "breaking up, disordering, disrupting," and "unmasking," rather than composing coherent and round characters. Like in the naked emperor's story, the humorist "looks at the world, perhaps not really naked, but at least in shirt sleeves." He is a little devil who enjoys taking a mechanism apart, "just to see how it is made inside." Contrary to ordinary artists, who focus on the representation of the body exclusively, the humorist is interested in both the body and its shadow, and sometimes more in the shadow than in the body.[19]

The Language of Science

Jakobson did not stop at the distinction between emotive and referential function of language. He also introduced a distinction between metaphoric and metonymic discourse – a dichotomy "of primal significance and consequence of all verbal behaviour and for human behaviour in general" (Jakobson, 1956, p. 79). Contrary to traditional work on rhetoric from Aristotle onward who regarded metonymy (and synecdoche) as subspecies of metaphor, Jakobson regarded them as polar opposites (Lodge, 1977, pp. 75–6). Different types of discourse are fundamentally characterized by the dominance of one trope over the other.[20] "Prose ... tends towards the metonymic pole ... poetry ... tends towards the metaphoric pole. Romantic and symbolist writing is metaphoric, and realist writing is metonymic" (Lodge, 1977, p. 80). "Metonymy ... is the favored trope of all *modern* scientific discourse," writes White.[21] At the linguistic level science was born at the expense of metaphorical discourse. Modern science privileged metonymy over metaphor, the concrete over the imaginative (Jakobson, 1960, p. 375). Metaphors (for example, "time is money," "Joan is a gem") link together, by association, things that belong to different orders. Abstract thinking may ultimately be nothing but a metaphor. For Huizinga (1949, p. 4), "behind every abstract expression, there lie the boldest of metaphors, and every metaphor is a play upon words. Thus, in giving expression to life man creates a second, poetic world alongside the world of nature."

Metaphors expand not only the number of linguistic objects (time *and* money, Joan *and* gem) but also the number of different worlds in which those objects find their place (for example, the human order of Joan and the mineral order of a gem). A proper understanding of metaphors requires a leap of the imagination. On the contrary, metonymy celebrates the concrete. When we represent London as "The Tube," Rome as the "Colosseum," or Paris as the "Eiffel Tower," we construct an image of these cities by focusing on a specific part. The language of metonymy is both concrete and "reductive," as Kenneth Burke posits (cited in White, 1978, p. 131). "The metaphoric mode," wrote Lodge (1977, p. 111), "bewilders us with a plethora of possible meanings. The metonymic text, in contrast, deluges us with a plethora of data, we seek to unite into one meaning." Again, Jakobson's remarks are right on target (1960, pp. 374–5):

> It is no mere chance that metonymic structures are less explored than the field of metaphor. ... [T]he study of poetic tropes has been directed mainly toward metaphor, and the so-called realistic literature, intimately tied with the metonymic principle, still defies interpretation, although the same linguistic methodology, which poetics uses when analyzing the metaphorical style of romantic poetry, is entirely applicable to the metonymical texture of realistic prose.

It was Aristotle who first laid the groundwork of the art of rhetoric. According to Aristotle, there are four basic ways for an orator to deliver a convincing argument: 1) Putting his character in a good light, "to make the speaker worthy of credence" (Aristotle, *Rhetoric*, 1.2.4); 2) working on the emotions of the audience; 3) using sound arguments; 4) using arguments only *apparently* sound (Aristotle, *Rhetoric*, 1.2.2–3). Indeed, travelers' accounts never fail to shed a positive light on their characters: Pilgrims do not tell us of the less than holy aspects of life on the road; voyagers of discovery are always victim rather than perpetrators of violence. Alchemists make it clear that it is not personal gain or lust of riches that motivates their quest of the alchemic transformation of vile metals into gold. Contrary to this, scientists are rather silent about their characters. Science does not like the personal. "Science," von Wiese tells us in his *Memoires*, "demands constant self-discipline, fighting against subjectivity and against the heart's desire for expression" (von Wiese, 1956, p. 25). Yet, the scientist may well fight against subjectivity, but in truth he is the only "subject"; he is the only one empowered to speak, and to speak with the voice of authority (the voice of the expert); the others are "objects" of inquiry; objectivity is the turning of others into objects. The social scientist's syntagms are no doubt syntagms of power: indeed, power, precision, rigor, objectivity. In the end, scientists do tell us a great deal about themselves, even through their silence. They do shed a positive light on their (collective) character. Merton best celebrated the positive characteristics of the ethos of science in his seminal essays on the sociology of science: intellectual honesty, universalism or communism of intellectual property, integrity, organized scepticism, disinterestedness, impersonality, humility.[22] Quite a different character from that humorously painted by David Lodge (for example, 1984) or by later critical developments in the sociology of science.

And, needless to say, scientists do use arguments – sound or only apparently sound as that may be. And those arguments must be coherent. They must have a point. Even quantitative statistical work shares these characteristics with narrative and other texts. No one knows this better than those of us who have struggled with uncooperative data – some of the statistical results of our estimates going one way and some others going another way, depending upon model specification, sample analyzed, and estimating method. As McCloskey has convincingly argued:

> If the results of the fitting to the data are 'reasonable' … the article is sent off to a journal for publication, and added to the resume of the economist. If the results are unreasonable, the hypothesis is consigned to do a loop, as they say at the computation center: The economic scientist returns to the hypotheses or the specifications, altering them until a publishable article emerges. (McCloskey, 1985, pp. 138–9)

The most prolific in the profession are, no doubt, those who learn quickly how to pick and choose among fluctuating results, how to impose order on chaos, ultimately providing coherent accounts. Ideally, we should also provide a punch line, give a point to our story, one that we can deliver succinctly like an advertising slogan. Knowing how to present one's findings in appropriate ways is part and parcel of the social scientist's professionalization. The fact that only statistically "significant" results are published adds to the pressure of this ritualized game.[23]

We build coherence between theory and data, between hypotheses and empirical evidence, between contradictory statistical results. That requires a subtle game of silence and emphasis: Backgrounding negative results and foregrounding positive ones, backgrounding discrepancies and foregrounding similarities. One thing is for sure. In our texts, "we are permitted to see only the finished play, never the actor as he really is, adjusting his make-up, rehearsing his lines" (Feuer, 1995, p. 253). Lazarsfeld tells us:

> I have repeatedly advocated that sociologists should give accounts of the way their interests and writings actually develop ... In my teaching, ... We [with students] read empirical research closely and try to reconstruct how the author was led from one step to the next: What data he might have inspected but not reported; how the order of his final presentation might have developed from an originally vague and quite different imagery. (Lazarsfeld, 1993, pp. 258–62)

It is unfortunate that Lazarsfeld's pedagogy is not standard practice in the social sciences.

In the literature review section of our articles we line up friends and foes, we masterfully set up our "straw man." In the literature review we also find that characteristic identified by Lévi-Strauss in historical writing: The thickening of the pace of narrative as we get closer to the narrated time – a measuring scale of events that is not invariant but changes with the historian's point of view (1972, pp. 258–60). Our bibliographical references similarly thicken the closer we get to the publishing date. There is typically nothing in between fleeting references to the "founding fathers" and a host of references to the most up-to-date articles, those not yet published, those delivered at yesterday's (if not tomorrow's) conference (Billig, 1987, pp. 1–2). We religiously update our references till the last minute, with our papers already in press, for fear those references may have become stale between the time of submission and the time of final publication. Like Danto's Ideal Chronicle, the writing of past historical events implies knowledge of future events, of what came after the event that made the event relevant or important in some respect. In light of future developments of scientific discourse much of these reverently and minutely up-to-date citations are likely to truly be a waste.

You do find a great deal of rhetoric in our scientific texts, against science's own rhetoric of antirhetoric. Even when we try our hardest to eschew rhetoric, close inspection will reveal the gamut of rhetorical devices we still, perhaps unconsciously, use. In a masterful analysis of Galileo's and Darwin's writing,

Marcello Pera shows the gamut of rhetorical devices that these two authors, fundamentally opposed to rhetoric, use (Pera, 1991). In several points of his book, Darwin relies on arguments based on analogy (1996, pp. 41, 48, 50, 116, 148, 177, 194, 206). More generally, not only is Darwin sympathetic to the use of analogy as a mode of scientific proof and argumentation, but he is very aware of the power of metaphors as well. Rather than being naive about metaphor, Darwin refers repeatedly to the "metaphorical sense" of his concepts. He writes: "I use the term Struggle for Existence in a large and *metaphorical sense* ... As the mistletoe is disseminated by birds, its existence depends on birds; and it may *metaphorically* be said to struggle ..."[24] The metaphor of the "tree of life" that Darwin used must be seen in the context of a long tradition in botany and zoology of metaphorical representations (the *ladder of nature*, Linnaeus's *map*, the *polygon*, the *tree of life*; see Ritvo, 1997, pp. 28–35; Gruber, 1978).

James Watson's remarks on language and style are quite revealing of a scientist's attitudes toward language. Of an article written by fellow biologist Linus Pauling, Watson says: "The only thing I was sure of was that is was written with style."[25] Of another article by Pauling, he similarly remarks: "Again the language was dazzling and full of rhetorical tricks." The apparent praises for Pauling's writing style are tempered by the increasing negativity expressed by such words as "dazzling," "rhetorical," and "tricks." Watson toys with Pauling's language and character. "One article started with the phrase, 'Collagen is a very interesting protein.' It inspired me to compose opening lines of the paper I would write about DNA ..." That line, as it appeared in a paper published in *Nature*, would finally be: "We wish to suggest a structure for the salt of deoxyribose nucleic acid (DNA). This structure has novel features which are of considerable biological interest." Quite a carefully understated opening, a teaser really, for someone well aware that he "had found the secrets of life," and that, through that discovery, he "would win the Nobel Prize." The painting of Pauling's character similarly mixes positive and negative traits. Of a talk given by Linus Pauling, Watson writes:

> Pauling's talk was made with his usual dramatic flair. The words came out as if he had been in show business all his life. ... This show, like all of his dazzling performances, delighted the younger students in attendance. There was no one like Linus [Pauling] in all the world. ... Several fellow professors, however, watched this performance with mixed feelings.

The youngsters may be gullible, but not the "professors." Watson calls Pauling "a genius" but one who "play[s] like a ten-year-old boy."

Indeed, scientific writing could hardly escape rhetoric. There is, I am afraid, no escape from it. The great literary critic Northrop Frye – notice my rhetoric – made this clear:

> Anything which makes a functional use of words will always be involved in all the technical problems of words, including rhetorical problems. The only road from grammar to logic, then, runs through the intermediate territory of rhetoric. (Frye, 1957, p. 331)

> Nothing built out of words can transcend the nature and conditions of words, and that the nature and conditions of *ratio* [reason], so far as *ratio* is verbal, are contained by *oration*. (Frye, 1957, p. 337)

> All structures in words are partly rhetorical, and hence literary, and that the notion of a scientific or philosophical verbal structure free of rhetorical elements is an illusion. (Frye, 1957, p. 350)

Rhetoric is constitutive of discourse, including scientific discourse, often in unconscious ways. As McCloskey wrote: "The most important example of economic rhetoric, however, falls outside the border of self-consciousness. It is the language economists use, and in particular their metaphors."[26] That language, in economics and, more generally, in the social sciences and history were systematically and consciously worked out in the early days, in the archeology of knowledge. The development of the professions and of academic disciplines meant *discipline* of language and method, among other things. "Every discipline ... is ... constituted by what it *forbids* its practitioners to do" (White, 1978, p. 126; emphasis in the original).

Novick, in a masterful analysis on the development of modern historiography, tells us how history professionalized as an academic discipline from an early start where "historical discussion was conducted in ordinary language, about comprehensive issues, and more or less in public" (Novick, 1988, p. 58). A move away from the lyrical tones of romantic historiography toward the more technical language of scientific history and a move away from metaphor toward metonymy were the basic ingredients of professionalism at the language level (White, 1978, pp. 94–6).

Albion W. Small, in an editorial of the *American Journal of Sociology* titled "What is a Sociologist?" reflected on what the Chicago press said about sociologists. The press complained about "the jargon in which sociologists expressed themselves. Sociologists use language which common people cannot understand" (Small, 1903, pp. 474–5). Rising to the defense of sociologists and of their language, Professor Small wrote:

> Scientific discussion is by no means a mere matter of rhetoric. ... [I]t will be necessary ... that men who are actually advancing knowledge shall talk to each other a great deal in language that says little or nothing to the layman. ... [S]cientific tasks are performed sooner and better if scientists address themselves exclusively to their kind ... The really flagrant sins that have been committed in the name of sociology in recent years have been *inflammatory utterances* ... Serious sociology is a deliberate plan to discredit that sort of thing ... Sound

learning will be promoted sooner and faster by discussing unsettled problems in the *technical language appropriate to problems* ... The worse enemy of the sociologists is defect of scientific patience.[27]

Of course, "the conclusion ... that all science is merely a game can be discarded as piece of wisdom too easily come by" (Huizinga, 1949, p. 203). But whatever else science is (for example, method, theory, adherence to "the strict demands of accuracy and veracity," in Huizinga's words; 1949, p. 204), it is also, fundamentally, a game of language played to underscore some of science's objectives (indeed, objectivity).

Poetry and Science

Back in 1667, Thomas Sprat, in his *The History of the Royal Society*, told the poets "that their interest is united with that of the Royal Society; and that if they shall decry the promoting of experiments, they will deprive themselves of the most fertil subject of fancy" (cited in Jones, 1966, p. 80). The poets did not heed immediately to the call. But over the next century and a half many of them did put science into perfectly mediocre verses (Jones, 1966, p. 212). The new inventions of the telescope and microscope, the new discoveries of Newton's laws in astronomy and Linnaeus's classification scheme in the natural sciences did strike the "fancy" of poets (Jones, 1966, pp. 2, 79, 181). But this *entente cordiale* between science and poetry was short lived. After all, the *entente* was to be on science's own terms. And if that weren't enough, the new philosophers of empiricism and utilitarianism were renewing an "old ... quarrel between philosophy and poetry," a quarrel, it appears, old already at the time of Plato (Plato, *Republic*, X.607b, 1963).

The way Bingham put it in the first issue of the *Westminster Review*, the journal founded by Bentham, best summarizes the philosophers' position: "Mr. Moore *is* a poet and therefore is *not* a reasoner" (cited in Mill, 1981, p. 114). And that is not good. Socrates had said as much two thousand years earlier. "The mimetic art [for example, painting, poetry] is far removed from truth," "easy to produce without knowledge of the truth" (Plato, *Republic*, X, 598b; X, 599, 1963). The poet, as "the creator of the phantom, the imitator ... knows nothing of the reality but only the appearance" (Plato, *Republic*, X, 601c, 1963). The new English philosophers toe very closely the Socratic and Platonic line. Locke's major work, *An Essay Concerning Human Understanding*, is full of references to Truth. "Truth has been my only aim," he tells us, "... Nothing being so beautiful to the Eye, as Truth is to the Mind; nothing so deformed and irreconcilable to the Understanding, as a Lye" (Locke, I, IV, 23, 35; IV, III, 20, 19–21; 1975, pp. 100, 552). As for poetry, its domain is the fanciful. Poetry is not constrained by reality. It has no relationship to truth. "All poetry is misrepresentation," would later write Bentham. "Between poetry and truth there is a natural opposition. ... Truth, exactitude of every kind, is fatal to poetry."[28]

>Wit and Fancy finds easier entertainment in the World, than dry Truth
>and real Knowledge … if we would speak of Things as they are, we
>must allow, that all the Art of Rhetorick, besides Order and Clearness,
>all the artificial and figurative application of Words Eloquence hath
>invented, are for nothing else but to insinuate wrong *Ideas,* move the
>Passions, and thereby mislead the Judgment; and so indeed are *perfect
>cheat.*[29]

The detractors of poetry typically bunch together poetry with rhetoric. To the extent that both poetry and rhetoric manipulate words, that they both use words as embellishments and ornaments, poetry *is* rhetoric. And rhetoric does not fare well with the philosophers. "My conception of rhetoric," says Socrates to Polus in Plato's dialogue *Gorgias* (Plato, *Gorgias,* 465e, 1963), "is the counterpart in the soul of what cookery is to the body"; and that is "a form of flattery … a mischievous, deceitful, mean, and ignoble activity which *cheats us* by shapes and colors, by smoothing and draping" (Plato, *Gorgias,* 465b, 1963; emphasis added).[30] "Rhetorick [is] that powerful instrument of Error and Deceit," Locke tells us.[31]

To the extent that rhetoric is the art that contributes to making arguments attractive, the poet rather than the reasoner, the skilled manipulator of words is the one to win arguments. "Victory … [is] adjudged not to him who had Truth on his side, but the last word in the Dispute" (Locke, III, X, 7, 16–17; 1975, p. 494). Pascal, in the chapter of his *De l'esprit géométrique* dedicated to "The Art of Persuasion," had written: "[E]very man is almost always led to believe not through proof, but through that which is attractive" (Pascal, 1995, p. 193). And what makes things attractive, against reason and proof, is rhetoric, with its "*Figurative Speeches,*" "allusion in Language," and "Ornaments."

Poetry and rhetoric can certainly win people over by appealing to their aesthetic sense, to their sense of the attractive and the beautiful. "Persuasion occurs through the arguments when we show the truth or the apparent truth" (Aristotle, 1.2.6; 1991, p. 39). *Pisteis,* the means of persuasion, include both nonartistic and artistic means, namely character, logical argument, and appeal to emotions. Writers of *Arts of Speech,* Aristotle tells us, have concentrated their attention exclusively on the appeal to people's emotions as a way to win arguments, but "it is wrong to warp the jury by leading them into anger or envy or pity."[32] Passions and emotions are a source of error against good Judgment and Reason (for example, Locke, IV, XX, 12, 1975, pp. 714–15). "Where is my reason at that time," asks Augustine, when at night, in his dreams, he succumbs ("like to the deed doing") to the passions, to the "lust of the flesh," to "carnal copulation?" (Augustine, X, XXX; 1912, pp. 151, 153).

Dangerous is this art of rhetoric, this skill in manipulating words when applied against the truth, appealing to people's passions and emotions rather than reason. And "a very useless Skill … the direct opposite to the ways of Knowledge" (Locke, III, X, 8, 18–9; 1975, p. 494). "Poetry and Gaming, which usually go together," Locke would write elsewhere, "are alike in this too, that they seldom bring any advantage but to those who have nothing else to live on."[33] Bentham, the utilitarian, would later become the champion of that view. What is the use of poetry? He would ask. Of course, poetry is useful, he would reply. After all, poetry is "put together, and commonly sent abroad for the purpose of affording what is called amusement; amusement – viz. an assemblage of pleasures of a particular sort, commonly termed pleasure of the imagination" (Bentham, VIII, XII, 4; 1843, p. 272). To the extent that poetry does give "amusement" to people it is useful. But its utility is limited, Bentham hastens to add. After all, push-pin gives as much amusement to people, but to a much larger number of them. "Everybody can play at push-pin: Poetry and music are relished only by a few."[34]

Plato, we know, had no room for the poets in his ideal Republic. They had no business there.

> If a man …who was *capable by his cunning of assuming every kind of shape and imitating all things* should arrive in our city, bringing with himself the *poems* which he wished to exhibit, we should … say to him that there is no man of that kind among us in our city, and *we should send him away* to another city, after pouring myrrh down over his head, and crowning him with fillets of wool … (Plato, *Republic*, III, 398, 1963; emphasis added)

Yet, Socrates (and Plato) are willing to keep an open mind, to reconsider the poets' admission into the Republic. And the conditions of entry are utilitarian.

> If the mimetic and dulcet poetry can show any reason for her existence in a well-governed state, we would gladly admit her … [if] she is not only delightful but *beneficial to orderly government and all the life of man* … if it can be shown that she *bestows not only pleasure but benefit*. (Plato, *Republic*, X, 607c–e, 1963; emphasis added)

Like Plato (or Socrates) before him,[35] Bentham was no poets' friend, as John Stuart Mill recalls in his *Autobiography* (1981, p. 114). But neither was Mill; not in his youth years at any rate. Mill tells us how he had been brought up by his father – a staunch utilitarian, Bentham's friend and collaborator – "to the undervaluing of feeling."[36] "The cultivation of feeling … had very little place in the thoughts of most of us, myself in particular," he records. "There was at that time an intermission in me of what is its natural source, poetical culture; while there was a superabundance of the discipline antagonistic to it, that of mere logic and analysis." But in the autumn of 1826, at the young age of twenty, Mill was struck by "a dull state of nerves … one of those moods in which what is pleasure at other times, becomes insipid and indifferent." Utilitarianism and logic lost their meaning to Mill. "I had nothing left to live for." "My education had failed." Oddly enough, in the autumn of 1828, it would be poetry to lead him out of "the dry heavy dejection of the melancholy winter of 1826–7." The reading of Wordsworth was "a medicine for my state of mind," he confesses. "I gradually but completely emerged from my habitual depression and was never again subject to it."

Perhaps, there is an irony in Wordsworth's victory over Mill, as told by Mill himself, in poetry's victory over philosophy, heart over reason, feelings and passion over logic.[37] For Mill, feelings and emotions had played no role in his education. For Wordsworth, "poetry is the overflow or expression of feeling in an integral and naturally figurative language" (Abrams, 1953, p. 298). For Wordsworth, the contrast is not between poetry and prose, as traditionally thought, as much as between "Poetry and Matter of Fact, or Science"[38] which is precisely how John Stuart Mill put it in his essay "What is Poetry?"[39] Poetry, for the romantics, became inextricably linked to emotions and passions, taking a path radically opposite to that of science. Coleridge wrote of the "union of passion with thought and pleasure ... which constitutes the essence of all poetry, as contradistinguished from science, and distinguished from history."[40] The solitary Italian romantic poet Giacomo Leopardi annotated in his *Zibaldone*: "Listen to what the philosophers say. One must ensure that man acts by reason, rather than by passion, in fact by reason alone ... Nonsense. ... One must not quell passion with reason; ... reason is neither live force nor moving force" (22 *Ottobre* 1820; I, 372, 1–19; 1937, p. 185). From then on, the litany of citations is endless. "For the man who takes up pen or chisel ... passion is his only business," wrote Yeats in his *Per Amica Silentia Lunae* (1918).

With Romanticism, art and science took on that stark contrast between mind and heart, reason and passion, the classic and the romantic, that has endured. In his *The Tragic Sense of Life*, Unamuno (1931, p. 103) wrote: "Science will be able to satisfy, and in fact does satisfy in an increasing measure, our increasing logical or intellectual needs, our desire to know and understand the truth; but science does not satisfy the needs of our heart ..." "Reason is certainly not a consoling faculty" and "yes, we must learn how to weep! Perhaps that is the supreme wisdom" (Unamuno, 1931, pp. 94, 17). The rationality that science pursues is not just the artist's enemy. It is "the enemy of life" altogether. "Rational truth and life stand in opposition to one another" (Unamuno, 1931, pp. 90, 103).

Science is emerging the winner in that "old ... quarrel between philosophy and poetry." And in these worldly quarrels fought with words, science makes its mark in language. The only poet and taleteller Socrates and Plato are willing to admit into the ideal Republic "for our soul's good," is "*the more austere and less delightful poet and taleteller*, who would imitate the diction of the good man and would tell his tale in the patterns which we prescribed in the beginning, when we set out to educate our soldiers."[41] Indeed, poetry, even in the best of cases, such as Homer, would only mollify the character of young boys.[42] Embellishments and ornaments, Locke would argue, "are certainly, in all Discourses that pretend to inform or instruct, wholly to be avoided; and where Truth and Knowledge are concerned, cannot but be thought a great fault, either of the Language or Person that makes use of them" (Locke, III, X, 34, 18–22; 1975, p. 508). Thus, the forging of *science* demanded not only an appropriate method, but also an appropriate language. There is no room in the Republic of Science for lyrical and poetic language, for emotional discourse, for embellishment, ornaments, and metaphors. These play no part in scientific language.[43] To be admitted in that all too concrete Republic of the modern science, you do need to be of some use to the Republic and to speak a "more austere and less delightful language." And although neither history nor sociology is without its passionate accounts,[44] by and large, the practitioners heeded to the canons. Northrop Frye best described the end result of these developments (1957, pp. 330–1; emphasis added):

> Passing over some intermediate stages, we eventually arrive, in this pursuit of *non-emotional rhetoric*, at conceptual jargon, otherwise known as gobble-dygook or officialese. ... The jargon of government reports, inter-office memoranda, and military instructions is motivated by a wish to be as impersonal as possible ... it is a disease of language ... It is found in most aspects of journalism and is the dress uniform of a large amount of professional writing, including that of humanists.

Heart and Mind

A focus on truth and utility leads to diverging paths where poetry and science, art and science will never meet. But a focus on creativity and genius is a more promising path for a rapprochement. That is the path T. S. Eliot trod. Indeed, for Eliot, passions and emotions are not the touchstone of great work not even in the arts and poetry. No doubt, he wrote, "the elements which enter the presence of the transforming catalyst, are of two kinds: emotions and feelings."[45] Yet, "poetry is not a turning loose of emotion, but an escape from emotion." Emotions must be filtered and transformed "in working them up into poetry, to express feelings which are not in actual emotions at all." In the end, "the emotion of art is impersonal," with an impersonality based on "a continual self-sacrifice, a continual extinction of personality." Eliot concludes: "It is in this depersonalization that art may be said to approach the condition of science."

So art and science do meet. They meet on the terrain of creativity and genius. For Nisbet, the sociologist, "there is no conflict between science and art." In fact, "in their psychological roots they are almost identical. The unity of science and art exists most luminously in the motivations, desires, rhythms, and itches which lie behind creativeness in any realm" (Nisbet, 1976, p. 4). The "creative act" gives the basic unit of art and science (Nisbet, 1976, p. 5). Popper, we know, is dismissive of this unity of art and science based on the creative act. "Every discovery contains 'an irrational element,' or a 'creative intuition,' in Bergson's sense," Popper admits.[46] But this is irrelevant to the process of science. "The initial stage, the act of conceiving or inventing a theory, seems to me," writes Popper, "neither to call for logical analysis nor to be susceptible of it." "I shall distinguish sharply between the process of conceiving a new idea, and the methods and results of examining it logically." "The task of the logic of knowledge – in contradistinction to the psychology of knowledge – ... *consists solely in investigating the methods employed in those systematic tests* to which every new idea must be subjected if it is to be seriously entertained."

And yet, we may get nowhere by means of these "systematic tests." Max Planck, the physicist, wrote that "science ... means unresting endeavour and continually progressing development towards an aim which *the poetic imagination may apprehend, but which the intellect can never fully grasp*" (1936, p. 77; emphasis added). Planck openly acknowledges the role of the imagination, "irrationality," he writes, "is a necessary component in the make-up of every intellect" (1936, p. 96). Only an "act of faith" can bridge the gap between raw empirical data and a postulated theoretical framework that might explain it (1936, p. 115).

Feuer's exploration into the lives of the *rationalist philosophers* – Spinoza, Kant, Descartes – reveals the *irrational* and unconscious underpinnings of their *rationalism* – Descartes's relationship with his father, Kant's obsession with his mother, Spinoza's trauma of excommunication. While Spinoza, Kant, and Descartes ignored the murky world of the irrational, Pascal, the philosopher and mathematician, explored it in an attempt to bridge the gap between heart and reason.[47] In the section on "The Art of Persuasion" of *De l'esprit géométrique*, he wrote that "divine truths ... enter from the heart into the mind, and not from the mind into the heart, in order to humiliate that proud power of reasoning which claims it ought to be the judge."[48] But the heart is no stranger even in the truth of "human matters." "We know the truth not only by means of the reason," he wrote in the *Pensées*, "but also by means of the heart. It is through the heart that we know the first principles, and reason ... has no part in this knowledge ..."[49] The heart is the seat of "the knowledge of first principles, such as space, time, movement, numbers ... It is on this knowledge by means of the heart and instinct that reason has to rely, and must base all its arguments." "The heart has its reasons which reason itself does not know ..." Pascal continues:

> The heart feels that there are three dimensions in space and that there is an infinite series of numbers, and then reason goes on to prove that there are no two square numbers of which one is double the other. The principles are felt, and the propositions are proved, both conclusively, although by different ways ...

It is to these irrational and unconscious aspects of scientific discovery that a new logic of mathematics has turned its attention. Italian logician and philosopher of science, Carlo Cellucci (1998, p. 382) concludes:

> The logic of discovery recognizes the delusion of any attempt to guarantee absolute certainty in mathematics and substitutes it with that

of building tools able to widen our knowledge, subject to that chance of error that is characteristic of all human endeavors. The purpose of knowledge is not to eliminate uncertainty but rather to teach mistrust in one's certainties, and this is the aim of the logic of discovery.

Perhaps, art and science meet. But, perhaps, art and science also meet on the terrain of that all too human faculty of appreciation of beauty, on the *a priori* category of aesthetic judgment. "The scientist [must] be seen in the light of what we call aesthetics," declares Nisbet (1976, p. 10). "Wordsworth's poems," acknowledged Mill, the one-time enemy of poetry, "expressed, not outward beauty but states of feeling, and of thought coloured by feeling, under the excitement of beauty" (Mill, 1981, p. 150). True. The work of the scientist is doomed to early death. Weber and Merton do not let us forget that. But the scientists' lives remain. And so do the lives of artists and poets, philosophers and generals. It is those lives, those "heroic" lives that generate a "reverential admiration" in the young Mill or Robert Merton.[50] These lives live on as exemplary lives.[51] One more time, history and biography intersect.

And the lives of those "heroic persons" are lives driven by passion. Max Weber wrote of the man without passion:

> [H]e ... may as well stay away from science. He will never have what one may call the 'personal experience' of science. Without this strange intoxication ... without this passion ... without this you have *no* calling for science and you should do something else. For nothing is worthy of a man unless he can pursue it with passionate devotion. (In Gerth and Mills, 1946a, p. 135; emphasis in the original)

Quite a plea from a man so square once described by a Viennese journalist as "one of the German stone masons of the Renaissance period ... [whose] words remind us of Cyclopic blocks."[52] Simmel had similarly written of the emotional underpinnings of all rational, "purposive action" (1978, p. 206, emphasis added):

> Purposive action involves the conscious interweaving of our subjective energies and the objective world, and a double impact of reality upon the subject; first, in an anticipation of the content of reality in terms of subjective intention, and second, in a retroactive effect of the realization of the object in terms of subjective *emotion*.

English historian George Trevelyan (1919, p. 56) wrote:

> The dispassionateness of the historian is a quality which it is easy to value too highly, and it should not be confused with the really indispensable qualities of accuracy and good faith. We cannot be at too great pains to see that our passions burn pure, but we must not extinguish the flame. Dispassionateness – *nil admirari* – may betray the most gifted historian into missing some vital truth in his history.

Notwithstanding these powerful voices, by and large, those dedicated to the pursuit of truth, particularly in the human sciences where one's emotions may get tangled up with the passions of those they study, were weary of emotions, weary of feelings and passion. Historians have long recommended keeping passions at bay. In his 1691 *Traité des Études Monastiques,* Jean Mabillon wrote of the need for the historian: "*Avoir le coeur dégagé des passions,*" a heart free of passions (cited in Momigliano, 1969, p. 27). Fernand Braudel in the Preface to his *The Mediterranean and the Mediterranean World in the Age of Philip II* wrote:

> Though by its nature the most exciting and richest in human interest of histories, it [narrative history of individual events] is also the most perilous. We must beware of that history which still simmers with the passions of the contemporaries who felt it, described it, lived it, to the rhythm of their brief lives, lives as brief as are our own. It has the dimensions of their anger, their dreams, and their illusions. ...

Among sociologists, to repeat Durkheim's words:[53]

> Our political and scientific beliefs and our moral standards carry with them an emotional tone that is not characteristic of our attitude toward physical objects; consequently, this emotional character infects our manner of conceiving and explaining them. ... Sentiment is a subject for scientific study, not the criterion of scientific truth.

Von Wiese (1932, p. 65) put it quite similarly:

> That we must take some account of motivation in order to "understand" actions is undeniable, but his does not mean that the sensations underlying the motives should be analyzed by the sociologist. This is the task of the psychologist; sociology deals with occurrences, events, processes taking place *between* human beings and plurality patterns; such happenings can be none other than social actions.

Definitely. The world of science is a heartless world.

Dialoghi Italiani[54]

GIORDANO BRUNO. Blah, blah, blah. But, in the end, my art lives on, Franzosi. I wasn't too far off the mark when I wrote of my "art": "[T]his is an instrument almost divine and pregnant of other possibilities ... And so this art annuls all others that have preceded it, and does not fear to be annulled by others that may be developed in the future. We believe, in fact, to have taken this to its limits ..." (Bruno, 1997, *De umbris idearum,* pp. 210–1). It seems to me that you are still playing with my wheels. Four hundred years later, my "art" has not been annulled, certainly not by you.

ROBERTO FRANZOSI. I am just as pleased to see that you haven't changed; four hundred years on and you are still every bit your same arrogant self.

GIORDANO BRUNO. Arrogant! We are back to that same old story. Have you listened carefully to what Kenneth Burke says, someone you cite approvingly, before you call *me* arrogant? Listen to this:

> We shall use five terms as generating principle of our investigation. They are: Act, Scene, Agent, Agency, Purpose. ... [A]ny complete statement about motives will offer *some kind of* answers to these five questions: What was done (act), when or where it was done (scene), who did it (agent), how he did it (agency), and why (purpose). ... [T]his pentad of key terms ... provide[s] us with a kind of simplicity that can be developed into considerable complexity, and yet can be discovered beneath its elaborations. We want to inquire into the purely internal relationships which the five terms bear to one another, considering their possibilities of transformation, their range of permutations and combinations ... (Burke, 1969, pp. xv–xvi)

Agents, actions, simplicity, complexity, combinations do you hear that? That's my "art," not some "Grammar of Motives!"

ROBERTO FRANZOSI. So, it's your art. After all, what you call *your* art, you took from Lull's *Clavis Magna*.[55] In any case, my own "art" is grounded in modern mathematics, in set theory, and matrix algebra, not wheels. My actors are social actors, my actions social actions, firmly grounded in reality, and not some mythological figures brought out for magical purposes. My purpose is to explain social reality, to build sociological theory, not magic!

GIORDANO BRUNO. Mathematics, modern mathematics you invoke. And where did that come from, pray tell? It is my art that Leibniz professed, it is my combinatorial wheels he too played with. Combinatorial and infinitesimal calculus came out of my wheels.[56] A sociologist you say you are? You are an ass, Franzosi, no doubt a grandchild of that ass saved on Noah's Ark to preserve the species.[57] And, perhaps, this is what a sociologist is in your times: an ass. You can't see farther than your nose, the pedantic grammarian ass you are. I can see that Oxford hasn't changed in over four hundred years.[58]

ROBERTO FRANZOSI. Leave Oxford out of this. You are being unfair to me. Yes, in your works, you do talk about agents, actions, instruments. There is a vague resemblance there with a story grammar. I have, after all, given you proper credit for it.

GIORDANO BRUNO. You think I care about your "proper credit"? Another ass took my arguments and ideas on the infinity of the universe.[59] And he wasn't the only one. You make me sick. These are your heroes. One saved his skin abjuring.[60] The other thought better than to publish his work.[61]

GALILEO GALILEI. "I have not held and do not hold as true the opinion which has been condemned, of the motion of the Earth and stability of the Sun." "I held, as I still hold, as most true and indisputable, the opinion of Ptolemy ... the stability of the Earth and the motion of the Sun." "I am here to submit." "I, Galileo, son of the late Vincenzo Galilei, Florentine, aged seventy years, ... have abjured, sworn, promised, and bound myself ... this twenty-second day of June, 1633."[62]

TOMMASO CAMPANELLA. "It is well to lie if good comes of it / ... Wisely they lived behind closed doors, / publicly applauding in words and deeds / others' mad and erroneous fancies."[63]

ROBERTO FRANZOSI. In any case, there is a world of difference between you and Galileo, not just a handful of years. You still believe that you can resolve the disputes over the size of the universe or geocentrism versus heliocentrism via purely *philosophical* arguments. For Galileo, those arguments are only tangential. Scientific questions must be resolved via observation.

GALILEO GALILEI. Salviati to Simplicio: "However, Mr. Simplicio, welcome are reasons and demonstrations, yours or Aristotle's, and not the texts and naked authorities, because our arguments ought to be around the empirical world, and not a paper world."[64]

ROBERTO FRANZOSI. Galileo ushers in the modern world of science. My story grammars belong to this new world. Your "wheels" are antiquarians' curiosities.

GIORDANO BRUNO. Franzosi, you truly are an ass, modern out of ignorance of the past; your "science" the result of untenable restrictions in the scope of what you look at. Each epoch has its games. You've got yours, but you don't know it.

PITIRIM SOROKIN. "Not knowing that a certain theory has been developed long ago, or that a certain problem has been carefully studied by many predecessors, a sociologist may easily devote his time and energy to the discovery of a new sociological America after it was discovered long ago" (Sorokin, 1928, pp. xviii–xix).

G. M. TREVELYAN. "The present is always taking us by surprise ... because we do not sufficiently know and consider the past" (Trevelyan, 1945, p. 21).

GIORDANO BRUNO. Who are these other asses? I don't need their approval! They don't belong here! Shut them up!

ROBERTO FRANZOSI. Shut them up! Do you think I control the plot? That I control who says what, where, when, and why? You've been out of the loop, my fellow countryman. Audiences are active; *they* are in control, not I!

Confessions of an Ass

And yet, I am in control of the plot. I have the last word in this imaginary, mostly Italian, dialogue. I succeed where even the almighty Inquisition failed: In shutting up Giordano Bruno. The few extant documents of Bruno's last hours have consigned to history the image of a most defiant man.[65] According to the German Gaspar Schopp, in Rome in February 1600, Bruno reproached the

Inquisition judges who had come to read him the death sentence with the following words: *"Maiori forsan cum timore sententiam in me fertis quam ego accipiam."* Perhaps you bring in this sentence against me with greater fear than I shall receive it. *"Eretico impenitente,"* unrepentant heretic, he did not yield to the final implorations and arguments of the Church fathers who had come to fetch him at the prison of Torre di Nona. "He persevered in his wretched obstinacy, picking his brain with thousand errors and fallacies."[66] "He was taken to the square of Campo di fiori and there he was undressed, tied to a pole, and burned alive." "Stubborn heretic, loose of tongue, for the horrible words he uttered, without wanting to listen to either those who wanted to comfort him or others." "A most obstinate heretic ... he kept saying that he was dying a martyr and willingly, and that his soul would climb to Heaven with that smoke."

I may succeed in shutting up Bruno. But I cannot shut up my own conscience. In the end, I have to agree with Bruno. I am an ass. I have not done my homework properly. Because, behind the issues of the last five years of the *American Journal of Sociology* and the *American Sociological Review* – "all a sociologist needs to know," in the creed of a former colleague at the University of Wisconsin-Madison – there is a tradition of work on narrative structures stretching back to Greek and Roman times. That tradition even came up with the jingle – *quis, quid, ubi, quibus auxiliis, cur, quomodo, quando* – that, in its English rendering, you still find in the handbooks of professional writing for journalists – the five W*s: who, what, when, where, why*, and *how*. Cicero laid the foundation of that tradition with his work on *argumentatio*, the *loci*, in particular: who, what, when, where, why, how, ...[67] While many classical texts, Greek and Latin, were unknown to the Middle Ages and were rediscovered only during Italian Humanism,[68] Cicero's texts on rhetoric (*De Inventione* and *Orator*) enjoyed great popularity. They were among the first to be printed after the invention of the press.[69] But that tradition, as all traditions, is dotted by many big and small names. Victorinus, in his commentary on the *De Inventione*, contributed to a discussion of rhetorical issues; so did Boethius in his *De topicis differentiis*, or the Spanish rethorician Martín de Córdova, not to mention Thomas Aquinas in the *Summa Theologiae* ("Quaestio 7. *De circumstanciis humanorum actuum*).[70] Giordano Bruno, like Aquinas, a fellow Dominican, refers to the *loci* as circumstances. He has his own rendering of Cicero's "jingle": *Quid? De quo? Quare? Quantum? Quale? Quando? Ubi? Quo modo?/cum quo?* (Tocco, 1889, p. 5).

In the end, when we dig deep into the archeology of knowledge, Bruno himself turns out to be not nearly as *original* as he would like to be; but with another four hundred years of history, I am certainly far less original than he was. Bruno is right: I am modern out of ignorance of the past. The path to modernity that "cutting-edge" social science traces is easy. Modernity takes on a physical meaning: the gap in the number of cited authors, between then and now, the handful of references to the father founders (Weber, Marx, Durkheim, Simmel) with nothing in between. The author, of course, makes a fundamental contribution in closing that gap. The standard rhetorical construction of our papers – as evidenced particularly in abstracts, introductions, literature reviews, conclusions – is meant to convey both characteristics. Consider this as an example:

> In recent years the literature on social movements has made giant leaps in knowledge (reference, reference, reference, reference). However, investigators have generally neglected to study the impact of the size of the participants' eyes and ears on protest outcomes (see, however, reference [typically to the author's own yet unpublished work]). This paper fills that gap in our knowledge. It shows that bigger eyes and ears do significantly contribute to positive protest outcomes.

Whether our modernity will survive into posterity, that is a different matter. Who ever heard of the many contemporaries that some of the surviving giants cite in their work, the poets, historians, and philosophers *en vogue* that we find in Seneca's or Pliny's, in Dante's, Bruno's, or Marx's writings? A collective process of silence and emphasis sifts and winnows the survivors. And that process is ongoing. Events in the past – and that includes artistic and scientific work – become important in light of sometimes distant events in the future. George Boole's binary mathematics may well have appeared as a curious and even ingenious oddity to his contemporaries back in 1854 when it was first published. How could they have suspected that electricity and computers – not to mention even comparative historical sociology[71] – would work on the basis of boolean, zero-one principles, of on and off switches? As Danto has argued, narrative sentences are made up of at least one pair of time-indexed sentences, a prior and posterior sentence. It is the second narrative sentence in the pair that determines the historical relevance of the first narrative sentence: "In 1854 George Boole published in London his book *An Investigation into the Laws of Thought, on Which Are Founded the Mathematical Theories of Logic and Probabilities*. During World War Two, COLOSSUS, perhaps the first example of computer, was developed."

As literary critic Northrop Frye put it: "It is clearly the simple truth that there is no real correlation either way between the merits of art and its public reception" (Frye, 1957, p. 4). Out of the past, history continuously selects and reselects its heroes of the moment. Giulio Camillo, heralded throughout the seventeenth century as the "divine Camillo," has all but disappeared from our collective memory. Giordano Bruno's name has waxed and waned over the last centuries with the fortunes of anticlerical thinking – the manner of his life, or, better, of his death perhaps often more telling than his work. Today's young sociologists may be surprised to find out that Georg Simmel, not Max Weber, enjoyed far greater fame in America in the early decades of the twentieth century.[72] For Gadamer (1997, p. 264), the interpretative act "is partly determined also by the historical situation of the interpreter and hence by the totality of the objective course of history." Interpretation, in that sense, depends upon one's position in the social structure, one's location in history, one's *point of view.*

> Whether a thing 'is' a work of art or not is one which cannot be settled by appealing to something in the nature of the thing itself. It is convention, social acceptance, and the work of criticism in the broadest sense that determines where it belongs. (Frye, 1957, p. 345)

Criticism, as much as the whole course of history, thus brings out, according to Northrop Frye, himself a literary critic, the truly deserving artists, teases out the *classics,* ensures that history deals a fair hand to authors. "Whatever popularity Shakespeare and Keats have *now* is equally the result of the publicity of criticism" (Frye, 1957, p. 4). The critic is "the pioneer of education and the shaper of cultural tradition" (Frye, 1957, p. 4). In the social sciences the counterpart of that literary or art critic would be the social theorist (Alexander, 1987). The social theorist constantly constructs and reconstructs "the classics," those "earlier works of human exploration which are given a privileged status *vis-à-vis* contemporary explorations in the same field" (Alexander, 1987, pp. 11–2).[73] Yet, even the social theorist does not have a monopoly in the construction of classics. All social scientists contribute to "make texts classical" "through their theoretical interests and their theoretical intentions" (Alexander, 1987, p. 33). The role of art or literary critic – wrongly thought of as "intellectuals who have a taste for art but lack both the power to produce it and the money to patronize it ... cultural middlemen ... parasites," in the words of Frye[74] – is here reevaluated (by critics themselves). The critic, not the artist or the social scientist, has the ultimate creative power: the power of life and death upon authors and scientists alike.

Content Analysis Myths (Back to Silence and Emphasis)

Content analysis has held on tight to some fundamental tenets of its science. Meaning is unproblematic, the practitioners of content analysis believe; and even if it weren't, content analysis should be concerned with manifest meaning *exclusively.*[75] As Cicourel (1964, p. 155) put it:

> the sociologist ... often assumes that the language of the materials he submits to content analysis contains 'obvious' meaning structures which simply require 'counting' under some set of *a priori* or *ex post facto* categories.

So confident are they that meaning is unproblematic and that context is irrelevant to text understanding, that content analysts (and sociologists are hardly alone) recommend that coding be organized so that no single reader works on a single subsample of coding material. The coded data may be otherwise affected by possible spurious trends due to coder idiosyncracies (for example, Hofstetter, 1976, p. 25). In any case, they believe, issues of meaning should be resolved on the basis of written instructions. No content analysis project worth its salt can get away without its "Handbook of coding," without the formulation of explicit coding rules.[76] The handbook is the coders' Bible, the talisman that provides a solution to any coders' discrepancy in interpretation, to any arguments about meaning. Roberts (1997), of lately, best expressed that approach. "Some coder disagreement is inevitable" in content analysis, Roberts concedes. Yet, "when coding rules have been conscientiously developed and applied, coders are likely to attain consistently high agreement in … encodings." "Disagreements among coders are, of course, the makings of poor interrater agreement," Roberts continues. "However, they are also the 'grist' in the development of explicit coding rules." And if any difficulties remain: "During regular meetings, the coders met to jointly resolve differences in their encodings in the light of an evolving set of consistent coding rules." Whatever the code book cannot achieve, consensual agreement on what the meaning should be will.[77] Cicourel (1964, pp. 154–5) best summarized this version of the coder:

> The coder of documents and mass media material must be, according to writers on the subject, a 'sensitive person' who can detect nuances in symbolic material. But ideally, the coder should also function as a automaton coding various responses, sentences, phrases, and comments according to a prearranged set of rules that provides for a precise correspondence between some expressed form and the object to which it refers.

In this view of the communication process, senders encode a set of meanings in a message and receivers unproblematically decode it.[78] Written instructions are meant to make the process even less problematic: "[T]here *is* a sense, that [sense] … is embedded or encoded in the text, and … it can be taken in at a single glance" (Fish, 1980, p. 158).

Within the field of content analysis, among the faithful and the believers, the voices of caution have been rare. Among the early definitions, Janis's comes closest to acknowledging "the role of the reader":

> 'Content analysis' may be defined as referring to any technique a) for the *classification* of the *sign-vehicles,* b) which relies solely upon the *judgments* (which theoretically may range from perceptual discrimination to sheer guesses) of an analyst or group of analysts as to which sign-vehicles fall into which categories, c) on the basis of *explicitly formulated rules*, d) provided that the analyst's judgments are regarded as the reports of a scientific observer. (Janis, 1949, p. 55, emphasis in the original)

Similarly, de Sola Pool (1959, p. 226) acknowledges that

> Most content analysis procedures use the coder as a judge of what
> lexical forms convey what meanings of interest. They have relied on
> the common sense of a coder who was, of course, a user of the
> language in which the analysis was being done. His common sense
> enables him to recognize, for example, that the phrases 'a man of
> courage,' 'a brave man,' and 'a guy with guts' all mean the same thing.
> But these concerns, even when rarely voiced, only took up the space of
> a sentence or a paragraph in a sea of text dedicated to "scientific"
> issues. The key words of most definitions of content analysis leave no
> doubt about that: "objective," "systematic," "scientific," "quantitative,"
> "replicable and valid inference," and "explicitly formulated rules." Yet,
> where is the science?

The science is a single-minded concern with method. Lasswell, one of the
"founding fathers" of the technique, concentrated his "scientific" efforts on such
issues as statistical sampling of texts, design of coding categories, validity and
reliability, unit of analysis, and methods of data analysis.[79] In that, his
achievement, and that of all the other developers of the technique that we have
encountered, is unsurpassed. In paying tribute to one of the early developers of
content analysis, G. C. Thompson (1886), Lasswell et al. (1949) describe the "2
fact-stuffed volumes" (1949, p. 45) a study "of great technical excellence"
(1949, p. 44), a "remarkable work" (1949, p. 44).

> Thompson's treatise is noteworthy for the unification of carefully
> defined abstractions with exhaustive data from sources. Nevertheless,
> the outcome of all the admirable intelligence and industry that went
> into this treatise does not yield maximum results, because of a basic
> failure: The problem of sampling, recording and summarizing sources
> was not solved. Hence, the entire foundation of the work rests on shaky
> ground ... (Lasswell et al., 1949, p. 44)

Lasswell, no doubt, did solve that problem. But in so doing, he brushed aside the
more intractable and unsolvable problems of the role of the reader. He brushed
aside critics, as well. And, at least for a while, he succeeded in silencing voices
of dissent.[80]

The "science," then, this new science of content analysis, was a curious result
of those same operations of foregrounding and backgrounding, of silence and
emphasis that we have seen at work in the media production of ideology (and
even in language). Content analysis foregrounded reliability, sampling, and
validity; it doubly backgrounded meaning, assuming that 1) only manifest
content counts; 2) the translation of that manifest content into coding categories
is unproblematic and can be achieved via coding instructions. It is not just the
pilgrims or early explorers that see reality in specific ways, that leave texts

behind where silence and emphasis are the main mechanisms involved in the construction of texts. Social scientists, as well, view reality in specific ways, construct their texts on the basis of these same mechanisms.

Debunking the Myths: What Is Meaning?

"What is the meaning of a word?" asks Wittgenstein in the very first sentence of *The Blue Book* (1958, p. 1). What is meaning? ask Ogden and Richards in a once very popular book titled *The Meaning of Meaning* (1946)?

"The meaning of words is the history of words," literary critics Wimsatt and Beardsley would answer (1954, p. 10). For Wittgenstein himself (1958, p. 5), "the sign (the sentence) gets its significance from the system of signs, from the language to which it belongs. Roughly: Understanding a sentence means understanding a language." As Simmel (1978, p. 87) put it: "Things receive their meaning through each other and have their being determined by their mutual relations." For Gadamer as well, "the truth of things resides in discourse – which means, ultimately, a unitary meaning concerning things – and not in the individual words, not even in a language's entire stock of words. ... It is not the word ... but the logos that is the bearer of truth ... [and logos is a] system of relations" (Gadamer, 1997, pp. 411–12). For Skinner, words and concepts gain their meaning from their relation to other words and concepts, from their position in a network of meaning. "A term ... gains its meaning from the place it occupies within an entire conceptual scheme" (in Tully, 1988, p. 124).

There is nothing simple, it appears, about meaning. Confronted with a text, how do readers extract meaning from it? How do they interpret it? Gadamer has no hesitation. "Understanding and interpretation are ultimately the same thing";[81] "*understanding occurs in interpreting*"; "all understanding is interpretation," he repeats. For Gadamer, "in understanding we are drawn into an event of truth" (Gadamer, 1997, p. 490). But what exactly goes into that event of truth? Nothing but the text itself, would be Wimsatt and Beardsley's answer (1954). In a seminal article titled "The Intentional Fallacy," Wimsatt and Beardsley argued that "the design or intention of the author is neither available nor desirable as a standard for judging the success of a work of literary art" (1954, p. 3). The meaning of a text has nothing to do with the intentions or the motives of the author. Paradoxically, the internal is public, the external is private: Only what is internal to the text itself should come under the interpretative act, should be public; anything else, the external circumstances of the text as expressed in notes, letters, confidences, is private (Wimsatt and Beardsley, 1954, p. 10). Skinner does not go along with that position. He writes: "[W]e need to know what a writer may have meant by what he wrote, and need (equivalently) to know his intentions in writing, in order to interpret the meaning of his works."[82] "In order to be able to interpret the meaning of a text, it *is* necessary to consider factors other than the text itself" (Skinner in Tully, 1988, p. 78; emphasis in the original). A text does not come in isolation from its context. What goes with the text (*cum* text or con.text) plays a fundamental role in the meaning of a text. Only by looking at the full historical and linguistic context in which texts are produced can we begin to understand their meaning.

So meaning is in context[83] and text understanding implies a "variety of interpretative operations."[84] Even the most rudimentary textual narratives open an entire discursive field within which a range of possible worlds are called into play. In order to understand a text, van Dijk wrote, "the reader needs not only the information expressed in the discourse, but also more general knowledge of the world" and of "meaningful action and interaction."[85] "No knowledge without foreknowledge," the hermeneutic scholars maintain (Diesing, 1991, p. 108). Our very ability to read stories seems to fundamentally depend upon our "foreknowledge" of story schemata.[86] To the process of text understanding, even the simplest of texts,[87] we bring a wealth of specialized knowledge of the subject matter and general knowledge as members of the larger culture, as participants in "a universe of shared meanings."[88]

The meaning of a word, sentence, or other – the *sign*.ificance of any *sign*, Wittgenstein argued, comes from practice, from "the use we make of it" (1958, p. 65; also pp. 4, 69). It is communities of discourse that assign meaning to things. "The practice of the use of language" in these communities is a "language-game" similar to that children play in order to learn their native language (Wittgenstein,1953, p. 5). Yet, make no mistake. This is no innocent game. The language of game and play mystifies the relations of power behind language itself.[89] That, for Marcuse, is the limit of Wittgenstein's philosophical work – "language games and academic boredom" being one and the same thing (Marcuse, 1964, p. 182); that would be the limit of a purely linguistic analysis of meaning that did not take into account the extralinguistic elements that push and pull in the determination of the meaning of a word (Marcuse, 1964, pp. 191–8). For Fish as well, the "language games" of "interpretative communities" are anything but innocent, because an "interpretative community ... as a bundle of interests, of particular purposes and goals, its perspective is interested rather than neutral" (Fish, 1980, p. 14).

Innocent or interested, these interpretative communities, these communities of discourse play a fundamental role in the production and reproduction of meaning. In Fish's words: "[T]here are no fixed texts, but only interpretative strategies making them." Texts do not hand over to the reader "ready-made or prefabricated meanings" somehow encoded in the text, and existing "in the world independently of the individuals."[90] In Fish's model, "meanings are not extracted but made not by encoded forms but by interpretative strategies that call forms into being." Yet, meaning is not entirely subjective in the sense of being up to the single individual to make it. The reader is not "a free agent ... but ... a member of a community whose assumptions about literature determine the kind of attention he pays and thus the kind of literature 'he' makes." As a result of a reader's membership in a community, "interpretative strategies are not natural, but learned." Fish (1980, p. 14) concludes: "The meanings and texts produced by an interpretative community are *not subjective* because they do not proceed from an isolated individual but from a public and conventional point of view".

How did we go from here to the simplistic view of meaning explicitly or implicitly held by the practitioners of content analysis? How could we have come to believe that a handbook of coding instructions could ever provide the "intertextual encyclopedia" upon which meaning is premised, without itself looking like the largest of encyclopedias (and even that would not be enough)?[91] The belief that a handbook can resolve the problems of meaning simply glosses over (and takes for granted) the wealth of background knowledge that readers consciously or unconsciously bring to the text in the construction of meaning. Content analysis practitioners have deluded themselves into thinking they are doing science by writing "handy instructions" and handbooks of coding rules. In fact, what they are doing, is relying on common sense knowledge shared between coders and researcher. Critics, such as Cicourel, are well aware that "most content analysis procedures use the coder as a judge of what lexical forms convey what meanings of interest. They have relied on the common sense of a coder ..."[92] Consciously or unconsciously, "the researcher relies upon his common-sense knowledge." The social scientist and his coders come from a common culture which leads to a common understanding of texts – "there is a strong tendency among sociologists to take the common culture and language for granted." It is coders that supply meaning from context. Indeed, if meaning were unproblematic, why should it have taken me years to explore the meaning of such simple a word as "journey"? And, speaking of journeys, how are we to read Columbus's diaries of his voyages? The exaltation of the hero? The research proposal that promises the world and delivers the word? The travel diary? How are we to read the pilgrims' accounts? More generally, how are we to read human action?

When looked upon under close scrutiny, *traditional* content analysis does not fare well. But debunking the myths of others is easy (and fun). It is indeed the way we rhetorically build our arguments. What about my own way of doing "content analysis," my own "science"? If traditional content analysis, retrieving into science, has fundamentally ignored issues of meaning, does the linguistics-based approach to content analysis peddled in these pages solve those problems? Caught in the web of my own rhetoric, I will have to honestly acknowledge the limits of this new "science" of content analysis based on linguistics, of the *novum organum*.

1. A linguistic approach to content analysis provides a more rigorous approach to text "coding." Rigor, however, comes at the expense of generality. The approach works well *only* for narrative texts and for the purely narrative clauses of narrative texts.

2. For all the rigor of story grammars, even when applied to structure purely narrative clauses of narrative texts, the process of text coding, of how coders derive meaning from the text, is as shrouded in mystery as in traditional content analysis. "The depths of the matter remained a sealed book" (Hegel, 1993, p. 39).

3. Story grammars do not eliminate the "role of the reader," that is, the role of the coder in the interpretation of text. Narrative texts are hardly ever made up of purely narrative clauses only. Narrative and nonnarrative clauses typically mix in a narrative text. Coding of nonnarrative clauses within the framework of the grammar will pose serious problems to the coders. Even purely narrative clauses may not necessarily conform to the simple template subject-action-object of the grammar. The greater the distance between the surface representation of these clauses and the deep structural representation of the grammar, the greater the interpretative role of the coder, in trying to squeeze one into the other (the simplest case being the linguistic operations required to convert passive forms to active).

4. It is one thing to structure narrative in order to extract basic information on *who* does *what, when, where, why,* and *how*; but quite another to expect that through this simple template we can capture the meaning of a text. That meaning, as conveyed through the choice of metaphors, syntactic structures, nouns, verbs, and adjectives, and by silence and emphasis on different aspects of an event (or authors and readers, for that matter), is well beyond the power of our tools.

5. Story grammars have nothing to offer to ease another problem: that of data aggregation. Once investigators have coded thousands of words (for example, actors, actions) how do they reduce these words to manageable sets, how do they classify them, how do they aggregate them for analysis? The way we go from words to numbers is, simply, by counting words. But what is being counted is not always clear. Another matter "the depths of ... [which] remained a sealed book."

So, these are the limits of my new "art." Cicourel is well aware of those limits:

> The 'rules' governing the use of language and the meanings conveyed by linguistic and nonlinguistic utterances and gestures are unclear and remain an almost untouched problem for empirical research. If the 'rules' governing the use of language to describe objects and events in everyday life and in sociological discourse are unclear, then the assignment of numerals or numbers to the properties of objects and events according to some relatively congruent set of rules will also reflect a lack of clarity. (Cicourel, 1964, p. 15)

"Our Knowledge being so narrow ... it will ... give us some Light into the present State of our minds, if we look a little into the dark side, and take a view of *our Ignorance:* ... infinitely larger than our Knowledge" (Locke, III, 22, 5–8, 1975, p. 553; emphasis in the original). Linguists, literary critics, and philosophers of language give us a glimpse of the extent of *our Ignorance.* Social scientists, of course, do not generally read the lucubrations of this assorted bunch. And the assorted bunch repays us with the same currency – but the few who have read content analysis monographs have nothing flattering to say about our approach to texts (for example, van Dijk, 1972). Here and there, voices of dissent against such crass views of texts and meaning have risen within the social sciences (for example, Cicourel, 1964, in particular, chapters 6 and 8; Mishler, 1986). But with so many people busy counting, busy sampling, busy measuring reliability and validity, busy designing coding categories, busy pretesting, busy writing handbooks of coding instructions, busy, in other words, "doing science," who had the time (or inclination) to listen to the mad raving of marginal voices going against the grain of the royal road of quantification?

True Believers

Raymond Cattell, the psychologist we met in Chapter 3 of Party 1 for his work on factor analysis, must certainly be considered one of the great social scientists of the twentieth century. A quick search through the citation index will reveal citation frequencies well into the hundreds for several of his articles with occasional peaks close to the thousands, a feat truly for the selected few. Let's read what this scientist wrote in 1950, at the time when he was making a bold entrance into the field of international conflict research, deeply influencing a strand of research in the field of content analysis that ran from Cattell to Guetzkow, Rummel, and Tanter. After analyzing eighty variables for sixty-nine countries through factor analysis, Cattell obtained twelve basic factors. These factors, Cattell informs the reader, have been isolated "by purely *objective* methods. ... [based on] *objective* statistical standards and I.B.M. methods."[93] This "objective" and "scientific" method is "more truthful" in what it delivers than what is held "in the eyes of the cultural anthropologist" (Cattell, 1950, p. 248). Cattell (1950, p. 248; emphasis added) concludes:

> The present quantitative approach to "civilizations" or "culture patterns" releases us from *prejudices* which enter into qualitative and often *intuitive appraisals* and, secondly, that our method has taken into account a wider array of dimensions than is commonly guaranteed by cultural anthropological or historical methods.

Only to find what? Cattell himself is not sure. He writes: "[I]t must be understood that the verbal labels [of the twelve factors] are purely tentative and that the interpretations are also hypothetical. ... We do not yet know what these dimensions mean in their entirety."[94] Not only does Cattell not know the real meaning of what he finds, but what he finds presents anomalies that seem to defy commonsense. "A single cluster," he points out to the reader, "sometimes includes countries which our preoccupations would not suggest to us as members of the same family" (Cattell, 1950, p. 233). *"This need not to worry us very much,"* Cattell reassures his readers. Anomalies should not be "taken too seriously." After all, "our preconceptions may be wrong and the present method stands on its own feet" (Cattell, 1950, p. 233). And in any case, "some of these apparent misclassifications [of countries] will be resolved ... as the data necessary for estimating the factor endowment of a particular country become more accurately available" (Cattell, 1950, p. 249).

Back in 1959, in his *The Sociological Imagination*, C. Wright Mills had scathing words for this form of "abstracted empiricism" where "The thinness of the results is matched only by the elaboration of the methods and the care employed" (Mills, 1959, p. 52). But what will *you* make of this, distant reader of 2520? To get an idea of how you might react to Cattell's work, let us face our own reactions of early twenty-first century readers to some of the vintage writing we came across in our journey. Thus, the anonymous Pilgrim of Bordeaux tells us that "there is Mount Syna where there is a spring, and women who wash in it become pregnant" (Wilkinson, 1981a, p. 153, lines 586.1–2). Antonino of Piacenza[95] in his *Itinerarium* similarly reports with no sign of critical spirit:

> On the Carmelo mountain there is a little round stone. If you shake it, it emits a sound, although it is of solid rock. Such are the miraculous virtues of the stone that, if is placed on a woman or on any animal, it will never abort.

> In the Synagogue [in Nazaret] there is the beam upon which Jesus sat with the other children. The beam can be moved and lifted by Christians, but Jews cannot nudge it; it will not let be taken out.

> In the place where Jesus was crucified you can still see the blood.

> In the Church is kept the column where the Lord was whipped. This column has the following characteristics: That when you hug it, it sticks to your chest and both hands and fingers and palms appear on the stone; this way, the stone takes your 'measurements' to diagnose any disease; then, you put it around your neck and you are cured.

Nikulas of Munkathvera, the Icelandic pilgrim, tells us without a doubt than in Lucca in the Church of Santa Maria "there is that crucifix that Nicodemo ordered made following the will of God himself. It has spoken twice: The first time it donated its shoe to a poor; the second time it testified in favor of a man unjustly accused" (in Stopani, 1991, p. 69). The anonymous author of the twelfth-century *The Pilgrim's Guide* to Santiago de Compostela tells of various miracles assuring us: "I have had personal experience of what I say."[96]

Why would twentieth-century social scientists laugh – or benevolently smile – at the pilgrims' words while taking those of Cattell very seriously – those same words that would make you, reader of 2520, benevolently smile as well? The answer, for once, is simple. We smile at the pilgrims' credulity because we, the scientists, do not share their world vision. And you smile because you do not share ours. We are willing to write about certain truths because we know that our readers will accept them without questioning. We operate within communities that share fundamental assumptions about the world. Problems lose their meaning outside these communities. New ways of seeing simply set old problems aside. Whatever arguments were used in the middle ages to show how many angels would fit on top of a pin are irrelevant in the context of subsequent scientific discourse. What will happen to our arguments? As Wittgenstein wrote:

> The new way of thinking is what is hard to establish. Once the new way of thinking has been established, the old problems vanish; indeed, they become hard to recapture. For they go with our way of expressing ourselves and, if we clothe ourselves in a new form of expression, the old problems are discarded along with the old garment.[97]

It is these "interpretative communities" that make sense of such different ways of writing texts. Interpretative communities "are made up of those who share interpretative strategies not for reading but for writing texts, for constituting their properties" (Fish, 1980, p. 14). Meaning, for Fish, is constantly being produced neither by writers or readers but by interpretative communities.

Science itself "presupposes the same way of looking at things" (Foucault, 1972, p. 33). And that is why no one smiles with benevolence, not at least around the time of my writing, at Cattell's text. Fish writes (1980, p. 15):

> Members of the same community will necessarily agree because *they will see (and by seeing, make)* everything in relation to that community's assumed purposes and goals; and conversely, members of different communities will disagree because from each of their perspective positions *the other "simply" cannot see* what is obviously and inescapably there.

> Thus, science and scientific method as means of viewing and obtaining knowledge about the world around us provide those who accept its tenets with a grammar that is not merely a reproducing instrument for describing what the world is all about, but also shapes our ideas of what the world is like, often to the exclusion of other ways of looking at the world. Language, then, and the cultural meanings it signifies, distorts, and obliterates, acts as a filter or grid for what will pass as knowledge in a given era. (Cicourel, 1964, p. 35)

The forging of academic disciplines involved the forceful construction of "discursive communities" that shared similar languages, similar assumptions, similar beliefs, similar outlooks on the world, increasingly based on formal training and credentials. Huizinga, some decades before the postmodern onslaught, put it this way:

> All esoterics presuppose a convention: We, the initiates, agree to take such and such a thing thus and thus, so we will understand it, so admire it. ... [E]soterics requires a play-community which shall steep itself in its own mystery. Wherever there is a catch-word ending in *-ism* we are hot on the tracks of a play-community. (Huizinga, 1949, p. 203)

Postmodern scholars have pushed the argument one step further, denying a reality existing outside the text. In Derrida's and Barthes's words:[98]

> [T]here is nothing outside the text. ... there has never been anything but writing; there has never been anything but supplements, substitutive significations which could only come forth in a chain of differential references. .... [It is] impossible to separate ... the signified from the signifier.

> A text is not a line of words releasing a single 'theological' meaning (the 'message' of the Author-God) but a multi-dimensional space in which a variety of writings, none of them original, blend and clash. *The text is a tissue of quotations drawn from the innumerable centres of culture.*

Nothing *outside* the text? Nothing *in* the text, except strings of quotations (acknowledged or unacknowledged?) Derrida's or Barthes's provocative posture is particularly worrisome for us in light of the textual strategies of this book. Indeed, when we start tracking precursors and their ways of seeing, we see them through their texts. Their words become our points of connection, our link to their worlds. With our data as words and our modes of explanation as more words, could these texts of ours, these scientific texts of ours, be nothing but signifiers? With a quote juxtaposed to another quote – and I have amply done that in this text – is a text only "a tissue of quotations?" Perhaps more dangerously, as we start chasing connections through the words of others, is there ever an end to that search? *Omne omne est*, everything is everything, the alchemists of old never tired to repeat. Is the end of a journey simply the place where a traveler decides to stop? Do we get on top of a scholarly problem, only to find ourselves at the bottom of another?

Modern Alchemists: What We Do with the Numbers

In 1980, David Hendry, appointed to the chair of econometrics at the London School of Economics and Political Science, delivered an inaugural lecture by the provocative title: "Econometrics – Alchemy or Science?" (Hendry, 1980; reprinted in 1993). Hendry was taking up a question raised some fifty years earlier by Keynes about Tinbergen's book *Statistical Testing of Business-Cycle Theories*. John Maynard Keynes had written (1940, p. 156; see also 1939):

> No one could be more frank, more painstaking, more free from subjective bias or *parti pris* than Professor Tinbergen. There is no one, therefore, so far as human qualities go, whom it would be safer to trust with *black magic*. That there is anyone I would trust with it at the present stage, or that this brand of *statistical alchemy* is ripe to become a branch of science, I am not yet persuaded. But Newton, Boyle, and Locke all played with Alchemy. So let him continue. (Emphasis added)

Hendry, the theoretical econometrician, ultimately believes in the scientific value of his discipline. He concluded his lecture on an optimistic note: "I believe that at this School [the LSE] we have attempted to tackle the subject scientifically." Not econometrics but *the practice of econometrics* is to be blamed for black magic and statistical alchemy. "The three golden rules of econometrics are test, test, and test; ... rules ... broken regularly in empirical applications." For Hendry, "Econometricians have found their philosophers' stone; it is called regression analysis and is used for transforming data into 'significant' results!" (Hendry, 1980, p. 388) – something McCloskey (1985, p. 167) would put more colorfully as: "Come, have a look at my new program, PUBPER ('publish or perish') which searches and researches the data until it finds statistically significant results."

It is hardly surprising that researchers should recur to the philosophers' stone for help. After all, one is much more likely to get manuscripts published if the findings reported are statistically significant.[99] And in the name of statistical significance, social scientists have become "data miners." "A Data Miner ... given a set of data ... will fit as many alternative equations as there are alternative subsets of potential explanatory variables and will choose the "best" equation."[100] And equations are "best" when they maximize R^2 and obtain statistically significant coefficients. Indeed, data mining is likely to lead to exaggerated claims of total explained variance and significance of individual coefficients (Lovell, 1983, pp. 3–4). And those claims may be further exaggerated by the presence of influential observations. Both measures of explained variance and significance of coefficients may be due to a single data point.[101] More dangerously, it is likely to lead to a warped view of theory as the set of variables in a regression equation that best explains a given outcome. In a passage written forty years ago and that has not lost any of its biting pessimism, C. Wright Mills (1959, p. 66) thus gave voice to his views on "abstracted empiricism": "'Theory' becomes the variables useful in interpreting statistical findings; 'empirical data' ... are restricted to such statistically determined facts and relations as are numerous, repeatable, measurable."[102]

Driven by a quest for scientific status, social scientists have turned to statistics for help. But we have treated it as an officiant of the rituals of "hypothesis testing," rather than as a precious tool for bringing out patterns in the data. "The community of researchers," Randall Collins wrote (1984, p. 339), "is less concerned with whether a given finding is true than with whether it can pass the hurdle of a very high level of ritual distrust imposed on it."

Social scientists' "noble dream" of theory building and rigorous formal approaches may well have turned into the nightmare of a ritualistic approach to the social science enterprise. As Malinowski and Mauss have shown,[103] magical rituals emphasize adherence to established procedures, steps taken in the right order, words used and pronounced in an accepted way. In our approach, theories are, at best, empirical generalizations and, at worst, literature reviews or variables in a statistical model.[104] Indeed, nowhere is theory more obsessively invoked than in quantitative social science work, along with the many words that form the basic vocabulary of science: "Data," "validity," "reliability," "test," "power," "model," "formal," "empirical," "rigorous," "novel," "innovative," "mathematical" ... (just reread Part I to get the full range of words in this vocabulary). "The most important element in magic," Malinowski tells us (1948, p. 73), "is the spell. ... the ritual centers round the utterance of the spell. The formula is always the core of the magical performance." Oddly enough, for believers in numbers, this obsessive invocation of a handful of words – "hypnotic nouns which evoke endlessly the same frozen predicates"[105] – is an ironic tribute to the power of words in a ritual that has more in common with magic than science.[106] For Freud (1950, p. 85) "the principle governing magic ... is the principle of the 'omnipotence of thoughts.'" To utter the word is to call up all its power. *Fiat lux* and *lux fuit*, we read in Genesis. "The riddle is a sacred thing full of secret power, hence a dangerous thing" (Huizinga, 1949, p. 108).

Paradoxically, in quantitative social science, theory has been elevated into a religion with statistics relegated to the ancillary role of an officiant of those rituals. The idol of "hypothesis testing" before which we kneel with religious fervor tends to obscure the invaluable role that good statistical work can play in bringing out patterns in the data. In Tukey's[107] words: "Exploratory data analysis can never be the whole story, but nothing else can serve as the foundation stone – as the first step." The discovery of patterns can indeed provide the first step toward understanding the causes behind those patterns. "One of the really valuable functions of empirical social research," wrote Lieberson (1985, p. 213), "is a descriptive one." "Regression models make it all too easy to substitute technique for work" (Freedman, 1991, p. 300). "Shoe leather," that is, a great deal of careful investigative work guided by good intuition and intelligence, is more likely to lead to sound scientific discoveries than any quick fix from high powered statistics.

Not surprisingly, we are neither doing good sociology (if that means building of social theories) nor good statistics (if that means discovering meaningful patterns in the data). Conformity to the social science rituals has led researchers to gloss over the many problems that both numbers and statistical modeling come with. Scientific *rigidity* has taken the place of scientific *rigor* (Bourdieu and Wacquant, 1992, pp. 225, 227). The close etymological connection between the two words (rigidity and rigor; consider the Latin expression *rigor mortis*, the rigidity of death) has long since been lost. Taken by our "noble dream" of theory building we have become completely unconcerned with the frail empirical and methodological bases upon which that dream rests. We have backgrounded two unsettling questions: What's in the numbers? What do we do with the numbers? What we do with the numbers is not at all uplifting. Lieberson's (1985, p. ix) words in the preface to his *Making it Count* cannot but resonate a strongly sympathetic chord:

> I am fully sympathetic with the empirical research goals found in much of contemporary American sociology, with its emphasis on rigor and quantification. However ... I have reluctantly reached the conclusion that many of the procedures and assumptions in this enterprise are of no more merit than a quest for a perpetual-motion machine. Even worse, whereas the latter search is innocuous, some of the normal current practices in empirical social research are actually counter-productive.

In this light, was the "good" pudding I baked in Part I more like one of Leamer's sausages?

What's to Be Done? Alchemists' Recommendations to the Novice

• *Recommendation 1.* "No one should begin operations without plenty of funds, so that he can obtain everything necessary and useful for this art: For if he should undertake them and lack funds for expenses then he will lose the material and everything" (Albertus Magnus, 1958, p. 14).

Costly, indeed, they are these alchemic transformations of words into numbers.[108] Fogel (1975, p. 337) wrote:

> One can divide the various methods of rigorous measurement currently employed in historical research into two categories-direct and indirect. The most common method of direct measurement in history is counting. My reference to counting as a rigorous method of measurement is not to be taken derisively. I use portentous language for what appears to be an elementary operation ... [yet] counting is rarely an easy task in historical work. ... [C]omplex, costly, and time consuming.

It is the costs of these "vast undertakings" that prompted Lawrence Stone to scoff at these "gigantic enterprises," to question "whether the concentration of such vast quantities of scarce resources of money and manpower on a few gigantic projects was altogether wise. ... Some of them may leave nothing behind them but miles of computer tape and mountains of printout" (Stone,

1987, p. 38). That is, indeed, possible.[109] But, before rejecting this approach to historical research as having "more in common with the modern scientific laboratory ... than with the traditional lonely scholar" (Stone, 1987, p. 37) consider the alternative: "Do not guess, try to count, and if you cannot count, admit that you are guessing" (Clark, 1962, p. 14). And if the difficulties involved rightly frighten you, follow Mills (1959, p. 205) when he admits: "Now I do not like to do empirical work if I can possibly avoid it. If one has no staff it is a great deal of trouble; if one does employ a staff, then the staff is often even more trouble."

• *Recommendation 2.*

> Do not presume to start the work unless you are very knowledgeable of natural principles, and experienced in the operations of distillation, dissolution, coagulation and, especially, in the workings of fire. Ignorant is the man who approaches alchemy out of personal greed, rather than discretion and care. (Thomas Aquinas, 1996, p. 42)[110]

Indeed, alchemic transformations, of any kind, are never easy. Albertus Magnus tells us how, "in the interest of the science called Alchemy," he "laboriously traveled to many regions and numerous provinces, likewise to cities and castles," how he "diligently consulted learned men and sages," how he "took down their writings and toiled again and again over their works" (Albertus Magnus, 1958, pp. 1–2). His own pupil, Thomas Aquinas, warns us that "It is useful to aid Nature with Art; this, however, is no simple matter, and because of these difficulties many have gone mad, wasting away their youth and their wealth" (Thomas Aquinas, 1996, p. 39).

The knowledge required in going from words to numbers is also "no simple matter": From linguistics, to computer science, and statistics, not to mention the historical and theoretical knowledge of the problem under scrutiny. Technical knowledge, in particular, comes at high cost; years of training in graduate schools and beyond. It should perhaps come as no surprise that, having acquired that level of technical and methodological competence, we should try to maximize the returns from our investment. In so doing, however, our research agenda becomes method driven, rather than theory or substantive driven. We displace the end for the means, the search for the actor becomes a search on ... how to search for the actor. As Bernard Bailyn put it in his presidential address to the 1981 annual meeting of the American Historical Association (Bailyn, 1982, p. 6):

> Many of the most energetic historians have forsaken the general goals of history for technical problem-solving, and not for trivial reasons. Anyone who has struggled with the mind-absorbing, soul-entrapping difficulties of subjecting scrappy social data of the prestatistical era to computer analysis will know how captivating and strangely satisfying, yet how severely vision-limiting, that kind of technical work can be.

• *Recommendation 3.*

> One should be on one's guard before all else against [associating oneself] with princes or potentates in any [of these] operations, because of two dangers: If you have committed yourself, they will ask you from time to time, 'Master, how are you succeeding? When will we see some good results?' and, not being able to wait for the end of the work, they will say that, it is nothing, it is trifling, and the like, and then you will experience the greatest dissatisfaction. And if you are not successful you will suffer continued humiliation because of it. If, however, you do succeed, they will try to detain you permanently, and will not permit you to go away, you will be ensnared by your own words and caught by your own discourses. (Albertus Magnus, 1958, pp. 13–14)

That advice is old. Over a millennium earlier, Seneca, in a beautiful and famous epistle, had given this last advice to those who "desire to scale the heights of greatness":[111]

> Do you behold yonder homes of the great, yonder thresholds uproarious with the brawling of those who would pay their respects? They have many an insult for you as you enter the door, and still more after you have entered. Pass by the steps that mount to rich men's houses, and the porches rendered hazardous by the huge throng; for there you will be standing, not merely on the edge of a precipice but also on a slippery ground. ... It is a rough road that leads to the heights of greatness; but if you desire to scale this peak, which lies far above the range of Fortune, you will indeed look down from above upon all that men regard as most lofty, but none the less you can proceed to the top over level ground. Farewell.

Perhaps, we all face the dilemma of being pure, but outsiders, or impure and insiders. John Berger (1972, p. 32) put it bluntly: "The idea of innocence faces two ways. By refusing to enter a conspiracy, one remains innocent of that conspiracy. But to remain innocent may also be to remain ignorant." Goethe gave that dilemma of the modern scientist its most powerful impersonation in the figure of Faust. "For from the desire of power the angels fell, and men from that of knowledge," reminds us Bacon in the preface to his *Novum Organum* (1831, p. 12). Our dreams of researchers are dependent on those who control the purse strings. And along with our dreams, those may also control our dignity. "The university is much like the church," wrote Peter Berger (1963, p. 195), "in its susceptibility to seduction by the powerful of this world." No one knew this better that one such dreamer, Christopher Columbus, who knocked on the doors of the powerful of Europe in pursuit of his dream: That beyond the great Ocean Sea, far out to the west, there lay the legendary lands of India, Cathay (China), and Chipangu (Japan) and that he could reach those lands by sailing west. He never tired to remind his readers of the humiliating and long years spent waiting for an answer from the Kings of Portugal and of Spain (I will spare "thee, reader," an account of humiliations of my own).

• *Recommendation 4.* Simmel, C. Wright Mills, Foucault, and Wittgenstein would probably add the following corollary to the previous advice: Beware of academic fads! Beware of academic disciplines! It is there that language games have achieved their most sophisticated refinement, their most constraining strength (indeed, as the very word "discipline" implies). In a letter of congratulations to his friend Norman Malcolm for finishing a Ph.D. at Harvard and getting a new job at Princeton, Wittgenstein wrote: "Because, unless I'm very much mistaken, *that's* what will be expected of you." *"Only by a miracle* will you be able to do decent work in teaching philosophy" (cited in Monk, 1991, p. 425). And true to his own advice, Wittgenstein resigned his professorship at Cambridge after only two years. Much earlier, soon after returning from the front, he had already given away to his sisters and brother his family's incredible wealth ("one of the wealthiest men in Europe"), till the end of his life returning unopened even Christmas presents from his family (Monk, 1991, pp. 171, 197, 220, 230).

• *Recommendation 5.* "Of all the operations of alchemy, the best is that which begins in the same way as nature" (Albertus Magnus, cited in Kibre, 1980, p. 193). Giordano Bruno extended that principle when he wrote:

> Every similar is produced by a similar, every similar can be known through its similar, every similar is contained in the similar. Furthermore, even a similar entity not close to another one tends to reach its far similar via an intermediate similar which is closer. ... Thus, he who will have known the intermediate entities more appropriate to reach the extremes, will be able to extract everything from everything, both in practice and in theory. (Bruno, *De umbris idearum*, 1997, p. 68)

Marsilio Ficino put this dictum even more succinctly: "One should not attempt to go from one extreme to another without a middle."[112] We have closely followed that advice in bridging the gap between such nonsimilar entities as words and numbers. We have gone from words to numbers in successive steps, starting with nature itself, with the words. These were the steps:

1. Structure narrative text within the relational categories of a story grammar (subjects related to actions, actions to objects, subjects, actions, and objects related to their respective modifiers).
2. Store in the computer within a relational database system (RDBMS) the textual information structured in the relational format of a story grammar.

3. Divide into subsets the set of words contained in each category of the grammar. For instance, divide all actions into spheres of actions of similar meaning: actions of conflict, of communication, of violence, and so on.
4. Rely on the power of the computer to easily manipulate and count the mass of information stored within each category and subcategory. The numbers at last!
5. Rely on network models to analyze the data statistically. Network models operate on numerical information for relational entities.

• *Recommendation 6.* "Persevere in your labors and do not become discouraged, knowing that great utility will follow your work" (Albertus Magnus, 1958, p. 4).

That, of course, may be something of an exaggeration, with no guarantee that "great utility will follow." After all, Albertus Magnus himself tells us that:

> Many learned men of wealth, abbots, bishops, canons, natural philosophers, as well as unlettered men, who expended much money and great effort in the interest of this art, and yet *they failed because they were not capable of tracking it down.* (Albertus Magnus, 1958, p. 2)

But in case perseverance may involve traveling "laboriously ... to many regions and numerous provinces, likewise to cities and castles," do not forget to pack plenty of David Freedman's "shoe leather." It will surely come in handy on a long journey. Alternatively, take Hendry's route: Work on *theoretical* problems.

6

Journeys' Ends

And in 77 days, after so many fatigues and dangers, we entered in this arbor [Lisbon] in the day of June 28 1504, thank God, where we were well received and beyond belief, because the entire city thought we were lost ...

Amerigo Vespucci (1984, p. 175)

I want you to be quite clear about these mountains, reverend ladies my sisters ... From there we were able to see Egypt and Palestine, the Red Sea and the Parthenian Sea ... as well as the vast lands of the Saracens – *all unbelievably far below us.*

Egeria (in John Wilkinson, 1981a, pp. 94–5; emphasis added)

The unity of these investigations does not lie, therefore, in an assertion about a particular content of knowledge and its gradually accumulating proofs but rather in the possibility – which must be demonstrated – of finding in each of life's details the totality of its meaning.

Georg Simmel (1978, p. 55)

Sta Viator

Sta viator, "stop wayfarer." We find that invitation in many Greek and particularly Roman tomb epitaphs (Lattimore, 1962, pp. 230–4). As burials within the city were prohibited, thoroughfares leading in and out of cities were a favorite choice. Still today, a line of tombs and dark pine trees on either side form a melancholic procession along the first few miles of the Appian way stretching south from Rome to Brindisi. Of this Roman road, the "queen of roads," the 1886 Baedecker guide to Italy – a faithful companion of British travelers to Italy – says:

we enjoy a magnificent prospect, embracing the *campagna*, the ruins of the aqueducts, and the mountains ... The ancient pavement is visible in many places, the road is skirted on both sides by continuous rows of ruined tombs, and the view becomes more extensive at every step. ... The scenery ... strikingly beautiful.[1]

"Take the time to read my story," would typically continue a tomb epitaph. "It will only take a few minutes." "It will give you an opportunity to take a break from dust and thirst, and to rest under the shade of this tree." Quickl_y_ approaching the end of our journey, we too should perhaps pause, for "a few minutes," to reflect upon the deeper meaning of our experience.

From Words to Numbers

From Thin Explanations to "Thick Descriptions"?

"To what kind of issues should quantitative methods be applied?" asked Robert Fogel (1975, p. 344). His answer was: "Formal quantitative methods have their most obvious application in the analysis of the behavior of groups." Like Hobbes's "orderly Method," based on Elements, Names, Assertions, Connexions, Syllogismes, and Consequences (Hobbes, 1985, p. 115), or the Lullian "method" of the art of memory, the "formal quantitative method" advocated by Fogel is no simple matter. Indeed, the "method" is a complex set of procedures; it requires a number of steps, carefully taken in the right order: 1) The development of a theoretical framework, from which 2) hypotheses are derived, and 3) are expressed in mathematical form as in Equation 6.1:

$$Y_t = \beta_0 + \beta_1 X_{1t} + \beta_2 X_{2t} + \ldots + \beta_k X_{kt} + \ldots \epsilon_i \qquad 6.1$$

where a "dependent" variable, Y, is a function of a set of "independent" variables, $X_1, X_2, \ldots, X_k$, according to a set of parameters $\beta_0, \beta_1, \beta_2, \ldots, \beta_k$. This mathematical model that specifies our hypotheses then 4) needs to be estimated via one kind or another of statistical technique. Finally, 5) on the basis of the empirical results obtained from the statistical procedures, hypotheses and theories will be accepted or rejected. This is precisely what we did in estimating the "red menace" hypothesis back in Chapter 3 ("Of Thin Threads and Other Threads").

Strikes are one type of group behavior to which economists, sociologists, and political scientists have most frequently applied formal quantitative methods. David Snyder[2] was among the sociology pioneers in the use of time-series econometric methods. In his study of the determinants of the temporal patterns of Italian strikes, he proposed a model where the dependent variable, Y, measured either the logged numbers of strikes or strikers (Gurr's event counts), and six independent variables, X, measured national income, a six-year lagged moving average of the percent change in real wages, union membership, number of cabinet changes in a year, election-year dummy, and a time trend variable. According to Snyder (1975, p. 272), the statistical results show that

> unionization is the strongest predictor of fluctuations in the frequency and size of industrial conflict ... [and that there is] no significant influence of Shorter and Tilly's indicators of political change or crisis on industrial conflict.

Snyder (1975, p. 274) concluded that organizational/political models explain the fluctuations of strikes better than economic/bargaining models.

The lure of this modern "method" is undeniable. The theory, the hypotheses, the mathematics, the statistics, all contribute to give the method the appeal of modernity and science. Yet, critics would argue that these models are typically based on a very limited number of explanatory variables, due to problems of data availability and of statistical estimation. As a result, not only the data upon which these models are based tend to be very "thin," highly aggregated as they are, but the explanations that those models provide also tend to be "thin."

Historian Elton[3] retorts to the quantitative "scientific" historians that they

> have found evidence and means for a meaningful study of a good many questions ... However, the very nature of their methods compels them to eliminate large areas of enquiry from their agenda ...

C. Wright Mills, a relentless sociological critic, put it no differently (1959, p. 57):

> the kinds of problems that will be taken up and the way in which they are formulated are quite severely limited by The Scientific Method. Methodology, in short, seems to determine the problem.

No doubt, quantitative research can only study what is quantifiable. Quantitative sociohistorical research is forced to concentrate on those social and historical processes and on the aspects of those processes that can profitably be submitted to statistical testing to the exclusion of others, which may well be more relevant but are not as easily quantifiable.

To that, the proponents of formal quantitative methods reply: True, our models do take into account only a limited number of factors. But, from a statistical viewpoint, that may not be a problem. Model misspecification (that is, the exclusion of significant variables or the adoption of the wrong functional form of the relationship between X and Y, for example, X^2 rather than X) is a potentially statistically serious problem; but, in reality, you can expect contrasting effects to cancel each other out. So, in the end, it does not really matter if you leave out some variables.

Unfortunately, there is no way to tell which variables will cancel each other out. So, in the end, it does matter which variables you include and which you exclude from your model. Let us go back to Snyder's model. The specification of the model includes union membership among the "independent" variables.

Yet, can we reasonably claim that, in fact, it is changes in the level of union membership that "cause" changes in the levels of industrial conflict? Is it not, rather, the other way around as I have argued in *The Puzzle of Strikes* for the Italian case in the postwar period (Franzosi, 1995, pp. 124–34)? Snyder also included a "time trend variable" in his model.[4] Yet, the inclusion of this variable in the model builds an artificial collinearity with national income and unionization that seriously distorts the statistical estimates; and the estimates are further distorted by the presence of one or two influential observations (Franzosi, 1995, pp. 237–40). So, in the end, our social science models upon which we have increasingly relied to explain social reality are not only thin but, often, altogether wrong.

Yet, at the core of that approach there is the explicit attempt to "explain" social phenomena by providing a causal framework, however crudely specified, however poorly operationalized, however wrongly estimated. And that is not always the case with research based on event properties rather than event counts – indeed, I am afraid, the type of research illustrated in this book. The very richness of the data may lure investigators into a purely descriptive approach, the narrative of the evidence imposing its form on the mode of explanation. The sheer quantity of available information on a wide range of event properties makes it possible to fully describe the events in terms of those properties. Yet, that wealth of information is deceitful. *We only have information on the dependent variable*, to use the language of traditional statistical models. We are only dealing with *Y*, where *Y*, instead of being measured by a simple count of number of strikes, is measured by thick descriptions of those same strikes. But we are still only dealing with strikes, albeit in terms of the complex network of social relationships involved. What happened to the set of independent variables, $X_1, X_2, X_3, ..., X_k$, the presumed "causes" of those strikes? As Braudel (1980, p. 67) argues: "[A]n event ... [occurs] within the context of a whole family of other events."

From Variables to Actors

The real problem with a narrowly focused statistical approach to history is that it encourages a view of history and social relations as "variables" rather than as social actors. The agents of history (whether individuals, institutions, social groups, or classes) are nowhere to be seen (Braudel, 1980, pp. 49, 79). Strike research is certainly a good case in point. The ready availability of government-collected aggregate strike statistics for over one-hundred years has made it all too easy for researchers to relate these figures to other readily available figures, in particular, economic figures: gross national product, unemployment, wages (Franzosi, 1987). But noneconomic factors are certainly at work. Perhaps not as readily quantifiable, but nonetheless present. In any case, quantitative strike research has predominantly, when not exclusively, focused only on one actor (workers) and on one action (strikes). Yet, "it takes two to tango." The employers and the state are actively involved in these struggles. Strikes emerged in the nineteenth century in most western countries as the predominant expression of grievances of a class generated by industrial capitalism (Thompson, 1978, pp. 146–50). They grew out of the incessant interactions among the main actors involved – workers, employers, and the state; it is this interaction that ultimately defined the rules and the acceptable forms of protest (Tilly, 1978, p. 161). It is not possible to understand what workers do without at the same time understanding what employers and the state do.

In a variable-based approach, the interaction between workers, employers, and the state – with all the passion and the emotional world of the red banners, the hammers and sickles, the police lines – become abstracted in the interaction between "number of strikes," "unemployment rate," "unionization," the handful of variables typically involved in a model of strikes. The interests of those actors, the actions they perform in the pursuit of those interests – the "stuff" of the "class struggle" – gets lost in technical definitions and problems. In omitting the variable "repression," for instance, from the specification of a regression model because we do not have adequate time-series measures of that variable, we do not just break statistical assumptions of the General Linear Model. Implicitly or explicitly, a model of strikes where repression is not part of the relevant causal structure is equivalent to a view of strikes and the "class struggle" where employers and the state do not exist!

A story grammar, this simple subject-action-object structure that I have pursued in this book, is fundamentally a template for the representation of a relationship between social actors mediated by an action. After all, the grammar "rewrites" the <subject> as <actor> and the <object> as well as an <actor>. It delivers data that under the guise of skeleton narrative sentences depict actors who do something, often for or against some other actors. We saw in Chapter 3 that it is quite possible to obtain variables from this type of data. In fact, this is precisely what researchers involved in the study of conflict events have typically done, even when they used narrative texts as sources of data and content analysis as a method of data collection. But the use of network models on these data safeguards the fundamental concern with agency over variables. Thus, our sources of information (newspaper narratives), the tool that we use to extract data from those sources (story grammar), the very data that we obtain as a result (skeleton narrative sentences), and the tools of statistical analysis of those data (network models) all have the social actor at the core of their concerns. In Bernard Bailyn's words:

> The numbers become signals to lead one far more deeply into human realities than one could otherwise have gone. It's just enumeration, it's not history; it's numbers. In the end, one must talk about people, their activities and concerns. (Bailyn, 1994, p. 38)

The techniques of data collection and data analysis used here never allow us to forget that "there are people behind numbers," in Michelle Perrot's expression

(Perrot, 1968, p. 120). Furthermore, one can always recapture the narratives of the people behind the numbers by zooming back into the narratives, as Bailyn would wish (1994, p. 38).

From Synchronic to Diachronic Time

"Interhuman relations," wrote von Wiese (1932, pp. 54, 65), "have, as *action* patterns, a decidedly dynamic aspect. ... Social actions are data which are dependent on time ..." If actors are nowhere to be seen in sociology's world, time is often no more than an excuse for statistical exercises – the dates in article titles (1920–1930, 1860–1980, 1960–1975) only providing the end points of a sample period for econometric models with remarkably little concern with history in the articles' content (Abbott, 1991, p. 205). These models are typically ahistorical, if not altogether antihistorical in their conception of time.

When quantitative sociologists approach issues of historical nature, their *time* is anything but the historian's time. In the quantitative sociologist's tool bag of time series analysis (whether Econometrics, ARIMA, or Spectral Analysis), time is an indexing mechanism $(t_1, t_2, \ldots t_i, \ldots t_n)$ for a series of equally spaced data points. Time refers to the position of a particular data point in this series. Statistical time is synchronic rather than diachronic time. The temporal flow of history, flux and change is (synchronically) fixed in one point (a coefficient). In historical narrative time flows (diachronically) with the narrative of an event (Abbott, 1990). At each time point the historian can provide a wide-angle picture, accounting for the broad range of factors that operate in a particular historical conjuncture.

The quantitative methods that sociology relies upon in its approach to the study of time are very effective in distancing sociology from history, both in discourse and in practice. Historians are typically concerned with agency, with actors and actions, and the relationships among various actors (the "event"). Time series analysis transfers that concern with actors to a concern with numbers and their properties (for example, estimating techniques, properties of estimators, statistical significance, percentage of explained variance). Events, with their matrix of actors and actions, become cases and observations. Points of historical breaks and change become problems of temporal stability of structural parameters. History tries to understand the social forces that bring out change. In the statistical analysis of time series, change is a statistical problem with measurable effects on the estimated coefficients. Change needs to be dealt with, typically, through the use of dummy variables and trend variables. For history, change is what needs to be explained. And historians rely on narrative to explain change or on simple exploratory techniques, such as plots and tables of raw data, where each time point has meaning.

Contrary to traditional quantitative aggregate historical data, with their organization by case and variable, our data have a built-in temporal dimension.

Our data are skeleton narrative sentences organized in chronological order. And contrary to traditional approaches to data analysis, with their synchronic view of time, the use of network models is premised on a diachronic view of time.

From Statistical Causality to Narrative Sequences

Narrative is characterized by simple SAO structures. These structures, in fact, are the very hallmark of narrative. If a text, or part of a text, is not reducible to a set of SAO structures, then, that text (or that part of a text) does not belong to the narrative genre. We have seen that the degree to which a text differs from an SAO structure causes problems of intercoder reliability, when coders choose different ways of fitting nonnarrative text into a narrative (SAO) structure.

The chronological ordered sequence of these structures provides the *story* of the narrative. The sequence of SAO structures adopted by the narrator for rhetorical effect is the *plot*. Perhaps, cognition, at its most elemental level, occurs in narrative form, proceeding from a sequence of SAO structures to higher and higher levels of abstractions. Thus, we look around and we see someone doing something. From there we extract propositions of higher level order into ever more abstracted principles.

This representation (or model) of social reality in sequence form is quite different from the more typical representation of statistical variables in a causal model, with a set of "independent" variables $X_1, X_2, ..., X_i, ..., X_k$ causing a "dependent" variable Y. Having data in SAO form shifts the emphasis from statistical causality to narrative sequences, where causality, perhaps, can only be understood in terms of its original narrative meaning. Thus, the types of models "scientists" adopt to represent social reality deeply shape the way they think of that reality, no less than everyday metaphors direct and constrain the ways in which we understand the social world around us (Lakoff and Johnson, 1980). Let there be no misunderstanding. Those models (whether variables in causal structures, or sequences of SAO structures) provide powerful tools for the analysis and understanding of social reality. They allow us to see patterns in an otherwise chaotic world. The patterns we ultimately see, however, are deeply influenced by the models we use to make order of chaos. In that sense, these models are not just *enabling* (that is, allowing us to see), they are also *constraining* (that is, they allow us to see only certain things and in certain ways).

The question before us is: If narrative is nothing but a sequence of SAO structures, can one find further patterns in these sequences? (Abbott, 1983; Abbott and Barman, 1997). Another way to say this is: Are there particular subgenres of the narrative genre, characterized by specific SAO sequences? Consider a restaurant scene, where a customer enters the restaurant expecting to be served dinner. It is a scene we are rather accustomed to in the modern world. We know what the "routine" is. We could translate that routine into a set of chronologically ordered SAO structures:

$(SAO)_1$ customer enters restaurant
$(SAO)_2$ customer waits to be seated
$(SAO)_3$ host approaches customer
$(SAO)_4$ host seats customer
$(SAO)_5$ waiter brings menu to customer
$(SAO)_6$ waiter leaves
$(SAO)_7$ customer looks at menu
$(SAO)_8$ waiter returns to customer
$(SAO)_9$ customer orders food

...

$(SAO)_i$ customer eats

...

$(SAO)_{n-1}$ customer pays bill
$(SAO)_n$ customer leaves

It is precisely the routine character of these sequences that has allowed computer scientists to build powerful artificial intelligence (AI) tools for computer understanding of natural languages. In AI these patterned routines have been called *scripts* (Schank and Riesbeck, 1981) or *protocols* (Ericsson and Simon, 1996). Needless to say there are problems with a view of social reality as scripts, the basic problems being that these scripts are repeated endlessly every day, infinitely rewritten but never quite in the same way. It is not just the fact that a customer could enter the restaurant and leave immediately without going through the entire sequence simply because there is a long line – in which case, not only sequences $(SAO)_2$ through $(SAO)_{n-1}$ would be missing, but the structure "there is a long line," intermediate between $(SAO)_1$ and $(SAO)_2$, is missing from the script. Or that the customer starts shouting that the food is inedible and leaves without paying the bill. In this case, the structure $(SAO)_{n-1}$ would not be present. All of that is, indeed, part of the script and can easily (well, not so easily, but it can) be accounted for. We can then move from script to script. Imagine that same scene in a restaurant on a busy street. Imagine that, all of a sudden, a car runs into the front window crashing through the tables and customers; or that a man enters with a machine gun and starts shooting randomly. The script now becomes that of an accident or of an act of violence (individual or political as it may be) with, perhaps, a parallel script of panic.

In fact, social reality is orderly even when it appears most disorderly and chaotic. Consider violent forms of collective behavior. Traditional social science interpretations of these forms of behavior stressed its irrational character (the "maddening crowd," the "moments of madness"). Yet, recent historical and sociological work on forms of collective action has shown that even this type of behavior shows "meaningful" patterns, both in terms of routines that are familiar to the actors involved and their unfolding over long stretches of time (for example, Burke, 1983; Sahlins, 1981). Just when we thought of such "moments of madness" as irrational and random, they become predictable, almost tamed and familiar under the grip of undercurrents of historical forces. Such seems to be the nature of our Red Years and Black Years.

The point is: If social reality is, indeed, orderly, if there are observable and repeatable patterns of behavior, if there are scripts of social reality, then the sequences of our SAO structures are not random. Rather, they are patterned in specific ways, in specific sequences. Within broader scripts, we can always, more or less, anticipate (predict) the proper and ordered sequence of SAO structures. These patterns, of course, are not rigid. There is always the possibility of innovation. But they are rigid enough to make social reality quite predictable, our daily routines reliable, our social life quite orderly (boring?).

From Structures to Events

A narrative is not just a collection of simple narrative sentences (of the SAO type), centered around a microaction ("On 31 October 1517, Dr. Martin Luther ... nailed a paper ... to the door of the Castle Church in that town [Wittenberg].").[5] A narrative also groups together in larger meaningful narrative units (the event) several individual narrative sentences chronologically ordered in structured sequences. And the event is typically expressed linguistically as yet another narrative sentence this time centered around a macroaction and, often, around abstract actors who act as "quasi-characters" in "quasi-events" narratively held together in "quasi-plots" (for example, the Reformation deeply changed northern and central European societies).[6] Through a process of abstraction, the historian progressively moves away from a focus on concrete, human agents and creates new historical agents. Martin Luther, the crowd, strikers, people – Ricoeur's "first-order entities" – are abstracted into "second-order entities" – imperialism – and "third-order entities" – Reformation, Classical Antiquity, Renaissance (Ricoeur, 1984, pp. 181–206). Even Braudel's structures are nothing but third-order entities, Braudel's history nothing but a history of a "major event: The retreat of the Mediterranean from general history." "Braudel has invented a new type of plot" based on this quasi-event, claims Ricoeur.[7] These quasi-events – like Burke's pentads and Danto's "project verbs" – provide overall organizing principles for the myriad of microactions through which history unfolds. No organizing principle, no history, only *temporal structures* to borrow Danto's expression.

I set out on this journey in search of the actor. In the end, what I really found was the action, or, better, the interaction between actors and actions, in other words, the event. Is the return of the actor inextricably linked to the return of the event? Perhaps. For one thing, a more or less numerous set of thick descriptions of events (such as strikes, rallies, or violence) provides the basic empirical material we now work with. Those events ultimately sow the weft of a larger cloth; they are subsumed under a bigger event, such as my Red Years and Black Years, or the "Reformation," or even the "Fall of the Roman Empire." It is those larger events that drive the overall narrative of the analyses. Thus, the event – whether the microevent or microaction that provides the basic building block of the thick descriptions (for example, "workers distribute leaflets," "employers send letters to union leaders"), the event proper (for example, strike, lockout, attack), or the macroevent – Danto's "project verb" or Le Roy Ladurie's "creative event"[8] – that sews together individual stories into broader meaningful units (for example, the Red Years, the Hot Autumn) – the event is back, claiming a place at the center of sociohistorical explanation.

Financial pressures also tend to direct scholarly attention toward a single transformative point, toward the macroevent. The high costs of collecting event properties rather than event counts and in ways that preserve much of the flavor and richness of the original narratives typically force researchers to target only a handful of years for investigation. And the temptation, of course, is to target years particularly rich in events, typically also years that can be subsumed under a macroevent. Thus, the sample period of this project is four years (1919–22), that of my other project on service sector versus industrial sector conflict is two years (1986–87), that of Tarrow (1989) on the Italian postwar cycle of protest is eight years (1966–73).[9]

Yet, Braudel had warned us a long time ago of the dangers of focusing solely on the event as a unit of historical analysis. To repeat Braudel's words (1980, pp. 3–4) of the *Preface* to his monumental, 1,100 page, 3 volume monograph, *The Mediterranean and the Mediterranean World in the Age of Philip II*:

> Though by its nature the most exciting and richest in human interest of histories, it [narrative history of individual events] is also the most perilous. We must beware of that history which still simmers with the passions of the contemporaries who felt it, described it, lived it, to the rhythm of their brief lives, lives as brief as are our own. It has the dimensions of their anger, their dreams, and their illusions.

Events, for Braudel, can only be understood in a broader temporal context, in the time span of several decades (*conjunctures*) and several centuries (*structures*). Those are the really significant temporalities for historical explanation.[10] Events are but "a surface disturbance, the waves stirred up by the powerful movement of tides ... sharp, nervous vibrations" (Braudel, 1980, p. 3). Structures, rather than events, are for Braudel the new units of historical analysis and "the whole of history is to be rethought" in light of the relation of events "to these expanses of slow-moving history." "All the stages, all the thousands of stages, all the thousand explosions of historical time can be understood on the basis of these depths, this semistillness. Everything gravitates around it."[11]

Our focus on the event prevents us from considering Braudel's longer time spans, that semistillness. Engrossed by our thick descriptions, we can certainly provide a rich texture for the unfolding of the event, but the event itself we cannot explain. To explain the event we would have to consider the event in the context of possibly other such events scattered in time.[12] "Resounding events often take place in an instant, and are but manifestations of that larger destiny by which alone they can be explained" (Braudel, 1980, p. 3).

Unexpected Crossings

Egeria tells us how the monks who accompanied her to the Sinai, "the Mount of God," "point[ed] out to us all the different places. ... They showed us the cave where holy Moses ... They showed us all the other places ... All this was pointed out to us by the holy men" (Wilkinson, 1981a, pp. 94–5). I had the good fortune of meeting holy men of my own along the way, on this journey from words to numbers: Computer scientists, statisticians, literary critics, economists, explorers, philosophers, psychologists, poets, and artists had plenty of things to show us, plenty of advice to give me. Even medieval alchemists were generous with their recommendations. Busy as they all were hurrying along toward destinations that were not mine, they always spared their time.

In his *Sentimental Journey* Laurence Sterne wrote: "*[A]n English man does not travel to see English men*" (1983, p. 38; emphasis in the original)."When I have been abroad," Montaigne similarly acknowledges (III, IX; 1892, p. 228), "I ... always frequented tables the most filled with foreigners." Myself a sociologist, I started parting ways from my fellow sociologists, increasingly seeking the company of the most diverse scholars. Yet, historians and linguists were my preferred companions. Unconsciously at first, with still much road to travel, it is the historians' and linguists' company I increasingly sought, as we journeyed on; it is their voices I strained to hear in that cacophony of sounds of the crowded roads of knowledge; it is their languages I made an effort to learn so that we could converse. Now, at last, after much journeying and conversing – carefully listening to what they all had to say – it is starting to dawn on me what we share together. To linguists and historians I am indebted for alerting me to the shortcomings of my single-minded pursuit of the numbers. It is linguists and literary critics who gave me the tools with which to understand and take apart our texts, our (social) scientific texts. And the tools unveiled the rhetoric buried in those texts, the rhetoric behind the numbers.

A paralyzing doubt at first gripped me. But the more we conversed, the more I was able to reconcile my point of view with theirs. "I am ashamed," says Montaigne (III, IX; 1892, p. 228), "to see my countrymen besotted with this foolish humour of quarrelling with forms contrary to their own; they seem to be out of their element when out of their own village: Wherever they go, they keep to their own fashion, and abominate those of strangers." In the end, I discovered the sheer joy of understanding my work in the context of other pursuits, of getting a glimpse, however feeble, of the invisible threads that link a knowledge that only in the academy comes in neatly divided and easily digestible chunks, the name of each chunk inscribed on different buildings: Psychology, Sociology, ... The choice, really, is that between being wise and doubtful, or ignorant and certain – silence and emphasis are still pursuing us, till the very end. But the three disciplines – sociology, linguistics, and history – also came together in more specific ways in this journey of ours.

Sociology Meets History[13]

"The story of history and sociology is the story of the mutual enlightenment that never happened," writes Abbott (1991, p. 230). After all, each discipline has its "founding fathers," its tradition, its language, its myths, metaphors, disciplinary mottos, and banners. However misguided myths may be, however distant may be what both historians and sociologists practice from what they preach, myths do function as powerful rallying banners. As Lasswell (1949, pp. 51–2) wrote:

> The dominant political symbols of an epoch provide part of the common experience of millions of men. There is some fascination in the thought of how many human beings are bound together by a thread no more substantial than the resonance of a name or the clang of a slogan. In war, men suffer pain, hunger, sorrow; the specific source of pain, the specific sensation of one's specific object of sorrow, may be very private. In contrast, the key symbol enters directly into the focus of all men and provide an element of common experience.

Alas, the "thread," the "key symbol," and the "common experience" are common only within and not across disciplines (and, increasingly so, within subdisciplines). Braudel puts it best: "There is hardly ever any real dialogue between sociologist and historian" (Braudel, 1980, p. 64).

Historians have long maintained that social-science formal models provide a representation of history without agency and without time. In Elton's (1983, pp. 118–19) words: "Despite attempts to deny this, it [scientific history] can effectively operate only by suppressing the individual – by reducing its subject matter to a collectivity of human data in which the facts of humanity have real difficulty in surviving." As for time, Braudel writes: "It is not history which sociologists, fundamentally and quite unconsciously, bear a grudge against, but historical time."[14] Elton (1983, p. 112) echoes: "The social science methods ... were designed to analyze structure (static conditions) and were thus ill-equipped to cope with the basic problem of history, that is, change through time." No doubt, sociology is a discipline of the present. While historians cannot avoid time, sociologists must look for it. In a paper delivered in 1948 at Oslo, Paul F. Lazarsfeld – one of "the more sophisticated spokesmen of this school [abstracted empiricism]" in C. Wright Mills's scathing words – acknowledged that "the sociologist will ... have a tendency to deal mainly with contemporaneous events for which he is likely to get the kind of data he needs."[15] For all the recent revival of historical sociology, a tabulation of published sociological works would reveal sociologists' overarching concern with current social problems.[16] The most popular method employed in sociology – perhaps sociology's very hallmark, the sample survey – can only by its very nature focus on the present.[17] If the methods used by quantitative sociologists lead them astray from history, qualitative sociologists may not fare better. Their method – "participant observation," as it was once called or the ethnographic method, as it is now called – is no more concerned with historical time than survey techniques.[18] On the contrary, "the historian never escapes from time," as Marc Bloch wrote (1953, p. 156). Braudel put it similarly: "The historian can never get away from the question of time in history: Time sticks to his thinking like soil to a gardener's spade." Sociologists' "time is not ours: It is never central to their problems and their thoughts."[19]

Not surprisingly, despite a common fundamental concern with (historical) social action, the two disciplines had little to say to each other. They kept each other at arm's length. Yet, as Braudel acknowledged, "It can hardly be denied that history and sociology come together, identify with each other, and merge often enough" (Braudel, 1980, p. 69). The marriage of history and sociology may have never come, but "some pre-marital intercourse seems to have had results."[20]

When opposition among German historians grew to the Rankian exclusive concern with political and military events, and with dominant historical figures at that, it consolidated around the *Kulturgeschichte*, a social history ante litteram that looked to social and economic structures for explanations. Max Weber fully embraced that manifesto and he himself contributed to *Kulturgeschichte* with such works as *The Agrarian Sociology of Ancient Civilizations* (1976). The French historians who congregated around the journal *Annales*, founded by Marc Bloch and Lucien Febvre in 1929, embraced a similar approach to the study of history. They turned their back on the event, with its emphasis on elite's actions, and put structures firmly under the spotlight. At around the same time, in England, Namier and Tawney similarly pleaded for a history based on the analysis of structures (Burke, 1991b, p. 233). It was Braudel who perhaps most clearly and most forcefully stated the new manifesto. Of the three temporalities of history – the fleeting event, the decades-long *conjuncture,* and the centuries-long *structure* – it is with structure that, according to Braudel, historians should concern themselves. And that structure, in Braudel's view, should provide the common ground between historians and social scientists. "The *long durée* appears to us ... as the most useful line to take toward a way of observing and thinking common to all social sciences" (Braudel, 1980, p. 50).[21]

With Braudel and the French *Annales*, that almost necessary link between history and narrative comes to an end, between the way history unfolds by actors and processes – the "event" – and the way we represent it as a narrative similarly centered around actors and actions – François Simiand's *histoire événementielle*, history of events.[22] Braudel's emphasis on structures rather than events broke the umbilical chord to which historians had been attached since Thucydides's times.

But once historians start toying with structures as objects of inquiry, with the interplay between the political, social, and economic spheres, they slowly step out of "the territory of the historian" to move into that of the social scientist, as Braudel is keenly aware. And in that territory, we find familiar concerns with quantification, model building, and theory. Braudel himself was not quantitative, and neither were the founders of the journal *Annales*, Marc Bloch and Lucien Febvre. Themselves "traditional" lonely scholars, trotting from archive to archive (Hexter, 1979, p. 93), they nonetheless welcomed exact measures whenever possible. Under their supervision, a number of quantitative studies of prices, climatic fluctuations, and population movements sprung up with the name of *histoire sérielle* (Chaunu, 1978; Furet, 1985). We met one such project carried out by Huguette and Pierre Chaunu (1955–59). As director of the *Centre de recherches historiques* in Paris, Braudel launched a series of huge projects of historical nature involving teams of scholars from various disciplines.[23]

The end of the line of a "structural" approach to history is a full-fledged adoption of social science modes of explanation. The French historians of the *histoire sérielle* and the American economic historians grouped under the label "Cliometrics" were pushing in that direction.[24] They insisted on the need for a quantitative grounding of one's arguments, whenever possible, for clear definitions, for an explicit statement of one's assumptions in mathematical/statistical behavioral models. For Fogel (1983, p. 24), "the common characteristic of cliometricians is that they apply the quantitative methods and behavioral models of the social sciences to the study of history." But, then, issues of interpretation recede to the background, in the name of exactness and measurement, in the name of science. By this route, the association between *storia* and *storia*, history and story is broken once and for all. History has ventured into the territory of science. The marriage of history and sociology has been celebrated at last. The title of a chapter of an edited volume that appeared in 1980 makes that clear: "Quantitative Analysis of Historical Material as the Basis for a New Cooperation Between Sociology and History" (Scheuch, 1980).

American cliometricians and the French exponents of *histoire sérielle* succeeded in putting quantitative methods on the map of historical work. As Bailyn put it (1982, p. 24): "No effective historian of the future can be innocent of statistics." But they hardly succeeded in displacing, once and for all, a narrative approach to history with statistical/mathematical modeling. Neither did Braudel succeed in dethroning the event, putting conjunctures and structures in its place. For all their might, Braudel's blows to the event and to the *histoire événementielle* were not fatal.

In the 1980s, the vision of history driven by a project of a social scientific mathematical/statistical representation of sociohistorical reality came under increasing attack from all sides. Among both social scientists and historians awareness increased of the limits of a purely quantitative approach to the study of social reality; awareness increased of the alchemic games – the search for a philosophers' stone and the rituals – in which "quantofrenics" delighted;

awareness increased of the rhetorical foundations of social science work – rhetoric to which a dominant culture of scientific discourse made them blind. Stone put it quite scornfully:

> It might be time for the historical rats to leave rather than to scramble aboard the social scientific ship which seems to be leaking and undergoing major repair. History has always been social, and it was attracted by the siren songs of the social sciences because it thought – perhaps somewhat mistakenly, it now appears – that they were also scientific. (Stone, 1981, pp. 32–3)

And those who shied away from the numbers and preferred to exorcize the event and narrative with the help of structures and conjunctures, in the end perhaps found themselves still telling stories, stories where the protagonists are not individual or collective human actors, but structures and conjunctures, quasi-characters involved in quasi-plots, a meta-history of history. "Historical narrative is dying," Barthes had written (Barthes, 1970, p. 155). But don't rush to the funeral. For the event came back, back with a vengeance.[25] And with the event, back came historical narrative, to give us such historical gems as Emmanuel Le Roy Ladurie's *Montaillou* (1979a), Carlo Ginzburg's *The Cheese and the Worms* (1982), Natalie Zemon Davis's *The Return of Martin Guerre* (1983). In sociology, not to mention anthropology, "tales from the field" and the study of culture also came back in fashion to give us more gems, from Kai Erikson's *Everything in Its Path* (1976) to Elliot Liebow's *Tell Them Who I Am* (1993). The "linguistic turn" of the 1980s was providing the new ground for interdisciplinary frolicking.

To which ground does the path between words and numbers, art and science traced in these pages lead us? The common ground, no doubt, is the tool we have used to structure narrative: story grammars. That structure of actors performing certain actions for or against other actors (or of agents involved in actions with patients and beneficiaries, in the language of semantic roles) is the way historians tell their "true" stories. Myself I use that structure to collect "data" on "true" historical events. But that structure was developed by linguists (Propp, in particular) as a template to understand "fictional" stories, namely Russian folktales. It fits indifferently true or fictional stories.[26] Narrative action – action that unfolds in time, involves animate human agents, and leads to many reversals of the original situation – resembles human action. To the extent that history deals with this temporal unfolding of human action, history, at heart, is nothing but narrative. The writing of history in narrative form is the necessary outcome of the very unfolding of historical events as human action. There is a "natural" link between the two. It is worth quoting at length a passage of Hayden White on this point (1987, p. 54).

> There is ... a certain necessity in the relationship between the narrative, conceived as a symbolic or symbolizing discursive structure, and the

representation of specifically historical events. This necessity arises from the fact that human events are or were products of human actions, and these actions have produced consequences that have the structures of texts – more specifically, the structure of narrative texts. The understanding of these texts, considered as the products of actions, depends upon our being able to reproduce the processes by which they were produced, that is, to narrativize these actions. Since these actions are in effect lived narrativizations, it follows that the only way to represent them is by narrative itself. Here the form of discourse is perfectly adequate to its content, since the one is narrative, the other what has been narrativized. The wedding of form with content produces the symbol, 'which says more than what it says' but in historical discourse always says the same thing: historicality.

And that fundamental link between history and narrative does not go away, if we are to believe in Ricoeur's critique of Braudel's structures, conceived to eschew narrative, but ultimately ending up in further narrative. "My thesis is," Ricoeur states, "that history the most removed from the narrative form continues to be bound to our narrative understanding by a line of derivation that we can reconstruct step by step and degree by degree ... without losing anything of its scientific ambition" (Ricoeur, 1984, p. 91).

In the end, history and sociology meet in this strange world of ours where numbers betray their close connection with the words: Our data *are* skeleton narrative sentences and even the statistical analyses of those data fundamentally preserve historical narrativity by producing representations based on the social interaction between human agents rather than variables and models of the general linear type. The narrativity of history mirrors the narrativity of social reality. Our SAO structure is a "syntax of social life."[27]

The Centrality of the Verb (Linguistics and Sociology)

Of Labov's seminal work on narrative, Toolan wrote:

> Labov works on the broad assumption that *what is said* ... will not be the core of a story; that, rather, *what is done* ... will be. The 'what is done' then becomes (or may become) the core narrative text of clauses – *actions* – while the 'what is said' becomes evaluative commentary on those actions. (Toolan, 1988, p. 157)

Indeed, this "doing versus saying" distinction, implicitly or explicitly, is at the core of linguistic theories of narrative structures. Genette (1980, pp. 164, 169) distinguishes between narrative of events and narrative of words. For Ricoeur (1984, p. 56) "there is no structural analysis of narrative that does not borrow from an explicit or implicit phenomenology of 'doing something.'" Bal similarly points out that "in general, narrative theorists rather tend to analyse the course of action to which they limit their *story*" (Bal, 1977, p. 89; emphasis in the original). It is this emphasis on action (on "doing something") that has led to the privileged position of actions/events over actors in poetics. We first find that subordination of character to action in Aristotle who wrote in his *Poetics*:[28]

> Tragedy is a representation not of people as such but of actions and of life and both happiness and unhappiness rest on action. ... [A]nd while men do have certain qualities by virtue of their character, it is in their actions that they achieve, or fail to achieve, happiness. ... [W]ithout action you would not have a tragedy, but one without character would be feasible.

We find it in Propp, the early twentieth-century Russian formalist,[29] who wrote: (1968, p. 20; emphasis in the original):

> The names of the dramatis personae change (as well as the attributes of each), but neither their actions nor functions change. ... The question of *what* a tale's dramatis personae do is an important one for the study of the tale, but the question of *who* does it and *how* it is done already fall within the province of accessory study.

We still find it in Greimas who proposed to describe and classify narrative characters according to what they do (hence the name *actants*) – once more reproducing the subordination of character to action despite Greimas's focus on *actants* (Greimas, 1966).

Even the linguists working on argument theory and theory of semantic roles defend the central role of verbs over nouns, of action over agents. In Chafe's (1970, p. 96) words:

> the total human conceptual universe is dichotomized initially into two major areas. One, the area of the verb, embraces states (conditions, qualities) and events; the other, the area of the noun, embraces "things" (both physical objects and reified abstractions). Of these two, the verb will be assumed to be central and the noun peripheral. There are various kinds of evidence which are best explained by assuming centrality for the verb.

Theta roles fundamentally assign a privileged position to verbs. Verbs contain, so to speak, the basic genetic information of the entire sentence. "The verb determines what the rest of the sentence will be like," writes Chafe (1970, p. 97). In comparison, "a noun is like a planet whose internal modifications affect it alone, and not the solar system as a whole" (Chafe, 1970, pp. 97–8). Not the noun, not the adjective, not the preposition, not any of the parts of speech, but the verb holds the key to language.

Wittgenstein approvingly cites Goethe *"Im Anfgang war die Tat"* (In the beginning was the Deed/Action).[30] But to Wittgenstein, it is action of a different kind that was in the beginning. His action is language use or practice.

Knowledge is the result of that action, a shared discourse in a community of users. Halliday takes that one step further. The process – the verb as action – constitutes a fundamental cognitive category, providing "the frame of reference for interpreting our experience of what goes on. ... [Processes] are semantic categories which explain in the most general way how phenomena of the real world are represented as linguistic structures" (Halliday, 1994, pp. 107, 109). And those processes are limited in number. In Toolan's view of Halliday's work: "By means of choices among a limited set of processes and participant roles, expressed in the grammar of the clause and, *in particular, its verb, we characterize our view of reality*" (Toolan, 1988, p. 112; emphasis added).

And yet, this distinction between actors and actions is clearly overdrawn. Because, surely, there cannot be action without actors. The Red Years are red because a working class tinted with the revolutionary color took center stage in history. The red flags were flying high on occupied factories during August 1920. The red guards stood vigil on factory rooftops and gates wearing red bands around their arms. The Black Years are black because the Fascists introduced a new color in Italian piazzas during the years 1921–22 with their black shirts. The network graphs of Figures 3.2 through 3.7 make one thing clear: That the fortunes of social actors swing on the stage of history.

But the two periods – Black Years and Red Years – are not only characterized by the centrality of different social actors as historical agents. They are also fundamentally characterized by different sets of actions. We go from the predominance of protest actions during the Red Years to that of violent actions during subsequent years. The relationship between agents and actions that the grammar brings out allows us to establish a direct link between protest events and the working class and violence and the Fascists.

Without agents there is no action. Without action there is no interaction, no relationship between social actors. French sociologist Alain Touraine (1984)[31] best expresses the dilemma between actor and action. In a book titled *The Return of the Actor*, Touraine's "return of the actor" ends up as "the return of the action," when he writes:

> All inquiries that refuse an analysis of relations among social actors are extraneous to sociology or even opposed to it. ... The sociology of action is at the core of sociological analysis. ... [T]he object of sociology is to explain the behavior of actors by the social relations in which they are placed ... It is the relation, not the actor, that we must study.

"To act is always to act 'with' others," wrote Ricoeur.[32] Action is fundamentally interaction. Interaction[33] – the *Oxford Dictionary* tells us – is action *inter* actors, action that binds together different social actors. The terms focus on the action. Actors can vary, but the action is fixed, a pivot around which actors turn, like in a merry-go-round. The very etymology of the term seems to privilege the role of action in relating social actors. Yet, for Ricoeur, "the very term 'action,' taken in the narrow sense of what someone does, gets its distinct meaning from its capacity for being used in conjunction with other terms of the whole network," a "conceptual network," made up of actors, actions, goals, motives, agents, circumstances, and outcomes. According to Ricoeur, "these terms or others akin to them occur in our answers to questions that can be classified as questions about 'what,' 'why,' 'who,' 'how,' 'with whom,' or 'against whom' in regard to any action." But this conceptual network is nothing other than a story grammar in its most basic representation, nothing but the journalists' five Ws.[34] Kenneth Burke, in his *Grammar of Motives*, similarly pays tribute to that simple structure, to "the five key terms of dramatism," the "pentad of key terms": Act, Scene, Agent, Agency, Purpose, "what was done (act), when or where it was done (scene), who did it (agent), how he did it (agency), and why (purpose)."[35]

Just like Touraine's return of the actor is, ultimately, a return of the action, my own search for the actor (remember? "it takes two to tango") seems to end up in the discovery of the action, if not altogether of the entire "conceptual network" of a story grammar. Linguistics and sociology cross paths at this unlikely juncture. But within sociology, a theoretical vision that privileged action over actors, or, better yet, interaction as a relation between social actors has much deeper roots than a casual reference to Touraine's work may highlight.

Sociology as the Study of Social Relations

"To those who regard sociology as the study of social relations," Peter Marsden (1992, p. 1887) wrote, "social networks are fundamental." Given my reliance on data organized as actors related to other actors (namely, as agents, patients, or beneficiaries) and on modes of statistical analysis based on social network models, could the reverse be true? Do my data and methods fundamentally imply a theoretical view of sociology as the study of social relations? But who are "those who regard sociology as the study of social relations?"

Tracing precursors is always a risky business. From a distance only the tallest trees are visible. The rich underworld, upon which those trees feed, disappears. And whomever you start with, there is bound to be someone before. So let me take an arbitrary cutoff point. Let me start with Saint Simon. Saint-Simon, no doubt, put the spotlight on social relations: "The form of government is but a form, and property relations are the basis; hence property relations are the real basis of the social edifice," of all social relations.[36] And through Saint-Simon, the idea filtered down to his disciples, Comte[37] and Marx. On social relations Marx has left behind some of his most cited passages:[38]

> The production of life, both of one's own in labour and of fresh life in procreation ... appears as a double relationship: On the one hand as a natural, on the other as a social relationship.

> Social relations are bound up with productive forces. In acquiring new productive forces men change their mode of production; and in changing their mode of production, in changing their way of earning a living, they change all their social relations. The hand-mill gives you society with the feudal lord; the steam-mill society with the industrial capitalist.

> The bourgeoisie cannot exist without continually revolutionising the instruments of production, and thereby the relations of production and all the social relations.

Weber dedicated several introductory pages of his *Economy and Society* to the issue of social relations.[39] Yet Weber hardly goes beyond the definitions and types of social relations that Simmel had considered in his *The Philosophy of Money* (conflictual, peaceful, competitive, communal, and associative social relations). After all, during a lull of the disease that crippled him for years, Weber took to reading literature and art, finally turning to Simmel's *Philosophy of Money* (Gerth and Mills, 1946b, p. 14). Of that book, Altmann (1903, pp. 47–8) wrote in his review for the *American Journal of Sociology*:

> [I]t is difficult to pass by so much beauty and so many new thoughts. ... [E]verything is seen in relation to everything else – that is the view that Simmel shows us in his *Philosophy of Money*. ... The man who wrote this book had to be more than a small prince over a narrow province of science; he had to be absolute master over the wide realm of human thought.

No doubt, it is to the name of this "absolute master" – Georg Simmel (1858–1918) – that is linked a view of sociology as the study of social relations.

Georg Simmel (1858–1918): "The Stranger in the Academy"[40]

In 1918, Max Weber, aged fifty four, delivered a speech at Munich University, a speech later published under the title "Science as a Vocation." Weber acknowledged to his audience:

> Academic life is a mad hazard. If the young scholar asks for my advice with regard to habilitation, the responsibility of encouraging him can hardly be borne. If he is a Jew, of course one says *lasciate ogni speranza*.[41]

Perhaps, Weber had Georg Simmel in mind, a man he had supported, strongly and unwaveringly, in his life-long quest for a permanent academic position. Indeed, we have disturbing evidence of the official antijewish climate of turn-of-the-century Germany. Listen to what Dietrich Schaefer wrote in a letter of reference[42] in relation to Simmel's application for a chair in philosophy at Heidelberg in 1908:

I will express my opinion about Professor Simmel quite frankly. I do not know whether or not he has been baptized, nor did I want to inquire about it. He is, at any rate, a dyed-in-the-wool Israelite, in his outward appearance, in his bearing, and in his manner of thinking. ... [A] Semitic lecturer – wholly, partially, or philo-Semitic, whatever he is ... (Schaefer, in Coser, 1965, pp. 37–8)

Not surprisingly, Schaefer concluded: "I regret that I must render an unfavorable judgment" (in Coser, 1965, p. 39). And not surprisingly, Simmel was not appointed to the chair, despite the support of the Heidelberg faculty, Gothein and Weber in particular.

Being Jewish certainly did not help Simmel's career. Nor did it help Simmel that he never conformed to the basic rules of the academy. A young student aged twenty two, Simmel submitted a doctoral thesis titled: "Psychological-ethnographic studies on the origins of music." The thesis was rejected. The examiners, Professors Zeller and Helmholtz, praised Simmel's intellectual self-confidence and brilliance, but they criticized the choice of a topic too broad and too ambitious for a young scholar. They also criticized the aphoristic character of the work (too many details given without supporting evidence), the large number of orthographic errors, and the carelessness in style.[43] Laas, the examiner of Simmel's second thesis (accepted *cum laude – eruditionis et sanii iudicii documentum laudabile*) similarly praised Simmel's brilliancy, but the praise verged on criticism: brilliancy as lack of self-discipline.[44]

Like a shadow, this mixture of positive and negative remarks would follow Simmel throughout his life. Again, in Schaefer's letter of reference we read: "Professor Simmel ... operates more by wit and pseudo-wit than by solid and systematic knowledge" (in Coser, 1965, p. 39). Ernst Bloch put it no differently:

> Simmel has the finest mind among all contemporaries. But beyond this, he is wholly empty and aimless ... He consumes himself in many quick and occasional fires and is most of the time nothing but dazzling in an ever repeated methodological pyrotechnic display, by which we are rapidly bored. He is coquettish ...[45]

Simmel's enemies were certainly vitriolic in their attacks. But even his strongest allies were dismayed by his style. Tönnies paid tribute to Simmel for the "multiplicity of charming observations, brilliant insights, and blinding dialectics," but, like Bloch, he also acknowledged that "these observations approach coquetry."[46] Even Weber wrote that Simmel's "mode of exposition strikes one at times as strange, and often it is at the very least uncongenial."[47]

Job application after job application, time and again, Simmel submitted himself to the predictable experience of humiliating rejections. He endured his professional isolation with a mixture of disbelief, indignation, and self-confidence. In a letter to Rickert, dated November 3, 1897, Simmel calls a "scandalous injustice" the appointment of a certain Dessoir to a post at Berlin

University he had competed for.[48] He reacted with passionate indignance to the rejection of his application in 1908 for a chair in Philosophy at Heidelberg.[49] Replying to a letter by Max Weber that presumably[50] must have informed him of the "behind-the-scene" reasons for the decision, an indignant Simmel wrote on March 18, 1908 (in Gassen and Landmann, 1958, pp. 128–9):

> That is a joke! That I should be refused a position, which I wanted to accept, because of such a perfidy – that is revolting, that is something one cannot accept without a feeling of indignation, whether one thinks the thing in question is important or not ...

After yet another rejection at Heidelberg in 1915, Simmel wrote to Rickert:

> I know, there are myths about me, what I am, and what I am not, can and cannot – and every time when faculties or governments consider me, it is either the one or the other myth which is prevalent: Sometimes I am too one-sided, sometimes I am too many-sided, here I am 'only a sociologist,' there I am 'only of talmudic astuteness,' most often 'only critical and negating,' etc. I stopped fighting against this nonsense, which does not touch the real shortcomings, of which I am very well aware.[51]

Tired and demoralized, Simmel never completely gave up his dream of a chair at Heidelberg, a chair that had been Hegel's. Eberhard Gothein, who visited Simmel in Strasbourg in 1918 right before Simmel's death, wrote: "Even on the stairs, when his wife could not hear us, he gave me several instructions on what we could still do," to get him a chair at Heidelberg.[52]

Simmel was fond of the Franciscan motto: "*Nihil habentes, omnia possidentes,*" those who have nothing, posses everything (Laurence, 1991, p. 37). In his treatise on *The Philosophy of Money* he wrote (1978, p. 254):

> In a higher and supreme sense, the world belongs to he who renounces, even though he does not really renounce; rather, in poverty he possesses the purest and finest extracts of things ... [T]he Franciscans were characterized as *nihil habentes, omnia possidentes.*

And yet, at least for some time, Simmel's family patrimony allowed him to be a refined aesthete who loved to surround himself with exquisite antiques and art objects.[53] Again, in *The Philosophy of Money* he acknowledged "the aesthetic possibilities that wealth provides" (Simmel, 1978, p. 276). His house had become the center of weekly meetings (the *jours*) that assembled the *creme* of Berlin intelligentsia, particularly artists. Of those *jours*, poet Margaret Susman recollects that

> conversation took on a form ... which floated in an atmosphere of intellectuality, affability and tact, detached from the ultimate burden of the personal element. ... Only exceptional people, distinguished by intellect or even by beauty, took part in these social events.[54]

In the memories of another participant: "With them [the Simmels] it is exquisite
… One does not speak of those things that are topical in Berlin but … about
other things of which no one else knows anything."[55]

It is the lack of a proper academic appointment throughout his life (*"nihil
habentes"*) that gave Simmel freedom[56] and intellectual independence (*"omnia
possidentes"*). In their letter of support for Simmel's application to the chair in
Heidelberg, the philosophy faculty made that point quite clear: "One cannot
locate him in any of the general currents; he has always gone his own way …"[57]
Simmel wrote of the social type of the stranger, himself a stranger to German
society and to the academy. A stranger, Simmel wrote in his *Soziologie* of 1908,

> is not bound by roots to the particular constituents and partisan
> dispositions of the group, he confronts all of these with a distinctly
> 'objective' attitude, an attitude that does not signify mere detachment
> and nonparticipation, but is a distinct structure composed of remoteness
> and nearness, indifference and involvement. … Objectivity can also be
> defined as freedom. The objective man is not bound by ties which
> could prejudice his perception, his understanding, and his assessment
> of data. This freedom … permits the stranger to experience and treat
> even his close relationships as though from a bird's-eye view …[58]

Oddly enough, Simmel never talks about the "cost" of being a stranger, *"come
sa di sale / lo pane altrui, e come è duro calle / lo scender e 'l salir per l'altrui
scale"* (How salty someone else's bread tastes, how hard a climb it is to go up
and down someone else's stairs).[59] And yet, Simmel's own freedom of a
stranger, his "going his own way" did come at a cost.[60] When he was finally
appointed to a chair of philosophy in 1914, it was in the peripheral university of
Strasbourg, where he found "some interesting minds but the faculty as a whole
a half-witted bunch," in Simmel's own assessment (in Frisby, 1984, p. 33). And
after another unsuccessful attempt in 1915 to obtain the vacant chairs of either
Wilhelm Windelband or Emil Lask in Heidelberg, Simmel's life of academic
isolation finally got to him (Frisby, 1984, p. 33). Weber (in Gerth and Mills,
1946a, p. 132) could have predicted that, or, again, he may have been thinking
of Simmel, when he declared in his 1918 Munich lecture:[61]

> [M]ediocrities undoubtedly play an eminent role at the universities. …
> Do you in all conscience believe that you can stand seeing mediocrity
> after mediocrity, year after year, climb beyond you, without becoming
> embittered and without coming to grief? … I have found that only a
> few men could endure this situation without coming to grief.

By the end of his life, Simmel had, indeed, come to grief. In 1918, he confessed
to a friend that professional isolation and the war "have had the effect of aging
me twice or three times what is normal."[62] The book that he wrote in 1918 in the
isolation of the Black Forest, already gravely ill with cancer of the liver –
Lebensanschauung, Interpretation of Life – will strike the reader for its "total

lack of optimism," Laurence remarked (1991, p. 39). According to Simmel's wife, Gertrud (cited in Wolff, 1950, p. xxii):

> During his last days, Georg no longer wanted the paper, and I did not want to bring it uncalled lest I disturb him in his thoughts. ... Before he died, Georg Simmel said emphatically and on more than one occasion that he had done his essential work; that he could merely have applied his way of looking at things farther and farther and to ever new objects – so to something really new it would not have come.

He died in the manner of the Greek philosophers of old (Spykman, 1964, p. xxix). Struck by cancer, he inquired with his doctor how much time he had left, because he wanted to finish his *Lebensanschauung*. A few days before dying, he wrote to a friend: "I am waiting for the Delos ship."[63]

If little is known of Simmel's private life,[64] we know a great deal about his writings, because he left over two hundred pieces of writing behind. His work ranges from philosophy, to psychology, to sociology, to music and art history.[65] In his writings no less than in his lectures[66] Simmel pursued relentlessly "the relationalism of all items ... which he found to haunt ever new territories – from sociology to history to ethics to epistemology to art" (Wolff, 1950, p. xxii). He pursued the alchemists' dream of *omne omne est*, of everything is everything. His sociology was a sociology of social relations both among people and among ideas. His two essays *Conflict* and *The Web of Group Affiliations* (1955) provide the theoretical basis for the abstract forms of social relations in traditional and modern societies, of single concentric affiliations versus intersecting, multiple affiliations. The *form* of sociation changed from traditional to modern societies from concentric to intersecting and partially overlapping, with the individual caught in this ever larger web of affiliations.[67] But the *forms* of sociation also involve for Simmel both conflict and cooperation, discord and unity. To give *content* to these forms, Simmel studied the relationships between men and women, between workers and employers; the relationships of conflict and cooperation between and within groups. In his *The Philosophy of Money* we even find the embryo of a graphical representation of a story grammar (or of a social relation): "The fundamental significance of purposive action is the interaction between subject and object. ... Our relationship to the world may be represented as an arc that passes from the subject to the object, incorporates the object and returns to the subject" (Simmel, 1978, p. 205).

Von Wiese's "*Specificum Sociologicum*"

Simmel once annotated in his diary (cited in Maus, 1959, p. 195):

> I know that I shall die without spiritual heirs (and this is good). The estate I leave is like cash distributed among many heirs, each of whom

puts his share to use in some trade that is compatible with *his* nature but which can no longer be recognized as coming from that estate.

Among the first to pick up his share of Simmel's cash was Leopold Max Walter von Wiese und Kaiserwaldau (1876–1969).[68] It would be von Wiese who, "more systematically than anybody else, pushed Simmel's formal conception of sociology to its logical end";[69] von Wiese who explored the full implications of a view of sociology as the study of social relations. Heralded in 1936 as "a leading expression of the present animus of post-Simmelism" by the editor of the *American Journal of Sociology*, Albion Small,[70] von Wiese died himself without leaving a trace in the discipline. His book *Systematic Sociology* translated into English and amplified by Howard Becker (von Wiese and Becker, 1932) was "widely regarded as an uninspired work of taxonomy, ... [and] had relatively little impact on sociology itself" (Levine et al., 1976b, pp. 825–6). Notwithstanding the uncertainty of a search in the Social Science Citation Index for von Wiese, the frequency, under any combinations of his names, does not go beyond the handful. It is by and large a forgotten name.

The last sentence of von Wiese's *Systematic Sociology* reads: "*The sole task of the systematic sociologist is the scientific study of interhuman behavior as such*" (von Wiese, 1932, p. 713; emphasis in the original).[71] And "the specifically 'social' or interhuman," he explains elsewhere (von Wiese, 1941, p. 25), "consists in an involved and entangled network of relations between men; each social relation is the product of one or more social processes." These few lines give us the core of von Wiese's approach to sociology. For von Wiese, the social process or action is the basic building block of the entire social construct. "The social consists only of processes" (von Wiese, 1941, p. 40). "What is a social process?" he asks. "It must be some kind of occurrence which can be shown as a basic happening in the whole interhuman sphere" (von Wiese, 1941, pp. 30–1). Social processes are basically actions (von Wiese, 1932, p. 71). Social processes lead to social relations, which are inherently unstable, for ever changing (von Wiese, 1941, pp. 30, 38, 40). Out of the accumulated repetitions of social processes come social relationships and plurality patterns, which "are merely the plural aspect of relationships" (von Wiese, 1932, p. 72). Social structures emerge out of the stable pattern of social processes, social relations and plurality patterns. "*Social structures* ... must be defined as *a number of social relations so bound together that they are understood as units or substances in daily life*" (von Wiese, 1941, p. 41; emphasis in the original). "There is no relation without a structure, and ... there is no structure without relations."[72]

Social life is characterized by a large variety of social processes.[73] But these processes lead to only two fundamental types of social relations: relations of association and relations of dissociation.

All social relations may be placed in one or another of three main classes: (1) those which are associative, (2) those which are dissociative, and (3) those which in certain aspects are associative and in others are dissociative. ... This division is characteristic of and peculiar to sociology; it determines the *specificum sociologicum.*

There are no other types of social relations for von Wiese: "In everything done by one human being with reference to another, the actions involved are classifiable as approach, avoidance, or a mixture of both." The task of sociology is that of systematizing "all the relations of association and dissociation ... nothing more and nothing less than this is the object-matter of sociology."

Von Wiese gives us the blueprint of his empirical agenda, as "(1) The analysis and classification of the social processes. (2) The analysis of the social structures by reducing them to social processes, and the classification of the social structures" (von Wiese, 1941, p. 43). Actions or social processes, not the relations, are the object of study of systematic sociology. Von Wiese writes: "The relation as such is not the chief point of sociological attention; this place is filled by the social process!" (von Wiese, 1932, p. 54). And again: "Social relationships are not the objects of observation; social actions or processes ... are" (von Wiese, 1932, pp. 71–2).

It is therefore the social action that we must study and classify "in accordance with one consistent method ... and with the sole purpose of determining the way and degree in which the human beings involved associate and/or dissociate."[74] And since these actions fundamentally express themselves in verbal form (for example, "strike," "demonstrate," "kill," "summon") "the fundamental categories of systematic sociology are *verbal* in nature." "The word society ... does not denote a thing, a being, but has a merely verbal character. It is a ceaselessly moving equilibrium generated and maintained by a multiplicity of processes."

True to his theoretical view, von Wiese spent years of his life as a professor of sociology at the University of Cologne classifying words (and not just verbs). In an attempt to systematize his sociology of action, he ranked ordered processes (for example, the action "kill" is stronger than "wound") (von Wiese, 1932, p. 69). He had the basic idea of a graphical representation of the network of social relations that link human beings, the "impenetrable network of lines between men."

> There is not only a line connecting *A* with *B, and B* with *C* etc., but *C* is directly connected with *A*, and moreover, *A, B* and *C* are enclosed within a circle. Not only is there *one* line connecting *A* with *B*, and not only *one* circle in which both are enclosed, but there are many connecting lines, some of which are stretched straight and some of which are in loose curves. ... These connections ... are called *social* relationship and the entire network is called the *social system of relations.*[75]

Simmel's Cash Among the Heirs

"*Nemo profeta in patria.*" No one is a prophet at home. That was certainly the case for Simmel. It was in the United States that Simmel became a success story, "being the only European scholar who has had a palpable influence on sociology in the United States throughout the course of the twentieth century."[76] Not Karl Marx, not Max Weber, the names that came to dominate the sociological scene of the decades of the 1960s and beyond, but Georg Simmel.[77] A number of early leading American sociologists met Simmel in Berlin either as Simmel's fellow students (Albion Small in 1880)[78] or as Simmel's own students when he began lecturing. Robert E. Park, who succeeded Small as the leading figure in Chicago sociology, was among them. In their *Introduction to the Science of Sociology*, Park and Burgess (1921) developed their analysis of social interaction, distance, and interaction processes (competition, conflict, accommodation, and assimilation) after Simmel.

By the 1930s, a view of sociology as processes and social relations had become common place in the discipline, on both sides of the Atlantic. Edward Ross, professor of Sociology at the University of Wisconsin-Madison, published a *Principles of Sociology* where the study of cooperation and conflict occupies a number of chapters. In the preface to the third edition Ross writes: "Here I go still further into social processes; for, with society as with organisms, it is insight into *processes* that counts" (Ross, 1938, p. xi). In England, Sidney and Beatrice Webb (1932, p. 17) wrote in 1932:

> [Social] phenomena are not matter, whether living or nonliving, but the relations formed to exist among human beings in their groupings. Such a relation can be known and described as such, irrespective of the human beings whom it concerns, though not without them.

And in spite of his scathing critique of Simmel's work and of the formal school of sociology,[79] Sorokin himself dedicated the first chapter of his third volume of *Social and Cultural Dynamics* to a detailed analysis of social interaction. In his words (1937, p. 5): "[A]ny real social group differs from a mere nominal conglomeration of individuals by the fact that its members are in the process of interaction." The very expression "network of social relationships" appears there several times (Sorokin, 1937, pp. 34, 39, 40). In 1946, when Talcott Parsons and Samuel Stouffer founded the sociology department at Harvard University, after serious disagreements with Sorokin, they gave it the unusual name "Department of Social Relations." James Coleman followed suit when he founded the Department of Social Relations at Johns Hopkins University in 1959.[80] "Society ... [is] a system of interaction," insisted Peter Berger in his classic *Invitation to Sociology*. That "is the stuff of sociological analysis." "The sociological problem is always the understanding of what goes on ... in terms of social interaction."[81] In the 1960s and 1970s, with the "network metaphor ... increasingly popular with social scientists" (White et al., 1976, p. 730), the cash inheritance of Georg Simmel was distributed among his many heirs more copiously than ever.[82]

"Fatti Maschi, Parole Femmine"

> Know Ye therefore, that We ... by this our present Charter ... do Give, Grant, and Confirm, unto ... Caecilius, now Baron of Baltimore, his Heirs, and Assigns, all that Part of the Peninsula ... lying in the Parts of America, between the Ocean on the East, and the Bay of Chesopeake on the west ...[83]

With the words of this charter issued on June 20, 1632, King Charles I of England granted to Cecil Calvert, second Lord Baltimore,[84] a territory in North America to be called Terra Mariae, Land of Mary, soon to become Maryland, in honor of Henrietta Maria, queen consort.

Soon after receiving his charter, Lord Baltimore set up to organize the settlement of his estate overseas. In a step typical of the early colonial enterprises, he advertised his *Mary-land* to prospective settlers in a seven-page tract titled *A Declaration of the Lord Baltemore's Plantation in Mary-land; Wherein is set forth how Englishmen may become Angels, the King's Dominions be extended and the adventurers attain Land and Gear; together with other advantages of that Sweet Land.* In the *Declaration,* dated "February, 10. anno 1633," Mary-land is described as the land of plenty: from fish to fowl, hogs and horses, berries, grass, corn, and trees. To each settler to join "in this first Voyage" due "to make Sayle ... about the middle of September" 1633, Lord Baltimore "proposeth many very large conditions ... besides honors ... a mannor of good Land, to the full quantity of 2,000. Akers ... and sundry other incouragements & priviledges ..."

Maryland was to remain in the Calvert family's hands for several generations.[85] But what King Charles I of England had sought to grant to Cecil Calvert "forever" was not meant to be. The sixth and last Lord Baltimore, Frederick Calvert, died in Naples in 1771 without heirs to the title. In an eccentric final act by an eccentric man, the last Lord Baltimore bequeathed the province of Maryland to Henry Hardford, a child. James Boswell annotates in his diary of his "grand tour" of Europe: "Berlin, 3 August 1764. A Swiss gentleman ... told me that Lord Baltimore was living at Constantinople as a Turk, with his seraglio around him. ... He lived luxuriously and inflamed his blood ... leading a strange, wild life ..." (Boswell, 1928[1764], p. 48). The sentiment expressed by the great German archeologist Johann Winckelmann, whom Lord Baltimore had hired as a private guide through the antiquities of Rome, was even harsher. In letters to friends, Winckelmann wrote:

> My Lord [Baltimore] is an original ... one of those sensual, unhappy Englishmen ... who has lost all moral and physical taste ... He finally

got so unbearable that I told him what I thought of him and shall have no more to do with him ... I could stand him no longer. (Cited in Boswell, 1928[1764], pp. 48–9; also Stephen and Lee, 1908, p. 720)

The American Revolution was to annul Frederick Calvert's bequest of Maryland to Henry Hardford. Yet, in those ironic paradoxes of history, the new state maintained in its flag and in its official seal what had been the coat of arms issued to Sir George Calvert, the first Lord Baltimore, by Richard St. George, Knt., Norroy King of Arms, on December 3, 1622.[86] As described in the original document deposited at the College of Arms in London, the Calvert coat consisted of a center shield ("escutcheon"), surrounded by twin leopards on either side, and surmounted by an earl's coronet crown, on which stood a full-faced helmet; on the helmet rested the Calvert crest.

A scroll that ran under the shield, the plowman, and the fisherman contained the following Italian proverb: "*Fatti Maschi Parole Femine.*"[87] They say that George Calvert had picked up the proverb during a visit to Italy. Quite possible. Young George had traveled extensively abroad after obtaining a degree from Trinity College, Oxford, in 1597 (Stephen and Lee, 1908, p. 721). Lawrence Stone, in his *The Crisis of the Aristocracy, 1558–1641*, confirms that the education of English nobility was not complete without a stay on the continent, France and Italy in particular – at least prior to the separation of the Anglican Church; thereafter, members of the aristocracy regarded with increasing suspicion their offsprings' trips to Italy, afraid of the "corrupting" influence of Roman Catholicism (so much so that the English government excluded Rome from the list of places English tourists were allowed to visit).[88]

It is more likely, however, that Calvert picked up the saying in England where it was made popular around those years by John Florio. In the *Epistle Dedicatorie*[89] of his English-Italian dictionary Florio writes (1598): "[A]s our Italians saie, *Le parole sono femine, & i fatti sono maschij*, Wordes they are women, and deeds they are men."[90] Florio's nationalistic claim to the saying may be something of an exaggeration. In those days, the saying seems to have been quite popular across a number of European languages. Bernal Díaz (1963, p. 395), in his *The Conquest of New Spain,* "remembers" that the Mexicans reject Cortés's offers of peace: "[W]ords are for women, arms for men."[91] Henry III, king of France, in a letter to Henri de Saint-Sulpice, François d'Épinay, and s[r] de Luc and Joachin de Dinteville dated October 1, 1575, assures his addressees of his good will toward them with the words: "*[L]es parolles sont femelles et les effects malles,*" indeed "words are female, deeds are male."[92]

There has been much debate over the exact spelling of the words in the Calvert's motto: *Maschii* or *maschi*? *femine* or *femmine*? No less contested has been the exact meaning of those words. The motto has been variously translated as "Manly deeds, womanly words"; "Words are masculine, deeds feminine"; "Words are women and deeds men." The sexist nature of the motto has not escaped Maryland women over the years. Protests have flared up. In times past, these protests were met (by men) with a great deal of acrimony and scorn. Writing in the Baltimore *Evening Sun*, on August 18, 1948, journalist Carroll Dulaney wrote:

> Only the feminist mind much addicted to both words and deeds, could contrive to discover anything slighting in the imputation that women are of gentler speech than men. Women with less time on their hands for tilting at windmills would react to the motto as the vast majority of men. That is, to speculate briefly as to just what the devil it *does* mean and to savor its cryptic, antique flavor. It is as well that the feminists, on this score, did not ring up yet another deed for the distaff side.

Recent protests have been unsuccessful in persuading Maryland state legislators to drop the motto from the official state seal, but they have at least succeeded in getting the state to adopt new, less sexist translations of the motto, such as "Strong deeds, gentle words"; "Courage and courtesy" (*The Washington Post*, March 25, 1993). These new translations of the motto may take some of the political heat off the Maryland legislature, but they do not alter in any way the real meaning of the original motto. Yet, why is that meaning sexist?

Structurally, the proverb of the motto belongs to the class of equational proverbs where A is made equal to B (Dundes, 1962, p. 37). There are many examples of this type of equational proverb: "Time is money"; "seeing is believing"; "business is business"; "first come, first served." In fact, in *"fatti maschi, parole femine"* we have a double equation, similarly to "finders, keepers, losers, weepers." A proper translation of the motto would have to reflect the linguistic structure of the original proverb, which would, therefore, bring us back to something like "Manly deeds, womanly words" or:

(1) men = deeds (2) women = words.

And what is wrong with that? To properly answer that question, we have to bring in another equational proverb: "Not words but deeds." This proverb implicitly (but clearly) implies the following equations:

(3) words = bad (4) deeds = good;

and if we then combine all four equations (1)–(4), we obtain a new set of identities that leave no doubt about the sexist nature of our motto:

(5) men = deeds = good (6) women = words = bad.

My question is: In going from words to numbers, am I implying – indeed, proposing – a vision of science that, implicitly or explicitly, embraces a male-biased vision of the world? When combined with the directional nature of the title *"from* words *to* numbers," does this mean that words are the origin but numbers the destination? Are numbers the way to go in the social sciences?

The Feminist Critique

"We are living in an *age of testocracy*," writes Sorokin[93] at the end of an ironic paragraph on the development of tests applied to human beings. We are living in an age of *testosterone*, feminist scholars rather claim. Or, better, testocracy and testosterone in the social sciences go hand in hand. Our science reeks of testosterone. Men control the wider context in which social research is produced. Men control the academy. Men control sociological discourse. "Women are outside the frame" (Smith, 1987, p. 63). Through their positions of power men set the scientific agenda: The appropriate theoretical concepts, the appropriate objects of inquiry, the appropriate methodologies – that is how androcentrism "subtly" manifests itself in science (Mies, 1983, p. 118). The language of science – the *hard* sciences and the human sciences – is a subtly gendered language. The epistemological tenets it embraces are subtly gendered.

Consider objectivity. Positivistic science portrays an image of itself as value free and neutral. But how can one seriously talk about objectivity when women's role in history has been silenced for so long, when their contribution to science has been systematically overlooked, when their world has been consistently undervalued? Objectivity rather smells of "a generalisation from the subjectivity of quite a small social group"; a group of men, white men, bourgeois men (Alcoff and Potter, 1993, p. 22). "Most social scientists are men and ... the masculine values of autonomy, separation and distance are embodied in 'objective,' quantitative research" (Jayaratne, 1983, p. 145). "We cannot uncritically use the positivist, quantitative research methodology" writes Mies (1983, p. 120). Feminist scholars rejected "quantitative analysis with its false promises of objectivity" (Jayaratne and Stewart, 1991, p. 89). They sought "to reduce or eliminate the use of quantitative research as a valid methodology for social scientists" (Jayaratne, 1983, p. 140).

But why? Why should a social science based on numbers be any more androcentric than one based on words? Feminist scholars address that question by taking a close look at the interviewing method based on close-ended questionnaires – the hallmark of that quantitative, scientific, and modern sociology ushered in by Lazarsfeld. Interviewing epitomizes an androcentric view of the social sciences. Interviewing is represented in the social science methodology textbooks as a context in which a detached scientist asks the questions and a passive respondent obediently answers those questions. This relationship between interviewer and interviewee is hierarchical. At its core, it is a relation of power. But the subordination of the interviewee parallels the subordination of women in society. How can female social scientists subject themselves and their female interviewees to research practices so laden with power? Those who speak of objectivity – men in positions of authority in the academy – probably do not have much direct experience of viewing the world from below, from a position of subordination.

Feminist scholars reject the hierarchical relationship between knower and known, interviewer and interviewee, subject and object. "Dichotomous oppositional differences invariably imply relationships of superiority and inferiority, hierarchical relationships that mesh with political economies of domination and subordination" (Collins, 1991, p. 42). And women, of course, are more likely to experience the world from a position of subordination. Not surprisingly, Oakley concludes that, for a woman, the paradigm of scientific interviewing is "a contradiction in terms" (Oakley, 1981, p. 49). "The entire paradigmatic representation of 'proper' interviews in the methodology textbooks, owe a great deal more to a masculine social and sociological vantage point than to a feminine one" (Oakley, 1981, p. 38).

Regarding quantitative methods with "deep suspicion" "as having concealed women's real experience," feminist social scientists embraced qualitative methods, in particular semistructured interviewing, personal narratives, and ethnography (Jayaratne and Stewart, 1991, p. 89). These methods are viewed as better suited to bring out women's experience, to shed light on women's world, to "focus on interpretation, rely on the researcher's immersion in social settings, and aim for intersubjective understanding between researchers and the person(s) studied" (Reinharz, 1992, p. 16). Qualitative methods "do not break living connections in the way that quantitative methods do" (Mies, 1991, p. 67). Qualitative research methods that allow a more meaningful relationship between knower and known are better suited to women's world. For Sandra Harding

> what it means to be scientific is to be dispassionate, disinterested, impartial, concerned with abstract principles and rules; but what it means to be a woman is to be emotional, interested in and partial to the welfare of family and friends, concerned with concrete practices and contextual relations. (Harding, 1991, p. 47)

If you did not know this passage came from a feminist scholar, you may think you are reading Sighele or Le Bon. Yet Harding continues:

> [T]hese features of womanliness are not the consequences of biology – let alone of inferior biology. Rather, they arise from a variety of social conditions that are more characteristics of women's lives than of the lives of men in the dominant groups. (Harding, 1991, p. 47)

And if being a woman means being emotional, empathetic, and partial, "must women renounce what they can know about nature and social relations from the perspective of their daily lives in order to produce what the culture is able to recognize as knowledge?" (Harding, 1991, p. 48). Feminist methodology stems from this acknowledgment of women's worlds. The emphasis on qualitative methods represents an emphasis on participation and empathy. "Formal methods and aggregate data ... separate one from people," Diesing (1991, p. 285) wrote, "and allow one instead to deal with numbers and mathematical objects ... The S[ubjects] need not be experienced as whole people but as future numbers ..." But a feminist researcher should not be aloof or elitist; she should be as much a participant subject as the objects of research through self awareness and emotional involvement. Interviews are not a one-way process.[94] Interviewers must be prepared to invest their own personal identity in the relationship

(Oakley, 1981, p. 41). The real goal of the social scientific enterprise is not just detached scientific knowledge, but knowledge that is empowering for both the knower and, more to the point, the known. "A masculine science," Diesing summarized (1991, p. 285), "is *predominantly* self-centered and externalizing, while a feminine science is *predominantly* other-centered and internalizing." Understanding and *verstehen* are the best way for a feminist social science to bring that about. Reason and action, theory and praxis, whichever came first "in the beginning," they are, once again, united.

Such empathetic relationship with one's objects of inquiry leads to a very different view of these subjects, "observer and observed ... in the same causal scientific plane" (Harding, 1991, p. 11). Marxist historian of African Americans Eugene Genovese and feminist Sandra Harding put it very similarly. "In view of how much conspired to thwart the maternal instincts of these women [black mothers]," wrote Genovese (1978, p. 500), "their achievement reached heroic proportions." "The slaves of the United States had always faced hopeless odds. ... [They] should not have to answer for their failure to mount more frequent and effective revolts; they should be honored for having tried at all under the most discouraging circumstances" (Genovese, 1978, p. 594). And Harding (1991, p. 23) wrote of early female scientists that "the success of the daily struggles for survival as a scientist in which these pioneers were forced to engage ... simply surviving against the odds was a remarkable achievement."

Like the earlier Marxist debate on methods, the feminist debate must be viewed in the context of a wider critique of capitalist or patriarchal societies (Jayaratne and Stewart, 1991, p. 101). Science represents the standpoint of men in a patriarchal society. How would "a sociology ... look," asks Dorothy Smith, "if it began from women's standpoint and what might happen to a sociology that attempts to deal seriously with that standpoint"? (Smith, 1990, p. 12). How would a science look like," Marcuse had asked, "if it weren't organized, funded, and promoted under the sponsorship of capitalist organizations (be these the state or the Foundations)? Marcuse, Smith, and Harding all would agree that sociology and science would certainly ask different questions. They would look at different aspects of social reality. They would focus on different social actors, different types of social relations. In so doing, they may have to adopt different methods. They would have to be critical, exposing the fallacies of dominant paradigms. In particular, they would have to view the research act in the context of wider social relations – the social conditions of the production of our texts – social relations of class, but also of gender because "gender is fundamentally a relation, not a thing" (Harding, 1991, p. 13). "Our picture of the world would indeed be different, if ... women's voices were powerful in shaping the general direction of scientific research" (Harding, 1991, p. 41). Marcuse had similarly claimed that the scientific project carried out under different social arrangements of class "would arrive at essentially different concepts of nature and establish essentially different facts" (Marcuse, 1964, p. 168).

Memorabilia

"There are pilgrims going to Canterbury with rich offerings, / and traders riding to London with fat purses," declares Poins in *Henry IV* (Shakespeare, 1994, Part I, Act I, Scene ii, Lines 122–3). No doubt, pilgrimages have always been a big business. Starting as early as the fourth century, a complex organizational machinery slowly rose around the pilgrimages: Monasteries, abbeys, hostelers, and hospices at convenient stopping points en route, and military orders to protect the pilgrims.[95] As early as the fourteenth centuries "all-inclusive package tours" were available for sea travelers from Venice to the Holy Land (Sumption, 1975, p. 188).

The biggest of businesses, surely, must have been the sale of indulgences, the partial or complete remission of sins. It was Pope Urban II who had first granted a plenary indulgence (complete remission of sins) to the first crusaders in 1095. Boniface VIII, under pressure from the Roman populace, declared the year 1300 a jubilee year, granting plenary indulgence to all Christians who spent fifteen continuous days in Rome visiting the cathedrals of St. Peter and St. Paul (Alfani, 1750, p. 5; Sigal, 1984, p. 76).[96] Even those who died on the way were promised admission to heaven – and the following year, cash payment, equivalent to the cost of the journey, was accepted instead.[97] According to Alfani (1750, pp. 7–8), an "infinite number of people, from Italy, Sicily, Sardinia, Corsica, France, Spain, Germany, Hungary, Poland, and England," came to Rome in 1300. "Thirty thousand people came in and out of Rome every day … two hundred thousand pilgrims" were present in the city. With so many people, the Romans took full advantage of the opportunity. The chronicler Guglielmo Ventura, a pilgrim to Rome that year, tells us: "I spent fifteen days in Rome. There was plenty of bread, wine, meat, fish, and hay; but everything was incredibly expensive," including a bed to sleep on (cited in Alfani, 1750, p. 13). In 1350, Pope Clement VI followed suit with the second Jubilee year.[98] Once again, the Romans plundered the pilgrims. "All Romans had become hostellers," we read in Alfani (1750, p. 32), "renting their houses to the pilgrims. To make a disorderly profit … they forbade merchants to bring in wine, or grain, or hay from the outside, in order to sell theirs at higher prices."

Other shrines, across Europe, soon realized that a promise of indulgences meant a surge in the number of pilgrims.[99] And they would apply to Rome for a license to offer such indulgences. And licenses have their cost. As Cardinal Campeggio referred back to the Englishman who had come to Rome to negotiate a jubilee for Canterbury for the year 1520: "[I]t is not possible that the pope [Pope Leo] will grant you this for no money or favour" (Loxton, 1978, p. 91).

By the end of the thirteenth century, shrines were outbidding each other in the length of remissions of sins they could offer. Special guidebooks known as the *Libri indulgentiarum*, detailing the number of indulgences at various shrines, began to appear.[100] Pilgrims' narratives started to include detailed accounts of indulgences gained in the various places.[101] The twelfth-century *The Pilgrim's Guide* to Santiago de Compostela reminds the pilgrim not to forget to visit the dean in order to receive the promised plenary indulgence (Davidson and Dunn-Wood, 1993, p. 160). And for those who could not afford going to a shrine there were always the "pardoners," authorized Church salesmen who walked the length of a country, promising the remission of sins in exchange of cash payments. Many were fraudulent, as masterfully portrayed in Boccaccio's and Chaucer's characters of Fra Cipolla and the Pardoner; but there were plenty of real names (for example, the German Dominican friar John Tetzel) (Loxton, 1978, p. 97). Little by little, even for the devout, the line between the religious and the mundane often blurred, with pilgrims keeping an accountant's eye on the indulgences gained at the various shrines.

Memorabilia – today's souvenirs – were part of the business, the trinkets pilgrims would buy as tangible records of their journeys. No one would leave Santiago de Compostela without having purchased the cockleshell, or Rome without the crossed keys, the Holy Land without the palms of Jericho.[102] The anonymous twelfth-century *The Pilgrim's Guide* to Santiago de Compostela tells pilgrims where they can buy "the shells which are the badges of St James" (Anonymous, 1992, pp. 70–1).

Seafarers on voyages of discovery were no less fond of bringing back *memorabilia* from distant lands. "Herewith you will receive," wrote Captain James Cook in a letter to the Admiralty Secretary dated August 13, 1771, "the bulk of the curiositys I have collected in the course of the voyage" (Cook, 1955, Vol. I, p. 638). In another letter to the Admiralty Secretary dated March 22, 1775, near the end of his second "Circuit of the Globe," Cook provides a detailed list of the new lands discovered, along with "Surveys, Views and other drawings" (Cook, 1961, Vol. II, p. 692). Columbus had similarly reminded the sovereigns of Spain of the riches in gold, pearls, spices, people, and lands that he has procured them through his discoveries: "[On my second voyage, 1493–6] by the Grace of God I discovered in a very short time 333 leagues of mainland, the end of the East, and 700 islands of importance in addition to those discovered on my first voyage" (Columbus, 1969, p. 206).[103] "Your Highnesses," he tells the sovereigns of Spain appealing to both their practical and spiritual sense, "have now another world in which our Holy Faith can be greatly extended and from which such great profits can be derived" (Columbus, 1969, p. 225). But what is this when compared to the discovery made on the Admiral's third voyage (1498–1500)? "Royal Majesties ... you are receiving information about these lands which I have newly discovered and in which I fervently believe the Earthly Paradise to lie" (Columbus, 1969, p. 226).

Voyage of pilgrimage or voyage of discovery or, more simply, academic armchair voyage, which *memorabilia* do I have on offer? Here is my list:

1. In a methodological field that has heard several pleas for the use of linguistics in the further development of content analysis, I illustrate here some

linguistic tools (story grammars and semantic roles) that can be profitably used in the quantitative analysis of textual information, narrative in particular.

2. I implement these linguistic tools in a computer environment. This implementation also has surface and deep structural representations. In Chapter 2, I tackle the problem of computer storage and retrieval of the narrative information structured within the categories of a story grammar (Relational DataBase Management Systems, RDBMS, and Structured Query Language, SQL). I also illustrate the surface manifestation of a computer-assisted approach to text coding (PC-ACE), focusing on the interface between text, coder, and computer, and on the basic characteristics of a data-entry software designed on the basis of a story grammar/semantic roles.

3. By counting the narrative information structured within the categories of a story grammar and stored in a RDBMS computer environment, words can be turned into numbers, quality into quantity. The alchemic transformation of words into numbers, in the end, is remarkably simple.

4. A story grammar (even in its modified version to reflect a theory of semantic roles) can be formally represented through a series of rigorous rewrite rules. That notation can be converted into a set theoretical notation. Set theory is the basic mathematical framework of Relational DataBase Management Systems. But set theory also provides the mathematical framework of network models, a statistical tool that looks at the interconnections between social actors. An elegant mathematical "thin thread" based on set theory thus runs from words to numbers.

5. The tools presented in this book are not just clever toys with interesting linguistic and mathematical properties. They can be used to tackle "real" historical problems, as shown by the analysis of narrative data on the rise of Italian fascism (1919–22) collected from over 15,000 newspaper articles.

6. This set of methodological tools has far-reaching implications, as revealed by the bird's-eye view of our journey taken in this chapter. The relational structure of the linguistic tool (with actors related to other actors via certain actions) encourages a statistical approach to the analysis of these data similarly based on a network representation. More to the point, this representation of data organization and analysis encourages a theoretical view of *sociology as the study of social relations,* as interactions of social actors around specific social processes. Social actors and actions, rather than variables or structures, populate the world we encounter at the end of our journey from words to numbers. Time is not "crunched" synchronically within a regression or econometric coefficient. It flows diachronically with the sequence of "skeleton narrative sentences" made available by a story grammar. This same narrative flow of before and after, of actions and events distributed in time and space forces upon us a rather different view of causality than the position of a variable in a multivariate statistical model.

7. From substance to method, from method to epistemology, from epistemology to theory, the journey in "search of the actor" takes us in rapid succession

across different academic disciplines and across different realms of knowledge. At the end of this tour de force we find not only the actor, but the action. And the action is even more crucial than the actor. In a journey characteristic for having forced us to tread along different but separate disciplinary routes, these routes (linguistics, sociology, and history, in particular) come together at an unexpected crossing, where verbs have a privileged position over nouns, actions over actors.

The *memorabilia* are numerous. Our "method" of going from words to numbers has served us well. Yet, there is more to this method than *technique*. More fundamentally, this method that I have been peddling is also a particular way of

1. looking at social reality and of constructing objects of scientific inquiry;
2. constantly turning objects of inquiry into one's hands in a systematic pursuit of connections and relations; method is a way of conceiving knowledge and understanding "which consists in seeing connections" (Wittgenstein, in Monk, 1991, p. 451). These are the "methods" and "methodology" to which Simmel refers to in his preface to *The Philosophy of Money* (1978, pp. 55–6);
3. engaging with the archeology of knowledge; understanding a word in the context of its own history and the history of other words (con.text; *cum* text);
4. looking at the very process of quantification – at this going from words to numbers – as a way of seeing, as the historical product of a specific constellation of social relations; and that implies asking the questions: Who benefits? How else could it be?
5. confronting the broader theoretical issues (not to mention social) hidden behind even pure methodological questions;
6. breaking the canon of scientific writing, so as to make explicit the rules and conventions of our language games, the unconscious assumptions upon which our science rests;
7. facing the dilemma of the pursuit of knowledge – vertically, in the bottomless and dehumanizing pit of specialization and, horizontally, in the hopeless dream of Renaissance scholarship;
8. approaching science as a self-reflexive practice – method as a way of pursuing honesty, away from academic fads and constraining rules of disciplines, as a way of understanding the *ritual acts* in which we partake.

More, no doubt, I could have told you about all the things I saw in this journey. But, like Mandeville (1983, p. 188):

> I do not want to say any more about marvels that there are there, so that other men who go there can find new things to speak of which I have not mentioned. For many men have great delight and desire in hearing of new things; and so I shall cease telling of the different things I saw.

Tales of Measurement

Measurement concerns the problem of linking abstract concepts to empirical indicants.

Richard Zeller and Edward Carmines (1980, p. 2)

Measurement is the assignment of numbers to represent properties.

Norman Campbell (1952, p. 110)

When historians cite 'typical' newspaper editorials and the beliefs of 'representative men,' or when they use terms such as 'significant,' 'widespread,' 'growing,' 'intense,' in effect they are making quantitative statements.

Lee Benson (1957, p. 117)

Quantification is *not* the essence.

Charles Tilly (1981, p. 35)

What matters is … the questions one asks.

Emmanuel Le Roy Ladurie (1979b, p. 3)

Tales of Horror

On October 22, 1707, four English warships and two thousand lives were lost at the Scilly Isles, just a few miles from home, because Admiral Sir Clowdisley Shovell and his officers had miscalculated their longitude (Sobel, 1996, pp. 11–12). They were not the first ships, not the first lives to be lost at sea because of the longitude problem. Neither would they be the last.[1] But, as more and more of Europe's wealth came to depend upon goods transported aboard ships that traveled the oceans, a solution to the problem became imperative. And "in the Atlantic ... knowledge of the longitude, however desirable, was less critical than in the Pacific and Indian oceans" (Landes, 1996, p. 25).

The meridians of longitude are the imaginary lines that slice the earth, vertically, north to south, passing through the poles. Together with the parallels of latitude, the lines that run horizontally from the equator to both poles, they provide a precise positioning system. To know one's longitude at sea requires knowledge of two times: aboard the ship and at the point of departure or another place of known longitude at the very same moment. The time difference can then be converted into a space difference. Unfortunately, early clocks were too rudimentary to work under the humid and rolling conditions of a ship; and no one had yet figured out how to use the stars, so helpful in computing one's latitude.[2]

Under pressure from various shipping interests in London, in 1714 the English Parliament passed the Longitude Act promising a £20,000 reward[3] for anyone who found a "practicable and useful" solution to an accuracy of half a degree of a great circle.[4] It was an enormous sum. The first prize of the lottery for the year 1726 was £20,000, by far the highest amount the lottery reached in those years. It attests to the seriousness of the problem and to the urgency of a solution in the eyes of the contemporaries. The half a degree difference required by the Longitude Act really seems like splitting hairs – but, in fact, it corresponds to a difference of sixty nautical miles at the equator (sixty-eight geographical miles) (Sobel, 1996, pp. 5, 53–4). Many harbors can be missed, many islands can go unnoticed on that distance in open sea.

It would be an obscure English clock maker, John Harrison (1693–1776), who eventually claimed the prize, winning a race that saw in competition some of Europe's finest minds of the time, perhaps, of any time.[5] While Galileo, Cassini, Newton, Halley, and others looked for a solution at the skies, at the universal clock of the universe, Harrison built a transportable mechanical clock – in fact, five clocks in his lifetime – that kept time on a ship within the three seconds in twenty-four hours equivalent to the half degree specification of the Longitude Act (Sobel, 1996, pp. 58–9). Harrison was eighty-two-years old when he finally pocketed the money in 1775, only a year before his death,[6] and "after forty struggling years of political intrigue, international warfare, academic backbiting, scientific revolution, and economic upheaval" (Sobel, 1996, p. 10). Captain James Cook had brought an exact replica of H-4, a pocket-size chronograph, commissioned to the clockmaker Larkum Kendall by the Board of Longitude aboard his ship *Resolution* on his second voyage of discovery in the Pacific Ocean (1772–75) as a way to test the accuracy of the clock. In a letter to the admiralty, Cook paid this indirect tribute to Harrison's ingenuity: "Mr. Kendal's Watch has exceeded the expectations of its most Zealous advocate, and by being now and then corrected by Lunar observations has been our faithfull guide through all the vicissitudes of climates" (Cook, 1961, Vol. II, p. 692). The clock is still on display at the National Maritime Museum in London, a marvel of engineering ingenuity in precision measurement of time, and of longitude.

Tales of Pressure

Down dropt the breeze, the sails dropt down, / 'Twas sad as sad could be; / And we did speak only to reak / The silence of the sea! / All in a hot and copper sky, / The bloody Sun, at noon, / Right up above the mast did stand, / No bigger than the Moon. / Day after day, day after day, / We stuck, nor breath nor motion; / As idle as a painted ship / Upon a painted ocean. / Water, water, every where, / And all the boards did shrink; / Water, water, every where, / Nor any drop to drink. / The very deep did rot: O Christ! / That ever this should be! / Yea, slimy things did crawl with legs / Upon the slimy sea. / About, about, in reel and rout / The death-fires danced at night; / The Water, like a witch's oils, / Burnt green, and blue and white.

These beautiful verses are the product of Coleridge's poetic imagination.[7] But reality was often ever more blood chilling and spell binding. Antonio Pigafetta, on Magellan's ship during its first voyage around the world, wrote in his diary:[8]

Wednesday, November 28, 1520, we debouched from the strait, engulfing ourselves in the Pacific Sea. We were three months and twenty days without getting any kind of fresh food. We ate biscuit, which was no longer biscuit, but powder of biscuits swarming with worms, for they had eaten the good. It stank strongly of the urine of rats. We drank yellow water that had been putrid for many days. We also ate some ox hides that covered the top of the mainyard ... Rats were sold for one-half ducato apiece, and even then we could not get them. The gums of both the lower and upper teeth of some of our men swelled, so that they could not eat and ... therefore died.

If Pigafetta's account is, perhaps, among the best known among the horror stories of sea voyages, there is no dearth of stories of this kind in the sea-travel literature. Only a few decades later, the French protestant Jean de Léry left an even more dramatic story of being lost at sea during his return voyage from "the land of Brazil" in 1558 (de Léry, 1990, pp. 208–13):

Because of this navigational error ... we had completely run out of all provisions. To get the last bits of food, we had to clean and sweep up the hold ... There we found more worms and rat droppings than crumbs of bread ... Those who had still monkeys and parrots ... made them serve as food. ... During that famine the tempest raged day and night for three weeks ... so that during this whole time ... we could not catch a single fish. ... Some took it into their heads to cut pieces of the shields made of the hide of the *tapiroussou* and boil them, intending to eat them this way ... [S]ome among us arrived at the point of eating their morocco collars and their shoe leather; even the pages and the cabin boys ... ate all the lantern horns ... and as many tallow candles as they could lay hands on. ... [R]ats and mice ... [were] sold at two, three, and even four crown apiece. ... [W]e had left not a trace either of wine or of fresh water ... we had nothing left but brazilwood, which has less moisture than any other; several, however, pressed to the limit, for lack of anything else began to gnaw on it. ... all this makes one ferocious, and engenders a wrath that can truly be called a kind of madness ... a person is mad with hunger. ... he will look with an evil eye upon his neighbor, even his wife and his children, and desire to eat them.[9] ... [W]e could scarcely speak to each other without getting angry, and what was worse (may God pardon us), glancing at each other sideways, harboring evil thoughts regarding that barbarous act.

For all the descriptions of rites of cannibalism that early travelers to unknown lands left us,[10] it was not uncommon among sailors to eat the flesh of dying men. The famous 1884 English court case of *Dudley and Stephens* attests to the survival of the practice well into our times.[11]

With little instrumentations and few reliable charts, the great sea captains of the modern era were "masters of the wind." Vasco da Gama, pushing his way south along the coast of Africa, when he met the contrary Oceanic currents beyond Cape Verde, swung west almost as far as Brazil and then back down toward the African southern tip, charting the optimal course of sail navigation around Africa (Ravenstein, 1898, pp. xviii–xix; Baker, 1937, pp. 68–9; Landes, 1996, p. 24). As a 1583 account put it (cited in Baker, 1937, p. 68):

Men must take heed and keep themselves from coming too near the coast to shun the calms and storms [in the waters facing Guinea]; and also not to hold out far off, thereby to pass the flats and shallows [of the Brazilian coast at 18° S]; wherein consisteth the whole Indian voyage.

When Magellan first sailed through the Pacific, he chose a course still recommended today by United States Government Pilot Charts for winter sailing from Cape Horn to Honolulu (Boorstin, 1986, p. 265). But even the greatest of captains could do little to move a sailing ship in no wind, no matter how well he knew his longitude. We know that Columbus, during the return to Spain from his second voyage (1493–96), "with little wind and many calms ... began to be in great trouble owing to shortage of food" (Columbus, 1969, p. 198). And chasing the winds – "for they had not the experience we have today by which we steer north to find the strong westerlies" (Columbus, 1969, p. 198) – they wandered about in the great ocean sea, with "all the pilots ... at a loss except the Admiral" as to their whereabouts (Columbus, 1969, p. 199). Alvaro Velho, a member of Vasco da Gama's 1497 expedition in the circumnavigation of Africa, annotated in his journal of the voyage (Velho, 1898, p. 87):

Owing to frequent calms and foul winds it took us three months less
three days to cross this gulf [the Arabian Sea], and all our people again
suffered from their gums, which grew over their teeth, so that they
could not eat. Their legs also swelled, and other parts of the body, and
these swellings spread until the sufferer died, without exhibiting
symptoms of any other disease. Thirty of our men died in this manner.

The steamboat would solve that last problem of sea navigation. George
Canning, the satirical poet and British Member of Parliament at the opening of
the nineteenth century, thus described the new steamship

> which walks the waters like a giant rejoicing in its course, stemming
> alike the tempest and the tide, accelerating intercourse, shortening
> distances, creating, as it were, unexpected neighborhoods, and new
> combinations of social and commercial relations, and giving to the
> fickleness of the winds and the faithlessness of waves the certainty and
> steadiness of a highway upon the land. (Cited in Smiles, 1997/1865,
> p. 455)

But before the steamboat could find a solution to the last problem of sea
navigation, other problems needed to be solved: Namely, a steam engine had to
be developed. It would be water, again, to put pressure on inventors for a
solution; inland water; in fact, underground water in mining pits.

English school children learn that James Watt invented his steam engine by
watching the lid of a kettle bubbling up and down under the pressure of steam-
hot water. Mantoux (1983, p. 319) reports the anecdote but knows better: "There
is no question here, of any precious or sudden inspiration." Watt was thoroughly
familiar with the earlier engines dating from 1698 onwards; he had studied
closely the Newcomen's engine (Landes, 1969, p. 100). Even so, the development of his first steam engine, patented in 1769, was no simple matter.[12]

The most pressing difficulty was that of securing a tight fit between the piston
and its chamber. Without that fit, pressure could not be built; efficiency would
be lost. Earlier models, in which the pumping piston was cold, were able to seal
the interstices between piston and chamber with a few drops of water, but Watt's
major innovation – that heating and pumping should occur in the same chamber
– meant that such water would instantaneously evaporate, leaving an air gap that
made maintenance of pressure impossible. With characteristic ingenuity and
imagination, Watt experimented with anything he could lay his hands on:

> he tried tin, copper, wood, and cast iron for his cylinders and pistons
> to see which materials could be worked to the closest tolerances ... He
> considered square pistons, round pistons, and flexible pistons ... He
> experimented with piston disks and rings of leather, pasteboard, cloth,
> cork, oakum, hemp, asbestos, a lead-tin alloy, and a copper-lead alloy.
> To help seal the piston he tried mercury, oil graphite, tallow, *horse*

dung, vegetable oil, and a variety of other materials. (Smiles, 1997, pp. 177–8; emphasis added)

But these endeavors were to no avail. That Watt should try even horse dung as a sealant for the piston may seem like a sign of utter desperation. Yet, the maceration of the philosophers' stone in warm horse dung is a crucial step in the alchemical transformation of gold (for example, Thomas Aquinas, 1996, pp. 47, 77; Albertus Magnus, cited in Kibre, 1980, p. 200). When even horse dung failed, clearly a new approach was required. Indeed, as Landes put it: "The steam engine required from the start a corresponding revolution in the relevant fields of metallurgy and construction" (Landes, 1969, p. 103). John Wilkinson, the Scottish iron-master, made that revolution. In 1774, Wilkinson obtained his first patent for a new method for boring cannons.[13] A year later, Wilkinson sent the first accurately measured piston cylinder to Boulton and Watt.[14] In Watt's words, the new technique could "promise upon a seventy-two inch cylinder being not farther distant from absolute truth than the thickness of a thin six-pence [say 0.05 in] in the worst part" (cited in Landes, 1969, p. 103). In an address to the Mechanics' Institute delivered in 1825 in Manchester, Sir Benjamin Heywood heralded the new invention as the most "beautiful and striking exemplification of the union of art and science."[15] The Manchester entrepreneurs of the Industrial Revolution rekindled, perhaps for the last time before the splintering of knowledge of modern times, the flame of that "consuming romance that all knowledge was one," the alchemists' dream that *omne omne est.*

The first steamboat, the *Charlotte Dundas*, was only a barge-tow, "launched" in 1788 (Buchanan, 1956, p. 13). The first crossing of the Atlantic took place thirty-one years later. By 1896 the north Atlantic could be traversed on a steamboat in just six days (Buchanan, 1956, p. 41). In the end, Wilkinson's closure of a few millimeters of measurement error opened up to the British ships of trade and empire thousands of miles of ocean waves.

Social Science Tales

I cannot help looking at the trickle of ideas that have come down from Bodart, to Sorokin, to Tilly and Gurr, from Propp, to Greimas, van Dijk, and Prince ... like thousands of ants each pushing the frontier a fraction of an inch, now one way now another. Under pressure to analyze larger and larger amounts of qualitative material, both historians and social scientists have shown even greater ingenuity in turning into numerical form some of their nonnumerical evidence.[16] In Charles Tilly's words (1972, p. 96): "Quantitative analysis strikes in unexpected places. Where it strikes depends more on the investigator's genius than on the intrinsic nature of the problem." Aydelotte (1969, p. 13) had similarly put it: "It has proved possible, again and again, to describe in quantitative terms things that were formally thought to fall beyond the reach of this net." Lazarsfeld tells us the story of "a methodologist who wanted to improve the walking efficiency of the centipede community." He concludes:

> When the methodologist finally published his findings, there was a general outcry that he had only reported facts which everyone already knew. Nevertheless, by formulating this knowledge clearly, and by adding hitherto unobserved facts at various points, he eventually enabled the average centipede community to walk better. After a generation or so, this knowledge was incorporated into textbooks, and so filtered down to students on a lower level of scholarship. *In retrospect this was the outstanding result.*[17]

Economics, no doubt, led the way in this scholarly race to help the centipede community. After all, as Schumpeter (1933) argued, economics is a more naturally quantitative science since many economic problems come up already in quantitative form. Other sciences had to invent their measurement process, but they have done so in greater or lesser degree. Even in history, as Stone argued, "it is a waste of time to argue whether or not one ought to permit quantification in historical writing since it is not possible to exorcize this demon" (Stone, 1987, p. 331). Certainly, it would have been hard to imagine, even some thirty years ago, that one day historians and social scientists would turn into numbers the narratives of newspaper articles and police reports. In fact, it would have been hard to even imagine that newspapers would be considered proper sources of historical data. You do not find them cited in that wonderful historian's *vademecum* by Langlois and Seignobos (1898), not in George (1909), and not even in Renier as late as 1950.[18]

No doubt, our *technical* ability to measure social phenomena has greatly risen. Our methods have become more and more refined and capable of bringing ever larger areas of social reality under quantifiable observation. Content analysis, in this respect, is no exception. Technological advances, typically located outside the domain of the social sciences, such as computers and communication, have been largely responsible for these advances. Like Galileo's telescope or the various laboratory contraptions that Watson describes in his "personal account of the discovery of the structure of DNA," these tools have allowed us to investigate *quantitatively* social phenomena once the typical purveyor of qualitative techniques. No doubt, we can expect more in the future. And more refined methods should lead to more knowledge. "At any given time knowledge depends on the particular state of methods in use; future knowledge will depend on the development of today's methods" (Cicourel, 1964, p. 7).

Yet, in the human sciences, methodological advances have not necessarily gone hand in hand with an increase in theoretical knowledge. With specific reference to issues of collective action and protest – those same ones that underpin the methodological developments described in this book – James Rule would argue that they have not (1988). If anything, technique has dangerously substituted theory, the mean has increasingly become the end – methodology as fetish and, ultimately, pestilence. Worse yet, in our spirit of modernity, we have become blind to our own rhetoric. "Quantification is *not* the essence," Tilly warns us, but rigor (1981, p. 35). Yet, rigor has often been replaced by rigidity. We may have lost the ability to ask the questions that would *fundamentally* challenge our *modus operandi*.

To measure is fundamentally to think relationally. As Max Born wrote apropos of the theory of relativity: "[A] measurable quantity is not a property of a thing, but a property of its *relation* to other things."[19] As such, different measurements of an object will lead to different relations of that object to other objects. Measurement will affect entire networks of relations. In the case of social objects, networks of social relations will fundamentally depend upon our measurements. Different measurements of workers' involvement in violent actions during protest events will tilt the social networks between workers, employers, the police, and other social actors (for example, the Fascists) whose graphical representations we saw in Chapter 3. Classification, one of the most important steps in the process of measurement, is similarly fundamentally relational. As Thomas Henry Huxley told an audience in 1860: "[C]lassification is the expression of the relationship which different animals bear to one another, in respect to their anatomy and their development" (cited in Ritvo, 1997, p. 37). A measurable quantity is not just characterized by its relation to other things, but, perhaps more fundamentally, by its relation to the measuring scientist. As Ritvo (1997, p. xii) put it: "[T]he classification of animals, like that of any group of significant objects, is apt to tell as much about the classifiers as about the classified." Thomas (1984, p. 52) similarly notes that the process of classification "involves the use of mental categories," which are linked to specific ways of seeing and are the result of historically-specific social and cultural arrangements. Research in cognitive psychology on principles of categorization reach substantially similar conclusions. Rosch and her collaborators write:

> Basic objects for an individual, subculture, or culture must result from an *interaction* between the potential structure provided by the world and the particular emphases and state of knowledge of the people who are categorizing. However, the environment places constraints on categorization.[20]

Classification, then, is the result of the interaction between the world and the word. As we have seen repeatedly, data depend upon the relation of the scientist to society as a whole, upon a particular form of social production of knowledge. Measurement (what we measure and how we measure it) is closely bound up with our view of social reality, bound up with a theory that purports to explain those social relations, bound up with a particular view of science. Our very *data*, far from *given*, are negotiated, contested, and fought over.[21]

Our involvement with the many disciplines that deal with issues of language and meaning – from linguistics, to the philosophy of language, history of ideas, literary criticism, or semiotics – has perhaps allowed us to pursue quantity and rigor *at the same time as* the very limitations of these pursuits and, better yet, an awareness of the broader social underpinnings of these pursuits. No doubt, the grounding of content analysis in a body of formal linguistic theory (story grammars and semantic roles) has given us a rigorous tool for the quantitative analysis of narrative texts. But that same body of knowledge has also clearly highlighted the many subtle ways in which language conveys meaning, ways that are fundamentally beyond the power of our tool. It has also linked issues of meaning to the broader social contexts in which knowledge is produced, to the social arrangements behind the scientific projects of quantification. It is those social arrangements, those hierarchies of power and interest that go a long way in explaining that fundamental game of silence and emphasis.

There is the answer to issues of measurement: In the pursuit of a production of knowledge that does not obscure the conditions of its own production. But to the extent that production occurs under specific arrangements of power, this answer to issues of measurement may ultimately be utopic or confined to the fringes of scientific work.

Wars of Words

Reader of 2520 what will you make of the acrimonious debate between quality and quantity, between words and numbers?[22] Wasn't Lee Benson (1957, p. 117), one of the early American proponents of quantitative history, right on target when he wrote

> When historians cite 'typical' newspaper editorials and the beliefs of 'representative men,' or when they use terms such as 'significant,' 'widespread,' 'growing,' 'intense,' in effect they are making quantitative statements.

And would anyone object to Kitson Clark's (1962, p. 14) famous words: "Do not guess, try to count, and if you cannot count, admit that you are guessing." Would anyone object to having clearly stated hypotheses and assumptions rather than muddled arguments? As Robert Fogel put it:

> Cliometricians [or 'scientific,' quantitative, historians] want the study of history to be based on explicit models of human behavior. They believe that historians do not really have a choice of using or not using behavioral models since all attempts to explain historical behavior … involve some sort of model. The real choice is whether these models will be implicit, vague, incomplete, and internally inconsistent, … or whether the models will be explicit, with all the relevant assumptions clearly stated, and formulated in such a manner as to be subject to rigorous empirical verification. (Fogel, 1983, pp. 25–6)

What is the objection, then, if we all agree with this? Why has such furious debate – quality versus quantity – raged in history and the social sciences?

• *The objection is* to the hegemonic drive of the quantitative approach. That, really, is what triggers angry (and in their anger, perhaps overly stated) reactions. Let Arthur Schlesinger Jr. do the talking (1962, p. 770), in the words of a brief intervention at the fifty-seventh annual meeting of the American Sociological Association in 1962 in honor of Paul Lazarsfeld:

> The humanist, let me repeat, does not deny the value of the quantitative method. What he denies is that it can handle everything which the humanist must take into account; what he condemns is the assumption that *things which quantitative methods can't handle don't matter.*

Or, however much they may matter "on principle," "in practice" they would still find no place in a quantitative research agenda. What is not quantifiable cannot be studied.[23] Period. Only what we can *count counts.* This way, our human sciences become method driven, rather than problem driven (Mills, 1959, p. 57).

• *The objection is* to the lure of numbers. Bailyn (1982, p. 6), in his presidential address to the 1981 annual meeting of the American Historical Association, warned his audience of "the mind-absorbing, soul-entrapping" seductions of the technical aspects of quantitative work. "It is only too easy to become absorbed in the gadgets and to forget the ideas" (Aydelotte, 1969, p. 21). Not that narrative history does not fall prey to the songs of its own sirens: The "mind-absorbing, soul-entrapping" lures of telling a good story, the seduction of history or sociology as art rather than science (White, 1987, pp. 26–57). Not dry technical issues, but style, good writing, plot and story are the key elements in this game.[24] But the "numbers" have a special lure. As McCloskey put it:

> A man who wishes to convince his modernist neighbor will show him numbers. Numbers are believed to tell. Numbers are believed to be objective, intersubjective, conclusive. Most people, and even most economists, believe that once you have reduced a question to numbers, you have it out of human conversation. The best quantitative scientists know that this is naive. (McCloskey, 1985, p. 141)

Naive and very insidious. Because like the everyday language mechanisms that produce meaning in typically unconscious ways, the rhetoric of numbers, formalism, and rigor in the social sciences also largely operates at the unconscious level in the members of the social scientific community (McCloskey, 1985, p. 74). In Fish's (1980, p. 167) words: "The moral is clear: The choice is never between objectivity and interpretation but between an interpretation that is unacknowledged as such and an interpretation that is at least aware of itself." Thus, Roberts (1997) speaks of "unambiguous encoding" of his "semantic approach to content analysis," but he is blind to the ambiguities that plague his work. Abbott and Barman (1997) speak of rhetorical rigidification of sociological journal articles, but are blind to the impressive array of rhetorical devises they muster.[25] McCarthy et al. (1996) question the validity of newspaper data on protest events, but measure it against the "objective" yardstick of police records.

• *The objection is* to an approach to issues of measurement where the real problems involved are systematically swept under the rug. That is particularly true for the methodology of content analysis where the relationship between numbers and issues of language and meaning is so close. Unfortunately, in our graduate training, statistics, culture, and language do not typically go hand-in-hand. And issues of meaning are likely to be ignored.

• *The objection is* to the ritualism of hypothesis testing, R-squares, significance levels, and data mining. When we come to accept numbers acritically and nonreflexively as the hallmark of science, we become dangerously blind to the rituals in which we are involved as a result of that view of the research enterprise. Lewis F. Richardson (1960, pp. xiii–xiv), himself a great mathematician and an outsider to the academic game, put it cogently:

> Mathematical expressions have, however, their special tendencies to pervert thought: The definiteness may be spurious, existing in the equations but not in the phenomena to be described; and the brevity may be due to the omission of the more important things, simply because they cannot be mathematized. *Against these faults we must constantly be on our guard.* It will probably be impossible to avoid them entirely, and so they ought to be realized and admitted.

But, again, how can one be on guard against faults so deeply entrenched in our scholarly culture as to have become unaccessible to our very conscience?

Let me end this war of words with more words, words taken from the introduction to a collection of quantitative studies of history by Price and Lorwin (1972, p. 10):

> Not all the quantitative work attempted will, of course, be elegant, rigorous, satisfying, or even necessary. Some, yielding perhaps unwittingly to what looks like a mode, will rush into numbers without a sufficient awareness of the problems inherent in the materials they are using or the methods they are attempting. Others, fascinated with the method mastered, may use it to play games that are not worth the candle. Nor may the technically proficient always sense the unnecessarily limited scope of the adequate work they are doing; thus they may fail to perceive the rich pastures waiting outside the walls of their carefully tended but limited quantitative gardens.

We seem to know the recipe for good puddings in the human sciences. That we should find so few served on our library shelves only begins to tell the tale of the difficulties involved: The requirements of substantive and technical knowledge, the task of overcoming the limits of specialism, the need for introspection to keep under check the unspoken assumptions of our personal and professional socialization, the determination to pursue the answers to our questions as guided by unfailing passions, all … within the limits of a life that is all too short.

What Have We Lost?

"What have we gained?" I asked at the closing of Chapter 1. Perhaps, in light of these wars of words, I should ask the more humbling question: "What have we lost?" To answer that question, consider this account of a strike that occurred in May 1921 in Italy, one of 237 that occurred that month.[26]

> It has happened again. The heartless arrogance of ACR management has resulted in a strike. Last Friday at the end of the day thirty workers were handed dismissal slips with their pay. When they marched in anger to the *padrone*'s office Mr. Faraglia was nowhere to be found – they should have known better; Friday afternoons are sacred to Mr. Faraglia who meets his mates for drinks at the employers' club. The accountant, Mr. Torregiani, talked about hard times, falling profits, impossibility of keeping the place afloat; that they were lucky when so many companies were closing down. Twenty five of these workers had served on the Adige front. And this is the 'thank you' they get. One of the dismissed workers, Nando Bertin, whose wife was in hospital with cancer and had enormous doctors' bills to pay, was quietly sitting in a corner holding his head between his hands. Paolo Poeri, the union leader at the factory, screamed with Mr. Torregiani that these were unfair dismissals, that these men were thrown out for being union men. Twenty of them had led the occupation of the factory last September. A delegation of workers marched to the town hall to meet the mayor. The rest of the workers assembled inside the factory. It was decided to occupy the factory in protest.

The data of Table 1 leave no doubt about the losses we incur in the process of going from words to numbers, from narratives to counts (compare columns 1 through 4). Through the reduction of the passage to skeleton narrative sentences, gone is the ideological point of view of the narrator. That point of view is made clear enough by the use of language: Heartless arrogance, *padrone*, the contrast in the images of Mr. Faraglia meeting his mates for drinks at the employers' club and of Nando Bertin who wonders in desperate solitude how he is going to pay the hospital's bills for his wife's cancer without a salary, the ingratitude of the country's elite toward men who had served in the war. Counting will hardly do

Table 1. *Loss of Information in Going from Words to Numbers*

Skeleton sentences	Actions	Events	Counts
Employer *dismisses* workers	Dismissal		
Accountant *justifies* dismissals	Justification		
Union Leader *accuses* management of unfair dismissals	Accusation		
Worker delegation *marches to* town hall	March	Strike	237
to *meet* mayor	Meeting		
Workers *assemble*	Assembly		
Workers *strike*	Strike		
Loss of ideology	*Loss of actors*	*Loss of microactions*	

justice to the subtleties through which language conveys meaning. Whether in its more crude or more sophisticated version, counting will not solve the problem of capturing the meaning of language. Moving further to the right in column 2, as we aggregate skeleton narrative sentences into microactions, we lose sight of the actors involved. We lose sight of "causality" as agency and "responsibility" (employer *dismisses* workers; employer causes workers to be dismissed). In column 3, by aggregating microactions into events we also lose sight of the microactions. Even events disappear under the numbers (column 4).

So, in the name of science, we promote techniques that leave much of reality out of reach of social science investigations and where, in any case, the stuff of social reality – social actors – disappears behind variables and statistical models for even that part of social reality under scrutiny. We become absorbed in the mind-trapping games of quantitative work where the study of social reality is forsaken in the pursuit of method – our means altogether becoming our end – we become unable to reach that level of consciousness where alternatives become accessible. And, in the end, in view of the losses incurred by our alchemic transformation of words into numbers, it appears that Barthes was right when he wrote: "[B]y reducing any quality to quantity, myth economizes intelligence" (Barthes, 1970, p. 153).

"Garçon, l'addition!" Counting What?

"Garçon, l'addition!" "Young man, the check!" screams out *le client*, the restaurant customer of Jacques Prévert's poem *L'addition*. But when *le garçon* starts preparing the check, the enraged customer bursts out:

> *Enfin, tout de même, de quoi se moque-t-on?* ... Whom are you kidding? ... You must be completely out of your mind to dare trying to 'add' veal with cigarettes, cigarettes with coffee, coffee with green almonds, hard-boiled eggs with green peas, and green peas with a telephone call ... Why not a green pea with an officer of the *Légion d'honneur*, while you are at it? ... No, my friend, believe me, do not insist, do not even try, nothing would come of it, you understand, nothing, absolutely nothing ... not even a tip for you![27]

You may be similarly inclined to scream at me. "What have you been adding here, Franzosi? What words did you add up together under the 'labels' of your tables and graphs, those 'communication,' 'political activists,' 'make claims,' 'violence,' or 'facilitation? What have you been hiding under the euphemism 'properly aggregated'?" And you, the reader, do not even have the option of *le client*'s reaction, to walk out on *le garçon* without paying the check, in fact, taking the napkin holder for good measure.

No doubt, it is time for me to go deeper into the secrets of my art. I have disclosed to you already that the way from words to numbers is simple: You count. More precisely, you count objects within a class. That much was clear since the early days of the development of the technique. "The operations of content analysis," Janis wrote (1949, p. 55; emphasis added), "consist in classifying the signs occurring in a communication into a set of appropriate categories. The results state the *frequency of occurrence of signs for each category in the classification scheme*." But if counting is of objects within a category or class, what you put in those categories or classes is of fundamental importance. It is the different words that we put in the various categories of actors, actions, or any of the modifiers that give us the numbers, ultimately determining our results. Beatrice and Sidney Webb made that clear:

> This work of classification, which the enquirer is perpetually revising and remaking as his observations and discoveries extend, is, in itself, an instrument of investigation. Every new fact placed in a particular class either fortifies or weakens the implicit assertion as to attributes and relations that has been provisionally made by the creation of that class. (Webb and Webb, 1932, pp. 59–60)

The classification of actions (namely, verbs and verb phrases) plays a particularly crucial role in the process of going from words to numbers through classifying and counting. After all, the categories of verbs, or the spheres of action in which we classify verbs, determine the types of social relations that we see (the network graphs of Chapter 3). So, let us focus on the classification of verbs to understand more clearly some of the problems of measurement.

Classification and the Numbers

The classification scheme behind my numbers is the result of a mixture of inductive and deductive reasoning, of empirical and theoretical considerations. I started out very close to home, looking into the social movement literature for guidance. While it is easy enough to find the basic categories in that literature, it is not as easy to find lists of the content of those categories. Tilly (1995a, pp. 414–15), in a rare example of published classification scheme and content – few of us dare disclosing the inner secrets of our alchemies – provides a scheme of actions on contentious events in England between 1758 and 1834 based on eight categories: claim, attack, control, cheer, communicate, deliberate, enter, and other. Unfortunately, Tilly does not provide clear definitions for these categories. Why is the verb "celebrate" classified under <other>, rather than <cheer>, or the verb "vote" under <other> instead of <deliberate>? And if "demonstrate" is classified under <other>, where would "strike" or "rally" go?

  Working with Tilly's scheme as my starting point, I began the slow process of classifying the 17,827 actions in my 1919–22 database, modifying and expanding the original scheme on an empirical basis, moving verbs now in this category, now in another, creating new categories and subcategories, or simply renaming old ones. In that sense, I was closely following Auguste Comte who, some two centuries ago, wrote (1896, Vol. 1, p. 22): "Classification must proceed from the study of the things to be classified, and must by no means be determined by *a priori* considerations. The real affinities and natural connections presented by objects being allowed to determine their order." But such ad hoc approach left me very uneasy. All the more so, because I was trying hard to abide by a fundamental principle of taxonomy: To achieve a classification based on mutually exclusive categories. Unfortunately, there were too many "real affinities" and "natural connections" among many verbs and different categories to be able to satisfy that principle. No doubt, what Eckstein wrote some forty years ago is as true today as back then:

> classification often seems essentially arbitrary ... Writings on internal war abound in disparate classificatory schemes, some completely unique to a particular writer, others overlapping, still others using much the same concepts to denote different events. Obviously this situation is not desirable. (Eckstein, 1964, p. 19)

In search of a more rigorous approach to issues of classification, I started looking beyond the social movement literature, in particular, in the field of content analysis (Namenwirth and Weber, 1987). But I did not find much help there, either. Further afield, in game theory[28] and network analysis,[29] I did find basic classification schemes of action – although you have to search very hard for them, pasting together definitions of actions scattered through many books and pages.[30] What is worse, there is no standard classification scheme. Game theory focuses on such actions as: promise, commitment, threat, delegation, mediation, communication, conflict (the latter ranging from such typically non-violent actions as strikes to wars).[31] The network analysis literature focuses on more general social processes. For Knoke and Kuklinski (1982, pp. 15–16), the more common types of relations investigated in the literature are: transaction (involving the exchange of physical or symbolic goods), communication, instrumental, sentiment, authority/power, and kinship.[32] With perhaps slightly different names, that basic list holds for Wasserman and Faust (1995, p. 18), with only a few additions of their own (namely, movement, both social and physical, and physical connection between points, such as a road or a bridge).

I also turned for help to linguistics[33] and philosophy (particularly philosophy of language and of human action).[34] No doubt, philosophers of language and linguists have done the most and the most rigorous work on word classification. They have provided stringent criteria of classification, typically based on inherent properties of the verb itself rather than context. Thus, Zeno Vendler (1957), proposed a system of verb classification based on the verbs' restrictions on time adverbials, tenses, and logical entailments. Unfortunately, the end product of Vendler's rigorous work – a scheme of four distinct classes of verbs – states, activities, accomplishments, and achievements[35] – is of limited value for sociological analysis. Knowing that a verb is either a state, an activity, an accomplishment, or an achievement would not help my understanding of the social relations of prefascist Italy. I stand a better chance with Austin's five-fold classification of verbs into verdictives, exercitives, commissives, behabitives, and expositives. After all, there is a broad correspondence between the substance of Austin's classes and some of mine;[36] but even Austin's classes – terminology aside – are too broad to be of concrete help.

Among linguists, Dowty (1979), Halliday (1994), and Levin (1993) have carried out the most extensive work on verbs and their classification. Dowty (1979, pp. 37–85) proposes a classification of verb based on aspect (or the relation of the verb to time, namely, the perfect aspect and the progressive aspect) that builds upon the work done by Aristotle, Ryle, Kenny, and Vendler, ultimately leading to a similarly unhelpful (for my purposes!) classification of verbs into states, activities, achievements, and accomplishments.[37] Halliday's classification is more promising (1994, pp. 106–44). For Halliday, the function of verbs in language is that of capturing men's and women's outer and inner experiences. That function fundamentally divides verbs ("processes" proper) into material and mental processes (doing and sensing), with the addition of a third category of relational processes (processes of being), used for classifying and identifying (for generalizing). At the boundaries between these three categories, we find further categories: behavioural (between material and mental processes), verbal (between mental and relational processes), and existential (between relational and material processes). Within these six categories of processes, you will find such subcategories as behaving, seeing, feeling, thinking, saying, symbolizing, having identity, having attribute, existing, happening, creating, and doing/acting (see Halliday's representation in concentric circles and the summary table, 1994, pp. 108, 143). Levin (1993, pp. 111–276), in her comprehensive classification of over three thousand English verbs into forty nine classes and subclasses, provides a scheme based on shared meaning and similar syntactic behavior. The great advantage of Levin's work is that, for each class, she gives a clear definition of the class and provides a comprehensive list of the verb members of that class. Her verb classes are also much closer in meaning to verb classes of interest to us: For example, communication, killing, motion, or change of possession – what Knoke and Kuklinski (1982, p. 15) and Wasserman and Faust (1995, p. 18) call transaction.

At the end of my search – which included perusals among naturalists and cognitive psychologists – I did not find a definitive solution to the problem of classification. So, I am left with the choice between the social scientists' bewildering variety of schemes offered with little justification or the linguists' just as varied classification schemes but rigorously derived and of little use to social scientists. As Shapiro and Markoff noted (1998, p. 81):

> At one extreme, we find a logically organized system of abstract categories deductively derived from a theoretical system; at the other, a loosely organized collection of concrete categories, inductively derived, primarily from a study of the documents.

Yet, there may be no escape from this duality. On the one hand, social scientists involved in content analysis projects should strive to achieve general classification schemes of more universal validity, based on intrinsic properties of the objects to be classified (linguistic or otherwise). On the other hand, social scientists may want (and will often need) to classify actions (and not just actions) in schemes designed upon theoretical criteria. Thus, Durkheim's suicides are egoistic, anomic, altruistic, or fatalistic (1951) and Inglehart's societal values are material or postmaterial (1977). An investigator working in the field of social movements may want to group together all the actions that are collective in nature (that is, actions where a group of people act together in some recognizable and meaningful fashion for some goals and objectives; Tilly, 1978, p. 276). These actions may cut across the entire range of categories of a more general scheme (for example, the action "scuff", "assembly", "meeting", and "strike," all <collective actions>, but perhaps individually classified under <violence against people>, <debate>, and <conflict>). Similarly, the investigator may be interested in classifying actions into <private> versus <public>, or <industrial> versus <service>, depending upon where the actions occur, in the private or public sphere, in the industrial or service sector of the economy (Franzosi, 1997c). The nature of the demands or grievances voiced by protest groups may suggest a basic classification of actions into reactive versus proactive or conservative versus radical (Tilly, 1978, pp. 143–51; Shapiro and Markoff, 1998, pp. 358–9). Thus, proper classification of actions may require the use of a dual scheme, a primary scheme based on intrinsic properties of the actions themselves or of the social world, and a secondary one based on the investigator's theoretical categories. We might as well accept this duality and to try make the underpinnings of each scheme more rigorous.

Within each group, we may also need to use multiple codes in order to classify cases of fuzzy meanings: Linguists and philosophers of language set me straight on the tenet that coding categories, however arrived at, should be mutually exclusive. Most words have too many, too fuzzy, and even contradictory meanings to be able to fit them tidily into one pigeon hole only. As Propp wrote in his seminal work on the structure of narrative: "Identical acts can have different meanings ... Functions [actions] can not be distributed around mutually exclusive axes." Oxford analytical philosopher John Austin later followed suit. In the concluding pages of his *How to Do Things with Words*, having eliminated one classification scheme after another, Austin (1962, p. 150) gave up on the idea of arriving at a system of mutually-exclusive classes, "in favour of more *general* families of related and overlapping speech acts." He even cautions the reader about the limits of his final scheme: "We should be clear from the start that there are still wide possibilities of marginal or awkward cases, or overlaps."[38] Levin put it quite similarly (1993, p. 18):

> [S]ince most verbs are characterized by several meaning component, there is potential for cross-classification, which in turn means that other, equally valid classification schemes might have been identified instead of the scheme presented in Part II of the book.

For Halliday (1994, p. 107), the boundaries between process categories are also fluid, with each category "sharing some features of each" adjacent category.

Linguistics not only helped me to solve problems of verb classification. It also offered tools to help me understand and solve some problems encountered in the classification of verbs: nominalization of processes and implicit objects.

• *Nominalization of processes.* Nominalization, in linguistics, refers to the transformation of certain verbs into nouns (for example, layoff or strike as verb and noun). The nominalization of verbs that refer to processes (something that people do) is of particular interest in the context of the research project described in these pages. Many actions in the 1919–22 database, in fact, contain nominalized processes. We find instances of nominalization in the <demand> or <outcome> category (both modifiers of the <action>), but also in the <action> category itself. Typical cases of the first type of nominalization found in the database are such triplets as: <subject> workers <action> strike <reason> layoff; <subject> employer <action> fire <object> workers <outcome> strike; <subject> Minister of Labor <action> summons <objects> parties <reason> mediation. The type of nominalization found in the <action> occurs because many actions in the database are not single verbs (or, at most, auxiliary/modal + verb) but verbs + a complement, as specified by the grammar of data collection (for example, "accept the mediation", "declare a strike", "reject a meeting", "announce the arrest"). When the verb's complement is not a thing (for example, a chair, a building) but an event, the complement is a nominalization of a process. It is really an action transformed into a noun (for example, "the mediation" = "to mediate", "a strike" = "to strike"). From a linguistic point of view, sentences that contain nominalized processes are both syntactically and semantically correct. But they can pose problems in going from words to numbers. After all, nominalization reduces the number of processes (<actions>) and of semantic triplets, and, as a result, the number of social relations. This way, nominalization can fundamentally distort the pictures of our network graphs of Figures 3.2 through 3.7. They can also distort the narrative sequence of actions, since the sequences of nominalized processes would be missing.[39] To avoid these problems, nominalized processes should be converted back into processes (as verbs); in other words, the implicit triplets of nominalized processes should be coded explicitly; for example: <subject> employer <action> fire (<reason> strike) <object> workers, recoded as a sequence of two triplets <subject> workers <action> strike; <subject> employer <action> fire <object> workers.

• *Implicit objects.* It was not long ago that the English verb "strike" would require a complement, as in "strike work" or "strike employer." But in today's use the verb strike has become intransitive, that is, it does not require a complement. Many verbs/actions in my 1919–22 database do not have an explicit object, although implicitly they do have some social actors as objects. Certainly, all actions of conflict or of solidarity have implicit objects (patients or beneficiaries), whether these are explicitly present in a triplet or not. For 1919, some four thousand triplets have no objects (and two thousand do). Of those four thousand, over three thousand are actions of <conflict> or <request> (therefore with an implicit object). Excluding the implicit object "employer" from such triplets as "workers strike" would greatly underestimate the intensity of conflict from workers to employers. Consider the following sentence: "Blue-collar workers strike. White collar workers do not participate in the strike." If the lack of an explicit <object> in the first sentence would lead to underestimating conflict relations between workers and employers, the lack of an explicit object in the second sentence (the implicit object is "blue-collar workers") would tend to underestimate the relations of conflict *within* the working class. The contrary is also true. The sentence "Management approves salary increases" is well formed and quite meaningful even without any explicit reference "in favor of workers." But the lack of an explicit object leads to underestimate actions of <facilitation>. Since network models operate on the basis of explicit relations between social actors, the lack of explicit codes for implicit objects, while syntactically correct and semantically meaningful, would greatly distort the matrix of social relations. To avoid bias in the estimation of network models, implicit objects must always be explicitly coded. For this reason, the specification of the grammar (see Appendix) calls for an <implicit object> in the rewrite rule for <object>.

Classification in Practice: The Secret of Secrets[40]

The process of classification means that each of the 17,827 action/verbs (and not just verbs) found in the 1919–22 database must be assigned to a handful of categories. Here is a step-by-step procedure:

• *Step 1.* Reduce all synonyms to a standard canonical form in order to avoid redundancies. Ericsson and Simon (1996, p. 265) give a similar advice. Although this procedure loses semantic content, it increases efficiency.

• *Step 2.* Obtain a frequency distribution of all "canonical" actions. Be ready to expect a highly skewed distribution of actions, a handful of which will occur with very high frequencies and the rest with a frequency of one. Ericsson and Simon (1996, pp. 265–6) note:

> A good rule of thumb for protocols of any considerable length is that the number of different words will be between five and ten per cent of the length of the text. Usually the different words will be distributed by frequency in a highly skewed way … This has the unfortunate consequence that about one-half of all the words that occur will occur only once in the text – a serious impediment to parsimonious encoding.

For our data, out of 17,827 action/verbs, 5,733 are unique (the other 12,094 are repeats), 465 occur twice, 173 occur three times, and only 292 occur with a frequency greater than three times.

• *Step 3.* Assign individual actions to the set of action categories, taking into account both primary and secondary classification schemes and fuzzy sets.

1. You may wish to use both *primary* and *secondary classification schemes*, one based on linguistic characteristics or on characteristics of the social world and the other based on theoretical characteristics.
2. Within each scheme, you may need to assign multiple codes to overcome problems of fuzzy meaning (fuzzy sets for fuzzy meaning).[41] Imputation of codes can often be done automatically (PC-ACE will make automatic

suggestions about the presumed classification codes). In some cases, however, disambiguation of meaning will require an understanding of the context,[42] in particular, 1) the actors involved (subjects and objects),[43] 2) the modifiers of the action (for example, instrument, causes, consequences),[44] and 3) the position of an action in a meaningful sequence.[45]

I could conclude, at this point, with Dowty (1979, p. 126), that "My suggestion as to how to approach this problem is tentative and problematic." But adepts in the alchemic art will know that the deeper secrets, the *secretum secretorum*, are never openly revealed. "Believest thou O fool that we plainly teach this secret of secrets?" asks the twelfth-century alchemist Artephius in *The Secret Book*.

• *Step 4*. Without breaking that alchemic tradition, let me at least give you an indication of where to look in the final step (Step 4) of the art.

1. The solution to the problem of verb classification lies at the intersection between some of the work done in game theory and network analysis, some of the definitions of social processes found in the early introductory texts in sociology (in particular, Park and Burgess, 1921; Ross, 1938), in the extensive work of verb classification carried out by von Wiese (over 600 processes classified; 1932, 1941), and, among linguists, in the work of Halliday (1994, pp. 106–44) or Levin (1993), which are based on semantic categories closer to what you find in the more sociological approaches. Don't expect a large number of classes.[46]

2. For each class, provide a definition of the class, a list of class members, and a list of members of all overlapping classes (fuzzy sets). Levin is a good model to follow for this practice (1993).
   Threat (non violent): To utter or otherwise express an intention to carry out *legal* and *legitimate* actions against an actor; to give signs or warnings to someone. The threat may or may lot be linked to specific conditions or requests (if ...).
   Verbs: admonish, ..., menace, ..., threaten, ..., warn, ...
   Fuzzy verbs: admonish, warn <control>; admonish, warn <disapproval>.

3. Wherever possible, place the spheres of action (or verb classes) along a continuum on a line. Thus, actions of <approval> can vary from minimum support (<approval> proper), to <acceptance>, and to <agreement>. Verbal utterances can vary, left to right, from <communication>, to <verbal threats>, to more serious <threats> (involving the use of threatening instruments such as a gun), and to <violence>. The precise metric may not be known. There may not be a one to one correspondence between a point on the line and a given action (as in the case with real numbers, for instance). Is the action "look with favor" more to the left/right or exactly on the same position as the action "welcome" along the continuous line of approval? But, at least, you will achieve a relative standing of verb classes.

4. Wherever possible, place the spheres of action (or verb classes), not just in a one-dimensional space (a line), but in a Cartesian, two-dimensional or even a n-dimensional space, perhaps linking actors and actions. Thus, in the two-dimensional space spanned by <membership> (on the x-axis) and <role> (on the y-axis),[47] we would have such actors as "unemployed" close to the origin (that is, low on both <membership> and <role>, "worker" high on <membership> and low on <role>, and "employer" high on both <membership> and <role>. Follow Dowty on this, who suggests "promising ways of proceeding," placing verbs in a logical space (1979, pp. 126–7):

> There will be as many axes of logical space as there are kinds of measurement; if the measurables were only weight, color and hardness, for example, a point in a logical space would be a triple representing a possible outcome of measurements of weight, color and hardness respectively. Each axis might have a different mathematical structure according to the discriminations that can appropriately be made in each case. For example tests for hardness give only a linear ordering – we can say that one thing is harder than another but not twice as hard – but in the case of weight, we can say that one thing weighs twice as much as another. Values on the space-axis would represent places, which would themselves be regions in Euclidian or some sort of space. It is not necessary at this stage to commit ourselves as to just what axes are to be included in logical space nor just what the mathematical structure of each axis is to be, as long as there are only a finite number of axes. A model for a language is then to include – in addition to a set of individuals, a set of worlds and a set of times – a function assigning to each individual at each index a value in logical space. Of course, certain individuals may lack values for certain axes at certain indices – for example some things are colorless – and this situation might best be handled by including a 'null position' on various axes.

Take these steps, and "great utility will follow" from the application of the art (Albertus Magnus, 1958, p. 4). But don't forget Thomas Aquinas's advice (1996, p. 39) to be guarded against the "many deceitful books, many trivialities, and many different procedures, that if you followed their indications, you would lose everything, and, doubting the science, you would achieve trifle results."[48]

The Words (and the Worlds) of Science and Metaphor

Our science promised rigor, formalism, exact measurement, power. What it delivered, in the end, was a curious object, fashioned out of the careful dosage of silence and emphasis, the selective use of given master tropes (for example,

Table 2. *The Words of Science and Metaphor*

Science's Words	Metaphor's Words
Rigor	Meaning
Power	Interpretation
Mathematics	Communities
Formalism	Subjectivity
Methods	Language games
Objectivity	Rhetoric
Reason	Unconscious
Logic	Emotions
Hypotheses	Passion
Truth	Silence and emphasis
	Point of view
	Aesthetics
	Play

metonymic versus metaphoric discourse), the reliance on specific literary devices, styles (for example, passive sentences), and types of persuasive arguments and modes of communication (for example, statistical argumentation), and the ritualistic use of the tools of the craft (for example, regression models and significance tests). Table 2 provides a list of the key words that we have encountered in Part I of the book (the words of science) and in Part II (the words of metaphor). They could not be more different. The two cultures, the humanistic and the scientific, the world of counting and recounting, clash here without a common language (Snow, 1993; Bernardini and De Mauro, 2003).

If *"the essence of metaphor is understanding and experiencing one kind of thing in terms of another,"*[49] then the metaphors of the journey and alchemy served us well. We discovered what science actually delivered by pursuing its metaphorical aspects. Understanding science ("one kind of thing") in terms of journeys and alchemy ("another kind of thing") forced me to relativize my quest – to view it comparatively in light of other quests – and to historicize it – as yet another human pursuit undertaken at a specific historical time in the context of broader social pursuits. Metaphor forced us to familiarize ourselves with different texts (travel accounts and alchemic tracts). We know about journeys and alchemy through the texts that voyagers and alchemists have left for us. We know about science through the texts that we write to disseminate our findings. As texts, our science texts have characteristics that are linguistically similar to those of travel accounts or alchemic tracts. Newspaper articles, pilgrims' and early voyagers' travel accounts, historical writing, our social scientific texts all rely on an impressive array of similar metaphorical and rhetorical devices.

In the end, not only our science, but the metaphor of the journey delivered knowledge. But why be surprised? "[T]he further one travels the more one learns," Columbus wrote to the sovereigns of Spain (Columbus, 1969, p. 224). The sixteenth-century alchemic doctor Paracelsus put it this way: "Universities do not teach everything ... We must discover for ourselves what is necessary for science, *travel*, run many adventures and learn all that may be useful along the way."[50] Real or imaginary, journeys were the alchemists' way to knowledge.[51] Knowledge acquired by reading the "book of the world" through traveling was dear to the medieval and Renaissance *homo viator* (Tucker, 1996, pp. 48, 53). When traveling, "the map of the world ceases to be a blank; it becomes a picture full of the most varied and animated figures. Each part assumes its true dimensions" (Darwin, 1989, p. 376). The travelers of Sterne's *Sentimental Journey* are "sailing and posting through the politer kingdoms of the globe in pursuit of knowledge and improvements. *Knowledge and improvements are to be got by sailing and posting* for that purpose ..." (Sterne, 1983, p. 34; emphasis added). Indeed, a journey forces us to question what we see, what we left behind at home, and to compare. Our ability to be innovative in science fundamentally depends upon taking a different perspective on our objects of inquiry, viewing our work if not with innocent eyes, with the eyes of a different discipline. Our very process of categorization, upon which our numbers are so dependent, are fundamentally shaped by mental categories that "make it very difficult for us to see the world in any other way" (Thomas, 1984, p. 52).

The metaphoric view of this book has inexorably pushed us along a path that we had hardly foreseen when we first set out. It has highlighted the power of metaphor in the construction of knowledge – including scientific knowledge so openly given to metonymy rather than metaphor – its conscious and unconscious pervasiveness in culture. A metaphoric view of the world paved the way to a relational view of that world – a metaphor being just a particular type of relation. From Locke to Simmel, from Wittgenstein to Gadamer, we have learned that understanding is relational. The temporal and spatial central features of narrative – from where we started our journey, from using narrative as data – have established the basic parallels, the common ground between journeys, play, and biography. Journeys not only involve displacement and movement in time and space – fundamental narrative categories – they also produce typical narrative accounts. And in these accounts, the temporality of narrative as "recovery of the past" becomes biography (Brooks, 1984, p. 321). The construction of biography is a narrative construction (Brooks, 1984, p. 36). The homologous relationship between narrative and history noted by White or Ricoeur is also an homologous relationship between narrative and biography. They both live in a world of action. They are both bound by time and space. But these biographies, conceived as our personal identities, are, for Locke, nothing but relations. In three chapters of *An Essay Concerning Human Understanding* dedicated to the study of Relations, Locke privileges Cause, Time, Space, and Identity as the fundamental relations (II, XXVI–XXVIII; 1975, pp. 319–62). Biographical narratives, for Somers (1994, p. 616), are nothing but "constellations of *relationships* ...

embedded in *time and space*, constituted by *causal emplotment … a social network* of relationship." Given this homologous relationship between narrative and biography, it is not surprising that those same mechanisms of silence and emphasis that are at play in narrative are also at play in biography under the guise of memory. "The past is malleable and flexible," writes Berger (1963, p. 71), "constantly changing, as our recollection reinterprets and reexplains what has happened. Thus, we have as many lives as we have points of view. We keep reinterpreting our biography …"

Denial of the metaphorical and rhetorical underpinnings of discourse may certainly be comforting. But it is perhaps "wiser simply to become aware of metaphor than to try to eradicate it" (Frye, 1957, p. 337). That awareness would ultimately produce better science. "Self-consciousness about the rhetoric of his statistics can raise the standard of the most technical arguments the economist uses" (McCloskey, 1985, p. 138). "Attempts to analyze metaphor solely to debunk an argument or suggest that it is 'nothing but' a metaphor are not to be encouraged. What is to be encouraged is the analysis itself" (Frye, 1957, p. 337). It is that analysis that Frye recommends, it is that conscious pursuit of metaphor and rhetoric in our journey that has highlighted the two general mechanisms that are characteristic of all texts, of all types of discourse: silence and emphasis, and ways of seeing (coupled with the question: Who benefits?).

With the hindsight of several hundred years of history and in light of a fundamentally different *weltanschauung*, we smiled at some of the things we read in those travel diaries of medieval pilgrims and renaissance voyagers of discovery. How could Antonino of Piacenza realistically believe that he had seen the blood of Jesus on the Golgotha? (only 500 years after the fact!) How could Columbus in all seriousness think that he had reached the Earthly Paradise? But if we can already smile at some of the things we read in the accounts of our social science journeys (only a few decades later), if we can already see our quest as having the characteristics of the alchemic philosophers' stone and of the alchemists' and travelers' rituals, what will you think reader of the year 2520? What will you think of Cattell, Blalock, and Snyder (and, perhaps more crucially, of Franzosi)?

Tales of Time and Space

Of Frederick Taylor, Braverman (1974, pp. 91–2) wrote in his *Labor and Monopoly Capital*: "An exaggerated example of the obsessive-compulsive personality … The picture of his personality … justifies calling him … a neurotic crank."[52] An avid athlete in his childhood, "even a game of croquet was a source of study and careful analysis with Fred," later recalled Birge Harrison, Fred's playmate and lifelong friend (in Copley, 1923, p. 57; Nelson, 1980, p. 24). Young Fred "worked out carefully the angles of the various strokes, the force of impact and the advantages and disadvantages of the understroke, the overstroke, etc." (in Copley, 1923, p. 57; Nelson, 1980, p. 24). There was nothing leisurely about cross-country walks. For Fred, these too were opportunities for experimentation and measurement, in search of that perfect stride that "would cover the greatest distance with the least expenditure of energy" (Kakar, 1976, p. 18). To young Fred, a stop in a train station was significant only for the times of arrival and departure, which he annotated carefully in the diary of his boyhood visit of Europe with his family (Kakar, 1976, p. 23). In Harrison's memories, young Fred insisted that all games should be played by "strict rules and exact formulas," that "the rectangle of ... [the] rounders' court should be scientifically accurate," wasting "the whole of a fine sunny morning ... in measuring it off by feet and inches" (in Copley, 1923, p. 56).

From all accounts, perhaps not a fun playmate – although always extremely fair in his competitiveness; "before going to a dance he would conscientiously and systematically list the attractive and unattractive girls with the object of dividing his time equally between them" (Kakar, 1976, p. 19). But, as an engineer, those neurotic obsessions served him well; this "man who wanted to measure everything"[53] ultimately went down in history as the "father" of scientific management.

Born in 1856 into a well-to-do Philadelphia family, Frederick Taylor grew up as a "privileged young man."[54] He traveled and lived in Europe with his family (1869–70). He attended an exclusive preparatory school, the Phillips Exeter Academy of New Hampshire, becoming "an outstanding student, the leader of his class" (Nelson, 1980, p. 25). Having been admitted into Harvard, severe, constant eye problems led Fred to abandon his college plans and to start working as a craft apprentice in a factory. In 1878, he took up a job as a common laborer at the Midvale Steel Works, owned by family friends. There, Taylor laid the foundations of his work on scientific management, as he tells us in several of his publications (particularly, his *Shop Management*, first published in 1903, and *The Principles of Scientific Management*, published in 1911). At Midvale, Fred was dismayed to discover the workers' practice of "soldiering," of "deliberately working slowly so as to avoid doing a full day's work ... The greatest evil," he calls it, "done by the men with the deliberate object of keeping their employers ignorant of how fast work can be done" (Taylor, 1911, pp. 20–1). Taylor himself tells us the story of how he followed a man to and from work, how he watched him closely on the job, and how he found out that this man walked at the speed of one mile per hour on the job and three to four miles per hour off the job (Taylor, 1911, pp. 31–2).

In a short time, after starting working at Midvale, Fred Taylor was promoted from clerk, to journeyman machinist, and gang boss in charge of the lathe department. He recalls how, after being promoted to gang boss, all his former fellow workers approached him with the following words:

> Now, Fred, we're very glad to see that you've been made gang-boss. You know the game all right, and we're sure that you're not likely to

be a piece-rate hog. You come along with us, and everything will be all right, but if you try breaking any of these rates you can be mighty sure that we'll throw you over the fence. (Taylor, 1911, p. 49)

Not Fred Taylor. He "told them plainly that he was now working on the side of the management, and that he proposed to do whatever he could to get a fair day's work out of the lathes."[55] He was convinced that it is possible to obtain productivity increases by "eliminating unnecessary motions and substituting fast for slow and inefficient motions." Thus, he who had spent his childhood accurately timing movements and their "best" representation in space, set out to accurately measure the motions of the human body for new purposes, to "develop a science for each element of a man's work." "Every single act of every workman can be reduced to a science," he wrote, namely through systematic and scientific time-study and motion-study.[56] Managers should "assume ... the burden of gathering together all of the traditional knowledge which in the past has been possessed by the workmen and then of classifying, tabulating, and reducing this knowledge to rules, laws, and formulae." "All possible brain work should be removed from the shop and centered in the planning department ...," in management's hands.[57] As a result of Taylor's work, output did eventually increase at Midvale, "in many cases doubled, and as a result the writer had been promoted to one gang-boss-ship to another until he became foreman of the shop." In that capacity as well, "he decided to make a determined effort to ... change the system of management," a system he would eventually call "scientific management."

Taylor assures us that "One of the marked advantages of scientific management lies in its freedom from strikes" (Taylor, 1911, p. 68, *Shop Management*). He was overstating his case, of course. Opposition to the spreading of Tayloristic practices grew throughout America to such an extent that a Special House of Representatives Committee on Labor had to be set up in 1911 to investigate the Taylor system, leading to "five years of public controversy over time study" (Nelson, 1980, p. 165). No doubt, with Frederick Taylor, the study of time and space, the fundamental categories of narrative with which we have concerned ourselves in this book, becomes a project of domination and control, revealing the seamy side of measurement. In Braverman's summary (1974, p. 100; emphasis added):

> The conclusion which Taylor drew from the baptism by fire he received in the Midvale struggle may be summarized as follows: Workers who are *controlled* only by general orders and discipline are not adequately *controlled*, because they retain their grip on the actual process of labor. So long as they *control* the labor process itself, they will thwart efforts ... *[C]ontrol* over the labor process must pass into the hands of management.

Faust and His World: What Was in the Beginning?

We read in Goethe's *Faust*:

> 'In the beginning was the Word [*Wort*]': Why, now / I'm stuck already! I must change that; how? / Is then the 'word' so great and high a thing? / There is some other rendering, / Which with the spirit's guidance I must find. / We read: 'In the beginning was the Mind [*Sinn*].' / Before you write this first phrase, think again; / Good sense eludes the overhasty pen. / Does 'mind' set worlds on their creative course? / It means: 'In the beginning was the Force [*Kraft*].' / So it should be – but as I write this too, / Some instinct warns me that it will not do. / The spirit speaks! I see how it must read, / And boldly write: 'In the beginning was the Deed [*Tat*]!' (Goethe, 1987, lines 1224–37)

So what was in the beginning? If not the Word – which, in any case, was at the beginning of our project – was it Reason/Mind, Force, Action/Deed? Faust does provide his own answer to the question when he acknowledges to Mephistopheles: "*Herrschaft gewinn ich, Eigentum! / Die Tat ist alles, nichts der Ruhm.*" "Power I shall achieve, and property! / Action is everything, fame is nothing."[58] Fame, posterity had been the obsession of the *philosophes* of the Enlightenment: Having dispossessed God and religion, why live otherwise?[59] Action is the romantics' new motto, action as producer of power and property.

Mussolini would agree with that: Action is power. In an article on fascism that appeared in 1932 in the *Enciclopedia italiana* he wrote: "[T]here was no specific doctrinal framework in my spirit. My doctrine ... had been the doctrine of action. Fascism ... was born out of a need for action and it was action" (cited in Chabod, 1961, p. 57). And power came soon after out of that action. So, the deed/action may have been at the beginning. And not just at the beginning of fascism. Freud's final sentence of his *Totem and Taboo* reads: "[W]ithout laying claim to any finality of judgement, I think that in the case before us[60] it may safely be assumed that 'in the beginning was the deed'" (Freud, 1950, p. 161). And that deed, for fascism, if not for Freud's primitive men and neurotics, was force. The network models of Chapter 3 made that clear enough. In the beginning, fascism was action and force.

But what about property, action leading to property? Here it is Marx who would agree with Faust. Property is the result of action, social action:

> Our owners of commodities think after the manner of Faust: 'In the beginning was the deed' – action comes first. They have therefore acted before they have thought. ... They cannot bring their commodities into relation with one another as values, except by comparing them with some other commodity as general equivalent. ... But the only way in which a particular commodity can become a

general equivalent is by a *social act*. The *social act* performed by all other commodities therefore sets apart a particular commodity in which they all express their values. Thereby the bodily form of this commodity becomes the form of the socially recognised equivalent. To be the general equivalent is, thanks to this social process, the specific function of the commodity thus set apart from the rest. In this way it becomes – money. (Marx, 1930, pp. 61–2, chap. 2; emphasis added)

To this issue of money Simmel dedicated one of his most ambitious works, *The Philosophy of Money*. Contrary to Marx, for Simmel, the study of money is an excuse for the study of the totality of life. "I am here concerned with the relation of money to the totality of human life," he tells us explicitly (Simmel, 1978, p. 211). "From the interaction of individuals, there develop objective institutions which become the junction of countless individual teleological sequences and provide an efficient tool for otherwise unattainable purposes" (Simmel, 1978, pp. 209–10). One such institution, one such tool is money, "the purest form of the tool" (Simmel, 1978, p. 210). Money, not being related to any specific purpose, is rather related to the totality of purposes. As such, it is the tool with the greatest possible number of unpredictable uses (Simmel, 1978, p. 212). "Its quantity is its only important determination ... *its quality consists exclusively in its quantity*" (Simmel, 1978, p. 259; emphasis in the original).

Indeed, for Simmel, money is "the most perfect representative of a cognitive tendency in modern science as a whole: *The reduction of qualitative determinants to quantitative ones*," the best "example ... of the modern emphasis on the quantitative moment" (Simmel, 1978, pp. 277, 279; emphasis added).

> Modern times as a whole are characterized throughout by a trend towards empiricism ... Empiricism replaces the single visionary or rational idea with the highest possible number of observations; it substitutes their qualitative character by the quantity of assembled individual cases. ... It would be easy to multiply the examples that illustrate the growing preponderance of the category of quantity over that of quality ... (Simmel, 1978, p. 278; emphasis added)

And so did Lukács who had attended Simmel's lectures in Berlin in 1909–10:[61]

> Rationalisation, the desire to reduce everything to signs and formulae, progressively increases however not only in the pure natural sciences but also in the more historical sciences (sociology) .... the category of the qualitative is superseded by that of the quantitative ... [62]

For Weber, "one can, in principle, master all things by calculation" (in Gerth and Mills, 1946a, p. 139). Simmel is not so sure. No doubt, there is a growing "tendency to dissolve quality into quantity ... [but] this tendency may never absolutely attain its goals by mortal means" (Simmel, 1978, p. 278). Quantification can never encompass the whole of social life, it always "leaves a qualitative determination of the elements intact and the question of quantity unanswered" (Simmel, 1978, p. 279)."Only money is free from any quality and exclusively determined by quantity"; money represents "the pinnacle of a cultural series of historical developments" (Simmel, 1978, p. 279). Those historical developments were traced plainly enough by one of Simmel's contemporaries. Sombart, in his classic portrayal of bourgeois spirit, *Der Bourgeois,* wrote: "The bourgeois spirit is composed of *calculation*, careful policy, reasonableness, and economy." "Put into two words, he [the bourgeois entrepreneur] must be able to *calculate* and to save," and where even saving involves calculation.[63] Money simply makes those calculations easier, the rational accounting of means and ends in the sequence of purposes (Simmel, 1978, pp. 204–80). Money is behind purposeful, rational action.

For Weber, the development of the money economy was at the basis of the development of bureaucracy (Weber, 1978, p. 968). "Bureaucracy is *the* means of transforming social action into rationally organized action" (Weber, 1978, p. 987; emphasis in the original). Rational action is, for Weber, action oriented toward "rationally pursued and calculated ends," action where "the end, the means, and the secondary results are all rationally taken into account and weighted."[64] But this is typical bureaucratic action. Weber continues: "[A] system of rationally debatable 'reasons' stands behind every act of bureaucratic administration, namely, subsumption under norms, or a weighing of ends and means" (Weber, 1978, p. 979). Bureaucracy, in Weber's vocabulary, means rationality. And rationality gives bureaucracy its "*technical* superiority over any other form of organization" (Weber, 1978, pp. 973, 987).

But bureaucracy was not "in the beginning." Rather, "the bureaucratic structure is everywhere a late product of historical development" (Weber, 1978, p. 1002; also p. 983). And to the extent that "bureaucracy has a 'rational' character," the "march of bureaucracy," its "rise and expansion" meant an "advance of *rationalism* in general" (Weber, 1978, p. 1002; emphasis in the original). Thus, rationalism and reason were not in the beginning. Reason was a late comer on the stage of history. On that, Weber and the *philosophes* of a century earlier would be in agreement. Where they would disagree is on timing: The *philosophes* saw their own age, the age of Enlightenment, as *the* age of Reason, in contrast to the darkness of any previous epoch, Middle Ages in particular. For Weber, the age of Reason spans the centuries of the rise of capitalism and the state. Its early days date back to the growth of a money economy in the medieval Italian city states.

Thus, the development of a money economy, the rise of capitalism, the drive to measure, calculate, and quantify go hand in hand. Marcuse asked the question: "Between the two processes of scientific and societal quantification, is there parallelism and causation, or is their connection simply the work of sociological insight?" (Marcuse, 1964, p. 157). The answer is: Quantification is a social project, a "specific mode of 'seeing' the world," in Husserl's words.[65] "And this 'seeing,' in spite of its pure disinterested character, is seeing within a purposive, practical context" (Marcuse, 1964, p. 164). Quantification is the way of seeing of specific social formations, specific social arrangements, and specific networks of social relations. "Efforts to mathematicize social science can only be efforts at disguising or promoting particular points of view," Alexander writes (1987, p. 21). "Science observes, calculates, and theorizes from a position in ... this universe [of discourse and action]" (Marcuse, 1964, p. 157). Theodore Porter would later put it in very similar way in an excellent book on the pursuit of objectivity:

> The appeal of numbers is especially compelling to bureaucratic officials who lack the mandate of a popular election, or divine right ... Quantification is a way of making decisions without having to decide. Objectivity lends authority to officials who have very little of their own. (Porter, 1995, p. 8)

In his essay "Objectivity in Social Science and Social Policy," Weber (1949, p. 72) acknowledged:

> There is no absolutely 'objective' scientific analysis of culture ... or ... of 'social phenomena' independent of 'special' and one-sided viewpoints according to which – expressly or tacitly, consciously or unconsciously – they are selected, analyzed and organized for expository purposes. (Weber, 1949, p. 72)

"All knowledge of cultural reality ... is always knowledge from *particular points of view*" (Weber, 1949, p. 81). "Scientific truth is the product of certain cultures and is not a product of man's original nature" (Weber, 1949, p. 110).

> In the empirical social sciences ... the possibility of meaningful knowledge of what is essential for us in the infinite richness of events is bound up with the unremitting application of viewpoints of a specifically particularized character, which, in the last analysis, are oriented on the basis of evaluative ideas. (Weber, 1949, p. 111)

The drive toward measurement and quantification far from being "innocent," is the result of the active involvement of certain social actors in the pursuit of their interests. The state – a prime example of that Weberian bureaucracy – played a fundamental role in this process. The very etymology of the word "statistics" betrays its close connection to the state's interest in counting and quantifying, to raise taxes and conscripts. "Princes are not only Powerful but Rich according to the number of their people," John Graunt had written in his 1661 *Natural and Political Observations on the London Bills of Mortality* (cited in Pearson, 1978, p. 34), "it is no wonder why States by encouraging Marriage and hindering Licentiousness, advance their own Interest." Sir William Petty built upon Graunt's measurement dream in his 1690 *Political arithmetick*.[66] The infancy of statistics in Great Britain, in the work of Galton, Pearson, and Fisher, was also linked to less savory projects of eugenics and racial improvement (MacKenzie, 1979, 1981). "Quantifiability is a prerequisite for the *domination* of nature," writes Marcuse (1964, p. 164). And when that nature is the social world? Porter (1995, p. 43) would answer: "[Q]uantification has been part of a strategy of intervention, not merely of description ... quantification is simultaneously a means of planning and of prediction." Or, in Starr's words (1987, p. 9), social statistics "serve an interest in social coordination and control."

This historical process of rationalization, measurement, and quantification bound up with wider social relations and interests, comes at a cost, and not just for those at the bottom of the social hierarchy. Simmel, the consumed aesthete, wrote of "the antagonism between an aesthetic tendency and money interests. Aesthetic interests are so much focused on pure form ... the aesthetic value of things remains attached to their form."[67] "Money is the most terrible destroyer of form." "The irreconcilable and, for all aesthetic interests, decisive antagonisms always remains in the emphasis placed on whether we value things according to their form or ask the amount of their value."

And one of the "things" we value for their form, for their pure pleasure, rather than utilitarian value, is certainly play. And like form, play has slowly been destroyed by the modern tendency toward rationalization and quantification. A play-element has been characteristic of all ages, perhaps reaching a peak in the seventeenth and eighteenth centuries, in the Baroque and, especially, Rococo periods (Huizinga, 1949, pp. 182–9). But with the nineteenth century this century-old civilizing play-element came to an abrupt end (Huizinga, 1949, pp. 191, 195). The advent of the Industrial Revolution, with its new culture of technical and scientific discourse, and the new entrepreneurial ethos ("I am not paying you to have fun!") run "directly counter to all that we mean by play" (Huizinga, 1949, p. 191). "Never had an age taken itself with more portentous seriousness" than the nineteenth century, writes Huizinga (1949, p. 192).

> More and more the sad conclusion forces itself upon us that the play-element in culture has been on the wane ever since the 18th century, when it was in full flower. Civilization to-day is no longer played, and even where it still seems to play it is false play ... (Huizinga, 1949, p. 206)

In the end, play too, along with beauty and form, was engulfed and destroyed by the tide of quantification. "The fate of our time," Weber wrote, "is characterized by rationalization and intellectualization and, above all, by the 'disenchantment of the world.'" "This above all is what intellectualization means": That "technical means and calculations perform the service," they are responsible for that disenchantment of the mysterious powers of a magical world (in Gerth and Mills, 1946a, p. 155).

And if play and aesthetics are characteristics of freedom, rationalization is ultimately a destroyer of freedom. Take bureaucracy, the best symbol, for Weber, of rationalization, bureaucracy with "its purely *technical* superiority over any other form of organization" (Weber, 1978, pp. 973, 987). But this technical superiority also provides "the most highly developed power instrument in the hands of its controller" (Weber, 1978, p. 991). Contrary to Marx, Weber sees no prospect for revolutionary action in this "practically indestructible" social system. "Once fully established, bureaucracy is among those social structures which are the hardest to destroy" (Weber, 1978, p. 987). The trouble is ... *it will be fully established*. Of that, Weber has no doubt. In the conclusion of his *The Agrarian Sociology of Ancient Civilizations*, Weber sadly annotated: "[I]n all probability some day the bureaucratization of German society will encompass capitalism too, just as it did in Antiquity" (Weber, 1976, p. 365). And that will mark the end of beauty, of form, of play, of freedom, and perhaps of all that is human, engulfed by the process of capitalist rationalization: The "irrational" element of human character, "anxiety, anger, ambition, envy, jealousy, love, enthusiasm, pride, vengefulness, loyalty, devotion, and appetites of all sorts" – all, in other words, that it means to be human (Weber, 1978, p. 6). In a wonderful little book, Albert Hirschman explored the close link between the rise of capitalism and the suppression of passion (1977, especially pp. 9–66). But, before him, Weber had made explicit that link. "Bureaucracy promotes a "rationalist" way of life ... the bureaucratization of all domination very strongly furthers the development of "rational matter-of-factness" (Weber, 1978, p. 998). No. There is no room for emotional and irrational elements in that world.

> The peculiarity of modern culture, and specifically of its technical and economic basis, demands this very 'calculability' of results. When fully developed, bureaucracy also stands, in a specific sense, under the principle of *sine ira ac studio*. Bureaucracy develops the more perfectly, the more it is 'dehumanized,' the more completely it succeeds in eliminating from official business love, hatred, and all purely personal, irrational, and emotional elements which escape calculation. This is appraised as its special virtue by capitalism. (Weber, 1978, p. 975)

With life utterly dominated "in his entire economic and ideological existence," by "the ever more bureaucratic organizations of capitalism," "the ruled ... cannot dispense with or replace the bureaucratic apparatus once it exists"; "the idea of eliminating... ['the ever more bureaucratic organizations of capitalism'] becomes more and more utopian" (Weber, 1978, p. 988). "Such an apparatus makes 'revolution,' ... more and more impossible" (Weber, 1978, p. 989).

The very development of productive forces that the entrepreneurial action brings about, the process of increasing rationalization that capitalism generates is not without its *irrational* consequences. In the 1940s, this Weberian theme of the irrational aspects of rationality was taken up by some of the exponents of the Frankfurt School. Echoing Weber, Marcuse writes that "reason ... is necessarily mastery, domination. Logos is law, rule, order by virtue of knowledge" (Marcuse, 1964, p. 167). "[T]here is no such thing as a purely rational scientific order; the process of technological rationality is a political process" (Marcuse,

1964, p. 168). "The web of domination has become the web of Reason itself, and this society is fatally entangled in it" (Marcuse, 1964, p. 169). For Marcuse (1964, pp. ix, xiii) there is a double meaning of rationalization: The greater and greater efficiency of capitalist enterprises goes hand-in-hand with a greater efficiency in exploiting and oppressing labor.[68] "Scientific-technical rationality and manipulation are welded together into new forms of social control." While domination of man by man is a historical continuum between societies characterized by pretechnological and technological Reason the base of domination has sinisterly changed from a personal one to an objective one ("the market"). "Something must be wrong with the rationality of the system itself." With Mussolini's (and Hitler's) actions, the separation between technical reason and moral reason, between Kant's theoretical and practical reason, the split in the Weberian process of rationalization may have just reached its pinnacle, ultimately leading to the eclipse of reason (Horkheimer, 1947). The triumph of reason marks its very eclipse, the triumph of theoretical reason, the eclipse of practical reason, and the triumph of irrationality.

Reason, it seems, was neither in the beginning nor in the end. "The rational society subverts the idea of Reason" (Marcuse, 1964, p. 167). And if a measure of this reason is calculation and quantification, what is scientists' role in this process, what is *my* role as I push to convert into quantity the ultimate and most sacred symbol of quality – the word? "Science," Marcuse writes, "*by virtue of its own method* and concepts, has projected and promoted a universe in which the domination of nature has remained linked to the domination of man" (Marcuse, 1964, p. 166; emphasis in the original). Is that my role? Do the *word* and the *deed* go hand in hand, *theoretical reason* entering into the service of *practical reason* by remaining pure and neutral (Marcuse, 1964, p. 158)?

Caught in the whirlwind of rationalization, quantification, and bureaucratization, prisoner of the *discipline* of academic disciplines, blinded by a language that does not allow him to step outside the path traced by language, the social scientist, with his ever-increasing specialized knowledge, becomes himself part and parcel of that process, "only *a small cog in a ceaselessly moving mechanism* which prescribes to him an essentially fixed route of march" (Weber, 1978, p. 988). Willingly or unwillingly, consciously or unconsciously, he himself comes to play a role "in the perpetuation of the apparatus and the persistence of its rationally organized domination" (Weber, 1978, p. 988; emphasis added). Do I and thousand other little Franzosis contribute to social projects of power and domination, ourselves perhaps unconscious victims of such projects? Is the domination of others *for* others the price we pay for *our* personal freedom? The path of knowledge is strewn with the bodies of innocent victims. Gretchen's life is the price that Mephistopheles exacts for Faust's freedom, for Faust's thirst for knowledge.

And After

No! In the beginning was emotion. The Word came next to replace emotion as the trot replaces the gallop. … They pulled man out of emotive poetry in order to plunge him into dialectics, that is, into gibberish, right!

Louis Ferdinand Céline (cited in Kristeva, 1980, p. 144)

Feeling is everything. Words are just sound and smoke, bedimming the light of heaven.

Johann Wolfgang Goethe (1970, p. 60)

Man is said to be a reasoning animal. I do not know why he has not been defined as an affective or feeling animal. Perhaps that which differentiates him from other animals is feeling rather than reason.

Miguel de Unamuno (1931, p. 3)

That summer fields grew high. We had wildflower fever. We had to lie down where they grew. How I've learned to hide, how I've locked inside, you'd be surprised if shown. But you'll never, you'll never know.

10,000 Maniacs (*Stockton Gala Days,* 1992)

"So Long as We Get Somewhere"

"Would you tell me, please, which way I ought to walk from here?" "That depends a good deal of where you want to get to," said the Cat. "I don't much care where—" said Alice. "Then it doesn't matter which way you walk," said the Cat. "—so long as I get *somewhere*," Alice added as an explanation. "Oh, you're sure to do that," said the Cat, "if you only walk long enough."[1]

Long enough we did walk across time and disciplines. And just like the wise Cat promised in *Alice's Adventures in Wonderland*, we surely did get *somewhere* in this journey from words to numbers. But *where?* What exactly is that object of scientific inquiry fashioned out of stories – newspaper articles – the validity of which I am not sure of and through methods of data collection the validity of which I am similarly not sure of? And upon closer inspection, do not the methods we use to analyze those numbers, however fashioned out of invalid stories and methods, bring out more stories, more words?

Indeed, we can read network graphs as grand narratives. A handful of graphs around a handful of relations (social actions) tell us the basic story of the "red" and "black" years, of who did what for or against whom. Each graph crunches together tens, hundreds, or even thousands of individual triplets; but each graph itself is yet another triplet, yet another skeleton narrative sentence. Seven such triplets provide a synthetic representation of the 1919–22 years, provide the grand narrative of those years. Four pages of network graphs summarize thousands of pages of historians' narrative work on the period. It is precisely this capacity of network models to tell a story of social actors and social relations that brings sociology and history closer together.[2]

A narrative representation is no doubt only below the surface of such statistical tools as network models. But other statistical tools fare no better. They simply more aptly conceal their narrative logic. Let us go back to econometric models, the statistical tool most typically used for the past thirty years in quantitative strike research.

$$STRIKES_t = \beta_0 + \beta_1 UNEMP_{1t} + \beta_2 UNIONIZ_{2t} + \epsilon_t \qquad\qquad 1$$

It is models of this kind that we use to estimate the effect, at time *t*, of the *UNEMP*loyment rate and the level of *UNIONIZ*ation on the number of *STRIKES*. It is in models of this kind that we plug that number – 237 – encountered in Table 1 of the Chapter "Tales of Measurement." Such models, we have seen, provide "thin," if not altogether wrong, explanations of social reality. But they also provide narrative explanations of social reality under disguise. They too tell us stories. How?

One of the clearest findings in strike research is the negative relationship between unemployment rate and number of strikes and the positive relationship between unionization and number of strikers[3] (in the language of Equation 1, we expect the estimated signs of the coefficients β_1 and β_2 to be respectively negative and positive). Another way to say this is that when unemployment is high, strikes tend to be less frequent; when union membership is high the number of strikes is also high. The typical "narrative" associated with the reading of the coefficient of the unemployment variable is then something like:

> There were many people out of jobs in the city. Not a day went by that
> you wouldn't hear of another factory closing down or letting more

workers go. Employers were not just cutting jobs, but wages as well. Union leaders fussed and screamed, but workers were simply too scared to listen. No one wanted to hear about strikes. With no jobs around to be had at any price, no one was willing to risk giving management an excuse for further cuts.

That is "a" narrative consistent with Equation 1. Unfortunately, this narrative is not consistent with the events at the ACR firm that we met in the chapter on "Tales of Measurement." Our statistical models not only still provide narrative representations of social reality in a different format, but those representations often clash with underlying stories. The numbers contain within them the traces of the words (sometimes distorting them). As Collins (1984, p. 351) put it: "Mathematics keep resurfacing into the world of words from which it starts its plunges. Words seem to be a necessary and inescapable frame within which mathematics is embedded." If a structural analysis of narrative allows us to go from words to numbers, the borders between the two worlds become fuzzier and more permeable than declarations of principle and programmatic positions of the qualitative and quantitative camps would have us believe.

But the journey from words to numbers is certainly not one way. Not only the realm of numbers is incomprehensible without words – we even need words to work through the successive steps of a mathematical theorem – but the statistical models that we have long applied on those numbers imply behavioral narratives that the seemingly mathematical appearance of those models lead us to forget. In any case, numbers need a context, something to go with the text (the numbers, actually) to make their interpretation possible. How else could we explain the persistent use of ritualistic literature review sections in social science quantitative journal articles? As quantitative audiences, don't we typically go straight for the tables, the numbers, the signs, the significance (not of problems, of course, but of coefficients)? Shouldn't we just collect all reviews in journals specializing in literature reviews and save precious journal space? Perhaps. Except ... those literature reviews are part of the scientific story telling. They guide the reader through the minefield of competing theories, approaches, and models. They set up straw men. They contextualize one's findings in a way that theory, method, and results present a coherent unity.

So ... in the end of our journey, did we arrive where we began, from words to numbers, and back to the words? Where did we arrive in this journey of ours?

> At the still point of the turning world. Neither flesh nor fleshless; / Neither from nor towards; at the still point, there the dance is, / But neither arrest nor movement. And do not call it fixity, / Where the past and future are gathered. Neither movement from nor towards, / Neither ascent nor decline. Except for the point, the still point, / There would be no dance, and there is only the dance. / I can only say, *there* we have been: But I cannot say where. (T. S. Eliot, *Burnt Norton*, 1963, p. 191)

But in the end, wherever we arrived, the journey remains. "But, at your age, you will never return from so long a journey," Montaigne's imaginary interlocutor objects to a journey (III, IX, 1892, p. 218). "What care I for that?" is Montaigne's reply. "I neither undertake it to return, nor to finish it: My business is only to keep myself in motion, whilst motion pleases me; I only walk for the walk's sake." Perhaps, our paths are straight only in retrospect. Social science journals are full of stories of pat solutions and straight paths; they rarely tell us of our meandering and groping; we always seem to know what we are doing (just read Watson's account of his discovery of DNA to set you straight on that; Watson, 1969). Perhaps, as Antonio Machado[4] writes in another gem of twentieth century poetry:

> *Caminante, son tus huellas / el camino, y nada más; / caminante, no hay camino, / se hace camino al andar. / Al andar se hace camino, / y al volver la vista atrás / se ve la senda que nunca / se ha volver a pisar. / Caminante, no hay camino, / sino estelas en la mar.*[5]

The journey alone is certain. Darwin, after enumerating a long list of negative aspects of long journeys, at the end of his *Voyage of the Beagle*, still concludes on a positive note: "I have too deeply enjoyed the voyage, not to recommend" it to others (1989, p. 377).

Poupinel and His World: In the Beginning Was Meaning

Let us go back to the beginning. Back to one of the dramatic opening scenes of our journey from words to numbers. Back to that Saturday morning of July 16, 1639. Back to Poupinel, *lieutenant particulier* of the Présidial at Coutances. History has preserved for us the record of the last horrific hours of this "wretched" man – the wrong man at the wrong time – who had come to Avranches to carry out business "which related to justice and had nothing to do with fiscal matters."

> An hour and a half later, four hundred people, mostly salt makers and wood porters, were kicking and punching Poupinel and beating him with sticks and stones. The wretched man, his flesh in shreds, died about half past twelve noon. The spinning women put out his eyes with their spindles. (Mousnier, 1970, p. 98)

As a narrative passage – of the five Ws type, of actors performing certain actions for or against other actors – a story grammar allows us to structure the information contained in the passage in ways that we can then analyze statistically. On the basis of hundreds or thousands of passages of this kind we could obtain frequency distributions of actors, actions, and attributes. We could display tables with "relational" information – who does what – after all, isn't that where the power of the technique lies? We could produce network graphs to map the patterns of social relations in which women, for instance, are enmeshed, the actors they are more likely to come in touch with, the actions they are more likely to perform.

Carefully lining up individual episodes, counting them, cataloguing them would (hopefully) bring out patterns in our data; patterns in the "repertoire of actions," in the matrix of interactions among actors, in the temporal and spatial distribution of events, just like they did for the 1919–22 project illustrated in Chapter 3 of Part I. Those patterns would allow us to understand Poupinel's ill fate as part and parcel of the intrusion of the state into the lives of ordinary people during several hundred years of European history. Anderson (1974), Tilly (1975), Poggi (1978), and others have told the bloody tale of state formation. As Mousnier (1970, pp. 306, 348) wrote: "[T]he revolts of the seventeenth century ... were reactions against ... the development of the state ... [against] the whittling away of customary local privileges and liberties ..." Then, a computer-based story grammar would have produced a "good pudding."

Yet, coding, cataloguing, and counting – the alchemic transformation of words into numbers – effectively lead us to forget that "there are people behind numbers"[6] – people driven by their emotions, their passions, their loves, their angers and hatreds. No doubt, once we get to the numbers and the tables, the passion of the original prose is gone, along with the savage fury of emotions of the quickly consumed drama of Avranches 1639. In the tedious process of doing science, of tracing historical patterns through the meticulous parsing of narrative episodes into sets of actors, actions, and their respective attributes, we lose sight of Poupinel and of the spinning women, we lose sight of the inner chords that moral outrage in people's encounters with unjust authority strikes in the meander of human psyches.[7]

"The paraphernalia of scientific research and ... the bloodless vocabulary that sociology has developed in its desire to legitimate its own scientific status" may ultimately obscure "what it means to be a man and what it means to be a man in a particular situation" (Berger, 1963, p. 189). Our science, with its "bloodless vocabulary," hardly helps us understand the bloody events of July 16, 1639 in Avranches. Neither our tools of data collection and analysis, nor our "cutting-edge" theories have anything to say about passion and emotion in collective action. In social movement "theory" we find such labels as "political opportunity structures," "resource mobilization," and "frame alignment." But of passion and emotion there is no mention.[8]

We have to dig deep into the archeology of knowledge to get a glimpse of that murky world of crowds and their passions. We have to go back to once popular names, like Gustave Le Bon (1841–1931), Gabriel Tarde (1843–1904), Scipio Sighele (1868–1913) who wrote extensively about crowd behavior. The work of these right-wing conservatives, once associated with the ideologies of European fascism, was discredited and the very memory of their work disappeared. Yet, it is to them that we have to turn to shed some light on a world of sudden and ferocious passions. For Tarde, Le Bon, Sighele, Rossi, and others, emotions are the moving force of crowd behavior. Crowds are fundamentally irrational.[9] For Le Bon crowds are "little adapted to reasoning ... quick to act." Fiercely intolerant, irritable, impulsive, and given to excessive sentiments, crowds are easy preys of violent propaganda. Individuals in crowds will do things they would never dare doing by themselves.[10] *"To unite in the human world means to get worse.* This is the principle to which we arrive" (Sighele, 1922, p. 145; emphasis in the original). Crowds do not operate at the level of conscious reason. The motives behind crowds' behavior are mostly unconscious.[11] Irresponsibility, contagion, and suggestibility are the key ingredients in crowd behavior (Le Bon, 1969, pp. 25–6, 27).[12]

But do we really need to understand emotions, to understand the fury of passions for sociology to be a science? Weber has no doubt about that. For Weber (1978, p. 4; emphasis added), "sociology ... is *a science concerning itself with the interpretative understanding of social action* ... We shall speak of 'action' insofar as the acting individual attaches a subjective meaning [*sinn*] to his behavior ... Action is 'social' insofar as its subjective meaning takes account of the behavior of others and is thereby oriented in its course."

"'In the beginning was the Mind,'" we earlier met Faust muttering to himself (Goethe, 1987, lines 1229–37). "I see how it must read." "In the beginning was Meaning [*sinn*]." Not *sinn* as Mind or Reason, but *sinn* as Meaning. Not Reason/Mind, Force, Action/Deed, then, in the beginning, but Meaning. That is what really was in the beginning. That, in any case, is what we find at the beginning of Weber's sociology, in the very opening pages of his *Economy and Society*, at the very foundation of his epistemology of the social sciences.

There are two fundamental ways for Weber of understanding social action of interpreting its meaning: rational and emotional/empathic. He writes:

> All interpretation of meaning, like all scientific observations, strives for clarity and verifiable accuracy of insight and comprehension ... The basis for certainty in understanding can be either rational, which can be further subdivided into logical and mathematical, or it can be of an emotionally empathic or artistically appreciative quality. Action is rationally evident chiefly when we attain a completely clear intellectual grasp of the action-elements in their intended context of meaning. Empathic or appreciative accuracy is attained when, through sympathetic participation, we can adequately grasp the emotional context in which the action took place. (Weber, 1978, p. 5)

Being ourselves human, being steeped into the same emotional world as our subjects of inquiry, made out of the same "anxiety, anger, ambition, envy, jealousy, love, enthusiasm, pride, vengefulness, loyalty, devotion, and appetites of all sorts" and being subject to the "irrational conduct that grows out of them" allows us to understand our subjects (Weber, 1978, p. 6). "The more we are ourselves susceptible to such emotional reactions ... the more readily we can empathize with them" (Weber, 1978, p. 6).

Weber turns into strength commonly perceived weaknesses in the social sciences when compared to the natural sciences.[13] "Subjective understanding is the specific characteristic of sociological knowledge" (Weber, 1978, p. 15). Weber (1978, pp. 15, 74) explains:

> [I]t is important to understand in order to explain a given phenomenon. ... In the case of social collectivities ... we are in a position to go beyond merely demonstrating functional relationships and uniformities. We can accomplish something which is never attainable in the natural sciences, namely the subjective understanding of the actions of the component individuals.

> Whereas in astronomy, the heavenly bodies are of interest to us only in their *quantitative* and exact aspects, the *qualitative* aspect of phenomena concerns us in the social sciences. ... [T]he empathic understanding of ... [social phenomena] is naturally a problem of a specifically different type from those which the schemes of the exact natural sciences in general can or seek to solve.

Weber, the humanist, the social historian steeped in a tradition of German historicism,[14] concludes: "[S]ociology ... is a science concerning itself with the interpretative understanding of social action and *thereby with a causal explanation of its course and consequences*" (Weber, 1978, p. 4). Understanding and explaining go hand-in-hand in the human sciences.[15] Understanding (*verstehen*) is a prerequisite for explaining (cause and effect). English historian George Trevelyan would ask: Can historians exclude emotion from their method simply because "history deals only with the science of cause and effect in human affairs"? Then, how could they "understand the emotions of others, which have none the less played a principal part in cause and effect"? After all, "*those by whom history was enacted were in their days passionate.*"[16] And so they were in Avranches, France, on that day of July 16, 1639. And so they were in Italy during the tumultuous Red Years and Black Years of 1919–22. Perhaps Céline was right after all when he screamed: "No! In the beginning was emotion. The Word came next," with all the rest ... including numbers.[17]

On the Road, Again

We are approaching the end of our journey from words to numbers. And numbers, Nobel Prize economist Robert Fogel tells us, are most appropriate "in the analysis of the behavior of groups" (Fogel, 1975, p. 344). Which is precisely what I have used our numbers for: To study the behavior of groups in post-First World War Italy. And that behavior manifests itself in actions. And if looking for "processes of actions" is the task of the historian, in Collingwood's words (1946, p. 215), that as well I have done. After all, those network models are nothing but processes of actions.

Yet, for Collingwood, this is certainly not enough. Through my numbers, I have barely scratched the surface of group behavior, I have contented myself with determining the external manifestations of the acts of the agents I am studying (Collingwood, 1946, p. 228). Actions, per se, are useless to the historian, who "is not concerned with events as such at all." The proper task of the historian "is not knowing what people did but understanding what they thought ... penetrating to the inside of events and detecting the thought which they express. ... For history, the object to be discovered is not the mere event, but the thought expressed in it." "All history is the history of thought."[18] And how does the historian penetrate inside the events? "By thinking for himself the thoughts of past people," by rethinking their same thoughts, in a "re-enactment of past thought in the historian's own mind," in order to understand the experience.[19] No experience, no history. "When all is said and done," Marc Bloch wrote (1953, p. 71), "a single word, 'understanding,' is the beacon light of our studies."[20] Writing during World War Two, where he was eventually taken prisoner by the Germans, tortured, and executed, Bloch left us a heart-felt description of that "word pregnant with difficulties" – understanding:

> I have many times read, and I have often narrated, accounts of wars and battles. Did I truly know, in the full sense of that word, did I know from within, before I myself had suffered the terrible, sickening reality, what it meant for an army to be encircled, what it meant for a people to meet defeat? (Bloch, 1953, p. 44)

But if that is so, through my numbers, I may be looking at action ("behavior") at the wrong level, at the surface, rather than at the deep level, at the outer manifestations of action, rather than at their inner meanings for the actors and at the cultural and ideological frameworks through which actors interpret their actions.

The debates surrounding the nineteenth-century psychological and realist novels provide a good parallel to these social-science dilemmas. In discussing Maupassant's preface to *Pierre et Jean*, indeed a manifesto of realism in novels, Genette best characterized the dilemma of the realist novel:

> It [Maupassant's preface] praises realism, which it contrasts with the novel of adventure ... But this realistic technique that aims to give 'a total illusion of truth' must choose between two paths: That of psychological analysis and that of 'objectivity'; the latter eschews all 'dissertation upon motives' and limits itself as a matter of methodology 'to showing us people and the things that happen,' leaving psychology 'concealed in the book as it is in reality behind the events of life.' We see that this delayed manifesto of the realistic or naturalistic novel is

also a very premature manifesto of the so-called behaviorist novel. (Genette, 1997, p. 228)

In similarly adopting a behaviorist model of social reality where only the actors and their actions count – *we can count them, therefore they count?* – have we forgotten the meaning of action? Has action come at the expense of motives? But if motives count, unfortunately, the measurement of those motives is well beyond the power of the tools we have developed to capture the surface manifestations of action. Having gone in search of the actor, when the actor we do find, it turns out that the action is even more telling than the actor. Several disciplines (linguistics, history, sociology) converge on this point, as we saw in Chapter 6. But the action can perhaps only be understood in terms of the meaning that the actors involved impose upon it.[21] That meaning is well beyond the power of the tools developed here. Among the losses due to formalism and abstraction, we have to add these: The loss of empathy, the loss of our ability to share human experience, to reach the depth of human emotions, the loss of empathetic understanding of the meaning of action.

And what about that very way of knowing that I have borrowed from Simmel, the relentless pursuit of "relations" between things? If knowledge is fundamentally the pursuit of relations in Simmel's way, we fared well in our journey. Yet, empiricism and modern science were born out of the rejection of those principles, of that way of knowing. Things must be looked at for what they really are, not in light of something else or, what amounts to the same thing, in light of metaphor (White, 1978, pp. 131–4). As early as 1690, in his *An Essay Concerning Human Understanding*, John Locke had thundered against metaphor. He wrote:

> Men who have a great deal of Wit, and prompt Memories, have not always the clearest Judgment, or deepest Reason. For *Wit* lying mostly in the assemblage of *Ideas,* and putting those together with quickness and variety, wherein can be found any resemblance or congruity, thereby to make up pleasant Pictures, and agreeable Visions in the Fancy: *Judgment,* on the contrary, lies quite on the other side, in separating carefully, one from another, *Ideas,* wherein can be found the least difference, thereby to avoid being misled by Similitude, and by affinity to take one thing for another. This is a way of proceeding quite contrary to Metaphor and Allusion, wherein, for the most part, lies that entertainment and pleasantry of Wit, which strikes so lively on the Fancy, and therefore so acceptable to all People; because its Beauty appears at first sight, and there is required no labour of thought, to examine what Truth or Reason there is in it. (Locke, II, XI, 2, 22–36; 1975, p. 156; emphasis in the original)

Against Locke's better *Judgement*, in these pages, I have pursued metaphoric discourse – the journey, the alchemy – at the expense of metonymic discourse, a discourse of poetry rather than science. Not only have I developed the wrong tool, but I seem to have led you, reader, altogether along the wrong path to science.

For all the road we have traveled, for all the marvelous things we have seen in our journey, we may have been looking at the wrong thing, we may have taken the wrong road. We are on the road again.

"Know Thyself": Notes on Reflexive Sociology

A search that started in pursuit of the actor has taken us quite far afield – although precisely where we do not know and the path trodden may have been misleading. What remains in the end is meaning: meaning of texts, meaning of science, meaning of action for the actors involved, ultimately meaning of this journey for this actor, for the "I/me." And I, no doubt, I am the "sentimental traveller," traveling "as much out of *Necessity*, and the *besoin de* Voyager,"[22] a combination of a Ulysses longing for home and a don Quixote longing for the road. Traveling, for the "sentimental traveller," is only an excuse to know oneself or "to know the others in ourselves," as Ugo Foscolo put it in the preface to his 1813 Italian translation of Sterne's work (Foscolo, in Sterne and Foscolo, 1983, p. 5).

Even for the alchemists of old the "Great Work" was only minimally concerned with the transformation of vile metals into gold.[23] The understanding of *oneself* and of celestial mysteries was far more important.[24] The material transformation was only an excuse for much more fundamental transformations – or a tangible sign of having reached the final step in the different levels of knowledge. "You will separate earth from fire, thin from thick ... with great industry. ... This way you will achieve all the glory in the world and you will dispel darkness," promised the *Tabula smaragdina*, an alchemic tract attributed in the Middle Ages to the legendary Hermes Trimegistus.[25] *Laboratorium* and *oratorium*: Medieval alchemic tracts dedicate as much attention to the chemical and physical transformations achieved in the laboratory as to the inner transformations in the adept's conscience achieved in the oratory (Hutin, 1991, pp. 32–3, 49, 82). The basic motto of alchemic practice is: "*Lege, lege, relege, ora, labora, et invenies*" (read, read, and read some more, pray, work, and you will discover) (Hutin, 1991, p. 82). There is a perfect correspondence between the inner and outer worlds, the spiritual and the physical, man's microcosmos and the macrocosmos. Knowledge of the microcosmos leads to knowledge of the macrocosmos. Still in the nineteenth century, John Stuart Mill firmly believed that knowledge of the laws of human nature would explain social institutions.

"Know thyself," had preached Pythagoras's teacher, Thales. Like the modern corporate logos set on the facades of corporate high rises, that dictum stood inscribed across the Delphi oracle. This preaching has not been without its followers. Thomas Aquinas acknowledges that inward looking and self-reflection brought him knowledge in the alchemic art: "I myself ... came to believe that this science would yield nothing. But, *looking inside myself* ... I then reflected on the natural principles and discovered what can be found through them."[26] Descartes in his *A Discourse on Method* (1960, pp. 44, 45) tells us: "[A]s soon as my age permitted me to pass from under the control of my instructors, I entirely abandoned the study of letters, and resolved no longer to *seek any other science than the knowledge of myself*, or of the great book of the world." It is that knowledge derived from the self, not knowledge derived from books, that delivers truth. Descartes concludes (1960, p. 45):

> I at length resolved to make myself the object of study, and to employ all the powers of mind in choosing the paths I ought to follow, an undertaking which was accompanied with greater success than it would have been had I never quitted my country or my books.

Traveling helps to acquire knowledge of oneself. In Montaigne's words:

> Travel is in my opinion a very profitable exercise; *the soul is there continually employed in observing new and unknown things*, and I do not know, as I have often said, a better school wherein to model life than by incessantly exposing to it the diversity of so many other lives, fancies, and usances, and by making it relish so perpetual a variety of forms of human nature. (Montaigne, III, IX; 1892, p. 213; emphasis added)

And knowledge of the self and the other go hand in hand. "Self-knowledge develops only through the knowledge of others," Simmel wrote (1978, p. 84). Traveling also helps to acquire "knowledge of others."

In the social sciences, the preachment of inner knowledge has never been popular. Minor voices could be heard here and there insisting that a social scientist

> needs first of all to *go deeper into himself and understand himself.* Without that understanding of the depth of his own mind, without that self-knowledge, he cannot perfectly understand other human beings. ... [A] social scientist must work pretty hard on himself, improving his own understanding of his own mind.[27]

Momigliano (1969, pp. 110–11), the Jewish Italian historian forced to leave fascist Italy, put it in very similar words: "Self-examination is a necessary step not only to personal redemption, but also to objective historical research" to the extent that it helps to clarify our own biases. But at the core of the social sciences, the "scientists" were too busy doing science – formulating hypotheses, collecting and analyzing data, accepting and rejecting theories – to have time for such introspective pleasantries. "Skilled at objectivizing others," sociologists are far less prone to "objectivize" themselves, to turn the observer into the observed, the subject into object (Bourdieu, in Bourdieu and Wacquant, 1992, pp. 66–70).

But why be surprised? The baring of one's heart, the confessional narrative, is rare, even among those accustomed to confessions. You will be hard pressed to find references to personal feelings in the very rich pilgrimage and religious literature – that is perhaps why Peter Abelard's (1079–1142) story of his misfortunes (*Historia Calamitatum*) and of his love relationship with Eloise is so powerfully moving. Not that pilgrimage sites were always favorable to solitude and silent introspection, if Pietro Della Valle's description of the Easter ceremony of the "holy fire"[28] in the Church of the Holy Sepulchre in Jerusalem in mid-seventeenth century, is anything to go by.[29]

> [People are] running headlong through the church all around the Chapel of the most Holy Sepulchre, shouting in a loud voice, while running, *Kyrie eleison*. And when they rush into people who get in their way … they collide with them and needlessly knock them to the ground. Very often this leads to brawls and fisticuffs so that *I swear to you I've never seen anything wilder in all my life*. … the crowded confusion … the people crying out with joy … all running to light their candles, jostling, trampling and beating each other.

Indeed, there must have been little room for silent solitude at the major shrines, at least at peak times of visitation. The death by trampling and suffocation of tens of pilgrims is a recurrent theme in Alfani's treatment of the Roman jubilees (1750, pp. 14, 30, 60, 63).

Yet, self-consciousness – reflexive sociology – does not need producing a kind of "confessional" literature fashionable in ethnography.[30] Self-consciousness and reflexivity are not synonyms of narcissism. Reflexivity should not be a path that leads us away from the object of inquiry to the self (see Bourdieu and Wacquant, 1992, p. 72). Rather, reflexivity is an understanding of social reality in terms of broad social relations, of understanding our own production of knowledge in terms of those social relations. Reflexivity is a way of understanding the rhetorical aspects of texts, of writing open texts, where knowledge is not delivered ready-made, wrapped, and packaged for the "'obedient' cooperation" on the part of the reader (Eco, 1979, p. 7). "A scientific practice that fails to question itself does not … know what it does."[31]

There is both a scientific and an aesthetic value in a confessional that does not become a substitute for one's real work. Historian Marc Bloch made that perfectly clear (1953, p. 71):

> Every historical work worthy of the name ought to include a chapter, or if one prefers, a series of paragraphs inserted at turning points in the development, which might almost be entitled: 'How can I know what I am about to say?' I am persuaded that even the lay reader would experience an actual intellectual pleasure in examining these 'confessions.' The sight of an investigation, with its successes and reverses, is seldom boring. It is the ready-made article which is cold and dull.

I fully agree with Bloch's recommendation. I made it mine in *The Puzzle of Strikes* where, chapter after chapter, I involved the reader in the shortcuts (and shortcomings) of my science. I have made it mine here again.

It is this kind of critical consciousness that Peter Berger sees as the very hallmark of sociology. "The sociologist," according to Berger, "does not look at phenomena that nobody else is aware of. But he looks at the same phenomena in a different way." And that different way of looking – the "sociological perspective" – is characterized by "a certain awareness that human events have different levels of meaning," by "a measure of suspicion about the way in which human events are officially interpreted by the authorities," by "seeing through," "seeing through the facade of social structures," "looking behind the scenes," "being up on all the tricks."[32] "The hallmarks of sociological consciousness"[33] are the three motifs of debunking (for example, of official interpretations of events), unrespectability (of middle class values), and relativizing (an awareness that "ideas are relative to specific social locations").[34] For Berger, "Sociology uncovers. ... Sociological understanding leads to a considerable measure of disenchantment ... a measure of suspicion." Sociology is "this very ability to look at a situation from the vantage points of competing systems of interpretation." Such critical consciousness, according to Berger, is "built in" the very methodology of sociology. Yet, Berger may have overstated his case. "To practice radical doubt, in sociology, is akin to becoming an outlaw," states Bourdieu (Bourdieu and Wacquant, 1992, p. 241). And outlaws, by definition, are outside the law, outside the norm. The norm is rather the scholar producing norm.al science rather than revolutionary science, to borrow Kuhn's dichotomy (1962). Academic *discipline.*s (in the sense best known to children or members of total institutions) are the modern sites of production (reproduction, should I say?) of normal science, sites of definition of norms and eradication of outlaws.

Today's knowledge is the knowledge of the specialist and the expert. "A really definitive and good accomplishment is today always a specialized accomplishment," insisted Weber (in Gerth and Mills, 1946a, p. 135). "The individual can acquire the sure consciousness of achieving something truly perfect in the field of science only in case he is a strict specialist" (in Gerth and Mills, 1946a, p. 134). But, when looked at from the specialist's perspective, the specialist's knowledge is one-sided and one-dimensional. It defies self-awareness. Weber asked his audience (in Gerth and Mills, 1946a, p. 139):

> Does it mean that we, today, for instance, everyone sitting in this hall, have a greater knowledge of the conditions of life under which we exist than has an American Indian or a Hottentot? ... The savage knows incomparably more ... The increasing intellectualization and rationalization do *not*, therefore, indicate an increased and general knowledge of the conditions under which one lives.

The specialist is not only unaware of the general "conditions of life," of "the conditions under which one lives." He is even unaware of the particular conditions of his profession, of the conditions under which he produces science. He is typically unaware of the social roots of objectivity and social "facts":

> If the notion that those standpoints can be derived from the 'facts themselves' continually recurs, it is due to the naive self-deception of the specialist who is unaware that it is due to the evaluative ideas with which he unconsciously approaches his subject matter, that he has selected from an absolute infinity a tiny portion with the study of which he *concerns* himself.[35]

It is these evaluative ideas, Weber insists, that "decide the 'conception' of a whole epoch," what is "significant or insignificant, 'important' or 'unimportant'" in our objects of inquiry.

> All research in the cultural sciences in an age of specialization ... will consider the analysis of the data as an end in itself. It will discontinue assessing the value of the individual facts in terms of their relationships to ultimate value-ideas. Indeed, it will lose its awareness of its ultimate rootedness in the value-ideas in general.

As Simmel put it (Simmel, 1978, p. 231; emphasis added):

> With increasing competition and increasing division of labour, the purposes of life become harder to attain; that is, they require an ever-increasing infrastructure of means. *A larger proportion of civilized man remains forever enslaved, in every sense of the word, in the interest in technics.* The conditions on which the realization of the ultimate object depends claim their attention, and they concentrate their strength on them, so that every real purpose completely disappears from consciousness. Indeed, they are often denied.

The end of the road is the one-dimensional man, where the depth of scholarship is as flat as a Romanesque mosaic. Beware of *the* expert who has lost all relations between threads of knowledge. And nothing is more insidious, nothing more dangerous (and yet, potentially, so very rewarding) than large-scale, long-term research projects. May this very journey from words to numbers serve as a reminder of both the good and the bad. The sequence of purposes, in these projects, the relationship between short-term means and long-term ends can become dangerously blurred, the sight of any end goal lost in too far a distance.

No doubt, exposure to the different points of view that come from traveling helps to relativize one's own position (and to write and rewrite one's biography), to construct Berger's critical sociological consciousness. "Travelling ought ... to teach ... distrust," wrote Darwin as a final remark to his *Voyage of the Beagle* (1989, p. 377). But travel is not the only form of rupture. The "social history of problems" – Foucault's archeology of knowledge or Gadamer's and Wimsatt and Beardsley's history of words – is, for Bourdieu, "one of the most powerful instruments of rupture" (Bourdieu and Wacquant, 1992, p. 238). For Marcuse, as well, the only way for critical sociology to transcend the limits of everyday language, is the history of words. Because people's language is also "the language of their masters ... Thus, they do not only express *themselves*, their own knowledge, feelings, and aspirations, but also something other than themselves."[36] Historicizing concepts "uncovers the *history* in everyday speech as a hidden dimension of meaning – the rule of society of its language." Such a historical analysis would uncover the struggles that, before the battle was over, closed the meaning of a noun against further inspection, closed "the universe of discourse ... against any other discourse which is not on its own terms," "made [the noun] immune against contradiction," fixed "the meaning in the recipient's mind" so that no "essentially different (and possibly true) explications of the noun" become possible. Historical consciousness is essentially critical thought. "Remembrance of the past may give rise to dangerous insights." It unveils "the subversive contents of memory ... [I]t projects the limits and the alternatives."

We have uncovered many meanings of the word "method" in this book. But method is also this way of searching deep into Augustine's "huge court of my memory," "these fields and spacious palaces of my memory," "those innumerable fields, and dens, and caves of my memory, innumerably full of innumerable kinds of things." Method, in *this* meaning, is a way of searching into one's past, a discipline's past, and society's past. The relational view of sociology that I have embraced in this book is a relation of present to past, of biography and history. And that view is a critical view. The antiquarian interest that has informed my quest throughout this book has its roots in that view of scientific knowledge. "History thus conceived," Bourdieu continues, "is inspired not by an antiquarian interest but by a will to understand why and how one understands. To avoid becoming the object of the problems that you take as your object, you must retrace the history of the *emergence* of these problems, of their progressive constitution."[37] For Gadamer, "a work of art never completely lose[s] the trace of its original function"; "the picture contains an indissoluble connection with its world" (Gadamer, 1997, pp. 120, 144). And if that is true of art, it is all the more true of science. My attempt to step outside history, my talking to you, reader of 2520, has landed me right back into history, into my own times, into ongoing current disciplinary debates, ongoing current concerns, ongoing current ways of seeing. Collingwood expressed that idea in a beautiful passage, quite appropriately at the end of a section of the book titled *The Historical Imagination* (1946, p. 248; emphasis added):

> This is not an argument for historical scepticism. It is only the discovery of a second dimension of historical thought, the history of history: The discovery that the historian himself, together with the here-and-now which forms the total body of evidence available to him, is a part of the process he is studying, has his own place in that process, and can see it only from the *point of view* which at this present moment he occupies within it.

And for all I know, dear reader, you may not even exist in flesh and bone. My appeals to heart and passion, to aesthetics and self-reflection are lost on you, an artificial intelligence machine who has not only solved, once and for all, many of the thorny issues involved in going from words to numbers, but even many of the thorny issues involved in "what it means to be a man" (or a woman). But this, dear AI machine, this "you'll never, you'll never know. You'll never, never know" (10,000 Maniacs, 1992, "Stockton Gala Days").

Origin and Origin.ality: Limits to Innovation[38]

So that was our voyage, which, in truth, if one considers that we sailed about seventy-three degrees, or about two thousand French leagues north-south, will not be regarded as one of the shortest. But to give honor where it is due, does it compare to the voyage of that excellent pilot, the Spaniard Juan Sebastián del Cano? (de Léry, 1990, p. 216)

The year was 1558. The writer was the French Huguenot Jean de Léry. He had just made a most adventurous return voyage to France from "the land of Brazil, otherwise called America," during which he had suffered "extreme famine, tempests, and other dangers."[39] De Léry's account of his experience in Brazil well deserves Lévi-Strauss's high praises as a "masterpiece of anthropological literature" – "in my pocket I carried Jean de Léry, the anthropologist's breviary," Lévi-Strauss tells us in his *Tristes Tropiques*, another account of an adventurous voyage to Brazil, another masterpiece of anthropological literature (1992, pp. 83, 81). But de Léry's voyage itself is certainly not worth recording in the annals of the voyages of discovery. By 1558, such transoceanic voyages had become routine occurrences (see Chaunu and Chaunu, 1955, Vol. VI, Tome VI). De Léry got it right when he gave honor where it was due, to the man who had brought back Magellan's ship in 1522, after its captain's death, in the first voyage around the globe.

But what about our journey from words to numbers? Was that a small or big accomplishment? And compared to what? To other ways of looking at texts? Content analysis? Discourse analysis? In the lack of such clear-cut standards as miles and months traveled, perhaps it is best to refrain from insidious comparisons. But the problem of originality remains.

"Let us be original," wrote Guy de Maupassant in a letter of January 17, 1877, "whatever the nature of our talent may be (not to confuse original with bizarre), let us be the *Origin* of something. What? I don't care what, as long as it is beautiful and that it is not part of a definite tradition" (Maupassant, 1938, p. 224; emphasis in the original). Original, then, as "the origin of something," and original as both "beautiful" and "not part of a definite tradition."

Only in the most trivial sense can we claim to be the origin of something: Producing something, such as this book that you have been kind enough to read

– I hate to think that I am talking to myself at this very moment; reader, human or AI machine as you may be, you are still there, aren't you? To go back to Temple Grandin, the autistic scientist who confessed to Oliver Sacks: "I'm not interested in power, or piles of money. I want to leave something behind" (Sacks, 1995, p. 282). Yet, in the short-run, power does help those who want to leave something behind, to be the origin of something, to get their message across, to focus the debate upon their work, to boost their citation index. C. Wright Mills (1959, p. 103) described the "academic entrepreneurs" whose "academic reputations rest upon their academic power." For as long as these "academic entrepreneurs" are alive, they can count on their work being "the origin of something." After all, "they are the members of The Committee; they are on The Board of Directors; they can get you the job, the trip, the research grant" (Mills, 1959, p. 103). In the long run, leaving "something behind" ... may be a different story. But "in the long run we are all dead," John Maynard Keynes said. Even a book on a library shelf is as dead as we all eventually are *unless* a reader picks it up. No doubt, our immortality lies in the hands of future generations, in *your* hands, reader, particularly if you are a "professional" critic, as Frye (1957, p. 4) or Alexander (1987) tell us. So, whether we are the origin of something, only time can tell. This may be a painful fact to acknowledge for the seeker of originality but: "Success or failure, whether in specific investigations or in an entire career may be almost accidental, with chance a major factor ... success may be determined by forces ... outside ... creative capacity or ... willingness to work hard."[40] By now we know that a narrative sentence is given its importance by a second narrative sentence at a later time.

The first view of originality – originality as the origin of something – seems to leave us at the mercy of almighty critics and capricious history. Short of renouncing our calling and becoming academic entrepreneurs, there is not much we can do to take charge of our own destiny. But what about Maupassant's second view of originality – originality as a break with the past, as "work recognized as distinct from that of other men" (Ruskin, 1903, Vol. 22, p. 145)? T. S. Eliot, in a (now) *classic* essay, questioned "our tendency to insist, when we praise a poet, upon those aspects of his work in which *he least resembles anyone else.* ... We dwell with satisfaction upon the poet's *difference from his predecessors*, especially his immediate predecessors ..." (Eliot, 1975, pp. 37, 38; emphasis added). " "The poet ... must be quite aware of the obvious fact that *art never improves* ..." (Eliot, 1975, p. 39; emphasis added). Furthermore, one cannot avoid being "part of a definite tradition"; poetry is "a living whole of all the poetry that has ever been written."[41] Italo Calvino (1991, pp. 13–14) expressed a similar idea in one of the fourteen propositions that characterize a "classic." "Classics are those books that come to us bearing the traces of the readings that have preceded them and leaving behind them traces in the culture or cultures that they traverse." "Classic," Calvino continued, "is what tends to relegate the up-to-date last-minute information to background noise but that, at the same time, cannot do without that noise" (Calvino, 1991, p. 18).

But "if art never improves" and poets and artists can never step outside a tradition, what about science? What about us, social *scientists?* It is science's hallmark, Merton argued, that it should improve (Merton, 1968, pp. 27–30). And scientific improvement implies that past scientific work quickly becomes obsolete, that scientific discoveries are constantly outdated and surpassed by new discoveries. "Classics" have no place in the sciences. The social scientists' "uncritical reverence toward almost any statement made by illustrious ancestors" places a misguided emphasis on the old-fashioned artistic roots of social science, rather than on its scientific vocation; it is a pathological response to the pressure of science (Merton, 1968, p. 30).[42] Such reverence only fosters erudition rather than originality, an emphasis on exegesis of classic texts, a conflation of "the systematics of sociological theory with its history"; all deplorable tendencies in sociology (Merton, 1968, p. 29).

In attempting to link art and science, I may have betrayed the scientific calling of the discipline, developing "deviant roles." Perhaps, like "most sociologists," I have "succumbed" to the cross-pressures that pull us between art and science (see Alexander, 1987, p. 13). I have clearly been unable to "adapt to these pressures by acting wholly the scientific role" (Merton, 1968, p. 29). I did reach the numbers, all the while longing for the words.

"Originality," Merton (1973, pp. 302, 305) continues, is "a major institutional goal of modern science, at times the paramount one." And with the institutional need for originality comes the individual need for recognition. But this way, "the institution of science ... incorporates potentially incompatible values: Among them, the value of originality ... leads scientists to want their priority to be recognized, and the value of humility ... leads them to insist on how little they have been able to accomplish." Darwin agonizes, in his personal correspondence, over this inner need for recognition. "I wish I could set less value on the bauble fame, either present or posthumous, than I do." "It is miserable in me to care at all about priorities."[43] If the dilemma of sociology as art or science brings out its specific pathological forms of deviance and maladaptation, so does this dilemma between originality and humility.[44]

"In the organized competition to contribute to man's scientific knowledge the race *is* to the swift, to him who gets there first with his contribution in hand" (Merton, 1973, p. 302; emphasis in the original). It helps, to get there first, to approach problems from a completely different perspective. But that, in itself, is no small feat, prisoners as we are of mental categories and cultural forms that make it difficult to see the world in any other way. So, the advice to the young scientist, really, should be: "Keep away from discursive communities, where similar ways of seeing give us the comfort of the familiar, but deprive us of the ultimate prize of science: innovation"; "traverse disciplinary lines"; "don't travel close to home" ... Yet, one ought to be aware that longer journeys are also the most risky and dangerous. In any case, to get there first, implies that there is a second, and a third ... and over that, we have little control.

So, in the end, what is my contribution? The breach of academic writing? The use of dialogues, the authorial voice, the acknowledgment of the presence of the reader, the narrative strategies? These are hardly new. Whatever Merton's views on mixing art with science – we can always turn to Nisbet for support – these strategies are part of twentieth-century literary experimentation with language and genres, in a tradition that is centuries old, from Plato, to Cicero, to the Italian Renaissance rediscovery of the genre.[45] Is my contribution, then, the "thin thread," my way of going from words to numbers? There as well, I am afraid, I can make no claim to originality. I have discovered nothing new. A good tinkerer (Lévi-Strauss's *bricoleur*; 1972, pp. 16–36), in putting together my machine, I searched through the academic scrapyards in this archeology of knowledge and just grabbed pieces here and there with the curiosity of an antiquarian seeking answers to questions of the present, rather than the past. The trickle of innovation in going from words to numbers that I have traced in this book through the "precursors" highlights each contribution in a line of other contributions. Behind each word, there is a "worlde of wordes." I am simply last in line. As Bernard de Chartres put it: "We are but midgets on the shoulders of giants" – an epigram Newton later made his own.[46] And I wouldn't even say that I "can see farther," as Bernard has it. Worse yet, this antiquarian curiosity of mine does not bid well for true originality. Listen to what Coser wrote of von Wiese's use of Simmel's formal method (Coser, 1965, p. 25; emphasis added):

> In this attempt [by von Wiese] to systematize Simmel's thought much of the sparkle and brilliance of his approach was lost. Formal sociology became *formalistic sociology* and the passion for cataloging and codifying social processes led to higher *sociological bookkeeping* rather than to fruitful investigation.

Even popular culture does not associate accountancy with brilliancy. In light of this critique, my own involvement in playing critic/God, in bringing von Wiese back to life, in putting his contributions under the spotlight, may seem nothing more than a desperate attempt to save my own skin of a sociological bookkeeper, the pedantic ass exposed by Bruno. Von Wiese himself seems to have had no illusion about the nature of his work, when he wrote that he had "purposely attempted to lay down a plan of classification with nothing less than scholastic pedantry" (von Wiese, 1932, p. 132). And to von Wiese's pedantry of classification I have added one of my own: the pedantry of (borrowed) erudition.[47]

So, where does this leave us? Was it a big or a small voyage, this voyage of discovery from words to numbers? "How far I may have succeeded," wrote Captain James Cook in a letter to the British Admiralty on March 22, 1775, at the end of his second voyage of discovery in the South Pacific, "I submit to their Lordships better judgment" (Cook, 1961, Vol. II, p. 693). Like Cook, let me submit that question to the reader's better judgement and move on.

"Murmure Againste Me"

Cornelius Agrippa, in the Preface to his *Of the Vanitie and Uncertaintie of Artes and Sciences* published in London in 1575, wrote:

> Cornelius Agrippa to the Reader
>
> …Will not this my enterprise (studious Reader) seeme unto thee valiant and adventurous, and almost comparable to the attemptes of Hercules, to take up weapons against all that Giaunts force of Sciences and Artes, and to chalenge into the field all these most hardie hunters of Artes and Sciences. The statelinesse of the Doctours, the learning of the Practicers, the authoritie of the Writers, the endeavours of the Bachelours, the enuie of all the Scholars, and the sedition of the Handicraftes men, will murmure againste me.

Will my enterprise similarly seem to you, studious reader, an attempt to take up weapons against *all* the giants in the sciences *and* the arts? Have I succeeded in displeasing everyone? Will C. Wright Mills's "sunshine moralists" murmur against me for having deprived them of the "happy ending" to which Hollywood-style films have accustomed them? Will the proponents of a quantitative approach to the social sciences murmur against me for investigating into the seamy side of their "noble dream?" Will qualitative scholars of any discipline murmur against me for even seriously considering this enterprise of quantifying quality, of performing an alchemic transformation of words into numbers? And will not historians be confirmed in their fear that social scientists (and, perhaps, even those historians who have succumbed to the lures of the social sciences) harness portentous research apparatuses, only to forget in this process the real historical questions? Whatever new or different did I have to say about the rise of Italian fascism?

Perhaps. But I doubt you are that kind of reader. You are *not* Agrippa's "studious reader." You are more like Calvino's clever reader of *If on a Winter's Night a Traveler*, the one who does not "expect anything in particular from this particular book."[48] You crave puzzles, charades, and brain teasers of all kinds (all the more so if you really are an AI machine). You are the sort of reader who loves being taken by surprise (albeit, after a temporary moment of disappointment, directed more at yourself, for not having been able to double guess the author). You would have closed this book many chapters ago, had you anticipated all its twists and turns. You are not bothered, one way or the other, by what I have to say about the originality of my work – the avid reader you are, you are all too familiar with the gamut of authors' rhetorical devices to exalt their work while declaring *propter infirmitatem*. You make up your own mind about what is and what is not original. You are all too aware that the most exciting (and frightening) developments in science at the turn of the second millennium – genetic research – come from that same tradition of natural history that spent centuries in the attempt to classify the natural world. Who knows where Durkheim's classification of suicides, or Simmel's, Weber's, von Wiese's classification of social relations will lead us? And, above all, you have a good sense of humor – "for it is the decay of humour that kills," assures us Huizinga (1949, p. 207). For Berger, "a sense of the comic in man's social carnival," including "that particular corner of the social carnival that we call scholarship," is part of the "sociological understanding."[49] Pirandello seems to think differently when he draws a sharp contrast between the sociologist and the humorist. "While the sociologist describes social life as it results from external observations," wrote Pirandello in his essay on *Humour* (1986, p. 156), "the humorist ... reveals how appearances are profoundly different." If so, the transgressive subversion of science of the second part of the journey, this childish taking apart a toy so painfully built, is not likely to get any sympathy from fellow sociologists. Of them, I beg forgiveness. But humor may just be my only way out of the dilemma between building and destroying, construction and deconstruction, my way of saying "Reader, I was just joking!" – hardly a fun game, if we are to believe Pirandello, for whom humor is "the result of a bitter experience with life and men."[50] Indeed, this playful and perhaps irreverent armchair journey in science, from words to numbers, has run parallel to more painful and humiliating journeys of mine – all too real – across countries and institutions, each new encounter bringing its peculiar way of seeing. And Pirandello is right again in believing that the humorist's special way of seeing things and their contrary, the outside and the inside, the body and its shadow, is the result of that "special activity of reflection"[51] – reflection upon those "bitter experiences," reconciling points of view, in one's attempt to find a home among strangers, one's place among different cultures, the "two" cultures, in particular (Snow, 1993). The break with tradition is necessarily self-reflexive. It implies an explicit rejection of the canon, a rejection of discipline in the name of freedom.

And yet that freedom is limited. Play or journey, the break with the past, adventure and transgression, are bound by time and space – "an intermezzo, an *interlude*" (Huizinga, 1949, p. 9). In play, "every child knows perfectly well that he is "only pretending," or that it was "only for fun" (Huizinga, 1949, p. 8). And unless we approach journeys in the way of St. Brendan[52] and other medieval Irish monks forever wondering in pilgrimages with no end, a journey implies a return home, an end to adventure. A scientific journey is doubly limiting, because "modern science, so long as it adheres to the strict demands of accuracy and veracity, is far less liable to fall into play" (Huizinga, 1949, p. 204). Only art enjoys complete freedom. "In the origination, as in the contemplation, of its creations," Hegel wrote in his *Introductory Lectures on Aesthetics*,[53] "we appear to escape wholly from the fetters of rule and regularity. ... Science, on the contrary ..."

So armed with a sense of humor, and persecuted by self-reflection and beauty – humor, don't forget, belongs to the realm of the aesthetics, and through beauty we rise to immortality like "rungs in a ladder" – we can perhaps appreciate that journeys, particularly long and difficult journeys, no doubt undertaken in the name of immortality, rarely end in the way we anticipate. Consider perhaps the most famous of all voyages: Christopher Columbus's first voyage to the Americas. The great admiral had *almost* made it back from a journey that was to change the course of history when he met a terrible storm at the Azores. Between Tuesday, February 12th and Thursday the 14th 1493, day after day, "the wind increased, the sea was most tremendous ... the cross sea grew more and more terrible ..." (Columbus, 1969, pp. 187–8). "All expecting to be lost, so furious was the rage of the hurricane" and "to be crushed" by the tremendous waves (Columbus, 1969, pp. 189, 188),

> the Admiral ordered that lots should be cast for one of them to go on a pilgrimage to St. Mary of Guadalupe and carry a wax taper of five pounds weight; he caused them all to take an oath that the one on whom the lot fell should perform the pilgrimage. For this purpose as many peas were selected as there were persons on board, one of them was marked with a cross, and the whole shaken together in a cap. The first who put his hand in was the Admiral, and he drew the crossed pea. So the lot fell upon him, and he looked upon himself as bound to accomplish the pilgrimage. Another lot was taken for a pilgrimage to St. Mary of Loretto ... A third lot was determined upon, for the selection of a person who should watch a whole night in St. Clara de Moguer ... After this, he and all the crew made a vow to go in procession, clothed in penitential garments to the first church dedicated to Our Lady which they should meet with on arriving at land ... (Columbus, 1969, pp. 188–9) ["barefoot and in their shirts," as stated in the account left to us by the Admiral's son Hernando; Columbus, 1969, p. 102)]

Columbus saw fame and glory slip through his fingers. Like later Protestants, he anxiously looked for signs of doom or salvation. Marco Polo (1955, p. 316) had concluded his travel book *Il Milione* with the words: "It was God's will that I should return, so that it could be known the things that are in the world." The admiral, who had read Polo's work – we have an extant copy annotated by Columbus in his own hand – similarly asked: How could "our Lord suffer them to perish ... and not allow the important information they were carrying to the King and Queen to be lost" (Columbus, 1969, pp. 189–90)? Why Polo and not him? What sins had he committed? Columbus was too religious to believe with Plato that "man is made God's plaything" (*Laws*, VII, 803, 1963). Had it been God's design to prevent this great discovery, why would He have "enabled him to conquer all his adversities and hindrances in Castile" (Columbus, 1969, p. 190)? Why would He have given him the strength to win over a mutinous crew during the outward journey? Las Casas's summary of Columbus's own navigation diary (now lost) gives us a most powerful portrayal of Columbus's inner feelings in those tremendous hours. "The apprehensions and the anguish of his mind would not allow him to rest" for several days (Columbus, 1969, pp. 190–1). Here is a man concerned not so much for his own life as for that of his crew and for "the state of his two sons whom he had left at their studies in Cordova ... left orphans in a foreign land" (Columbus, 1969, p. 191). More to the point, Las Casas tells us, the admiral

> seems to have felt the most anxious desire to have his great discovery known, so that the world might be convinced the assertions made by him had been correct, and that he had accomplished what he professed himself able to do; *the thought of this not being done, gave him the greatest inquietude, and he was perpetually in apprehensions as the smallest trifle might defeat his whole undertaking.* (Columbus, 1969, p. 190; emphasis added)

In a disparate attempt to let the world know "that Our Lord had granted success to the enterprise in the discovery of the Indies," he wrote upon parchment an account of his voyage, "as full as possible." "The parchment was rolled up in a waxed cloth, and well tied; a large wooden cask being then produced, he placed it within, and threw it into the sea, none of the crew knowing what it was, but all taking it for some act of devotion" (Columbus, 1969, p. 191).

On Monday, February 18, 1493, they finally land on the island of St. Mary in the Azores. "The inhabitants ... declared that they had never witnessed a storm like that which had endured for fifteen days past, and wondered how the Spaniards had escaped" (Columbus, 1969, p. 193). The next day, Columbus, mindful of "the vow they had made during the storm," sends half of his crew on pilgrimage. Barefoot and in shirt sleeves as they are, the sailors/pilgrims are ambushed by the Portuguese, Spain's rivals in oceanic explorations, literally caught with their pants down! After more difficulties, Columbus manages to negotiate with the Portuguese Captain the release of his men. He takes again to the sea for the last short stretch of navigation, back to an anticipated triumphant arrival in Seville. He can hardly wait.

But a most capricious destiny is not done playing with the great admiral. On Wednesday, February 27, Columbus meets once again with "contrary wind and heavy sea" (Columbus, 1969, p. 201). "He was much afflicted," Las Casas annotates, "at meeting with such a storm so near home" (Columbus, 1969, p. 201). Once again, the storm does not seem to abate for days ("such a stormy winter had never been known," he would be told upon landing; Columbus, 1969, p. 202). The *Niña* was "near meeting with destruction from the cross sea, the fury of the wind, which seemed to carry them up to the sky" (Columbus, 1969, pp. 201–2). The crew renews to the Lord vows of pilgrimage and fasting. And the Lord listens, but delivers them to a "lonely place" near Lisbon, into the land of the king of Portugal whom Columbus had first approached in vain in search of patronage for his dreams. Columbus worries that "some avaricious persons, imagining that the vessel contained much gold might in that lonely place attempt some deed of violence" (Columbus, 1969, p. 203). Columbus, no doubt, worries about what may happen to him when he is summoned to the court of the king of Portugal. After all, Portuguese historian Joam de Barros (1496–1570) in his *Asia* tells us that "many of the nobles ... offered [the king] to prevent his return to Castile by assassinating him."[54]

You do need a good sense of humor to appreciate the irony of the ending to such a momentous journey!

Farewell to the Reader

With Columbus's ritual of the pilgrimage, "as it is the custom of sailors," assures us Amerigo Vespucci,[55] voyages of pilgrimage and discovery, the metaphoric threads of this book, come together at last. And with voyages of discovery ending in voyages of pilgrimage, here comes to an end my own voyage from words to numbers. You may not trust this solemn declaration of mine. After all, I have announced the end of the journey too many times. In a voyage from words to numbers, it seemed that the voyage was over when we got to the numbers, at the end of Part 1. Instead, in Chapters 4 and 5, I started retracing our steps, questioning every step and turn, only to come to a safe landing again in Chapter 6. And yet, we have now discovered, we may have landed altogether in the wrong place – Columbus *still* believed that he had landed in India sailing westward, when he reached the coasts of America, as it had been the purpose of his voyage. De Léry (1990, pp. 213–14) tells us of a similar distrust by crews and passengers at the announcement "Land! Land!"

> By His [God's] grace ... the twenty-fourth day of that month of May [1558] ... we sighted Lower Brittany. However, the pilot had deceived us so many times, showing us passing clouds instead of land, that although the sailor in the crow's nest cried out two or three times, 'Land! Land!' we still thought that it was all a hoax.

But this *is* the end of our journey – time, not leagues, the measure of distance traveled ("we had sailed fourteen thousand four hundred and sixty leagues, and completed the circuit of the world from east to west," tells us Pigafetta [1969, p. 148]). Twenty years spent on this road from words to numbers: Three years of preparation (we know that Columbus had studied extensively the available maps of the world before embarking upon his voyages and Vasco da Gama was equipped with the most up-to-date maps and scientific equipment of the time in his first voyage round Africa to India); five years of data collection; three years of data analysis. Even the final act of the journey – writing this fair account of what I saw along the way – took several more years of hard work. I was not as lucky (or clever) as John Bunyan who wrote in the preface to his *The Pilgrim's Progress,* an immensely popular book: "Thus, I set pen to paper with delight, /

And *quickly* had my thoughts in black and white. / ... / *Still as I pulled it came,* and so I penned / It down, until it came at last to be / For length and breadth the bigness which you see" (Bunyan, 1965, p. 4; emphasis added). True to the alchemists' dictum *omne omne est* – everything is everything – I could have pulled words for ever, more words behind each word, "a worlde of wordes" for each word, in a unity of knowledge lost in the archeology of knowledge. That is the danger of a relational view of the world. As Locke warned: "The *nature* therefore *of Relation*, consists in the referring, or comparing two things, one to another; ... There is *no one thing ... which is not capable of almost an infinite number of* Considerations, in reference to other things" (Locke, II, XXV, 7, 31–4; 1975, p. 321; emphasis in the original).

So, I stopped pulling. I stopped journeying – the thought of having to be on the road again a daunting prospect for me at the moment, in this end of a journey as the beginning of a new one. "I am tired of writing about battles," wrote Bernal Díaz (1963, p. 392), "and was even more tired when I had to take part in them, and my readers may well be tired of my prolixity. For ninety-three days we were fighting continuously." He remembers the deafening sound of silence after victory.

> [A]ll we soldiers became as deaf as if all the bells in a belfry had been ringing and had then suddenly stopped. ... during the whole ninety-three days of our siege of the capital, Mexican captains were yelling and shouting night and day ... Then there was the unceasing sound of their accursed drums and trumpets, and their melancholy kettle-drums in the shrines and on their temple towers. Both day and night the din was so great that we could hardly hear one another speak. But after Guatemoc's capture, all the shouting and the other noises ceased ... (Díaz, 1963, pp. 404–5)

And he remembers the nauseating stench of victory.

> All the houses and stockades in the lake were full of heads and corpses. ... We could not walk without treading on the bodies and heads of dead Indians. ... Indeed, the stench was so bad that no one could endure it ... (Díaz, 1963, p. 405)

"We soldiers," of course, "gained no profit, but plenty of arrows ... I had never felt such fear" (Díaz, 1963, pp. 406, 408). Pigafetta, aboard Magellan's ship in the first circumnavigation of the globe, having just been spared death by scurvy in the "three months and twenty days ... four thousand leagues across the Pacific Sea," fearing they had all been lost "in this very great sea," annotated in his diary: "I believe that *nevermore will any man undertake to make such a voyage*" (Pigafetta, 1969, p. 57; emphasis added). He was wrong, of course. Vespucci came closer to the mark when he wrote to Piero Soderini after his fourth voyage of "discovery of new lands":

> And in 77 days, after so many fatigues and dangers, we entered in this arbor [Lisbon] in the day of June 28 1504, thank God. Where we were well received and beyond belief, because the entire city thought we had gotten lost ... At the present I am here in Lisbon and I do not know what the king will want to do of me, because I would really want to rest. (Vespucci, 1957, pp. 86–7, lines 1376–85)

Alchemists seem to feel no differently at the end of their quest for the philosophers' stone, if we are to believe Thomas Aquinas (1996, p. 53).

> You will find in books many other operations, almost an infinite number, of them, but confused and leading men to error and to financial losses; these books, in particular, provide false guidelines for preparations about which it would take me too long to talk. ... This work is true and perfect, but great labor and stench I had to endure, and I suffer from the infirmity of the body, that in no way would I want to undertake this work again unless compelled by necessity.

This work of mine is neither true nor perfect. And despite some financial losses and great labor (not to mention career disasters), I had to endure no scurvy, no stench, and no arrows. Alchemist or voyager, I am a lucky man after all; all the luckier, for having successfully completed a journey most thought impossible, for still being alive, when most feared I had been lost at sea, for having been able to count on many friends and supporters during the crossing, and for not having lost sight of the entire "sequence of purposes," despite so long a journey. As the German pilgrim Arnold von Harff wrote at the end of his pilgrimage's account (von Harff, 1946, p. 295):

> Praise be to God the Almighty Father, the Son, and the Holy Ghost that I have completed these pilgrimages in good health, returning to Coellen on St. Martin's eve, as one writes after the birth of Christ 1499, and fulfilling the vow that I made at my departure to seek out again the Three Kings. May they preserve us from harm. *Amen.*

With these words of a good Christian – "science ... can afford no guidance for the life of man," only religion can[56] – my own journey ends where it began: with words. And as we part ways, do fare well, most kind of readers, faithful companion of travel transgressions and dreams. At least, "farewell if thou meane well; els fare as ill, as thou wishest me to fare."[57]

Ricorditi di me. Remember me.

Here ends the book of Roberto Franzosi.

Ad Anna Giulia,
con questo libro nata e cresciuta insieme.

Ulisse

Nella mia giovinezza ho navigato
lungo le coste dalmate. Isolotti
a fior d'onda emergevano, ove raro
un uccello sostava intento a prede,
coperti d'alghe, scivolosi, al sole
belli come smeraldi. Quando l'alta
marea e la notte li annullava, vele
sottovento sbandavano più al largo,
per fuggirne l'insidia. Oggi il mio regno
è quella terra di nessuno. Il porto
accende ad altri i suoi lumi; me al largo
sospinge ancora il non domato spirito,
e della vita il doloroso amore.

Umberto Saba (From *Mediterranee*, 1963)

In my youth I sailed along the Dalmatian coasts. Islets, where rare birds stopped
to prey, covered with algae, slippery and in the sun as beautiful as emeralds,
emerged from the wave crest. When the high tide and the night annulled them,
leeward sails kept afar to avoid their danger. Today, my kingdom is that no
man's land. For others, the harbor turns on its lights; me – the untamed spirit and
the painful love of life still pushes out to sea. (My translation)

Appendix: A Complete Story Grammar for the Collection of Sociohistorical Data from Text Sources on Protest and Violent Events

<dispute>	→	{<event>} [<comment>] {<document key>}
<document key>	→	<newspaper name> <date> <page> [<page title>] <column> <position in column>
<newspaper name>	→	(*New York Times* | *Il Lavoro* | ...)
<date>	→	<definite date>
<page>	→	<digit> <digit>
<page title>	→	(*Cronaca di Genova* | *Pagine economiche* | ...)
<column>	→	<digit> <digit>
<position in column>	→	<digit> <digit>
<event>	→	{<semantic triplet>} [<comment>] {<document key>}
<semantic triplet>	→	{<subject>} {<action>} [{<object>}] [<comment>] {<document key>}
<subject>	→	<actor> <semantic role> [{<actor modifier>}] [<comment>] {<document key>}
<actor>	→	<individual> | <set of individuals> | <institution>
<individual>	→	<improper name> [<proper name>] [<comment>] {<document key>}
<improper name>	→	(mayor | president | ...)
<proper name>	→	(Agnelli | Giolitti | Mussolini | ...)
<set of individuals>	→	(group | mob | ...)
<semantic role>	→	(agent | patient | beneficiary | ...)
<actor modifiers>	→	[{<type>}] {<organization>} <number> {<space>} [<comment>] {<document key>}
<type>	→	(male | young | black | skilled | ...)

\<organization\>	→	\<simple organization\> \<complex organization\> [\<comment\>] {\<document key\>}
\<simple organization\>	→	(FIAT | Pirelli | Romeo | …)
\<complex organization\>	→	[\<number of units\>] \<improper name of unit\> [\<level of aggregation\>] [\<number of individuals in unit\>] [\<location of unit\>]
	→	\<proper name of unit\> [\<level of aggregation\>] [\<number of individuals in unit\>] [\<location of unit\>]
\<number of units\>	→	\<quantitative expression\>
\<improper name of unit\>	→	(assembling | painting | automobile | mechanic | …)
\<proper name of unit\>	→	(Mirafiori | Bicocca | …)
\<level of aggregation\>	→	(shop | office | plant | department | firm | division | economic sector | …)
\<number of individuals in unit\>	→	\<quantitative expression\>
\<location of unit\>	→	\<space\>
\<space\>	→	\<territory\> | \<city\> [\<comment\>]
\<territory\>	→	{[\<quantitative expression\> \<improper name of territory\>] [{\<proper name of territory\>}]}
\<improper name of territory\>	→	(state | county | …)
\<proper name of territory\>	→	\<name of non-administrative unit\> | \<name of administrative unit\>
\<name of non-administrative unit\>	→	(North | North-East | South | …)
\<name of administrative unit\>	→	\<state\> | \<county\> | \<commune\> | …
\<state\>	→	(Wisconsin | Michigan | …)
\<county\>	→	(Dane | Door | …)
\<commune\>	→	(Madison | Green Bay | …)
\<city\>	→	\<commune\> [\<neighborhood\>] [\<street/square\>] [\<in front of …\>]
\<neighborhood\>	→	(Park Heights | Roland | …)
\<street\>	→	(State | Columbus | …)
\<number\>	→	\<quantitative expression\> [\<comment\>] {\<document key\>}
\<quantitative expression\>	→	\<single value\> | \<range\>
\<qualifier\>	→	(probably | circa | about | …)
\<single value\>	→	\<comparative\> & \<numeral\> | \<vague quantifier\>

<comparative>	→	(more than | less than | at least | ...)
<numeral>	→	{<digit>}
<digit>	→	(0 | 1 | 2 | 3 | ... | 9)
<vague quantifier>	→	(tens | hundreds | thousands | millions | ... | few | some | many | several | ...)
<range>	→	<single value> <single value>
<action>	→	<action phrase> [<negation>] [<modality>] [<tense>] [{<action modifier>}] [<comment>] {<document key>}
<action phrase>	→	(strike | demonstrate | hand out leaflets | ...)
<negation>	→	(not)
<modality>	→	(can | could | may | might | will | would | shall | should | must | ought)
<tense>	→	(past | present | future)
<action modifiers>	→	[{<time>}] [{<space>}] [<modality>] [{<case>}] [{<type>}] [{<instrument>}] [{<reason>}] [{<outcome>}] [{<duration>}] [<number>] [<comment>] {<document key>}
<time>	→	[<date>] [<time of day>]
<date>	→	<definite date> | <indefinite date>
<definite date>	→	[<day>] [<month>] [<year>]
<day>	→	<digit> [<digit>] | <day word>
<day word>	→	(Monday | Tuesday | ... | Sunday)
<month>	→	<digit> [<digit>] | <month word>
<month word>	→	(January | February | ... | December)
<year>	→	<digit> <digit> [<digit>] [<digit>]
<indefinite date>	→	([<quantitative expression>] [<unit of time>] <temporal qualifier> <temporal direction> <time of reference>) | <other time reference>
<other time reference>	→	(on a market day | ...)
<unit of time>	→	(second | minute | hour | day | ... | time)
<temporal qualifier>	→	(early | mid | late | ...)
<temporal direction>	→	<past> | <future>

<past>	→	<past tense of verb> | <temporal adverb>
<future>	→	<future tense of verb> | <temporal adverb>
<temporal adverb>	→	(ago | before | then | next | after | ...)
<time of reference>	→	<definite date> | <time of another triplet>
<time of another triplet>	→	<time>
<time of day>	→	<definite time of day> | <indefinite time of day>
<definite time of day>	→	[<qualifier>] <hour> <minute>
<hour>	→	<digit> [<digit>]
<minute>	→	<digit> <digit>
<indefinite time of day>	→	[<qualifier>] [<temporal qualifier>] <part of day>
<part of day>	→	(dawn | morning | noon | afternoon | evening | night | ...)
<type>	→	(general | sit-down | ...)
<instrument>	→	(baton | tear gas | letter | horns | ...)
<reason>	→	(economic | union right | ...)
<outcome>	→	(positive | negative | settlement | ...)
<duration>	→	<quantitative expression> <time unit>
<object>	→	(<actor> | <inanimate object> | <implicit object> | <semantic triplet>) <semantic role>
<inanimate object>	→	(factory, road, car, ...)

Notes

Before

1. I am grateful to Jackson Toby for this "Harvard" story.
2. Closer to us, Tilly (1981, p. 34) and Lieberson (1985, pp. 6–12) repeated these warnings with specific reference to a quantitative approach to social reality.
3. Robinson and McKie (1976, p. 233).
4. Tilly (1995a); Franzosi and Centis (1988).
5. In reality, in 1984, I submitted the proposal to the National Science Foundation. The proposal was not funded. With hindsight, and having internalized the norms of the profession, I myself would not have recommended funding: The project was too broad, too ambitious, too "risky," in other words. But the University of Wisconsin Graduate School provided backup funds. David Ward, professor of geography, later Chancellor of the University of Wisconsin-Madison campus, came around to interview the candidates who had submitted proposals, with a characteristic brisk style of a very sharp mind. He quickly went over with me the figures in my budget and raised them considerably, saying that I would need every penny of it and it wouldn't be enough. With my (also characteristic) enthusiasm and lack of realism, I thought I could do twenty projects with that kind of money. I was wrong and David Ward was right, a mistake that would prove to be very, very costly, at least in the short to medium run; thank God, life is long!
6. Lakoff and Johnson (1980, pp. 5, 36, 171; emphasis in the original).
7. Leopardi (1937, p. 497); *Zibaldone*, June 10, 1822, IV, 258, 1: 2–5, 9.
8. Leopardi (1937, p. 497); *Zibaldone*, June 10, 1822, IV, 258, 1: 12–13.
9. Turner and Turner (1978, p. 34). In their work, Turner and Turner apply some of the concepts from the anthropology of van Gennep to the study of pilgrimages. Van Gennep had argued that rites of passage in "primitive" cultures involved a transition between two communities which confer different social roles (for example, rites of passage mark transitions from girl to woman, boy to man, single to married, living to dead). The structure of the rite of passage is a preliminary phase, in which the individuals are prepared for change, ask for the blessings of ancestors, and so on; a liminal phase in which the social and cultural relations defining the community are temporarily abandoned and individuals are in a social space where very unusual rituals and laws apply. This is the phase of transition where the old community is left behind but the new one has not yet been joined. It is often characterized by taboos on certain types of food, communication, physical activity, and so on that would not normally apply to members of any social group in the population at large; finally there is the postliminal period where new social roles are adopted.
10. Cited in Ciliberto (1986, pp. 9, 23) as referring to French composer Pierre Boulez (1975).
11. The title of one of Derrida's essays (Derrida, 1992).
12. On the "laws of genre" see Derrida (1992).
13. Without that creative freedom, our social science works look more and more alike, and are more and more standardized in their format. That is particularly true for journal articles (see Abbott and Barman, 1997).
14. Of course, Mills was hardly the first to embrace this manifesto. Marx, before him, had similarly called for the integration of theory and praxis. Nor, was he to be the last. Both Marxist and feminist historians and social scientists of the 1960s wholeheartedly embraced the manifesto.
15. On Weber's position on methods, see Oakes (1977). Writing in the late nineteenth century, French historians Langlois and Seignobos (1898, p. xi) pointed out in a wonderful early book on historical method "the two dangers of the [methodological] genre: obscurity and banality."
16. References in this paragraph are to an amazing page of Simmel's *Philosophy of Money* (1978,

p. 231; emphasis added).
17. The argument, for instance, was advanced by the Cambridge mathematician E. W. Barnes with regard to theories of gravitation (cited in Feuer, 1995, p. 6).
18. Bourdieu and Wacquant (1992, p. 149).
19. Lévi-Strauss (1992, p. 53) similarly acknowledges his antiquarian spirit.
20. 1811–12, cited in Stern (1970, p. 49).
21. Cited in Sorokin (1956, p. 300).
22. Cited in Laurence (1991, p. 35).
23. Rossi (1960, p. 255); Yates (1992, pp. 365–73).
24. Brooks (1984, pp. 316, 320).
25. The medieval poetics assigned four different levels of meaning in any work of art: literal, allegorical, moral, and anagogic (Frye, 1957, p. 72; see the discussion, pp. 73–128). Meaning is always manifold or "polysemous," as Dante put it. Jean de Meung, the author of the *Romance of the Rose*, warned his readers: "In my words there is a different meaning than what you think, and those who go deeper into the text will find the exact meaning of the narrative" (cited in Hutin, 1991, p. 92). Cesare Ripa's *Iconologia overo Descrittione dell'Imagini universali cavate dall'antichità et da altri luoghi Da Cesare Ripa Perugino* (iconology or the description of the universal images taken from the antiquity and from other places by Cesare Ripa from Perugia; the title varied slightly with the various editions) has left us a rich graphical representation to the complex symbolism of Medieval culture in a set of plates (Ripa, 1971). In each plate, Ripa represented a concept, arranged in alphabetical order by their names (for example, *obedientia, peccatum*). For each concept, he provided a picture and a verbal description of the allegorical figure that embodied the concept, giving the type and color of its clothing and its varied symbolic paraphernalia, along with the reasons why these were chosen (reasons often supported by references to literature). The *Iconologia* was first published in Rome in 1593 and "was received with great enthusiasm" (see Maser's "Introduction" to Ripa, 1971, pp. ix–x). The book continued to be immensely popular even after Ripa's death, as shown by the many editions that followed in France, Germany, and the Netherlands, as well as in Italy. The *Iconologia* became the standard reference work for the representation of allegories, providing examples of how to represent abstract ideas in visual terms. The *Mutus Liber*, another book of great popularity first published in La Rochelle in 1677, was, as the title suggests, a book of figures without words where each figure has several different ways of reading (Hutin, 1991, pp. 83–5).
26. On the death of the author, see Foucault (1977) and Barthes (1977b, 1977c). From there, the idea that texts do not exist in themselves but only in the continuously recreative process of interpretation (albeit in the less individualistic mode of "interpretative communities") spread to literary criticism (for example, see Fish, 1980, pp. 147–80). "It is the reader who 'makes' literature," Fish tells us categorically (1980, p. 11).
27. Cited in Wolff (1950, p. xvii).
28. Schlegel (1967, p. 38) fragment 108 from *Lyceum*. See also fragment 48 (p. 27).
29. Berger (1963, p. 187).
30. C. Wright Mills (1959, p. 78).
31. Cited in Levine (1971, p. xii; emphasis added).
32. Cited in Hutin (1991, p. 49).
33. Lieberson (1985, p. 171).
34. On Hegel's views on prefaces and introductions, see Derrida (1981, pp. 9–31).
35. Paratexts are those texts that accompany the main body of a book: titles, tables of contents, prefaces, prologues, epilogues, and so on (Genette, 1997, pp. 161–236).
36. Genette (1997, p. 197).
37. Cited in Genette (1997, p. 230).
38. Brody (1987); Adorno (1992).
39. Ruskin (1903, Vol. VII, Chapter III "The Rule of the Greatest," p. 230).
40. In the fall of 2003, with research grants from the University of Reading and the University of Trento, and a Windows version of PC-ACE supported by a grant from the Nuffield Foundation, I resumed data collection on the 1919–22 period from *L'Avanti!* and archival material.
41. Intercoder reliability is usually measured through a coefficient of intercoder reliability (see Budd, Thorp and Donohew, 1967, p. 68; for further measures of reliability, see Krippendorff,

1980, pp. 129–54). Intercoder reliability is a problem that affects all content analysis projects; potentially, even the ones that report high coefficients of intercoder reliability (Krippendorff, 1980, p. 74). For this reason, practitioners claim, "reliability in one study should be compared with similar studies" (Budd, Thorp and Donohew, 1967, p. 67). Intercoder reliability also depends upon the way the coding categories have been designed, the type of instructions given to the coders, and the clarity with which the coding rules have been written. Coefficients of intercoder reliability should then be computed for each coding category (Budd, Thorp and Donohew, 1967, p. 67).

42. Thompson (1990, p. 7; emphasis in the original).
43. Columbus (1969, p. 198).
44. Wilkinson (1981a, p. 115).
45. Fragment 8, Schlegel (1967, p. 20).
46. Genette (1997, p. 197; emphasis in the original).
47. de Man (1979, p. 922); on autobiography, see also Lejeune (1989, in particular, pp. 3–30; 1996); Goodwin (1993).
48. Fiske (1990, pp. 62–83); Morley (1992, pp. 18–41); Seaman (1992).

Chapter 1 *"In the Beginning Was the Word"*

1. From *The Gospel according to John* (1:1).
2. The passages have been taken from Mousnier (1970, pp. 97–8), Rudwick (1964, pp. 44–9), Rudé (1959, pp. 73–4), and Thompson (1991, p. 475).
3. Walter William Skeat (1835–1912), the great nineteenth century English etymologist, is the author of *An Etymological Dictionary of the English Language*, which underwent several editions.
4. See the entries for "count" and "recount" in *The Oxford English Dictionary* (Simpson and Weiner, 1989). See also the entry *"conter"* in the *Dictionnaire historique de la langue française* (Rey, 1992) where one reads that the link between the two different meanings of the word *conter* (to count and to narrate) "was often confused in the medieval mind, is the common idea of 'enumerating,' 'drawing up a list'" (Rey, 1992, p. 485). The Italian words *contare* and *raccontare* have a similar etymology from the Latin (see, the book title of Bernardini and De Mauro, 2003)
5. In the fourteenth century, the two verbs *reconter* and *conter* were converted into *raconter* and *compter*.
6. On the two cultures, see Snow (1959) and Bernardini and De Mauro (2003).
7. Definitions taken from Kaplan (1943, p. 230), Janis (1949, p. 55), Kaplan and Goldsen (1949, 83), Berelson (1952, p. 18), Cartwright (1953, p. 424), Stone et al. (1966, p. 5), Krippendorf (1980, p. 21). For a quick summary of definitions, see Holsti (1969, pp. 2–3); Shapiro and Markoff (1997).
8. The Experimental Division had been set up at the beginning of the war in the basement of the Library of Congress in Washington, D.C. The Division was part of the War Communications Research Project sponsored by the Rockefeller Foundation (Lasswell, 1941; Lasswell, Leites, and Associates, 1949, p. v; Berelson, 1952, p. 23). Harold D. Lasswell, then a professor of political science at the University of Chicago, became its director.
9. Lasswell (1941); Willey (1926), a sociologist, talks about "newspaper analysis" (or "press analysis") and so does Woodward (1930, pp. 39–64; 1934).
10. Lasswell (1941); Lasswell (1942); Lasswell and Associates (1942); Lasswell, Geller, and Kaplan (1942). See the volume by Smith, Lasswell, and Casey (1946) for a good compendium of annotated bibliographies.
11. Janis and Fadner (1943), Kaplan (1943).
12. See Lasswell, Leites, and Associates (1949). Individual members of the War Timep. Communication project had already published their work, first as documents of the Experimental Division, then in journals (for example, Janis and Fadner, 1942, 1943, 1949).
13. de Sola Pool (1959); Budd, Thorp, and Donohew (1967); Holsti (1969); Krippendorf (1980); Weber (1990).
14. See the volumes of annotated bibliographies by Smith, Lasswell, and Casey (1946) and

Lasswell, Casey, and Smith (1935).

15. Various government agencies in the United States set up their own projects for the systematic study of war propaganda (for a brief introduction and further references, see Berelson, 1952, pp. 23–4). Hans Speier had started a project on totalitarian communication at the New School for Social Research (Krippendorf, 1980, p. 16).

16. For an evaluation of this early literature, see Willey (1926, pp. 24–32).

17. On the history of quantification in the early period, see Woodward (1930, pp. 39–64, Chap. II, "Quantitative Method in Measuring Newspaper Content").

18. A similar procedure is applied to one month of two Connecticut weekly newspapers.

19. The book was published posthumously in 1960. At a young age, in 1922, Richardson had already published a seminal contribution to the mathematical weather forecast.

20. 1618 for Austria-Hungary and 1614 for France.

21. There is hardly any discussion of method in Bodart's work, with the exception of a handful of pages where he laments the lack of reliable sources for the earlier centuries (Bodart, 1916, pp. 11–12).

22. For each recorded instance of war and internal disturbance, as taken from various published sources, particularly by historians, Sorokin measures the location, the duration, and the intensity. In an appendix, he provides bullet descriptions of each event. As Sorokin (1937, p. 282) writes: "Are there quantitative aspects to the phenomena of war that can be counted? Evidently! ... [S]ize of the army ... casualties ... – individuals killed and wounded – ... [and] the duration of the war."

23. Against Brinton's (1937) scathing review of the book, Tilly and Rule (1965, pp. 35, 36) wrote: "[Sorokin] has performed the work of a pioneer, and too few others have sought to tame the territory he opened up ... We find Sorokin's work a bold attempt to face real problems." An impassionate tribute to a mentor by someone who was to dedicate a lifetime to seeking to tame Sorokin's territory.

24. Tilly (1975; 1985).

25. The "Enigma" project in England led to build "a remarkable mechanism about the size of three large wardrobes codenamed COLOSSUS. ... regard[ed] as ... the first electronic computer" (Kahn, 1980, p. 631).

26. Eckstein (1962); see also Rummel (1966).

27. For definitions of these measures, see Eckstein (1962, Appendix I) and Rummel (1966).

28. See Rummel's (1963) work on domestic conflict for seventy-seven nations in the period 1955–57 with data collected from *The New York Times Index, Facts on File, Keesing's Contemporary Archives, Britannica Book of the Year,* and *New International Yearbook.* Tanter (1966) extended Rummel's work from the years 1955–57 to 1958–60. Rummel's conflict behavior included the following eight actions: assassination, general strike, guerrilla war, major government crisis, purge, riot, antigovernment demonstration, and revolution. In addition, the total number killed in domestic violence was also collected. Tanter's measures replicate Rummel's exactly.

29. For instance, the U.S. Department of Defense (DOD) funded directly Gurr's work through its Advanced Research Project Agency (see the acknowledgments in Gurr, 1968, 1970). DOD similarly funded parts of the Dimensionality of Nations Project initiated by Guetzkow and continued by Rummel and Tanter (personal communication by Professor Rummel).

30. Tilly and Rule (1965, pp. 93–100); Gurr (1969, Appendix A; 1972, pp. 94–7).

31. For some examples, see Paige (1975, Appendix 3); McAdam (1981, Appendix 1); Tarrow (1989, Appendix A).

32. Markoff et al. (1975). See also Shapiro and Markoff's (1998) more recent book-length treatment of the same methodological and substantive issues.

33. The term "scene," used to provide background information, particularly circumstantial information as time and space, is found across many authors (for example, Colby, 1973, p. 654; Burke, 1969, p. xv). Rumelhart uses the term "setting" (1975, p. 213), and so do those scholars influenced by his seminal work, for example, Mandler and Johnson (1977, p. 117); Throndyke (1977, p. 79); Mandler (1982, p. 307); Wilensky (1983, p. 580).

34. Contrary to Markoff et al.'s scheme, Franzosi and Centis's scheme allows coders to place the information supplied by subordinate clauses in individual coding categories, no differently from the coding of either single or main clauses.

35. Roberts (1989, p. 167).

36. The rules listed here are only meant to provide an example of rewrite rules. They are only a subset of the complex set of rules necessary to generate all the sentences of English.
37. For an introduction to semantic text grammars, see van Dijk (1972); for a brief introduction to the relationship between syntax and semantics from a Chomskyian viewpoint, see Bierwisch (1970).
38. Kintsch and van Dijk (1978, p. 366).
39. See Kintsch and van Dijk (1978, p. 374). On titles as superordinate macrostructures, see also Kozminsky (1977).
40. "Eidons" are sequences of narrative thought. Colby's analysis is concerned with finding recurrent sequences of narrative elements, rather than simply identifying those elements (as in Propp's original work). Only a handful of the functions found by Propp in Russian folktales are also found in Eskimo folktales. Colby concludes: "the narrative elements and rules resulting from this analysis appear to apply to the folktales of all Eskimo, but not to the folktales of neighboring peoples. ... [T]he set of Eskimo eidons is culture specific, not universal" (Colby, 1973, pp. 645–6).
41. Dundes (1962) similarly tried to find an invariant narrative structure in folktales of native Americans.
42. See also Bremond (1964; 1966); Lakoff (1972); Prince (1973).
43. Rumelhart (1975); Mandler (1978; 1982; 1983; 1987); Mandler and Goodman (1982); Mandler and Johnson (1977); Thorndyke (1977); Stein and Glenn (1979); Stein (1982a; 1982b); Stein and Policastro (1984); Wilensky (1983); Shen (1988); Bower and Morrow (1990). From the field of psychology and cognitive psychology, story grammars were also picked up in the field of education, as a way of understanding children's ability to comprehend stories (see Schumm, 1992; Montague et al., 1990; Lehr, 1987; Bereiter, 1983). For an evaluation of story grammars, see Black and Wilensky (1979); de Beaugrande (1982); Weaver and Dickinson (1982).
44. References in this paragraph are to Rumelhart (1975, pp. 211, 213, 213–14, 235). Rumelhart mixes the terms "schema" (in the title of the paper) and "grammar" (in the title of the main section and throughout) for his approach to stories (on this point, see de Beaugrande, 1982, p. 388). Prince (1973) had already used the term "grammar of stories," following Todorov (1968). The label "story grammar," however, was the one to become popular in psychology.
45. See de Baugrande's critique (1982, p. 388).
46. See also Thorndyke (1977) who, around the same time and for similar purposes as Mandler, proposes a story grammar "similar to one [sic] suggested by Rumelhart (1975)" to study the effect of story structures on comprehension and memorization of narrative discourse (Thorndyke, 1977, p. 79).
47. The paper was coauthored with Johnson (Mandler and Johnson, 1977). References in this paragraph are to Mandler and Johnson (1977, pp. 113, 113–14), unless otherwise noted.
48. For Mandler's version of a story grammar, see Mandler and Johnson (1997); Mandler (1984, pp. 17–30) where, however, it is referred to as "story structure."
49. Thorndyke (1977); Mandler and Johnson (1977); Stein and Glenn (1979); Mandler and Goodman (1982); Stein and Policastro (1984); Wilensky (1983); Mandler (1987).
50. Mandler (1982, pp. 307–8). For the psychologists' experimental work, see Mandler and Johnson (1977); Throndyke (1977); Mandler (1978); Stein and Glenn (1979); Stein and Policastro (1984); Mandler (1987).
51. Labov and Waletzky (1967); Labov (1972, particularly Chapter 9, "The Transformation of Experience in Narrative Syntax," pp. 354–96. For a comparison of Greimas's and Labov and Waletzky's schema, see van Dijk (1972, p. 293).
52. Todorov (1969, pp. 27–8). See also Chatman's discussion of Todorov's work (Chatman, 1978, p. 91). Todorov also presents the plot recurrence of *Decameron* stories in algebraic form.
53. Formalizations of this kind based on predicate calculus have been popular in cognitive science and computer science. Thus Ericsson and Simon (1996, p. 266) write: "Usually the encodings o f segments [of text] can be somewhat formalized by using functional notation: R(x,y,...), where the R's are relations, and the x, y, etc., arguments. ... The relations in such an encoding are generally derived from the verbs, prepositions, and adjectives of the protocol [text under investigation], while their arguments often take the form of nouns and noun phrases."
54. Subscripts and superscripts are used by van Dijk to indicate the degree of predicates and arguments higher than one (2-place, 3-place, ... n-place predicates and arguments) (van Dijk, 1972, p. 145).

55. Strictly speaking, one of the action modifiers, <time>, is not optional. There can be no narrative without time.
56. Rewrite rules are represented via the symbol →. Nonterminal symbols are notationally represented as being enclosed in angular brackets < >. Terminal symbols are enclosed in parenthesis. Dots at the end of a string of terminal symbols indicate open sets; dots between terminal symbols indicate closed sets (see Lyons, 1970, p. 120). Symbols enclosed in square brackets [ ] are optional, that is, they may be repeated zero or one time, while those enclosed in curly brackets { } may be repeated one or more times. A vertical bar | between symbols indicates an exclusive "or"; a comma or a blank are to be interpreted as inclusive "and."
57. In output, events and triplets are organized in chrono-logical order (temporal *and* logical), and passive sentences are turned into the active form; Sager (1987, p. 4) calls this type of text coding "information formatting." When transforming passive sentences into active forms a question mark (?) is used to denote an unknown subject. When the subject can be inferred from context, this is put in parenthesis with a question mark.
58. Early work by computer scientists on computer understanding of natural languages was based on a very similar simplified story grammar. Schank and Riesbeck (1981, p. 11) write: "At the heart of any meaning representation system is the representation for events. CD [Conceptual Dependency, their representational theory] uses a simple structure to represent the core of an event, that is invariant across descriptions. That is, no matter what form an utterance describing that event may take, the form of the CD used to represent it is always the same. This works as follows: Every EVENT has: An ACTOR an ACTION performed by that actor an OBJECT that the action is performed upon a DIRECTION in which that action is oriented."
59. At each level (from the high-level nonterminal symbols, such as <dispute> or <event>, to the low-level terminal symbols, such as the <subject> "workers") the grammar should also specify the information that allow to identify a source document: <document key>. This set of information varies with the type of sources used. For instance, when using newspapers, the document key is made up of the newspaper name, the section, the page and column number, and the position of the article in the column; when unpublished documents available in the archives are used, the document key is given by the name of the archive, the city/state where the archive is located, the series name or number of the specific collection, and the box or folder name or number where the particular document may be found. At each level, the grammar allows coders to introduce free <comments> as well.
60. I have not rewritten the nonterminal symbols <quantitative expression> and <organization> because the set of rules for these symbols are quite long (see the Appendix of this book).
61. The most comprehensive account of narrative time is Genette's treatment (1980). Ricoeur's (1984) three volume treatment is more ambitious, but not as crisp as Genette's. Ricoeur deals with linguists', philosophers', and historians' views of time. Ricoeur's work provides a comprehensive review of each author's position in a very lucid and clear language. For brief introductions to the issues, see Rimmon-Kenan (1983, pp. 43–58); Cohan and Shires (1988, pp. 84–9); Toolan (1988, pp. 48–61).
62. The narrativists' duration and frequency do not just refer to the duration and frequency of the narrated (real-life) events. More generally, duration and frequency refer to the relationship between narrative clauses and narrated events. A narrator can sum up in one sentence events that took place over a long period of time ("After the fall of the Roman empire ..."), or dwell for many pages on fleeting events lasting a few minutes (Geertz's thick description, 1973, pp. 3–30). A narrator can recount the same event several times (frequency). And that game is by no means confined to purely fictional narrative. Claude Lévi-Strauss argued that chronology is the distinctive characteristic of history: Without chronology ("dates"), there is no history (Lévi-Strauss, 1972, pp. 258–60; see also Barthes, 1970; White, 1987, pp. 1–25). But different periods of history are characterized by different densities of dates. There are "hot" chronologies, such as World War Two, where the historian closely follows the events day by day, hour by hour; and chronologies where the historian quickly jumps over long spans of thousands of years. This selection of dates and events (the "facts" of the historian), these narrative strategies are not "innocent." They reflect the historian's conscious or unconscious intentions, they serve a fundamental ideological function (Barthes, 1970; White, 1987, p. 35).
63. And for good reason. After all, you cannot have a narrative without some timevarying characteristics, while you can have a narrative where space is immutable (think of the many theater pieces where the scene never changes, only the actors and the actions do, through time).

64. I have not rewritten <space> and <time> down to their terminal symbols. The sets of rewrite rules for both of these action modifiers are quite cumbersome (see Appendix). One problem is that, in verbal accounts, indefinite temporal expressions are just as common as definite ones. The temporal forms "at 11:45 P.M.," "on March 3, 1976" are definite; "a few days ago," "from three to five days ago," "in approximately one week," and "some months ago" are indefinite. Furthermore, the timing of events and actions is often reported, not in terms of the same temporal standards (namely the Gregorian Calendar and the Christian era), but in terms of the timing of other events or phases of an event. The mixture of use of standard and nonstandard temporal expressions, along with the use of different yardsticks of reference – Gregorian Calendar and other events – makes it impossible to obtain a complete time ordering of events or actions; only partial time ordering may be achieved. The rewrite rules for <time>, however, not only allow coders to code both definite and indefinite temporal forms (for both date and time of day); they also require coders to specify the time of reference of vague temporal expressions in terms of either a standard date or the time of another action or event. Take the following sentence. "A few days after the deadly lynching, the body of a young man was found hanging from a tree." The time of the second event is given in relation to the time of the first one, whose timing itself may not necessarily be expressed in terms of a standard yardstick.

65. For other examples of coding see Franzosi (1989b; 1990a; 1990b; 1990c; 1994a; 1997b; 1997c; 1998b).

66. Watt (1765); inscribed on one of the internal walls of the Science Museum of London.

67. Labov (1972, pp. 359–60); see also Labov and Waletzky (1967, p. 20).

68. Rimmon-Kenan (1983, pp. 2–3); Cohan and Shires (1988, pp. 52–3); Toolan (1988, p. 7).

69. Halliwell (1987, p. 37, Chapter 6).

70. See Benveniste (1971, pp. 206–8); Barthes (1977). This terminology was then exported to the English world as *story* versus *discourse*, see Chatman (1978, p. 19); on story/plot, story/discourse, see Toolan (1988, pp. 11–12).

71. See Toolan (1988, pp. 10–11); Genette (1980, p. 27).

72. Bal (1977, pp. 5–6) speaks of a "three-level hierarchy *histoire, récit, narration*"; Rimmon-Kenan (1983, pp. 3–4) of the "three aspects of narrative": story, text, and narration (see also Cohan and Shires, 1988, p. 53). There are subtle differences among authors not only in the narrative levels and labels, but also in definitions that make ploughing through the literature an unnecessarily difficult task (see Toolan, 1988, pp. 9–11, on this point). Nonetheless, we could summarize the linguists' distinctions in the following way:

Narrative
- Story/*fabula*/*histoire* (Genette's second meaning)
- Plot
  - Text/*sjužet*/discourse (Genette's first meaning)
  - Narrating/narration (Genette's third meaning)

73. Tomashevski (1965, p. 70); Labov (1972); Prince (1973, p. 23); Bal (1977, p. 7); Todorov (1977, p. 111); Rimmon-Kenan (1983, p. 19); Cohan and Shires (1988, pp. 53–4).

74. Although, as Chatman argues (1978, pp. 47, 49), readers will typically attempt to make a story out of even temporally sequenced but logically unrelated clauses by implicitly supplying logical connectives.

75. Bremond (1964; 1966); Todorov (1981, pp. 52–3); Rimmon-Kenan (1983, p. 23).

76. Most change would involve no such reversal of polarity, just an "after" different from the "before" but neither necessarily better nor worse.

77. See also Prince (1973, p. 23). On the reversal of situation, see Tomashevski (1925, pp. 70–1) and Todorov (1977, pp. 111–2; 1981, p. 51); see also Aristotle who first introduced the concept of reversal in his *Poetics* (Halliwell, 1987, p. 42, Chapter 11). Bremond (1964; 1966) also believed that all sequences are either sequences of improvement or deterioration (see the discussion by Rimmon-Kenan, 1983, p. 27).

78. Halliwell (1987, p. 51, Chapter 18); on Aristotelian reversals, see Chatman (1978, p. 85); Ricoeur (1984, pp. 43–4).

79. Some sociologists have introduced formal structural analyses of narratives based on the sequential properties of narrative texts and on the difference between kernel and satellite events, between sequential and consequential events (see Heise, 1989; Corsaro and Heise,

1990).

80. Danto (1985, pp. 143–81) similarly talks about "narrative sentences."
81. Labov (1972, p. 360). In 1925, Tomashevski had already made the distinction between *bound motifs* and *free motifs*, where a *motif* is basically a unit of narrative. Bound motifs are those that may be safely omitted from a story "without destroying the coherence of the narrative"; while *free motifs* are those whose deletion would disturb "the whole causal-chronological course of events" (Tomashevski, 1965[1925], p. 68). As Todorov notes (1981[1968], pp. 52–3) "optional ('free') propositions … are such only from the point of view of sequential construction; they are often what is most necessary in the text as a whole." Indeed, it is likely that it is at the level of free motifs that the telling of the story (the plot) would differ (Tomashevski, 1965[1925], p. 68). Barthes (1977[1966], pp. 93–4) similarly distinguishes between *cardinal functions* (or *nuclei*) and *catalysers*. Catalysers "merely fill in the narrative space," while cardinal functions alter current state of affairs, either by bringing them to a new equilibrium or by disrupting an existing equilibrium. Again, in Barthes's words: "Catalysers are only consecutive [that is, chronologically ordered] units, cardinal functions are both consecutive and consequential" (1977[1966], p. 94).
82. Renier (1950, pp. 22–3); Elton (1967, pp. 118–23, 126–41).
83. Tomashevski (1965[1925], p. 66); Bal (1977, p. 13); Rimmon-Kenan (1983, pp. 14–5).
84. Bal (1977, p. 13) correctly points out that a theory of narrative presupposes a theory of text genres. She proposes three types of texts: lyrical, dramatic, and narrative (Bal, 1977, p. 12). The narrative text tells a story (just like drama, but unlike lyrical texts), in a complex way (contrary to the other two types of texts), and where the ratio of narrator's discourse to actor's discourse is maximized (contrary to both lyrical and dramatic texts).
85. Todorov (1990[1978], p. 28).
86. Chatman (1978, pp. 31–2; emphasis in the original). Chatman also distinguishes events into *actions* and *happenings*, where actions are nonverbal physical acts, speeches, and feelings, perceptions, and sensations (Chatman, 1978, pp. 44–5). Prince similarly distinguishes *stative* and *active* events, the former being events which describe a state, the latter an action (Prince, 1973, p. 29). Furthermore, a stative event, for Prince, is expressed in a story by a stative sentence, that is, a sentence "which is not paraphrasable by a sentence of the form *NP's V-ing NP Aux be an act*" (Prince, 1973, p. 30; emphasis in the original). The sentence "John was happy" is stative because it cannot be paraphrased by "John's being happy was an act." Van Dijk also distinguishes between two types of predicates, static versus dynamic (1972, p. 142).
87. See, for example, Paige (1975, Appendix 3); Tarrow (1989, Appendix A).
88. For more general advantages of a grammar-based approach, see van Dijk (1983, p. 26–27).

Chapter 2 Ars Memoriae

1. Idea of the work. Explanation of the frontispiece painting that serves as introduction to the work.
2. He was the first, however, to make such extensive use of an allegorical painting, taking up close to forty pages for its description (Vico, 1959, pp. 239–76).
3. Quintilian rather believes in the old-fashioned way of committing things to memory (1922, 26, p. 227) based on "practice and industry" (1922, 39, p. 235), namely learning by heart as much as possible and with daily practice. Nonetheless he also suggests a practical way of increasing one's memory and that he directly quotes from Cicero in his *De Oratore* (ii, lxxxvi, 354, lxxxvii, 358).
4. On the fascinating story of the art of memory, see two wonderful books by Rossi (1960) and, in English, by Yates (1992).
5. Camillo refers to the Cabala several times in the essay *L'idea del theatro* (for example, Camillo, 1554, pp. 61, 66). In a letter addressed to a loved woman, certain Lucretia, he refers to the "ancient Hebrew theology" as "marvellous" (*"antica hebraica theologia … meravigliosa"*; Camillo, 1554, p. 344).
6. Few remember Giulio Camillo today. Even Italian school children, who are still familiar with the name of one of his contemporaries, Pico della Mirandola, for his famed and prodigious memory, will not have heard of him. Yet, Giulio Camillo "was one of the most famous men

of the sixteenth century" (Yates, 1992, p. 135).

7. And, apparently, from what Lodovico Dolce tells us, Camillo did not write the essay himself but, rather, he "dictated this essay called '*Idea*' in the course of eight mornings" (Dolce, *Ai lettori*, in Camillo, 1554, p. 57).

8. Taken from Dolce's introduction to Camillo's essay *L'idea del Theatro, Ai lettori* ("to the readers"), contained in Camillo (1554, p. 57).

9. See Ricci (1990, pp. 16–8) on Bruno's similar view of the art as *theatrum mundi*.

10. See Rossi (1968, in particular pp. 49–78).

11. See Rossi (1960, p. 255); Yates (1992, pp. 365–72).

12. On the work of Lull, see Yates (1992, pp. 175–96).

13. Date (1981, p. 3). In a computer database this information is stored in files. Files are collections of records. Records contain one or more fields where different types of information are stored (Ullman, 1980, p. 20).

14. Ullman (1980, p. 11); Date (1981, p. 8).

15. There is no single or "best" way of organizing complex data structures, the number and types of individual files depending upon the specific needs and requirements of each application.

16. Ullman (1980, p. 13). Relationships can be one-to-one, that is, for each entity in either set there is at most one entity in the other set. More common, though, is the many-to-one relationship, where one entity in entity set S_2 is associated with zero or more entities in the set S_1, but each entity in S_1 is associated with at most one entity in S_2 (in this case, the relationship is called many-to-one from S_1 to S_2). The different types of relationships correspond to different types of data organization in the computer (data models), the most common being the hierarchical (many-to-one relationships), the network and the relational models (many-to-many relationships) (Ullman, 1980, p. 13). Data models differ in the way they deal with relationships among the entities of different entity sets (that is, among data in various files) (Date, 1981, p. 78). All data models consist of two elements: 1) a mathematical framework and notation for expressing data and relationships; and 2) operations that express queries and other manipulation of the data (data entry and editing) (Ullman, 1980, p. 18). In the hierarchical and network models relationships are represented via pointers – integer values that correspond to the physical location of a record in a file where a particular item of information is stored. In the relational model, relationships between files (or "tables," as they are called in relational terminology) are represented by at least one common field (or "column") in two different files (Date, 1981, p. 65).

17. Around the mid 1980s, social scientists had slowly started applying relational DBMSs to analyze such textual material as medical records (Sager et al., 1987; Sager, 1981, pp. 213–39), questionnaire responses such as SIPP (Survey of Income and Program Participation) (Sager et al., 1987; David, 1989), longitudinal household data such as PSID (Panel Study of Income Dynamics) (Solenberger, Servais and Duncan, 1989), or cross-sectional data (National Study of Families and Households) (Winsborough, 1989).

18. The hierarchical features of the grammar (semantic triplets under events, events under disputes) would seem to translate naturally into a hierarchical data model; yet, its relational characteristics (subjects related to actions, actions to objects) would seem to rather call for a relational model. In translating a grammar of data collection into a computer data model we need to carefully weigh pros and cons of the two types of data models. On balance, a relational data model fares better than a hierarchical one.

19. Within a relational database, one does not need to start data collection with a fully specified grammar. All the hierarchies and all the modifiers need not be known in advance. One can add complexity to the grammar as necessity calls for, and as data collection proceeds, by simply adding new relations (Winsborough, 1989, p. 246).

20. A number can be attached to the entities of different entity sets (subjects, actions, and objects). In order to be able to pin down the entity set to which the number attribute refers, we need an identifier for the tables that stand on higher nodes than numbers (that is, subjects, actions, and objects).

21. Alternatively, each hierarchy could be set up as a separate table, providing one overlapping field only between contiguous tables in the tree structure. This data model lowers disk overheads but severely taxes query performance. In an environment where disk space is not an issue, I strongly recommend the first type of database design. To understand this, consider the following problem. Suppose that you wanted to find out whether different unions (where

<trade union> is an attribute of the <subject>) make different claims (<demand>, an attribute of <action>). In a database, where every entity set is stored in an appropriate table, a query that addressed that question would require joining several tables, upward and downward. Upward, we would have to join the union_table and the subject_table using the subject_id (to obtain the triplet_id); the triplet_table and the event_table on the basis of the triplet_id to obtain the event_id; and so on. Downward, we would have to join the action_table to the demand_table using the triplet_id as a relation between the two tables. Several joins could be saved if each table carried the identifiers of each of the upper-level nodes in the tree. Although this approach requires more disk storage, it makes queries much faster.

22. The link between the number_table and any of the other three tables (subject_table, action_table, or object_table) is more complex. According to the specifications of the grammar of data collection, subjects, actions, and objects can all have a number as attribute. As a consequence, for any number stored in the number_table we need to be able to identify not only the entity to which the number refers but also the entity set (that is, we need to identify both tuple and table). In other words, we need to be able to identify in the tree the specific node above the attribute <number>. Thus, the value of 3 found in the upper_table_id of the number_table would indicate that the quantitative expression found in the column number_value refers to an object. The upper_tuple_id would further identity the specific entity to which the number_value refers. Thus, a value of 1 would link the number_value "all" to the object_name "technical personnel," precisely as it reads in the original newspaper article.

23. Arkwright, however, was no inventor; it appears that he stole his invention; a very successful businessman, yes, the man who "really created the modern factory," but no inventor (Mantoux, 1983, pp. 221, 227–34).

24. Technological innovation went hand-in-hand with falling prices. Mantoux (1983, p. 253) tells us that the price in shillings per pound of No. 100 cotton yarn kept falling from 38 in 1786, 35 in 1788, 15 in 1793, 9.5 in 1800, and 7.10 in 1804.

25. In a rapidly changing field, see Weitzman and Miles (1995); Dohan and Sánchez- Jankowski (1998); Richards and Richards (2000).

26. "Coding" is the term traditionally used in content analysis for recording information taken from a printed source to a coding scheme. "Tagging" is an alternative term used in conjunction with information already available on a computer. Either way, coding or tagging require human intervention.

27. More generally, the coder needs to record the information that uniquely identifies a source document. If that document is taken from historical archives, this information will differ from newspapers. But the principle is the same: Keep track of the sources of information.

28. In a computer environment, the precoded lexicon of the particular content analysis application expands as the project proceeds. This eliminates the need for extensive prereading of the material, a particularly time consuming step in large-scale projects (see Sudman, 1983, p. 222; Ericsson and Simon, 1996). But the alternative of using open-ended categories had serious drawbacks in a paper environment, since these had to be recoded (on open-ended categories, see Budd, Thorp, and Donohew, 1967, p. 54).

29. The large majority of random errors are immediately detected by the person committing the error (van Nes, 1976, p. 166). Direct data entry into the computer, however, greatly enhances the detection of random error in large scale data collection projects. The spelling of names of localities, industrial sectors, major firms, and organizations can be checked on-line; dates, too, can be checked and constrained within the historical boundaries of the period under study; cross consistency of coded categories can be monitored (for example, checking the actions that certain actors perform). Acceptance tests for individual or combined fields (for example, a "range test" rejecting numeric values for month outside the range one to twelve; Naus, 1975, p. 12) can be conveniently organized in dictionaries (Naus, 1975, pp. 7–31).

30. On titles and their biasing effect, see Kozminsky (1977).

31. Kintsch (1974); Kozminsky (1977).

32. The amount of material to be read and analyzed for the purpose of coding is called "context unit" in content analysis. It refers to the portion of the symbolic material that has to be analyzed in order to characterize the recording unit, that is, the items and symbols to be coded. It is within the broader context unit that one must search for the recording units: a word, a sentence, a paragraph, a theme, and so on. Recording units are wholly contained in the context units. Context units in turn can be recording units within larger contexts (Budd et al., 1967,

p. 47; Krippendorf, 1980, pp. 61–2). Articles constitute the typical context units. Syntactical units – subject, action, object/target – and thematic units are the elementary recording units for any given event. Coding categories provide the basic thematic units for collection. An article usually is a well-identifiable unit with a title (headline) and, often, a subtitle; a short news item that appears under such captions as "News Brief," "Update," "News Roundup," and the like, qualifies as an article; an article could even be the caption of a photograph, if the information contained there does not appear in an article proper.

33. The software should link each item of information to a specific article key in order to be able to identify the source of information for any data item in the database.

34. Mandler and Johnson (1977); Mandler (1978); Stein and Glenn (1979); Stein and Policastro (1984); Mandler (1987).

35. If the text material is in machine-readable form, automatic searches of keywords (for example, strike, rally, riot) can make the identification of qualifying articles, that is, the first pass, very speedy. But my experience with processing text material stored on microfilms suggests that the first pass does not require more than two or three minutes per article (depending upon the number of articles per newspaper issue).

36. Again, the repetition of tasks is independent of the type of computer-assisted content analysis used. Whether text is in machine-readable form or not, coders still have to read the qualifying article and either tag or enter the appropriate text.

37. A way to reduce the inefficiency of two-pass coding in the presence of multiple dispute articles, is to code contemporaneously a set of disputes, rather than a single dispute. This strategy helps to reduce costs without sacrificing quality. Depending upon the number of multiple-dispute articles in the set, this approach to coding could greatly reduce costs, while maintaining data quality. The data-entry software should compute the number of collective disputes to be coded simultaneously since this involves a complex iterative procedure between articles and disputes. It should then advise the coder whether to code the dispute separately or together with others.

38. Mintz (1949, pp. 144–5). "Generally speaking, samples consisting of consecutive days can be expected to be less accurate than samples consisting of days separated by regular intervals" (Mintz, 1949, p. 143). The accuracy of every fifth-day and every second-day samples is "distinctively better" than the weekly samples (Mintz, 1949, p. 145).

39. A second sampling strategy is to code only part of the information provided by each qualifying article. Within qualifying articles, coding time varies with the amount of information to be coded, which depends upon the complexity of the coding scheme. Simplifying the coding scheme, that is, cutting down on the number of coding categories, will reduce coding time and data collection costs. Unfortunately, it will also reduce data available for analysis. On sampling in content analysis, see Budd, Thorp, and Donohew (1967, pp. 4–9); Krippendorff (1980, pp. 65–70).

40. Rucht and Neidhardt (1999) and Koopmans (1995b; 1999, p. 102) avoid that problem by tracing back in time any event encountered in a Monday issue and coding every article that deals with the event regardless of day of the week.

41. Stratifying the sample of disputes to be coded by the number of articles that deal with the dispute assumes that the "importance" of events, in terms of severity and intensity, and newspaper coverage of these events are directly related. Unfortunately, this is not always the case.

42. The software could help by providing the basic sampling framework, allowing the investigator to select a sample of disputes perhaps stratified by the number of articles cross-referenced (as a measure of the relative importance of the dispute).

43. Van Dijk (1985, p. 86; 1986; 1988, p. 55; see also 1983; 1986).

44. Tuchman (1978, pp. 82–103).

45. The formulation "doing some actions" may be sufficient, without the need to add the qualification "or saying something." After all, Austin and Searle would argue that "to say" is "to act," that is, to issue an utterance is a speech act. "[To] say anything must always be to do something," although different speech acts will carry different weights, will have different and increasingly serious consequences from locutionary, to illocutionary, and perlocutionary (Austin, 1975, pp. 92, 109). Searle similarly argues that "Speaking a language is engaging in a … rule-governed form of behavior" (1969, pp. 12, 16).

46. In enchaining events in these chronological sequences of past and future events, reporters

attempt to provide reading frameworks for events characterized by temporal (and perhaps spatial) proximity, by similarity of reasons and demands, by a continuity of social actors. Altheide (1987), for instance, has shown how news articles often come in "mini-series" of several days. But in their attempt to conceptualize events and to impose meaning on an otherwise seamless stream of events, news reports often try to link current events not only to immediately preceding events but quite distant ones in time as well (a category of news information that van Dijk would place in the *history* category of his schema). Such enchaining of events has profound epistemological implications for historiography – even mere description in historical narrative becomes explanation through the choice and sequence of events.

47. With direct computer entry, coders have available on-line all previously coded information to help them check that a given item of information has not been coded already. This implies that coders must be able to perform keyword searches within coding categories and to display coded material in a variety of ways for readability. Relying on memory alone, in fact, is quite risky (see Loftus, 1979).

48. Information provided under the category *consequences/reactions*, particularly *events/acts*, may also provide information that will lead to further developments in subsequent articles.

49. If all events and disputes were reported in one article only, there would not be any savings in coding time. All the "background" information provided in the article would have to be coded, since no previous articles with this information would be available. This, however, is unlikely. It is in the very nature of collective events (for example, strikes, rebellions, wars) to stretch over time – often, over several months if not years. Second, only major events are likely "to make the papers." These events are precisely the ones that last longer. But the larger the percentage of disputes made up of several articles (multiple-article disputes) relative to the one-article disputes, the larger the savings in coding time.

50. We can safely expect the amount of new information in each article to increase with every new event in a dispute. After all, a new event entails a new set of actions and a new time framework; perhaps, even new actors and locations (Franzosi, 1995b). Furthermore, a short and isolated event, however severe, may not receive extensive coverage simply because it does not reach the information network in time. With events of longer duration and/or with repeated occurrences of an event, the media will have enough time to send reporters to the scene for in-depth coverage. News reports, then, become longer, denser with information, and richer in detail. The proportion of new material in each article is thus likely to decrease with the temporal position of the article in the sequence of articles that report an event. Other types of documents share these characteristics. Personal narrative, as found in open-ended interviews and life stories, is similarly characterized by a set of temporally successive documents (interviews); in each interview, a person narrates one or more events of her/his life; summaries, repetitions, commentaries, and evaluations of one's past are very much part of these documents as of newspaper articles. The same is true for medical records. In summary: 1) The larger the number of multiple-article disputes, the greater the potential savings in coding time; 2) the greater the number of multiple-event disputes, the greater the likelihood of repeated information, and the greater the likelihood of savings in coding time. Comparative data for the years 1919 and 1972, taken from two of my protest-event projects, show that a large number of disputes (around 40% in both periods) is covered in only one article. This suggests that a data collection strategy in which only new information is recorded would lead to savings in coding time for about 60% of the articles. These savings would increase for larger disputes. In both periods there is a tendency toward some very large disputes (3% of the disputes between thirty to one hundred articles). This is all the more true for 1972. Although the ratio of small-to-large disputes seems to be constant over time, the absolute number of large disputes quadrupled in 1972. It is the very large disputes that are more likely to lead to real savings in coding time.

51. Error prevention should be the first step in a data quality strategy. Error prevention demands an understanding of the factors that affect human performance, that is, the probability that a coder will commit an error in the process of performing the coding task. Identification of these factors will allow investigators to eliminate the very sources of errors. Human engineers have classified these factors (Performance- Shaping Factors, or PSFs, as they call them) as internal and external (Miller and Swain, 1987, p. 223). On these issues see Franzosi (1990a).

52. Human engineers have introduced a distinction between two basic types of errors committed

in the process of recording information: errors of omission and errors of commission (Miller and Swain, 1987, p. 221). In content analysis, errors of omission occur when an operator fails to record relevant items of information (entire documents – document omission – or individual items of information within a document – item omission). Errors of commission "occur when an operator does the task, but does it incorrectly" (Miller and Swain, 1987, p. 221).

53. On these issues see Franzosi (1990a, 1990b, 1990c, 1995b).
54. On coherence, see Agar and Hobbs (1982); van Dijk (1983, p. 25). Agar and Hobbs (1982) posited three kinds of textual coherence: global, local, and themal.
55. Not always are these surface relational mechanisms present. When they are not, a competent language user must infer intersentence well formedness not from syntactical rules but from semantic rules about the meaning of one sentence in relation to the meaning of its preceding and following sentences (local coherence), and in relation to the general meaning of the text as a whole (global coherence).
56. On the temporal ordering of sentences, see also van Dijk (1972, pp. 84 ff., 290 ff.).
57. The software of data collection should allow users to specify the number of levels of aggregation desired (for example, dispute and event, or dispute, subdispute, event, and subevent) and the appropriate labels for the various coding categories. For example, the category <dispute> may be labeled <life history> in a project involving narratives of personal life histories. Similarly, the label <trade union> may be unnecessary in a study of lynching of American blacks.
58. See Mishler (1986, p. 74). In event history analysis, temporal aggregation of individual actions into macroactions is always a problem. Part of the problem stems from the fact that "event data" is likely to be both "left and right censored." In newspapers, for example, events usually become newsworthy well after their beginning, often at the point of intervention of public authorities, particularly the police, and they are typically dropped well before their resolution. The narrative thus misses both head and tail of the event (on censorship and its effects in event history data, see Cox and Oakes, 1984; censorship will also introduce bias of sample selection; see Heckman, 1979). Events can be censored not only along the time dimension, but also by location and sector, as the contours of events become blurred and as no information is provided on peripheral locations and/or marginal sectors. Aggregation can be problematic even in the absence of censorship and with full information. Still, some guidelines that are generally applicable to aggregation suggest themselves. By and large, a macroaction, such as event or dispute, should 1) involve the same actors; 2) center on the same demands; 3) have temporal and spatial proximity among the events (see van Dijk, 1982; on episodes as semantic units, see also Hinds, 1979; Chafe, 1980).
59. To signal the presence of extra information on the subject, action, or object, the software could produce different color displays for subjects, actions or objects that have modifiers. Coders could then choose to display the extra information. In this example, both subject and action ("people" and "march") would need to be marked as having modifiers.
60. The software should also allow coders to get printouts of the different versions of a story. This presupposes that coders can flag information that are in contradiction with each other (for example, because they come from different documents). This could be done at any level: single coding item or aggregates, such as triplet, event, or collective dispute.
61. Task complexity has been found to be positively related to the likelihood of error (Kammeyer and Roth, 1971; Crittenden and Hill, 1971; Morrissey, 1974).
62. One drawback of input versus output verification is that coder's and verifier's coding are not independent. The verifier may be affected by the previous coding he/she is inspecting. Minton argued that operators in keypunching verification are often influenced by the interpretation of the original puncher (cited in Naus, 1975, p. 90). Thus, while a log of errors encountered during verification can be quite useful for assessing coders' and categories' performance, it cannot be used to infer the extent of intercoder reliability. To avoid this problem, and still be able to monitor intercoder reliability, as the project proceeds, the whole team should periodically and independently code the same newspaper article(s).
63. On data verification, see Avenhaus and Canty (1996). The data-entry software should perform all the tasks involved. It should allow verifiers to select the population to sample (a single coding session, a week's worth of coding, and so on), the unit to be sampled for inspection (for example, a dispute, an event, an article, a single coding category), and the percentage of units to be sampled. The software should then randomly draw the sample of units to be verified and

keep track of the status of each sampling unit (sampled, unverified, verified with no errors found, verified with errors found, and so on).

64. These two types of errors can be verified and rectified independently of each other. One can verify and rectify information entered for a given document even if over half of the relevant documents have been missed; similarly, one can check whether any documents have been missed from coding, regardless of whether or not the information coded within each coded document is accurate.

65. The data-entry software should file all the remarks written by verifiers under semantic coherence verification and all errors (additions, deletions, and editing) found during input versus output verification. Through routine inspection of these files, the researcher can monitor the performance of coders and coding categories and take timely corrective actions, if required.

66. When working on material not directly stored in the computer but on paper or on microfilms, readers of the coded output may not have easy access to the original. When a verifier detects an error (from the lack of internal consistency of the data or from the discrepancy between coded information and their knowledge of the world) the verification routines should prevent verifiers from changing codes. They should restrict verifiers' intervention to entering only free remarks at any point where the semantic coherence of the code appears to break down. Only the coder could take appropriate corrective action after inspecting the verifier's remarks.

67. On acceptance sampling, see Freeman et al. (1948); American Statistical Association (1959); Naus (1975, pp. 89–106).

68. Ideally, one should verify all coded output, perhaps not just once but several times (multiple-pass verification). In fact, single-pass verification, even of 100% of the output, will not detect all errors (see Naus, 1975, pp. 91, 92, 165). Yet multiple-pass verification is prohibitively expensive.

69. Date (1981, pp, 145–58). See also Date (1986); Date (1987); Fleming and van Halle (1989).

70. Technically, a "query" is the set of commands necessary to perform an operation of data retrieval.

71. C. Wright Mills (1959, p. 104).

72. Le Roy Ladurie (1979b, p. 3); see also Elton (1967, pp. 30–9).

73. Ericsson and Simon (1996, pp. 265–6) remark that with large bodies of text "the different words will be distributed by frequency in a highly skewed way ... [A]bout one-half of all the words that occur will occur only once in the text."

74. On the limitations of these data, see Shalev (1978).

75. As Fascists are also known from the black shirts they wore as part of their uniform.

76. The Socialists scored a major victory in those elections. They won 2,162 communes out of 8,059 and 25 out of 69 provinces; compare this to 300 communes and 22 provinces in the previous local elections of 1914.

77. Snowden (1986, pp. 80, 158–60, 165).

78. For Ferrara, see Corner (1975, pp. 138–43); for Bologna, see Cardoza (1982, pp. 308, 314, 346–8). On the role of violence in early fascism, see De Felice (1995a, pp. 3–99).

79. See Maier (1975, p. 177); Corner (1975, pp. 119–20); Kelikian (1986, pp. 142–3); Snowden (1989, p. 198).

80. The query that addresses that question is more complex than the ones previously encountered because the English language offers several choices on how to build a syntactically well-formed sentence centering on the verb "clash." Thus, the three sentences "Fascists and Communists clashed," "Fascists clashed with Communists," and "Communists clashed with Fascists" are all properly formed, but, in the first case, both Fascists and Communists occupy the subject position and the sentence has no object, and in the second and third cases, the Fascists and the Communists interchange their position as subjects and objects of the two sentences. A search for those actors with whom the Fascists clash would then require us to look in both the subject_table and object_table, with the Fascists as both subjects and objects.

81. For evidence, see also Corner (1975, pp. 119–20, 201–2); Cardoza (1982, p. 348); Kelikian (1986, pp. 142–3); Snowden (1989, p. 198).

82. For similar evidence, see Lyttleton (1973, p. 80); Maier (1975, pp. 335–7); Kelikian (1986, pp. 157–8).

83. For an easy introduction to set theory, see Halmos (1960).

84. Cohn (1985, pp. 83–4, 87).

85. Weitzman and Miles (1995); Dohan and Sánchez-Jankowski (1998); Richards and Richards

(2000). I am less impressed with the marketing pitch of some of these new products, as "tools of theory building and hypothesis testing." Their real value is both more modest and more important at the same time: To allow researchers to store and retrieve in a systematic and quick way large volumes of qualitative data.

86. Unamuno (1931, p. 90).
87. References in this paragraph are to Plato (*Symposium*, 201d–212c, 1963).
88. For these quotes, see Unamuno (1931, pp. 36, 36, 48, 52, 37, 55, 292, 55, 53).
89. Burckhardt (1979, pp. 278–9).
90. This eighteenth-century botanist wrote a poem of over 165 pages, *The Loves of Plants*, (Darwin, 1991) on the reproduction of plants. Each section of the poem is about a different species or genus, and about half of each page is taken up by Darwin's "philosophical notes" which help to explain his poetry.
91. Díaz (1963, pp. 37, 71, 199); see also Vasco da Gama (cited in Boorstin, 1986, pp. 257–8).
92. Cited by Beer in her "Introduction" (Darwin, 1996, p. xvi).
93. References in this paragraphs are to Merton (1973[1957], pp. 286–7, 287, 288, 289, 294).
94. Unamuno (1931, pp. 39, 45).
95. Unamuno (1931, p. 51).

Chapter 3 *"Everything is Number"*

1. Dedieu (cited in Monter, 1990, p. 30).
2. Seville or Aragon were not alone. In other cities the Inquisition had a similar harder time. In Venice, for instance, where *primi gentiluomini, huomini grandi* (first gentlemen, great men), the aristocratic elite of the city itself, had embraced evangelical beliefs (Martin, 1993, p. 74). Antonio de la Bastida, a young French immigrant into Spain, is recorded to have told his cell mate, Juan García, in the Inquisition jail in the city of Cuenca, that, would he ever get out of it alive, he would immediately set out for Venice (Griffin, 1997, pp. 315–6, 321, 340). Antonio's information, however, was slightly out of date. By the mid 1500s, the screw of the Inquisition had started tightening up even in Venice. In any case, Antonio did not keep good to his words; he hung around Spain; came under the Inquisition's axe a second time; and was lucky enough to escape never to be heard again (Griffin, 1997, pp. 340–1).
3. For a clear, non-technical introduction to network analysis, see Scott (1991); for a statistical treatment, see Wasserman and Faust (1994).
4. Peter Abell's formal work on comparative narratives is based on a similar underlying set theoretical approach to structure the relation between social actors and their actions (Abell, 1987; 1993). There is no reference in Abell's work to the large body of linguistic literature on narrative. Issues of meaning and of how to map surface sentence structures onto Abell's grammar are neglected. The work stands mostly as a highly formalized way to structure narrative, all the more so for the lack of substantive applications by Abell himself or others (see Heise's critique, 1993).
5. The arrow does not refer to the linguists' rewrite rule but to the statisticians' directed *i j* relation from *n* to *n*.
6. A large number of relations implies a large number of directed graphs – one graph per relation. But a large number of actors may imply graphs with poor readability – too many nodes, with too many arcs cluttering the graph. Again, aggregation may be required in order to reduce the number of actors. With the actors and actions properly aggregated, we can then place the arcs of the directed graphs on several figures (one for each relation), or on a single figure containing points representing the actors and arcs or lines for all relations, simultaneously (a *multivariate directed graph*).
7. The application of network models in sociohistorical research, particularly in the study of social movements and collective action, has become increasingly popular with both methodological and substantive contributions; for examples, see Laumann and Pappi (1976); Burt and Lin (1977); Laumann and Knoke (1989); Gould (1991; 1995); Padgett and Ansell (1993); Diani (1995); Diani and McAdam (2003); see also the many titles in this Cambridge University Press series "Structural Analysis in the Social Sciences."
8. The information contained in Fig. 3.2 must to be taken with a grain of salt. After all, my

reliance on a socialist newspaper is likely to distort the real amount of communication for actors other than workers and unions (for example, Fascists, Communists). Nonetheless, the fact that the information contained in Fig. 3.2 as provided by a working-class paper points to an increasing isolation of the working class, that, in my opinion, can be taken as serious evidence of the increasing difficulties of the Italian working class.

9. One could view the appearance and disappearance of social actors during the temporal span of mobilization in light of Tarrow's concept of "cycles of protest." According to Tarrow, the rapid diffusion of collective action from more to less mobilized groups, the faster innovation in forms of collective action, the combination of organized and unorganized protest and the intensified interaction between challengers and authorities indicate the rise of such a cycle (Tarrow, 1994, pp. 153–69). The result is a period of heightened and widespread collective action, in which protest spreads rapidly and across traditional cleavages (center/periphery, rural/urban, and so on). During cycles of protest, particular groups typically at the forefront of protest are joined at the peak by less insurgent groups. Different groups join the mobilization process at different points. However, the mobilization of different groups rarely heads in the same direction as the initiators. Early risers trigger a variety of processes of diffusion, imitation, and reaction among other groups (Tarrow, 1994, pp. 155–6). McAdam argues that there is a certain lack of logic in Tarrow's claim that a protest cycle increases the leverage of all potential challengers. He suggests that the demands of the early riser would seem to preclude the possibility of much leverage for other groups (early risers gain most public and institutional attention; latecomers must confront a state already preoccupied with and accustomed to collective action pressures). McAdam suggests that it is more likely that latecomers benefit only from the diffusion of early risers' tactical and organizational lessons, rather than from a more open political opportunity structure (McAdam, 1996, pp. 31–3).

10. For Apulia, see Colarizi (1977, pp. 55–9, 94–116) and Snowden (1989); for Tuscany, see Snowden (1986, pp. 80, 158–60, 165, 186–7); for the province of Ferrara, see Corner (1975, pp. 121, 138–43); for the province of Bologna, see Cardoza (1982, pp. 308, 314, 317–20, 346–8); for Brescia, see Kelikian (1986, pp. 133, 142–3); for Friuli, see Fabbro (1977, p. 42).

11. Salvemini (1928, pp. 72–4); De Felice (1995a, p. 17).

12. Fabbro (1974, pp. 38, 43); Cardoza (1982, pp. 317–20); Snowden (1986, pp. 186–7); Kelikian (1986, p. 133).

13. Unemployment office.

14. Union leader.

15. Salvemini (1928, pp. 113–14); Snowden (1986, p. 80).

16. Salvemini (1961, p. 39, ff.); De Felice (1995a, pp. 27–34); Maier (1975, pp. 177, 316–17); Corner (1975, pp. 119–20); Kelikian (1986, pp. 119–20, 142–3, 201–2); Del Carria (1975, pp. 184, 194, 200); Cardoza (1982, pp. 308–9, 354–5); Fabbro (1974, pp. 43–4); Colarizi (1977, pp. 98–101, 108–9, 112–16).

17. The data prepared by the *Direzione Generale di Pubblica Sicurezza* (General Direction of Police) on the cases of violence that occurred in Italy up to May 8, 1922 strongly confirm these findings (data reported in De Felice, 1995a, pp. 36–9).

18. For a strong defense of Giolitti's role, see De Felice (1995a, pp. 25–6); see also Chabod (1961, p. 67). Less sympathetic is Salvemini who holds Giolitti responsible for the dictatorship (1928, p. 71). Yet, even Salvemini spares Giolitti the words he uses for Bonomi and Facta, two of the other prime ministers of the time. Salvemini (1928, p. 129) writes: "It might have seemed impossible to discover a Prime Minister more incapable than Bonomi. But one was found in *Signor* Facta." And again: "Facta – one of the biggest idiots of all times and all countries" (Salvemini, 1928, p. 156). Chabod (1961, p. 48) is kinder in words toward Facta, but no less severe in his judgement when he writes: "[A]n honest provincial lawyer, but without the qualities necessaries to be a head of state."

19. De Felice (1995a, p. 29).

20. Plato (*Timaeus*, 34 c–36 d, 1963).

21. Consider this. "6=1+2+3. But 1, 2, 3 are all the numbers less than 6 that divide 6 without remainder. That is, 6 is the sum of all its divisors less than itself." Indeed, a perfect number (Bell, 1946, p. 157)!

22. The system is based on correspondences between the Hebrew and the western alphabets; there are no letters for the numerical value 9, because the Hebrew letter that stood for it has no equivalents in the western alphabet. Alternatively, we could assign numeric values to the letter

of the western alphabet in the order in which the letters appear in that alphabet. Different numerologists prefer different methods, although the Hebrew system is typically preferred because of its antiquity.

23. Giulio Camillo (1554, p. 344).
24. Although, recognizing the "doability" of a problem may be part of the genius.
25. In modern numerology each one of us bears three numbers known as the *ambition* number, the *personality* number, and the *expression* number (Anderson, 1979, pp. 23–4).
26. YHVH, in the Jewish tradition, is the sacred name of God. In Hebrew this "four-letter word" or symbol, called Tetragrammaton, corresponds to yod-ye-vau-he (YHWH) and signifying Yahweh. Pronounced in Hebrew as "Adomai," it is written as JHYH, or JHVH, or YHVH. In English it became Jehovah. Yahweh is the name of the Almighty Father commonly referred to as The Lord" or "God." The reason for using such words as "Lord" or "God" is because of a Jewish tradition that the name Yahweh was not to be spoken for fear that the name be blasphemed. "Shemhamforash" is a Hebrew word that means "the specific name." It is the 72-letter-word used instead of the name of God (JHVH).
27. Similarly awe struck was Jasso (2000, pp. 492–4) when she discovered a mathematical function of justice evaluation, function that she later extended to further sociological problems (Jasso, 1997).
28. Grants NSF-G24827, NSF-GS224, and NSF-GS536.
29. Rummel (1963, pp. 9, 3).
30. See also Rummel (1966) for similar results based on the analysis of twelve measures of domestic conflict originally collected by Eckstein (1962).
31. I have translated the two actions *dimostrazione* and *manifestazione* as "demosntration 1" and "demonstration 2." The Italian words both refer to public forms of collective action, something akin to a rally or a demonstration. I translated the Italian word *comizio* as "public meeting with speech making" and the Italian *agitazione* as "agitation." It is not always clear exactly what newspapers mean when they write: "Fiat workers agitate." It probably means that workers are in a state of protest, although it does not necessarily lead to specific forms of collective action (for example, strike, demonstration).
32. Rummel (1963, p. 4).
33. Eckstein (1962); on Eckstein's data, see Rummel (1966). In Tanter's (1966) replication of Rummel's work, eighty-three nations are used for the same twenty-two measures.
34. Thirty-six provinces were excluded from the analyses, because of missing measurements on two of the variables in the model (nineteen missing on fascist violence; twenty nine missing on protest from below). The fifty-seven provinces on which the regression model was run are: Alessandria, Ancona, Arezzo, Bari, Benevento, Bergamo, Bologna, Brescia, Cagliari, Caltanissetta, Catanzaro, Cremona, Cuneo, Ferrara, Firenze, Foggia, Forlì, Frosinone, Genova, Grosseto, Imperia, L'Aquila, La Spezia, Lecce, Livorno, Lucca, Mantova, Massa Carrara, Milano, Modena, Napoli, Novara, Padova, Palermo, Parma, Pavia, Perugia, Piacenza, Pisa, Pistoia, Pordenone, Potenza, Roma, Rovigo, Savona, Siena, Siracusa, Taranto, Terni, Torino, Treviso, Trieste, Udine, Varese, Venezia, Verona, Vicenza.
35. As Propp observed (1968, pp. 21–2): "If functions are delineated, a second question arises: In what sequence are these functions encountered? ... The sequence of events has its own laws."
36. De Felice (1995b). One such interpretation that has enjoyed considerable popularity in both Germany and Italy is that advanced by Croce and Meinecke. For Croce, fascism represents a moral malaise of the postwar times, the catastrophe of civilization, as Meinecke put it (De Felice, 1995b, pp. 29–41). Perhaps, Gobetti (1948, p. 193) put it best when he wrote that "Mussolini was the representative hero of that weariness and of that aspiration to rest [of the times]." Fascism, according to Croce, is not just an Italian phenomenon but a universal phenomenon. It is not the product of specific social classes, but of all social classes. Fascism can strike anywhere, at any time. Such an interpretation, no doubt, helps to appease the feelings of guilt in those societies who experienced fascism and to widen to others the historical responsibility of dictatorship. Unfortunately, it leaves unresolved the problem of pinning down the active role of different social actors in bringing out fascism.
37. The first fascist programs were "catalogues of petty bourgeois grievances" (Poulantzas, 1970, p. 250). Petty bourgeois ideology fused several themes together: Nationalism, anti-parliamentarism, and a preference for strong aggressive governments, anticapitalism and antiworking-class fears (Poulantzas, 1970, pp. 251–2). It was the common ideological themes

of nationalism and anticommunism that masked the contradictions inherent in an alliance of petty bourgeoisie and big capital. Fascism was an urban phenomenon: Its supporters and its militant wing came from the cities and the industrial sector. Other groups joined in tow, and may have seemed dominant, but this was only as a result of concessions made to cover up contradictions within the mass movement (Poulantzas, 1970, pp. 87, 281). For Poulantzas, fascism found its first milieu in the upper and middle strata of the urban petty bourgeoisie severely hit by a profound postwar crisis. The acceleration of capital concentration threatened the existence of small-scale ownership and war reconversion created unemployment among white-collar workers (Poulantzas, 1970, p. 246).

38. The following "necessary factors" contribute to this coalition: A politically dominant landlord class that holds power through the period of industrialization and early democracy; the existence of peasant agriculture geared to the market but employing political rather than market forms of labor control (this "labor repressive agriculture" leads the landlords to seek an alliance with the state in order to secure control over state coercive apparatuses and to oppose democracy as this undermines repressive forms of labor control); sufficient industrialization for the bourgeoisie to be a significant political actor, but ideologically subordinate to the landlords and dependent upon the state for the maintenance of its economic position (through protective policies, state credit, and so on); a sufficiently strong state and autonomous from the subordinate classes, a tendency increased by participation in wars and by aspiration to great power status (Moore, 1966, pp. 433–41). Where this antidemocratic alliance existed, no other coalition could muster sufficient strength to overthrow it.

39. Rueschemeyer, Stephens, and Stephens (1992) have rejected Barrington Moore's claim that fascism is necessarily one of three "paths to the modern world"; the class alliances that produce fascism are too inherently unstable for that (Rueschemeyer et al., 1992, p. 152). Industrialists can be antidemocratic in light of their own interests, and not only when they are politically subordinate to the landed elite. Conversely, landlords need not necessarily be labor repressive, just "dependent on a large supply of cheap labor." Notwithstanding these criticisms, even Rueschemeyer et al. in the end agree with Barrington Moore that fascism is the result of an antidemocratic alliance among landlords, industrial bourgeoisie, and the state.

40. Unfortunately, there is no universal agreement on what elements constitute the political opportunity structure. McAdam has synthesized the works of Brockett (1991), Kriesi et al. (1992), Rucht (1996), and Tarrow (1994) to construct a basic consensual list: 1. The relative openness/closure of the institutionalized political system (a system in which formal access is closed is more likely to channel discontent into extrainstitutional movement activity). 2. Stability/instability of that broad set of elite alignments that typically undergird a polity (power bloc disunity creates uncertainty amongst its supporters, encourages elite fractions to compete for outside support, and activates outside challengers). 3. Presence/absence of elite allies (activity is encouraged when groups have allies who can act as friends in court, guarantors against repression or acceptable negotiators). 4. State capacity/propensity for repression (repression increases the costs of collective action, relative to potential gains) (McAdam, 1996, pp. 26–7).

41. They may also be relevant to movement form. Rucht (1996) outlines some aspects of a group's political opportunity structure and their likely impact: 1. Open access invites movements to attempt to influence the party/policy system by building formal and institutionalized structures (for example, political parties). 2. Weak state policy implementation capacity, typically connected with high legislative/judicial power and/or high administrative decentralization, encourages formal organizations to exert continuous pressure at institutional leverage points. Conversely, strong executive power invites fundamental critiques of bureaucracy and encourages decentralized structures. 3. A weak alliance system forces a movement to develop its own bases of organization and action, while those with strong allies can remain informal and profit from a division of labor (Rucht, 1996, p. 13). 4. A strong conflict system encourages the creation of formal organizations best suited for immediate and strategic response (Rucht, 1996, pp. 191–2).

42. Snow et al. (1986, pp. 464–81) outline a number of ways in which movements try to align the frames of potential members with their programs, ranging from the manipulation of particular aspects of common views to the total transformation of world views. Zald (1996) points out that movements exist in a larger societal context and must draw upon existing cultural frameworks, particularly what is perceived to be just and what are deemed to be acceptable

forms of protest and organization. In doing this, however, movements come into competition not only with other movements, but with the authorities and ruling class interests, which often have powerful cultural weapons to hand (Tarrow, 1994, pp. 122–3). In any case, not all movements have equal access to cultural stock. Members are differentially located in the social structure, which allows movements to draw on a variety of skills and orientations, as well as on economic resources (Zald, 1996, p. 267). Social movements also create cultural feedback. Frames of successful movements are translated into public policy and their slogans, symbols, and methods are likely to serve as models for other movements. Even movements that failed provide networks of affiliation and reservoirs of experience, which can be drawn upon by later movements (Zald, 1996, pp. 270–1).

43. Sorokin (1928, pp. xxii–xxiii; emphasis added).
44. Palmer (1994, p. 4) writes: "These [roles] are sometimes referred to as 'semantic roles', but the less precise term 'notional roles' is to be preferred."
45. One can also look at the difference between Agent and Patient "in terms of causation, the Agent being essentially the cause or 'initiator' of the action and the Patient the one directly affected by it or its 'endpoint.' This notion of causation makes it possible to extend the notion of agent beyond that of animate beings acting in a deliberate fashion" (Palmer, 1994, p. 25). Examples are: "The tree fell and killed the man"; "The famine of that year decimated some 10% of the population."
46. Goal has also been used for Beneficiary (Croft, 1991, p. 157), but *goal* has been used in the past to refer to the Patient-Object (Palmer, 1994, p. 33).
47. Palmer (1994, pp. 10, 33, 36). "Generally one gives, buys, etc. something to or from some other person" (Palmer, 1994, p. 33).
48. See Chafe (1970, pp. 144–66) on secondary roles. Unfortunately, there is no general agreement on either the number or the names of semantic roles. It "rests largely on the judgment of the investigator" (Palmer, 1994, p. 6).
49. It was Fillmore who first attracted the linguists' attention to semantic roles. In his *Case for Case*, Fillmore provided the following list of roles (1968; see also the revised and augmented set of such "cases" in Fillmore, 1971, p. 376). *Agent*, the instigator of the event; *Counteragent*, the force or resistance against which the action is carried out; *Object*, the entity that moves or changes or whose position or existence is in consideration; *Result*, the entity that comes into existence as a result of the action; *Instrument*, the stimulus or immediate physical cause of the event; *Source*, the place from which something moves; *Goal*, the place to which something moves; *Experiencer*, the entity which receives or accepts or experiences or undergoes the effect of the action. Radford (1988, p. 373) gives the following list of roles: Theme (Patient), Agent (Actor), Experiencer, Benefactive, Instrument, Locative, Goal, Source. For other lists, see Palmer (1994, p. 5).
50. "Perceivers are not agents, for perceivers are in no sense causers or instigators of the perception; on the contrary, it would seem that the thing perceived is more like the cause" (Palmer, 1994, p. 9).
51. Yet, in the grammar, the instrument of an action is typically inanimate. Even in the grammar, then, animate instruments could be better dealt with as a semantic role (as in the sentence "the government sent in troops" where troops is clearly an instrument of government repression).
52. In active sentences, semantic and grammatical roles coincide; the subject is also the agent, and the patient is also the object (Palmer, 1994, p. 19). As for the beneficiary, its most familiar use is that usually referred to in traditional grammars as the "indirect object," where it is the third term in a three-way construction (the others being Agent- Subject and Patient-Direct Object).
53. See Halliday (1994, pp. 143, 166) for a complete summary table of his processes, participants, and circumstances; see p. 151 for a summary table of all circumstantial elements.
54. Cited in Chandrasekhar (1987, p. 52).
55. We find Pythagoras's mysticism influence even in medicine, for example in William Harvey's work on blood circulation. The *cycle* of blood was a new concept, and Harvey admired its mystical aesthetics. In one passage he writes: "The heart, consequently, is the beginning of life; the sun of the microcosm, even as the sun in his turn might well be designated the heart of the world; for it is the heart by whose virtue and pulse the blood is moved, perfected, made apt to nourish, and is preserved from corruption and coagulation; it is the household divinity which, discharging its function, nourishes, cherishes, quickens the whole body, and is indeed the foundation of life, the source of all action" (cited in Debus, 1978, p. 69).

56. A most intractable mathematical object involving links between number theory and something called "the monster," which exists in 196,883 dimensions.
57. From *The Sunday Times*, January 10, 1999, p. 6 of "News Review" column 7, "The brains behind the twenty-first century," by Steve Farrer "on the scientists who are going to revolutionise our lives in the course of the next 100 years."
58. Dirac (1980, p. 44). On aesthetic grounds Dirac moves a criticism to Einstein's equation of the invariant distance in a four-dimensional space:

$$ds^2 = c^2 dt^2 - dx^2 - dy^2 - dz^2$$

(where s refers to invariant distance, t time, and x, y, and z the three spatial dimensions). For Dirac, Einstein's theory "is not quite perfect. The lack of complete symmetry lies in the fact that the contribution from the time direction $(c^2 dt^2)$ does not have the same sign as the contributions from the three spatial dimensions $(- dx^2, - dy^2$ and $- dt^2)$" (Dirac, 1963, p. 50).
59. In every day social scientific discourse the use of such expressions as "well-crafted paper" betrays the implicit adoption of aesthetic criteria in the evaluation of scientific production. Presumably, a "well-crafted paper" is one constructed out of the proper handling of the methods and procedures of the craft in a "competent" way, ultimately to fashion a product that also has some aesthetic appeal: "well" crafted.
60. Darwin (1996, pp. 51, 51, 90, 138). On Darwin's aesthetic sense, see Gruber (1978).
61. Darwin (1996, p. 107; emphasis added).
62. Weisskopf (1990, p. 311).
63. Cited in Chandrasekhar (1987, p. 60).
64. Watson (1969, p. 120; emphasis added; see also, pp. 30, 139 for occurrences of the word "beautiful").
65. Cited in Baggott (1994, 68–9, 70; emphasis added).
66. References in this paragraph are to Jasso (2000, pp. 492, 494, 493, 496).
67. For a number of other associations with beauty, see Ogden and Richards (1946, pp. 142–3).
68. Plato (*Symposium*, 201c, 1963). For a discussion of Plato's conception of beauty, see Gadamer (1997, pp. 474–91).
69. Current psychological research shows that, in experimental situations, more physically attractive individuals are typically perceived as being happier, more successful, and socially more skillful (for example, Goldman and Lewis, 1977). More to the point, attractive defendants receive shorter sentences in real life jury decisions than unattractive ones (see DeSantis and Wesley, 1997).
70. That follows an older Judaic tradition, where the devil is a goat (*serizzim*): The prince of evil spirits takes the form of an unclean animal. In the Bible, Satan is portrayed as a worm and a dragon (Revelations) and a snake (Genesis).
71. Dante, *Inferno*, xxxiv. The Chester *Play of Antichrist* calls the devil "grisly and grim" (indeed the mortality players usually went to great lengths to make the devils look as ugly and horrifying as possible). Crashaw, a seventeenth-century Renaissance Catholic, also has a particularly ugly Satan near the end of his *Herode*. Milton is the first to suggest that the devil, in *Paradise Lost*, remains beautiful, even after his fall. The devil's parliament is composed of "a thousand demigods on golden seats" (I.794), "their visage and their stature as of gods" (II.570). Satan "…in shape and gesture proudly eminent / Stood like a tower; his form had yet not lost / All its original brightness, nor appeared / Less than archangel ruined" (II.590–3). But if the devil is ugly, he is also able to hide his ugliness, thus resolving a redoubtable theological problem, namely, if the devil is ugly, and sin transparently bad, why would anyone sin? Thus, Augustine, in the *Civitatis Dei* says that devils often appear as "angels of light." For Shakespeare "the devil hath power to assume a pleasing shape" (*Hamlet*, II.2.628). Marlowe's *Doctor Faustus* finds the doctor summoning a demon, who turns out to be "too ugly to attend on (him). / Go and return as an old Franciscan friar, / That holy shape befits a devil best." *Faustus* also has the doctor summoning a demonic Helen of Troy, "fairer than the evening air / Clad in the beauty of a thousand stars." Burton, in the *Anatomy of Melancholy* (I.2.i.2) says that devils can "represent castles in the air, spectrums, prodigies, and such strange objects to mortal men's eyes … The devil reigns and in a thousand several shapes." There is, though, no suggestion that these writers thought that the devil really *was* beautiful, only that he could make himself *appear* to be so.
72. Melville (1929).

Journeys

1. From Wordsworth's autobiographic poem *The Prelude* (1805 edition, Book VI, line 428). William Wordsworth undertook his youth voyage through France to Italy, described in lines 332–705 of *The Prelude* with his life-long friend Robert Jones right after their college years at Cambridge.
2. Goethe (1987, 550–5).
3. Calvino (1993, pp. 105, 106).
4. Calvino (1993, pp. 3–4).
5. The number of pilgrims' accounts on Holy Land travels is much larger than anything produced for other places – Rome and Santiago in particular (Richard, 1984, p. 144). The number of lay people writing increased particularly starting with the thirteen century (Richard, 1981, p. 38). By no means is that tradition of writing personal accounts of pilgrimages dead. It has continued to flourish right up to the present day.
6. The word "pilgrimage" (Latin, *peregrinatio)* comes from the Latin *per agere,* "to go through land, countries." In classical Latin it indicated vagabondage. Adopted by early Christianity, the term took on a new meaning to refer to those faithful who left their normal life in order to search for salvation in an endless wandering. Early Celtic (Irish) pilgrims of the sixth and seventh centuries wandered all their life through continental Europe without a specific place in mind (Geary, 1984, p. 265; Sigal, 1984, p. 76; Grabois, 1988, p. 65; Sumption, 1975, pp. 96–7). Pilgrimages to the Holy Land, starting in the fourth century, and, toward the end of the millennium to Santiago de Compostela, changed that pattern. Pilgrimages became attached to specific places.
7. In his *Vita Nuova* (XL), Dante Alighieri thus distinguishes the various types of pilgrims: "In a wide sense, whoever is outside the fatherland is a pilgrim; in the narrow sense, none is called a pilgrim save he who is journeying to or from the sanctuary of St James. They are called palmers, in so far as they journey over the sea, there, whence many times they bring back palm branches; they are called pilgrims in so far as they journey to the sanctuary of Galicia, because the tomb of St James was farther from his own country than that of any other apostle."
8. The early proliferation of shrines and holy places across Europe, must be seen in light of a "careful program of Carolingian ecclesiastical policy carried out by the leading bishops and abbots of the Frankish Church" (Geary, 1984, p. 267). Sacred places could be created where "politically" needed by moving relics around. With the capturing and sacking of Constantinople, in 1215 after the Fourth Crusade, the flood of Byzantine relics that spilled into the West no longer made it necessary to travel long distance to worship the relics of a saint (Geary, 1984). A number of local places of worship emerged out of the fame of new local saints (Thomas Beckett in Canterbury, Saint Francis in Assisi). Local shrines started competing fiercely with the traditional great pilgrimage sites in their offers of indulgences (Coleman and Elsner, 1995, pp. 109–10; Geary, 1984, p. 265).
9. For examples of luxury travel to the Holy Land by Roman aristocrats, see Hunt (1984, pp. 76–82).
10. Even towns, during droughts or famine, may pay someone to go on a pilgrimage (Davidson and Dunn-Wood, 1993, p. 68). Professional pilgrims developed out of these practices, who got half of their money upon departure and half upon return (Sigal, 1984, pp. 82–3), and who may embellish their cloaks with cross-shaped patches to denote their "professional" status (Loxton, 1978, p. 113). In the fifteenth century in England, proxy pilgrimage became a purely commercial transaction (Loxton, 1978, p. 96).
11. Wilkinson (1981a, p. 153); Davidson and Dunn-Wood (1993, p. 106); Richard (1981, p. 16). For the original Latin, see Tobler (1869) or Cuntz (1929, pp. 86–102). For an English translation of the handful of pages where the pilgrim provides more information on a place than a name and a distance in miles, see Wilkinson (1981a, pp. 153–63). Although the Bordeaux pilgrim was the first Christian pilgrim to leave us a diary of his journey, he was not the first Christian to travel to the Holy Land. But he certainly was among the very first ones. Church historian Eusebius left us a description of Helena's visit to the Holy Land in 326–27 A.D. in his *Vita Costantini.* The empress Helena, the mother of Constantine, was no pilgrim, however. She went to Jerusalem in the "full magnificence of royal power" to put the imperial stamp on the grand construction works of churches and monasteries sponsored by the newly

converted emperor (Eusebius, in Hunt, 1984, p. 35). Even before Helena, history has recorded a handful of names who had traveled to the Holy Land (for example, Melito of Sardis, Origen) (Hunt, 1984, p. 83; Wilkinson, 1981b, pp. 11–12). Helena's trip, however, paved the way to a new era of travel to the Holy Land (Hunt, 1984, p. 28).

12. That was not so unusual, particularly for the earlier centuries. In his study of medieval guidebooks and travel accounts, Richard (1981, pp. 38–9) tells us that guidebooks proper were typically anonymous (for example, *The Pilgrim's Guide* to Santiago de Compostela; although Burchard de Mont-Sion left his name on a work that was meant to simply describe the Holy Land; for the original account, see Laurent, 1864). Pilgrims of the fourteenth and fifteenth centuries typically signed their work. The twelfth-century travelers to the Holy Land, Saewulf and John of Würzburg, start their travel diaries with the classical stamp of authorship: *"Ego Saewulf ..."* and *"Iohannes, dei gratia in Wirziburgensi aecclesia ..."* (Huygens and Pryor, 1995, pp. 59, 79).

13. See the *Itinerarium Provinciarum* (Cuntz, 1929, p. 70).

14. We know that from the names of the Roman consuls in office that he has left us (Wilkinson, 1981a, p. 153).

15. Wilkinson (1981a, p. 154); original account also found in Tobler (1869). With its detailed recording, the document provides invaluable information about the organization of travel in the fourth-century Roman Empire; so much so, that it was included among the handful of extant maps and cosmographic material collected under the title of *Itineraria Romana* (Cuntz, 1929, pp. 86–102; Hunt, 1984, p. 57).

16. Hunt (1984, p. 56). His journey must have taken him over a year, much of it spent on the road, at an average of twenty-one miles a day on horseback, when he was lucky, otherwise on foot. Traveling privately, he had no right to assistance by the imperial Roman travel system (he often had to wait patiently for a ride to the next staging post; Hunt, 1984, p. 58); being among the first Christians to embark upon the journey, he could not rely on a Christian system of hospitality yet to come (Hunt, 1984, p. 63). Even only a century later it was a different story, with the establishment, along the way, of many hostels supervised by clergy and monks (Hunt, 1984, p. 63). "An alternative, and explicitly Christian, framework for travel around the Roman empire" slowly became available (Hunt, 1984, p. 65).

17. Wilkinson (1981a, p. 115). She came from the Atlantic coast of Western Europe, perhaps Spain or France (A. Palmer, 1994, pp. 40–5).

18. References in this paragraph are to Wilkinson (1981a, pp. 111–12, 121–2, 95, 98, 113).

19. "How should I your true love know / From another one? / By his cockle hat and staff / And his sandal shoon," sang Ophelia, mad with love for Hamlet. Shakespeare's reference (*Hamlet*, Act IV, scene 5, lines 23–6) is to the stereotypical pilgrim's attire: a large-brimmed hat, a staff, a long cloak, a gourd, a scrip or pouch, and a symbol of the pilgrimage goal: The cockleshell of Compostela or the crossed keys for Rome (Davidson and Dunn-Wood, 1993, p. 69; Loxton, 1978, p. 113). According to tradition, pilgrims were to journey barefoot, not to sleep twice in the same place, not to set iron on hair or nail – men typically wore a long beard parted in two (see Holloway, 1987, p. 8; Hunt, 1984, p. 68; Sumption, 1975, pp. 127, 171–5). Pilgrims were also to fast and pray. And, above all, they were to be chaste.

20. Richard (1984, pp. 145, 146, 147); Grabois (1988, pp. 66, 74).

21. Quotes taken from Jerome's *epitaphium* for his friend Paula (Hunt, 1984, p. 87).

22. For Thietmar's account, see Tobler (1851) or Laurent (1852). Burchard de Mont-Sion invites his readers to go themselves to the Holy Land, although his own account may allow those who cannot travel to visit the Holy Land "vicariously" (for these and other examples, see Richard, 1981, p. 21; for the original account, see Laurent, 1864). Jean de Wurzbourg, who traveled to the Holy Land around 1170, addresses his brief account to his friend Dietrich so that he may feel encouraged by Jean's faithful description to go to the Holy Land to see for himself Jerusalem and the other places of Jesus's life (Huygens and Pryor, 1995, p. 79; the original account is also in Tobler, 1874).

23. Richard (1981, pp. 39–40); Davidson and Dunn-Wood (1993, pp. 43, 103). Typical is the case of the sixth-century *Itinerarium Antonini Piacentini*, parts of which were incorporated in later texts (Milani, 1977, pp. 42–3). In later periods, some authors compiled travel books to the Holy Land without ever having been there and solely on the basis of existing written accounts (Milani, 1977, p. 45). The pilgrim von Harff could not have possibly seen all the places he describes (1946, p. xvi). There is a long tradition of "plagiarism" in the travel literature. Marco

Polo in his *Il Milione* describes monsters that come all the way from Pliny and that you still find in Columbus. Mandeville takes abundantly from a number of earlier accounts (see Moseley's introduction to Mandeville's *Travels*, contributing to raise the suspicion that "Mandeville's longest journey was to the nearest library" (Mandeville, 1983, p. 12). Seneca (1920, p. 266) in one of his epistles uses three metaphors to approach plagiarism (imitation, in the classic tradition): The bee and honey, digestion and food, the chorus; out of the plurality of flower pollens comes a new creation of honey, out of the variety of food ingested, if properly digested, comes nourishment for the individual, out of the plurality of voices comes a new and single creation. On imitation see McLaughlin's wonderful essay (1995).

24. Pilgrims' views of the world had vast echo in Europe, as witnessed by the repeated editions of many of these works through the centuries. Audiences would gathered to hear the pilgrims' story of their journey in vernacular language. These stories, oral or written, roused much interest in European society (Grabois, 1988, p. 74; Richard, 1984, p. 145).

25. Richard (1981, p. 18). On the development of the guidebook, see de Beer (1952). Indeed, "the combination of inventory and itinerary, is the decisive feature of the class" (de Beer, 1952, p. 36).

26. Richard (1981, p. 16). The original Latin is also known by other names: *Codex Calixtinus, Codex Compostelanus, Liber Sancti Iacobi,* or *Jacobus.*

27. Anonymous (1992, pp. 17–18, 18, 19, 23). In fact, the text continues "faithless, dishonourable, corrupt, lustful, drunken, skilled in all forms of violence, fierce and savage, dishonest and false, impious and coarse, cruel and quarrelsome, incapable of any good impulses, past masters of all vices and iniquities" (Anonymous, 1992, p. 23).

28. Saewulf (in Huygens and Pryor, 1995, lines 13–14; 110–148); see also Richard (1981, pp. 22, 40, 77).

29. Huygens and Pryor (1995, pp. 75–6, lines 565–77, p. 76, line 590); Coleman and Elsner (1995, p. 97). In self-defense, pilgrims started traveling in large groups, even thousands strong (Sumption, 1975, pp. 196–8; Alfani, 1750, p. 29). But such large bands of unarmed pilgrims often made them easier targets, with hundreds dying in sudden attacks (for example, see Sumption, 1975, p. 183).

30. Hunt (1984, p. 71); Loxton (1978, p. 78).

31. Pietro Della Valle (1989, p. 3); see also Hunt (1984, p. 72). Claude Lèvi-Strauss, in his *Tristes Tropiques,* left a similar description of a twentieth-century crowded sea journey (1992, pp. 22–8).

32. Cited in Grabois (1988, p. 71). Whatever were the pilgrims' motives for travel, for the crusader it was not faith and religion that attracted them to the Holy Land, but glory and adventure (Richard, 1984, p. 150).

33. Some, of course, had no choice. The Church and local governments often sentenced individuals to walk a pilgrimage route in order to atone for a crime or a sin, the socalled penitential pilgrimage. The practice probably started in the Netherlands in the late Middle Ages and soon spread to France and Italy. By the thirteenth century, both lay and Inquisition tribunals were sentencing convicts to pilgrimages, the distance to be traveled being commensurate to the severity of the crime committed (Sigal, 1984; Loxton, 1978, p. 98; Geary, 1984). Sometimes, expiation pilgrims were ordered to make the pilgrimage in chains, with the murder weapon suspended from the chains (Loxton, 1978, p. 98).

34. We have no extant records of their numbers. It was probably many, particularly during the heyday of Christian travel, between the twelfth and fourteenth century. According to Daniel-Rops, half a million pilgrims a year traveled to Compostela (although he does not tell us when), and two million to Rome for the jubilee of 1300 (cited in Davidson and Dunn-Wood, 1993, p. 64). Alfani, in his history of the Roman jubilee years, tells us repeatedly of the incredible crowds, coming from all over Europe, with a recurring number of 200,000 pilgrims present in Rome and 30,000 coming and going on any given day (Alfani, 1750, pp. 8, 13, 30). A sixteenth-century description of the shrine of Regensburg in Bavarian Germany tells us that "the pilgrims came in thousands, often whole villages together" (cited in Coleman and Elsner, 1995, p. 84).

35. This would become a recurrent theme in pilgrims' accounts (for example, see Thietmar, in Laurent, 1852, lines I–4–6). Paula left an account of her journey found in Tobler (1869).

36. See Davidson and Dunn-Wood (1993, p. 71). Pilgrims, in any case, before undertaking their journey needed to acquire permission from the bishop or the overlord (Davidson and Dunn-

Wood, 1993, p. 71). In England, those going on pilgrimage overseas had to gain permission from the crown, taking an oath that they would do nothing contrary to their obedience and fealty to the king or take out more money or bullion than was needed for the expenses of the journey, and there was sometime a clause promising not to reveal "the secrets of the kingdom" (Loxton, 1978, pp. 101–2).

37. Hospitality was sacred (Sumption, 1975, pp. 198–203). Pilgrims were to be given bread, water and lodging for twenty-four hours in the communities through which they went (Holloway, 1987, p. 6). *The Pilgrim's Guide* insisted that "All pilgrims should, for the love of God and the Apostle, receive full hospitality in the hospice on the night following their arrival. The sick should be charitably cared for in the hospice until their death or complete restoration to health" (Anonymous, 1992, pp. 85–6). "Pilgrims, whether poor or rich, returning from St James or going there must be received with charity and compassion; for whoever receives them and gives them hospitality has for his guest not only St James but our Lord Himself. As the Lord says in His Gospel, 'He that receiveth you receiveth me'" (Anonymous, 1992, p. 86). The anonymous author then goes on to list the terrible things that have happened to people in various towns for not complying. Both state criminal codes and Church's bulls became increasingly harsh on those who molested travelers, pilgrims in particular (Sumption, 1975, pp. 177–8).

38. Coleman and Elsner (1995, p. 117); see also Holloway (1987, p. 42). For the figure of the merchant, Chaucer ambiguously states in his *Canterbury Tales*: "[T]heir wiste no wight that he was in dette" (there knew no man that he was in debt).

39. Jünger (1930, p. 1; emphasis added). Ernst Jünger is one of Germany's most controversial figures of the twentieth century. A right-wing publicist and writer, during World War One, Jünger had volunteered for the front at the young age of nineteen, as an officer with the Prussian Army. He wrote a very apologetic account of the war, *The Storm of Steel* (1930). Nietzsche echoes through the pages of the diary.

40. This is just a matter of degree. Bathing, after all, was not common even in ordinary life. Even the rich were averse to bathing. Davidson and Dunn-Wood (1993, p. 160) tell us how inside a shrine "persons milled about, devout and tourists alike. It was often noisy, and more circus-like than religious, with pilgrims singing, fighting, pushing and shoving to move closer to the tomb. Bathing was infrequent, and often the stench of the unwashed bodies and of the diseased visitors was difficult to overcome." The typical remedy against stench was the burning of incense (Davidson and Dunn-Wood (1993, p. 160).

41. A sixteenth-century description of the shrine of Regensburg tells us that "some [pilgrims] elected to come naked, others on their knees; visions and wonders increased ... crowds danced howling around the statue [of the saint]" (cited in Coleman and Elsner, 1995, p. 84).

42. Michel de Montaigne, a young man at the time of the trial (1603), left us the romantic and tragic story of one such soldier by the name of Martin Guerre who ended up losing his life not in war but for being condemned of taking the wife, children, and property of a dead fellow soldier (see the more recent account of Zemon Davis, 1983).

43. Sumption (1975, pp. 98–113); Holloway (1987, p. 8); Loxton (1978, p. 94). On the categorization of pilgrimages, see Sigal (1984). Cesare Ripa in his *Iconologia* gives an iconographic representation of the political exile as a pilgrim with the label *Esilio*, exile (Ripa, 1971).

44. Columbus was the first to deliver the news of the discovery in a series of letters, probably five and probably quite similar in content, that he dispatched to the sovereigns of Spain, Ferdinand and Isabel, and others (Thacher, 1903, vol. 2, p. 15). Until recently, only one of these letters had survived in various copies, probably addressed to Santángel, a court official who had helped him with the financing of his voyage (four in Spanish, three in Italian, and one in Latin). A new letter to the sovereigns of Spain, although of questioned authenticity, came to light in the 1980s (Ife, 1992, p. 13). On Columbus's work, see Jane's introduction to his collection of Columbus's work (Columbus, 1930, vol. 1, pp. cxxiii–cxliii); see also Thacher (1903, vol. 2, pp. 3–72) and West (1992, pp. 267–76). Columbus also wrote a log-book of his first voyage, unfortunately lost. All we have is a summary written by Bartolomé de Las Casas on the basis of the original document, as Las Casas himself tells us (1925; also in Columbus, 1969). Direct quotes taken from the lost log-book are also found in the Columbus's biography, *The Life of the Admiral by His Son, Hernando Colón* (in Columbus, 1969; also Colón, 1959).

45. See Chaunu (1979, pp. 67–92). It is the thirteenth century, according to Chaunu, that saw "the

development of the tools of discovery and conquest: ships for world exploration, the compass and the means for using it, and the tentative tools of early capitalism" (Chaunu, 1979, p. 62). For the story of the Vivaldi brothers, see Chaunu (1979, p. 82).

46. The boats that the Portuguese had used in the fourteenth century in their explorations of the African west coast were even smaller, thirty to fifty tons, propelled by oars and sails, keeping close to the coast as a result (Chaunu, 1979, p. 243). Huguette and Pierre Chaunu, on the basis of data uncovered at the *Casa de la Contratación*, show that tonnage of ships remained low (at around one hundred tons) for the first couple of decades of the sixteenth century, to increase steadily thereafter (see the tonnage data for individual ships by year in Vol. VI, *Ports, Routes, Trafics, Tome II, Le Trafic, de 1504 a 1560* of Chaunu and Chaunu, 1955).

47. Henry ("The Navigator," 1391–1460), son of King João of Portugal, from his secluded life on the promontory of Cape St.Vincent, was the real master mind of Portugal's oceanic adventure to the south. His chronicler, Azurara, tells us that "he had a wish to know the land that lay beyond the Isles of Canary and that cape called Bojador" (cited in Baker, 1937, p. 63). Henry gathered information, even sending his brother Pedro in a tour of Europe to collect books and maps; he trained pilots; he encouraged explorers (Baker, 1937, p. 64).

48. Ravenstein (1898, pp. xviii–xix); Baker (1937, pp. 68–9); Landes (1996, p. 24); Chaunu (1979, pp. 104–42).

49. References in this paragraph are to Columbus (1933, pp. 2, 2–3 and 1969, p. 302).

50. The letter was addressed to the sovereigns of Spain after Columbus's fourth and final voyage and was printed in Venice in 1505.

51. For an introduction to early accounts, see Hirsch (1976).

52. Pigafetta (1969, p. 51). A ceremonial planting of a cross or a flag, the circling of a harbor, the pronunciation of ritualistic formulas ... ah, the power of words! (For example, Vasco da Gama, in Boorstin, 1986, pp. 257–8).

53. Columbus had found shelter in the Franciscan community of La Rábida with his fiveyear- old son and an avalanche of debts after his failure to convince the king of Portugal to finance a voyage of discovery (Chaunu, 1979, p. 151).

54. For these passages, see Díaz (1963, pp. 222 and 32; see also p. 81).

55. For example, Columbus (1969, pp. 66, 69, 72, 73, 86, 87, 93, 117, 122, 156, 157, 190, 268, 270, 273); Pigafetta (1969, pp. 69, 95).

56. Cited in von Martels (1994, p. vii) from the Latin inscription under an engraving plate by Theodorus de Bry in *Americae pars quarta, sive insignis et admiranda Historia de reperta primum Occidentali India a Christophoro Columbo anno MCCCCXCII scripta ab Hieronimo Bezono mediolanese* published in Frankfurt in 1594.

57. Even so, recruitment was not always easy (Skelton's note to Pigafetta, 1969, p. 150). Pigafetta (1969, p. 38) informs us that Magellan "did not wholly declare the voyage which he wished to make, lest the people from astonishment and fear refuse to accompany him on so long a voyage."

58. The diaries of the first "voyages of discovery" tell the stories of these types of "unequal exchange." Columbus knows all too well that bells and glass beads will typically establish a friendship that will get him gold (Columbus, 1969, p. 71). "Some of them wore pieces of gold hanging from their noses, which they happily exchanged for little bells ... and glass beads, but the amount was a mere trifle" (Columbus, 1969, p. 72). Dr. Chanca, who accompanied the Admiral on his second voyage, tells us how "Guacamari presented the Admiral with eight and a half marks of gold" (Columbus, 1969, p. 150). He tells us how "the Indians barter gold and provisions and all that they bring for tags of laces, beads, pins and bits of dishes and plates" (Columbus, 1969, pp. 153–4). Vespucci leaves a similar account of a transaction with local people: "We stayed there for 47 days and came away with 119 marks of pearls with trifles in exchange, that I do not think they cost us more than 40 *ducati*, because we only gave them rattles, mirrors, little balls, and brass leaves; for a rattle they gave us as many pearls they had" (Vespucci, 1957, p. 60).

59. "But ships are but boards, sailors but men; there be land-rats and water-rats, water-thieves and land-thieves – I mean pirates; and then there is the peril of waters, winds, and rocks," the rich Shylock protests as he bargains with Bassanio over insurance rates in Shakespeare's *The Merchant of Venice* (Shakespeare, 1994, act I, scene iii, lines 19–24).

60. The French Bertrandon de la Broquière tells in the account of his voyage to the Holy Land how he and several other pilgrims boarded two galleys in Venice in 1432. "We always sailed

through islands," he wrote, "and reached the Slav city of Sebenich which is also Venetian. And we sailed on among islands until we came to the isle of Corfu ... also Venetian. And from there we came to another Venetian city ... by the name of Moudon ... And from there we reached the isle of Candy ... with a governor of seignory of Venice ..." (in Stopani's anthology, 1991, p. 142; my translation).

61. Chaunu (1969, pp. 283–4) discusses the security but also the economic advantages and disadvantages of this practice.

62. As in Vasco da Gama's expedition (see Velho, 1898, pp. 25, 40, 88) or Magellan's (see Pigafetta, 1969, pp. 71, 113, 127).

63. Familiar routes, unfortunately, were familiar not only to the captains of commercial vessels and to the admirals of warships. Pirates traveled along those same crowded routes. Pirates knew all too well where to wait for their precious preys (Landes, 1996, pp. 21, 25–6; Sobel, 1996, p. 15). By Tenenti's reconstruction (1959, pp. 32–3), the number of Venetian ships that fell into corsairs' hands between 1592 and 1609 was over two hundred. Traveling in convoys reduced the risks (or just spread them) – there is comfort in numbers ... – but it meant idling in wait for a number of ships to be ready to travel.

64. This was later collected and published in the *Book of Privileges* (or *Codex Diplomaticus*). On the *Book of Privileges*, see Thacher (1903, vol. 2, pp. 530–65). The sovereigns of Spain themselves conveniently forgot their dues and they had to be reminded from time to time. Till the end of his life, Columbus battled with the crown for his privileges, obstinately claiming his due (Thacher, 1904, vol. 3, pp. 493–7). In a typically self-pitying style, he wrote to them: "I came to serve at the age of twenty eight and today I have not a hair on my head that is not grey. My body is sick and wasted. All that I and my brothers had has been taken from us, down to our very coats ... I am ruined ... Of worldly possessions, I have not even a farthing to offer for my spirit's good. ... [A]lone in my trouble, sick, in daily expectation of death, and surrounded by a million hostile savages full of cruelty ... Weep for me, whoever has charity, truth, and justice!" (Columbus, 1969, pp. 303–4).

65. *Universalis Cosmographia* is the first known map to show the new world comprised of two continents. These continents are very narrow and separated by a strait into two (a northern and southern continent). The Pacific Ocean is also represented as very narrow. In *Universalis Cosmographia* the southern continent is labeled "America," the first appearance of the name "America" on a map. Waldseemüller argued that, since the three continents then known, Europa, Asia, and Africa, had names of women, it was proper to give the newly-discovered continent also the name of a woman, taking it from the baptismal name of the discoverer of the new continent, Amerigo Vespucci. Amerigo Vespucci had published the account of his third voyage in 1503 with the title *Mundus novus*, the New World. A year later, in 1504, the German humanist Matthew Ringmann, a friend of another Florentine friend of Vespucci, Pico della Mirandola, edited the *Mundus novus* with the new title *De ora antartica per regem Portugalliae pridem inventa*. In 1507, the geographer Martin Waldseemüller, a friend of Ringmann, published *Universalis Cosmographia*, a large world map designed to fold into a globe, along with the expository book *Cosmographiae Introductio*. A small set of friends was unconsciously to decide the fate of history, the strength of weak ties! (Granovetter, 1973). On the first geographical representations of the new world, see Quinn (1976) and Thrower (1976).

66. Columbus's believes about the Earthly Paradise must be read in the context of the medieval world views, in which Columbus was deeply steeped. Mandeville's last few chapters of his travel book are dedicated to a description of two lands on earth that captured the imagination of medieval people: the kingdom of the mythical Prester John and the Earthly Paradise, although of this "I cannot speak properly, for I have not been there; and that I regret" (1983, p. 184).

67. Columbus (1969, p. 221; see also p. 226). Columbus had already made a reference to the Earthly Paradise in his log of the first voyage; in the entry for February 21, Columbus claims that theologians and learned philosophers had been right in placing the Earthly Paradise at the extremity of the East, a region that he has just discovered. Over the next ten years he must have more seriously thought that he had indeed discovered it. On Columbus's convictions about the Earthly Paradise, see Thacher (1903, vol. 2, pp. 409–16).

68. The content of the letter is intriguing. It may even seem that Columbus was trying hard to conceal from others the possible discovery if not of the Pacific Ocean, perhaps, of gold. Some of the unusual remarks he makes seem to point in that direction. "I had with me on this voyage

150 men, among whom were some very capable pilots and fine sailors. But none of them can give a certain account of where I went or from where I came ... Let them state if they can the position of Veragua. ... [A] land where there is much gold ... But they do not know by what route they could return to it. ... In order to return they would have to make a new voyage of discovery" (Columbus, 1969, p. 296). On the issue of Columbus's presentiment of another sea, see Thacher (1903, vol. 2, pp. 589–93); on the issue of Columbus's belief about India or Cathay, see Thacher (1903, vol. 2, pp. 616–21).

69. Cited by Pozzi in his introduction to Vespucci (1984, p. 11).
70. See Cohen's introduction to the collection of documents on Columbus's voyages in Columbus (1969, p. 13).
71. For examples, see Columbus (1969, pp. 59, 66, 70, 75, 76, 116).
72. To give a sense of the popularity of these two travel books, some seventy manuscripts of Polo's book have survived and three hundred of Mandeville's (from Moseley's introduction, Mandeville, 1983, p. 10). John Mandeville incorporates many descriptions found in another fourteenth-century travel book by the friar Odoric of Pordenone, *The Travels of Friar Odoric of Pordenone*. Although Odoric of Pordenone is today a forgotten name, his travel book enjoyed great popularity.
73. For examples, see Mandeville (1983, pp. 53, 55, 57, 64, 163, 165, 169 173, 181, 188).
74. References in this paragraph are to Columbus (1969, pp. 116, 121, 117, 118, 119, 121, 122).
75. On travel fact and fiction, see the collection by von Martels (1994); with specific reference to Columbus's voyages, see Flint (1994); see also Quinn (1976).
76. In Thacher (1903, vol. 1, pp. 55–6; emphasis added). The very first published account of the discovery, other than letters, is found in Bergoma's 1503 *Chronicle* (Thacher, 1903, vol. 2, p. 73).
77. Citations and references in this paragraph are to Vespucci (1984, pp. 57, 109, 62, 70, 66).
78. References in this paragraph are to Vespucci (1984, pp. 99–103); quotes are on page 101.
79. Bernal Díaz's *Historia Verdadera de la Conquista de Nueva España*, although written in the second half of the sixteenth century, it was not published until 1632 in Madrid.
80. Given such descriptions, how could the Spaniards debate the issue at Valladolid of whether the American Indians were men like themselves, with reason and souls, and capable of government? The self-serving interests for Spain of Sepúlveda's position at Valladolid are all too clear.
81. Wilkinson (1981b, p. 4); Hunt (1984, p. 84); Richard (1984, pp. 145–6); Grabois (1988, p. 66).
82. In Milani (1977, p. 238, line 5.4; emphasis added). Although Antonino is probably from Piacenza in central Italy, as he himself tells us, the name Antonino comes from an erroneous reading of the Latin text (Milani, 1977, pp. 34–5). The pilgrim must be considered anonymous.
83. Pilgrims' views of Saracens were widely diffused through European medieval society (Grabois, 1988, pp. 72–3).
84. Richard (1981, p. 21). Starting in the fourteenth and fifteenth centuries, pilgrimage accounts became more complex and more autobiographical (Richard, 1981, p. 22; 1984, p. 150).
85. Pigafetta (1969, p. 88). And in spite of their heroic dimensions, these valiant admirals and captains were not devoid of humility. Of Cortés, Díaz (1963, pp. 46–7) wrote: "I will henceforth ... speak of him ... as Hernando Cortés. ... The valiant Cortés himself preferred simply to be called by this name than by any lofty titles." Díaz, however, also tells us that, no sooner had Cortés been appointed general "he began to adorn himself and to take much more care of his appearance than before. He wore a plume of feathers, with a medallion and a gold chain, and a velvet cloak trimmed with loops of gold. In fact he looked like a bold and gallant Captain" (Díaz, 1963, p. 47). "It is there in Havana that Cortés began to form a household and assume the manners of a lord" (Díaz, 1963, p. 55).
86. Díaz (1963, p. 408).
87. The letter is contained in Columbus (1969, pp. 129–57). References in this paragraph are to Columbus (1969, pp. 138, 151, 144, 145, 150, 143, 145, 147, 149, 133, 148, 132, 134, 148, 149, 152, 150, 151).
88. Columbus (1969, p. 190). Columbus continues: "That is to say: In the province of Cibao, where the goldfields lay, every person over the age of fourteen would pay a large bell-full of gold dust, and everywhere else twenty-five pounds of cotton. And in order that the Spaniards should know what person owed tribute, orders were given for the manufacture of discs of brass or copper, to be given to each every time he made payment, and to be worn around the neck.

Consequently if any man was found without a disc, it would be known that he had not paid and he would be punished" (Columbus, 1969, p. 190).

89. Pigafetta (1969, p. 87; emphasis added). "Then our captain summoned all the chief men of the king, and told them that *if they did not obey the king (as he himself did) he would have them all killed, and would give all their goods to the king*" (Pigafetta, 1969, p. 81; emphasis added). "[A]ll those of this island, and of some others were baptized. And *we burned a village which refused to obey the king or us*" (Pigafetta, 1969, p. 82).

90. Having informed the reader a few lines above that "we found some very pretty Indian women and much spoil" Díaz is careful not to tell us what came of either (1963, p. 338).

91. The travel literature of the fourteenth and fifteenth century had already aroused the Europeans' interest in the sexual practices, real or fictional, of people in far away lands. Mandeville (1983, p. 176) tells his readers of a country where men "marry their own daughters, and their sisters, and their female relatives, and live ten or twelve or more together in one house. Each men's wife shall be common to the others who live there; each of them takes other wives, one on one night, one on another."

92. See Carman (1992) for a discussion of the voice of Lopéz de Gómara in his *Historia de la Conquista de México*.

93. Ruskin similarly writes: "Originality in expression does not depend on invention of new words; nor originality in poetry on invention of new measures; nor, in painting, on invention of new colours, or new modes of using them. ... [goes on to discuss van Eyck's technical invention] Originality depends on nothing of the kind. A man who has the gift will take up any style that is going, the style of his day, and will work in that, and be great in that, and make everything that he does in it look as fresh as if every thought of it had just come down from heaven" (Ruskin, 1903, Vol. VIII, Chapter III "The Seven Lamps of Architecture," p. 253).

94. In that sense, technology is not an "independent" variable. It is shaped by the interests of those who have the power to control its development (see Noble, 1977; Lazonick, 1979, 1981).

95. Ruskin (1903, Vol. III of *Modern Paintings*, pp. 294–5, 255; also pp. 249, 253–5) "Dread of mountains." "Mountain scenery ... is always introduced as being proper to meditate in, or to encourage communion with higher beings" (Ruskin, 1903, Vol. III of *Modern Paintings*, p. 249). "The idea of retirement from the world for the sake of self-mortification, of combat with demons, or communion with angels, and with their King ... gave to all mountain solitude at once a sanctity and a terror, in the medieval mind ..." (Ruskin, 1903, Vol. III of *Modern Paintings*, pp. 253–4).

96. The English movement of the "Gothic" novel (for example, Mathew Lewis's *The Monk*, Horace Walpole's *The Castle of Otranto*, Mary Shelley's *Frankenstein*) or the poetic of the German *Sturm und Drang* are good examples of the romantic rehabilitation of the medieval world.

97. Milani (1977, lines 3.3 of the *recensio altera* p. 236 of the Italian translation; 22.4-5 pp. 247-8; 5.2 p. 238).

98. Cited in Pendle (1963, p. 17). The anonymous *Capitolo, qual narra tutto l'essere d'un mondo nuovo, trovato nel mar Oceano, cosa bella, et dilettevole* puts it this way (cited in Ginzburg (1982, pp. 82–3): "A new and beautiful place has been discovered / By sailors in the Ocean Sea / Which had never before been seen, and never heard about ... / A mountain of grated cheese / Is seen standing alone in the middle of the plain ... / A river of milk gushes forth from a cave / and goes flowing through the town / Its embankments are made of ricotta ... / When it rains it rains ravioli ... " As much as there is plenty to satisfy one's belly, in the new world even social relations are unencumbered by any types of restrictions. "Neither skirts nor cloaks are needed there, / Nor shirts, nor pants at any time: / They all go naked ... / Everybody sees and touches the other as much as he desires ... / Nor about their girls and marrying them off / Is there any worry, since they go as booty, / Everyone satisfies his own appetites."

99. As Ife wrote about Columbus's first letter: "Most of the time he [Columbus] wrote because he wanted something. What he wanted at the beginning of March 1493 was more time and more money" (Ife, 1992, p. 18).

100. Columbus never mentions in his writings the disaster of Navidad (see Ife's introduction to Columbus's letters on this point, Ife, 1992, pp. 16–18). During his first voyage, on Christmas Eve, 1492, Columbus grounded and sank the flagship Santa María on a reef. With the remains of the ship, Columbus had a fort built on shore, named *La Navidad* (Christmas). As the tiny Niña could not hold all of the remaining crew, Columbus left about forty men behind. Upon

return from Spain during the second voyage, all men had been killed and the fort destroyed.
101. On rituals, see Malinowski (1948, pp. 70–4); Mauss (1972, pp. 44–60).

Part II. Looking Back: What's in the Numbers?

1. Like the alchemic tract attributed to Thomas Aquinas (1996), this tract is probably not a work by Albertus Magnus himself. Many alchemists wrote under false and famous names.
2. The conception of life either as a pilgrimage and or a labyrinth was quite widespread. Francesco Colonna, a sixteenth-century Italian monk, in his epistle dedicatoria to the Duke of Urbino of his bizarre book between the mystic and the art of memory, *Hypnerotomachia Poliphili*, first published in Venice in 1499, tells the reader "that if he wishes to have a brief summary of what the book contains, he should know that Poliphilo tells to have seen in a dream marvelous things (*mirande cose*) ... Three gardens, one made out of glass, one of silk, and one as *a labyrinth, which is human life*" (Colonna, 1980, pp. ix, xii; emphasis added).
3. Berger (1963, p. 186). See also Malinowski (1948, p. 73) on the power of words in rituals.
4. Cited in Huizinga (1949, p. 156).

Chapter 4 The Word and the World

1. See also Mulkay's book title *The Word and the World* (Mulkay, 1985); see also Foucault (1970), which in the original French reads *Les mots et les choses* (the words and the things).
2. Coser (1971, p. 3); Rex (1961, pp. 1–26).
3. The Law of the Three Stages (or Law of Human Progress) and his Hierarchy of the Sciences (we still find that terminology and that hierarchy in Webb and Webb, 1932, pp. 8–17). Each stage grows out of the previous one (an idea that both Comte and Marx borrowed from Saint-Simon). The law of the three stages stated that each branch of knowledge passes successively through three different stages: theological or fictitious, the metaphysical or abstract (which reached its peak in the Middle Ages and Renaissance), and the scientific or positive (just beginning at the time of Comte's writing).
4. Weber is less categorical on the issue of "general laws" and "causal explanation." In the first few pages of his *Economy and Society* (1978, pp. 11–12, 18–22), Weber acknowledges that it is possible to provide adequate causal explanations of empirical uniformities, but these "Statistical uniformities constitute understandable types of action, and thus constitute sociological generalizations, only when they can be regarded as manifestations of the understandable subjective meaning of a course of social action" (Weber, 1978, p. 12).
5. The expression is used by Novick (1988, pp. 132, 28) in reference to Ranke's words *wie es eigentlich gewesen* (tell the story the way it actually happened).
6. Cited in Tolman (1902, pp. 805–6).
7. Writing in 1902, in the first of a series of articles that appeared in the *American Journal of Sociology* on "The Study of Sociology in Institutions of Learning in the United States," Tolman identified three different periods in the development of Sociology in the United States: 1) From 1880 to 1890 is the period of the so-called social science; 2) from 1890 to 1900 is marked by the ascendancy of social philosophy; 3) the first decade of the twentieth century characterized by a reaction, based on "analytic sociology, in which the statistical and psycho-sociologic method shall be largely used" (Tolman, 1902, p. 798).
8. On the role of Albion Small in American sociology, see Barnes (1948).
9. Park and Burgess (1921). Quote taken from Levine et al. (1976b, p. 817).
10. In England, Sidney and Beatrice Webb, in their book *Methods of Social Study*, similarly wrote (1932, pp. 2–3): "Sociology ... belongs, like botany and zoology, physiology and psychology to what may be termed the biological group of sciences, as distinguished from the group of physical sciences." A science of the living, in other words, but a science, nonetheless.
11. Bottomore and Frisby, from their "Introduction" (Simmel, 1978, p. 7).
12. Berger (1963, p. 24).
13. Simmel (1978, pp. 231–2).

14. For these citations, see Trevelyan (1919, pp. 22, 22, 23, 23).
15. The novelist and the historian, Collingwood would argue honoring that long tradition, differ in this "that the historian's picture is meant to be true" (Collingwood, 1946, p. 246). The novelist's only task is "to construct a coherent picture." But the historian confronts a double task: Construct a coherent picture *and* "a picture of things as they really were" (Collingwood, 1946, p. 246). He has no responsibility to truth. The historian, contrary to the storyteller, has to confront "two orders of events" what *really* went on in history and what is being told (White, 1987, p. 3). The storyteller does not have to worry about these two planes of action. The artist "is his own master" (Collingwood, 1946, p. 237).
16. Notable are Jean Le Clerc's *Ars Critica*, published in 1697, one of the most important early works on textual criticism (authenticity and emendation of texts) and Jean Mabillon's *De re diplomatica*, published in 1681.
17. Langlois and Seignobos call this erudition "external critique" or "erudits' critique" (1898).
18. In Germany, that approach was represented by idealist philosophy, Hegel in particular. For Hegel, history was the incarnation of the Spirit. Not surprisingly, Hegel despised Niebuhr as much as Voltaire had despised Mabillon (Momigliano, 1969, p. 105). Beethoven, born in the same year as Hegel, had been luckier. He was spared an open attack. Hegel, who did not rank music among the great arts, simply never mentioned him in his work, positively or negatively. On the concept of scientific history, see Berlin (1960).
19. Novick (1988, pp. 132, 28); see also Carr (1990, p. 8) and Braudel (1980, p. 11).
20. Langlois and Seignobos (1898, p. 144). They also write: "The detailed analysis of the arguments that lead from the material appraisal of documents to knowledge of facts is one of the main aspects of historical methodology" (1898, p. 45). "In order to know the relationship between document and fact, one must reconstruct the whole series of intermediary causes that have produced the document. ... [T]hat is the goal and the journey of critical analysis" (1898, p. 46). "One should go through the successive acts that have produced a document ... [and analyze] the conditions under which the document has been produced" (1898, pp. 118–19).
21. Elton (1967, pp. 65, 73–83); Bloch (1953, pp. 48–137). Elton insists on the importance of understanding "the historical circumstances behind their [documents] production" and argues that "the historian's primary task will always consist in discovering the circumstances in which his evidence came to be born – the circumstances, intentions, influences attending occasion of its creation" (Elton, 1983, pp. 117, 88; 1967, p. 77).
22. Other disciplinary mottos divided historians from the social scientists, in particular, the time-honored distinction between the particular and the general. French historian Paul Mantoux states: "The particular, whatever occurs only once is the domain of history" (cited in Braudel, 1980, p. 66). The Dutch historian Huizinga wrote: "By reason of its natural bent historical sense always inclines toward the particular, the graphic, the concrete, the unique, the individual. ... Knowledge that has lost sight of actual men and actual events may be worthwhile, but it is no longer history" ([1934] in Stern, 1970, pp. 297–8). Lawrence Stone echoes: "The discipline of history ... deals with a *particular* problem and a *particular* set of actors at *particular* time in a *particular* place" (Stone, 1987, p. 31; see also Elton, 1967, p. 26). Not surprisingly, social scientists have taken their distance from such a view. For Durkheim, the particular is only the first step, not the last, a means rather than a goal. He asked rhetorically: "Is it not the rule in science to rise to the general only after having observed the particular ...?" (Durkheim, 1938, p. 78). Even Max Weber (1978, p. 19) echoed in *Economy and Society*: "We have taken for granted that sociology seeks to formulate type concepts and generalized uniformities of empirical processes. This distinguishes it from history, which is oriented to the causal analysis and explanation of individual actions, structures, and personalities possessing cultural significance." No, the particular is not for the social scientists. They full heartedly embrace Alain René Lesage's (1668–1747) declaration in his *Gil Blas*: "I publicly avow that my purpose is to represent life as we find it: But God forbid that I should undertake to delineate any man in particular!" (Cited in Genette, 1997, p. 216). The German philosophers of history of the turn of the century fixed that time-honored distinction going all the way back to Aristotle into the cultural traditions of modern history and the social sciences. Rickert (1962, p. 55) wrote: "There are sciences that do *not* aim at the discovery of natural laws or even at the formation of *general* concepts. These are the *historical* sciences in the broadest sense of the term. They do not *want* to produce 'ready-made' clothes that fit Paul just as well as they do Peter; they propose to represent reality, which is never general, but always

individual, in its *individuality*." Those philosophers even came up with labels that were to become quite popular. Science is "nomothetic," wrote Windelband (1980[1894]), Rickert's teacher, that is, science is dedicated to the discovery of general laws, while history is "idiographic," that is, focused on the particular and the individual (on these terms, see also Rickert, 1962, pp. xii, 55–6; Elton, 1967, p. 8). On generalization in historiographical writing, see the collection of essays edited by Gottschalk (1963).

23. Collingwood (1946, p. 237); Langlois and Seignobos (1898, pp. 140–1).

24. On the idea of a "noble dream," at least for historians, see Beard (1935) and Novick (1988).

25. Selection is partly the result of time and space constraints in the daily production of news (Breed, 1955; Epstein, 1973; Gans, 1980, pp. 78–80; Gitlin, 1980, pp. 249–52), of the limitations imposed by the organizational structure of news rooms (Altheide, 1976; Tuchman, 1972, 1973; Molotoch and Lester, 1974; Gans, 1980, pp. 78–80; Gitlin, 1980, pp. 249–52), of the dominant culture and values in a society (for example, "anticommunism as a national religion," in Herman and Chomsky's words, 1988, pp. 2, 29–31; van Dijk, 1983), of the professionalization of journalists, with their own standards of objectivity reinforced by autonomous criteria for training, recruitment and promotion and of commercial imperatives. Media companies are large, profit-seeking, mostly family-controlled corporations (on the structure of media ownership, see Herman and Chomsky, 1988, pp. 5–8; Bagdikian, 1987; Compaine et al., 1982; Dreier, 1982; Murdock and Golding, 1974, 1977, 1978). For Herman and Chomsky the overall consequence of the "economic imperative" of media companies is that in Western "democratic" societies mass media operate as large-scale propaganda machines (Herman and Chomsky, 1988). The economic imperatives of mass media tend to restrict the scope of television programs to relatively "safe" issues. Even aggressive journalism is often over relatively localized and safe issues (see Barnouw, 1978, pp. 123–47). Documentaries avoid criticism of corporate activities, as well as in-depth explanations of the historical causes of events when these may prove to be controversial or disturbing to the "selling and buying spirit" (for examples, see Barnouw, 1978; Herman and Chomsky, 1988). Reciprocal investments, shareholdings, and interlocking directorships link media companies to other large industrial concerns and to the wider economic context in which they operate. Other mechanisms, however, reinforce these links, in particular, advertising. Advertising is the principal source of revenue for both the press and commercial television, and hence both are directly vulnerable to adverse changes in general economic conditions. Even the publishing, cinema, and record industry that gain little or no revenue from advertising, are affected by the business cycle through higher costs and lower sales. The mechanism of advertisement, the reliance of media companies on sponsors for profitability, give sponsors a great deal of power on what the media write, say, or show. As Barnouw (1978, p. 151) writes, with regard to U.S. television: "[S]ponsors – mainly global corporations that form the large majority of leading network sponsors – dominate our programming far more extensively than most viewers suppose" (see also Powell and Friedkin, 1983). But even more typical than either overt or subtle censorship, is self-censorship (Barnouw, 1978, p. 137; Herman and Chomsky, 1988, p. xii; Altheide, 1976, p. 58). As the vicepresident of the McCann-Erickson advertising agency, C. Terence Clyne, said in an interview: "There have been few cases where it has been necessary to exercise a veto, because the producers involved and the writers involved are normally pretty well aware of what might not be acceptable" (cited in Barnouw, 1978, p. 54). Certainly, negative experiences with media management and sponsors (experiences that get reflected in one's career opportunities) help to foster conformity among media personnel (the "to not give a shit [and] just do my job" attitude, Altheide, 1976, p. 58). Whether as journalists (Breed, 1955) or editors of publishing houses (Powell, 1985, p. 152), in a "sink or swim" approach to in-house, informal training, the newcomers learn very quickly to interpret the bosses' "frowns, impatience, blue-penciling memos or highlighting words and repeating them" (cited in Powell, 1985, p. 152). Behavior that is rewarded tends to be repeated; behavior that is chastised tends to be abandoned (Powell, 1985, p. 151). In-house socialization is a continuous process, although most visible with new members or with members that have undergone status changes within the organization (promotions or demotions) (Powell, 1985, pp. 148–9). Thus, even without any formal, in-house training, newcomers learn the ropes almost "by osmosis," the "must" and the "may" of their roles (Breed, 1955; Thorntorn and Nardi, 1975). The expectations attached to a role are as far reaching as to include personal behavior, styles of dress, mannerisms of speaking, laughing, joking, and interacting (Powell,

1985, p. 152; Ouchi, 1980). Members of an organization develop similar internal vocabularies and behavior (Cicourel, 1970; Powell, 1985, p. 151). In most cases, however, accommodation and conformity is the result of "professional" training. Professional schools (of education, of journalism, of management, and so on) create and transmit the standards that regulate professional behavior. In these schools, one learns what is and what is not acceptable. One learns to babble the professional mottos of truth and objectivity, "the news, and only the news, that's fit to print." Disciplines are disciplines, in more than one way. Occasional breaking of the rules only serves to reinforce these rules and to legitimate the overall system as "free." As Herman and Chomsky put it: "Media leaders [and school teachers] do similar things because they see the world through the same lenses, are subject to similar constraints and incentives" (Herman and Chomsky, 1988, p. xii).

26.   Molotoch and Lester (1974, p. 111); van Dijk (1983); Barnouw (1978, p. 126); Hall (1977); Gitlin (1980, p. 11); Herman and Chomsky (1988).

27.   Snyder and Kelly (1977); Jenkins and Schock (1992); McCarthy et al. (1996); Mueller (1997); Oliver and Myers (1999); Oliver and Maney (2000).

28.   Glasgow University Media Group (1976, p. 169); see also Beharrell and Philo (1977) and Morley (1976).

29.   Press censorship within a country is likely to lead to underreporting of protest and conflict worldwide (Gunther and Snyder, 1992). In a specific test of this hypothesis, however, Gurr (1968) found that censorship scores were positively correlated with four dimensions of civil strife: persistence, duration, intensity, and total magnitude. That is, press censorship within a country did not prevent the world press from discovering and reporting incidents of civil strife at higher levels of magnitude on critical dimensions. More recent studies have duplicated these findings for other countries with heavy press censorship like South Africa in the mid-1980s (Singer and Ludwig, 1987).

30.   More recent studies suggest that these criteria for press coverage remain the same, although the rank order of attention to any specific country may change in relative importance over time.

31.   Downs (1972); Medalia and Larsen (1958).

32.   Some issue attention cycles are closely tied to dramatic events (Watergate, the Iraq wars), but others (for example, poverty, environmental pollution) are not so obviously linked to objective trends (Gamson and Modigliani, 1989).

33.   For Danzger (1975, pp. 570, 581), this probability is higher in the former case, while for Snyder and Kelly (1977, pp. 119–20) it is exactly the opposite. See also McAdam (1982, p. 235).

34.   *The New York Times* has been extensively used as a data source in both national, U.S., and international projects on conflict, largely because of the ease of use through its extensive index of news. There has been considerable debate over the validity of its data, particularly for international conflicts. After all, *The New York Times* has served as the main source for enumeration lists of worldwide conflict/protest and strife in the three editions of the *World Handbook of Political and Social Indicators* (Russett, et al. 1964; Taylor and Hudson, 1972; Taylor and Jodice, 1983). Although an additional local or regional source has always been used in the *Handbook* to supplement *The New York Times,* early critics (Azar et al., 1972; Azar, 1975, p. 4; Hayes, 1973; Weede, 1973) argued that use of *The New York Times* as the basis of event enumeration results in a regionally biased listing of world protest events. The authors of the *Handbook* (Jodice, 1980; Taylor and Jodice, 1983) as well as other scholars (Jackman and Boyd, 1979) have defended the use of *The New York Times* by insisting that its listings are checked for accuracy, consistency and reporting against a variety of regional and international sources (Jodice, 1980, p. 188). In defending its use as the enumeration source for the third edition of the *Handbook,* Taylor and Jodice (1983) present data showing the proportion of unique events contributed by seven international news compendia for 1968–77. The vast majority (78.8%) were contributed by *The New York Times Index;* Keesing's contributed the second highest (12.2%). The *Middle East Journal,* the *Asian Record* and *African Diary,* generally regarded as the best of the regional news compendia, offered only 3.4, 2.3 and 2.2% percent respectively, with *Current Digest* and *Archive der Gegenwort* contributing less than 1% each.

35.   Jenkins and Perrow (1977), however, found few differences in the coverage of California migrant farm workers' collective actions in the 1960s by *The New York Times* and in *The Los Angeles Times.*

36. Contrary to Paige and Lehman-Wilzig and Ungar, Olzak (1992), in her study of ethnic mobilization in Quebec, found that *The New York Times* was superior to either the *Montreal Gazette* or *La Presse*, the key English and French language dailies in Montreal (see comments in Olzak, 1987, pp. 193–4, n4).

37. Hocke's comparison between national and local (in the town of Freiburg) newspapers in Germany shows a similar neglect by national papers of small, local protest events (1999, pp. 150, 159).

38. Russett et al. (1964); Taylor and Hudson (1972); Taylor and Jodice (1983).

39. For an analysis of the news on industrial relations and strikes, see Capecchi and Livolsi (1971); Nedzynski (1973); Glasgow University Media Group (1976, 1980, 1987); Morley (1976); Beharrell and Philo (1977); Murdock and Golding (1977); Hartmann (1975/1976; 1979); van den Berg et al. (1984); Downing (1980, pp. 47–8). Even when a plurality of views on conflict is expressed, these are confined to a narrow spectrum; they exclude more radical interpretations (van den Berg and van der Veer, 1989).

40. "The press," writes Stevenson (1992, p. 16), "are a staple source of popular disturbances in both eighteenth- and nineteenth-century England." But reporting was "exiguous and erratic," albeit with many variations over time and between large cities and the rural countryside. For Harrison, who relied on newspapers as sources of data for his study of English crowds between 1790 and 1835,"Local crowd gathering occasions were, perhaps, the single most newsworthy subject in the eyes of most newspaper proprietors and editors. *The history of crowds in this period is indirectly a history of newspapers also*" (Harrison, 1988, p. 45; emphasis added). But Wells is less optimistic. Among the different sources for data on riots in eighteenth-century England – police records, legal records, or the press – "The Press, even at the end of the eighteenth century, is an inconclusive source. Despite the fact that riots made good copy," the unspoken rule was rather to "maintain[ed] a conspiracy of silence" (Wells, 1978, p. 69). Censer agrees with that evaluation even with regard to the late eighteenth-century French press: "[D]omestic news was related to nothing but the most innocuous happenings" (1994, p. 25). But systematic comparative analyses of early press coverage of different news are rare. The work by a team of French scholars on the year 1778 is quite unique in this respect (Jansen et al., 1982). In particular, Favre's chapter on the coverage of different types of news (for example, catastrophe, crime, protest, custom, and so on) provides an opportunity to assess the wight of protest events in the early French press. Although the number of protest events reported is high, they mostly occur outside France – after all, "The subject is delicate for a French periodical controlled by the authorities" (Favre, 1982, p. 126).

41. Lieberson and Silverman (1965, p. 892); see also Tilly (1969, p. 23) and Danzger (1975, pp. 574, 582).

42. Paige (1975, p. 135); see also Eisinger (1973, p. 15).

43. See Jacobs (1967, pp. 37–40); see also, Danzger (1975, p. 574); Opp and Gern (1993); Fillieule (1999, p. 205).

44. For an analysis of the reporting of the same event by two newspapers of opposite political views, see Franzosi (2003).

45. More surprising are the arguments made by Tarrow or McCarthy, McPhail, and Smith. Tarrow (1989, p. 30), in defending his choice of *Corriere della Sera* as a source of data for his study of the 1966–73 cycle of protest in Italy, writes: "Italian critics may worry that the *Corriere* is an arm of the establishment. Although the criticism is partially just, it is actually an explanation of the newspaper's utility; for since we posit that the responses of elites and authorities to protest are conditioned by previous protests, what better instrument could we want than the newspaper that they read?" Yet, none of the sixteen tables and thirty-seven figures presented in the book are about elites' responses. Neither are they interpreted in that light. Each one of those tables, each one of those graphs is for Tarrow a window on social reality. I pick at random (Tarrow, 1989, pp. 79–80): "Figure 3.3. plots the average number of tactical forms that were observed in each protest event for each semester for 1966–73. The graph shows that tactical versatility rose very rapidly during the early years of the cycle and declined slowly thereafter, in contrast to the total number of events, which reached their peak only in 1971. Putting together the results of Figure 3.3 with those of Table 3.1 shows that, as the presence of known organizations was declining, people were learning to use more and more varied forms of collective action." The elites here are nowhere to be seen. The statement of page 30 forgotten on page 80, what we see here is "real" people learning the ropes of "real" collective

action, "history as it actually happened" (*wie es eigentlich gewesen*). And what about McCarthy, McPhail, and Smith? They (1996, p. 496) write: "[J]udging from our comparison, the national print media provides an amazingly stable portrait of the churning mixture of protest forms, purposes, and contexts in Washington, D.C., during 1982 and 1991." Surprising conclusion in light of all the evidence they provide on the extent of media bias. Churning, no doubt, there is but, sticking to the food metaphor, the amounts of each ingredient are unrecognizably altered to produce food with little resemblance to the original recipe.

46.   According to a comparison of Italian newspapers that I carried out prior to data collection, *Avanti!*, the official paper of the Italian Socialist Party, provides the largest number of articles on industrial conflict and violence and the largest number of information per article, followed by *Il Lavoro*, a local socialist newspaper published in Genoa – historians Maione (1975) and Spriano (1964) relied heavily on *Avanti!* as a source of information for their books. Unfortunately, *Avanti!* was not available in any of the libraries in Genoa where I carried out data collection. Not having the resources to purchase microfilmed copies of newspapers or to photocopy all articles, I had to rely on *Il Lavoro* as data source since this was available at the Berio public library.

47.   Capecchi and Livolsi (1971, p. 270); Eco (1971); Dardano (1973); Hartley (1982); Trew (1979a); van Dijk (1985a, 1985b, 1986, 1987, 1988). On the biasing effect of titles, see Kozminsky (1977).

48.   On racism and the media, see Hartman and Husband (1973); van Dijk (1987b). On women and the media, see Hobson (1980); Hartley (1982, pp. 28–30, 163). The portrayal of powerful groups (for example, corporations, government), on the contrary, is rarely critical or negative. For one thing, corporations represent an indispensable source of revenue to profit-seeking media. And media certainly "do not want to kill (or even harm) the goose that lays the golden egg." In any case, these organizations can harness great resources to avoid adverse publicity. The very fear of "flack" – the negative reactions to media statements or programs, in the form of letters, petitions, boycott campaigns, withdrawal of advertisement support, lawsuits, and so on – tends to ensure that the media tend to tread familiar ground and avoid potentially controversial issues (Herman and Chomsky, 1988, pp. 18–25). The more organized and powerful a group (such as, indeed, corporations and the government), the more threatening its use of flack for a media company. The same fear of flack and the cost of acquiring and verifying information independently, further conditions the media to rely heavily on a handful of experts with "established broadcasting reputations" (Westergaard, 1977, p. 107) and corporate and government sources for information (Herman and Chomsky, 1988, pp. 18–25). This way, the interpretation of events by these sources tends to become the media interpretation as well (Hartley, 1982, p. 73; van den Berg and van der Veer, 1989).

49.   Since entertainment sells, entertainment became the imperative of television programming early on. Furthermore, since many media companies had become internationalized, "entertainment [had to be] packaged for world markets" (Barnouw, 1978, p. 108; Murdock and Golding, 1977). "Action-adventure proved the most transplantable of forms": cowboy, crime, or secret agent series (Barnouw, 1978, p. 108). The emphasis on action, rather than dialogues, minimized dubbing costs. Furthermore, the good versus evil, us versus them plots transcended cultural barriers and "could be understood everywhere" (Barnouw, 1978, p. 108). Entertainment programs, however, do not simply provide entertainment to people. Entertainment and the apparatus of commercial television sells "a way of life, a view of man himself, a vision of the future" (Barnouw, 1978, p. 151): Communism as the enemy (Communists are always the "bad guys"), violence as a natural and normal fact of life (most action stories are all about violence), capitalism as the economic system that can provide such plentiful production of desirable commodities – and this desire is constantly being created and recreated via commercials. News has increasingly become entertaining, "consumed by much of the American public (and by publics everywhere) largely as a form of entertainment. As such, it competes with other types of entertainment for a share of each person's time" (Downs, 1972, p. 42).

50.   Barnouw (1978, p. 121); on ideology as a process of naturalization, see Barthes (1972 [1957], 1990 [1967]).

51.   New discoveries, new technologies typically create new opportunities for their use (an array of choices). Different groups struggle to affect the direction and use of innovation (Noble, 1977). Without historical memory of these struggles, though, the final outcome is made to

appear as the only possible avenue, as the "natural" way to use a new technology. The advent of television opened up such new possibilities and opportunities. Barnouw (1978) describes the struggles that surrounded early television programming: the sources of revenue (private or public), the format of television programs (serial versus open anthology), their content (entertainment, culture, documentaries, and so on), their scheduling (day, evening, night, weekdays, weekends, and so on), and the structure of advertisement (during or after the programs, and so on). What eventually emerged out of a struggle that involved government regulatory agencies, the public, the media personnel, and the media companies and "sponsors" (that is, corporate interests at large) was a television system that was popular, profitable, and "above all noncontroversial" (Barnouw, 1978, p. 120), "a huge selling machine" in Barnouw's words (Barnouw, 1978, p. 151; for an account of the struggles that surrounded the birth of television in England, see Connell, 1978). The history of the struggles that surrounded the introduction of radio programs are even more indicative of the available choices and of the interests and power of those who ultimately succeeded in imposing their standards (McChesney, 1990). By the time the television was introduced in the early 1950s, many of the structures and formats that were adopted were already in place, the radio having provided them some fifty years earlier (McChesney, 1990).

52. The sample of firms whose data one could use – regardless of the firms' willingness to disclose such data – most likely would be biased in favor of large firms. Small or even medium-sized firms are less likely to keep information on strikes.

53. Police archives are generally not open to the public for the most recent decades.

54. Cited in Krieger (1977, p. 105). See also von Ranke's words in von Ranke (1981, p. 70).

55. For the 1919–22 period in Italy, see Colarizi (1977) and Snowden (1986) for Apulia; Snowden (1989) for Tuscany.

56. The general purpose of gathering control data does not differ much in spirit from techniques commonly used in survey research aimed at gathering as much information as possible about nonrespondents. Careful investigations of respondents' versus nonrespondents' characteristics are very helpful in assessing the validity of one's inferences. Such investigations are standard practice in survey research, but are rarely encountered in studies of historical events.

57. Weede (1973, pp. 122, 109, 108, 125); on the effect of distributions and outliers, see also Belsley et al. (1980); Franzosi (1994b).

58. From the title of Hanke's book (1959): "Aristotle and the American Indians."

59. See Hanke (1959, pp. 15, 17, 23, 27, 47, 49, 59, 66, 90, 99–101).

60. Porter (1995, pp. 33–4); Starr (1987, pp. 32–3); Petersen (1987).

61. Krippendorf qualifies his critique by adding "in the past" (1980, p. 155).

62. Leamer (1983, p. 36).

63. In Nunnally's classic definition: "Reliability concerns the extent to which measurements are *repeatable* – by the same individual using different measures of the same attribute or by different persons using the same measure of an attribute" (1967, p. 172).

64. On newspaper reporting of crowd sizes, see Jacobs (1967, pp. 37–40); see also, Danzger (1975, p. 574); Opp and Gern (1993); Fillieule (1999, p. 205).

65. Krieger (1977, p. 6); Benzoni (1990, p. 51).

66. Cited in Krieger (1977, p. 105).

67. Cited in Krieger (1977, p. 105).

68. "In different places," he tells us, "I gathered together 48 reports relating to Rome: The oldest date from the year 1500; 19 are of the sixteenth century; and 21 of the seventeenth" (von Ranke, 1981, p. 63).

69. The reference is to the protagonist of Ariosto's *Orlando Furioso*.

70. Benzoni (1990, p. 50).

71. Miles and Ervine (1979). On French unemployment statistics, see Salais et al. (1986). On Canadian vital statistics, see Emery (1993).

72. Perrot (1974); in Italy, however, strike statistics are still collected through local police departments.

73. Lay, Marucco, and Pesante (1973, pp. 108–9); more generally, see Starr and Corson (1987) on the politics of the distribution of statistical information.

74. From a statistical viewpoint, the lack of measures on theoretically relevant variables is likely to lead to model misspecification (on the problems of estimation due to model misspecification, see Johnston, 1984, pp. 287–91, 309–13). Repression is certainly one such

variable. After all, resource mobilization theory claims that repression reduces the likelihood of collective action (for example, strikes) by raising the cost of collective action (see Tilly, 1978, p. 100).

75. von Ranke would have probably not regarded as proper data for historical use the Inquisition records that have given such beautiful works of history as *The Cheese and the Worms* (Ginzburg, 1982) and *Montaillou* (Le Roy Ladurie, 1979a) or the autobiographical accounts of ordinary people that social history has made ample use of.

76. Bloch (1953, p. 61).

77. Historian Hayden White explored the role on historical narratives of story and plot. Historians' narratives, no differently from purely fictional narratives, according to White, can be analyzed in terms of two basic linguistic components: Story and plot, *fabula* and *sjužet* – those same linguistic components worked out by the Russian formalists and the French structuralists. The three basic forms of historical representations – annals, chronicle, history proper – differ in their mix of story and plot: Pure story in the annals, story with minimal plot in the chronicles, a balance between story and plot in history proper – pure plot being characteristic only of philosophy of history (White, 1987, pp. 4, 21). Annals, for White, make no attempts at narrativity; they consist of a list of events in chronological order. The chronicle, by contrast, does tell a story; it "aspires to narrativity, but typically fails to achieve it" (White, 1987, p. 5; see also p. 16 – Danto strongly rejects this "distinction between history and chronicle, or between plain and significant narratives, or, what comes to the same thing, between explaining and describing in historical narration"; 1985, p. 119). Furthermore, for White, story and plot coincide, the narrative organization of events – the plot – coincides with the chronological order of events, in the order of their occurrence – the story. It is only history proper that develops the plot component that is in embryo in chronicles. In history proper, events are concatenated in a meaningful way, they have a beginning, a middle, and end. There is closure to history where there is none (or little) to chronicle. "The chronicle ... does not so much conclude as simply terminate; typically it lacks closure" (White, 1987, p. 16).

78. The next few citations are taken from Barthes (1970, pp. 145, 153, 155).

79. Danto (1985, p. 18); see also p. 169 and Danto's whole discussion of the Ideal Chronicler who is always dependent on knowledge of the future to write a perfect chronicle of the past (Danto, 1984, pp. 149–81). "A narrative sentence, referring as it does to a time-ordered pair of events E-1 and E-2, will then be a prediction if used by the Ideal Chronicler. For he will write it down *when* E-1 takes place (narrative sentences being about the earliest of the events they refer to), and so temporally earlier than E-2" (Danto, p. 170; emphasis in the original).

80. Carr (1990, p. 12; also 22, 23, 29, 30, 105, 107, 120); see also Abrams (1982, p. 194).

81. Danto (1985, p. 236). Not an easy task. Because a middle may be nested within another beginning and end, with its own middle nested, in its turn, in another pair of beginning and end. "Changes are nested within changes, and stories require increasingly complex middles to explain the outmost change" (Danto, 1985, p. 241).

82. Danto (1985, p. 115; see also p. 119).

83. Brooks (1984, p. 10); Danto (1985, p. 237; emphasis in the original; see also pp. 117, 140, 141, 233, 237, 251).

84. Danto (1985, pp. 141, 251, 255).

85. "Any narrative, every narrative, implies explanation, a reference to causes, motives, effects and results," wrote Renier (1950, pp. 22–3). Even the purest of narrative accounts cannot be entirely devoid of analysis and interpretation, Abrams would confirm in his seminal book on historical sociology (1982, pp. 309–12).

86. Collingwood argues that the "historical imagination" works constructively to fashion a coherent story out of the facts historians select for their stories (Collingwood, 1946, pp. 240–4). In and of themselves, the myriads of history's facts make no sense. It is the "idea of history" a Cartesian or Kantian *a priori*, that imposes order and coherence upon history's facts (Collingwood, 1946, p. 248).

87. Danto (1985, pp. 248–51).

88. See Bloch (1953, pp. 157–8).

89. Herder, Carlyle, Michelet, Niebuhr, Mommsen, and Trevelyan are examples of the romantic/formist/anarchist combination; Buckle, Taine, Marx, and Tocqueville of the tragic/mechanistic/radical strategy; von Ranke of the comic/organicist/conservative strategy. But Michelet combined a Romantic emplotment to a Formist argument in an explicitly liberal

ideology; Burckhardt combined a satirical emplotment and a contextualist argument in a conservative, even reactionary, ideological framework (White, 1973, pp. 29–30).
90. Cicourel (1964, p. 173; emphasis added).
91. Durkheim (1951, p. 310; emphasis added); Barthes (1970, p. 155).

Chapter 5 *"A Worlde of Wordes"*

1. The title of John Florio's first Italian-English dictionary published in London in 1598 and expanded and reprinted in 1611 under the new title *Queen Anne's Worlde of Wordes*.
2. For a history of the tutorial system at the University of Oxford see Moore (1968, p. 2).
3. Paraphrased by Sparrow (1967, pp. 92–3).
4. Sparrow (1967, p. 110).
5. See Harrison (1994, pp. 28, 727, 225) for these quotes. After World War One, English universities, including Oxford, increased their science courses, which were typically based on public lectures. The report of the 1964–65 Franks Commission acknowledged that "Tutorials had ceased to be informal meetings of scholarly minds … instead they had become surrogates for formal lectures, in which tutors frantically tried to cover the bloated factual content of entire subjects" (Harrison, 1994, p. 230).
6. The Oxford undergraduates involved in tutorials with me, through good and bad examples, also gave me a daily reminder of the virtues of creative writing. As Lévi- Strauss (1992) writes: "We all learn to write cookie cutter essays with a thesis, antithesis and synthesis."
7. For the two representations, see Jakobson (1960, p. 353).
8. They correspond to the three poetic genres of traditional models of language (for example, see in particular Bühler, 1990; Frye, 1957, pp. 243–337): Lyric (centered on the addresser, on the *I*), poetry of the second person, supplicatory or exhortative (centered on the second person, the *you* or *thou*), and epic poetry (centered on the third person, on the *he*) (Jakobson, 1960, pp. 355, 357).
9. Jakobson (1960, p. 357). Strictly speaking, Jakobson is talking here about the poetic function of language. This function of language emphasizes the characteristics of the message itself; it refers to a privileged focus on the language of the message. Yet, one cannot understand *any* message without paying attention to the poetic function of language. Again, Jakobson writes (1960, p. 356): "Any attempt to reduce the sphere of poetic function to poetry or to confine poetry to poetic function would be a delusive oversimplification. Poetic function is not the sole function of verbal art but only its dominant, determining function, whereas in all other verbal activities it acts as a subsidiary, accessory constituent."
10. On narrators, see Genette (1980; 1988).
11. Calvino (1993, p. 11; emphasis added).
12. Cited in Genette (1997, p. 231).
13. Gadamer (1997, pp. 105–6); Pirandello (1986, p. 61).
14. Cited in Brooks (1984, p. 313).
15. Kant (1911, p. 42, heading of second paragraph; emphasis in the original; p. 80; emphasis in the original). See Meredith's introductory essay on "The Beautiful" (Kant, 1911, p. lii).
16. See the discussion in Abrams (1953, p. 327); see also Abrams (1971, pp. 201–17, 433).
17. Cited in Pirandello (1986, p. 32).
18. References in this paragraph are to Pirandello (1986, pp. 166, 166, 135, 57, 156, 166, 166, 146–7).
19. Pirandello (1986, p. 168). It is Freud's emphasis on playful characteristics that, in Flieger's view, explain Freud's success among postmodern scholars (Flieger, 1991, p. 84; more generally, pp. 57–84).
20. "These terms – metaphoric, metonymic – are however (it has to be emphasized) relative. Any prose narrative, however 'metaphorical,' is likely to be more tied to metonymic organization than a lyric poem. … [W]e have a kind of spectrum of discourse extending from the metonymic to the metaphoric poles" (Lodge, 1977, pp. 103–4). We are not dealing with "two mutually exclusive types of discourse, but a distinction based on dominance" (Lodge, 1977, p. 111). "Most such [metonymic] texts, certainly most realistic fiction, contain a good deal of local metaphor" (Lodge, 1977, p. 111). "We would expect the writer who is working in the

metonymic mode to use metaphorical devices sparingly" (Lodge, 1977, p. 113).
21. White (1978, p. 131; emphasis in the original).
22. See Merton's 1942 essay "The Normative Structure of Science" for a detailed treatment; but see also Merton's continuous references to the characteristics of that ethos (1973[1938], p. 259; 1973[1957], p. 303).
23. Denton (1985, 1988); McCloskey (1985, p. 139); Moore and McCabe (1993, pp. 472–7).
24. Darwin (1996, p. 53; emphasis added; see also pp. 70, 392). White is simply wrong when he claims that "Darwin insists that the source of all error is semblance. Analogy, he [Darwin] says again and again, is always a 'deceitful guide'" (White, 1978, p. 131). In fact, only once does Darwin refer to analogy as a "deceitful guide." In another passage, in discussing the difficulties "a young naturalist" faced with "organisms quite unknown to him" (1996, p. 43), Darwin warns that "he will have to *trust almost entirely to analogy, and his difficulties rise to a climax*" (Darwin, 1996, p. 44; emphasis added). In all other references to analogy, "again and again" Darwin relies on analogy to support his arguments.
25. References in this paragraph are to Watson (1969, pp. 31, 31, 31, 140, 126, 127–8, 30, 51).
26. McCloskey (1985, p. 74); see also Bicchieri (1988, p. 104); Pera (1991).
27. Small (1903, pp. 475–7, *passim*; emphasis added).
28. Bentham (cited in Abrams, 1953, p. 301).
29. Locke (III, X, 34, 6–16; 1975, p. 508; emphasis in the original for *Ideas*; emphasis added otherwise).
30. "So mighty is the spell that these adornments naturally exercise, though when they are stripped bare of their musical coloring and taken by themselves, I think you know what sort of showing these saying of the poets make" (Plato, *Republic*, X, 601b, 1963).
31. Locke (III, X, 34, 28–9; 1975, p. 508).
32. Aristotle (1.1.3; 1991, pp. 29, 30). In Chapters 2–11 of Book 2, however, Aristotle gives a much more positive account of the role of rhetoric in the arousal of emotions.
33. Cited in Abrams (1953, p. 300).
34. Bentham; cited in Abrams (1953, p. 301).
35. See Socrates's arguments against Homer in Plato's *Republic*, Book III (1963).
36. References in this paragraph are to Mill's *Autobiography* (1981, pp. 112, 112, 112,136,138, 142; see also pp. 139–40, 142, 150, 152).
37. The poets' counterattack against science and philosophy was first led by William Blake. For Blake, the materialistic world of science – of Bacon, Locke, and Newton – had killed the spiritual world of imagination of Chaucer, Milton, and Shakespeare (Jones, 1966, p. 2).
38. Wordsworth (cited in Abrams, 1953, p. 299).
39. Cited in Abrams (1953, p. 299).
40. Cited in Abrams (1953, p. 299).
41. Plato (*Republic*, III, 398b, 1963; emphasis added).
42. See Socrates's arguments in the very beginning of Book III of Plato's *Republic* (1963).
43. See Bicchieri (1988, pp. 101–2).
44. Thus, Genovese (1976, in particular pp. 115, 117, 371, 500, 594) provides a passionate defense of American slaves and a powerful indictment of southern whites. Among sociologists, notable for their emotive power are Liebow's narrative of homeless women (1993) or Erikson's painful story of the devastation of a mining community in the Appalachian mountains (1976, in particular, pp. 28–9, 40, 162, 164–6).
45. References in this paragraph are to Eliot (1975, pp. 41, 43, 43, 44, 40, 40).
46. References in this paragraph are to Popper (1972, pp. 32, 31, 31; emphasis added).
47. For a discussion of Pascal's work in the context of Kant's and Frege's work on intuition, see Cellucci (1998, pp. 84–112).
48. Pascal (1995, 3, p. 192).
49. References in this paragraph are to Pascal's *Pensées* (1995, VII, 142, XLV, pp. 35, 36, 158, 36).
50. Mill (1981, p. 114); Merton (1994).
51. The "great men of history" pursue in their separate ways the goal at the very core of their existence. For artists, it is the creation of beauty. For economic, political and military leaders, quantity is the way to immortality: "piles of money," of land, of people. For voyagers and scientists, explorers and discoverers of worlds already there, the only way is to get there first. Their life achievements are celebrated as exemplary lives. Every epoch has its scores of

exemplary lives. The hagiographic production of the middle ages remains unsurpassed. The Renaissance had saints of its own: The artists, so brilliantly portrayed by Vasari (1942). With the Industrial Revolution in England, we leave behind that heavenly world of saints and beauty to celebrate a more earthly and prosaic hero: the capitalist entrepreneur, the industrialist. A myriad of biographies and autobiographies celebrated the new "hero" most of them completely fabricated if we are to believe Bendix who investigated the matter (1974, pp. 22–34). In the nineteenth and twentieth centuries, scientists have not done too bad for themselves in this parade of history. The late twentieth century has added women to the great men of history. Different times, different cultures, different values, different exemplary lives. Biography, this all too mortal and transient experience, is our link to immortality. Plutarch's *lives*, Bede's *lives*, Vasari's *lives*. The ways to achieve immortality are varied, and once achieved it is always precarious – hardly immortal – in this roller coaster of values and cultures.

52. Cited in Gerth and Mills (1946b, p. 26).

53. Durkheim (1938, pp. 28, 32, 34). Social things, for Durkheim, are independent of the social consciousness. Sentiments ultimately stand in the way of creating an objective reality, "out there," outside human consciousness; on Durkheim's process of objectification, see Durkheim (1951, p. 310; 1938, pp. 32–3); "our method is objective," he writes in the 'Conclusion' to his *The Rules of Sociological Method*, "It is dominated entirely by the idea that social facts are things and must be treated as such" (Durkheim, 1938, p. 143). See Berger (1963, p. 146) on the difference between Weber and Durkheim.

54. From the title of Giordano Bruno's collection of Italian dialogues (1958).

55. As Bruno himself acknowledges in his repeated references to the *Clavis Magna* (Bruno, 1997, *De umbris idearum*, pp. 108, 112, 118, 119, 122, 126, 128, 129, ff.).

56. Rossi (1960, p. 255); Yates (1992, pp. 365–73).

57. These are the exact words spoken by Filotimo in the "preliminary dialogue" of the *De umbris idearum* (Bruno, 1997, p. 48). The theme of ignorance (*asinità*) (asses and, worse yet, pedantic asses, *pedanteria*) runs through Bruno's thought and life (see Ciliberto, 1986, pp. 24–66; pedantic and grammarians, Bruno thought, were the Oxford Aristotelian philosophers anchored to tradition and to a literal interpretation of Aristotle). Indeed, the summary of the trial of Giordano Bruno – a trial that lasted seven years till the death sentence pronounced on February 8, 1600 – starts with the accusations laid against him by Giovanni Mocenigo in Venice in 1592: "I heard Bruno say a few times in my house that he does not like any religion. ... and he said that ... monks are all *asses,* and that our opinions are *asses'* doctrines (Mercati, 1942, p. 55). On the trial, see Firpo (1949).

58. Bruno's reference here must be to his brief and disastrous experience at the University of Oxford during the spring and summer of 1583. We have little information on his stay (Limentani, 1937; Yates, 1991, pp. 205–56; Ciliberto and Mann, 1997). Bruno himself gives an account of the events – with a scathing critique of the university and, more generally, of England – in one of his *Italian Dialogues, La cena de le ceneri* (dialog. 4; Buno, 1958, pp. 133–4). Allegedly, Bruno was invited to leave the university under the disgraceful accusation of plagiarism (he gave public lectures taking the lectures straight from Marsilio Ficino's work; Aquilecchia, 1971, pp. 31–2; see also, Yates, 1982, pp. 134–50; 1991, pp. 205–56). The real reason behind Bruno's sudden departure from Oxford, however, must be linked to his staunch defense of a Copernican and heliocentric view of the world against the dominant conservative Aristotelian and geocentric position of Oxford theologians and philosophers. In the end, his public anti-English stance lost him the few friends and supporters he had made (John Florio being a notable exception) (Spampanato, 1923/24, in particular, *fascicolo* 4, pp. 249–50; Yates, 1934, pp. 87–123, particularly, p. 123).

59. Bruno's reference is to Galileo. "There is no doubt about Galileo's knowledge of Bruno's thoughts," wrote Badaloni (1955, p. 289). But Galileo defended his scientific discoveries against the Inquisition by denying any link with Bruno's philosophy (Badaloni, 1955, pp. 291–2). Galileo, for instance, used Bruno's argument (but Campanella did the same) against the dominant Aristotelian view on the finite nature of the universe. For Bruno, the universe is infinite because infinite is the capacity of its Maker, as he argues against the Oxford philosophers in his *La cena de le ceneri.* Galileo in the third day of his *Dialogo dei massimi sistemi* makes a similar argument twice, once via Salviati, (p. 70) and a second time via Sagredo (p. 143). Sagredo says: "Great seems to me the stupidity of those who would want God to have made the universe more commensurate to the small capacity of their arguments,

than to His immense, in fact infinite, power." In a well-known letter to Fortunio Liceti, an Aristotelian academic from Padua, of September 24, 1639, Galileo declares his inability to reach a definitive conclusion on the infinity of the universe (Ricci, 1990, pp. 100–1). For an analysis of the relationship between Bruno's astronomic and physical ideas and Galileo's, see Tocco (1889, pp. 223–310); Ricci (1990, pp. 96–100).

60. See Galileo's letters to his inquisitors.

61. Bruno's reference is to Descartes who decided not to publish his ideas on the universe, after Galileo's 1616 trial. Descartes himself, in his *A Discourse on Method*, tells us that story: "Three years have now elapsed since I finished the treatise containing all these matters [*Monde*]; and I was beginning to revise it with the view to put it into the hands of a printer, when I learned that persons to whom I greatly defer [among them, Mersenne, whom Descartes had consulted on the issue; on Bruno, Mersenne, and Descartes see Badaloni (1955, pp. 292–300); Ricci (1990, pp. 92, 101)] … had condemned a certain doctrine in physics, published a short time previously by another individual [Galileo] … [T]his led me to fear lest among my own doctrines one might be found in which I had departed from the truth, notwithstanding the great care I had always taken … This has been sufficient to make me alter my purpose of publishing them" (Descartes, 1960, p. 83).

62. From the records of Galileo's trial, see de Santillana (1961, pp. 256, 302, 303, 312–3).

63. "*Bello è il mentir, se a far gran ben si trova / … Vissero col senno a chiuse porte, / in pubblico applaudendo in fatti e nome / all'altrui voglie forsennate e torte.*" From "*L'amor essenziale,*" *Poesie*, Campanella (madr. 9; son. 13, cited in Spampanato (1921, p. 590). At least from 1597, in his lectures, public or private, Galileo himself always professed a Tolemaic creed, despite his deep beliefs in the Copernican revolution (Spampanato, 1921, pp. 272–3).

64. *Dialogue*, Second day, (Galileo, 1964, p. 265). And elsewhere, "Empirical evidence – *sensate esperienze* – must be put before any argument fabricated by the human mind"; "empirical evidence must come before … anything put forward by human argument"; "what experience and sense demonstrate must be put before any argument, however sound this may seem" (Galileo, 1964, pp. 130, 150, 165).

65. For these documents, see in Spampanato, Schopp's letter of February 17, 1600, to Rittershausen, and *Documenti Romani*, IX, X, XI (Spampanato, 1921, pp. 798–805, 785–6). The quotes come from these documents, pp. 801, 785, 785–6, 786, in this order. On the history of the ill-fated relationship between the famous jurist Rittershausen and the young Schopp, see Spampanato (1921, pp. 787–98).

66. My translation from Italian.

67. Cicero (*De Inventione*, I, XXVI, 37–XXVIII, 43; 1949, pp. 75–83); see also Thomas Aquinas in his *Summa Theologiae* (1970, pp. 42–3, I-II q. 7 a. 3) where Thomas reports and debates Cicero's seven circumstances: *quis, quid, ubi, quibus auxiliis, cur, quomodo, quando* (who, what, where, by what aids, why, how, when); for a brief treatment of *loci*, see Lausberg (1998, p. 173).

68. See Weiss (1969).

69. *De oratore* and *Orator* in 1465; *De inventione* and the *Rhetorica ad Herennium*, falsely attributed to Cicero, in 1470. See Kennedy (1980, p. 195); for a listing of the printing dates of classical Greek and Latin works see Sandys (1908, pp. 103–5).

70. Victorinus (I, 24, 1863, p. 213); Boethius (IV, 8, 14-10, 6; 1990, p. 85); Martín de Córdova, in Faulhaber (1972, p. 131); Thomas Aquinas (1970, pp. 42–3, I-II q. 7 a. 3).

71. See Ragin's application of boolean algebra to the solution of historical-comparative problems (1987).

72. Jennifer Platt, in a study of citations in the *American Journal of Sociology* and the *American Sociological Review* between 1955 and 1970, shows that Weber was not even among the twenty-six most cited authors in 1955, but then was the fifth most cited author by 1970 (Platt, 1985, p. 454). It was Parsons, and particularly his *The Structure of Social Action*, according to Platt, that made "Weber's ideas salient to the general sociological public in America" (Platt, 1985, p. 454). Indeed, the swinging pendulum of Parsons's fortunes would be a good recent case in point (see Alexander's discussion, 1987, pp. 34–46).

73. For a beautiful essay on "the classics," see Calvino's introduction "*Perché leggere i classici*" – why read the classics – to the collection of essays by that same title (1991, pp. 11–19).

74. Frye (1957, p. 3).

75. That led to a rift between quantitative and qualitative content analysis, with quantitative

analysts focusing strictly on manifest content, and qualitative analysts focusing on both manifest and latent content (George, 1959). For Rosengren (1981, p. 11), that split refers to a European (qualitative) versus a North-American (quantitative) use of the technique.

76. Budd, Thorp, and Donohew (1967); Krippendorff (1980, p. 4).

77. For a critique of Roberts's work, see Franzosi (1997a).

78. For a recent rendering of "unambiguous" decoding, see Roberts (1997); for a critique, see Franzosi (1997a).

79. See the many chapters in *Language of Politics* dedicated to methodological issues (Lasswell et al., 1949).

80. Krippendorff (1980, pp. 17–18) tells us that Lasswell's position led to scathing criticisms of the technique. But Lasswell ignored them and plowed ahead.

81. References are to Gadamer (1997, pp. 388, 389; emphasis in the original).

82. In Tully (1988, p. 76). Skinner (in Tully, 1988, p. 70) distinguishes between three types of meaning: 1) "What do certain specific words or sentences mean, in this work?" 2) "What does this work mean to me?" 3) "What does the writer mean by what he says in this work?" In this passage, he is referring to the third type of meaning.

83. See van Dijk (1977); LaCapra (1983); Mishler (1986); Skinner in Tully(1988).

84. Culler (1975, pp. 113–30, 129). Kintsch and van Dijk (1978) have argued that text comprehension is based on a reader's (or listener's) ability to organize discourse in hierarchical macropropositions starting from more basic (surface level) micropropositions. Macrorules of macrostructure formation are repeatedly applied to obtain higher-level macrostructures; these higher level structures are the ones most easily remembered and most easily recalled by an individual. The higher the level of a macroproposition, the higher the number of times macrorules would have been applied, and the more remote the resulting proposition from its surface proposition(s).These tasks are performed by the coders whether they are specified by a written set of rules or not; in fact, written instructions simply cannot provide, as I have previously argued, all the world knowledge necessary to perform these tasks. What these tasks amount to is basically rewriting a discourse several times, through the operations of deletion, generalization, and construction. But the coder's role does not stop at that. The surface sentences that semantically belong to a given macrostructure are rarely organized at the surface level in the same sequence required by the macrostructural organization. Personal remarks and observations are interspersed with factual information. Facts concerning the current event are mixed in with those concerning previous events. "The characteristic discontinuous ordering of news discourse," for instance, is the rule, rather than the exception in newspaper reporting practices (see van Dijk, 1985, p. 89). What this all means is that a reader has to selectively organize each sentence into the appropriate macrostructure. To the extent that time is an important dimension of macrostructural organization, and to the extent that surface sentences of a source document are not time ordered, the reader will also have to sort along the time dimension the surface sentences or the macropropositions derived from them. A reader (and therefore a coder) is, thus, constantly selecting, sorting, and rewriting. These tasks are performed unconsciously. They are simply part of the process of text understanding. They are performed by a coder when using a traditional coding scheme as much as a story grammar, and with or without a set of written coding instructions. The grammar presented here, as we have seen, makes these tasks explicit, as the coder has to sort semantic triplets along the time dimension, convert passive forms into active ones, synthesize long clauses or sets of clauses into thematic units, eliminate paraphrases and synonymous expressions, and sift out comments from facts. Although these may seem like formidable tasks, and ones that would jeopardize some basic scientific principles of repeatability, in fact, they are no more than what we normally do every morning when reading a newspaper. When using highly abstract coding schemes, however, coders' tasks do not stop at the ones outlined here (and normally involved in the process of text understanding). Coders have to make not only linguistic judgements based on their world knowledge; they also have to make substantive/theoretical judgements, as to whether, for instance, a given demand is particularistic or universalistic, inner directed or etero directed, and so on. This process requires the coders to make decisions that involve a great deal of substantive and theoretical knowledge about the central hypotheses of the project. In this case, coders, indeed, come to play the role of "surrogate scientist" (Markoff et al., 1975, p. 37; Shapiro and Markoff, 1998, p. 64). It is not at the level of data collection that substantive/theoretical decisions should be made; it is not (and should not be) up to the coder

to make these decisions. There is a dangerous mixing of empirical and substantive/theoretical problems.

85. Van Dijk (1983, p. 34), for the first citation; van Dijk (1980, p. 13) for the second citation.

86. "Code" is the concept used by Barthes in his *S/Z* (1990). Eco talks about "intertextual frames" (1979) and Perry (1979, p. 36) of "frames." This process of assimilating the meaning of a text through the familiar is called "naturalization" by Culler (1975, p. 138).

87. Out of context, even a simple sentence like "John is standing up" is semantically ambiguous: Does the sentence mean that John has been standing up and continues to do so, or does it mean that John is in the process of getting up?

88. Agar (1980, p. 234).

89. See Marcuse's critique of Wittgenstein (1964, pp. 181–3; 189–91).

90. References in this paragraph come from Fish (1980, pp. 172–3). On the reader as the center of interpretive strategies, see also (Fish, 1980, pp. 11, 13, 14, 171).

91. Eco (1979, pp. 7, 208); see also Johnston (1985, pp. 985–97); van Dijk, (1980, pp. 3–4); Mishler (1986, pp. 92, 116). Eco also talks about "network of different messages" and "intertextual frames." For Mishler, interviews are socially constructed products, meaning defined in the context of the social interaction between interviewer and interviewee.

92. References in this paragraph are to Cicourel (1964, pp. 153, 21, 19, 23).

93. Cattell (1950, pp. 220, 228; emphasis added).

94. Cattell (1950, pp. 220, 226).

95. Quotes taken from Milani (1977, line 3.3. of the *recensio altera*, p. 236 of the Italian translation, 5.2 p. 238, 19.3 p. 246, 22.4–5 pp. 247–8).

96. Anonymous (1992, p. 30).

97. From *Vermischte Bermekungen*, cited in Bourdieu and Wacquant (1992, p. 1).

98. Derrida (1974, pp. 158–9); Barthes (1977b, p. 146; emphasis added).

99. Denton (1985, 1988); McCloskey (1985, p. 139); Moore and McCabe (1993, pp. 472–7).

100. Denton (1985, 1988). See also Lovell (1983, p. 1) and Leamer (1983, p. 36).

101. Belsley et al. (1980) and Franzosi (1994b). Unfortunately, every time you add new variables to a model, you add potential troubles. You increase the chances of adding idiosyncratic behavior into the model due both to the process of generation of the data concerning that variable and to its relationship with other similarly constructed variables. Adding a new variable to a model requires a deep understanding *both* of the theoretical reasons for the inclusion of the variable in the model and of the empirical behavior of the new variable. The latter involves an understanding of data definitions and collecting procedures, the plotting and replotting of the variable in question, by itself and in relation to other variables in the model, with an eye to the behavior of each individual data point. Each new variable added to a model thus requires a great deal of theoretical and empirical work. This is precisely what the practitioners of the "throw-it-all-in-the-hopper" approach want to avoid. Furthermore, under the kind of publishing pressures academics increasingly find themselves in, this type of work is a luxury that few can afford or are willing to pay the price it requires. Thus, it seems, we not only need a theory that provides a causal understanding of the social processes under investigation, and a theory of the data, but we also need a theory of the social relations of scientific production and academic knowledge.

102. See also Lieberson (1985, pp. 88–99, 223–7).

103. Malinowski (1948, pp. 70–4); Mauss (1972, pp. 54–60).

104. Just as the models and representations we use to understand social reality give us the illusion of built-in causal relationships among variables, the format of journal production gives us the illusion that the game we play in quantitative sociology is a theoretical one. After all, isn't theory built into the very format under which we produce our work? (Introduction, *theory and hypotheses*, data and methods, empirical results, conclusions). On these points, see the brilliant, early observations by C. Wright Mills in the chapter titled "Abstracted Empiricism" of his *The Sociological Imagination* (Mills, 1959, pp. 50–75). On the "theory" sections or chapters, see, in particular, p. 69.

105. Marcuse (1964, p. 100).

106. On the power of words, see the chapter "The Power of Words" in Ogden and Richards (1946, pp. 24–47).

107. Tukey (1977, p. 3).

108. My own alchemic experimentation cost several grants over the years, from several agencies,

totaling several hundred thousand U.S. dollars, to which one should add a year of unpaid leave for me to set up the project in Italy and, later, in 1990 and beyond, the money that I personally poured into the project to see it to its end.

109. Yet, would Professor Stone belittle physics, for instance, for running costly experiments (in comparison to which even the most "gigantic" and "vast" of historical enterprises pale), when projects like the supercolliding superconductor have to be scrapped with two billion dollars of sunk costs? See Hendry (1980) for a similar observation. Closer to home, do many question the cost of running large-scale surveys?

110. This is most certainly not a work by Thomas Aquinas himself. Many alchemists wrote alchemic tracts under false and famous names.

111. Seneca (Epistle LXXXIV, 12–13, 1920, pp. 283–4).

112. Cited in Bruno (1997, p. 69, note 49).

Chapter 6 Journeys' Ends

1. Quotes taken from Baedecker (1886, pp. 11, 344, 346).

2. Snyder (1975); for a similar test on Italian data for the same period, see Bordogna and Provasi (1979).

3. Elton (1983, p. 80); see also Stone (1987, p. 36) and Bailyn (1982, p. 9).

4. That is a widespread practice, one that Ashenfelter and Johnson (1969) also adopted in their seminal econometric model of U.S. strikes. Snyder neither gives the reasons for the inclusion of this variable in his model, nor he discusses the estimates of the coefficient. That is true for all the three countries Snyder analyses: United States, France, and Italy.

5. From the opening sentence of Elton's *Reformation Europe 1517–1559* (Elton, 1963).

6. On quasi-characters, quasi-events, and quasi-plots, see Ricoeur (1984, pp. 200–25).

7. Ricoeur (1984, pp. 216–17).

8. Danto (1985, p. 161). See also Ricoeur (1984, pp. 143–9). See Burke's discussion (1991b, pp. 233–48).

9. The alternative, that of using narrative data over long time spans for statistical analysis, requires a great deal of resources and long-term commitment to a project. Tilly's (1995a) *Popular Contention in Great Britain, 1758–1834* is the best example (perhaps the only example) of the kind of scholarship that this alternative has to offer, of what is in stock for us when we do not sacrifice a concern with the long term to the rich narratives of individual events. But researchers should be aware of the unintended consequences of methodological choices.

10. On temporalities, see also Le Roy Ladurie (1979b, pp. 111–31) and Sewell (1996).

11. Braudel (1980, p. 33).

12. Where the "event" here refers to the macroevent (the Red Years, the Hot Autumn), not the individual actions or microevents; that is the real crux of the explanation.

13. My version of Tilly's *As Sociology Meets History* (1981).

14. Braudel (1980, pp. 49, 79); see also De Felice (1995b, pp. 113–14).

15. Mills (1959, pp. 59, 62).

16. Lieberson (1985, p. 179); Braudel (1980, pp. 35–6).

17. See Braudel (1980, p. 35); see also Elton (1983, p. 112).

18. One can only participate in and observe current social reality. Through interviews and oral histories, however, ethnographers can gain insights into the past.

19. Braudel (1980, pp. 77, 47; also pp. 78, 79–80).

20. On the "marriage," see Abbott (1991, p. 230); on the "pre-marital intercourse," see Abrams (1982, pp. 300–1).

21. Paradoxically, Braudel's emphasis on structures may end up faring no better on issues of agency. The problem is: What is the capacity of human actors to intervene in the "semistillness" of *structures*, to change a "history that stands still" in Le Roy Ladurie's words (1981, p. 1; see also Le Roy Ladurie, 1979b, pp. 111–31 for an excellent discussion of issues of temporality; see also Sewell, 1996).

22. Even historians who cling to a traditional view of history in their manifestos, such as Elton, adopt quite a different approach in their own historical research (Abrams, 1982, pp. 312–14);

a case of: "Don't do as I preach, do as I practice!" After all, it is in the realm of practice that we have to look for clues of rapprochement "in the light of what working sociologists and historians actually do" (Abrams, 1982, pp. 220–1).

23. See Hexter (1979, pp. 67, 81, 90). As director of the *Centre de recherches historiques* in Paris Braudel fulfills his dream of unifying history and the social sciences under one roof. Hexter (1979, p. 63) tells us of Braudel's surprise that "area study" programs in the United States had been set up in the aftermath of World War Two on an interdisciplinary basis across various social sciences, except history. One certainly does not find in Braudel any of the fastidious scorn that Lawrence Stone displayed toward large scale historical projects, the "vast undertakings" the "gigantic enterprises" with their dozens of "helots" and with "more in common with the modern scientific laboratory ... than with the traditional lonely scholar" (Stone, 1987, p. 37).

24. *Histoire sérielle,* serial history, mostly deals with time series data (Chaunu, 1978; Furet, 1985). Cliometrics, after the goddess of history, *Clio,* was founded by American economic historians as the historians' equivalent of the economists' econometrics.

25. On the return of the event, see Morin (1969); Nora (1974); Stone (1979); Hobsbawm (1980); White (1987).

26. The way linguists and historians talk about this basic narrative structure is very similar. Both acknowledge that narrative is made up of basic "narrative sentences" (our semantic triplet). Similar is also the way linguists and historians (or philosophers of history) look at events and macrostructures. Again, both acknowledge that events provide organizing principles for sets of individual narrative sentences. The difference between Collingwood, Danto, White, Genette, Rimmon-Kenan, Cohan, Shires, and Toolan is not one of quality but of quantity. The linguists explore the narrative properties of their texts (true or fictional) to a much greater depth and extent than the historians and philosophers of history do (or probably care to do).

27. For the "natural" link between narrative and history, see White (1987, p. 54). On the "syntax of social life" see Abell (1987).

28. Halliwell (1987, pp. 37–8, Chapter 11); on the subordination of character to action in Aristotelian poetics, see also Ricoeur (1984, p. 37); Barthes (1977a, p. 104); Rimmon-Kenan (1983, p. 34).

29. In his study of Russian folktales, Propp (1968) identified thirty-one basic functions (namely, spheres of action) that are invariant across different tales. After spending the good part of a book discussing these functions and their roles in narrative sequences, Propp dedicated only a handful of pages to a quick discussion of characters (1968, pp. 79–91). All story characters can be reduced to a simple typology of seven "character roles" based on the unity of actions assigned to them by the narrative: the villain, the donor, the helper, the sought-for-person and her father, the dispatcher, the hero, and the false hero.

30. *Della certezza* (proposition 402). See also Monk (1991, p. 579) to put the statement in context.

31. "*Toutes les démarches qui refusent une analyse des relations entre acteurs sociaux sont étrangères à la sociologie ou même opposées à elle. ... la sociologie de l'action est au centre de l'analyse sociologique.*" (p. 107) "*... l'object de la sociologie est d'expliquer les conduites des acteurs par les relations sociales dans lequelles ils se trouvent placés. ... C'est la relation, non l'acteur, qu'il faut étudier*" (p. 111).

32. For Ricoeur's citations, see Ricoeur (1984, pp. 54–5).

33. The term *interaction* first came into English use relatively recently, in the 1800s, when compared to another noun we typically use today as synonym, *relation.* This latter word has been around since the medieval period and came straight from Latin.

34. Who, what, when, where, why and how (the "where" is missing from Ricoeur's representation). The five Ws constitute the basic set of information that should be provided right at the beginning of any news story.

35. Burke (1969, p. xv).

36. Cited in Coser (1971, p. 75). "J. A. Barnes (1954)," informs us Marsden (1992, p. 1888), "is generally credited with the first use of the term *social network.*"

37. Comte talks about "social relations" in his *Cours de philosophie positive* (for example, 1896, vol. 2, p. 248).

38. The three extracts are cited in Cohen (1978, pp. 92–3, 143–4, 145). The quotes come, respectively, from *German Ideology, Poverty of Philosophy,* and *The Communist Manifesto.*

39. Weber (1978, pp. 26–8, 38–46).

40. Coser (1965, p. 29), title of chapter.
41. In Gerth and Mills (1946a, p. 134). "*Lasciate ogni speranza o voi che entrate*" (leave every hope, you who enter here); these are the words inscribed in the entrance to Dante's Inferno.
42. The reference had been solicited by the Kulturministerium of Baden in regard to Simmel's application to a chair in philosophy at the University of Heidelberg in 1908.
43. Landmann (1958, pp. 16–17). Indeed, writing came so easy to Simmel that he never went over what he had written. He wrote "as if he saw the work before his inner eyes" (Landmann, 1958, p. 13). Given Simmel's way of writing, the "ability to associate the intellectually close ideas especially when they were at a certain distance from one another in the text," noted by Laas, the examiner of his second thesis, must be truly remarkable (in Landmann, 1958, p. 19). For an analysis of Simmel's writing style, see Coser (1965, pp. 34–7) and Frisby (1984, p. 23).
44. Landmann (1958, pp. 18–19).
45. Cited in Maus (1959, pp. 194–5).
46. Cited in Coser (1965, pp. 51, 52). Durkheim, who translated some of Simmel's work into French contributing to Simmel's renown beyond Germany, wrote: "Simmel's proofs generally consist only of explanations by example; some facts, borrowed from the most disparate fields, are cited but they are not preceded by critical analysis, and they often offer us no idea of how to assess their value. For sociology to merit the name of a science, it must be something quite different from philosophical variations on certain aspects of social life, chosen more or less at random according to the leanings of a single individual" (cited in Coser, 1965, pp. 48–9).
47. Cited in Levine (1971, p. xlvi). Altmann, the American reviewer of *The Philosophy of Money*, acknowledged that "Simmel's language is rich in analogies ... [and that] an intellect in which the tendency to analogies and similarities is so strong as in Simmel's is easily led to overrate the argumentative power." Yet, he concludes: "Only the narrow pride of a scientific bureaucracy can refuse to accept the installment of knowledge which is presented here in the form of scientific intuition" (Altmann, 1903, p. 68).
48. Gassen and Landmann (1958, p. 93). Only Dessoir, and none of the other candidates, Simmel included, had been told that the post was in the philosophy of aesthetics. Dessoir lectured on aesthetics, a factor which was decisive for his appointment.
49. Simmel was rejected, in spite of an official report that praised him as "the most original academic of his generation"; praised him for his independence; praised him for his broad-ranging knowledge, his penetrating intellectual energy, his originality, inspiring force, and brilliance as a lecturer (Landmann, 1958, p. 25).
50. Weber's letter, unfortunately, is lost.
51. December 26, 1915. Simmel had a point. When he competed in 1920 for a chair in philosophy at the small Prussian University of Greifswald, an official inquired why Simmel had not been given the chair. Elster (possibly the minister or an important civil servant) replied that Simmel was not appropriate for a small university; but had Simmel been proposed for a prestigious university, he (Elster) would have appointed him with the greatest pleasure (Letter to Edmund Husserl, quoted in Gassen and Landmann, 1958, p. 87).
52. Reported by Marie Luise Gothein in her biography of her husband written from his letters (in Gassen and Landmann, 1958, p. 145).
53. Himself a jew and a stranger he wrote that "the stranger as a person is predominantly interested in money ... The fact that jew was a stranger ... directed to trade and its sublimation in pure monetary transactions" (Simmel, 1978, pp. 224–5). And yet, Simmel did not take that route.
54. Cited in Frisby (1984, pp. 35–6).
55. Elly Heuss-Knapp, cited in Frisby (1984, p. 36).
56. "The absence of firm social ties promotes intellectual freedom" (Levine, 1971, p. xiii).
57. Landmann (1958, p. 25); Frisby (1984, p. 31).
58. Simmel (1971, pp. 145–6). There is a long literary tradition on the advantages of being a "stranger," from Seneca, to Plutarch, from medieval to Renaissance figures (Tucker, 1996, p. 37). Even political exile is liberty. "What is called exile is escape from countless cares," wrote Petrarch. Throughout the deeply religious middle ages, *patria*, home, is not of this world, so it really does not matter where you live. On these issues, see the illuminating pages in Tucker (1996).
59. Dante (*Paradise*, XVII, 58–60).
60. See also Levine (1971, p. lix) on this point.
61. In Gerth and Mills (1946a, pp. 133, 134).

62. Cited in Frisby (1984, p. 33).
63. Landmann (1958, p. 13). The reference is to Socrates's death, as described in Plato's *Crito* and *Phaedo*. In *Crito*, Socrates asks his friend Crito: "Has the boat come in from Delos – the boat which ends my reprieve when it arrives?" (Plato, *Crito*, 43c–d, 1963). The explanation for that question is given in the opening lines of *Phaedo*, where Phaedo, one of Socrates's devoted pupils, explains Echecrates why Socrates's execution had been delayed after the trial. "The Athenians ... send a solemn mission to Delos [to the temple of Delos] every year ... They have a law that as soon as this mission begins the city must be kept pure, and no public executions may take place until the ship has reached Delos and returned again, which sometime takes a long time, if the winds happen to hold it back. This is why Socrates spent such a long time in prison between his trial and execution" (Plato, *Phaedo*, 58b–c, 1963).
64. We know surprisingly little about Simmel's life, the little we know collected in 1958 by Gassen and Landmann for the one-hundred-year anniversary of Simmel's birth. All his personal correspondence, and even some unpublished manuscripts, were contained in a suitcase that his wife, Gertrud, was carrying on her way back to Berlin on a train (Laurence, 1991, p. 47). The suitcase was stolen and never recovered, despite the fact that newspapers across the country published invitations to the thief to return the suitcase. Of Max Weber's wife, Ann, who wrote her husband's biography and who dedicated her life to publishing Max's unpublished work, Carlo Antoni (1962, p. 119) wrote: "[O]ne of the most impressive tributes of love and devotion ever rendered by a woman to the memory of her husband." That would surely apply to Gertrud Simmel. But she was not as lucky.
65. Simmel, however, mainly saw himself as a philosopher. "It is in fact somewhat painful to me," he wrote to Durkheim's collaborator Célestin Bouglé in 1899, "to find that I am only recognised abroad as a sociologist – whereas I am indeed a philosopher, I see philosophy as my life-task and engage in sociology really only as a subsidiary discipline" (in Frisby, 1984, p. 25). In that same letter he added: "[W]hen I have at last fulfilled my obligation to it [sociology], namely that I publish a comprehensive sociology – which indeed will occur in the course of the next five years – I shall probably never again come back to it" (in Frisby, 1984, p. 30). See also his refusal to Max Weber's invitation to take the presidency of the Sociological Association (Frisby, 1984, p. 32).
66. Theodor Tagger, a student in a class when Simmel was still a young lecturer in Berlin, gives us a good example not only of Simmel's style of lecturing, but of his relentless pursuit of relations (Tagger, 1914). Tagger remembers that, during the lecture, a band playing military music passed on the street. Perhaps unconsciously, Simmel immediately started talking about medieval court music, weaving it into point he was making.
67. Simmel wrote: "The medieval group in the strict sense was one which did not permit the individual to become a member in other groups ... These patterns [of group affiliation] had the peculiarity of treating the individual as a member of a group rather than as an individual, and of incorporating thereby in other groups as well. ... The modern pattern differs sharply from the concentric pattern of group-affiliations as far as a person's achievements are concerned. Today someone may belong, aside from his occupational positions, to a scientific association, he may sit on a board of directors of a corporation and occupy an honorific position in the city government. Such a person will be more clearly determined sociologically, the less his participation in one group by itself enjoins upon him participation in another. He is determined sociologically in the sense that the groups 'intersects' in his person by virtue of his affiliation with them" (Simmel, 1955, pp. 140, 141, 150).
68. Von Wiese was not alone. Among the first heirs we also find Theodor Litt and Alfred Vierkandt (Maus, 1959, p. 196).
69. Sorokin (1928, p. 495).
70. Cited in Sorokin (1928, p. 495).
71. See also von Wiese (1932, pp. 10, 11, 23, 25, 65; 1941, pp. 25, 27, 30, 39, 43, 49, 59).
72. Von Wiese (1941, p. 42).
73. Von Wiese (1932, p. 71); references in this paragraph are to von Wiese (1932, pp. 37, 38; emphasis in the original; [also 1941, p. 58]; 38, 49, 50).
74. References in this paragraph are to von Wiese (1932, pp. 72 [also, 1941, p. 36], 131, 672).
75. Von Wiese (1941, pp. 29–30). There is a close link here with Moreno's sociometrix approach to the study of social action (1951, 1953). Von Wiese has left a personal memory of a curious episode. "Supposedly the last book that reached me from the United States before the

beginning of the war was Dr. Moreno's book *Who Shall Survive?* ... I only received it in 1939 or 1940. I still remember that I was put off by the title ... By a lucky chance, Moreno's book ... was one that survived the war in my cellar. In 1945, I got it out of the ruins" (my translation).

76. Levine et al. (1976b, p. 813).

77. Levine et al. (1976b, p. 813–14, 818). Levine et al. base their evaluation on the frequency of citations of European sociologists in American "general treatises on sociology and social psychology." The same pattern emerges from a study originally conducted by Luther L. Bernard in 1927. The study provided a frequency distribution of the names of the most influential sources of intellectual development given by 258 American sociologists in autobiographical statements. Simmel fares best on both scales.

78. It was, in fact, Albion Small who, as first editor of the *American Journal of Sociology*, contributed to the spreading of Simmel's work in America by publishing fifteen of his essays between volumes 2 and 16 of the journal (see Levine, 1971, pp. xlviii–xlix).

79. Sorokin (1928, pp. 495–507). Sorokin wrote: "Thus, we come to the conclusion that Simmel's conceptions of form and content are either meaningless and inapplicable to social phenomena; or that they lead to the conception of sociology as a generalizing science, which conception contradicts Simmel's pretensions of building sociology as a specific science" (Sorokin, 1928, p. 501). Von Wiese, who took Simmel's formal sociology to its most rigorous conclusions, without ever having been his disciple, left a more sympathetic and fair obituary: "Systematization of Simmel's thought is an extremely difficult and discouraging task. Since he had no idea of forming either a philosophical or sociological 'school,' and since in his works he but rarely makes reference to the productions of others, we are compelled to think of him as a unique scientific phenomenon, for whom, in his own words, 'the personal attitude toward the world' was decisive. He was no soldier in the rank and file, nor of course was he a leader in the proper sense, but a brilliant and stimulating scout, full of ideas and suggestions. He never attempted, however, to construct a system (a Spencer reversed). He was always inclined to say freely what he thought, and to say it without strict adherence to a formulated plan. He was always independent of academic rules and all artistic and traditional conventions. If we divest the term of all its disparaging and derogatory connotations, we may call this gifted writer a man of letters, one of the greatest, indeed, of all time."

80. The Harvard department of social relations included sociology, social anthropology, clinical psychology, and social psychology; at Johns Hopkins, it similarly included sociology, social anthropology, and social psychology. Both departments have since changed their names to the common "Department of Sociology." Harvard led the way in 1970/71 (when the department was closed down to reopen later under a more traditional name) and Hopkins followed in 1983.

81. Berger (1963, pp. 38–9, 49).

82. On Simmel's influence upon American sociology, see Levine (1971, pp. xlviii–lxi) and Levine et al. (1976a, 1976b). French sociologist Pierre Bourdieu insists: *"[T]he real is the relational"*; "One must *think relationally*"; "The real is relational" (Bourdieu and Wacquant, 1992, pp. 97, 228, 232; emphasis in the original). Italian sociologist Paolo Donati, in his textbook *Lezioni di Sociologia*, similarly privileges the social relation (Donati, 1998, p. 6).

83. For a reprint of the entire charter in both Latin and English, see Thorpe (1906, pp. 1669–77, Latin, and 1677–89, English); for selected passages of the English charter, see Steele Commager (1973, pp. 21–2).

84. Cecil Calvert was the son of George Calvert, the first Lord Baltimore, a Catholic Yorkshireman who had been in search of profit in the new world and of a safe haven from Protestant prosecution (Middleton, 1992, pp. 73–4). It was George Calvert who had applied for a charter to the new land but died shortly before receiving it.

85. George Calvert had sought the widest possible sovereignty from both the monarchy and the settlers in the administration of his overseas estate. He found a precedent of such extensive powers in the palatinate of Durham in the 1300s and framed the wording of his own charter after the palatinate (Jordan, 1987, pp. 2–4; Middleton, 1992, pp. 74–5). The anachronistic feudal character of Calvert's charter, however, generated constant controversies and open conflict in the context of the free spirit of the American colonies.

86. In England, the Kings of Arms have granted and are still granting arms to people since the fifteenth century by Letters Patent from under authority delegated to them by the Sovereign. A right to arms requires registration in the official records of the College of Arms of a pedigree

showing direct male descent from an ancestor already appearing therein as being entitled to arms, or by making application through the College of Arms for a Grant of Arms. The college is the official repository of the arms and pedigrees of English, northern Irish, and Commonwealth families and their descendants.

87. No doubt, the proverb comes from an earlier Latin one (*facere virorum est, loqui mulierum*). One finds it in many different romance and even Germanic languages. Dr. Johnson, who single handedly succeeded in putting together the *Dictionary of the English Language* where in France and Italy a team of scholars worked for years at a similar task, reports the following proverb in his preface to the dictionary: "Words are the daughters of earth, and ... things are the sons of heaven."

88. Stone (1967, pp. 316–17).

89. The book is dedicated "To the Right Honorable Patrons of Vertue, Patterns of Honor, Roger Earle of Rutland, Henrie Earle of Southampton, Lucie Countesse of Bedford.

90. "But let such know," Florio hastens to add, "that *Detti* and *fatti*, wordes and deeds with me are all of one gender." The saying was probably the result of Florio's collection of Italian proverbs published in England in 1591 under the name of *Giardino di ricreatione* (Florio, 1951b).

91. In the Spanish original: "*Las palabras son para las mujeres y las armas para los hombres!*" (Díaz, 1960, Tome 2, p. 52).

92. See also Arthaber (1989) on the proverb.

93. Sorokin (1956, p. 52; emphasis in the original).

94. Andreski (1972, pp. 119–20). For Zweig, interviewing is a two-way traffic not an external thing, an "object"; interviewing is a social act.

95. Coleman and Elsner (1995, p. 110); Hunt (1984, p. 67).

96. The number of days required for the visit would often be reduced by the Popes, when providing food for the thousand of pilgrims became a problem (Alfani, 1750, pp. 14, 31, 99).

97. Loxton (1978, p. 97). In England, in 1500, the Jubilee indulgence was sold for 1s. 4d (6.5 p) for those with an income of £20 a year or less, rising to £3.6 s. (£3.30) for those with more than £2,000.

98. The practice of jubilees soon became institutionalized with one every twenty-five years.

99. Loxton (1978, p. 91). Yet, the income gained from the surge of pilgrims had to be offset against the expenses incurred by monasteries. On July 7, 1220 the remains of St. Thomas at Canterbury were "translated" to a new shrine. For the occasion, with thousands of pilgrims visiting the shrine, Canterbury obtained from the pope the right to offer a plenary indulgence (Loxton, 1978, p. 88). Despite the tremendous income that this generated for the monastery, the cost of providing free lodging and food for thousands of pilgrims nearly bankrupted the monastery (Loxton, 1978, p. 89). In 1320, the year of Canterbury first jubilee, again Canterbury suffered a deficit of £83 (Loxton, 1978, p. 114).

100. Davidson and Dunn-Wood (1993, p. 59); Coleman and Elsner (1995, p. 110).

101. Coleman and Elsner (1995, pp. 109–10); Geary (1984, p. 265); Richard (1984, p. 149).

102. Loxton (1978, p. 114). Indeed, a prosperous merchant economy flourished behind the shrines, with the manufacture of badges usually local and licensed by the Church. Typically, the Church collected a commission on sales. For Canterbury, see Loxton (1978, p. 114).

103. We know from letters, circulating in Europe right after Columbus's first voyage, that he had "returned bearing substantial proofs in the shape of many precious things and particularly of gold" (Peter Martyr's letter, cited in Thacher, 1903, vol. 1, p. 54) and that he had "taken six men with him" (Hanibal Januarius's letter, cited in Thacher, 1903, vol. 2, p. 8).

Tales of Measurement

1. For a story of shipwrecks, see the seventeenth-century narratives of Bernardo Gomes de Brito (three of the original eighteen narratives are available in English as selected and translated by Boxer; see Brito, 1959).

2. For a brief introduction to the history of the measurement of longitude, see Taylor (1956, pp. 245–63); see also the Proceedings of the Longitude Symposium held at Harvard University, November 4–6, 1993, edited by Andrews (1996). See also Sobel's popular account (1996).

3. The Act also set up two additional prizes of £15,000 for a method accurate to within two-third of a degree, and a third prize of £10,000 for a method accurate to within one degree.

4. This was not the first time a European power had set up handsome rewards for a solution (Sobel, 1996, p. 25; Landes, 1996, p. 25). For the longitude story, see Sobel (1996, in particular, pp. 51–60).

5. On Harrison's life, see Gould (1935); Hobden and Hobden (1988).

6. Part of the reward had already been awarded to Harrison; on this story, see Taylor (1956, pp. 260–2).

7. *The Rime of the Ancient Mariner*, Coleridge (1912, pp. 190–1).

8. Cited in Boorstin (1986, p. 265).

9. Dante left a powerful poetic version of this hellish vision when he described the Conte Ugolino imprisoned with his son in Pisa in the tower of Gualandi: "*La bocca sollevò dal fiero pasto/quel peccator, forbendola a' capelli*" (Dante, *Inferno*, XXXIII, 1–3). Gericault similarly left a powerful painting of a the shipwreck of the Medusa that ended in cannibalism (Gericault, 1819, *The Raft of the Medusa*).

10. See de Léry's own chapter "How the Americans treat their Prisoners of War and the Ceremonies they Observe Both in Killing and in Eating Them" (1990, pp. 122–33). But, we do find descriptions of men eating human flesh in Mandeville (1983, p. 174), Columbus (1969, p. 121), Vespucci (1984, pp. 64, 103, 139).

11. Three men and a boy of the crew of a yacht (the "Mignonette") were shipwrecked and the weakened boy was killed and eaten. After being rescued and fetched to England, the surviving men were tried and convicted of murder, but the sentence was commuted to six month's imprisonment (Simpson, 1984).

12. Both technical and personal problems plagued Watt's development of his steam engine. Throughout his life Watt suffered from poor health and intense headaches that made work nearly impossible (Mantoux, 1983, p. 318). During his prolonged experimentation with the design of his engine, Watt endured the death of his wife and the death of his best mechanic (Smiles, 1997, p. 137), the failure of his first large prototype (Smiles, 1997, p. 323), the bankruptcy of his first partner, and the economic necessity of tiresome, plodding work as a surveyor (Mantoux, 1983, pp. 322–3). By 1773, four years after his first patent, "a combination of unfortunate circumstances threatened to overwhelm him. No further progress had yet been made with his steam engine, which he almost cursed as the cause of all his misfortunes" (Smiles, 1997, p. 158). Partnership with Boulton, whose wealth was as fantastic as the technical skill of his engineers and craftsmen, was a turning point for Watt's fortunes. The ambitious and energetic Boulton provided not only the money but the political support and personal encouragement that Watt needed (Robinson and McKie, 1976, pp. 13–14).

13. It involved rotating the casting itself rather than the lathe blade (Ashton, 1969, p. 63).

14. It was the beginning of a long-term partnership; one that created a great deal of discontent among competitors. Only three or four engines were built to Watt's design without Wilkinson cylinders between 1775 and 1795 (Smiles, 1997, p. 178).

15. Cited in Joyce (1994, p. 169). See Joyce for the industrialists' pursuit of the "consuming romance that all knowledge was one" (Joyce, 1994, p. 171).

16. For an introduction to the history of quantification in various natural and social sciences, see the collection of essays edited by Woolf (1961), that includes a chapter by Lazarsfeld on quantification in Sociology (Lazarsfeld, 1961).

17. Lazarsfeld (1993, p. 253; emphasis added). Also reported in Lazarsfeld's and Rosenberg's "Introduction" to their edited collection *The Language of Social Research* (1955, p. 1).

18. It is the "new history" inaugurated in the twentieth century that required attention to a much broader range of evidence than traditionally used by historians – namely, official state documents (Burke, 1991a, pp. 12–15). To get a sense of how much history changed in relations to the type of evidence considered as valid historical source, one only has to read a little book on historical evidence written in 1909 by H. B. George, fellow of New College in Oxford. One will be hard pressed to find there an anticipation of the explosion in the type of sources and material used by historians of just one or two generations later: from oral testimonies, to military conscription records, newspapers, Inquisition trial records, photographs, and more. In the words of Marc Bloch (1953, p. 66): "Everything that man says or writes, everything that he makes, everything that he touches can and ought to teach us about him." Indeed, historians have shown a great ingenuity in their use of sources. Think, for instance, of the use of the

transcripts of the trials of heretics by the Inquisition. Two wonderful pieces of history were written on the basis of those sources (Ginzburg, 1982; Le Roy Ladurie, 1979a).

19. Cited in Marcuse (1964, p. 149).

20. Rosch et al. (1976, p. 430). On classification and categorization as seen by cognitive psychologists, see, besides Rosch et al. (1976), Tversky (1977), Rosch and Lloyd (1978), in particular, the essays by Rosch (1978) and Tversky and Gati (1978), and Billig (1987, pp. 118–55). For a sociological approach to culture and cognition, see DiMaggio (1997).

21. Ritvo's work on the development of systems of classification in natural history is exemplar in tracing the struggle over the last few centuries over definitions and classifications between "experts" and scientists and various other social groups, the struggle between expert knowledge and lay knowledge (Ritvo, 1997, pp. 49–50, 187).

22. On the relation between quality and quantity in the social sciences, see Bryman (1988).

23. Critics are numerous, in history and the social sciences (for example, Ginzburg, 1979; Elton, 1983, p. 80; Stone, 1987, p. 36; Bailyn, 1982, p. 9).

24. Elton (1967) dedicates to these issues the longest chapter (appropriately titled "Writing") of his book on *The Practice of History*. The danger is that the "how" rather than the "why" questions, the form rather than content may become the overarching concerns of the researcher (White, 1987, pp. 142–68). The good narrativist may very well remain at the surface of human and historical action (the "how" question) seduced by the "nervous vibrations" of the event, without doing (or at least attempting to do) the much harder work of explaining (the "why" question) (White, 1987, p. 60). A master story-teller of the caliber of Trevelyan admits: "Writing history well is no child's play. The rounding of every sentence and of every paragraph has to be made consistent with a score of facts, some of them known only to the author, some of them perhaps discovered or remembered by him at the last moment to the entire destruction of some carefully erected artistic structure. In such cases there is an undoubted temptation to the artist to neglect such small, inconvenient pieces of truth. That, I think is the one strong point in the scholar's outcry against 'literary history'" (Trevelyan, 1913, pp. 42–3). Centuries before Trevelyan, Diodorus Siculus had already warned his readers that "some writers by excessive use of rhetorical passages have made their entire historical work into an appendage of oratory" (in Grant, 1992, p. 247).

25. For a critique of Roberts's and Abbott and Barman's articles, see Franzosi (1997a).

26. This is a purely fictitious account, but one of many similar accounts you encounter in *Il Lavoro* or *L'Unità*.

27. From *L'addition* in the collection titled *Histoires* (my translation).

28. Luce and Raiffa (1957); Nicholson (1970); Schelling (1980); Rangarajan (1985); Kreps (1990).

29. Knoke and Kuklinski (1982); Laumann and Knoke (1989); Wasserman and Faust (1995).

30. See, for example, Schelling (1980, pp. 43, 123–4, 142–4, 147).

31. Rangarajan (1985, p. 22) introduces the distinction between bargaining and negotiation, the first viewed as "An agreement between two parties settling how much each gives and takes, or what each performs and receives in a transaction between them"; the second defined as "To hold communication or conference (with another) for the purpose of arranging some matter by mutual agreement; to discuss a matter with a view to some settlement or compromise."

32. Laumann and Knoke (1989, p. 25), further reduce the list, claiming that, in the organizational and political community literature, "three generic relationships are especially significant in identifying social structure: information transmission, resource transactions, and boundary penetration."

33. In particular, Propp (1968); Greimas (1966); van Dijk (1972); Dowty (1979); Levin (1993).

34. In particular, Kenny (1963); Austin (1975); Vendler (1957); Davidson (1980).

35. Vendler (1957) proposes the following examples: states (know, believe, have, desire, love), activities (run, walk, swim, push a cart, drive a car), accomplishments (paint a picture, make a chair, deliver a sermon), achievements (recognize, spot, find, lose, reach, die).

36. *Verdictives* involve the giving of a verdict (by a jury or arbitrator), including the process of reaching a verdict, such as estimate, reckoning, or appraisal. They correspond to my categories of <authority> or <decision making>. *Exercitives* are the exercising of powers, right, or influence. Examples are appointing, voting, ordering, urging, advising, warning. They correspond to my categories of <authority> or <exhortative>. *Commissives* are typified by promising or otherwise undertaking; they commit you to doing something, but include also

declarations or announcements of intention, which are not promises, and also rather vague things which we may call espousals, as for example, siding with. They correspond to my categories of <promise> or <solidarity>. *Behabitives* have to do with attitudes and social behavior. Examples are apologizing, congratulating, commending, condoling, cursing, and challenging. They broadly correspond to my categories of <approval> or <disapproval>. *Expositives* have to do with the expository needs of arguments or conversations (e.g., "I reply", "I argue", I concede", "I illustrate", "I assume", "I postulate").

37.   Aristotle had introduced the distinction between verbs of *kinesis* ("movements") and *energiai* ("actualities"). Ryle distinguished between achievements (for the resultative verbs) and activities (irresultative). For Kenny verbs are divided into activities and performances (can occur in progressive tenses) and states (cannot occur in progressive tense). Finally, as we have seen, Vendler distinguished between states (know, believe, have, desire, love), activities (run, walk, swim, push a cart, drive a car), accomplishments (paint a picture, make a chair, deliver a sermon), and achievements (recognize, spot, find, lose, reach, die). For a thorough review, see Dowty (1979, pp. 51–71). For a critique of Dowty's work, see Pustejovsky (1995). Among linguists, Chafe (1970, pp. 95–104) also classified verbs into states, processes, and actions.

38.   Austin (1962, p. 152).

39.   Nominalization, like the passive sentence constructions that we saw in the section "Silence and Emphasis Revisited" of Chapter 4 as analyzed by Trew (1979a), also fundamentally backgrounds responsibility, as the agent of a nominalized process is eliminated, yet another way in which subtle manipulations of language can fundamentally alter meaning.

40.   *The Secret of Secrets* is the English title of the Arab work *Sir al-Asrar* written by the Islamic mystic and philosopher Abd al-Qadir al-Jilani. *Secretum secretorum*, the secret of secrets, for the alchemists, referred to the most sacred and never openly revealed aspects of their art.

41.   Markoff et al. (1975, p. 37) and Shapiro and Markoff (1998, p. 64) have correctly argued that when coders use coding schemes based on highly abstracted categories they come to play the role of "surrogate scientist." Indeed, as I have argued in endnote 83 of Chapter 5, it is not at the level of data collection that substantive/theoretical decisions should be made; it is not (and should not be) up to the coder to make these decisions. Should not that principle apply to classification, as well? Why should the coders be involved in it? The basic difference is that, when using abstract coding categories, once the coder has coded the information, the original information is irretrievable, and the code cannot easily be checked. When using a story grammar approach, the original information is stored as part of the semantic triplet; all the coder is doing is help PC-ACE disambiguate ambiguous cases that require knowledge of a triplet or an entire sequence of triplets. At a later stage, all codes should be verified both automatically and manually.

42.   In principle, classification codes can be imputed automatically at a later stage, after data collection, during the data analysis phase. However, in many cases, disambiguation of meaning requires knowledge of the context. It is precisely that knowledge that coders acquire as part of their involvement with the narrative material. For that reason, I would have coders assign preliminary codes during data collection. These codes can be later checked either by automatic imputation or by independent coders.

43.   Many exhortative actions could be classified as either <request> or <authority> depending upon the role of the actor: Whether the actor is uttering an exhortation from a position of power or moral authority (perhaps somewhat independently of the direct contenders) or whether it is a request for solidarity (from a position of weakness rather than power). Thus, the action "solicit the payment of back salaries" could be either a <request> or an <exhortative> depending upon whether the subject of the action is acting on behalf of the self (for example, "workers solicit …") or on behalf of others; furthermore, in the latter case, the action could be one of either <solidarity> or <facilitation>, <exhortative>, depending upon the position of power of the subject vis-a-vis the object (same power position for subjects and objects in the case of <solidarity>, for example, "FIAT workers solicit the payment of back salaries for Alfa Romeo workers," and position of power of the subject in the case of <facilitation> and <exhortative> (for example, "the Ministry of Labor solicits the payment of back salaries"). More generally, a classification of actions in such categories as <authority>, <conflict>, or <request> implies, if not direct consideration to the position of the actor in the process of classification, at least an indirect weight given to certain actors. Thus, it is more likely that those in a position of power will perform actions of <authority> (in particular, political and

state actors or employers and managers, perhaps with an emphasis on the former). Actions of <request>, on the other hand, are more likely to be performed by individuals and groups in subordinate positions: they would not be asking if they already had. The sphere of <market> actions is more likely to encompass actions by employers and managers. After all, that is their main sphere of actions. But political actors may occasionally perform actions oriented toward the market. Thus, our classification of actions broadly implies a classification of actors, political and economic actors in particular.

44. Consider the following examples. The action "strike," by itself, would be classified as "conflict." If, on the other hand, we have the information "strike in solidarity of the Russian people," the reason for the strike (<cause> solidarity) allows us to classify the strike not just as a form of conflict but as an action of solidarity. Similarly, such actions as "cancel flights" or "suppress trains" could be <conflict> if the action is carried out by workers and unions as part of their conflict strategies, or <market> if the airline or railroad company take action on the basis of market mechanisms of profitability, or <control> or <authority> if the action is taken for reasons of security or other. In all these examples, reference to the cause of the action allows us to be more precise about the classification of the action. Finally, in the triplet "employers warn unions," the action "warn" is a <threat (non violent)> but if the action contains the <instrument> modifier "press release," then the action should also be classified under <communication>.

45. Consider the action "suspends the application of the decree." What kind of action is it? The presence of such words as "suspends" and "decree" point to an action of <authority>. If "government" were the <subject> of the triplet, inspection of the subject would validate that interpretation. Even so, would it be an action of control or facilitation? To answer that question we would have to inspect the <case> modifier that links actions to objects in our semantic grammar and the <object>. Perhaps, we could find the code "against" for the <case> and the code "strikers" as <object>. The action could then be classified as "facilitation" since the government is helping out workers by revoking a decree unfavorable to strikers, as underscored by the <case> against. But, what if there is no <object> coded for the triplet? In that case, previous triplet(s) in the event may provide helpful clues for resolving the ambiguity between <control> and <facilitation>. For example, if the previous triplet reads (<subject>: workers <action>: strike <reason> government decree) then, the government's action of revoking the decree must be seen as a direct response to workers' demands and it is therefore an act of <facilitation> or <acceptance>/<agreement>. Alternatively, if no information is provided, one would need to have knowledge of the decree itself in order to know whether the effects of the decree on specific actors are negative (control) or positive (facilitation).

46. I have tentatively worked with the following set of spheres of action: <Membership> ∪ <Role> ∪ <Building> ∈ <INSTITUTIONS> (where the sum of the three subsets of actions make up the set of <institutions>); {{<Law> ∪ <Control> ∪ <Facilitation> ∈ <authority>} ∪ <Planning> ∪ <Rights> ∪ <Delegate>} ∈ <Power>; {{<Exhortative> ⊂ <Communication>} ∪ {<Negotiation> ⊂ <Debate>} ∪ <Request>} ∈ <Messages>; {{<Solidarity>∪<Acceptance (unilateral)>} ∈ <Approval>} ∪ {{<Obstruction>∪<Rejection (unilateral)>} ∪ <Disapproval>} ∪<Appraisal>} ∈ <Evaluation>; {<Promise>∪<Mediation> ∪ {{<Violation> ∪ <Compliance>} ∈ <Agreement (bi- or multi-lateral)>} ∈ <Bargaining>; {{<Violence against people> ∪ <Violence against things> ∪ <Violence against unknown object>} ∈ <Violence> } ∪ {{<Threat against people> ∪ <Threat against things> ∪ <Threats against unknown object>} ∈ <Threat>} ∪ <Collective actions>} ∈ <Conflict>; <Conjuncture> ⊂ <Market>; <Movement>; <Sentiments/Rituals>; <Temporal>.

47. Verbs of <membership> and <role>, together with <building>, are subclasses of the sphere of actions of <institutions>. *Membership:* The fact of belonging to an organization or an institution. *Verbs:* belong, is/are member(s), work, … *Role:* The position and/or role that individuals occupy within an institution or organization. *Verbs:* head, is/are, preside, run, … *Building:* The actions involved in the process of setting up administrative structures, organization and institution building. *Verbs:* build, create, establish, institute, found, …

48. Thomas Aquinas (1996, p. 39).

49. Lakoff and Johnson (1980, pp. 5, 36, 171; emphasis in the original).

50. Cited in Hutin (1991, p. 202).

51. Hutin (1991, pp. 86, 89, 102). The great fourteenth century Parisian alchemist Nicolas Flamel annotated in his diary how he went on a pilgrimage to Santiago de Compostela, how he met

an old Jew on his way home, and how this stranger revealed to him the secrets that would allow Flamel to achieve the Great Work "on a Monday, January 17 of the year 1382 around noon" (Hutin, 1991, p. 152).

52. In this paragraph Braverman is summarizing the work of Sudhir Kakar (1976) who used psychoanalytic techniques to unravel Taylor's personality.

53. The expression is used by Calvino (1991, p. 138) in a short essay on "Giammaria Ortes." Ortes (1713–1790), an eighteenth-century Italian monk, had an early education in music and poetry, followed by philosophy, theology, history and poetry. Between 1734 and 1738, he learned mathematics and geometry at the University of Pisa (Ortes himself gives us this sketch in a handful of autobiographic pages; 1984, pp. 47–51). Later in life, Ortes wrote many essays where he attempted to measure "everything." Using probability calculus, he attempted to calculate outcomes of card games, and extended these calculations to measuring truth in history, human beliefs, pleasures and pains of human life, virtues and vices. His essays on these calculations (Ortes, 1984) are not terribly innovative, but well in line with the spirit of times of *political arithmetick*. He signed most of his essays with the motto: "*Chi mi sa dir s'io fingo?*" (Who can tell me if I lie?).

54. Frederick Taylor's father was a lawyer who had graduated from Princeton in 1840. The Taylor family belonged to the "Quaker aristocracy," to the "Philadelphia elite" (Nelson, 1980, p. 22).

55. References in this paragraph are to Taylor (1911, pp. 49, 24, 36, 36, 98, 52, 52).

56. Taylor (1911, p. 64). On time-study and motion-study, see also (Taylor, 1911, pp. 45, 46, 58 of *Shop Management* and pp. 53, 64, 77, 114, 117).

57. Braverman (1974, pp. 113, 114, 119; emphasis in the original) summarizes Taylor's work in three principles: 1) "*Dissociation of the labor process from the skills of the workers*"; 2) "*separation of conception from execution*"; 3) "*use of this monopoly over knowledge to control each step of the labor process and its mode of execution.*"

58. Goethe, *Faust, The Second Part of the Tragedy*, (Act IV, lines 10187–8).

59. See Diderot, in Becker (1932, pp. 130, 150).

60. The "case before us" is Freud's distinction between thinking and doing in the neurotics and the primitive men. Both blur the line. Yet, while the neurotics are *inhibited* in their actions – "the thought is a complete substitute for the deed" – primitive men are *uninhibited* – "thought passes directly into action" and the deed is a substitute for the thought.

61. Cited in Bottomore and Frisby's "Introduction" to *The Philosophy of Money* (Simmel, 1978, p. 15).

62. Cited in Bottomore and Frisby's "Introduction" to *The Philosophy of Money* (Simmel, 1978, p. 17).

63. Sombart (1967, pp. 22, 102; emphasis added).

64. Weber (1978, pp, 24, 26); on the various types of social action, see Weber (1978, pp. 24–6).

65. Cited in Marcuse (1964, p. 164).

66. It would be Edmund Halley, the astronomer, and an unlikely player in these earthly matters, who provided the first reliable measures of mortality, thus laying "the foundation of modern actuarial science" (Pearson, 1978, p. 80).

67. References in this paragraph are to Simmel (1978, pp. 273, 272, 273).

68. Marcuse (1964, p. 146); for the references and citations to Marcuse's work in this paragraph, see Marcuse (1964, pp.144, 146).

And After

1. Carroll (1933, p. 64).

2. Social scientists are not necessarily happy about that. Social *scientists* may in fact regard these narratives as suspect – description as detracting from explanation. To distance themselves from description, network theorists have been quick to develop structural network models. Like factor analysis, this type of models "crunch" together the different social actors and social relations – these layers in a cube, each layer representing a specific type of relation – to find structural equivalents between social actors. Thus, in their introduction to a collection of essays on network analysis, Wellman and Berkowitz (1988) argue that network analysis provides explanatory mechanisms of behavior.

3. Franzosi (1995a).
4. Machado (1940, p. 37; CXXXVI, *"Proverbios y cantares"* XXIX).
5. "Wayfarer, your steps are the way, and nothing more; there is no way / the way is made as you walk / as you walk you make the way / and when you look back / you see the path that you shall never hollow again. / Wayfarer, there is no way / only waves in the sea."
6. Perrot (1968, p. 120).
7. Moore (1978); Gamson, Fireman, and Rytina (1982).
8. See Goodwin et al. (2000); Goodwin et al. (2001).
9. Freud gave these theories his stamp of approval in his 1921 *Group Psychology and the Analysis of the Ego* (Freud, 1967).
10. Le Bon (1969, p. 10). For the characteristics of Le Bon's crowds see Le Bon (1969, pp. 22–3, 34, 45, 47, 48, 59).
11. Le Bon (1969, pp. 4–5, 23, 24, 27, 31, 35, 49, 52).
12. For Le Bon, Tarde, or Sighele these crowd characteristics are essentially feminine. "Among the special characteristics of crowds there are several – such as impulsiveness, irritability, incapacity to reason, the absence of judgment and the critical spirit, the exaggeration of sentiments, and others besides – which are almost always observed in beings belonging to inferior forms of evolution – in women, savages, and children, for instance" (Le Bon, 1969, p. 31; also pp. 28, 34, 36, 44). At around the same time, Sighele (1922, p. 139) similarly wrote, in an exchange with Tarde, that "the crowd – like a woman – has an extreme psychology, capable of every excess, perhaps only capable of excess, frightful often in its ferocity."
13. From Comte to Mill, Windelband and Rickert, the positivist and antipositivist debate raged throughout the nineteenth century: Should (and could) the social sciences be modeled on the natural sciences, on principles of cause and effect and generalization? One of the arguments against the positivist claim was that the historical and social sciences could not clearly separate between subject and object of inquiry, between investigator and investigated.
14. It has become standard practice among qualitative sociologists, ethnographers in particular, to appeal to Weber's authority in defending the role of *verstehen* and empathy in the social sciences. Yet, as Jennifer Platt clearly shows (1985), Max Weber did not become generally known in American sociology until well into the 1940s. Early American qualitative sociologists, particularly the Chicago School, were influenced by Mead, in turn influenced by Cooley and Dilthey (Platt, 1985, pp. 456–7). Indeed, as Outhwaite (1975, p. 24) wrote: "The central figure in the history of the concept of *verstehen* is of course Wilhelm Dilthey," himself being strongly influenced by Droysen, Schleiermacher, and Kant. For Dilthey, "life as a starting point and abiding context provides the first basic feature of the structure of the human studies; for they rest on experience, understanding and knowledge of life. Social science, in other words, cannot simply be learned by imitating and empirical problem solution. Because its object is life, it depends on the scientist's own ability to understand life. It depends upon idiosyncratic abilities to experience, to understand and to know" (cited in Alexander 1987, p. 29). On *verstehen*, see Weber (1978, pp. 4–22); Skinner in Tully (1988, pp. 79–96); Abel (1953); Oakes (1977); Outhwaite (1975); Platt (1985); Diesing (1991, p. 141).
15. The role of *verstehen* in historical or social explanation has been hotly contested. For Durkheim social things are independent of the social consciousness (Durkheim, 1938, pp. 28, 32, 34; 1951, p. 310). Hempel similarly argues that it is quite possible to explain historical phenomena without *verstehen*. In fact, he would add: The alleged method of understanding is not a method at all (Ricoeur, 1984, p. 114). Frankel conceded that interpretation is a necessary moment of historical knowledge, the first moment in fact when the historians appraise and attribute value to historical phenomena. But interpretation plays no part in explanation, which involves establishing causal relations between events (Ricoeur, 1984, pp. 117–18).
16. For these quotes, see Trevelyan (1919, pp. 15, 19, 19, 31; emphasis added).
17. Cèline (cited in Kristeva, 1980, p. 144).
18. For these quotes, see Collingwood (1946, pp. 217, 214, 215; see also pp. 117, 120, 217, 304, 317).
19. Collingwood (1946, p. 215; also pp. 218, 228, 282, 283, 302). And this reenactment of past experience, Collingwood adds, is necessarily critical, because "the historian not only re-enacts past thought, he re-enacts it in the context of his own knowledge and therefore, in re-enacting it, criticizes it, forms his own judgement of its value, corrects whatever errors he can discern in it" (Collingwood, 1946, p. 215; also p. 216).

20. "History," Carr similarly wrote (1990, p. 24), "cannot be written unless the historian can achieve some kind of contact with the mind of those about whom he is writing." And that "contact" requires "imaginative understanding," if not "empathy."

21. For two masterful analyses of meaning and action, see Sahlins's (1981) account of captain James Cook's death or Burke's (1983) analysis of Masaniello's eighteenth-century revolt in Naples. Closer to home, how are we to read pilgrimages? With the confusion of pilgrims of penance and pilgrims of penalty, with some shrines taking on a political meaning (for example, Canterbury came to symbolize resistance to royal authority), with the journey providing opportunities to break away from the drudgery of everyday life (including the temporary relief of debts, or walking naked to the shrines, as we read in a sixteenth-century description of the shrine of Regensburg in Bavarian Germany) (Coleman and Elsner, 1995, pp. 84, 111, 112), with the poor and the rich, like Pietro Della Valle going on a pilgrimage in the full pump of his aristocratic status. It is these characteristics that have led some authors to talk about pilgrimage in terms of liminal experiences (for example, Turner and Turner, 1978, pp. 231–7; for a critique of Turner and Turner, see Eade and Sallnow who point to the persistent maintenance of social differences during pilgrimages, in fact, the pilgrimage as a "realm of competing discourses" [1991, p. 5]).

22. Sterne and Foscolo (1983, p. 32).

23. Hutin (1991, pp. 72–5, 85).

24. Hutin (1991, pp. 51, 56, 70, 88, 101).

25. Cited in Hutin (1991, p. 70); my translation.

26. Thomas Aquinas (1996, p. 39; emphasis added). Thomas's mentor, Albertus Magnus had put it strikingly similarly when he wrote: "I have expended infinite labor and expense, ever going from place to place, observing, considering, ... I persevered in studying, reflecting, laboring over works of this same subject until finally *I found what I was seeking, not by my own knowledge, but by the grace of the Holy Spirit*" (Albertus Magnus, 1958, pp. 1–2; emphasis added).

27. Zweig (cited in Andreski, 1972, p. 119; emphasis added).

28. When "the holy fire come[s] down from heaven (as they say) and [people light] their candles from it with their own hands" (Della Valle, 1989, p. 78).

29. Della Valle (1989, pp. 80–2; emphasis added).

30. For some examples of "confessional literature" in anthropology, see Marcus and Cushman (1982); Clifford and Marcus (1986); Marcus and Fisher (1986); Geertz (1987); Rosaldo (1989).

31. Bourdieu and Wacquant (1992, p. 236).

32. Berger (1963, pp. 40–3, *passim*).

33. Berger (1963, p. 51; for a development of the three motifs, see pp. 51–66).

34. Citations taken from Berger (1963, pp. 66, 178, 184, 41, 51, 51).

35. References in this paragraph are to Weber (1949, pp. 82, 82, 112; emphasis in the original).

36. References in this paragraph are to Marcuse (1964, pp. 193, 181, 90, 88, 91, 98, 100).

37. Bourdieu and Wacquant (1992, p. 238; emphasis in the original); Foucault's insistence on the "archeology of knowledge" and Gadamer's emphasis on the history of words belong here.

38. See Lethbridge's chapter title "Origins and Originality" (1984, p. 70).

39. Quotes taken from the title of the book and of the last Chapter (Chapter XXII, p. 208).

40. Kubie, cited in Merton (1973[1957], p. 320).

41. Eliot (1975, p. 40). For Eliot "No poet, no artist of any art, has his complete meaning alone. His significance, his appreciation is the appreciation of his relation to the dead poets and artists. You cannot value him alone; you must set him, for contrast and comparison, among the dead" (Eliot, 1975, p. 38).

42. For a critique of Merton's position and an appraisal of the role of the classics in sociology and the social sciences see Alexander (1987).

43. Cited in Merton (1973, pp. 306–7).

44. On the dilemma between originality and humility, see Merton's essays "Priorities in Scientific Discovery" and "The Ambivalence of Scientists" (1973[1957], pp. 286–324; [1963], pp. 383–412).

45. Some academic writers, particularly in the sociology of science, have experimented with creative writing, introducing dialogues, addresses to the reader, vignettes (see, Mulkay, 1985, 1991; Latour, 1987). Even a scientist like Richardson, as we saw in Chapter 1, interspersed his

text with dialogues, decades in advance of postmodernist experimentation (1960). No doubt, Foucault's dialogue between critics and himself at the end of his *Archeology of Knowledge* (1972, pp. 199–211) deeply influenced this fashion. But dialogues, of course, have a long history in scholarly writing. Between twenty to twenty-five percent of Thucydides's *History of the Peloponnesian War* is made up of direct speeches (Sloane, 1895–96, p. 5). In philosophy, Plato's work is in dialogue form. Cicero also put many of his works in dialogue form (for example, *De Amicitia*). Even medieval writes (for example, Dante and Petrarch) continued to use the genre. The rediscovery of the classics during the Italian Humanism and Renaissance, the privileged position that Cicero's work acquired – Cicero's *De Imitatione* was among the very first books to be published in 1470 after the invention of the printing press (Kennedy, 1980, p. 195; for a listing of the printing dates of classical Greek and Latin works see Sandys, 1908, pp. 103–5) – and the popularity of the dialogues written by the humanists Bruni and Alberti brought the dialogue form to prominence in the modern era (on Italian Humanism and Renaissance dialogues, see Marsh, 1980 and Cox, 1992). Giordano Bruno's *De Umbris Idearum* (The Shadow of Ideas), a text we have considered in this book, mixes dialogues to descriptive writing (Bruno, 1997). Galileo's *Dialogo dei due massimi sistemi del mondo* and *Discorsi e dimostrazioni matematiche intorno a due nuove scienze*, two masterpieces of modern science, are in dialogue form and so is Campanella's *City of God*.

46. Cited in Le Goff (1982, p. 147); cited in Merton (1973, p. 303).
47. Against the accusation of pedantry of classification, I could embrace von Wiese's line of defense when he wrote: "Those aware of the pressing need of present-day sociology – namely, of permeation with strictly defined concepts – will not sneer at this effort. We are laying foundations; above all else these must be firm and schematic" (von Wiese, 1932, p. 132). Indeed, we have met many others in our journey who spent a great deal of their lives observing and classifying, from Spencer to Sorokin, from Halley to Darwin. There is comfort in numbers, after all! As for the pedantry of erudition I could attempt a defense of my own: That erudition played a fundamental heuristic role in this book. It allowed me to construct a particular type of text, to break the law of genres, to make explicit the foundations of our science in words.
48. From Calvino's *If on a Winter's Night a Traveler* (1993, p. 4).
49. Berger (1963, pp. 184, 186). Andreski (1972, pp. 93–4) similarly stressed that a social scientist's "sense of humor is a fair indicator of [his] … value as an observer of human affairs … of the likelihood of immunity from … [the] folly [of mystifying jargon]."
50. Pirandello (1986, p. 146).
51. Pirandello (1986, p. 168).
52. The twelfth-century poem *The Voyage of St. Brendan* masterfully turns into the Christian world ancient pagan themes of voyages without a goal, as ends to themselves, as challenges to gain entrance into the world of heroes or saints. Waters, the curator of a modern critical edition of the poem, wrote: "The conversion of these romantic, often poetic, but entirely pagan stories into an edifying tale of saintly endeavour, suitable for monastic reading, is one of the most remarkable *tours de force* in the history of literature" (Waters, 1928, p. lxxxii).
53. Hegel (1993, p. 7).
54. In Las Casas (1925, p. 250) from Barros's *Asia* (First Decade, Book III, Chapter XI).
55. From Vespucci's 1504 letter to Piero Soderini (Vespucci, 1984, p. 170). Columbus, in a letter to the Sovereigns of Spain written "in the Indies on the island of Jamaica, 7 July 1503," states: "I beg your Highnesses' leave if it pleases God to bring me back from this place, to go to Rome and other places of pilgrimage" (Columbus, 1969, p. 304). Pigafetta tells us that Magellan's first voyage around the globe, as brought to an end by that Juan Sebastián del Cano who was de Léry's hero, ended with the ritual of the pilgrimage. "On Saturday the sixth of September, one thousand five hundred and twenty-two, we entered the Bay of San Lúcar, and we were only eighteen men, the most part sick … We all went, in our shirts and barefoot, and each with a torch in his hand, to visit the shrine of Santa Maria de la Victoria and that of Santa Maria de Antigua" (Pigafetta, 1969, p. 148). Jean de Léry (1990, p. 209) during his horrific return journey from "the land of Brazil" in 1558, similarly tells us: "You need hardly ask if our Papist sailors, seeing themselves reduced to such extremities, promised Saint Nicholas a waxen image as big as a man if he would get them safely to land, and made marvelous vows."
56. Tolstóy (1934, p. 229).
57. John Florio's farewell to the reader in his 1591 *Second Frutes*. Signed by Florio as: The "resolute I. F. The last of April, 1591" (Florio, 1591a).

References

Abbott, Andrew. 1983. "Sequences of Social Events: Concepts and Methods for the Analysis of Order in Social Processes." *Historical Methods,* Vol. 16, pp. 129–47.

1990. "Conceptions of Time and Events in Social Science Methods." *Historical Methods*, Vol. 23, No. 4, pp. 140–50.

1991. "History and Sociology: The Lost Synthesis." *Social Science History*, Vol. 15, No. 2, pp. 201–38.

Abbott, Andrew and Emily Barman. 1997. "Sequence Comparison Via Alignment and Gibbs Sampling: A Formal Analysis of the Emergence of the Modern Sociological Article." In: pp. 47–87, Adrian E. Raftery (ed.), *Sociological Methodology*, Vol. 27. Oxford: Blackwell.

Abel, Theodor. 1953. "The Operation Called *Verstehen.*" In: pp. 158–65, Edward H. Madden (ed.), *The Structure of Scientific Thought*. Cambridge, MA: The Riverside Press.

Abell, Peter. 1987. *The Syntax of Social Life. The Theory and Method of Comparative Narratives*. Oxford: Clarendon Press.

1993. "Some Aspects of Narrative Method." In: pp. 93–134, Peter Abell (ed.), "Narrative Methods." Special issue of *The Journal of Mathematical Sociology*, Vol. 18, Nos. 2–3.

Abrams, M. R. 1953. *The Mirror and the Lamp: Romantic Theory and the Critical Tradition*. Oxford: Oxford University Press.

1971. *Natural Supernaturalism. Tradition and Revolution in Romantic Literature*. New York: W. W. Norton & Company.

Abrams, Philip. 1982. *Historical Sociology*. Near Shepton Mallet: Open Books.

Adorno, Rolena. 1992. "The Discursive Encounter of Spain and America: The Authority of Eyewitness Testimony in the Writing of History." *The William and Mary Quarterly*, Vol. 49, No. 2, pp. 210–28.

Agar, Michael. 1980. "Stories, Background Knowledge and Themes: Problems in the Analysis of Life History Narrative." *American Ethnologist*, Vol. 7, No. 2, pp. 223–39.

Agar, Michael and Jerry R. Hobbs. 1982. "Interpreting Discourse: Coherence and the Analysis of Ethnographic Interviews." *Discourse Processes*, Vol. 5, pp. 1–32.

Agrippa von Nettesheim, Heinrich Cornelius. 1575. *Of the Vanitie and Uncertaintie of Artes and Sciences*. London: Henrie Bynneman.

Albertus Magnus. 1958. *Libellus de Alchimia. Ascribed to Albertus Magnus*. Translated from the Borgnet Latin Edition, Introduction and Notes by Sister Virginia Heines with a Foreword by Pearl Kibre. Berkeley: University of California Press.

Alcoff, Linda and Elizabeth Potter (eds.). 1993. *Feminist Epistemologies*. New York: Routledge.

Alexander, Jeffrey C. 1987. "The Centrality of the Classics." In: pp. 11–57, Anthony Giddens and Jonathan H. Turner (eds.), *Social Theory Today*. Cambridge: Polity Press.

Alfani, Tommaso Maria. 1750. *Istoria degli Anni Santi dal loro principio fino al presente del MDCCL. Tratta in gran parte da quella del P L. F. Tommaso Maria Alfani dell'Ordine de' Predicatori da Domenico Maria Manni accademico fiorentino con aggiunte notabili del medesimo di memorie, d'iscrizioni, di medaglie.* Florence: Stamperìa di Gio: Batista Stecchi alla Condotta.

Alonso, William and Paul Starr (eds.) 1987. *The Politics of Numbers*. New York: Russell Sage Foundation.

Altheide, David. L. 1976. *Creating Reality*. Beverly Hills, CA: Sage.

1982. "Three-in-one News: Network Coverage of Iran." *Journalism Quarterly*, Vol. 48, pp. 476–90.

1985. "Format and Ideology in TV News Coverage of Iran." *Journalism Quarterly*, Vol. 62, pp. 346–51.

1987. "Ethnographic Content Analysis." *Qualitative Sociology*, Vol. 10, No. 1, pp. 65–77.

Altmann, S. P. 1903. "Simmel's Philosophy of Money." *American Sociological Review*, Vol. 9, No. 1, pp. 46–68.

Alwin, Duane. 1977. "Making Errors in Surveys." *Sociological Methods and Research*, Vol. 6, No. 2, pp. 131–50.

American Statistical Association. 1959. *Acceptance Sampling*. Washington, DC.

Anderson, Mary. 1979[1972]. *Numerology. The Secret Power of Numbers. The Numerical Guide to the Secrets of Life.* Wellingborough, Northamptonshire: The Aquarian Press.

Anderson, Perry. 1974. *Lineages of the Absolutist State*. London: Verso.

Andreski, Stanislav. 1972. *Social Sciences as Sorcery*. Harmondsworth: Penguin.

Andrews, William J. H. (ed.). 1996. *The Quest for Longitude. The Proceedings of the Longitude Symposium. Harvard University, Cambridge, Massachusetts, November 4–6, 1993.* Cambridge, MA: Collection of Historical Scientific Instruments, Harvard University.

Anonymous. 1992[12th century]. *The Pilgrim's Guide*. Translated from the Latin by James Hogarth. London: Confraternity of St. James.

Antoni, Carlo. 1962[1940]. *From History to Sociology. The Transition in German Historical Thinking.* London: Merlin Press.

Aquilecchia, Giovanni. 1971. *Giordano Bruno*. Rome: Istituto della Enciclopedia italiana.

Aristotle. 1981. *Aristotle on Rhetoric. A Theory of Civic Discourse.* Newly Translated, with Introduction, Notes, and Appendices by George A. Kennedy. Oxford: Oxford University Press.

Arthaber, Augusto. 1989. *Dizionario comparato di proverbi e modi proverbiali in sette lingue.* Milan: Hoepli.

Ashenfelter, Orley and George E. Johnson. 1969. "Bargaining Theory, Trade Unions and Industrial Strike Activity." *American Economic Review*, Vol. 59, No. 40, pp. 35–49.

Ashton, Thomas S. 1969. *The Industrial Revolution, 1760–1830.* Oxford: Oxford

University Press.

Atkinson, Anthony C. 1988. "Transformations Unmasked." *Technometrics*, Vol. 30, No. 3, pp. 311–18.

Auerbach, Erich. 1953. *Mimesis: The Representation of Reality in Western Literature.* Princeton, NJ: Princeton University Press.

Austin, John L. 1975[1962]. *How to Do Things with Words.* Second Edition. Edited by J. O. Urmson and Marina Sbisà. Cambridge MA: Harvard University Press.

Avanti! 1963. *Fascismo. Inchiesta socialista sulle gesta dei fascisti in Italia.* Milan: Edizione Avanti!

Avenhaus, Rudolf and Morton John Canty. 1996. *Compliance Quantified: An Introduction to Data Verification.* Cambridge: Cambridge University Press.

Aydelotte, William O. 1969. "Quantification in History." In: pp. 3–22, Don K. Rowney and James Q. Graham (eds.), *Quantitative History: Selected Readings in the Quantitative Analysis of Historical Data.* Homewood, IL: The Dorsey Press.

Azar, Edward E., Stanley H. Cohen, T. O. Jukam, and J. M. McCormick. 1972. "The Problem of Source Coverage in the Use of International Events Data." *International Studies Quarterly*, Vol. 16, No. 3, pp. 373–88.

Azar, Edward E. 1975. "Ten Issues in Events Research." In: pp. 1–17, Edward E. Azar and Joseph D. Ben-Dak (eds.), *Theory and Practice of Events Research.* New York: Gordon and Breach.

Bacon, Francis. 1831. *The Works of Francis Bacon, Lord Chancellor of England, A New Edition by Basil Montagu, Esq. Vol. XIV.* London: William Pickering.

Badaloni, Nicola. 1955. *La filosofia di Giordano Bruno.* Florence: Parenti.

Baedeker, Karl. 1886. *Italy: Handbook for Travelers. Second Part. Central Italy and Rome.* 9th Revised Edition. Leipsic: Karl Baedeker.

Bagdikian, Ben. 1987. *The Media Monopoly.* Boston: Beacon Press.

Baggott, James E. 1994. *Perfect Symmetry: The Accidental Discovery of Buckminsterfullerene.* Oxford: Oxford University Press.

Bailyn, Bernard. 1982. "The Challenge of Modern Historiography." *American Historical Review*, Vol. 87, No. 1, pp. 1–24.

1994. *On the Teaching and Writing of History. Responses to a Series of Questions. Edited by Edward Connery Lathem.* Hanover, NH: University Press of New England.

Bain, Read. 1929. "Trends in American Sociological Theory." In: pp. 72–114, George A. Lundberg, Read Bain, and Nels Anderson (eds.), *Trends in American Sociology.* New York: Harper & Brothers Publishers.

Baker, J. N. L. 1937. *A History of Geographical Discovery and Exploration.* London: George G. Harrap & Co.

Bal, Mieke. 1977. *Narratologie. Essais sur la signification narrative dans quatre romans modernes.* Paris: Editions Klincksieck.

Barnes, Harry Elmer (ed.). 1948. "Albion Woodbury Small: Promoter of American Sociology and Expositor of Social Interests." In: pp. 766–92, Harry Elmer Barnes (ed.), *An Introduction to the History of Sociology.* Chicago, IL: The University of Chicago Press.

Barnes, J. A. 1954. "Class and Committees in a Norwegian Island Parish." *Human Relations*, Vol. 7, pp. 39–59.

Barnes, Samuel H., Max Kaase, et al. 1979. *Political Action: Mass Participation in Five Nations.* Beverly Hills, CA: Sage.

Barnouw, Erik. 1978. *The Sponsor.* Oxford: Oxford University Press.

Barthes, Roland. 1970[1967]. "Historical Discourse." In: pp. 145–55, Michael Lane (ed.), *Structuralism: A Reader*. London: Cape.

1977a[1966]. "Introduction to the Structural Analysis of Narratives." In: pp. 79–124, Roland Barthes, *Image Music Text*. Essays Selected and Translated by Stephen Heath. London: Fontana Press.

1977b[1966]. "The Death of the Author." In: pp. 142–8, Roland Barthes, *Image Music Text*. Essays Selected and Translated by Stephen Heath. London: Fontana Press.

1977c[1966]. "From Work to Text." In: pp. 155–64, Roland Barthes, *Image Music Text*. Essays Selected and Translated by Stephen Heath. London: Fontana Press.

1990[1970]. *S/Z*. Oxford: Blackwell.

Beard, Charles. 1935. "Noble Dream." *American Historical Review*, Vol. 40, pp. 74–87.

Bearman, Peter S. and Katherine Stovel. 2000. "Becoming a Nazi: A Model For Narrative Networks." *Poetics*, Vol. 27, Nos. 2–3, pp. 69–90.

Beaugrande, Robert de. 1982. "The Story of Grammars and the Grammar of Stories." *Journal of Pragmatics*, Vol. 6, Nos. 5–6, pp. 383–422.

1985. "Text Linguistics in Discourse Studies." In: pp. 41–70, Teun A. van Dijk (ed.), *Handbook of Discourse Analysis. Vol. 1. Disciplines of Discourse*. London: Academic Press.

Becker, Carl L. 1932. *The Heavenly City of the Eighteenth-Century Philosophers*. New Haven, CT: Yale University Press.

Beer, E. S. de. 1952. "The Development of the Guide-Book Until the Early Nineteenth Century." *Journal of the British Archeological Association*, Vol. 15, No. 3, pp. 35–46.

Beharrell, Peter and Greg Philo (eds.). 1977. *Trade Unions and the Media*. London: Macmillan.

Bell, Donald H. 1986. *Sesto San Giovanni: Workers. Culture and Politics in an Italian Town, 1880–1922*. New Brunswick, NJ: Rutgers University Press.

Bell, Eric Temple. 1991[1946]. *The Magic of Numbers*. New York: Dover.

Belsley, David, Edwin Kuh, and Roy Welsch. 1980. *Regression Diagnostics, Identifying Influential Data and Sources of Collinearity*. New York: John Wiley & Sons.

Bendix, Reinhard. 1974[1959]. *Work and Authority in Industry. Ideologies of Management in the Course of Industrialization*. Berkeley: University of California Press.

Benson, Lee. 1957. "Research Problems in American Political History." In: pp. 113–83, Mirra Komarovsky (ed.), *Common Frontiers of Social Sciences*. Glencoe, IL: Free Press.

Bentham, Jeremy. 1843. *"Essay on Logic."* In: pp. 213–93, Jeremy Bentham, *Works*. Edited by John Bowring. Vol. 8. Edinburgh: W. Tait.

Benveniste, Emile. 1971[1966]. *Problems in General Linguistics*. Coral Gables, FL: University of Miami Press.

Benzoni, Gino. 1990. "Ranke's Favorite Source." In: pp. 45–57, Georg G. Iggers and James M. Powell (eds.), *Leopold von Ranke and the Shaping of the Historical Discipline*. Syracuse, NY: Syracuse University Press.

Bereiter, Carl. 1983. "Story Grammar as Knowledge." *Behavioral and Brain Sciences*, Vol. 6, No. 4, pp. 593–4.

Berelson, Bernard. 1952. *Content Analysis in Communication Research*. New York: Free Press.

Berezin, Mabel. 1997. *Making the Fascist Self: The Political Culture of Interwar Italy.*

Ithaca, NY: Cornell University Press.

Berg, H. van den, H. F. Glastra, and C. G. van der Veer. 1984. "Television Images of an Industrial Dispute: The Structure and Function of News Coverage." *Gazette*, Vol. 33, pp. 37–50.

Berg, H. van den and C. G. van der Veer. 1989. "Ideologies in the News: On the Measurement of Ideological Characteristics of News Reports." *Gazette*, Vol. 14, pp. 159–94.

Berger, John. 1972. *Ways of Seeing: Based on the BBC Television Series with John Berger*. Harmondsworth: Penguin.

Berger, Peter. 1963. *Invitation to Sociology. A Humanistic Perspective*. Harmondsworth: Penguin.

Berlin, Isaiah. 1960. "The Concept of Scientific History." *History and Theory*, Vol. 1, No. 1, pp. 1–31.

Bernardini, Carlo and Tullio De Mauro. 2003. *Contare e raccontare. Dialogo sulle due culture*. Bari: Laterza.

Bicchieri, Cristina. 1988. "Should a Scientist Abstain from Metaphor?" In: pp. 163–83, Arjo Klamer, Donald N. McCloskey, and Robert M. Solow (eds.), *The Consequences of Economic Rhetoric*. Cambridge: Cambridge University Press.

Bierwisch, Manfred. 1970. "Semantics." In: pp. 166–84, John Lyons (ed.), *New Horizons in Linguistics*. Harmondsworth: Penguin.

Billig, Michael. 1987. *Arguing and Thinking. A Rhetorical Approach to Social Psychology*. Cambridge: Cambridge University Press.

Binkley, Robert, Richard Bronaugh, and Ausonio Marras. 1971. *Agent, Action, and Reason*. Toronto: Toronto University Press.

Black, John B. and Robert Wilensky. 1979. "An Evaluation of Story Grammars." *Cognitive Science*, Vol. 3, pp. 213–29.

Blalock, Hubert M. (ed.). 1971. *Causal Models in the Social Sciences*. Chicago, IL: Aldine.

Bloch, Marc. 1953. *The Historian's Craft*. New York: Vintage Books.

Bodart, Gaston. 1916. *Losses of Life in Modern Wars*. Oxford: Clarendon.

Boethius. 1990. *De topicis differentiis*. Athenai: Akademia Athenon.

Boissevain, Jeremy. 1974. *Friends of Friends. Networks, Manipulators and Coalitions*. Oxford: Basil Blackwell.

Bonaventura da Bagnoregio. 1994[1259]. *Itinerario della mente verso dio. Introduzione, traduzione e note di Massimo Parodi e Marco Rossini. Testo latino a fronte*. Milan: Rizzoli.

Boorstin, Daniel J. 1986. *The Discoverers*. Harmondsworth: Penguin.

Bordogna, Lorenzo and Giancarlo Provasi. 1979. "*Il Movimento degli scioperi in Italia (1881–1973).*" In: pp. 169–304, Gian Primo Cella (ed.), *Il movimento degli scioperi nel XX secolo*. Bologna: Il Mulino.

Bosman, Leonard. 1932. *The Meaning and Philosophy of Numbers*. London: Rider & Co.

Boswell, James. 1928[1764]. *Boswell on the Grand Tour. Germany and Switzerland*. Edited by Frederick A. Pottle. New York: McGraw-Hill.

Boudon, Raymond. 1993. "Introduction." In: pp. 1–29, Paul F. Lazarsfeld, *On Social Research and Its Language*. Edited and with an Introduction by Raymond Boudon. Chicago: The University of Chicago Press.

Boulez, Pierre. 1975. *Par volonté et par hasard: Entretiens avec Célestin Deliège*. Paris: Éditions du Seuil.

Bourdieu, Pierre and Loïc J. D. Wacquant. 1992. *An Invitation to Reflexive Sociology.* Cambridge: Polity Press.

Bower, Gordon and Daniel Morrow. 1990. "Mental Models in Narrative Comprehension." *Science.* No. 247, pp. 44–8.

Braverman, Harry. 1974. *Labor and Monopoly Capital: the Degradation of Work in the Twentieth Century.* New York: Monthly Review Press.

Braudel, Fernand. 1980. *On History.* Chicago, IL: The University of Chicago Press.

Breed, Warren. 1955. "Social Control in the Newsroom: A Functional Analysis." *Social Forces,* Vol. 33, pp. 326–35.

Bremond, Claude. 1964. *"Le message narratif."* *Communications,* Vol. 4, pp. 4–32.

1966. *"La logique des possibles narratifs."* *Communications,* No. 8, pp. 60–76.

Brinton, Crane. 1937. "Socio-Astrology." *The Southern Review,* Vol. 3, pp. 243–66.

Brito, Bernardo Gomes de. 1959. *The Tragic History of the Sea, 1589–1622: Narratives of the Shipwrecks of the Portuguese East Indiamen Sao Thomé (1589), Santo Alberto (1593), Sao Joao Baptista (1622), and the Journeys of the Survivors in South East Africa.* Edited by Charles R. Boxer. Cambridge: Hakluyt Society.

Brockett, Charles D. 1991. The Structure of Political Opportunities and Peasant Mobilization in Central America." *Comparative Politics,* Vol. 23, No. 3, pp. 253–74.

Brody, Robert. 1987. "Bernal's Strategies." *Hispanic Review,* Vol. 55, No. 3, pp. 323–36.

Brooks, Peter. 1984. *Reading for the Plot: Design and Intention in Narrative.* New York: A. A. Knopf.

Bruno, Giordano. 1958. *Dialoghi Italiani.* Florence: Sansoni.

1997. *Le ombre delle idee. Il canto di Circe. Il sigillo dei sigilli. Introduzione di Michele Ciliberto. Traduzione e note di Nicoletta Tirinnanzi.* Milan: Rizzoli.

Brustein, William. 1991. "The Red Menace and the Rise of Italian Fascism." *American Sociological Review,* Vol. 56, pp. 652–64.

Bryman, Alan. 1988. *Quantity and Quality in Social Research.* London: Unwin Hyman.

Buchanan, Lamont. 1956. *Ships of Steam.* New York: McGraw-Hill.

Budd, Richard, Robert Thorp, and Lewis Donohew. 1967. *Content Analysis of Communications.* New York: Macmillan.

Bühler, Karl. 1990[1934]. *Theory of Language: The Representational Function of Language.* Translated by Donald Fraser Goodwin from the German Original *Sprachtheorie; die darstellungsfunktion der sprache.* Amsterdam: Benjamins.

Bunyan, John. 1965[1678]. *The Pilgrim's Progress.* Edited with an Introduction and Notes by Roger Sharrock. Harmondsworth: Penguin.

Burckhardt, Jakob. 1979. *Reflections on History.* Indianapolis, IN: Liberty Classics.

Burke, Kenneth. 1969[1945]. *A Grammar of Motives.* Berkeley: University of California Press.

Burke, Peter. 1983. "The Virgin of the Carmine and the Revolt of Masaniello." *Past and Present,* Vol. 99, pp. 3–21.

1991a. "Overture: The New History, its Past and its Future." In: pp. 1–23, Peter Burke (ed.), *New Perspectives on Historical Writing.* Cambridge: Polity Press.

1991b. "History of Events and the Revival of Narrative." In: pp. 233–48, Peter Burke (ed.), *New Perspectives on Historical Writing.* Cambridge: Polity Press.

Burt, Ronald and Nan Lin. 1977. "Network Time Series From Archival Records." In: pp. 224–54, David R. Heise (ed.), *Sociological Methodology,* Vol. 8. San Francisco, CA: Jossey-Bass.

Calvino, Italo. 1991. *Perchè leggere i classici*. Milan: Mondadori.

1993. *If on a Winter's Night a Traveler*. London: David Campbell.

Camillo, Giulio Delminio. 1554. *Tutte le opere. Introdotte da Lodovico Dolce*. Venice: Gabriel Giolito de Ferrari et fratelli.

Campbell, Norman. 1952. *What is Science?* New York: Dover.

Capecchi, Vittorio and Marino Livolsi. 1971. *La stampa quotidiana in Italia*. Milan: Bompiani.

Cardoza, Anthony L. 1982. *Agrarian Elites and Italian Fascism: The Province of Bologna 1901–1926*. Princeton, NJ: Princeton University Press.

Carman, Glen. 1992. "The Voices of the Conqueror in López de Gómara's *Historia de la Conquista de Mexico*." *Journal of Hispanic Philosophy*, Vol. 16, No. 2, pp. 223–36.

Carr, Edward H. 1990[1961]. *What is History?* Harmondsworth: Penguin.

Carroll, Lewis. 1933. *Alice's Adventures in Wonderland*. London: J. Coker.

Cartwright, Dorwin P. 1953. "Analysis of Qualitative Material." In: pp. 421–470, Leon Festinger and Daniel Katz (eds.), *Research Methods in the Behavioral Sciences*. New York: Holt, Rinehart & Winston.

Cattell, Raymond B. 1949. "The Dimensions of Cultural Patterns by Factorization of National Characters." *Journal of Abnormal and Social Psychology*, Vol. XLIV, pp. 443–69.

1950. "The Principal Culture Patterns Discoverable in the Syntal Dimensions of Existing Nations." *Journal of Social Psychology*, Vol. 32, pp. 215–53.

1952. *Factor Analysis; an Introduction and Manual for the Psychologist and Social Scientist*. New York: Harper.

Cellucci, Carlo. 1998. *Le ragioni della logica*. Bari: Laterza.

Censer, Jack R. 1994. *The French Press in the Age of the Enlightenment*. London: Routledge.

Chabod, Federico. 1961. *L'Italia contemporanea (1918–1948)*. Turin: Einaudi.

1992[1969]. *Lezioni di metodo storico*. Bari: Laterza.

Chafe, Wallace L. 1970. *Meaning and the Structure of Language*. Chicago, IL: The University of Chicago Press.

Chafe, Wallace L. (ed.). 1980. *The Pear Stories*. Norwood, NJ: Ablex.

Chandrasekhar, Subrahmanyan. 1987. *Truth and Beauty*. Chicago, IL: The University of Chicago Press.

Charlesworth, Andrew. 1979. "Social Protest in a Rural Society: The Spatial Diffusion of the Captain Swing Disturbances of 1830–1831." *Historical Geography Research Series*, Vol. 1, University of East Anglia. Norwich: Geo Abstracts Ltd.

Chatman, Seymour. 1978. *Story and Discourse. Narrative Structure in Fiction and Film*. Ithaca, NY: Cornell University Press.

Chaunu, Huguette and Pierre Chaunu. 1955–59. *Séville et l'Atlantique, 1504–1650*. Paris: Institut des hautes études de l'Amérique latine.

Chaunu, Pierre. 1969. *Conquête et exploitation des nouveaux mondes (XVIe siècle)*. Paris: Presses universitaires de France.

1978. *Histoire quantitative, histoire sérielle*. Paris: A. Colin.

1979[1969]. *European Expansion in the Later Middle Ages*. Amsterdam: North-Holland.

Chierchia, Gennaro and Sally McConnell-Ginet. 1990. *Meaning and Grammar. An Introduction to Semantics*. Cambridge, MA: MIT Press.

Chiurco, Giorgio Alberto. 1929. *Storia della rivoluzione fascista*. Florence: Vallecchi.

Chomsky, Noam. 1957. *Syntactic Structures*. The Hague: Mouton.

1976. *Reflections on Language*. Glasgow: Fontana/Collins.

Cicero. 1949. *De Inventione, De Optimo Genere Oratorum, Topica*. With an English Translation by H.M. Hubbell. Cambridge, MA: Harvard University Press.

Cicourel, Aaron. 1964. *Method and Measurement in Sociology*. New York: The Free Press.

1970. "The Acquisition of Social Structure: Toward a Developmental Sociology of Language." In: pp. 136–68, Jack D. Douglas (ed.), *Understanding Everyday Life*. Chicago, IL: Aldine.

1973. *Cognitive Sociology. Language and Meaning in Social Interaction*. Harmondsworth: Penguin.

Ciliberto, Michele. 1986. *La ruota del tempo: Interpretazione di Giordano Bruno*. Rome: Editori.

Ciliberto, Michele and Nicholas Mann. 1997. "Giordano Bruno, 1583–1585: The English Experience; *L'esperienza inglese.*" *Atti del Convegno, Londra, 3–4 giugno 1994*. Istituto nazionale di studi sul Rinascimento and Warburg Institute. Florence: Leo S. Olschki.

Clark, George N. 1944. *Historical Scholarship and Historical Thought. An Inaugural Lecture Delivered at Cambridge on 16 May 1944*. Cambridge: Cambridge University Press.

Clark, Kitson G. 1962. *The Making of Victorian England*. London: Methuen.

Clifford, James and George E. Marcus (eds.). 1986. *Writing Culture. The Poetics and Politics of Ethnography*. Berkeley: University of California Press.

Cohan, Steven and Linda M. Shires. 1988. *Telling Stories: A Theoretical Analysis of Narrative Fiction*. New York: Routledge.

Cohen, Gerald A. 1978. *Karl Marx's Theory of History, A Defense*. Princeton, NJ: Princeton University Press.

Cohn, Samuel. 1985. *The Process of Occupational Sex-Typing. The Feminization of Clerical Labor in Great Britain, 1870–1936*. Philadelphia, PA: Temple University Press.

Colarizi, Simona. 1977. *Dopoguerra e fascismo in Puglia, 1919/1926*. Bari: Laterza.

Colby, Benjamin N. 1973. "A Partial Grammar of Eskimo Folktales." *American Anthropologist*, Vol. 75, No. 3, pp. 645–62.

Coleridge, Samuel Taylor. 1912. *The Complete Poetical Works of Samuel Taylor Coleridge*. Edited by Ernest Hartley Coleridge in two volumes, Vol. 1. Oxford: Clarendon Press.

Coleman, Simon and John Elsner. 1995. *Pilgrimage. Past and Present. Sacred Travel and Sacred Space in the World Religions*. London: British Museum Press.

Collingwood, R. G. 1946. *The Idea of History*. Oxford: Oxford University Press.

Collins, Randall. 1. 1984. "Statistics Versus Words." In: pp. 329–62, Randall Collins (ed.), *Sociological Theory*. San Francisco, CA: Jossey-Bass Publishers.

Collins, Patricia Hill. 1991. "Learning From the Outsider Within: The Sociological Significance of Black Feminist Thought." In: pp. 35–59, Mary Margaret Fonow and Judith A. Cook (eds.), *Beyond Methodology: Feminist Scholarship as Lived Research*. Bloomington, IN: Indiana University Press.

Colón, Fernando. 1959. *The Life of the Admiral Christopher Columbus by His Son, Ferdinand*. Translated by Benjamin Keen. London: Folio Society.

Colonna, Francesco. 1980[1499]. *Hypnerotomachia Poliphili. Edizione critica e commento a cura di Giovanni Pozzi e Lucia A. Ciapponi. Volume Primo, Testo.* Padua: Editrice Antenore.

Columbus, Christopher. 1930–33. *Selected Documents Illustrating the Four Voyages of Columbus.* Including Those Contained in R. H. Major's Select Letters of Christopher Columbus. Translated and Edited with Additional Material, and Introduction and Notes by Cecil Jane. Vol. 1, The First and Second Voyages. Vol. 2, The Third and Fourth Voyages. London: Hakluyt Society.

1969. *The Four Voyages of Christopher Columbus.* Edited and Translated by J. M. Cohen. Harmondsworth: Penguin

1992. *Letters from America. Columbus's First Accounts of the 1492 Voyage.* Edited and Translated by B. W. Ife. King's College London: Shool of Humanities.

Commager, Henry Steel (ed.). 1973. *Documents of American History. Vol. 1 to 1898.* Englewood Cliffs, NJ: Prentice-Hall.

Compaine, Benjamin et al. 1982. *Anatomy of the Communications Industry: Who Owns the Media?* White Plains, NY: Knowledge Industry Publications.

Comte, Auguste. 1896. *Cours de philosophie positive. The Positive Philosophy of Auguste Comte.* Freely Translated and Condensed by Harriet Martineau; with an Introduction by Frederic Harrison. 3 Vols. London: George Bell.

Condorcet, de Antoine-Nicolas. 1955[1795]. *Sketch for a Historical Picture of the Progress of the Human Mind.* Translated by June Barraclough with an Introduction by Stuart Hampshire. London: Weidenfeld and Nicolson.

Connell, Ian. 1978. "Monopoly Capitalism and the Media." In: pp. 69–98, Sally Hibbin (ed.), *Politics, Ideology, and the State.* London: Lawrence & Wishart.

Cook, James. 1955. *The Journals of Captain James Cook on His Voyages of Discovery. Vol. I. The Voyages of the Endeavour, 1768–1771.* Edited by John C. Beaglehole. Cambridge: Cambridge University Press.

1961. *The Journals of Captain James Cook on His Voyages of Discovery. Vol. II. The Voyage of the Resolution and Adventure, 1772–1775.* Edited by John C. Beaglehole. Cambridge: Cambridge University Press.

Copley, Frank Barkley. 1923. *Frederick W. Taylor. Father of Scientific Management.* 2 vols. New York: Harper and Brothers.

Corner, Paul. 1975. *Fascism in Ferrara 1915–1925.* Oxford: Oxford University Press.

Corsaro, William and David R. Heise. 1990. "Event Structure Models from Ethnographic Data." In: pp. 1–57, Clifford C. Clogg (ed.), *Sociological Methodology,* Vol. 20. Oxford: Blackwell.

Cortázar, Julio. 1967[1963]. *Hopscotch.* Translated by Gregory Rabassa from the Spanish Original *Rayuela.* London: Harvill Press.

Coser, Lewis A. (ed.). 1965. *George Simmel.* Englewood Cliffs, NJ: Prentice-Hall.

Coser, Lewis A. 1971. *Masters of Sociological Thought. Ideas in Historical and Social Context.* New York: Harcourt Brace Jovanovich.

Cox, David R. and D. Oakes. 1984. *Analysis of Survival Data.* London: Chapman and Hall.

Crittenden, S. Kathleen and Richard J. Hill. 1971. "Coding Reliability and Validity of Interview Data." *American Sociological Review,* Vol. 36, pp. 1073–80.

Croce, Benedetto. 1923. "*Sulla natura dell'allegoria.*" *La Critica,* Vol. XXI, Fascicolo 1, pp. 51–6.

Croft, William. 1991. *Syntactic Categories and Grammatical Relations.* Cambridge:

Cambridge University Press.

Culler, Jonathan. 1975. *Structural Poetics. Structuralism, Linguistics and the Study of Literature*. London: Routledge & Kegan Paul.

Cuntz, Otto (ed.). 1929. *Itineraria Romana*. Lipsiae: B. G. Teubneri.

Dante Alighieri. 1948. *The Divine Comedy of Dante Alighieri*. With Translation and Comment by John D. Sinclair. London: John Lane The Bodley Head.

Danto, Arthur C. 1985. *Narration and Knowledge*. New York: Columbia University Press.

Danzger, Herbert M. 1975. "Validating Conflict Data." *American Sociological Review*, Vol. 40, No. 5, pp. 570–84.

Dardano, Maurizio. 1973. *Il linguaggio dei giornali italiani*. Bari: Laterza.

Darwin, Charles. 1989[1839]. *Voyage of the Beagle*. Harmondsworth: Penguin.

 1996[1859]. *The Origin of Species*. Edited with an Introduction and Notes by Gillian Beer. Oxford: Oxford University Press.

Dascal, Marcelo and Avishai Margalit. 1974. "A New Revolution in Linguistics: Text Grammars vs. Sentence Grammars." *Theoretical Linguistics*, Vol. 1, No. 2, pp. 195–213.

Date, C. J. 1981. *An Introduction to Database Systems*. Reading, MA: Addison Wesley.

 1986. *Relational Database Selected Writings*. Reading, MA: Addison Wesley.

 1987. *A Guide to the SQL Standard*. Reading, MA: Addison Wesley.

David, Martin. 1989. "Managing Panel Data for Scientific Analysis: The Role of Relational Data Base Management Systems." In: pp. 226–41, Daniel Kasprzyk, Greg Duncan, Graham Kalton, and M. P. Singh (eds.), *Panel Surveys*. New York: John Wiley & Sons.

Davidson, Linda Kay and Maryjane Dunn-Wood. 1993. *Pilgrimage in the Middle Ages. A Research Guide*. New York: Garland Publishing, Inc.

Davis, Natalie Zemon. 1971. "The Reasons of Misrule: Youth Groups and Charivaris in Sixteenth-Century France." *Past & Present*, No. 50, pp. 41–75 (also in Natalie Zemon Davis. 1975. *Society and Culture in Early Modern France*. Stanford, CA: Stanford University Press).

de Andrè, Fabrizio. 1999. *I testi e gli spartiti di tutte le canzoni*. Milan: Mondadori. (Fabrizio de Andrè and Maurizio Pagani. 1983. *Creuza de mä*. Milan: Ricordi).

Debus, Allen G. 1978. *Man and Nature in the Renaissance*. Cambridge: Cambridge University Press.

De Felice, Renzo. 1995a[1966]. *Mussolini il Fascista. La conquista del potere, 1921–1925*. Turin: Einaudi.

 1995b[1969]. *Le interpretazioni del Fascismo*. Bari: Laterza.

Del Carria, Renzo. 1975. *Proletari senza rivoluzione. Storia delle classi subalterne italiane dal 1860 al 1950. Vol. III*. Milan: Savelli.

Della Valle, Pietro. 1989[1650–1663]. *The Pilgrim: The Travels of Pietro Della Valle*. Translated, Abridged, and Introduced by George Bull. London: Hutchinson.

de Man, Paul. 1979. "Autobiography as De-facement." *MLN (Modern Language Notes)*, Vol. 94, No. 5, pp. 919–30.

Denton, Frank T. 1985. "Data Mining as an Industry." *The Review of Economics and Statistics*, Vol. 67, No. 1, pp. 124–7.

 1988. "The Significance of Significance: Rhetorical Aspects of Statistical Hypothesis Testing in Economics." In: pp. 163–83, Arjo Klamer, Donald N. McCloskey, and Robert M. Solow (eds.), *The Consequences of Economic Rhetoric*. Cambridge:

Cambridge University Press.

Derrida, Jacques. 1974[1967]. *Of Grammatology*. Baltimore, MD: The Johns Hopkins University Press.

1981[1972]. *Dissemination*. London: Athlone Press.

1992. "The Law of Genre." In: pp. 221–52, Derek Attridge (ed.), *Acts of Literature*. London: Routledge.

DeSantis, A. and A. K. Wesley. 1997. "Defendants' Characteristics of Attractiveness, Race, and Sex and Sentencing Decisions." *Psychological Reports*, Vol. 81, pp. 679–83.

Descartes, René. 1960. In: *The Rationalists*. Garden City, NY: Doubleday & Company, Inc.

de Sola Pool, Ithiel (ed.). 1959. *Trends in Content Analysis*. Urbana: University of Illinois Press.

Diani, Mario. 1995. *Green Networks. A Structural Analysis of the Italian Environmental Movement*. Edinburgh: Edinburgh University Press.

Diani, Mario and Doug McAdam (eds.). 2003. *Social Movements and Networks. Relational Approaches to Collective Action*. Oxford: Oxford University Press.

Díaz (del Castillo), Bernal. 1960. *Historia verdadera de la conquista de la Nueva España*. 5th Edition Based on the 1944 Edition with Introduction and Notes by Joachin Ramìrez Cabañas, Tome 1 and 2. Mexico: Editorial Porrúa.

1963. *The Conquest of New Spain*. Harmondsworth: Penguin.

Diesing, Paul. 1991. *How Does Social Science Work? Reflections on Practice*. Pittsburgh, PA: University of Pittsburgh Press.

Dietze, Gottfried. 1979. "Introduction." In: pp. 9–57, Jacob Burckhardt, *Reflections on History*. Indianapolis, IN: Liberty Classics.

Dijk, Teun A. van. 1972. *Some Aspects of Text Grammars: A Study in Theoretical Linguistics and Poetics*. Paris: Mouton.

1977. *Text and Context*. London: Longman Group Ltd.

1980. "Story Comprehension: An Introduction." *Poetics*, Vol. 9, pp. 1–21.

1982. "Episodes as Units of Discourse Analysis." In: pp. 177–95, Deborah Tannen (ed.), *Analyzing Discourse: Text and Talk*, Washington, DC: Georgetown University Press.

1983. "Discourse Analysis: Its Development and Application to the Structure of News." *Journal of Communication*, Spring, pp. 20–43.

1985. "Structures of News in the Press." In: pp. 69–93, Teun A. van Dijk (ed.), *Discourse and Communication, New Approaches to the Analyses of Mass Media, Discourse and Communication*. Berlin: Walter de Gruyter.

1986. "News Schemata." In: pp. 155–86, Charles R. Cooper and Sidney Greenbaum (eds.), *Studying Writing: Linguistic Approaches*, Beverly Hills, CA: Sage.

1987b. "Mediating Racism. The Role of the Media in the Reproduction of Racism." In: Ruth Wodak (ed.), *Language, Power, and Ideology*. Amsterdam: Benjamins.

1988. *News as Discourse*. Hillsdale, NJ: Lawrence Erlbaum Associates, Publishers.

DiMaggio, Paul. 1997. "Culture and Cognition." *Annual Review of Sociology*, Vol. 23, pp. 263–87.

Dirac, Paul A. M. 1963. "The Evolution of the Physicist's Picture of Nature." *Scientific American*, Vol. 208, No. 5, pp. 45–53.

1980. "The Excellence of Einstein's Theory of Gravitation." In: pp. 42–6, Maurice Goldsmith, Alan L. Mackay, and James Woudhuysen. *Einstein, the First Hundred*

Years. Oxford: Pergamon Press.

Dohan, Daniel and Martín Sánchez-Jankowski. 1998. "Using Computers to Analyze Ethnographic Field Data: Theoretical and Practical Considerations." *Annual Review of Sociology*, Vol. 24, pp. 477–98.

Downing, John. 1980. *The Media Machine.* London: Pluto Press.

Downs, Anthony. 1972. "Up and Down with Ecology–The Issue Attention Cycle." *The Public Interest*, Vol. 28, pp. 38–50.

Dowty, David R. 1979. *Word Meaning and Montague Grammar: The Semantics of Verbs and Times in Generative Semantics and in Montague's PTQ.* Dordrecht: Reidel.

Doyle, Pat. 1989. "Data Base Strategies for Panel Surveys." In: pp. 163–89, Daniel Kasprzyk, Greg Duncan, Graham Kalton, and M. P. Singh (eds.), *Panel Surveys.* New York: John Wiley & Sons.

Dreier, Peter. 1982. "The Position of the Press in the U.S. Power Structure." *Social Problems*, Vol. 29, No. 3, pp. 298–310.

Dundes, Alan. 1962. "Trends in Content Analysis: A Review Article." *Midwest Folklore*, Vol. XII, No. 1, pp. 31–8.

1964. *The Morphology of North American Indian Folktales.* Academia Scientiarum Fennica. Helsinki: Helsingen Liikerijapaino Oy.

Durkheim, Emile. 1898. *"Préface." Année Sociologique,* Vol. 1, No. 1, pp. i–vii.

1938[1895]. *The Rules of Sociological Method.* New York: Free Press.

1951[1897]. *Suicide. A Study in Sociology.* New York: Free Press.

Eade, John and Michael J. Sallnow (eds.). 1991. *Contesting the Sacred. The Anthropology of Christian Pilgrimage.* London: Routledge.

Eckstein, Harry. 1962. *Internal War. The Problem of Anticipation.* Report submitted to Research Group in Psychology and the Social Sciences, Smithsonian Institution, January 15.

Eckstein, Harry (ed.). 1964. *Internal War. Problems and Approaches.* New York: The Free Press.

Eco, Umberto. 1971. *"Guida all'interpretazione del linguaggio giornalistico."* In: pp. 165–87, Vittorio Capecchi and Marino Livolsi (eds.), *La stampa quotidiana in Italia.* Milano: Bompiani.

1979. *The Role of the Reader. Explorations in the Semiotics of Texts.* Bloomington, IN: Indiana University Press.

Einstein, Albert. 1973. *Ideas and Opinions.* Based on Mein Weltbild, Edited by Carl Seelig, and Other Sources, New Translations from the German and Revisions by Sonja Bargmann. London: Souvenir Press.

Eisinger, Peter. 1973. "The Conditions of Protest Behavior in American Cities." *American Political Science Review*, Vol. 67, pp. 11–28.

Eliot, Thomas S. 1963. *Collected Poems 1909–1962.* London: Faber and Faber.

1975[1919]. "Tradition and the Individual Talent." In: pp. 37–44, *Selected Prose of T. S. Eliot.* Edited with an Introduction by Frank Kermode. London: Faber and Faber.

Elliott, John H. 1976. "Renaissance Europe and America: A Blunted Impact?" In: pp. 11–23, Fredi Chiappelli, Michael J. B. Allen, and Robert Louis Benson (eds.), *First Images of America: The Impact of the New World on the Old.* Berkeley: University of California Press.

Elton, Geoffrey R. 1963. *Reformation Europe 1517–1559.* London: Collins.

1967. *The Practice of History.* Sidney: Sidney University Press (London: Methuen & Co.).

1983. "Two Kinds of History." In: pp. 71–121, Robert William Fogel and Geoffrey R. Elton, *Which Road to the Past? Two Views of History.* New Haven, CT: Yale University Press.

Emery, George. 1993. *Facts of Life. The Social Construction of Vital Statistics, Ontario 1869–1952.* Montreal: McGill-Queen's University Press.

Emirbayer, Mustafa. 1997. "Manifesto for a Relational Sociology." *American Journal of Sociology*, Vol. 103, pp. 281–317.

Epstein, Edward J. 1973. *News From Nowhere.* New York: Random House.

Ericsson, K. Anders and Herbert Simon. 1996. *Protocol Analysis: Verbal Reports as Data.* 2nd Edition. Cambridge, MA: MIT Press.

Erikson, Kai. 1976. *Everything in Its Path.* New York: Simon and Schuster.

Fabbro, Mario. 1974. *Fascismo e lotta politica in Friuli (1920-1926).* Padua: Marsilio.

Faulhaber, Charles. 1972. *Latin Rhetorical Theory in Thirteenth and Fourteenth Century Castile.* Berkeley: University of California Press.

Favre, Robert. 1982. "*Le fait divers en 1778: Permanence et précarité.*" In: pp. 113–46, Paule Jansen (ed.), *L'Année 1778 à travers la presse traitée par ordinateur.* Paris: Presses universitaires de France.

Febvre, Lucien. 1932. *A Geographical Introduction to History.* London: Kegan Paul, Trench, Trubner & Co.

Fenby, Jonathan. 1986. *The International News Services.* New York: Schocken.

Feuer, Lewis S. 1995. *Varieties of Scientific Experience. Emotive Aims in Scientific Hypotheses.* New Brunswick, NJ: Transactions.

Fillieule, Olivier. 1999. "'*Plus ça change, moins ça change.*' Demonstrations in France During the Nineteen-Eighties." In: pp. 199–226, Dieter Rucht, Ruud Koopmans, and Friedhelm Neidhardt (eds.), *Acts of Dissent. New Developments in the Study of Protest.* Berlin: Sigma.

Fillmore, Charles J. 1968. "The Case for Case." In: pp. 1–88, Emmon Bach and Robert T. Harms (eds.), *Universals in Linguistics Theory.* New York: Holt, Rinehart, and Winston.

1971. "Types of Lexical Information." In: pp. 370–92, Danny D. Steinberg and Leon A. Jakobovits, *Semantics: An Interdisciplinary Reader in Philosophy, Linguistics, and Psychology.* Cambridge: Cambridge University Press.

Firpo, Luigi. 1949. *Il processo di Giordano Bruno.* Naples: Edizioni scientifiche italiane.

Fish, Stanley. 1980. *Is There a Text in this Class? The Authority of Interpretative Communities.* Cambridge, MA: Harvard University Press.

Fiske, John. 1990. *Television Culture.* London: Routledge.

Fleming, Candace C. and Barbara van Halle. 1989. *Handbook of Relational Database Design.* Reading, MA: Addison Wesley.

Flieger, Jerry A. 1991. *The Purloined Punch Line. Freud's Comic Theory and the Postmodern Text.* Baltimore, MD: The Johns Hopkins University Press.

Flint, Valerie I. J. 1994. "Travel Fact and Travel Fiction in the Voyages of Columbus." In: pp. 94–110, Zweder von Martels (ed.), *Travel Fact and Travel Fiction. Studies on Fiction, Literary Tradition, Scholarly Discovery and Observation in Travel Writing.* Leiden: E. J. Brill.

Florio, John. 1591a. *Second Frutes.* London: Thomas Woodcock.

1591b. *Giardino di ricreatione.* London: Thomas Woodcock.

1598. *A Worlde of Wordes, or Most Copious, and Exact Dictionaire.* In Italian and English, collected by John Florio. London: Arnold Hatfield.

Fogel, Robert W. 1975. "The Limits of Quantitative Methods in History." *The American Historical Review,* Vol. 80, No. 2, pp. 329–50.

1983. "'Scientific' History and Traditional History." In: pp. 5–70, Robert William Fogel and Geoffrey R. Elton, *Which Road to the Past? Two Views of History.* New Haven, CT: Yale University Press.

Fogel, Robert W. and Stanley L. Engerman. 1974. *Time on the Cross.: Evidence and Methods–a Supplement.* Boston: Little, Brown, and Company.

Foucault, Michel. 1970. *The Order of Things: An Archaeology of the Human Sciences.* London: Tavistock.

1972. *The Archaeology of Knowledge.* Translated from the French by Alan Sheridan Smith. London: Tavistock.

1977. "What is an Author?" In: pp. 113–38, Michel Foucault, *Language, Counter-Memory, Practice.* Edited by Donald F. Bouchard and Sherry Simon. Ithaca, NY: Cornell University Press.

1979. *Discipline and Punish. The Birth of the Prison.* New York: Vintage Books.

Fowler, Roger, Robert Hodge, Gunther Kress, and Anthony Trew. 1979. *Language and Control.* London: Routledge & Kegan Paul.

Francis of Assisi, Saint. 1957. *I Fioretti di San Francesco. Le Considerazioni sulle Stimmate. La Vita di frate Ginepro.* Milan: Rizzoli.

Franzosi, Roberto. 1987. "The Press as a Source of Socio-Historical Data: Issues in the Methodology of Data Collection from Newspapers." *Historical Methods,* Vol. 20, No. 1, pp. 5–16.

1989a. "One Hundred Years of Strike Statistics: Methodological and Theoretical Issues in Quantitative Strike Research." *Industrial and Labor Relations Review,* Vol. 42, No. 3, pp. 348–62.

1989b. "From Words to Numbers: A Generalized and Linguistics-Based Coding Procedure for Collecting Event-Data from Newspapers." In: pp. 263–98, Clifford Clogg (ed.), *Sociological Methodology,* Vol. 19. Oxford: Basil Blackwell.

1990a. "Strategies for the Prevention, Detection and Correction of Measurement Error in Data Collected from Textual Sources." *Sociological Methods and Research,* Vol. 18, No. 4, pp. 442–71.

1990b. "Computer-Assisted Coding of Textual Data: An Application to Semantic Text Grammars." *Sociological Methods and Research,* Vol. 19, No. 2, pp. 224–56.

1990c. "Qualità e quantità: Un gioco tradizionalmente a somma zero. Nuove prospettive nell'analisi del contenuto." *Quaderni di Sociologia,* No. 13.

1994a. "From Words to Numbers: A Set Theory Framework for the Collection, Organization, and Analysis of Narrative Data." In: pp. 105–36, Peter Marsden (ed.), *Sociological Methodology,* Vol. 24. Oxford: Basil Blackwell.

1994b. "Outside and Inside the Regression Black Box: A New Approach to Data Analysis." *Quality and Quantity,* No. 28, pp. 21–53.

1994c. *Il gioco delle parti: attori e azioni nei conflitti di lavoro.* Rome: SIPI.

1995a. *The Puzzle of Strikes. Class and State Strategies in Postwar Italy.* Cambridge: Cambridge University Press.

1995b. "Computer-Assisted Content Analysis of Newspapers: Can We Make an Expensive Research Tool More Efficient?" *Quality and Quantity,* No. 29, pp. 157–72.

1997a. "Comment: On Ambiguity and Rhetoric in (Social) Science." In: pp. 135–44, Adrian E. Raftery (ed.), *Sociological Methodology,* Vol. 27. Oxford: Blackwell.

1997b. "Mobilization and Counter-Mobilization Processes: From the 'Red Years'

(1919–20) to the 'Black Years' (1921–22) in Italy. A New Methodological Approach to the Study of Narrative Data." In: pp. 275–304, John Mohr and Roberto Franzosi (eds.), "New Directions in Formalization and Historical Analysis." Special issue of *Theory and Society*, Vol. 26, Nos. 2–3.

1997c. "Labor Unrest in the Italian Service Sector: An Application of Semantic Grammars." In: pp. 131–45, Carl W. Roberts (ed.), *Text Analysis for the Social Sciences: Methods for Drawing Statistical Inferences from Texts and Transcripts.* Hillsdale, NJ: Lawrence Erlbaum Associates, Publishers.

1998a. "Narrative Analysis – Why (And How) Sociologists Should Be Interested in Narrative." In: pp. 517–54, John Hagan (ed.), *The Annual Review of Sociology.* Palo Alto: Annual Reviews.

1998b. "Narrative as Data. Linguistic and Statistical Tools for the Quantitative Study of Historical Events." In: pp. 81–104, Marcel van der Linden and Larry Griffin (eds.), "New Methods in Historical Sociology/Social History." Special issue of *International Review of Social History*, Vol. 43.

1999. "The Return of the Actor. Networks of Interactions Among Social Actors During Periods of High Mobilization (Italy, 1919–22)." In: pp. 131–49, Dieter Rucht and Ruud Koopmans (eds.), "Protest Event Analysis." Special issue of *Mobilization*, Vol. 4, No. 2.

Franzosi, Roberto and Annella Centis. 1988. *Nuove frontiere nell'analisi del contenuto.* Genova: ECIG (Quaderni dell'Istituto di Scienza Politica, Università di Genova, Sociologia, Vol. 7).

Freedman, David A. 1991. "Statistical Models and Shoe Leather." In: pp. 291–313, Peter V. Marsden (ed.), *Sociological Methodology*, Vol. 21. Oxford: Basil Blackwell.

Freeman, H. A., Milton Friedman, Frederick Mosteller, and W. Allen Wallis (eds.). 1948. *Sampling Inspection.* New York: McGraw-Hill.

Freud, Sigmund. 1950[1913]. *Totem and Taboo. Some Points of Agreement between the Mental Lives of Savages and Neurotics.* Authorized Translation by James Strachey. London: Routledge & Kegan Paul.

1967[1921]. *Group Psychology and the Analysis of the Ego.* New York: Livewright Publishing.

1991[1905]. *Jokes and Their Relation to the Unconscious.* Translated from the German and Edited by James Strachey. Harmondsworth: Penguin.

Frisby, David. 1984. *Georg Simmel.* London: Ellis Horwood Limited and Tavistock Publications.

Frye, Northrop. 1957. *Anatomy of Criticicism.* Harmondsworth: Penguin.

Furet, François. 1985. "Quantitative Methods in History." In: pp. 12–27, Jacques Le Goff and Pierre Nora (eds.), *Constructing the Past. Essays in Historical Methodology.* Cambridge: Cambridge University Press.

Gadamer, Hans-Georg. 1997[1960]. *Truth and Method.* Second Revised Edition. Translation Revised by Joel Weinsheimer and Donald G. Marshall. New York: Continuum.

Galilei, Galileo. 1964. *Opere.* Con note di Pietro Pagnini. Florence: Salani.

Gallie, W. B. 1963. "The Historical Understanding." *History and Theory*, Vol. 3, No. 2, pp. 149–202.

Gamson, William A., Bruce Fireman, and Steven Rytina. 1982. *Encounters with Unjust Authority.* Homewood, IL: The Dorsey Press.

Gamson, William A. and Andre Modigliani. 1989. "Media Discourse and Public Opinion on Nuclear War." *American Journal of Sociology*, Vol. 95, No. 1, pp. 1–37.

Gans, Herbert J. 1980. *Deciding What's News. A Study of CBS Evening News, NBC Nightly News, Newsweek and Time*. New York: Vintage Books.

Gassen, Kurt and Michael Landmann (eds.). 1958. *Buch des Dankes an Georg Simmel: Briefe, Erinnerungen, Bibliographie*. Berlin: Duncker und Humboldt.

Geary, Patrick J. 1984. "The Saint and the Shrine. The Pilgrim's Goal in the Middle Ages." In: pp. 265–73, Lenz Kriss-Rettenbeck and Gerda Möhler (eds.), *Wallfahrt kennt keine Grenzen*. Munich: Verlag Schnell & Steiner München.

Geertz, Clifford. 1973. *The Interpretation of Cultures: Selected Essays*. New York: Basic Books.

1987. *Works and Lives: The Anthropologist as Author*. Stanford, CA: Stanford University Press.

Genette, Gerard. 1980[1972]. *Narrative Discourse: An Essay in Method*. Ithaca, NY: Cornell University Press.

1988. *Narrative Discourse Revisited*. Ithaca, NY: Cornell University Press.

1997[1987]. *Paratexts. Thresholds of Interpretation*. Cambridge: Cambridge University Press.

Genovese, Eugene D. 1976. *Roll, Jordan, Roll. The World the Slaves Made*. New York: Vintage Books.

Gentile, Emilio. 1989. *Storia del Partito Fascista, 1919–1922. Movimento e militanza*. Bari: Laterza.

George, Alexander L. 1959. "Quantitative and Qualitative Approaches to Content Analysis." In: pp. 7–32, Ithiel de Sola Pool (ed.), *Trends in Content Analysis*. Urbana: University of Illinois Press.

George, H. B. 1909. *Historical Evidence*. Oxford: Clarendon Press.

Gerard, Genette. 1980. *Narrative Discourse: An Essay in Method*. Ithaca, NY: Cornell University Press.

1988. *Narrative Discourse Revisited*. Ithaca, NY: Cornell University Press.

1997[1987]. *Paratexts: Thresholds of Interpretation*. Cambridge: Cambridge University Press.

Gerth, Hans H. and C. Wright Mills (eds.). 1946a. *From Max Weber: Essays in Sociology*. Translated, Edited, and with an Introduction by Hans H. Gerth and C. Wright Mills. Oxford: Oxford University Press.

1946b. "Introduction: The Man and his Work." In: pp. 3–74, Hans H. Gerth and C. Wright Mills (eds.), *From Max Weber: Essays in Sociology*. Translated, Edited, and with an Introduction by Hans H. Gerth and C. Wright Mills. Oxford: Oxford University Press.

Giddings, Franklin H. 1894. "The Theory of Sociology." *Annals of the American Academy of Political and Social Science, Supplement*, Vol. V, No. 1, pp. 7–80.

1924. *The Scientific Study of Human Society*. Chapel Hill: University of North Carolina Press.

Ginzburg, Carlo. 1979. "Roots of a Scientific Paradigm." *Theory and Society*, Vol. 7, No. 3, pp. 273–88.

1982. *The Cheese and the Worms. The Cosmos of a Sixteenth-Century Miller*. Harmondsworth: Penguin.

Gitlin, Todd. 1980. *The Whole World is Watching*. Berkeley: University of California Press.

Glasgow University Media Group. 1976. *Bad News*. London: Routledge and Kegan Paul.

1980. *More Bad News*. London: Routledge and Kegan.

1987. *Really Bad News*. New York: Writers and Readers.

Gobetti, Piero. 1948. *La rivoluzione liberale: Saggio sulla lotta politica in Italia*. Turin: Einaudi.

Goethe, Johann Wolfgang. 1987. *Faust*. Part I. Translated with an Introduction by David Luke. Oxford: Oxford University Press.

Goldman, W. and P. Lewis. 1977. "Beautiful is Good: Evidence that the Physically Attractive are more Socially Skillful." *Journal of Experimental Social Psychology*, Vol. 13, pp. 125–30.

Goodwin, James. 1993. *Autobiography. The Self Made Text*. New York: Twayne Publishers.

Goodwin, Jeff, James M. Jasper, and Francesca Polletta. 2000. "The Return of the Repressed: The Fall and Rise of Emotions in Social Movement Theory." *Mobilization*, Vol. 5, No. 1, pp. 65–84.

Goodwin, Jeff, James M. Jasper, and Francesca Polletta (eds.). 2001. *Passionate Politics: Emotions and Social Movements*. Chicago, IL: The University of Chicago Press.

Gottschalk, Louis (ed.). 1963. *Generalization in the Writing of History*. Chicago, IL: The University of Chicago Press.

Gould, Roger V. 1991. "Multiple Networks and Mobilization in the Paris Commune, 1871." *American Sociological Review*, Vol. 56, No. 6, pp. 716–29.

1995. *Insurgent Identities: Class, Community, and Protest in Paris from 1848 to the Commune*. Chicago, IL: The University of Chicago Press.

Gould, Rupert T. 1935. *John Harrison and his Timekeepers*. Greenwich: National Maritime Museum.

Grabois, Aryeh. 1988. "Medieval Pilgrims, the Holy Land and its Image in European Civilisation." In: pp. 65–79, Moshe Sharon (ed.), *The Holy Land in History and Thought*. Papers Submitted to the International Conference on the Relations Between the Holy Land and the World Outside it; Johannesburg 1986. Leiden: E. J. Brill.

Granovetter, Mark. 1973. "The Strength of Weak Ties." *American Journal of Sociology*, Vol. 78, pp. 1360–80.

Grant, Michael. 1992. *Readings in the Classical Historians*. New York: Charles Scribner's Sons.

Greimas, Algirdas Julien. 1966. *Semantinque structurale. Recerche de methode*. Paris: Larousse.

1971. "Narrative Grammar: Units and Levels." *Modern Language Notes*, Vol. 86, pp. 793–806.

Griffin, Clive. 1997. "Antonio de la Bastida y la Inquisición de Cuenca." In: pp. 315–41, Vol. II, *Pre-Actas: Ia Conferencia Internacional "Hacia un Nuevo Humanismo." El hispanismo angloamericano: Aportaciones, problemas y perspectivas sobre historia, arte y literatura españolas (siglos XVI–XVIII)*, 2 vols. Córdoba: Universidad de Córdoba and CajaSur.

Gruber, Howard E. 1978. "Darwin's 'Tree of Nature' and Other Images of Wide Scope." In: pp. 121–40, Judith Wechsler (ed.), *On Aesthetics in Science*. Cambridge, MA: M.I.T. Press.

Gunther, Anthony C. and Leslie B. Snyder. 1992. "Reading International News in a Censored Press Environment." *Journalism Quarterly*, Vol. 69, No. 3, pp. 591–9.

Gurr, Ted Robert. 1968. "A Causal Model of Civil Strife: A Comparative Analysis Using New Indices." *American Political Science Review*, Vol. 62, pp. 1104–24.

1969. "A Comparative Study of Civil Strike." In: pp. 572–631, Hugh Davis Graham and Ted Robert Gurr (eds.), *Violence in America: Historical and Comparative Perspectives*. New York: FA Praeger.

1970. *Why Men Rebel*. Princeton, NJ: Princeton University Press.

1972. *Polimetrics. An Introduction to Quantitative Macropolitics*. Englewood Cliffs, NJ: Prentice-Hall.

1974. "The Neo-Alexandrians: a Review Essay on Data Handbooks in Political Science." *American Political Science Review*, Vol. 68, pp. 243–52.

Haegeman, Liliane. 1991. *Introduction to Government and Binding Theory*. Oxford: Blackwell.

Hall, Stuart. 1977. "Culture, the Media and Ideological Effect." In: pp. 315–48, James Curran, Michael Gurevitch, and Janet Woollacott (eds.), *Mass Communication and Society*. London: Edward Arnold.

Halliday, M. A. K. 1970. "Language Structure and Language Function." In: pp. 140–65, John Lyons (ed.), *New Horizons in Linguistics*. Harmondsworth: Penguin.

1994[1985]. *An Introduction to Functional Grammar*. London: Arnold.

Halliwell, Stephen. 1987. *The Poetics of Aristotle*. Translation and Commentary. London: Duckworth.

Halmos, Paul R. 1960. *Naive Set Theory*. Princeton, NJ: D. Van Nostrand.

Handlin, Oscar. 1979. *Truth in History*. Cambridge, MA: Belknap Press.

Hanke, Lewis. 1959. *Aristotle and the American Indians: A Study in Race Prejudice in the Modern World*. London: Hollis & Carter.

Hankins, Frank H. 1939. "A Comtean Centenary: Invention of the Term 'Sociology.'" *American Sociological Review*, Vol. 4, No. 1, p. 16.

Hanks, William F. 1987. "Discourse Genres in a Theory of Practice." *American Ethnologist*, Vol. 14, No. 4, pp. 668–92.

Harding, Sandra. 1991. *Whose Knowledge? Whose Science? Thinking from Women's Lives*. Ithaca, NY: Cornell University Press.

Harff, Arnold von. 1946. *The Pilgrimage of Arnold von Harff, Knight, from Cologne, Through Italy, Syria, Egypt, Arabia, Ethiopia, Nubia, Palestine, Turkey, France and Spain, Which He Accomplished in the Years 1496 to 1499*. Translated from the German and Edited with Notes and an Introduction by Malcom Letts. London: Hakluyt Society.

Harrison, Brian H. (ed.). 1994. *The History of the University of Oxford*, Vol. VIII. Oxford: Clarendon Press.

Harrison, Mark. 1988. *Crowds and History: Mass Phenomena in English Towns, 1790–1835*. Cambridge: Cambridge University Press.

Hartley, John. 1982. *Understanding News*. London: Methuen.

Hartley, John and Martin Montgomery. 1985. "Representations and Relations: Ideology and Power in Press and TV News." In: pp. 233–69, Teun A. van Dijk (ed.), *Discourse and Communication*, Berlin: Walter de Gruyter.

Hartmann, Paul. 1975/1976. "Industrial Relations in the News Media." *Industrial Relations Journal*, Vol. 6, No. 4, pp. 4–18.

1979. "News and Public Perceptions of Industrial Relations." *Media, Culture & Society*, Vol. I, No. 3, pp. 255–70.

Hartmann, Paul and Charles Husband. 1973. "The Mass Media and Racial Conflict." In: pp. 270–84, Stanley Cohen and Jock Young (eds.), *The Manufacture of News: Deviance, Social Problems and the Mass Media*. London: Constable.

Hayes, Richard E. 1973. "Identifying and Measuring Changes in the Frequency of Event Data." *International Studies Quarterly*, Vol. 17, No. 4, pp. 471–93.

Hays, David G. 1969. "Linguistics Foundations for a Theory of Content Analysis." In: pp. 57–67, George Gerbner et al. (eds.), *The Analysis of Communication Content*. New York: John Wiley & Sons.

Heckman, James. 1979. "Sample Selection Bias as a Specification Error." *Econometrica*, Vol. 47, pp. 153–61.

Hedström, Peter. 1994. "Contagious Collectivities: On the Spatial Diffusion of Swedish Trade Unions, 1890–1940." *American Journal of Sociology*, Vol. 99, No. 5, pp. 1157–79.

Hegel, Georg Wilhelm Friedrich. 1993[1835]. *Introductory Lectures on Aesthetics*. Translated by Bernard Bosanquet. Edited with an Introduction and Commentary by Michael Inwood. Harmondsworth: Penguin.

Heise, David R. 1989. "Modeling Event Structures." *Journal of Mathematical Sociology*, Vol. 14, pp. 139–69.

2003. "Narratives Without Meaning?" In: pp. 183–9, Peter Abell (ed.), "Narrative Methods." Special issue of *The Journal of Mathematical Sociology*, Vol. 18, Nos. 2–3.

Hendry, David F. 1980. "Econometrics–Alchemy or Science?" *Economica*, Vol. 47, No. 188, pp. 387–406.

1993. *Econometrics: Alchemy or Science? Essays in Econometric Methodology*. Oxford: Blackwell.

Henry III, King of France. 1959[1574–1589]. *Lettres de Henri III, roi de France. Récueillies par Pierre Champion publiées pour la Societé de l'histoire de France par Michel François*. Vol. II. Paris: C. Klincksieck.

Herman, Edward S. and Noam Chomsky. 1988. *Manufacturing Consent, The Political Economy of the Mass Media*. New York: Pantheon House.

Hexter, Jack H. 1979. *On Historians: Reappraisals of Some of the Makers of Modern History*. Cambridge, MA: Harvard University Press.

Hinds, John. 1979. "Organizational Patterns in Discourse." In: pp. 135–58, Talmy Givon (ed.), *Syntax and Semantics*, Vol. 12, *Discourse and Syntax*. New York: Academic Press.

Hirsch, Rudolf. 1976. "Printed Reports on the Early Discoveries and Their Reception." In: pp. 537–62, Fredi Chiappelli, Michael J. B. Allen, and Robert Louis Benson (eds.), *First Images of America: The Impact of the New World on the Old*. Berkeley: University of California Press.

Hirschman, Albert O. 1977. *The Passions and the Interests. Political Arguments for Capitalism before its Triumph*. Princeton, NJ: Princeton University Press.

Hobbes, Thomas. 1843. "Of the Life and History of Thucydides." *English Works*, edited by W. Molesworth. Vol. 8. London: John Bohn.

1985[1651]. *Leviathan*. Harmondsworth: Penguin.

Hobden, Heather and Mervyn Hobden. 1988. *John Harrison and the Problem of Longitude*. Lincoln: Cosmic Elk.

Hobsbawm, Eric. 1980. "The Revival of Narrative: Some Comments." *Past and Present*, No. 86, pp. 3–8.

Hobsbawm, Eric and George Rude. 1969. *Captain Swing*. London: Lawrence and Wishart.

Hobson, Dorothy. 1980. "Housewives and the Mass Media." In: pp. 105–14, Stuart Hall,

Dorothy Hobson, Andrew Low, and Paul Willis (eds.), *Culture, Media and Language*. London: Hutchinson.

Hocke, Peter. 1999. "Determining the Selection Bias in Local and National Newspaper Reports on Protest Events." In: pp. 131–63, Dieter Rucht, Ruud Koopmans, and Friedhelm Neidhardt (eds.), *Acts of Dissent. New Developments in the Study of Protest*. Berlin: Sigma.

Hoffman, Paul. 1998. *The Man Who Loved Only Numbers. The Story of Paul Herdõs and the Search for Mathematical Truth*. London: Fourth Estate.

Hofstetter, C. Richard. 1976. *Bias in the News*. Columbus: Ohio State University Press.

Holloway, Julia Bolton. 1987. *The Pilgrim and the Book. A Study of Dante, Langland and Chaucer*. New York: Peter Lang.

Holsti, Ole. 1969. *Content Analysis for the Social Sciences and Humanities*. Reading, MA: Addison Wesley.

Horkheimer, Max. 1947. *Eclipse of Reason*. Oxford: Oxford University Press.

Huizinga, Johan. 1949. *Homo Ludens. A Study of the Play-Element in Culture*. Translated by R. F. C. Hull. London: Routledge & Kegan Paul.

Hunt, Edward D. 1984. *Holy Land Pilgrimage in the Later Roman Empire AD 312–460*. Oxford: Clarendon Press.

Hutin, Serge. 1991[1977]. *La vita quotidiana degli alchimisti nel Medioevo*. Milan: Rizzoli.

Huygens, Robert B. and John Pryor. 1995. *Peregrinationes tres: Saewulf, Johannes Wirziburgensis, Theodericus*. Turnhout, Belgium: Brepols.

Inglehart, Ronald. 1977. *The Silent Revolution: Changing Values and Political Styles Among Western Publics*. Princeton, NJ: Princeton University Press.

Inwood, Michael. 1993. "Introduction." In: pp. ix–xxxvi, Georg Wilhelm Friedrich Hegel, *Introductory Lectures on Aesthetics*. Translated by Bernard Bosanquet. Edited with an Introduction and Commentary by Michael Inwood. Harmondsworth: Penguin.

Jackman, Robert W. and William A. Boyd. 1979. "Multiple Sources in the Collection of Data on Political Conflict." *American Journal of Political Science*, Vol. 23, No. 2, pp. 434–58.

Jacobs, Herbert A. 1967. "To Count a Crowd." *Columbia Journalism Review*, Vol. 6, pp. 37–40.

Jakobson, Roman. 1956. "Two Aspects of Language and Two Types of Aphasic Disturbances." In: pp. 53–82, Roman Jakobson and Morris Halle (ed.), *Fundamentals of Language*. The Hague: Mouton & Co.

1960. "Closing Statement: Linguistics and Poetics." In: pp. 350–77, Thomas A. Sebeok (ed.), *Style in Language*. Cambridge, MA: The MIT Press.

Janis, Irving L. 1949. "The Problem of Validating Content Analysis." In: pp. 55–82, Harold D. Lasswell, Natham Leites, and Associates, *Language of Politics: Studies in Quantitative Semantics*. New York: George W. Stewart.

Janis, Irving L. and Raymond H. Fadner. 1942. "A Coefficient of Imbalance for Content Analysis." *Experimental Division for the Study of War Time Communications*, Document No. 31, Nov. 1. Washington, DC: Library of Congress.

1943. "The Coefficient of Imbalance." *Psychometrika*, Vol. 8, pp. 105–19.

1949. "The Coefficient of Imbalance." In: pp. 153–69, Harold D. Lasswell, Natham Leites, and Associates, *Language of Politics: Studies in Quantitative Semantics*. New York: George W. Stewart.

Jansen, Paule (ed.). 1982. *L'Année 1778 à travers la presse traitée par ordinateur*. Paris:

Presses universitaires de France.

Jasso, Guillermina. 1997. "The Common Mathematical Structure of Disparate Sociological Questions." *Sociological Forum,* Vol. 12, No. 1, pp. 37–51.

2000. "How I Became a Theorist." *Sociological Theory.* Vol. 18, No. 3, pp. 490–7.

Jayaratne, Toby Epstein. 1983. "The Value of Quantitative Methodology for Feminist Research." In: pp. 140–61, Gloria Bowles and Renate Duelli Klein (eds.), *Theories of Women's Studies.* London: Routledge & Kegan Paul.

Jayaratne, Toby Epstein and Abigail J. Stewart. 1991. "Quantitative and Qualitative Methods in the Social Sciences: Current Feminist Issues and Practical Strategies." In: pp. 85–106, Mary Margaret Fonow and Judith A. Cook (eds.), *Beyond Methodology: Feminist Scholarship as Lived Research.* Bloomington, IN: Indiana University Press.

Jenkins, Craig J. and Charles Perrow. 1977. "Insurgency of the Powerless: Farm Worker Movements (1946–1972)." *American Sociological Review,* Vol. 42, No. 2, pp. 249–68.

Jenkins, Craig J. and Kurt Schock. 1992. "Global Structures and Political Processes in the Study of Domestic Political Conflict." *Annual Review of Sociology,* Vol. 18, pp. 161–85.

Jodice, David A. 1980. "Notes on the Quantification of Political Events." In: Charles Lewis Taylor (ed.). *Indicator Systems for Political, Economic, and Social Analysis.* Cambridge, MA: Oelgeschlager, Gunn, and Hain.

Johnston, J. 1984. *Econometric Methods.* New York: McGraw-Hill.

Johnston, Judith. 1985. "Cognitive Prerequisites: The Evidence from Children Learning English." In: pp. 961–1004, Dan Isaac Slobin (ed.), *The Crosslinguistic Study of Language Acquisition,* Hillsdale, NJ: Lawrence Erlbaum Associates, Publishers.

Jones, William Powell. 1966. *The Rhetoric of Science: A Study of Scientific Ideas and Imagery in Eighteenth-Century English Poetry.* London: Routledge & Kegan Paul.

Jordan, David William. 1987. *Foundations of Representative Government in Maryland, 1632–1715.* Cambridge: Cambridge University Press.

Joyce, Patrick. 1994. *Democratic Subjects. The Self and the Social in Ninetenth-century England.* Cambridge: Cambridge University Press.

Jünger, Ernst. 1930. *The Storm of Steel. From the Diary of a German Storm-Troop Officer on the Western Front.* London: Chatto and Windus.

Kahn, David. 1980. "Codebreaking in World Wars I and II: The Major Successes and Failures, Their Causes and Their Effects." *The Historical Journal,* Vol. 23, No. 3, pp. 617–39.

Kakar, Sudhir. 1970. *Frederick Taylor: A Study in Personality and Innovation.* Cambridge, MA: MIT Press.

Kammeyer, Kenneth and Julius Roth. 1971. "Coding Responses to Open-Ended Questions." In: pp. 60–78, Herbert L. Costner (ed.), *Sociological Methodology,* Vol. 3. San Francisco, CA: Jossey-Bass.

Kant, Immanuel. 1911[1790]. *Critique of Judgement. Kant's Critique of Aesthetic Judgment.* Translated, with Seven Introductory Essays, Notes, and Analytical Index by James Creed Meredith. Oxford: Clarendon Press.

Kaplan, Abraham. 1943. "Content Analysis and the Theory of Signs." *Philosophy of Science,* Vol. 10, pp. 230–47.

Kaplan, Abraham and Joseph M. Goldsen. 1949. "The Reliability of Content Analysis Categories." In: pp. 83–112, Harold D. Lasswell, Natham Leites, and Associates, *Language of Politics: Studies in Quantitative Semantics.* New York: George W.

Stewart. (Revised from documents 40 and 41 of the Experimental Division for the Study of Wartime Communications, Washington, DC: Library of Congress, n.d.).

Kelikian, Alice A. 1986. *Town and Country Under Fascism: The Transformation of Brescia, 1915–1926*. Oxford: Oxford University Press.

Kennedy, George A. 1980. *Classical Rhetoric and its Christian and Secular Tradition from Ancient to Modern Times*. London: Croom Helm.

Kenny, Anthony. 1963. *Action, Emotion, and Will*. London: Routledge & Kegan Paul.

Keynes, John Maynard. 1939. "The League of Nations. Professor Tinbergen's Method." *The Economic Journal*, Vol. 49, pp. 558–68.

1940. "Comment." *The Economic Journal*, Vol. 50, pp. 154–6.

Kibre, Pearl. 1980. "Albertus Magnus on Alchemy." In: pp. 187–202, James A. Weisheipl (ed.), *Albertus Magnus and the Sciences. Commemorative Essays, 1980*. Toronto: Pontifical Institute of Medieval Studies.

Kintsch, Walter. 1974. *The Representation of Meaning in Memory*. Hillsdale, NJ: Lawrence Erlbaum Associates, Publishers.

Kintsch, Walter and Teun A. van Dijk. 1978. "Towards a Model of Text Comprehension and Production." *Psychological Review*, Vol. 85, No. 5, pp. 363–94.

Knoke, David and James Kuklinski. 1982. *Network Analysis*. Beverly Hills, CA: Sage.

Koopmans, Ruud. 1995a. "Appendix: The Newspaper Data." In: pp. 247–63, Ruud Koopmans, *Democracy from Below. New Social Movements and the Political System in West Germany*. Boulder, CO: Westview Press.

1995b. "Appendix: The Newspaper Data." In: pp. 253–73, Hanspeter Kriesi et al. (eds.), *The Politics of New Social Movements in Western Europe. A Comparative Analysis*. Minneapolis: University of Minnesota Press.

1999. "The Use of Protest Event Data in Comparative Research: Cross-National Comparability, Sampling Methods and Robustness." In: pp. 89–110, Dieter Rucht, Ruud Koopmans, and Friedhelm Neidhardt (eds.), *Acts of Dissent. New Developments in the Study of Protest*. Berlin: Sigma.

Kozminsky, Ely. 1977. "Altering Comprehension: The Effect of Biasing Titles on Text Comprehension." *Memory and Cognition*, Vol. 5, No. 4, pp. 482–90.

Kreps, David Marc. 1990. *Game Theory and Economic Modelling*. Oxford: Clarendon Press.

Kress, Gunther and Robert Hodge. 1979. *Language as Ideology*. London: Routledge & Kegan Paul.

Krieger, Leonard. 1977. *Ranke: The Meaning of History*. Chicago, IL: The University of Chicago Press.

Kriesi, Hanspeter, Ruud Koopmans, Jan Willem Duyvendak, and Marco G. Giugni. 1992. *New Social Movements and Political Opportunities in Western Europe*." European Journal of Political Research, Vol. 22, pp. 219–44.

Kriesi, Hanspeter, René Levy, Gilbert Ganguillet, and Heinz Zwicky. 1981. *Politische Aktivierung in der Schweiz, 1945–1978*. Diessenhofen: Verlag Rüegger.

Krippendorf, Klaus. 1980. *Content Analysis. An Introduction to its Methodology*. Beverly Hills, CA: Sage.

Kristeva, Julia. 1980. *Desire in Language: A Semiotic Approach to Literature and Art*. New York: Columbia University Press.

Kuhn, Thomas. 1962. *The Structure of Scientific Revolutions*. Chicago: IL: University of Chicago Press.

Labov, William. 1972. *Language in the Inner City*. Philadelphia: University of

Pennsylvania Press.

Labov, William and Joshua Waletzky. 1967. "Narrative Analysis." In: pp. 12–44, June Helm (ed.), *Essays on the Verbal and Visual Arts*. Seattle: University of Washington Press.

LaCapra, Dominick. 1983. *Rethinking Intellectual History: Texts, Contexts, Language*. Ithaca, NY: Cornell University Press.

Laffi, Domenico. 1673. *Viaggio in ponente a San Giacomo di Galitia e finis terrae per Francia e Spagna*. Bologna: Giovanni Battista Ferroni.

Lakoff, George P. 1972. "Structural Complexity in Fairy Tales." *The Study of Man*, Vol. 1, pp. 128–90.

Lakoff, George and Mark Johnson. 1980. *Metaphors We Live By*. Chicago, IL: The University of Chicago Press.

Lambert, Wallace E. 1972[1956]. "The Use of Pareto's Residue-Derivation Classification as a Method of Content Analysis." In: pp. 38–50, Wallace E. Lambert, *Language, Psychology, and Culture*. Essays by Wallace E. Lambert, Selected and Introduced by Anwar S. Dil. Stanford, CA: Stanford University Press.

Landes, David S. 1969. *The Unbound Prometeus. Technological Change and Industrial Development in Western Europe from 1750 to the Present*. Cambridge: Cambridge University Press.

1996. "Finding the Point at Sea." In: pp. 20–30, William J. H. Andrews (ed.), *The Quest for Longitude. The Proceedings of the Longitude Symposium. Harvard University, Cambridge, Massachusetts, November 4–6, 1993*. Cambridge, MA: Collection of Historical Scientific Instruments, Harvard University.

Landmann, Michael. 1958. *"Bausteine zur biographie."* In: pp. 11–33, Kurt Gassen and Michael Landmann (eds.), *Buch des Dankes an Georg Simmel: Briefe, Erinnerungen, Bibliographie*. Berlin: Duncker und Humboldt.

Langlois, Charles Victor and Charles Seignobos. 1898. *Introduction aux études historiques*. Paris: Hachette.

Lanphier, Vernard A. 1975. "Foreign Relations Indicator Project (FRIP)." In: pp. 161–79, Edward E. Azar and Joseph D. Ben-Dak (eds.), *Theory and Practice of Events Research*. New York: Gordon and Breach.

Las Casas, Bartolomé de. 1925. *Christopher Columbus: The Journal of His First Voyage to America*. With an Introduction by Van Wyck Brooks; from Bartolomé de Las Casas's Summary. London: Jarrolds.

1992. *A Short Account of the Destruction of the Indies*. Edited and Translated by Nigel Griffin; with an Introduction by Anthony Pagden. Harmondsworth: Penguin.

Lasswell, Harold D. 1941. "The Technique of Symbol Analysis (Content Analysis)." *Experimental Division for the Study of War Time Communications*, Washington, DC: Library of Congress.

1942. "Analyzing the Content of Mass Communication: A Brief Introduction." *Experimental Division for the Study of War Time Communications*, Document No. 11. Washington, DC: Library of Congress.

1965[1949]. "Why Be Quantitative?" In: pp. 40–52, Harold D. Lasswell, Natham Leites, and Associates, *Language of Politics: Studies in Quantitative Semantics*. Cambridge, MA: MIT Press.

Lasswell, Harold D. and Associates. 1942. "The Politically Significant Content of the Press: Coding Procedures." *Journalism Quarterly*, Vol. 19, No. 1, pp. 12–24.

Lasswell, Harold D., Ralph D. Casey, and Bruce Lannes Smith. 1935. *Propaganda and*

Promotional Activities; An Annotated Bibliography. Minneapolis: University of Minnesota Press.

Lasswell, Harold D., A. Geller, and D. Kaplann. 1942. "An Experimental Comparison of Four Ways of Coding Editorial Content." *Journalism Quarterly*, Vol. IV, No. 1.

Lasswell, Harold D., Natham Leites, and Associates. 1949. *Language of Politics: Studies in Quantitative Semantics.* New York: George W. Stewart.

Lasswell, Harold D., Daniel Lerner, and Ithiel de Sola Pool. 1952. *The Comparative Study of Symbols.* Stanford, CA: Stanford University Press.

Latour, Bruno. 1987. *Science in Action. How to Follow Scientists and Engineers Through Society.* Cambridge, MA: Harvard University Press.

Lattimore, Richmond A. 1962. *Themes in Greek and Latin Epitaphs.* Urbana: University of Illinois Press.

Laumann, Edward O. and David Knoke. 1989. "Policy Networks of the Organizational State: Collective Actions in the National Energy and Health Domains." In: pp. 17–55, Robert Perrucci and Harry Potter (eds.). *Networks of Power: Organizational Actors at the National, Corporate, and Community Levels.* New York: Aldine De Gruyter.

Laumann, Edward O. and Franz U. Pappi. 1976. *Networks of Collective Action.* New York: Academic Press.

Laurence, Alfred E. 1991. "Georg Simmel: Triumph and Tragedy." In: pp. 23–43, Larry Ray (ed.), *Formal Sociology. The Sociology of Georg Simmel.* Aldershot, England: Edward Elgar. Reprinted from the *International Journal of Contemporary Sociology*, 1975, Vol. 12, Nos. 1–2, pp. 28–48.

Laurent, J. C. M. 1852. *M. Thietmari. Historia de dispositione terre sancte.*

1864. *Preregrinatores Medii Aevi Quatuor. Burchardus de Monte Sion, Ricoldus de Monte Crucis, Odoricus de Foro Julii, Wilbrandus de Oldenborg.* Lipsiae: J. C. Hinrichs Bibliopola.

Lausberg, Heinrich. 1998. *Handbook of Literary Rhetoric: A Foundation for Literary Study.* Edited by David E. Orton and R. Dean Anderson. Leiden: Brill.

Lay, Adriana, Dora Marucco, and Maria Luisa Pesante. 1973. "*Classe operaia e scioperi: Ipotesi per il periodo 1880–1923.*" *Quaderni storici*, Vol. VIII, No. 22.

Lazarsfeld, Paul F. 1961. "Notes on the History of Quantification in Sociology–Trends, Sources and Problems." In: pp. 147–203, Harry Woolf (ed.), *Quantification. A History of the Meaning of Measurement in the Natural and Social Sciences.* Indianapolis, IN: The Bobbs-Merrill Company.

1993. *On Social Research and Its Language.* Edited and with an Introduction by Raymond Boudon. Chicago: The University of Chicago Press.

Lazonick, William. 1979. "Industrial Relations and Technical Change: The Case of the Self-Acting Mule." *Cambridge Journal of Economics*, Vol. 3, pp. 231–62.

1981. "Production Relations, Labor Productivity, and Choice of Technique: British and U.S. Cotton Spinning." *Journal of Economic History*, Vol. 41, pp. 491–516.

Leamer, Edward E. 1983. "Let's Take the Con Out of Econometrics." *American Economic Review*, Vol. 73, No. 1, pp. 31–43.

Le Bon, Gustave. 1969[1895]. *The Crowd. A Study of the Popular Mind.* New York: Ballantine.

Lefebvre, George. 1947. *The Coming of the French Revolution.* Princeton, NJ: Princeton University Press.

1973. *The Great Fear of 1789. Rural Panic in Revolutionary France.* New York: Pantheon Books.

Lehman-Wilzig, Sam and Meyer Ungar. 1985. "The Economic and Political Determinants of Public Protest Frequency and Magnitude: The Israeli Experience." *International Review of Modern Sociology*, Vol. 15, pp. 63–80.

Lehnert, W. G. 1980. "The Role of Scripts in Understanding." In pp. 79–95, Dieter Metzing (ed.), *Frame Conceptions and Text Understanding*. Berlin: Walter de Gruyter.

Lehr, F. 1987. "Story Grammar." *Reading Teacher*, Vol. 40, No. 6, pp. 550–2.

Leites, Nathan and Ithiel de Sola Pool. 1942. "On Content Analysis." *Experimental Division for the Study of War Time Communications*, Document No. 26, Sep. 1. Washington, DC: Library of Congress.

Lejeune, Philippe. 1989. *On Autobiography*. Edited and with a Foreword by Paul John Eakin; Translated by Katherine Leary. Minneapolis: University of Minnesota Press.

1996. *Le pacte autobiographique*. Paris: Éditions du Seuil.

Leopardi, Giacomo. 1937. *Opere. Vol. III, Zibaldone scelto*. Edited by Giuseppe de Robertis. Milan: Rizzoli.

Le Roy Ladurie, Emmanuel. 1979a[1975]. *Montaillou. The Promised Land of Error*. New York: Vintage Books.

1979b. *The Territory of the Historian*. Chicago, IL: The University of Chicago Press.

1981. "History That Stands Still." In: pp. 1–27, Emmanuel Le Roy Ladurie, *The Mind and Method of the Historian*. Translated by Siân Reynolds and Ben Reynolds. Chicago, IL: The University of Chicago Press.

Léry, Jean de. 1990[1580]. *History of a Voyage to the Land of Brazil, Otherwise Called America. Containing the Navigation and the Remarkable Things Seen on the Sea by the Author; the Behavior of Villegagnon in That Country; the Customs and Strange Ways of Life of the American Savages; Together with the Description of Various Animals, Trees, Plants, and Other Singular Things Completely Unknown over Here."* Translation and Introduction by Janet Whatley. Berkeley: University of California Press.

Lethbridge, Robert. 1984. *Maupassant. Pierre et Jean*. London: Grant & Cutler Ltd.

Levin, Beth. 1993. *English Verb Classes and Alternations. A Preliminary Investigation*. Chicago: The University of Chicago Press.

Levine, Donald N. 1971. "Introduction." In: pp. ix–lxv, Donald N. Levine (ed.), *Georg Simmel. On Individuality and Social Forms. Selected Writings*. Chicago, IL: The University of Chicago Press.

Levine, Donald N., Ellwood B. Carter, and Eleanor Miller Gorman. 1976a. "Simmel's Influence on American Sociology. I" *American Journal of Sociology*, Vol. 81, No. 4, pp. 1112–32.

1976b. "Simmel's Influence on American Sociology. II" *American Journal of Sociology*, Vol. 81, No. 5, pp. 813–41.

Lévi-Strauss, Claude. 1992[1955]. *Tristes Tropiques*. New York: Penguin Books.

1972[1962]. *The Savage Mind*. London: Weidenfeld & Nicolson.

Lieberson, Stanley. 1985. *Making it Count. The Improvement of Social Research and Theory*. Berkeley: University of California Press.

Lieberson, Stanley and Arnold R. Silverman. 1965. "The Precipitants and Underlying Conditions of Race Riots." *American Sociological Review*, Vol. 30, No. 6, pp. 887–98.

Liebow, Elliot. 1993. *Tell Them Who I Am. The Lives of Homeless Women*. New York: Free Press.

Limentani, Ludovico. 1937. "Giordano Bruno a Oxford." *Civiltà Moderna*, Vol. IX, Nos. 4–5, pp. 3–29.

Lipset, Seymour Martin. 1968. "History and Sociology: Some Methodological Considerations." In: pp. 20–58, Seymour Martin Lipset and Richard Hofstadter (eds.), *Sociology and History: Methods*. New York: Basic Books Inc.

1981[1959]. *Political Man. The Social Bases of Politics*. Baltimore, MD: The Johns Hopkins University Press.

Locke, John. 1975[1690]. *An Essay Concerning Human Understanding*. Edited with an Introduction, Critical Apparatus, and Glossary by Peter H. Nidditch. Oxford: Clarendon.

Lodge, David. 1977. *The Modes of Modern Writing: Metaphor, Metonymy, and the Typology of Modern Literature*. Ithaca, NY: Cornell University Press.

1984. *Small World: An Academic Romance*. London: Secker & Warburg.

Loesberg, Jonathan. 1983. "Narratives of Authority: Cortés, Gómara, Diaz." *Prose Studies*, Vol. 6, No. 3, pp. 239–63.

Loftus, Elizabeth. 1979. *Eyewitness Testimony*. Cambridge, MA: Harvard University Press.

Lovell, Michael C. 1983. "Data Mining." *The Review of Economics and Statistics*, Vol. 65, No. 1, pp. 1–12.

Loxton, Howard. 1978. *Pilgrimage to Canterbury*. Vancouver: David & Charles.

Luce, Robert Duncan and Howard Raiffa. 1957. *Games and Decisions. Introduction and Critical Survey*. New York: John Wiley & Sons.

Lundberg, George A. 1929. "The Logic of Sociology and Social Research." In: pp. 389–425, George A. Lundberg, Read Bain, and Nels Anderson (eds.), *Trends in American Sociology*. New York: Harper & Brothers Publishers.

1942[1929]. *Social Research. A Study in Methods of Gathering Data*. New York: Longman.

Lyons, John. 1970. "Generative Syntax." In: pp. 115–39, John Lyons (ed.), *New Horizons in Linguistics*. Harmondsworth: Penguin.

1970. "Introduction." In: pp. 7–28, John Lyons (ed.), *New Horizons in Linguistics*. Harmondsworth: Penguin.

Lyttleton, Adrian. 1973. *The Seizure of Power: Fascism in Italy. 1919–1929*. New York: Charles Scriber and Sons.

1977. "Revolution and Counter-revolution in Italy, 1918–1922." In: Charles Bertrand (ed.), *Revolutionary Situations in Europe, 1917–1922: Germany, Italy, Austria-Hungary*. Montreal: Interuniversity Centre for European Studies.

Machado, Antonio. 1940. *Poesías Completas*. Madrid: Espasa-Calpe, S.A.

Machiavelli, Niccolò. 1958. *The Prince*. Translated by W. K. Marriott. London: J. W. Dent & Sons Ltd.

MacKenzie, Donald. 1979. "Eugenics and the Rise of Mathematical Statistics in Britain." In: pp. 39–50, John Ervine, Ian Miles, and Jeff Evans (eds.), *Demystifying Social Statistics*. London: Pluto Press.

1981. *Statistics in Britain 1865–1930: The Social Construction of Scientific Knowledge*. Edinburgh: Edinburgh University Press.

Maier, Charles S. 1975. *Recasting Bourgeois Europe*. Princeton, NJ: Princeton University Press.

Maione, Giuseppe. 1975. *Biennio rosso. Autonomia e spontaneità operaia nel 1910–1920*. Bologna: Il Mulino.

Malinowski, Bronislaw. 1948. *Magic, Science and Religion and Other Essays by Bronislaw Malinowski.* With an Introduction by Robert Redfield. Garden City, NY: Doubleday Anchor Books.

Mandeville, John. 1983. *The Travels of Sir John Mandeville.* Translated with an Introduction by C. W. R. D. Moseley. Harmondsworth: Penguin.

Mandler, Jean M. 1978. "A Code in the Node: The Use of Story Schema in Retrieval." *Discourse Process*, Vol. 1, pp. 14–35.

——— 1982. "Some Uses and Abuses of a Story Grammar." *Discourse Processes,* Vol. 5, Nos. 3–4, pp. 305–18.

——— 1983. "What a Story Is." *Behavioral and Brain Sciences,* Vol. 6, No. 4, pp. 603–4.

——— 1987. "On the Psychological Reality of Story Structure." *Discourse Processes,* Vol. 10, No. 1, pp. 1–29.

Mandler, Jean M. and Marsha S. Goodman. 1982. "On the Psychological Validity of Story Structure." *Journal of Verbal Learning and Verbal Behavior,* Vol. 21, No. 5, pp. 507–23.

Mandler, Jean M. and Nancy S. Johnson. 1977. "Remembrance of Things Parsed: Story Structure and Recall." *Cognitive Psychology,* Vol. 9, No. 1, pp. 11–151.

Mantoux, Paul. 1983[1928]. *The Industrial Revolution in the Eighteenth Century. An Outline of the Beginnings of the Modern Factory System in England.* Chicago, IL: The University of Chicago Press.

Marangoni, Matteo. 1964[1933]. *Saper vedere. Come si guarda un'opera d'arte.* Milan: Garzanti.

Marcus, George E. and Dick Cushman. 1982. "Ethnographies as Texts." *Annual Review of Anthropology,* Vol. 11, pp. 25–69.

Marcus, George E. and Michael M. J. Fisher. 1986. *Anthropology as Cultural Critique: An Experimental Moment in the Human Sciences.* Chicago, IL: The University of Chicago Press.

Marcuse, Herbert. 1964. *One-Dimensional Man. Studies in the Ideology of Advanced Industrial Society.* Boston: Beacon Press.

Markoff, John, Gilbert Shapiro, and Sasha Weitman. 1975. "Toward the Integration of Content Analysis and General Methodology." In: pp. 1–58, David R. Heise (ed.), *Sociological Methodology,* Vol. 6. San Francisco, CA: Jossey-Bass.

Marsden, Peter V. 1992. "Social Network Theory." In: pp. 1887–94, Edgar F. Borgatta and Marie L. Borgatta (eds.), *Encyclopedia of Sociology,* Vol. 4. New York: Macmillan.

Martels, Zweder von (ed.). 1994. *Travel Fact and Travel Fiction. Studies on Fiction, Literary Tradition, Scholarly Discovery and Observation in Travel Writing.* Leiden: E. J. Brill.

Martin, John. 1993. *Venice's Hidden Enemies. Italian Heretics in a Renaissance City.* Berkeley: University of California Press.

Martindale, Carolyn. 1985. "Coverage of Black Americans in Five Newspapers Since 1950." *Journalism Quarterly,* Vol. 62, pp. 321–8.

Marx, Karl. 1930[1867]. *Capital.* Volume One. Translated from the Fourth German Edition by Eden and Cedar Paul. Introduction by G. D. H. Cole. Everyman's Library. London: J. M. Dent & Sons.

Maupassant, Guy de. 1938. *Chroniques, Études, Correspondance de Guy de Maupassant.* Recueillies, Préfacées et Annotées par René Dumesnil. Paris: Gründ.

——— 1982[1888]. *Pierre et Jean.* Paris: Gallimard.

Maus, Heinz. 1959. "Simmel in German Sociology." In: pp. 180–232, Kurt H. Wolff (ed.), *Georg Simmel, 1858–1918. A Collection of Essays with Translations and a Bibliography*. Edited by Kurt H. Wolff. Columbus: The Ohio State University Press.

Mauss, Marcel. 1972[1950]. *A General Theory of Magic*. London: Routledge & Kegan Paul.

McAdam, Doug. 1982. *Political Process an the Development of Black Insurgency, 1930–1970*. Chicago, IL: The University of Chicago Press.

——— 1996. "Conceptual Origins, Current Problems, Future Directions." In: pp. 23–40, Doug McAdam, John D. McCarthy, and Mayer N. Zald (eds.), *Comparative Perspectives on Social Movements: Political Opportunities, Mobilizing Structures, and Cultural Framings*. Cambridge: Cambridge University Press.

McAllister, James W. 1996. *Beauty and Revolution in Science*. Ithaca, NY: Cornell University Press.

McCarthy, John, Clark McPhail, and Jackie Smith. 1996. "Images of Protest: Estimating Selection Bias in Media Coverage of Washington Demonstrations, 1982–1991." *American Sociological Review*, Vol. 61, No. 3, pp. 478–99.

McChesney, Robert. 1990. "The Battle for the U.S. Airwaves, 1928–1935." *Journal of Communication*, Vol. 40, No. 4, pp. 29–57.

McCloskey, Donald N. 1985. *The Rhetoric of Economics*. Madison: University of Wisconsin Press.

McLaughlin, Martin L. 1995. *Literary Imitation in the Italian Renaissance. The Theory and Practice of Literary Imitation in Italy from Dante to Bembo*. Oxford: Clarendon Press.

Medalia, Nahum Z. and Otto N. Larsen. 1958. "Diffusion and Belief in a Collective Delusion: The Seattle Windshield Pitting Epidemic." *American Sociological Review*, Vol. 23, No. 1, pp. 180–6.

Melville, Sir James. 1929. *Memoirs of Sir James Melville of Halhill*. Edited by Francis Stuart. London: George Routledge and Sons.

Mercati, Angelo. 1942. *Il sommario del processo di Giordano Bruno, con appendice di documenti sull'eresia e l'Inquisizione a Modena nel secolo XVI*. Vatican City: Biblioteca Apostolica Vaticana.

Merton, Robert K.1968[1949]. *Social Theory and Social Structure*. New York: Free Press.

——— 1973. *The Sociology of Science. Theoretical and Empirical Investigations*. Edited and with an Introduction by Norman W. Storer. Chicago, IL: The University of Chicago Press.

——— 1994. *A Life of Learning*. American Council of Learned Societies. ACLS Occasional Paper, No. 25.

Middleton, Richard. 1992. *Colonial America. A History, 1607–1760*. Oxford: Blackwell.

Mies, Maria. 1983. "Towards a Methodology for Feminist Research." In: pp. 117–39, Gloria Bowles and Renate Duelli Klein (eds.), *Theories of Women's Studies*. London: Routledge & Kegan Paul.

——— 1991. "Women's Research or Feminist Research? The Debate Surrounding Feminist Science and Methodology." In: pp. 60–84, Mary Margaret Fonow and Judith A. Cook (eds.), *Beyond Methodology: Feminist Scholarship as Lived Research*. Bloomington, IN: Indiana University Press.

Milani, Celestina. 1977. *Itinerarium Antonini Piacentini. Un viaggio in Terra Santa del 560–570 D.C.* Milan: Vita e Pensiero.

Miles, Ian and John Ervine. 1979. "The Critique of Official Statistics." In: pp. 113–29, John Ervine, Ian Miles, and Jeff Evans (eds.), *Demystifying Social Statistics*. London: Pluto Press.

Mill, John Stuart. 1897. "What is Poetry?" In: pp. 201–36, *Early Essays*. Selected from the Original Sources by J. W. M. Gibbs. London: George Bell and Sons.

1981[1873]. *Autobiography and Literary Essays*. Edited by John M. Robson and Jack Stillinger. Collected Works of John Stuart Mill. London: Routledge & Kegan Paul.

Miller, Dwight P. and Alan D. Swain. 1987. "Human Error and Human Reliability." In: pp. 219–50, Gavriel Salvendy (ed.), *The Handbook of Human Factors*. New York: John Wiley & Sons.

Mills, C. Wright. 1959. *The Sociological Imagination*. Oxford: Oxford University Press.

Ministero di agricoltura, industria e commercio (Direzione generale della statistica e del lavoro, Ufficio del censimento). 1913. *Censimento degli operai e delle imprese industriali al 10 Giugno 1911. Volume I. Dati riassuntivi concernenti il numero, il personale e la forza motrice delle imprese censite*. Rome: Tipografia nazionale di G. Bertero e C.

Mintz, Alexander. 1949. "The Feasibility of the Use of Samples in Content Analysis." In: pp. 127–1522, Harold D. Lasswell, Natham Leites, and Associates. *Language of Politics: Studies in Quantitative Semantics*. New York: George W. Stewart. (Revised from document 49, August 1, 1943, of the Experimental Division for the Study of Wartime Communications, Washington, DC: Library of Congress).

Mishler, Elliot. 1986. *Research Interviewing, Context and Narrative*. Cambridge, MA: Harvard University Press.

Molotoch, Harvey L. and Marilyn Lester. 1974. "News as Purposive Behavior: On the Strategic Use of Routine Events, Accidents and Scandals." *American Sociological Review*, Vol. 39, pp. 101–12.

Momigliano, Arnaldo D. 1969[1966]. *Studies in Historiography*. London: Weidenfeld and Nicolson.

Monk, Ray. 1991. *Ludwig Wittgenstein. The Duty of Genius*. London: Vintage.

Montague, Marjorie, Cleborne D. Maddux, and Mary I. Dereshiwsky. 1990. "Story Grammar and Comprehension and Production of Narrative Prose by Students with Learning Disabilities." *Journal of Learning Disabilities*, Vol. 23, No. 3, pp. 190–7.

Montaigne, Michel de. 1892[1580]. *The Essays of Michel de Montaigne*. Translated by Charles Cotton, Edited With Some Account of the Life of the Author, and Notes by W. Carew Hazlitt. Second Edition, Revised, Vol. III. London: George Bell & Sons.

Montale, Eugenio. 1948. *Ossi di seppia*. Milan: Mondadori.

1965. *Selected Poems*. Translated by Glauco Cambon. Edinburgh: Edinburgh University Press.

Monter, William. 1990. *Frontiers of Heresy*. Cambridge: Cambridge University Press.

Moore, Barrington. 1966. *Social Origins of Dictatorship and Democracy*. Boston: Beacon Press.

1978. *Injustice. The Social Bases of Obedience and Revolt*. White Plains: NY: M. E. Sharpe.

Moore, David S. and George P. McCabe. 1993. *Introduction to the Practice of Statistics*. New York: W. H. Freeman and Company.

Moore, Will G. 1968. *The Tutorial System and Its Future*. London: Pergamon Press.

Moreno, Jacob L. 1951. *Sociometry. Experimental Method and the Science of Society. An Approach to a New Political Orientation*. Beacon, NY: Beacon House Inc.

1953[1934]. *Who Shall Survive? Foundations of Sociometry, Group Psychotherapy and Sociodrama.* Beacon, NY: Beacon House Inc.

Morin, Edgar. 1969. *La rumeur d'Orléans.* Paris: Editions du Seuil.

Morley, David. 1976. "Industrial Conflict and the Mass Media." *Sociological Review,* Vol. 24, No. 2, pp. 245–68.

1992. *Television, Audiences and Cultural Studies.* London: Routledge.

Morrissey, Elizabeth. 1974. "Sources of Error in the Coding of Questionnaire Data." *Sociological Methods and Research,* Vol. 3, No. 2, pp. 209–32.

Mousnier, Roland. 1970. *Peasant Uprisings in Seventeenth-Century France, Russia, and China.* New York: Harper & Row.

Mueller, Carol. 1997. "International Press Coverage of East German Protest Events, 1989." *American Sociological Review,* Vol. 62, No. 5, pp. 820–32.

Mulkay, Michael. 1985. *The Word and the World.* London: Allen & Unwin.

1991. *Sociology of Science. A Sociological Pilgrimage.* Milton Keynes: Open University Press.

Murdock, Graham. 1973. "Political Deviance: The Press Presentation of a Militant Mass Demonstration." In: pp. 156–76, Stanley Cohen and Jock Young (eds.), *The Manufacture of News: Deviance, Social Problems and the Mass Media.* London: Constable.

Murdock, Graham and Peter Golding. 1974. "For a Political Economy of Mass Communications." In: pp. 205–34, Ralph Miliband and John Saville (eds.), *The Socialist Register 1973.* London: The Merlin Press.

1977. "Capitalism, Communication and Class Relations." In: pp. 12–43, James Curran, Michael Gurevitch, and Janet Wollacott (eds.), *Mass Communication and Society.* London: Edward Arnold.

1978. "The Structure, Ownership and Control of the Press: 1914–1976." In: pp. 130–48, George Boyce, James Curran, and Pauline Wingate (eds.), *Newspaper History: From the Seventeenth Century to the Present Day.* London: Constable.

Myers, Daniel J. 1997. "Racial Rioting in the 1960s: An Event History Analysis of Local Conditions." *American Sociological Review,* Vol. 62, No. 1, pp. 94–112.

Namenwirth, J. Zvi and Robert P. Weber. 1987. *Dynamics of Culture.* Boston: Allen & Unwin.

Naus, Joseph I. 1975. *Data Quality Control and Editing.* New York: Marcel Dekker, Inc.

Nedzynski, Stefan. 1973. "Inequality in access to Communication Facilities for Working Class Organizations." In: pp. 413–23, George Gerbner, Larry Gross, and William Melody (eds.), *Communications, Technology and Social Policy.* New York: John Wiley & Sons.

Nelson, Daniel. 1980. *Frederick W. Taylor and the Rise of Scientific Management.* Madison: University of Wisconsin Press.

Nicholson, Michael. 1970. *Conflict Analysis.* London: English Universities Press.

Nietzsche, Friedrich. 1954[1883–85]. "Thus Spoke Zarathustra." In: pp. 103–439, Walter Kaufmann (ed.), *The Portable Nietzsche.* Selected and Translated with an Introduction, Prefaces, and Notes by Walter Kaufmann. Harmondsworth: Penguin.

Nisbet, Robert A. 1976. *Sociology as an Art Form.* London: Heinemann.

Noble, David F. 1977. *America by Design: Science, Technology, and the Rise of Corporate Capitalism.* New York: Knopf.

Nora, Pierre. 1974. *"Le retour de l'événement."* In: Jacques Le Goff and Pierre Nora (eds.), *Faire de l'histoire. Première Partie, Nouveaux Problèmes.* Paris: Gallimard.

Novacco, Domenico (ed.). 1967. *Storia del parlamento italiano.* Vol. 12. Palermo: Flaccovio.

Novick, Peter. 1988. *That Noble Dream. The "Objectivity Question" and the American Historical Profession.* Cambridge: Cambridge University Press.

Nunnally, Jum C. 1967. *Psychometric Theory.* New York: McGraw-Hill.

Oakes, Guy. 1977. "The *Verstehen* Thesis and the Foundations of Max Weber's Methodology." *History and Theory,* Vol. 16, No. 1. pp. 11–29.

Oakley, Ann. 1981. "Interviewing Women: A Contradiction in Terms." In: pp. 30–61, Helen Roberts (ed.), *Doing Feminist Research.* London: Routledge & Kegan Paul.

Ogden, Charles K. and Ian A. Richards. 1946. *The Meaning of Meaning. A Study of the Influence of Language upon Thought and of the Science of Symbolism.* London: Kegan Paul, Trench, Trubner & Co.

Oliver, Pamela E. and Daniel J. Myers. 1999. "How Events Enter the Public Sphere: Conflict, Location, and Sponsorship in Local Newspaper Coverage of Public Events." *American Journal of Sociology,* Vol. 105, No. 1, pp. 38–87.

2003. "Networks, Diffusion, and Cycles of Collective Action. In: pp. 173–203, Mario Diani and Doug McAdam (eds.), *Social Movement Analysis: The Network Perspective.* Oxford: Oxford University Press.

Oliver, Pamela E. and Gregory M. Maney. 2000. "Political Processes and Local Newspaper Coverage of Protest Events: From Selection Bias to Triadic Interactions." *American Journal of Sociology,* Vol. 106, No. 2, pp. 463–505.

Olzak, Susan. 1987. "Causes of Ethnic Protest and Conflict in Urban America, 1877–1889." *Social Science Research,* Vol. 16, pp. 185–210.

1989. "Analysis of Events in the Study of Collective Action." *Annual Review of Sociology,* Vol. 15, pp. 119–41.

1992. *The Dynamics of Ethnic Competition and Conflict.* Stanford, CA: Stanford University Press.

Opp, Karl-Dieter and Christiane Gern. 1993. "Dissident Groups, Personal Networks, and Spontaneous Cooperation: The East German Revolution of 1989." *American Sociological Review,* Vo. 58, pp. 659–80.

Ortes, Giammaria. 1984. *Calcolo sopra la verità dell'istoria e altri scritti. A cura di Bartolo Anglani. Presentazioni di Italo Calvino e Giampaolo Dossena.* Genoa: Costa & Nolan.

Osgood, Charles E. 1959. "The Representational Model and Relevant Research Methods." In: pp. 33–88, Ithiel de Sola Pool (ed.), *Trends in Content Analysis.* Urbana: University of Illinois Press.

Outhwaite, William. 1975. *Understanding Social Life: The Method Called Verstehen.* London: George Allen & Unwin.

Padgett, John and Christopher Ansell. 1993. "Robust Action and the Rise of the Medici, 1400–1434." *American Journal of Sociology,* Vol. 98, No. 6, pp. 1259–319.

Paige, Jeffrey. 1975. *Agrarian Revolution.* New York: The Free Press.

Palmer, Andrew. 1994. "Egeria the Voyager, or the Technology of Remote Sensing in Late Antiquity." In: pp. 39–53, Zweder von Martels (ed.), *Travel Fact and Travel Fiction. Studies on Fiction, Literary Tradition, Scholarly Discovery and Observation in Travel Writing.* Leiden: E. J. Brill.

Palmer, Frank R. 1994. *Grammatical Roles and Relations.* Cambridge: Cambridge University Press.

Park, Robert E. and Ernest W. Burgess. 1921. *Introduction to the Science of Sociology.*

Chicago, IL: The University of Chicago Press.

Pascal, Blaise. 1995. *Pensées and Other Writings*. Translated by Honor Levi. Edited with an Introduction and Notes by Anthony Levi. Oxford: Oxford University Press.

Pearson, Egon S. (ed.). 1978. *The History of Statistics in the 17ʰ and 18ʰ Centuries Against the Changing Background of Intellectual, Scientific and Religious Thought: Lectures by Karl Pearson Given at University College London During the Academic Sessions of 1921–1933*. London: Charles Griffin and Company Ltd.

Pendle, George. 1963. *A History of Latin America*. Harmondsworth: Penguin.

Pera, Marcello. 1991. *Scienza e retorica*. Bari: Laterza.

Perrot, Michelle. 1968. "*Grèves, grévistes et conjoncture. Vieux problem, travaux neufs.*" *Le mouvement social*, No. 63, pp. 109–24.

1974. *Les ouvriers en grève (France 1871–1890)*. Paris: Mouton.

Perry, Menakhem. 1979. "Literary Dynamics: How the Order of a Text Creates its Meanings." *Poetics Today*, Vol. 1, No. 1, pp. 35–64.

Petersen, William. 1987. "Politics and the Measurement of Ethnicity." In: pp. 187–233, William Alonso and Paul Starr (eds.), *The Politics of Numbers*. New York: Russell Sage Foundation.

Pigafetta, Antonio. 1969[1524 ca.]. *Magellan's Voyage. A Narrative Account of the First Circumnavigation*. Translated and Edited by R. A. Skelton. New York: Dover.

Pirandello, Luigi. 1986[1908]. *L'umorismo. Introduzione di Salvatore Guglielmo*. Milan: Mondadori.

Piven, Frances and Richard Cloward. 1977. *Poor People's Movements: How They Succeed, Why They Fail*. New York: Vintage.

Planck, Max. 1936. *The Philosophy of Physics*. London: George Allen and Unwin Ltd.

Plato. 1963. *The Collected Dialogues of Plato, Including the Letters*. Edited by Edith Hamilton and Huntington Cairns. With Introduction and Prefatory Notes. New York: Pantheon Books.

1994. *Symposium*. Translated by Robin Waterfield. Oxford: Oxford University Press.

Platt, Jennifer. 1985. "Weber's *Verstehen* and the History of Qualitative Research: The Missing Link." *The British Journal of Sociology*, Vol. 36, No. 3, pp. 448–66.

1996. *A History of Sociological Research Methods in America, 1920–1960*. Cambridge: Cambridge University Press.

Poggi, Gianfranco. 1978. *The Development of the Modern State: A Sociological Introduction*. Stanford, CA: Stanford University Press.

Poincaré, Jules-Henri. 1997[1908]. *Scienza e metodo (Sciences et méthodes)*. Turin: Einaudi.

Polo, Marco. 1955. *Il Milione* (a cura di Ettore Camesasca). Milan: Rizzoli.

Pool, de Sola Ithiel (ed.). 1959. *Trends in Content Analysis*. Urbana: University of Illinois Press.

Popper, Karl R. 1972[1959]. *The Logic of Scientific Discovery*. 6th Revised Impression. London: Hutchinson & Co.

Porter, Theodore M. 1995. *Trust in Numbers. The Pursuit of Objectivity in Science and Public Life*. Princeton, NJ: Princeton University Press.

Poulantzas, Nicos. 1979[1970]. *Fascism and Dictatorship*. London: Verso.

Powell, Walter W. 1985. *Getting Into Print. The Decision-Making Process in Scholarly Publishing*. Chicago, IL: The University of Chicago Press.

Powell, Walter W. and Rebecca Friedkin. 1983. "Political and Organizational Influences on Public Television Programming." In: pp. 413–38, Ellen Wartella and Charles D.

Whitney (eds.), *Mass Communication Review Yearbook*, Vol. 4. Beverly Hills, CA: Sage.

Prévert, Jacques. 1963. *Histoires et d'autres histoires*. Paris: Gallimard.

Price, Jacob M. and Val R. Lorwin. 1972. "Introduction." In: pp. 1–11, Val R. Lorwin and Jacob M. Price (eds.), *The Dimensions of the Past. Materials, Problems and Opportunities for Quantitative Work in History*. New Haven, CT: Yale University Press.

Prince, Gerald. 1973. *A Grammar of Stories; an Introduction. De proprietatibus litterarum*; Series minor; Vol. 13. Paris: Mouton.

Propp, Vladimir. 1968[1928]. *Morphology of the Folktale*. Austin: University of Texas Press.

Pustejovsky, James. 1995. *The Generative Lexicon*. Cambridge, MA: The MIT Press.

Quinn, David Beers. 1976. "New Geographical Horizons: Literature." In: pp. 635–58, Fredi Chiappelli, Michael J. B. Allen, and Robert Louis Benson (eds.), *First Images of America: The Impact of the New World on the Old*. Berkeley: University of California Press.

Quintilian. 1922. *The Institutio Oratoria of Quintilian*. With an English Translation by H. E. Butler. London: Heinemann.

Radford, Andrew. 1981. *Transformational Syntax*. Cambridge: Cambridge University Press.

1988. *Transformational Grammar: A First Course*. Cambridge: Cambridge University Press.

Ragin, Charles. 1987. *The Comparative Method. Moving Beyond Qualitative and Quantitative Strategies*. Berkeley: University of California Press.

2000. *Fuzzy-Set Social Science*. Chicago: The University of Chicago Press.

Rangarajan, L. N. 1985. *The Limitation of Conflict: a Theory of Bargaining and Negotiation*. London: Croom Helm.

Ranke, Leopold von. 1981. *The Secret of World History: Selected Writings on the Art and Science of History*. Edited and Translated by Roger Wines. New York: Fordham University Press.

Ravenstein, Ernest G. 1898. " Introduction." In: pp. xi–xxxvi, Alvaro Velho. *A Journal of the First Voyage of Vasco da Gama, 1497–1499*. Translated and Edited, with Notes, an Introduction, and Appendices by E. G. Ravenstein. London: Hakluyt Society.

Reinharz, Shulamit. 1992. *Feminist Methods in Social Research*. Oxford: Oxford University Press.

Renier, Gustaaf Johannes. 1950. *History. Its Purpose and Method*. London: George Allen & Unwin.

Rex, John. 1961. *Key Problems of Sociological Theory*. London: Routledge & Kegan Paul.

Rey, Alain. 1992. *Dictionnaire historique de la langue française*. Paris: Dictionnaires Le Robert.

Ricci, Saverio. 1990. *La fortuna del pensiero di Giordano Bruno (1600–1750). Prefazione di Eugenio Garin*. Florence: Le Lettere.

Richard, Jean. 1981. *Les récits de voyage et de pèlerinage*. Turnhout, Belgium: Brepols.

1984. *"Les relations de pèlerinages au Moyen Age et les motivations de leurs auteurs."* In: pp. 143–54, Lenz Kriss-Rettenbeck and Gerda Möhler (eds.), *Wallfahrt kennt keine Grenzen*. Munich: Verlag Schnell & Steiner München.

Richards, Thomas J. and Richards Lyn. 2000. "Using Computers in Qualitative Research." In: pp. 445–62, Norman K. Denzin and Yvonna S. Lincoln (eds.), *Handbook of Qualitative Research*. 2nd Edition. Thousand Oaks, CA: Sage.

Richardson, Lewis F. 1922. *Weather Prediction by Numerical Process*. Cambridge: Cambridge University Press.

1960. *Statistics of Deadly Quarrels*. Edited by Quincy Wright and Carl C. Lienau. Chicago, IL: Quadrangle.

Rickert, Heinrich. 1962[1902]. *Science and History. A Critique of Positivistic Epistemology*. Edited by Arthur Goddard. Princeton, NJ: D. Van Nostrand.

Ricoeur, Paul. 1984, 1985, 1988. *Time and Narrative*. Vols. 1, 2, and 3. Translated by Kathleen McLaughlin and David Pellauer. Chicago, IL: The University of Chicago Press.

Riley, Gail L. 1993. "A Story Structure Approach to Narrative Text Comprehension." *The Modern Language Journal*, Vol. 77, No. 4, pp. 417–32.

Rimmon-Kenan, Slomith. 1983. *Narrative Fiction: Contemporary Poetics*. London: Methuen.

Ripa, Cesare. 1971[1593]. *Baroque and Rococo Pictorial Imagery. The 1758–60 Hertel Edition of Ripa's 'Iconologia' with 200 Engraved Illustrations*. Introduction, Translations and 200 Commentaries by Edward A. Maser. New York: Dover.

Ritvo, Harriet. 1997. *The Platypus and the Mermaid and Other Figments of the Classifying Imagination*. Cambridge, MA: Harvard University Press.

Roberts, Carl W. 1989. "Other Than Counting Words: A Linguistic Approach to Content Analysis." *Social Forces*, Vol. 68, No. 1, pp. 147–77.

1997. "A Generic Semantic Grammar for Quantitative Text Analysis: Applications to East and West Berlin Radio News Content from 1979." In: pp. 89–130, Adrian E. Raftery (ed.), *Sociological Methodology*, Vol. 27. Oxford: Blackwell.

Robinson, Eric and Douglas McKie. 1976. *Partners in Science: Letters of James Watt and Joseph Black*. Edited with Introductions and Notes by Eric Robinson and Douglas McKie. London: Constable.

Rosaldo, Renato. 1989. *Culture and Truth: The Remaking of Social Analysis*. Boston: Beacon Press.

Rosch, Eleanor. 1978. "Principles of Categorization." In: pp. 27–48, Eleanor Rosch and Barbara B. Lloyd (eds.), *Cognition and Categorization*. Hillsdale, NJ: Lawrence Erlbaum Associates, Publishers.

Rosch, Eleanor and Barbara B. Lloyd (eds.). 1978. *Cognition and Categorization*. Hillsdale, NJ: Lawrence Erlbaum Associates, Publishers.

Rosch, Eleanor, Carolyn B. Mervis, Wayne D. Gray, David M. Johnson, and Penny Boyes-Braem. 1976. "Basic Objects in Natural Categories." *Cognitive Psychology*, Vol. 8, pp. 382–439.

Rosengren, Karl Erik (ed.). 1981. *Advances in Content Analysis*. Beverly Hills, CA: Sage.

Ross, Edward A. 1938[1929]. *Principles of Sociology*. 3rd Edition. New York: D. Appleton-Century Company Incorporated.

Rossi, Paolo. 1960. *Clavis Universalis*. Bologna: Il Mulino.

1968. *Francis Bacon: From Magic to Science*. Chicago, IL: The University of Chicago Press.

Rowney, Don K. and James Q. Graham Jr. (eds.). 1969. *Quantitative History. Selected Readings in the Quantitative Analysis of Historical Data*. Homewood, IL: The

Dorsey Press.

Rucht, Dieter and Friedhelm Neidhardt. 1999. "Methodological Issues in Collecting Protest Event Data: Units of Analysis, Sources and Sampling, Coding Problems." In: pp. 64–89, Dieter Rucht, Ruud Koopmans, and Friedhelm Neidhardt (eds.), *Acts of Dissent. New Developments in the Study of Protest.* Berlin: Sigma.

Rucht, Dieter and Thomas Ohlemacher. 1992. "Protest Event Data: Collection, Uses, and Perspectives." In: pp. 76–106, Marco Diani and Ron Eyerman (eds.), *Studying Collective Action.* London: Sage.

Rucht, Dieter. 1996. "The Impact of National Contexts on Social Movement Structures: A Cross-Movement and Cross-National Comparison." In: pp. 185–204, Doug McAdam, John D. McCarthy, and Mayer N. Zald (eds.), *Comparative Perspectives on Social Movements: Political Opportunities, Mobilizing Structures, and Cultural Framings.* Cambridge: Cambridge University Press.

Rudé, George. 1959. *The Crowd in the French Revolution.* Oxford: Clarendon Press.

Rudwick, Elliot M. 1964. *Race Riot at East St. Louis, July 2, 1917.* Carbondale, IL: Southern Illinois University Press.

Rueschemeyer, Dietrich, Evelyne Huber Stephens, and John D. Stephens. 1992. *Capitalist Development and Democracy.* Chicago, IL: The University of Chicago Press.

Rule, James B. 1988. *Theories of Civil Violence.* Berkeley: University of California Press.

Rumelhart, David. 1975. "Notes on a Schema for Stories." In: pp. 211–36, Daniel Bobrow and Allan Collins (eds.), *Representation and Understanding.* New York: Academic Press.

Rummel, Rudolph. 1963. "Dimensions of Conflict Behavior Within and Between Nations." *General Systems. Yearbook of the Society for General Systems Research,* Vol. VIII, pp. 1–50.

1965. "A Field Theory of Social Action with Applications to Conflict Within Nations." *General Systems. Yearbook of the Society for General Systems Research,* Vol. X, pp. 183–211.

1966. "Dimensions of Conflict Behavior Within Nations, 1946–59." *Journal of Conflict Resolution,* Vol. 10, No. 1, pp. 65–73.

Ruskin, John. 1903. *The Works of John Ruskin.* Edited by Edward T. Cook and Alexander Wedderburn. London: G. Allen.

Russett, Bruce M., Hayward Alker, Karl W. Deutsch, and Harold D. Lasswell. 1964. *World Handbook of Political and Social Indicators.* New Haven: Yale University Press.

Saba, Umberto. 1963. *Antologia del canzoniere.* Turin: Einaudi.

Sacks, Oliver. 1995. *An Anthropologist on Mars. Seven Paradoxical Tales.* New York: Alfred A. Knopf.

Sager, Naomi. 1987. "Computer Processing of Narrative Information." In: pp. 3–22, Naomi Sager, Carol Friedman, and Margaret S. Lyman (eds.), *Medical Language Processing, Computer Management of Narrative Data.* Reading, MA: Addison Wesley.

Sager, Naomi, Paul Jr. Mattick, Carol Friedman, and Emile C. Chi. 1987. "Information Structures in Survey Instruments." *American Statistical Association, Proceedings of the Section on Survey Research Methods,* pp. 267–70.

Sahlins, Marshall D. 1981. *Historical Metaphors and Mythical Realities: Structure in the*

Early History of the Sandwich Islands Kingdom. Ann Arbor: University of Michigan Press.

Salais, Robert, Nicolas Baverez, and Bénédicte Reynaud. 1986. *L'Invention du chômage. Histoire et transformations d'une catégorie en France des années 1890 aux années 1980.* Paris: Presses Universitaires de France.

Salvatorelli, Luigi and Giovanni Mira. 1964. *Storia d'Italia nel periodo fascista.* Turin: Einaudi.

Salvemini, Gaetano. 1928. *The Fascist Dictatorship in Italy.* London: Jonathan Cape.

Sandys, John Edwin. 1908. *A History of Classical Scholarship. From the Revival of Learning to the End of the Eighteenth Century. Vol. 2.* Cambridge: Cambridge University Press.

Santillana, Giorgio de. 1961. *The Crime of Galileo.* London: Mercury Books.

Saporta, Sol and Thomas A. Sebeok. 1959. "Linguistics and Content Analysis." In: pp. 131–50, Ithiel de Sola Pool (ed.), *Trends in Content Analysis.* Urbana: University of Illinois Press.

Schank, Roger C. and Christopher K. Riesbeck (eds.). 1981. *Inside Computer Understanding.* Hillsdale, NJ: Lawrence Erlbaum Associates, Publishers.

Schelling, T. C. 1980. *The Strategy of Conflict.* Cambridge, MA: Harvard University Press.

Schlegel, Frierich. 1967. *Frammenti critici e scritti di estetica. Introduzione e traduzione di Vittorio Santoli.* Florence: Sansoni.

Schlesinger Jr. Arthur. 1962. "The Humanist Looks at Empirical Social Research." *American Sociological Review,* Vol. 27, pp. 768–71.

Schumm, J. S. 1992. "Using Story Grammar with At-Risk High-School Students." *Journal of Reading,* Vol. 35, No. 4, p. 296.

Schumpeter, Joseph. 1933. "The Common Sense of Econometrics." *Econometrica,* Vol. 1, No. 1, pp. 5–12.

1954. *History of Economic Analysis.* Edited from Manuscript by Elizabeth Boody Schumpeter. London: George Allen & Unwin.

Scott, John. 1991. *Social Network Analysis: A Handbook.* London: Sage.

Seaman, William R. 1992. "Active Audience Theory: Pointless Populism." *Media, Culture and Society,* Vol. 14, pp. 301–11.

Searle, John R. 1969. *Speech Acts. An Essay in the Philosophy of Language.* Cambridge: Cambridge University Press.

Seneca. 1920. *Ad Lucilium. Epistulae Morales.* Vol. II. With an English Translation by Richard M. Gummere. London: Heinemann.

Sewell, William H. Jr. 1996. "Three Temporalities: Toward an Eventful Sociology." In: pp. 245–80, Terrence J. McDonald (ed.), *The Historic Turn in the Human Sciences.* Ann Arbor: University of Michigan Press.

Shakespeare, William. 1994. *Complete Works of William Shakespeare.* Glasgow: Harper Collins.

Shalev, Michael. 1978. "Lies, Damned Lies and Strike Statistics: The Measurement of Trends in Industrial Conflicts." pp. 1–20, in Colin Crouch and Alessandro Pizzorno (eds.), *The Resurgence of Class Conflict in Western Europe Since 1968. Volume 1. National Studies.* New York: Holmes & Meier.

Shapiro, Gilbert and John Markoff. 1997. "A Matter of Definition." In: pp. 9–31, Carl W. Roberts (ed.), *Text Analysis for the Social Sciences: Methods for Drawing Statistical Inferences from Texts and Transcripts.* Hillsdale, NJ: Lawrence Erlbaum

Associates, Publishers.

1998. *Revolutionary Demands: A Content Analysis of the Cahiers de Doléances of 1789*. Stanford, CA: Stanford University Press.

Shaw, George Bernard. 1959. *Man and Superman: A Comedy and a Philosophy*. New York: Bantam Books.

Shen, Yeshayahu. 1988. "Schema Theory and the Processing of Narrative Texts–The X-Bar Story Grammar and the Notion of Discourse Topic." *Journal of Pragmatics*, Vol. 12, Nos. 5–6, pp. 639–76.

Shorter, Edward and Charles Tilly. 1974. *Strikes in France, 1830–1968*. Cambridge University Press.

Sigal, Pierre André. 1984. *"Les différents types de pèlerinage au Moyen Age."* In: pp. 76–86, Lenz Kriss-Rettenbeck and Gerda Möhler (eds.), *Wallfahrt kennt keine Grenzen*. Munich: Verlag Schnell & Steiner München.

Sighele, Scipio. 1922. *L'intelligenza della folla*. 2nd Edition. Turin: Fratelli Bocca Editori.

Simmel, Georg. 1950. *The Sociology of Georg Simmel*. Translated, Edited, and with an Introduction by Kurt H. Wolff. Glencoe, IL: Free Press.

1955. *Conflict and The Web of Group-Affiliations*. Translated by Kurt H. Wolff and Reinhard Bendix. Forward by Everett C. Hughes. New York: Free Press.

1959. *Georg Simmel, 1858-1918. A Collection of Essays*. With Translations and a Bibliography. Edited by Kurt H. Wolff. Columbus: The Ohio State University Press.

1978. *The Philosophy of Money*. Translated by Tom Bottomore and David Frisby. London: Routledge & Kegan Paul.

Simpson, Alfred W. B. 1984. *Cannibalism and the Common Law: The Story of the Tragic Last Voyage of the Mignonette and the Strange Legal Proceedings to Which it Gave Rise*. Chicago, IL: The University of Chicago Press.

Simpson, John A. and Edmund S. C. Weiner (ed.). 1989. *The Oxford English Dictionary*. Second edition. Oxford: Clarendon Press.

Singer, Eleanor and Jacob Ludwig. 1987. "South Africa's Press Restrictions. Effects on Press Coverage and Public Opinion Toward South Africa." *Public Opinion Quarterly*, Vol. 51, No. 3, pp. 315–34.

Sloane, William M. 1895–96. "History and Democracy." *American Historical Review*, Vol. 1, No. 1, pp. 1–23.

Small, Albion W. 1903. "What is a Sociologist?" *American Journal of Sociology*, Vol. 8, No. 4, pp. 468–77.

Smiles, Samuel. 1997[1865]. *Lives of Boulton and Watt*. London: Routledge.

Smith, Bruce Lannes, Harold D. Lasswell, and Ralph D. Casey. 1946. *Propaganda, Communication, and Public Opinion. A Comprehensive Reference Guide*. Princeton, NJ: Princeton University Press.

Smith, Dorothy E. 1987. *The Everyday World as Problematic: A Feminist Sociology*. Toronto: University of Toronto Press.

1990. *The Conceptual Practices of Power: A Feminist Sociology of Knowledge*. Boston: Northeastern University Press.

Snow, C. P. 1993. *The Two Cultures*. Cambridge: Cambridge University Press.

Snow, David A., E. Burke Rochford, Jr., Steven K. Warden, and Robert D. Banford. 1986. "Frame Alignment and Mobilization." *American Sociological Review*, Vol. 51, No. 4, pp. 464–81.

Snowden, Frank M. 1986. *Violence and the Great Estates in the South of Italy: Pulia,*

1900–1922. Cambridge: Cambridge University Press.

1989. *The Fascist Revolution in Tuscany. 1919–1922*. Cambridge: Cambridge University Press.

Snyder, David. 1975. "Institutional Setting and Industrial Conflict: Comparative Analysis of France, Italy and the United States." *American Sociological Review*, Vol. 40, No. 3, pp. 259–78.

Snyder, David and William Kelly. 1977. "Conflict Intensity." *American Sociological Review*, Vol. 42, No. 1, 105–23.

Sobel, Dava. 1996. *Longitude. The True Story of a Lone Genius Who Solved the Greatest Scientific Problem of His Time*. London: Fourth Estate.

Solenberger, Peter, Marita Servais, and Greg J. Duncan. 1989. "Data Base Management Approaches to Household Panel Studies." In: pp. 190–225, Daniel Kasprzyk, Greg Duncan, Graham Kalton, and M. P. Singh (eds.), *Panel Surveys*. New York: John Wiley & Sons.

Sombart, Werner. 1967[1913]. *The Quintessence of Capitalism. A Study of the History and Psychology of the Modern Business Man*. Translated and Edited by M. Epstein. New York: Howard Fertig.

Somers, Margaret R. "The Narrative Constitution of Identity: A Relational and Network Approach." *Theory and Society*, Vol. 23, No. 5, pp. 605–49.

Sorokin, Pitirim A. 1928. *Contemporary Sociological Theories*. New York: Harper & Brothers.

1937. *Social and Cultural Dynamics. Fluctuation of Social Relationships, War, and Revolution. Vol. III*. New York: American Book Company.

1956. *Fads and Foibles in Modern Sociology*. Chicago, IL: Henry Regnery Company.

Spampanato, Vincenzo. 1921. *Vita di Giordano Bruno: Con documenti editi e inediti*. Messina: G. Principato.

1923–24. "*Giovanni Florio. Un amico del Bruno in Inghilterra*." *La Critica*, Vol. XXI; *Fascicolo* 1, pp. 56–60, *Fascicolo* 2, pp. 113–25, *Fascicolo* 3, pp. 189–92, *Fascicolo* 5, pp. 313–71; Vol. XXII, *Fascicolo* 1, pp. 56–61, Fascicolo 2, pp. 116–24, Fascicolo 4, pp. 246–53.

Sparrow, John H. 1967. *Mark Pattison and the Idea of a University*. Cambridge: Cambridge University Press.

Spengler, Oswald. 1926. *The Decline of the West. Volume One. Form and Actuality*. Authorized Translation with Notes by Charles Francis Atkinson. New York: Alfred A. Knopf.

Spooner, Frank C. 1983. *Risks at Sea. Amsterdam Insurance and Maritime Europe, 1766–1780*. Cambridge: Cambridge University Press.

Spriano, Paolo. 1964. *L'occupazione delle fabbriche*. Turin: Einaudi.

Spykman, Nicholas J. 1964. *The Social Theory of Georg Simmel*. New York: Russell & Russell.

Starr, Paul. 1987."The Sociology of Official Statistics." In: pp. 7–58, William Alonso and Paul Starr (eds.), *The Politics of Numbers*. New York: Russell Sage Foundation.

Starr, Paul and Ross Corson. 1987. "Who Will Have the Numbers? The Rise of the Statistical Services Industry and the Politics of Public Data." In: pp. 415–48, William Alonso and Paul Starr (eds.), *The Politics of Numbers*. New York: Russell Sage Foundation.

Stein, Nancy L. 1982a. "The Definition of a Story." *Journal of Pragmatics*, Vol. 6, pp. 487–507.

1982b. "What's in a Story: Interpreting the Interpretations of Story Grammars." *Discourse Processes*, Vol. 5, Nos. 3–4, pp. 319–35.

Stein, Nancy L. and Christine G. Glenn. 1979. "An Analysis of Story Comprehension in Elementary School Children." In: pp. 53–120, Roy Freedle (ed.), *New Directions in Discourse Processing*. Norwood, NJ: Ablex.

Stein, Nancy L. and Margaret Policastro. 1984. "The Concept of a Story: A Comparison Between Children's and Teacher's Perspectives." In: pp. 113–55, Heinz Mandl, Nancy L. Stein, and Tom Trabasso (eds.), *Learning and Comprehension of Text*. Hillsdale, NJ: Lawrence Erlbaum Associates, Publishers.

Stephen, Leslie and Sidney Lee (eds.). 1908. *Dictionary of National Biography*. London: Smith, Elder, & Co.

Stern, Fritz (ed.). 1970[1956]. *The Varieties of History. From Voltaire to the Present*. London: Macmillan.

Sterne, Laurence and Ugo Foscolo. 1983[1813]. *Viaggio sentimentale di Yorick lungo la Francia e l'Italia. Introduzione e note di Marisa Bulgheroni e Paolo Ruffilli*. Milan: Garzanti.

Stevenson, John. 1992. *Popular Disturbances in England, 1700–1870*. London: Longman.

Stone, Philip J., Dexter C. Dunphy, Marshall S. Smith, and Daniel M. Ogilvie. 1966. *The General Inquirer: A Computer Approach to Content Analysis*. Cambridge, MA: MIT Press.

Stone, Lawrence. 1967. *The Crisis of the Aristocracy, 1558–1641*. Oxford: Oxford University Press.

1979. "The Revival of Narrative: Reflections on a New Old History." *Past and Present*, No. 85, pp. 3–24.

1981. *The Past and the Present*. Boston: Routledge & Kegan Paul.

1987. *The Past and the Present Revisited*. New York: Routledge & Kegan Paul.

Stopani, Renato. 1991. *Le vie di pellegrinaggio del medioevo. Gli itinerari per Roma, Gerusalemme, Compostella. Con una antologia di fonti*. Florence: Le Lettere.

Sudman, Seymour. 1983. "Survey Research and Technological Change." *Sociological Methods and Research*, Vol. 12, No. 2, pp. 217–30.

Sumption, Jonathan. 1975. *Pilgrimage. An Image of Medieval Religion*. London: Faber & Faber.

Tagger, Theodor. 1914. "Georg Simmel." *Die Zukunft*, Vol. 89. Berlin: Verlag der Zukunft.

Tanter, Raymond. 1966. "Dimensions of Conflict Behavior Within and Between Nations, 1958–1960." *Journal of Conflict Resolution*, Vol. 10, No. 1, pp. 41–64.

Tarnas, Richard. 1996. *The Passion of the Western Mind: Understanding the Ideas That Have Shaped Our World View*. London: Pimlico Press.

Tarrow, Sidney. 1989. *Democracy and Disorder. Protest and Politics in Italy, 1965–1975*. Oxford: Clarendon Press.

1994. *Power in Movement*. Cambridge: Cambridge University Press.

Tasca, Angelo. 1995[1950]. *Nascita e avvento del fascismo. A cura di Sergio Soave*. Florence: La Nuova Italia.

Taylor, Charles Lewis and Michael C. Hudson (eds.). 1972. *World Handbook of Political and Social Indicators*. 2nd Edition. New Haven, CT: Yale University Press.

Taylor, Charles Lewis and David A. Jodice. 1983. *World Handbook of Political and Social Indicators*. 3rd Edition. New Haven, CT: Yale University Press.

Taylor, Eva Germaine R. 1956. *The Haven-Finding Art. A History of Navigation from Odysseus to Captain Cook.* London: Hollis & Carter.

Taylor, Frederick Winslow. 1911. *Scientific Management.* Comprising *Shop Management, The Principles of Scientific Management, Testimony Before the Special House Committee.* With a Foreword by Harlow S. Person. New York: Harper & Brothers Publishers.

Tenenti, Alberto. 1959. *Naufrages: Corsaires et assurances maritimes à Venise, 1592–1609.* Paris: S.E.V.P.E.N.

1961. *Venezia e i corsari, 1580–1615.* Bari: Laterza.

10,000 Maniacs. 1992. *Our Time in Eden.* New York: Elektra Entertainment.

Thacher, John Boyd. 1903–04. *Christopher Columbus: His Life, His Works, His Remains: As Revealed by Original Printed and Manuscript Records, Together with an Essay on Peter Martyr of Anghera and Bartolomé De Las Casas, the First Historians of America.* New York: G.P. Putnam's Sons.

Thomas Aquinas. 1970. *Summae Theologiae.* Volume 17, Psychology of Human Acts. Latin Text. English Translation, Introduction, Notes, Appendices & Glossary. Edited by Thomas Gilby. London: Eyre & Spottiswoode (New York: McGraw-Hill Company).

1996. *L'alchimia ovvero Trattato della pietra filosofale.* Cura e traduzione di Paolo Cortesi. Rome: Newton.

Thomas, Keith. 1984. *Man and the Natural World. Changing Attitudes in England 1500–1800.* Harmondsworth: Penguin.

Thompson, E. P. 1978. "Eighteenth-Century English Society: Class Struggle Without Class?" *Social History,* Vol. 2, pp. 133–66.

1991. *Customs in Common.* New York: The New Press.

Thompson, G. Carslake. 1886. *Public Opinion and Lord Beaconsfield: 1875–1880,* 2 Vols. London: Macmillan.

Thompson, John B. 1990. *Ideology and Modern Culture.* Stanford, CA: Stanford University Press.

Thorndyke, Perry W. 1977. "Cognitive Structures in Comprehension and Memory of Narrative Discourse." *Cognitive Psychology,* Vol. 9, pp. 77–110.

Thorp, Robert K. and Lewis Donohew. 1966. *Content Analysis of Communications.* New York: Macmillan.

Thorpe, Francis Newton (ed.). 1906. *The Federal and State Constitutions. Colonial Charters, and Other Organic Laws of the States, Territories, and Colonies Now and Heretofore Forming the United States of America. Vol. III, Kentucky–Massachusetts.* 7 Vols. Washington, DC: Government Printing Office.

Thornton, Russell and Peter M. Nardi. 1975. "The Dynamics of Role Acquisition." *American Journal of Sociology,* Vol. 80, pp. 870–85.

Thrower, Norman J. W. 1976. "New Geographical Horizons: Maps." In: pp. 659–74, Fredi Chiappelli, Michael J. B. Allen, and Robert Louis Benson (eds.), *First Images of America: The Impact of the New World on the Old.* Berkeley: University of California Press.

Tilly, Charles (ed.). 1975. *The Formation of National States in Western Europe.* Princeton, NJ: Princeton University Press.

Tilly, Charles. 1964. *The Vendée.* Cambridge, MA: Harvard University Press.

1969. "Methods for the Study of Collective Violence." In: pp. 15–43, Ralph Conant and Molly Apple Levin (eds.), *Problems in Research on Community Violence.* New

York: Praeger.

1972. "Quantification in History, as Seen from France." In: pp. 93–126, Val R. Lorwin and Jacob M. Price (eds.), *The Dimensions of the Past: Materials, Problems, and Opportunities for Quantitative Work in History*. New Haven, CT: Yale University Press.

1978. *From Mobilization to Revolution*. Reading, MA: Addison Wesley.

1981. *As Sociology Meets History*. New York: Academic Press.

1983[1969]. In: pp. 5–34, Leon Friedman (ed.). "Collective Violence in European Perspective." *Violence in America. Volume 2: Historical and Comparative Perspectives*. New York: Chelsea House Publishers.

1985. "War Making and State Making as Organized Crime." In: pp. 169–91, Peter Evans, Dietrich Rueschemeyer, and Theda Skocpol (eds.), *Bringing the State Back In*. Cambridge: Cambridge University Press.

1986. *The Contentious French*. Cambridge, MA: Harvard University Press.

1995a. *Popular Contention in Great Britain, 1758–1834*. Cambridge, MA: Harvard University Press.

1995b. "State-Incited Violence, 1900–1999." *Political Power and Social Theory*, Vol. 9, pp. 161–225.

Tilly, Charles and James Rule. 1965. *Measuring Political Upheaval*. Princeton, NJ: Center of International Studies.

Tilly, Charles, Louise Tilly, and Richard Tilly. 1975. *The Rebellious Century, 1830–1930*. Cambridge, MA: Harvard University Press.

Tobler, Titus (ed.). 1851. *Magistri Thetmari Iter ad Terram Sanctam anno 1217*. St. Gallen: Huber & Comp.

1869. *Palaestinae Descriptiones ex Seculo IV., V. et VI. Itinerarium Burdigala Hierosolymam, Peregrinatio S. Paulae, Eucherius de Locis Sanctis, Theodorus de Situ Terrae Sanctae*. St. Gallen: Verlag von Huber & Comp.

1874. *Descriptiones Terrae Sanctae ex Seculo VIII. IX, XII. et XV. S. Willibaldus, Commemoratorium de casis Dei. Bdrnardus Monacus, Innominatus VII, Johannes Wirziburgensis, Innominatus VIII, La Citez de Iherusalem. Johannes Poloner*. Leipzig: J. C. Hinrichs'sche Buchhandlung.

Tocco, Felice. 1889. *Le opere latine di Giordano Bruno esposte e confrontate con le italiane*. Florence: Le Monnier.

Todorov, Tzvetan. 1968. "*La Grammaire du récit*." *Langages*, No. 12, pp. 94–102.

1969. *Grammaire du Décaméron*. Paris: Mouton.

1977[1971]. *The Poetics of Prose*. Oxford: Basil Blackwell.

1981[1968]. *Introduction to Poetics*. Sussex: The Harvester Press.

1990[1978]. *Genres in Discourse*. Cambridge: Cambridge University Press.

Tolstóy, Leo. 1934. *On Life and Essays on Religion*. Translated with an Introduction by Aylmer Maude. Oxford: Oxford University Press.

Tomashevski, Boris. 1965[1925]. "Thematics." In: pp. 61–95, Lemon Lee and Marion Reis (eds.), *Russian Formalist Criticism: Four Essays*. Lincoln: University of Nebraska Press.

Toolan, Michael. 1988. *Narrative: A Critical Linguistic Introduction*. London: Routledge.

Topalov, Christian. 1994. *Naissance du chômeur, 1880–1910*. Paris: Albin Michel.

Touraine, Alain. 1984. *Le retour de l'acteur: Essai de sociologie*. Paris: Fayard.

Toynbee, Arnold J. 1946. *A Study of History*. Abridgement of Volumes I–VI by David

C. Somervell. Oxford: Oxford University Press.

Trevelyan, George Macaulay. 1919. *The Recreations of an Historian*. London: Thomas Nelson and Sons.

1945. *History and the Reader*. Cambridge: Cambridge University Press.

Trew, Anthony. 1979a. "Theory and Ideology at Work." In: pp. 94–116, Roger Fowler, Robert Hodge, Gunther Kress, and Anthony Trew (eds.), *Language and Control*. London: Routledge & Kegan Paul.

1979b. "What the Papers Say: Linguistic Variation and Ideological Difference." In: pp. 117–56, Roger Fowler, Robert Hodge, Gunther Kress, and Anthony Trew (eds.), *Language and Control*. London: Routledge & Kegan Paul.

Tuchman, Gaye. 1972. "Objectivity as a Strategic Ritual." *American Journal of Sociology*, Vol. 77, pp. 660–79.

1973. "Making News by Doing Work: Routinizing the Unexpected." *American Journal of Sociology*, Vol. 79, pp. 110–31.

1978. *Making News. A Study in the Construction of Reality*. New York: The Free Press.

Tucker, George Hugo. 1996. "*Homo Viator* and the Liberty of Exile." *EMF: Studies in Early Modern France*. Vol. 2, pp. 29–65.

Tukey, John. 1977. *Exploratory Data Analysis*, Reading, MA: Addison Wesley Publishing Co.

Tully, James (ed.). 1988. *Meaning and Context: Quentin Skinner and His Critics*. Edited and Introduced by James Tully. Princeton, NJ: Princeton University Press.

Turner, Victor and Edith C. B. Turner. 1978. *Image and Pilgrimage in Christian Culture*. New York: Columbia University Press.

Tversky, Amos. 1977. "Features of Similarity." *Psychological Review*, Vol. 84, No. 4, pp. 327–52.

Tversky, Amos and Itamar Gati. 1978. "Studies in Similarity." In: pp. 79–98, Eleanor Rosch and Barbara B. Lloyd (eds.), *Cognition and Categorization*. Hillsdale, NJ: Lawrence Erlbaum Associates, Publishers.

Ullman, Jeffrey D. 1980. *Principles of Database Systems*. Rockville, MD: Computer Science Press.

Unamuno, Miguel de. 1931. *The Tragic Sense of Life in Men and in Peoples*. Translated by J. E. Crawford Flitch With an Introductory Essay by Salvador de Madariaga. London: Macmillan.

van Nes, F. L. 1976. "Analysis of Keying Errors." *Ergonomics*, Vol. 19, No. 2, pp. 165–74.

Vasari, Giorgio. 1942. *Le Vite dei più eccellenti pittori, scultori e architetti*. Vol. I. Edited by Carlo L. Ragghianti. Milan: Rizzoli.

Velho, Alvaro. 1898[16th century]. *A Journal of the First Voyage of Vasco da Gama, 1497–1499*. Translated and Edited, with Notes, an Introduction and Appendices by E. G. Ravenstein. London: Hakluyt Society.

Vendler, Zeno. 1957. "Verbs and Times." *Philosophical Review*, Vol. 56, pp. 143–60. Also in: pp. 97–121, Zeno Vendler, 1967, *Linguistics in Philosophy*, Ithaca, NY: Cornell University Press.

Vespucci, Amerigo. 1984. *Il mondo nuovo. A cura di Mario Pozzi*. Milan: Serra e Riva Editori.

Vico, Giambattista. 1959. *Opere. A cura di Paolo Rossi*. Milan: Rizzoli.

Victorinus, Marius. 1863. "Explanationum in Rhetoricam. Tullii Ciceronis, Libri Duo." In: pp. 153–304, Carl Halm (ed.), *Rhetores Latini Minores*. Lipsiae: B. G. Teubner.

Waples, Douglas and Bernard Berelson. 1941. *What the Voters Were Told: An Essay in Content Analysis*. Chicago: Graduate Library School, University of Chicago, 77 pages, Mimeographed.

Wasserman, Stanley and Katherine Faust. 1994. *Social Network Analysis in the Social and Behavioral Sciences*. Cambridge: Cambridge University Press.

Waters, E. G. R. 1928. *The Anglo-Norman Voyage of St. Brendan by Benedeit. A Poem of the Early Twelfth Century*. Edited with Introduction, Notes and Glossary by E. G. R. Waters. Oxford: Clarendon Press.

Watson, James D. 1969. *The Double Helix: A Personal Account of the Discovery of the Structure of DNA*. Harmondsworth: Penguin.

Weaver, Phyllis A. and David K. Dickinson. 1982. "Scratching Below the Surface Structure: Exploring the Usefulness of Story Grammars." *Discourse Processes*, Vol. 5, Nos. 3–4, pp. 225–43.

Webb, Sidney and Beatrice Webb. 1932. *Methods of Social Study*. London: Longmans, Green, and Co.

Weber, Max. 1949. *The Methodology of the Social Sciences*. Translated and Edited by Edward A. Shils and Henry A. Finch. With a Foreword by Edward A. Shils. New York: The Free Press.

1976[1909]. *The Agrarian Sociology of Ancient Civilizations*. Translated by R. I. Frank. London: NLB.

1978[1922]. *Economy and Society. An Outline of Interpretative Sociology*. Berkeley: University of California Press.

Weber, Robert Philip. 1990. *Basic Content Analysis*. Newbury Park, CA: Sage.

Weede, Erich. 1973. "The Myth of Random Measurement Error in International Conflict Data Analysis." *Quality and Quantity*, Vol. 7, pp. 107–30.

Weiss, Roberto. 1969. *The Renaissance Discovery of Classical Antiquity*. Oxford: Basil Blackwell.

Weisskopf, Victor F. 1990. *The Joy of Insight: Passions of a Physicist*. New York: Basic Books.

Weitzman, Eben and Matthew B. Miles. 1995. *Computer Programs for Qualitative Data Analysis: A Software Sourcebook*. Newbury Park, CA: Sage.

Wellman, Barry and Stephen D. Berkowitz (eds.). 1988. *Social Structures: A Network Approach*. Cambridge: Cambridge University Press.

Wells, Roger. 1978. "Counting Riots in Eighteenth-Century England." *Society for the Study of Labour History*, Bulletin No. 37, pp. 68–72.

West, Delno. 1992. "Christopher Columbus and His Enterprise to the Indies: Scholarship of the Last Quarter Century." *The William and Mary Quarterly*, Vol. 49, No. 2, pp. 254–77.

Westergaard, John. 1977. "Power, Class and the Media." In; pp. 95–115, James Curran, Michael Gurevitch, and Janet Wollacott (eds.), *Mass Communication and Society*. London: Edward Arnold.

White, David M. 1950. "The Gatekeeper: A Case Study in the Selection of News." *Journalism Quarterly*, Vol. 27, pp. 383–90.

White, Harrison, Scott A. Boorman, and Ronald L. Breiger. 1976. "Social Structure from Multiple Networks: Part I. Blockmodels of Roles and Positions." *American Journal of Sociology*, Vol. 81, pp. 730–80.

White, Hayden V. 1973. *Metahistory. The Historical Imagination in Nineteenth-Century Europe*. Baltimore, MD: The Johns Hopkins University Press.

1978. *Tropics of Discourse: Essays in Cultural Criticism*. Baltimore, MD: The Johns Hopkins University Press.

1987. *The Content of the Form. Narrative Discourse an Historical Representation*. Baltimore, MD: The Johns Hopkins University Press.

Wiese, Leopold von. 1932. *Systematic Sociology, on the Basis of the Beziehungslehre and Gebildelehre of Leopold von Wiese*. Edited by Howard P. Becker. New York: John Wiley & Sons.

1941. *Sociology*. New York: O. Piest.

1949/49. "*Soziometrik*." *Koelner Zeitschrift fuer Soziologie, Neue Folge der Koelner Vierteljahreshefte fuer Soziologie*, Vol. 1, No. 1.

1956. Erinnerungen. Köln: Westdeutscher Verlag.

Wilensky, Robert. 1983. "Story Grammars Versus Story Points." *The Behavioural and Brain Science*, Vol. 6, No. 4, pp. 579–623.

Wilkinson, John. 1981a. *Egeria's Travels to the Holy Land*. Revised Edition. Newly Translated with Supporting Documents and Notes by John Wilkinson. Jerusalem: Ariel Publishing House.

1981b. "Introduction." In: pp. 3–88, John Wilkinson (ed.), *Egeria's Travels to the Holy Land*. Revised Edition. Newly Translated with Supporting Documents and Notes by John Wilkinson. Jerusalem: Ariel Publishing House.

Willey, Malcom Macdonald. 1926. *The Country Newspaper. A Study of Socialization and Newspaper Content*. Chapel Hill: University of North Carolina Press.

Wimsatt, William K. and Monroe C. Beardsley. 1954. "The Intentional Fallacy." In: pp. 3–18, William K. Wimsatt (ed.), *The Verbal Icon*. Lexington: University of Kentucky Press.

Windelband, Wilhelm. 1980 [1894]. "History and Natural Science." *History and Theory*. Vol. 19, No. 2, pp. 165–85.

Winsborough, Halliman H. 1989. "Data Base Management: Discussion." In: pp. 242–8, Daniel Kasprzyk, Greg Duncan, Graham Kalton, and M. P. Singh (eds.), *Panel Surveys*. New York: John Wiley & Sons.

Wittgenstein, Ludwig. 1958. *The Blue and the Brown Books*. Oxford: Blackwell.

1961 [1921]. *Tractatus Logico-Philosophicus*. Translated by D. F. Pears and B. F. McGuiness with an Introduction by Bertrand Russell. London: Routledge.

Wolff, Kurt H. 1950. "Introduction." In: pp. xvii–lxiv, Kurt H. Wolff (ed.), *The Sociology of Georg Simmel*. Translated, Edited, and with an Introduction by Kurt H. Wolff. Glencoe, IL.: Free Press.

Woodward, Julian L. 1930. *Foreign News in American Morning Newspapers. A Study in Public Opinion*. New York: Columbia University Press.

1934. "Quantitative Newspaper Analysis as a Technique of Opinion Research." *Social Forces*, Vol. XII, pp. 526–37.

Woolf, Harry (ed.). 1961. *Quantification. A History of the Meaning of Measurement in the Natural and Social Sciences*. Indianapolis, IN: The Bobbs-Merrill Company.

Wright, Georg Henrik von. 1971. *Explanation and Understanding*. London: Routledge & Kegan Paul.

Wright, Quincy. 1942. *A Study of War*. Chicago, IL: The University of Chicago Press.

Yates, Frances Amelia. 1934. *John Florio: The Life of an Italian in Shakespeare's England*. Cambridge: Cambridge University Press.

1982. *Lull & Bruno. Collected Essays*. Volume I. London: Routledge & Kegan Paul.

1991 [1964]. *Giordano Bruno and the Hermetic Tradition*. Chicago, IL: The University of Chicago Press.

1992[1966]. *The Art of Memory*. London: Pimlico.

Zadeh, Lotfi A. 1987. *Fuzzy Sets and Applications: Selected Papers*. New York: John Wiley & Sons.

Zagare, Frank C. 1984. *Game Theory. Concepts and Applications*. Newbury Park, CA: Sage.

Zald, Mayer N. 1996. "Culture, Ideology, and Strategic Framing." In: pp. 261–74, Doug McAdam, John D. McCarthy, Mayer N. Zald (eds.), *Comparative Perspectives on Social Movements: Political Opportunities, Mobilizing Structures, and Cultural Framings*. Cambridge: Cambridge University Press.

Zeller, Richard and Edward Carmines. 1980. *Measurement in the Social Sciences. The Link Between Theory and Data*. Cambridge: Cambridge University Press.

Zemon Davis, Natalie. 1983. *The Return of Martin Guerre*. Cambridge, MA: Harvard University Press.

Index

Abbott, Andrew 248, 284
Abelard, Peter 320
Abell, Peter 252, 357 n. 4
academy 9, 247, 257, 259, 267
  mediocrity of 259
  see also discipline, academic
Access, Microsoft 67, 70
accounts 82, 298
  travel 6–9, 23, 132–4, 141, 145,
    149, 150–1, 155, 203, 224, 276,
    296, 324, 331, 334, 363 n. 5, 364
    n. 12, 365 nn. 23, 35, 367 n. 58,
    369 n. 84
  see also emphasis; seeing, ways of;
    silence; writing, ways of
accuracy 34, 78, 207, 213, 275, 314,
  329, 353 n. 38, 374 n. 34
  see also bias; errors, detection of;
    reliability; validation; verification
actants 45, 253
  see also actors/agents
action(s) 5, 19, 23, 38, 39, 44–57,
  60–1, 67, 71, 77–8, 85–89, 99,
  114, 120, 122–3, 149, 152, 172,
  180, 215, 235–6, 242, 245, 249,
  251, 252–5, 269, 272–3, 287, 302,
  306, 313, 315–17, 341, 398 n. 21
  boundaries of 77, 290, 291
  see also event, macroaction
  canonical 46–7, 71, 293
  classification of 16, 262, 287,
    289–90
  collective 86, 106, 114, 120, 280,
    313
  research 15, 16, 38, 43, 103, 244
  see also movement, social,
    literature
  human 251

philosophy of 288
meaning of 19, 316–17
narrative 45, 251
network of 100, 101, 107, 255
processes 254, 261–2, 316
purposive/rational 213, 260, 304
sequence of 25, 38, 44, 58, 117,
  190, 291
  see also analysis, sequence of;
    purpose, sequence of
sets of 23, 67, 254
social 214, 261, 273, 302, 310, 314,
  315
sociology of 254, 262
spheres of 99, 100, 101, 109, 199,
  236, 287, 293–4
  see also calculation; control;
    guessing; measurement;
    quantification; rigor
  see also interaction; macroaction;
    microaction; reaction; relations,
    social
activism/activists 84–5, 87, 104, 287
Acton, John, Lord 183
actors/agents 3, 4, 5, 19, 25, 38, 39,
  43, 45, 47, 49, 51, 54, 61, 67, 71,
  72, 75, 82–5, 88, 89, 99–100, 101,
  103, 104, 106, 122, 157, 159, 174,
  215, 233, 240–2, 244, 245, 249,
  251, 253–5, 269, 272–3, 286,
  292–5, 304, 310, 312–13, 316–17,
  339, 348 n. 58, 357 n. 4, 358 n. 9,
  361 n. 49, 385 n. 21, 393 n. 43,
  395 n. 2
acts 37, 215, 273, 291, 316, 350 n. 86
  official 185
  speech 291, 353 n. 45
addressee/addresser 196–7

Other books in the series (*continued from page iii*)

14. David Wank, *Commodifying Communism: Business, Trust, and Politics in a Chinese City*
15. Rebecca Adams and Graham Allan, *Placing Friendship in Context*
16. Robert L. Nelson and William P. Bridges, *Legalizing Gender Inequality: Courts, Markets and Unequal Pay for Women in America*
17. Robert Freeland, *The Struggle for Control of the Modern Corporation: Organizational Change at General Motors, 1924–1970*
18. Yi-min Lin, *Between Politics and Markets: Firms, Competition, and Institutional Change in Post-Mao China*
19. Nan Lin, *Social Capital: A Theory of Social Structure and Action*
20. Christopher Ansell, *Schism and Solidarity in Social Movements: The Politics of Labor in the French Third Republic*
21. Thomas Gold, Doug Guthrie, and David Wank, eds., *Social Connections in China: Institutions, Culture, and the Changing Nature of Guanxi*